Evidence

Carolina Academic Press Context and Practice Series
Michael Hunter Schwartz
Series Editor

Administrative Law
Richard Henry Seamon

Advanced Torts
Alex B. Long and Meredith J. Duncan

Animal Law—New Perspectives on Teaching Traditional Law
Kathy Hessler, Joyce Tischler, Pamela Hart, and Sonia S. Waisman

Antitrust Law
Steven Semeraro

Civil Procedure
Gerald F. Hess, Theresa M. Beiner, and Scott R. Bauries

Civil Procedure for All States
Benjamin V. Madison, III

Complex Litigation
James M. Underwood

Constitutional Law, Second Edition
David Schwartz and Lori Ringhand

A Context and Practice Global Case File:
An Intersex Athlete's Constitutional Challenge,
Hastings v. USATF, IAAF, and IOC
Olivia M. Farrar

A Context and Practice Global Case File:
Rossi v. Bryce, **An International Embryo and Surrogacy Dispute**
Olivia M. Farrar

A Context and Practice Global Case File:
Thorpe v. Lightfoot, **A Mother's International Hague Petition**
for the Return of Her Child
Olivia M. Farrar

Contracts, Second Edition
Michael Hunter Schwartz and Adrian Walters

Criminal Law
Steven I. Friedland, Catherine Carpenter,
Kami Chavis, and Catherine Arcabsacio

Current Issues in Constitutional Litigation, Second Edition
Sarah E. Ricks, with co-author Evelyn M. Tenenbaum

Employment Discrimination, Second Edition
Susan Grover, Sandra F. Sperino, and Jarod S. Gonzalez

Energy Law
Joshua P. Fershee

Evidence, Second Edition
Pavel Wonsowicz

International Business Transactions
Amy Deen Westbrook

International Women's Rights, Equality, and Justice
Christine M. Venter

The Lawyer's Practice
Kris Franklin

Professional Responsibility
Barbara Glesner Fines

Property
Alicia Kelly and Nancy Knauer

Sales, Second Edition
Edith R. Warkentine

Secured Transactions
Edith R. Warkentine and Jerome A. Grossman

Torts
Paula J. Manning

Workers' Compensation Law, Second Edition
Michael C. Duff

Your Brain and Law School
Marybeth Herald

Evidence

A Context and Practice Casebook
SECOND EDITION

Pavel Wonsowicz
UCLA School of Law

Carolina Academic Press
Durham, North Carolina

ISBN 978-1-5310-0703-4
LCCN 2017945200
e-ISBN 978-1-53100-704-1

Carolina Academic Press, LLC
700 Kent Street
Durham, NC 27701
Telephone (919) 489-7486
Fax (919) 493-5668
www.cap-press.com

Printed in the United States of America

To Joy,
    All the other stars seem dim around you.

To Eva and Charles,
    Deep in their roots, all flowers keep the light.

Contents

Table of Principal Cases

xix

Series Editor's Preface

Welcome to a new type of law text. Designed by leading experts in law school teaching and learning, Context and Practice casebooks assist law professors and their students to work together to learn, minimize stress, and prepare for the rigors and joys of practicing law. **Student learning and preparation for law practice are the guiding ethics of these books.**

Why would we depart from the tried and true? Why have we abandoned the legal education model by which we were trained? Because legal education can and must improve.

In Spring 2007, the Carnegie Foundation published *Educating Lawyers: Preparation for the Practice of Law* and the Clinical Legal Education Association published *Best Practices for Legal Education*. Both works reflect in-depth efforts to assess the effectiveness of modern legal education, and both conclude that legal education, as presently practiced, falls quite short of what it can and should be. Both works criticize law professors' rigid adherence to a single teaching technique, the inadequacies of law school assessment mechanisms, and the dearth of law school instruction aimed at teaching law practice skills and inculcating professional values. Finally, the authors of both books express concern that legal education may be harming law students. Recent studies show that law students, in comparison to all other graduate students, have the highest levels of depression, anxiety and substance abuse.

The problems with traditional law school instruction begin with the textbooks law teachers use. Law professors cannot implement *Educating Lawyers* and *Best Practices* using texts designed for the traditional model of legal education. Moreover, even though our understanding of how people learn has grown exponentially in the past 100 years, no law school text to date even purports to have been designed with educational research in mind.

The Context and Practice Series is an effort to offer a genuine alternative. Grounded in learning theory and instructional design and written with *Educating Lawyers* and *Best Practices* in mind, Context and Practice casebooks make it easy for law professors to change.

I welcome reactions, criticisms, and suggestions; my e-mail address is mschwartz@pacific.edu. Knowing the author(s) of these books, I know they, too, would appreciate your input; we share a common commitment to student learning. In fact, students, if your professor cares enough about your learning to have adopted this book, I bet s/he would welcome your input, too!

Michael Hunter Schwartz, Series Designer and Editor
Consultant, Institute for Law Teaching and Learning
Dean and Professor of Law, University of the Pacific, McGeorge School of Law

Preface and Acknowledgments

People learn best when they answer their own questions and receive feedback on their efforts. They achieve their best insights when they fight through confusion through thought, reflection, and problem solving. In this way, knowledge is constructed, not received.

In this book, most of our focus will be on the ambiguity and uncertainty in evidence law—what I often refer to as the "gray area." In each section, the core tests and rules are presented right up front, as clearly as I could write them. The rest of the section explores uncertainty: What are the ambiguities in the rules? How do courts apply the test? Upon what does the court rely in making its determination? By recognizing these gray areas, grappling with them, rethinking our assumptions, and examining our mental models of reality, we can turn confusion into insight.

It is my hope that this book will help you construct knowledge through a natural, critical learning environment in your classroom. By "natural," I mean that you will explore authentic, real-world application of evidence law. By "critical," I mean that you will not only examine your understanding of the law, its application, and its synthesis, but also have the opportunity to provoke an imagination that leads to possibilities and solutions. I hope it will help you develop all the skills that a practitioner must possess, such as creativity, practical judgment, fact finding, persuasive advocacy, strategic planning, passion, and engagement.

Most of all, I hope that journey is a good one for you. Have fun with this book: actively engage in the motivations of the parties and lawyers in the cases, try to predict the outcome of the problems, and do not ignore the emotions that arise in you as you go through these materials. In other words, dive into the ambiguity and make the knowledge your own.

Acknowledgments

Tremendous thanks go to my wife, Joy, who supported me in writing this book in every way imaginable. This book would not exist without her love, patience, and hard work. I also owe so much to my children, Eva and Charles—yes, the book is done, and, yes, I now have more time to play. Words simply cannot express my love and gratitude to you all.

I am very grateful to Michael Hunter Schwartz for his faith and patience. I would also like to thank the excellent people at Carolina Academic Press for their hard work on this book and commitment to this series.

Denis Poncet and Jean-Xavier de Lestrade created a remarkable documentary in "The Staircase," and I thank them for use of excerpts of their work.

Many research assistants have their fingerprints all over this book. Roni Pomerantz deserves special mention, as her excellent work served as a model for me and for all the other research assistants. I would also like to thank Andrea Alarcon, Adam Beshara, Michael Sier, Kimberlina McKinney, Lindsey Harms, Rosie Kim, and Amira Hasenbush.

My Evidence classes at UCLA School of Law in 2010 and 2011 had to suffer through drafts of this book. They did so with grace and good humor. I thank them for their insights and constructive criticism.

Pavel Wonsowicz
July, 2012

Acknowledgments for the Second Edition

I would like to thank my wife and children for their continued support as this book evolved into a second edition. Their encouragement and patience made this book possible. Their insights proved invaluable, although my daughter Eva's request that I re-name the book "EVAdence" was ultimately rejected.

Thanks also to my students who made thoughtful suggestions about the first edition. In particular, Rebecca Rosen provided wonderful revisions and very clever flowchart ideas for this edition.

Pavel Wonsowicz
March, 2017

Evidence

Chapter 1

An Introduction to Evidence

I. Introduction

We heard the Sermon on the Mount and I knew it was too complex
It didn't amount to anything more than what the broken glass reflects
—Bob Dylan*

Two teams of advocates exist. Both are looking at the same facts. In this gray world, one team will argue that the facts are black. The other team will argue that the facts are white. A factfinder, typically a jury, will decide who has better marshaled the facts to support their vision. Each team of advocates will craft a narrative that best encompasses the facts to support their vision of reality. The party with the better narrative, that is the party that weaves the facts most compellingly in their narrative, wins.

The preceding paragraph is one vision of a trial. But it ignores a critical component — the advocates have limits as to facts they may use. Those limits are evidence law. Evidence law puts limits on what a jury may hear due to a fear that the jury will not be able to properly weigh the evidence. Is it not relevant to the dispute? Is it too prejudicial for the jury to use it fairly? Is it too unreliable to allow the jury to rely on it? Is there a policy consideration that should counteract its relevance and keep it from the jury? Thus the narrative flow, your own as well as your opponents', is filled with landmines — evidence that evidence law will not allow you to use.

This book will explore evidence law from the eyes of an advocate. What are the meanings of these rules? What policies underlie them? And, perhaps most importantly, when an advocate approaches a gray line in the law of evidence, how do courts determine, both factually and legally, whether that evidence is admissible?

Each section of this book will begin with a rule of evidence from the Federal Rules of Evidence. We will then deconstruct its language. Then, the hard part begins: what factors determine admissibility from inadmissibility? When will our narrative be interrupted, and how do we best craft arguments that it should not be?

---

* Copyright © 1974 by Ram's Horn Music; renewed 2002 by Ram's Horn Music.

The Staircase

To aid our comprehension of the Federal Rules of Evidence (which 42 states have adopted as their evidence code), we will be relying on case materials and video footage from a 2001 murder trial that took place in North Carolina, State v. Michael Iver Peterson. To best illustrate evidence principles, it helps to have a single thread that runs through a textbook. *The Staircase* is that thread.

An award-winning documentary, *The Staircase* was directed by Academy Award-winning documentary filmmaker Jean-Xavier de Lestrade. We will be able to follow the trial, including the strategies undertaken by counsel and the battles of evidentiary issues that shaped both sides' narrative in the trial. Let us begin with the factual backdrop to this case, in which Michael Peterson was charged with the murder of his wife Kathleen, whose body was discovered lying in a pool of blood on the stairway to her home. As you read through the facts of this case from the appellate court opinion, ask yourself: What evidence should not be admitted in the trial of this case? Then ask yourself, why do I think that a jury could not handle this evidence? Is it because it is not relevant? Is it not reliable? Is there a policy argument against the evidence? Is it too prejudicial?

State v. Peterson

179 N.C.App. 437, 634 S.E.2d 594
(N.C.App., 2006)

On 9 December 2001, at 2:40 a.m., defendant called the City of Durham's 911 center from his residence. He stated that his wife, Kathleen Peterson (Kathleen), had fallen down the stairs. Defendant further stated that she was unconscious but was still breathing. Defendant hung up and then called back to 911 a short time later, claiming that Kathleen was not breathing. Approximately seven to eight minutes after defendant's initial 911 call, James Rose and Ron Paige—paramedics with the Durham County Emergency Medical Services—arrived at the Peterson residence. Defendant's son, Todd Peterson (Todd), arrived at the same time as the paramedics.

The Peterson house is a large estate home with an open foyer entrance. The paramedics found the front door open and noticed blood on it. Straight ahead through the front door is the large, main staircase leading to the second floor. Immediately to the left after entering, however, is a front hallway leading down to the kitchen. Off of this hallway near the kitchen is an enclosed, narrow stairwell also leading to the second floor. Upon entering the house, the paramedics observed Kathleen lying at the bottom of this stairwell. Her legs were out into the hallway and her head was just inside the encased, open doorframe where the first few steps are located. The stairwell runs parallel to the hallway, but has a few angled steps at the bottom designed to open up the staircase perpendicular to the hallway. Defendant was seen standing over Kathleen in a "semi-knees-bent position" with blood on his hands, arms, legs, and feet; he wore shorts and a t-shirt partially blood-soaked with splatter spots.

When paramedics arrived at Kathleen's body, Todd tried to pull defendant away, stating, "Dad, she's dead, the paramedics are here." Paramedics Rose and Paige quickly determined that Kathleen had no pulse and was not breathing. Defendant stated that he had gone outside to turn off the lights, came back in, and found her at the bottom of the steps. Paramedic Rose testified that there was an "enormous amount of blood involved." He saw "dried blood on the steps, and also on the wall. And it also looked like it had been wiped away or wiped on. It had been smeared, instead of just blood droplets just soaking down the wall." He testified that based on his experience there was an unusual amount of blood for a fall, and the most severe injury he had seen from a fall was a broken neck. The blood under Kathleen's head had already clotted and started to harden.

Later that day, Dr. Deborah Radisch, a pathologist with the Office of the North Carolina Medical Examiner, performed an autopsy on Kathleen's body and determined the cause of death to be blunt force trauma of the head. The autopsy revealed multiple contusions and abrasions on the head and neck; seven distinct lacerations on the posterior scalp; and contusions and abrasions on the arms, wrists, and hands.

Also on that day, Investigator A.H. Holland, Jr., a member of the Criminal Investigation Division of the Durham Police Department, applied for and received a search warrant to search the Peterson residence at 1810 Cedar Street, Durham, North Carolina. The warrant stated that the property to be seized included, *inter alia,* fingerprints, bloodstains, physical layout and measurements of the premises, documentary evidence indicating ownership, and moving pictures, video, and still pictures to preserve the nature of the crime scene. Investigator Holland's affidavit supporting probable cause included the following underlying facts:

> This applicant has been a law enforcement officer for more than nineteen years. I am currently assigned to the Homicide Unit of the Criminal Investigation Division of the Durham Police Department. I have been an Investigator with the Durham Police Department since 1989. During this time I have been assigned to conduct follow-up investigations of Child Sexual Abuse, Adult Rape, Aggravated Assault and Homicide.
>
> On December 9, 2001, 0309 hrs., I, Inv. A.H. Holland, Jr., was paged by On-Call CID Supervisor Sgt. Fran Borden in reference to a Death Investigation at 1810 Cedar St. Sgt. Borden advised that the victim, age 47, fell down a flight of stairs and there was a large amount of blood present at the scene. At 0359 hrs., this investigator arrived at 1810 Cedar St. Prior to entering the front door, I observed blood on the sidewalk that leads to the front door. Upon entering the front door, I observed blood on the inside of the door. Sgt. Terry Wilkins advised that the victim's husband had blood all over his person. I saw the victim at a distance, but did not approach. At this point, this investigator made the decision to obtain this Search Warrant.

On 10 December 2001 Investigator Holland applied for and received a second search warrant. This warrant stated the premises to be searched as defendant's residence along with four vehicles not on the first warrant. The probable cause for the second warrant simply repeated the probable cause from the affidavit for the first warrant.

On 12 December 2001 Investigator Holland applied for and received a third search warrant to search defendant's residence. That warrant stated that the property to be seized included all items from the previous warrant as well as "computers, CPUs, files, software, accessories and any and all other evidence that may be associated with this investigation." The only additional probable cause listed in Investigator Holland's application for the search warrant was the following statement: "After conferring with the District Attorney's Office and the State Medical Examiners Office, this applicant has probable cause to believe that additional evidence remains at the residence."

On 20 December 2001 defendant was indicted on the charge of first-degree murder for the death of Kathleen. Before trial, the court denied defendant's motion to suppress all evidence seized as a result of the 9, 10, and 12 December 2001 search warrants.

At trial, the State's evidence relative to motive tended to show that Kathleen had worked at Nortel Networks. Helen Prislinger, a process analyst and project manager for Nortel Networks, reported directly to Kathleen. Ms. Prislinger testified that Kathleen telephoned her on 8 December 2001, at 11:08 p.m. Ms. Prislinger informed Kathleen that she had documents to e-mail her for a meeting the coming Sunday in Canada. Kathleen asked someone in the room for an e-mail address and gave it to Ms. Prislinger.

Todd Markley, a lead consultant at CompuSleuth which performs forensic processing and investigation, testified as an expert in forensic computer examination. He examined a disk drive from defendant's computer and identified an e-mail sent 8 December 2001 at 11:53 p.m. from Ms. Prislinger. He could not determine if the e-mail had been read, but was "pretty confident" that the attached documents were not extracted. Mr. Markley also testified that he recovered a large volume of pictures of sexual activity that were on the computer as a result of web browsing. The State introduced numerous e-mails between defendant and Brent "Brad" Wolgamott, a male escort. In these e-mails with Mr. Wolgamott, defendant attempted to set a time to "hook up" with Mr. Wolgamott and also indicated that defendant understood he would be paying for sexual services. The State further introduced an e-mail dated 23 February 2001 from Dirk Yates, an operator of a web service dealing in homosexual pornography.

The State also introduced numerous papers that were collected by the police from defendant's den or study area. This paperwork included naked photographs of Mr. Wolgamott, escort reviews of Mr. Wolgamott, and printouts of e-mails between defendant and Mr. Wolgamott discussing defendant paying Mr. Wolgamott for sexual services. This paperwork was intermingled with other various paperwork including a tax appraisal of defendant's residence, Kathleen's cell phone bill from Sprint, and Kathleen's flex benefit confirmation statement from Nortel.

Regarding the Petersons' finances and Kathleen's job status at Nortel Networks, Raymond Young, a special agent, certified public accountant, and certified fraud examiner with the North Carolina State Bureau of Investigation, testified that at the time of Kathleen's death, the value of the Petersons' major assets was $1,618,369.00. In 1999, $276,790.00 was received into the Petersons' bank account and $461,400.00 left the account. In 2000, $203,390.00 was received into the account and $300,760.00 left the account. In 2001, $180,480.00 was received into the account and $288,000.00 left the account. On the Petersons' 1999, 2000, and 2001 tax returns, defendant had no taxable income from employment.

Katherine Kayser, an administrative assistant at Nortel Networks, testified that in 2001, Kathleen earned $145,000.00 plus a bonus of $10,750.00. At Nortel, she obtained the following stock options: In 1994, 4,800 shares at $3.94 per share and she had 1,600 shares outstanding; in 1995, 5,600 shares at $4.2113 per share; in 1996, 4,800 shares at $5.6175 per share; in 1997, 5,600 shares at $8.8513 per share; in 1998, 6,000 shares at $11.29 per share; in 1999, 4,000 shares at $17.43 per share; in January 2000, 2,000 shares at $37.94; in April 2000, 2,000 shares at $57.41 per share; and in July 2000, 2,000 shares at $80.69 per share, and all were outstanding. In September 2000, Nortel's stock plunged. All of Kathleen's stock options from 2000 were cancelled as the market price fell below the option price; she was going to trade them in; however, upon her death they were reinstated. Kathleen exercised 3,200 shares of options with a purchase price of $3.94 in five separate transactions of 500, 800, 500, 200, and 1,200 shares with market prices of $36.75, $32.75, $37.625, $31.94, and $19.40 respectively, for a total profit of $80,431.50, less $31,054.05 in taxes for a net profit of $49,377.45. She exercised her last option in March 2001.

Ms. Kayser also testified that as Kathleen's beneficiary, defendant received $29,360.38 after taxes from her 401(k) plan; $94,455.75 after taxes from her retirement benefits; and $223,182.46 from her deferred compensation fund. Kathleen also had a life insurance policy for which she had filled out a "Life Insurance Beneficiary Designation Form" listing defendant as the beneficiary; however, she had neither signed nor dated that form.

Kim Barker, a human resource employee at Nortel, testified that from the fourth quarter of 2000 through 2001 Nortel laid off employees, described by Nortel as "optimization." In November of 2001, Kathleen was placed on the "optimization list" for three days. However, Ms. Barker did not know if Kathleen knew that she was on the list. Ms. Barker testified that a terminated employee is not entitled to continue a company life insurance policy.

John Huggard, an expert in the field of estate planning, testified as to how Kathleen's estate would be divided, pursuant to the laws of intestate succession, between defendant and Kathleen's daughter [from a previous marriage,] Caitlin Atwater.

E-mails recovered from defendant's computer also related to the Petersons' finances. One e-mail was from defendant to his ex-wife, Patty Peterson, asking her to pay a portion of their sons' living expenses. Another was an e-mail from Thomas Ratliff to defendant on 19 April 2001, responding to defendant's request that Thomas pay $5,000.00 per semester for Martha Ratliff's college expenses.

The trial court also allowed the State to present evidence related to the death of Elizabeth Ratliff, a friend of defendant and his first wife who died under circumstances with factual similarities to the death of Kathleen....

Defendant presented evidence tending to support the theory that Kathleen died as a result of an accidental fall down the stairs. He presented several expert witnesses who testified regarding the blood splatter patterns and the biomechanics of a fall to support his theory of accident.

II. The Anatomy of a Trial

As an advocate prepares for trial, the rules of evidence play a central role. The pleadings will define the legal issues of consequence and will therefore determine what evidence is relevant. Discovery in a civil case focuses on matters "reasonably calculated to lead to admissible evidence," and, therefore, is directly dependent on evidence rules. Perhaps more importantly, an advocate's knowledge of which evidence will ultimately be admissible allows her to gauge the strength of her case, the strength of her opponent's case, and the settlement value. Therefore, even before the advocates step into the courtroom, evidence law is shaping the narrative of the case.

What follows is a breakdown of how a trial unfolds and the degree to which the rules of evidence play a part. Each jurisdiction will possess its own variations, but a jury trial usually breaks down as follows:

Pretrial Motions. Before a trial begins, lawyers will begin the battle over evidentiary issues. Typically, the lawyers will file "motions in limine" ("at the threshold") with the court in order to exclude inadmissible evidence before the trial begins. The motions may also request that the proponent of certain evidence at trial raise the admissibility of the evidence outside of the jury's presence before attempting introduction. Motions in limine are not restricted to the opponent of evidence; the proponent may make a motion to clarify the scope of admissible evidence.

Let us look at an example. Suppose you represent a client charged with murder. Your client had previously been convicted of manslaughter, served his time in prison, and was released seven years ago. As an advocate, you desperately do not want this information in front of the jury, as there is a huge risk of jurors lapsing into a "once a murderer, always a murder" line of thought. So you make a motion in limine to exclude this evidence. The judge might rule in your favor or she might decide that she does not want to rule on the motion in the abstract. Instead, she may decide to defer her ruling until the trial, when the factual record is more developed and the context of the evidence in the scope of the trial is clearer. If the judge defers her ruling, you should make a motion that the prosecutor should not offer this evidence in front of the jury until the judge has ruled on your motion. After all, a prosecution cross-examination of your client that leads off "This isn't the first time you've killed a man, is it?" will have a great effect on the jury. Even if you immediately object, and the judge decides that, indeed, the evidence is inadmissible now that the record is clearer, it will be hard for the jury to forget about that question. Even if the judge instructs the jury to disregard the question, it is very hard for jurors to "unring the bell."

Jury Selection and Instruction. Depending on the rules of the jurisdiction, the judge, the attorneys, or both ask questions of potential jurors to determine their impartiality through a process called "voir dire." All trial attorneys begin jury selection with a vision of their ideal jury. They use jury selection to come as close as they can to the ideal. Toward this end, potential jurors can be dismissed for cause if, for example, they demonstrate an inability to be impartial. The attorneys may also use "peremptory" challenges to remove a juror. No reason need be given when using a peremptory challenge, but they may not be used to discriminate based on race or gender. After the jury has been selected, a judge often will instruct the jury as to their role in the trial (e.g., that the jury will decide questions of fact and must keep an open mind throughout the trial).

Opening Statements. The party with the burden of proof (usually the plaintiff/prosecutor) offers their opening statement first. The defense may offer their opening statement either directly after the plaintiff/prosecutor's opening or the defense may wait until the plaintiff/prosecutor has rested her case-in-chief. The opening statement offers a roadmap of what the evidence will demonstrate. Although a lawyer is not allowed to argue inferences stemming from the evidence during an opening, a trial judge has a great deal of latitude in defining the scope of an opening. Some judges allow themes or theories of the case during opening statement as long as they are not excessively argumentative. Thus, stating what a witness will state or what an exhibit will show is proper, but characterizing the evidence or trying to persuade the jury about a point is inappropriate during an opening statement. The line between merely stating the evidence and making arguments about it is a blurry one, and attorneys, eager to craft their narrative at the outset, tend to walk as close to the line as a judge will allow.

Plaintiff/Prosecutor's Case-in-Chief. After the opening statement(s), the party with the burden of proof begins their case-in-chief by presenting evidence. As will be discussed in greater detail later, witness testimony, "real evidence" (i.e., tangible items, such as a document or murder weapon), "demonstrative evidence" (i.e., evidence that illustrates the testimony of a witness, such as a diagram or summary), stipulations between the parties, and facts that are judicially noticed by the court may all be used as long as they are admissible pursuant to the rules of evidence. In other words, the evidence must survive any objections raised by defense counsel.

For live testimony, the plaintiff/prosecutor will call a witness and conduct a direct examination of those witnesses. Defense counsel may then cross-examine the witness, if she desires to do so. The judge may allow re-direct examination by the plaintiff/prosecutor, but redirect is limited to responding to new points raised on cross-examination. Likewise, again at the discretion of the judge, defense counsel may recross-examine on new points raised on re-direct.

The narration that was planted during the opening statement takes shape during the examination and cross-examination of witnesses. For direct examination, it is the witness, not the attorney, who is the star of the show. The witness must be allowed to tell her version of the story in a credible manner in order for the jury to have faith in her version. Thus, counsel for the plaintiff/prosecutor will use open-ended questions rather than leading questions (i.e., questions that require a yes/no answer) in order that the witness can best express herself. Cross-examination, on the other hand, makes the attorney the star. Through leading questions, the witness is controlled and, ideally, doubts about her credibility emerge.

The advocate who is not examining the witness can object on admissibility grounds (e.g., hearsay, relevancy, etc.) or can object to the form of the question. Objections as to form, which will not be a focus in this book, focus on improper questioning: the question may be leading (which is not allowed on direct examination), ambiguous, duplicative, assuming facts not in evidence, or argumentative, to name but a few of the common objections. Regardless of whether the objection relates to admissibility or form, the goal is to break up the narration of the witness and to assure that all her testimony is relevant and reliable. Most objections occur in front of the jury, but if the risk of prejudice is high, counsel can request to be heard at "sidebar." At sidebar, counsel will approach the bench and argue the merits of the objection in hushed tones that the jury cannot hear. The judge, at her discretion, can also order the jury to be removed so that counsel can argue the merits of an objection outside of their presence.

A judge will either sustain or overrule the objection. When the judge overrules the objection, the evidence is admissible. If the objection is sustained, the judge may give a cautionary instruction to the jury to disregard the objectionable question. If a judge sustains an objection to a witness' answer to a question, an attorney will move to strike the answer of the witness, and the judge will again issue a cautionary instruction to the jury to disregard the answer.

Motion for Acquittal or Directed Verdict. At the close of the plaintiff/prosecutor's case-in-chief, a defendant may ask the court to dismiss the case on the grounds that the plaintiff/prosecutor has not met her burden of producing sufficient evidence to establish every element of its case. In the criminal context, defendant would move for an acquittal, while in the civil context the defendant would move for a directed verdict. At this stage, the judge need only determine whether sufficient evidence exists that could justify a jury verdict in the prosecution/plaintiff's favor. In other words, could a rational factfinder determine that the element is met? If the answer is yes, the motion will be denied.

Defendant's Case-in-Chief. The defendant presents her evidence after the prosecution/plaintiff has rested its case. The same procedures in presenting evidence as in the plaintiff/prosecution's case-in-chief govern. At the conclusion of her presentation of the evidence, the defendant then rests her case. If the defendant has presented an affirmative defense, the defendant usually has the burden to produce sufficient evidence to survive a plaintiff/prosecution motion to dismiss the affirmative defense as a matter of law. In a civil case, the plaintiff may also move for a directed verdict against the defendant. In a criminal case, the prosecution may not receive a judgment as a matter of law due to a defendant's Sixth Amendment jury right.

Rebuttal and Surrebuttal. The plaintiff/prosecutor may now offer rebuttal evidence, but this evidence is confined to responding to the defendant's evidence. Likewise, a judge may allow the defendant to offer surrebuttal evidence, which is again limited to evidence that responds to the plaintiff/prosecutor's rebuttal evidence.

Directed Verdict Motions. After each party has finally rested its case, either party in a civil case and the defendant in a criminal case may move for a directed verdict on the whole case or on specific issues, such as affirmative defenses.

Closing Arguments. Normally, the party with the burden of proof offers the first closing argument. Defendant follows, and then the plaintiff/prosecutor ordinarily is given an opportunity for a rebuttal. The goal of the closing argument is to sum up the evidence for the jury, so every argument by counsel must be supported by evidence in the record. In the closing argument, the advocate is free to argue interpretations of the evidence in order to convince the jury that their narrative is the correct one. Therefore, the advocate urges the jury to accept her view of the appropriate inferences presented by the evidence.

Jury Instructions. As the jury is the fact finder in a case, the judge will instruct the jury on the application of law (substantive, procedural, evidentiary) to fact in the case. The parties will often submit proposed jury instructions to the judge, but it is the judge who determines how the jury will be instructed. If they disagree with the judge's charge, attorneys may object to the charge.

Jury Deliberations. The jury then deliberates in secrecy. Usually, the jurors may examine exhibits in the jury room. Should they wish to review testimony, a judge will typically call them back into the jury room and have the transcript of the testimony read to the jurors. Should they have questions about the jury instructions, they may ask the judge their questions.

The jury may be asked to reach a general verdict or a special verdict. The general verdict, as the name implies, asks the jury to decide who wins and, if applicable, what remedy should result. A special verdict answers a series of questions crafted by the judge; the court will use the answers to the questions to determine the verdict.

Post-Trial Motions and Entry of Judgment. The loser in a civil case, as well as a criminal defendant who loses her case, may move for a judgment as a matter of law or for a new trial. After ruling on this motion, the court will enter judgment on the verdict, which is an appealable order for any type of party except for the government in criminal cases.

III. Witnesses

As mentioned previously, a party can present different types of evidence: witness testimony, real evidence, demonstrative evidence, stipulations between the parties, and facts that are judicially noticed by the court may all be used as long as they are admissible pursuant to the rules of evidence. How advocates elicit testimony from witnesses will be a major focus of the chapters to come. Initially, we need to focus on what qualifies a witness to testify. FRE 601, 602, and 603 set forth the threshold mandates that allow a witness to testify.

A. Competency

Relevant Rule[1]
FRE 601

Competency to Testify in General

Every person is competent to be a witness unless these rules provide otherwise. But in a civil case, state law governs the witness's competency regarding a claim or defense for which state law supplies the rule of decision.

The FRE sets a very low threshold for competency: almost any witness with relevant testimony will be deemed competent. Almost all matters that call into question the witness' *credibility* (e.g., "how could she see that far without her glasses?" or "she was inebriated at the time she witnessed the accident, so I don't trust her testimony") are matters of *weight rather than admissibility*. This is a crucial concept in evidence. Just because we have very good reason to question the veracity or accuracy of testimony does not mean that the witness is silenced. Instead, those issues of veracity or accuracy are left for cross-examination, where an able advocate can illuminate those issues for the jury. Consider it the "Gazelle Theory": all evidence that merits little weight (i.e., the slow-moving gazelles) will be exposed on cross-examination (i.e., devoured by the predator).

So, you may be asking, can a mental incompetent testify? Can a four-year-old child testify? The answer is generally "yes," as long as the witness meets the mandates of FRE 602 (possess personal knowledge) and 603 (ability to take an oath to be truthful) and is minimally capable of observing, recalling, and communicating the source of their testimony. A judge will typically question a witness outside the presence of a jury in order to establish that the threshold for competency is met.

The FRE do provide some limitations to the general rule that those who can perceive, recollect, and communicate can testify. For example, FRE 605 prevents the judge who is presiding at trial to testify. Similarly, FRE 606(a) prevents a member of the jury from testifying at the trial. The second sentence of FRE 601 also presents a limitation as to who may be competent to testify. FRE 601 mandates that *state* competency law, rather than the FRE rules on competency, apply when (i) the issue arises in a civil action, (ii) the issue concerns an element of a claim or defense, and (iii) the claim or defense is one as to which state law applies the applicable substantive rule. Essentially, this is an application of the *Erie* doctrine — in a civil action brought in federal court under diversity jurisdiction the state's competency rules apply. We will not focus on state exceptions to

---

1. In 2011, the Federal Rules of Evidence were "restyled" in an effort to simplify them, clarify them, and make them more uniform. No substantive changes were meant to be undertaken; the changes were meant to be stylistic only. Obviously, all pre-2011 case law applied the "old" version of the Federal Rules of Evidence. **Thus, do not be surprised if FRE language cited in a case differs from the FRE included in the text.** Despite the differing language, the foundational elements of a given FRE remain the same, as the intent of the drafters of the restyled FRE was not to change the substance of the FRE.

competency in this book, in part because most state competency law mirrors that of the FRE.

Problem 1-1

Allen J., a fifteen year-old male, was charged with aggravated sexual abuse for allegedly raping his then twelve-year-old cousin. Prior to trial, Allen J. filed a motion challenging the victim's competence to testify and requesting a competency examination. In the motion, Allen J. offered documents indicating that the victim may have suffered from Fetal Alcohol Syndrome and mild retardation or learning disabilities. The first document (from an unknown source) stated that the victim had learning disabilities and had to repeat the first grade and that her mother drank frequently during her pregnancy. The second document was a report by a pediatrician, in which the doctor mentioned that the victim suffered from developmental delay and mild mental retardation, although she could not conclude that those problems resulted from Fetal Alcohol Syndrome. Both documents were completed several years before the trial.

In reviewing the motion, the district court judge stated that even if the then thirteen year-old victim had a minor learning disability, she would be at least as capable of testifying as much younger children who had testified in previous cases before the court. Allen J.'s attorney suggested a competency examination was necessary because the victim had poor verbal skills and could not accurately relate what took place the evening of the alleged rape. The court asked the government's case agent, who had interviewed the victim, if he had any trouble understanding her, to which the case agent said he did not. The judge then denied the defendant's motion.

During trial, the court asked the victim a series of questions seeking to confirm she understood the importance of the oath, such as, "Do you know the difference between the truth and a lie?" However, the victim did not respond to the judge's questioning. The court then asked the prosecutor to try questioning the witness. The victim gave correct answers to simple questions such as "What is your name?" and "Where do you live?" The prosecutor then asked the victim a series of questions, which established the victim knew the difference between a truth and a lie, knew she was to tell the truth in court, and knew she would be punished if she told a lie. However, the victim had difficulty responding to some of the prosecutor's questions. For instance, she paused for long periods of time before answering certain questions. She also gave wrong answers to some questions (e.g., she said she was eleven when she was thirteen) and nonsensical answers to others (e.g., when asked, "Is it good or bad to tell a lie?" she answered, "True").

Allen J. was found guilty. On appeal, he argued that the district court erred in finding the victim competent to testify. How should the appeals court have ruled?

Problem 1-2

In 1998, a fire started in a home at 528 Buckeye Street in Toledo, Ohio. Prior to the fire the Amersons had lived in the home for a number of years. The week before the fire the family had purchased two Black and Decker battery chargers.

The Monday after the chargers were hooked up to their space heater, Mr. Amerson turned on the heater and went to work. Mrs. Amerson remained at home with their children, Nathaniel (who was five years-old) and Samuel (who was three years-old). Sometime within the next two hours a fire broke out within the home. Mrs. Amerson was able to escape with her children unscathed, but the home was destroyed by the fire.

Four days after the fire, Investigator Sbrocchi spoke to Samuel and Nathaniel about what they remembered about it. Investigator Sbrocchi was not diligent in his note taking and did not write in his report the specific responses of each child.

The Amersons sued Black and Decker for selling faulty batteries, and, three years after the fire, the case went to trial. Samuel and Nathaniel were both questioned separately to establish if they were competent to testify. Both children were able to correctly tell their ages, the names of their teachers, and where they attended school. They also both told the court that it was wrong to tell a lie, and, when asked if it would be a lie to say that the judge was wearing a blue robe (she was wearing a black robe), they both responded that that would be a lie. When asked specifically about the fire, both Samuel and Nathaniel were only able to provide vague answers and sometimes gave inconsistent answers about details that had previously been given to fire investigators and were stipulated to by both parties.

Ohio state law applied in this case. Ohio state law looks to the following factors to assess a child's competency: (1) the child's ability to receive accurate impressions of fact or to observe acts about which he or she will testify, (2) the child's ability to recollect those impressions or observations, (3) the child's ability to communicate what was observed, (4) the child's understanding of truth and falsity, and (5) the child's appreciation of his or her responsibility to be truthful. Based on this standard, should the children be allowed to testify?

B. Personal Knowledge

Relevant Rule
FRE 602

Need for Personal Knowledge

A witness may testify to a matter only if evidence is introduced sufficient to support a finding that the witness has personal knowledge of the matter. Evidence to prove personal knowledge may consist of the witness's own testimony. This rule does not apply to a witness's expert testimony under Rule 703.

A witness can only testify as to a matter if she has personal knowledge of the matter obtained through one or more of her senses. Thus, seeing a light turn red, hearing a car screeching its brakes or feeling a rear end collision will all allow a witness to testify as to an accident. One thing the witness is not permitted to do is *speculate*. Thus, hearing the screeching sound of a car's brakes will not allow the witness to speculate that the driver attempted to run a red light unless the witness in fact saw the red light. Similarly, hearing Sally state, "John just ran a red light!" does not allow the listener/witness to testify that the light was red; it only allows the witness to testify that Sally *said* that John ran a red light because hearing the statement is all the witness perceived.

Personal knowledge also requires that a witness be able to comprehend the event, remember it, and be able to communicate what she perceived. Without these abilities, the proponent of the witness cannot satisfy its burden under FRE 602. As the rule states, the proponent of the witness must introduce evidence "sufficient to support a finding" that the witness has personal knowledge of the matter. What this means is that if a *reasonable juror could believe* that the witness perceived the matter of her testimony and possesses the ability to comprehend, remember and communicate, then the burden is met. We shall encounter this "could a reasonable juror believe" standard repeatedly throughout the FRE, but, for our present purposes, realize that it is a very low threshold. As long as the judge believes that a reasonable juror could reach the conclusion, then the evidence is admissible. Of course, admissibility is not the same as weight. As we have seen, even admissible evidence can be attacked on cross-examination to demonstrate that the evidence should be afforded very little probative value.

Finally, note the exception in the last sentence of FRE 602: FRE 703 sometimes permits an expert to testify based on facts which she did not perceive. As we shall see later in the book, an expert can learn about a matter from examining reports or speaking to eyewitnesses, yet they still may provide an expert opinion on the facts that they learned secondhand.

Problem 1-3

Corporal Robert Frazier, of the United States Army, was charged in military court with conspiracy to steal and larceny of military property of the United States. Frazier had stolen two Claymore Mines (military explosives), two wire and blasting cap sets, and a firing device. At trial, defense counsel focused on Frazier's excellent military character and his benign motivation for committing the crimes (namely, that he intended to sell the items in order to help resolve his mother's financial and medical problems). As part of its case, the defense called Master Sergeant Harold Richards to testify as to Frazier's outstanding military service.

On cross-examination of Richards, the prosecutor elicited Richards' familiarity with the Claymore Mine and its purpose, as follows:

Q: What's [the Claymore Mine] used for?

A: It's for killing people, sir.

[Questions omitted]

Q: Okay, is there a [civilian] counterpart for the Claymore Mine out there?

A: There is no such thing as a counterpart for the Claymore Mine, sir.

Q: So its one and only use is to kill people, is that correct?

A: Yes, sir.

Q: Now let me ask you this: You heard the accused say he was going to sell it?

A: Yes, sir.

Q: What type of people do you sell Claymore Mines to?

Defense Counsel: Objection. That's speculative and it's not something this witness is likely to have knowledge of.

Prosecutor: Your Honor, I think the individual can use his common sense and say.

Defense Counsel: Sir, he's asking him to speculate as to what type of people might make a certain purchase. I don't see that as probative.

Judge: The objection is overruled.

Q: What type of people do you think would have a need for a Claymore Mine out in the civilian world?

A: My own personal opinion, sir, would be anybody that's deranged in the mind to a point to where he wants to do bodily [sic] to something or someone.

Q: Terrorists maybe?

A: A good possibility, sir.

Q: Maybe drug dealers?

A: A good possibility, sir, anybody.

Frazier also objected to the portion of the prosecutor's argument that was based on the disputed portion of the cross-examination. That objection was also overruled. Frazier was convicted and sentenced to a bad-conduct discharge, a three-year confinement, a $500 fine each month for 36 months, and a reduction in rank. Frazier appealed his conviction and sentence to the Court of Military Appeals. He based his appeal specifically on the disputed portion of the cross-examination and the ensuing argument. How should the Court of Appeals have ruled?

C. Oaths and Affirmations

Relevant Rule
FRE 603

Oath or Affirmation to Testify Truthfully

Before testifying, a witness must give an oath or affirmation to testify truthfully. It must be in a form designed to impress that duty on the witness's conscience.

FRE 603 mandates that every witness must give an oath or affirmation prior to testifying. The rule serves two purposes. First, it is meant to "impress … the witness's conscience" in order to stress to the witness the importance of testifying truthfully. Second, it lays the groundwork for a potential perjury prosecution, which requires that a witness falsely testifies after giving an oath or affirmation.

The witness may choose between an "oath," which typically invokes God, or an "affirmation," which invokes a promise to tell the truth without reference to God. If a witness refuses to make the oath or affirmation, their testimony is excluded. Furthermore, if a witness cannot appreciate the oath or affirmation or cannot tell the difference between the truth and lie (e.g., a mental incompetent, a young child, etc.), then a judge may find that the witness is incapable of taking the oath and will exclude the testimony.

Problem 1-4

Wallace Ward was the president of I&O Publishing Company, a mail-order house and publisher located in Boulder City, Nevada. On March 29, 1990, a grand jury indicted Ward of tax evasion and failure to file income tax returns.

At trial, the government presented evidence that despite having substantial income, neither I&O nor Ward filed tax returns or paid income taxes for the years 1983, 1984 and 1985.

Ward represented himself at trial. He made a lengthy opening statement and actively cross-examined government witnesses. Ward maintained his innocence and wished to testify on his own behalf but did not want to take the standard oath because, he said, compelling him to testify under the "truth" oath would "profoundly violate his freedom of belief and run counter to the convictions that are the central theme of all his published books and writings for the past 22 years." Ward, who believed "that honesty is superior to truth," proposed an alternative oath that would read: "Do you affirm to speak with fully integrated Honesty, only with fully integrated Honesty and nothing but fully integrated Honesty?"

Ward offered to take both the standard oath and his oath so that he could testify. The prosecutor was amenable to the compromise, but the district court judge refused to allow it, saying, "The oath or affirmation which has been administered in courts of law throughout the United States to millions of witnesses for hundreds of years should not be required to give way to the defendant's idiosyncratic distinctions between truth and honesty." Consequently, Ward was not permitted to testify. At the close of the government's case, Ward asked once again to testify under his oath, but the judge again refused. As such, Ward did not testify, and he also presented no witnesses. The jury convicted Ward of all counts after an hour's deliberation.

Ward appealed. Assume for the purposes of this question that Ward's beliefs are protected as religious beliefs. Should the trial judge have allowed him to take both oaths?

IV. The Role of the Jury

Relevant Rule
FRE 606(b)

(b) During an Inquiry into the Validity of a Verdict or Indictment.

(1) *Prohibited Testimony or Other Evidence.*

During an inquiry into the validity of a verdict or indictment, a juror may not testify about any statement made or incident that occurred during the jury's deliberations; the effect of anything on that juror's or another juror's vote; or any juror's mental processes concerning the verdict or indictment. The court may not receive a juror's affidavit or evidence of a juror's statement on these matters.

(2) *Exceptions.* A juror may testify about whether:

(A) extraneous prejudicial information was improperly brought to the jury's attention;

(B) an outside influence was improperly brought to bear on any juror; or

(C) a mistake was made in entering the verdict on the verdict form.

FRE 606(b) highlights an important concept inherent throughout evidence law: we should be extremely careful about what evidence we allow the jury to see and hear, but, once that information is before the jury, its deliberations must remain private. But exceptions exist. What is an improper "outside influence"? What "extraneous prejudicial information" would allow a jury to testify about what goes on in the black box of the jury room? *Tanner v. United States* explores these issues.

Focus Questions: *Tanner v. United States*

- The Supreme Court crafted a distinction between external and internal influences. How would you define the difference?

- Create a hypothetical that focuses on an external or internal influence—is there a bright line between the two?

- What rationales does the Court rely on to justify its decision? Try to articulate at least four rationales.

Tanner v. United States

483 U.S. 107 (1987)

O'CONNOR, J., delivered the opinion for a unanimous Court with respect to Parts III and IV and the opinion of the Court with respect to Parts I and II, in which REHNQUIST, C.J., and WHITE, POWELL, and SCALIA, JJ., joined. MARSHALL, J., filed an opinion concurring in part and dissenting in part, in which BRENNAN, BLACKMUN, and STEVENS, JJ., joined.

Justice O'CONNOR delivered the opinion of the Court.

Petitioners William Conover and Anthony Tanner were convicted of conspiring to defraud the United States in violation of 18 U.S.C. § 371, and of committing mail fraud.... Petitioners argue that the District Court erred in refusing to admit juror testimony at a post-verdict hearing on juror intoxication during the trial....

I

The day before petitioners were scheduled to be sentenced, Tanner filed a motion, in which Conover subsequently joined, seeking continuance of the sentencing date, permission to interview jurors, an evidentiary hearing, and a new trial. According to an affidavit accompanying the motion, Tanner's attorney had received an unsolicited telephone call from one of the trial jurors, Vera Asbul. Juror Asbul informed Tanner's attorney that several of the jurors consumed alcohol during the lunch breaks at various times throughout the trial, causing them to sleep through the afternoons. The District Court continued the sentencing date, ordered the parties to file memoranda, and heard argument on the motion to interview jurors. The District Court concluded that juror testimony on intoxication was inadmissible under Federal Rule of Evidence 606(b) to impeach the jury's verdict. The District Court invited petitioners to call any nonjuror witnesses, such as courtroom personnel, in support of the motion for new trial. Tanner's counsel took the stand and testified that he had observed one of the jurors "in a sort of giggly mood" at one point during the trial but did not bring this to anyone's attention at the time.

Earlier in the hearing the judge referred to a conversation between defense counsel and the judge during the trial on the possibility that jurors were sometimes falling asleep. During that extended exchange the judge twice advised counsel to immediately inform the court if they observed jurors being inattentive, and suggested measures the judge would take if he were so informed:

"MR. MILBRATH [defense counsel]: But, in any event, I've noticed over a period of several days that a couple of jurors in particular have been taking long naps during the trial.

"THE COURT: Is that right. Maybe I didn't notice because I was-

"MR. MILBRATH: I imagine the Prosecutors have noticed that a time or two.

"THE COURT: What's your solution?

"MR. MILBRATH: Well, I just think a respectful comment from the Court that if any of them are getting drowsy, they just ask for a break or something might be helpful.

"THE COURT: Well, here's what I have done in the past—and, you have to do it very diplomatically, of course: I once said, I remember, 'I think we'll just let everybody stand up and stretch, it's getting a little sleepy in here,' I said, but that doesn't sound good in the record.

"I'm going to—not going to take on that responsibility. If any of you think you see that happening, ask for a bench conference and come up and tell me about it and I'll figure out what to do about it, and I won't mention who suggested it.

"MR. MILBRATH: All right.

"THE COURT: But, I'm not going to sit here and watch. I'm—among other things, I'm not going to see—this is off the record.

"(Discussion had off the record.)

" … [T]his is a new thing to this jury, and I don't know how interesting it is to them or not; some of them look like they're pretty interested.…

"And, as I say, if you don't think they are, come up and let me know and I'll figure how-either have a recess or-which is more than likely what I would do."

As the judge observed during the hearing, despite the above admonitions counsel did not bring the matter to the court again.

The judge also observed that in the past courtroom employees had alerted him to problems with the jury. "Nothing was brought to my attention in this case about anyone appearing to be intoxicated," the judge stated, adding, "I saw nothing that suggested they were."

Following the hearing the District Court filed an order stating that "[o]n the basis of the admissible evidence offered I specifically find that the motions for leave to interview jurors or for an evidentiary hearing at which jurors would be witnesses is not required or appropriate." The District Court also denied the motion for new trial.

While the appeal of this case was pending before the Eleventh Circuit, petitioners filed another new trial motion based on additional evidence of jury misconduct. In another affidavit, Tanner's attorney stated that he received an unsolicited visit at his residence from a second juror, Daniel Hardy. Despite the fact that the District Court had denied petitioners' motion for leave to interview jurors, two days after Hardy's visit Tanner's attorney arranged for Hardy to be interviewed by two private investigators. The interview was transcribed, sworn to by the juror, and attached to the new trial motion. In the interview Hardy stated that he "felt like … the jury was on one big party." Hardy indicated that seven of the jurors drank alcohol during the noon recess. Four jurors, including

Hardy, consumed between them "a pitcher to three pitchers" of beer during various recesses. Of the three other jurors who were alleged to have consumed alcohol, Hardy stated that on several occasions he observed two jurors having one or two mixed drinks during the lunch recess, and one other juror, who was also the foreperson, having a liter of wine on each of three occasions. Juror Hardy also stated that he and three other jurors smoked marijuana quite regularly during the trial. Moreover, Hardy stated that during the trial he observed one juror ingest cocaine five times and another juror ingest cocaine two or three times. One juror sold a quarter pound of marijuana to another juror during the trial, and took marijuana, cocaine, and drug paraphernalia into the courthouse. Hardy noted that some of the jurors were falling asleep during the trial, and that one of the jurors described himself to Hardy as "flying." Hardy stated that before he visited Tanner's attorney at his residence, no one had contacted him concerning the jury's conduct, and Hardy had not been offered anything in return for his statement. Hardy said that he came forward "to clear my conscience" and "[b]ecause I felt ... that the people on the jury didn't have no business being on the jury. I felt ... that Mr. Tanner should have a better opportunity to get somebody that would review the facts right."

The District Court ... denied petitioners' motion for a new trial.

The Court of Appeals for the Eleventh Circuit affirmed. We granted certiorari, to consider whether the District Court was required to hold an evidentiary hearing, including juror testimony, on juror alcohol and drug use during the trial....

II

Petitioners argue that the District Court erred in not ordering an additional evidentiary hearing at which jurors would testify concerning drug and alcohol use during the trial. Petitioners assert that, contrary to the holdings of the District Court and the Court of Appeals, juror testimony on ingestion of drugs or alcohol during the trial is not barred by Federal Rule of Evidence 606(b). Moreover, petitioners argue that whether or not authorized by Rule 606(b), an evidentiary hearing including juror testimony on drug and alcohol use is compelled by their Sixth Amendment right to trial by a competent jury.

By the beginning of this century, if not earlier, the near-universal and firmly established common-law rule in the United States flatly prohibited the admission of juror testimony to impeach a jury verdict.

Exceptions to the common-law rule were recognized only in situations in which an "extraneous influence," *Mattox v. United States,* 146 U.S. 140, 149 (1892), was alleged to have affected the jury. In *Mattox,* this Court held admissible the testimony of jurors describing how they heard and read prejudicial information not admitted into evidence. The Court allowed juror testimony on influence by outsiders in *Parker v. Gladden,* 385 U.S. 363, 365 (1966) (bailiff's comments on defendant), and *Remmer v. United States,* 347 U.S. 227, 228-230 (1954) (bribe offered to juror). In situations that did not fall into this exception for external influence, however, the Court adhered to the common-law rule against admitting juror testimony to impeach a verdict.

Lower courts used this external/internal distinction to identify those instances in which juror testimony impeaching a verdict would be admissible. The distinction was not based on whether the juror was literally inside or outside the jury room when the alleged irregularity took place; rather, the distinction was based on the nature of the allegation. Clearly a rigid distinction based only on whether the event took place inside or outside the jury room would have been quite unhelpful. For example, under a distinction based on location a juror could not testify concerning a newspaper read inside the jury room.

Instead, of course, this has been considered an external influence about which juror testimony is admissible. Similarly, under a rigid locational distinction jurors could be regularly required to testify after the verdict as to whether they heard and comprehended the judge's instructions, since the charge to the jury takes place outside the jury room. Courts wisely have treated allegations of a juror's inability to hear or comprehend at trial as an internal matter.

Most significant for the present case, however, is the fact that lower federal courts treated allegations of the physical or mental incompetence of a juror as "internal" rather than "external" matters. In *United States v. Dioguardi*, 492 F.2d 70 (2nd Cir. 1974), the defendant Dioguardi received a letter from one of the jurors soon after the trial in which the juror explained that she had "eyes and ears that ... see things before [they] happen," but that her eyes "are only partly open" because "a curse was put upon them some years ago." *Id.,* at 75. Armed with this letter and the opinions of seven psychiatrists that the letter suggested that the juror was suffering from a psychological disorder, Dioguardi sought a new trial or in the alternative an evidentiary hearing on the juror's competence. The District Court denied the motion and the Court of Appeals affirmed. The Court of Appeals noted "[t]he strong policy against any post-verdict inquiry into a juror's state of mind," and observed:

> "The quickness with which jury findings will be set aside when there is proof of tampering or *external* influence, ... parallel the reluctance of courts to inquire into jury deliberations when a verdict is valid on its face.... Such exceptions support rather than undermine the rationale of the rule that possible *internal* abnormalities in a jury will not be inquired into except 'in the gravest and most important cases.'" *Id.,* at 79, n. 12....

Substantial policy considerations support the common-law rule against the admission of jury testimony to impeach a verdict. As early as 1915 this Court explained the necessity of shielding jury deliberations from public scrutiny:

> "[L]et it once be established that verdicts solemnly made and publicly returned into court can be attacked and set aside on the testimony of those who took part in their publication and all verdicts could be, and many would be, followed by an inquiry in the hope of discovering something which might invalidate the finding. Jurors would be harassed and beset by the defeated party in an effort to secure from them evidence of facts which might establish misconduct sufficient to set aside a verdict. If evidence thus secured could be thus used, the result would be to make what was intended to be a private deliberation, the constant subject of public investigation-to the destruction of all frankness and freedom of discussion and conference." *McDonald v. Pless,* 238 U.S. 264, 267-268 (1915)....

There is little doubt that postverdict investigation into juror misconduct would in some instances lead to the invalidation of verdicts reached after irresponsible or improper juror behavior. It is not at all clear, however, that the jury system could survive such efforts to perfect it. Allegations of juror misconduct, incompetency, or inattentiveness, raised for the first time days, weeks, or months after the verdict, seriously disrupt the finality of the process. Moreover, full and frank discussion in the jury room, jurors' willingness to return an unpopular verdict, and the community's trust in a system that relies on the decisions of laypeople would all be undermined by a barrage of postverdict scrutiny of juror conduct....

Petitioners have presented no argument that Rule 606(b) is inapplicable to the juror affidavits and the further inquiry they sought in this case, and, in fact, there appears to be virtually no support for such a proposition. Rather, petitioners argue that substance abuse constitutes an improper "outside influence" about which jurors may testify under Rule 606(b). In our view the language of the Rule cannot easily be stretched to cover this circumstance. However severe their effect and improper their use, drugs or alcohol voluntarily ingested by a juror seems no more an "outside influence" than a virus, poorly prepared food, or a lack of sleep.

In any case, whatever ambiguity might linger in the language of Rule 606(b) as applied to juror intoxication is resolved by the legislative history of the Rule.... The House Judiciary Committee described the effect of the version of Rule 606(b) transmitted by the Court as follows:

> "As proposed by the Court, Rule 606(b) limited testimony by a juror in the course of an inquiry into the validity of a verdict or indictment. He could testify as to the influence of extraneous prejudicial information brought to the jury's attention (e.g. a radio newscast or a newspaper account) or an outside influence which improperly had been brought to bear upon a juror (e.g. a threat to the safety of a member of his family), but he could not testify as to other irregularities which occurred in the jury room. Under this formulation a quotient verdict could not be attacked through the testimony of juror, *nor could a juror testify to the drunken condition of a fellow juror which so disabled him that he could not participate in the jury's deliberations.*" H.R.Rep. No. 93-650, pp. 9-10 (1973), U.S.Code Cong. & Admin.News 1974, p. 7083 (emphasis supplied).

The House Judiciary Committee, persuaded that the better practice was to allow juror testimony on any "objective juror misconduct," amended the Rule so as to comport with the more expansive versions proposed by the Advisory Committee in earlier drafts, and the House passed this amended version.

The Senate Judiciary Committee did not voice any disagreement with the House's interpretation of the Rule proposed by the Court, or the version passed by the House. Indeed, the Senate Report described the House version as "considerably broader" than the version proposed by the Court, and noted that the House version "would permit the impeachment of verdicts by inquiry into, not the mental processes of the jurors, but what happened in terms of conduct in the jury room." S.Rep. No. 93-1277, p. 13 (1974), U.S.Code Cong. & Admin.News 1974, p. 7060. With this understanding of the differences between the two versions of Rule 606(b)—an understanding identical to that of the House—the Senate decided to reject the broader House version and adopt the narrower version approved by the Court. The Senate Report explained:

> "[The House version's] extension of the ability to impeach a verdict is felt to be unwarranted and ill-advised.

> "The rule passed by the House embodies a suggestion by the Advisory Committee of the Judicial Conference that is considerably broader than the final version adopted by the Supreme Court, which embodied long-accepted Federal law. Although forbidding the impeachment of verdicts by inquiry into the jurors' mental processes, it deletes from the Supreme Court version the proscription against testimony 'as to any matter or statement occurring during the course of the jury's deliberations.' This deletion would have the effect of opening verdicts up to challenge on the basis of what happened during the jury's internal deliberations, for example, where a juror alleged that the jury refused to follow the trial judge's instructions or that some of the jurors did not take part in deliberations.

"Permitting an individual to attack a jury verdict based upon the jury's internal deliberations has long been recognized as unwise by the Supreme Court....

"As it stands then, the rule would permit the harassment of former jurors by losing parties as well as the possible exploitation of disgruntled or otherwise badly-motivated ex-jurors.

"Public policy requires a finality to litigation. And common fairness requires that absolute privacy be preserved for jurors to engage in the full and free debate necessary to the attainment of just verdicts. Jurors will not be able to function effectively if their deliberations are to be scrutinized in post-trial litigation. In the interest of protecting the jury system and the citizens who make it work, rule 606 should not permit any inquiry into the internal deliberations of the jurors." *Id.,* at 13-14, U.S.Code Cong. & Admin.News 1974, p. 7060.

The Conference Committee Report reaffirms Congress' understanding of the differences between the House and Senate versions of Rule 606(b): "[T]he House bill allows a juror to testify about objective matters occurring during the jury's deliberation, such as the misconduct of another juror or the reaching of a quotient verdict. The Senate bill does not permit juror testimony about any matter or statement occurring during the course of the jury's deliberations." H.R.Conf.Rep. No. 93-1597, p. 8 (1974), U.S.Code Cong. & Admin.News 1974, p. 7102. The Conference Committee adopted, and Congress enacted, the Senate version of Rule 606(b).

Thus, the legislative history demonstrates with uncommon clarity that Congress specifically understood, considered, and rejected a version of Rule 606(b) that would have allowed jurors to testify on juror conduct during deliberations, including juror intoxication. This legislative history provides strong support for the most reasonable reading of the language of Rule 606(b)—that juror intoxication is not an "outside influence" about which jurors may testify to impeach their verdict....

Petitioners also argue that the refusal to hold an additional evidentiary hearing at which jurors would testify as to their conduct "violates the sixth amendment's guarantee to a fair trial before an impartial and *competent* jury." Brief for Petitioners 34 (emphasis in original).

This Court has recognized that a defendant has a right to "a tribunal both impartial and mentally competent to afford a hearing." *Jordan v. Massachusetts,* 225 U.S. 167 (1912)....

Petitioners' Sixth Amendment interests in an unimpaired jury ... are protected by several aspects of the trial process. The suitability of an individual for the responsibility of jury service, of course, is examined during *voir dire.* Moreover, during the trial the jury is observable by the court, by counsel, and by court personnel. See *United States v. Provenzano,* 620 F.2d 985, 996-997 (3rd Cir. 1980) (marshal discovered sequestered juror smoking marijuana during early morning hours). Moreover, jurors are observable by each other, and may report inappropriate juror behavior to the court *before* they render a verdict. See *Lee v. United States,* 454 A.2d 770 (DC App.1982), cert. denied *sub nom. McIlwain v. United States,* 464 U.S. 972 (1983) (on second day of deliberations, jurors sent judge a note suggesting that foreperson was incapacitated). Finally, after the trial a party may seek to impeach the verdict by nonjuror evidence of misconduct. See *United States v. Taliaferro,* 558 F.2d 724, 725-726 (4th Cir. 1977) (court considered records of club where jurors dined, and testimony of marshal who accompanied jurors, to determine whether jurors were intoxicated during deliberations). Indeed, in this case the District Court held an evidentiary hearing giving petitioners ample opportunity to produce nonjuror evidence supporting their allegations.

In light of these other sources of protection of petitioners' right to a competent jury, we conclude that the District Court did not err in deciding, based on the inadmissibility of juror testimony and the clear insufficiency of the nonjuror evidence offered by petitioners, that an additional post-verdict evidentiary hearing was unnecessary....

Justice MARSHALL, with whom Justice BRENNAN, Justice BLACKMUN, and Justice STEVENS join, concurring in part and dissenting in part....

Every criminal defendant has a constitutional right to be tried by competent jurors. This Court has long recognized that "[d]ue process implies a tribunal both impartial and mentally competent to afford a hearing," *Jordan v. Massachusetts*, 225 U.S. 167 (1912), "a jury capable and willing to decide the case solely on the evidence before it." *Smith v. Phillips*, 455 U.S. 209, 217 (1982). If, as is charged, members of petitioners' jury were intoxicated as a result of their use of drugs and alcohol to the point of sleeping through material portions of the trial, the verdict in this case must be set aside. In directing district courts to ignore sworn allegations that jurors engaged in gross and debilitating misconduct, this Court denigrates the precious right to a competent jury. Accordingly, I dissent from that part of the Court's opinion....

II

Despite the seriousness of the charges, the Court refuses to allow petitioners an opportunity to vindicate their fundamental right to a competent jury. The Court holds that petitioners are absolutely barred from exploring allegations of juror misconduct and incompetency through the only means available to them—examination of the jurors who have already voluntarily come forward. The basis for the Court's ruling is the mistaken belief that juror testimony concerning drug and alcohol abuse at trial is inadmissible under Federal Rule of Evidence 606(b) and is contrary to the policies the Rule was intended to advance.

I readily acknowledge the important policy considerations supporting the common-law rule against admission of jury testimony to impeach a verdict, now embodied in Federal Rule of Evidence 606(b): freedom of deliberation, finality of verdicts, and protection of jurors against harassment by dissatisfied litigants. It has been simultaneously recognized, however, that "simply putting verdicts beyond effective reach can only promote irregularity and injustice." If the above-referenced policy considerations seriously threaten the constitutional right to trial by a fair and impartial jury, they must give way.

In this case, however, we are not faced with a conflict between the policy considerations underlying Rule 606(b) and petitioners' Sixth Amendment rights. Rule 606(b) is not applicable to juror testimony on matters *unrelated* to the jury's deliberations. By its terms, Rule 606(b) renders jurors incompetent to testify only as to three subjects: (i) any "matter or statement" occurring during deliberations; (ii) the "effect" of anything upon the "mind or emotions" of any juror as it relates to his or her "assent to or dissent from the verdict"; and (iii) the "mental processes" of the juror in connection with his "assent to or dissent from the verdict." ...

The Court's analysis of legislative history confirms the inapplicability of Rule 606(b) to the type of misconduct alleged in this case. As the Court emphasizes, the debate over two proposed versions of the Rule—the more restrictive Senate version ultimately adopted and the permissive House version ... focused on the extent to which jurors would be permitted to testify as to what transpired *during the course of the deliberations themselves*. Similarly, the Conference Committee Report ... compares the two versions solely in terms of the admissibility of testimony as to matters occurring during, or relating to, the jury's deliberations: "[T]he House bill allows a juror to testify about objective matters occurring during the jury's deliberation, such as the misconduct of another juror or the reaching of a quotient verdict. The Senate bill does not permit juror testimony about any matter or statement occurring *during the course of the jury's deliberations.*" H.R.Conf.Rep. No. 93-1597, p. 8 (1974), U.S.Code Cong. & Admin.News 1974, p. 7102 (emphasis added). The obvious conclusion ... is that *both* versions of Rule 606(b) would have permitted jurors to testify as to matters not involving deliberations. The House Report's passing reference to juror intoxication during deliberations is not to the contrary. Reflecting Congress' consistent focus on the deliberative process, it suggests only that the authors of the House Report believed that the Senate version of Rule 606(b) did not allow testimony as to juror intoxication during deliberations.

In this case, no invasion of the jury deliberations is contemplated. Permitting a limited postverdict inquiry into juror consumption of alcohol and drugs *during trial* would not "make what was intended to be a private deliberation, the constant subject of public investigation-to the destruction of all frankness and freedom of discussion and conference." *McDonald v. Pless,* 238 U.S., at 267-268 ... "Allowing [jurors] to testify as to matters other than their own inner reactions involves no particular hazard to the values sought to be protected." Advisory Committee's Notes of Fed.Rule Evid. 606(b), 28 U.S.C.App., p. 701.

Even if I agreed with the Court's expansive construction of Rule 606(b), I would nonetheless find the testimony of juror intoxication admissible under the Rule's "outside influence" exception. As a common-sense matter, drugs and alcohol *are* outside influences on jury members.... The Court suggests that, if these are outside influences, "a virus, poorly prepared food, or a lack of sleep" would also qualify. Distinguishing between a virus, for example, and a narcotic drug is a matter of line-drawing. Courts are asked to make these sorts of distinctions in numerous contexts; I have no doubt they would be capable of differentiating between the intoxicants involved in this case and minor indispositions not affecting juror competency....

III

The Court acknowledges that "postverdict investigation into juror misconduct would in some instances lead to the invalidation of verdicts reached after irresponsible or improper juror behavior," but maintains that "[i]t is not at all clear ... that the jury system could survive such efforts to perfect it." Petitioners are not asking for a perfect jury. They are seeking to determine whether the jury that heard their case behaved in a manner consonant with the minimum requirements of the Sixth Amendment. If we deny them this opportunity, the jury system may survive, but the constitutional guarantee on which it is based will become meaningless.

I dissent.

Focus Questions: *Pena-Rodriguez v. Colorado*

- According to the majority opinion, how is this case distinguishable from *Tanner* and *Warger*? Why do those cases not risk "systemic injury to the administration of justice" in a similar manner to this case?

- How can an attorney root out potential racial bias in a jury? What methods would work best? What risks exist for the attorney who explores these issues with the jury?

- How much discretion does the majority opinion give to a trial court judge?

Pena-Rodriguez v. Colorado
580 U.S. ___ (2017)

KENNEDY, J., delivered the opinion of the Court, in which GINSBURG, BREYER, SO-TOMAYOR, and KAGAN, JJ., joined. THOMAS, J., filed a dissenting opinion. ALITO, J., filed a dissenting opinion, in which ROBERTS, C. J., and THOMAS, J., joined.

The jury is a central foundation of our justice system and our democracy. Whatever its imperfections in a particular case, the jury is a necessary check on governmental power. The jury, over the centuries, has been an inspired, trusted, and effective instrument for resolving factual disputes and determining ultimate questions of guilt or innocence in criminal cases. Over the long course its judgments find acceptance in the community, an acceptance essential to respect for the rule of law. The jury is a tangible implementation of the principle that the law comes from the people....

Like all human institutions, the jury system has its flaws, yet experience shows that fair and impartial verdicts can be reached if the jury follows the court's instructions and undertakes deliberations that are honest, candid, robust, and based on common sense. A general rule has evolved to give substantial protection to verdict finality and to assure jurors that, once their verdict has been entered, it will not later be called into question based on the comments or conclusions they expressed during deliberations. This principle, itself centuries old, is often referred to as the no-impeachment rule. The instant case presents the question whether there is an exception to the no-impeachment rule when, after the jury is discharged, a juror comes forward with compelling evidence that another juror made clear and explicit statements indicating that racial animus was a significant motivating factor in his or her vote to convict.

I

State prosecutors in Colorado brought criminal charges against petitioner, Miguel Angel Peña-Rodriguez, [alleging that he] ... sexually assaulted two teenage sisters.... .The State charged petitioner with harassment, unlawful sexual contact, and attempted sexual assault on a child. Before the jury was empaneled, members of the venire were repeatedly asked whether they believed that they could be fair and impartial in the case. A written questionnaire asked if there was "anything about you that you feel would make it difficult for you to be a fair juror." The court repeated the question to the panel of prospective jurors and encouraged jurors to speak in private with the court if they had any concerns about their impartiality. Defense counsel likewise asked whether anyone felt that "this is simply not a good case" for them to be a fair juror. None of the empaneled jurors expressed any reservations based on racial or any other bias. And none asked to speak with the trial judge.

After a 3-day trial, the jury found petitioner guilty of unlawful sexual contact and harassment, but it failed to reach a verdict on the attempted sexual assault charge. When the jury was discharged, the court gave them this instruction, as mandated by Colorado law:

> "The question may arise whether you may now discuss this case with the lawyers, defendant, or other persons. For your guidance the court instructs you that whether you talk to anyone is entirely your own decision.... If any person persists in discussing the case over your objection, or becomes critical of your service either before or after any discussion has begun, please report it to me."

Following the discharge of the jury, petitioner's counsel entered the jury room to discuss the trial with the jurors. As the room was emptying, two jurors remained to speak with counsel in private. They stated that, during deliberations, another juror had expressed anti-Hispanic bias toward petitioner and petitioner's alibi witness. Petitioner's counsel reported this to the court and, with the court's supervision, obtained sworn affidavits from the two jurors.

The affidavits by the two jurors described a number of biased statements made by another juror, identified as Juror H. C. According to the two jurors, H. C. told the other jurors that he "believed the defendant was guilty because, in [H. C.'s] experience as an ex-law enforcement officer, Mexican men had a bravado that caused them to believe they could do whatever they wanted with women." The jurors reported that H. C. stated his belief that Mexican men are physically controlling of women because of their sense of entitlement, and further stated, "'I think he did it because he's Mexican and Mexican men take whatever they want.'" According to the jurors, H. C. further explained that, in his experience, "nine times out of ten Mexican men were guilty of being aggressive toward women and young girls." Finally, the jurors recounted that Juror H. C. said that he did not find petitioner's alibi witness credible because, among other things, the witness was "'an illegal.'" (In fact, the witness testified during trial that he was a legal resident of the United States.)

After reviewing the affidavits, the trial court acknowledged H. C.'s apparent bias. But the court denied petitioner's motion for a new trial, noting that "[t]he actual deliberations that occur among the jurors are protected from inquiry under [Colorado Rule of Evidence] 606(b)." Like its federal counterpart, Colorado's Rule 606(b) generally prohibits a juror from testifying as to any statement made during deliberations in a proceeding inquiring into the validity of the verdict. *See* Fed. Rule Evid. 606(b). [The Colorado Court of Appeals and Supreme Court both affirmed the trial court's decision.]....

II

A

At common law jurors were forbidden to impeach their verdict, either by affidavit or live testimony.... The Mansfield rule, as it came to be known, prohibited jurors, after the verdict was entered, from testifying either about their subjective mental processes or about objective events that occurred during deliberations.

American courts adopted the Mansfield rule as a matter of common law, though not in every detail. Some jurisdictions adopted a different, more flexible version of the no-impeachment bar known as the "Iowa rule." Under that rule, jurors were prevented only from testifying about their own subjective beliefs, thoughts, or motives during deliberations. *See Wright* v. *Illinois & Miss. Tel. Co.*, 20 Iowa 195 (1866). Jurors could, however, testify about objective facts and events occurring during deliberations, in part because other jurors could corroborate that testimony.

An alternative approach, later referred to as the federal approach, stayed closer to the original Mansfield rule. *See Warger* [v. *Shauers*, 574 U.S. ___ (2016)]. Under this version of the rule, the no-impeachment bar permitted an exception only for testimony about events extraneous to the deliberative process, such as reliance on outside evidence — newspapers, dictionaries, and the like — or personal investigation of the facts....

The common-law development of the no-impeachment rule reached a milestone in 1975, when Congress adopted the Federal Rules of Evidence, including Rule 606(b). Congress ... rejected the Iowa rule. Instead it endorsed a broad no-impeachment rule, with only limited exceptions....

This version of the no-impeachment rule has substantial merit. It promotes full and vigorous discussion by providing jurors with considerable assurance that after being discharged they will not be summoned to recount their deliberations, and they will not otherwise be harassed or annoyed by litigants seeking to challenge the verdict. The rule gives stability and finality to verdicts....

C

... [S]ince the enactment of Rule 606(b), the Court has addressed the precise question whether the Constitution mandates an exception to it in just two instances.

In its first case, *Tanner* [v. *United States*], 483 U. S. 107 (1987), the Court rejected a Sixth Amendment exception for evidence that some jurors were under the influence of drugs and alcohol during the trial. *Id.*, at 125. Central to the Court's reasoning were the "long-recognized and very substantial concerns" supporting "the protection of jury deliberations from intrusive inquiry." *Id.*, at 127. The *Tanner* Court [expressed] concern that, if attorneys could use juror testimony to attack verdicts, jurors would be "harassed and beset by the defeated party," thus destroying "all frankness and freedom of discussion and conference." 483 U. S., at 120 (quoting *McDonald* v. *Pless*, 238 U.S. 264 (1915)). The Court was concerned, moreover, that attempts to impeach a verdict would "disrupt the finality of the process" and undermine both "jurors' willingness to return an unpopular verdict" and "the community's trust in a system that relies on the decisions of laypeople." 483 U. S., at 120–121.

The *Tanner* Court outlined existing, significant safeguards for the defendant's right to an impartial and competent jury beyond post-trial juror testimony. At the outset of the trial process, *voir dire* provides an opportunity for the court and counsel to examine members of the venire for impartiality. As a trial proceeds, the court, counsel, and court personnel have some opportunity to learn of any juror misconduct. And, before the verdict, jurors themselves can report misconduct to the court. These procedures do not undermine the stability of a verdict once rendered. Even after the trial, evidence of misconduct other than juror testimony can be used to attempt to impeach the verdict. *Id.*, at 127. Balancing these interests and safeguards against the defendant's Sixth Amendment interest in that case, the Court affirmed the exclusion of affidavits pertaining to the jury's inebriated state. *Ibid.*

The second case to consider the general issue presented here was *Warger*. The Court again rejected the argument that, in the circumstances there, the jury trial right required an exception to the no-impeachment rule. *Warger* involved a civil case where, after the verdict was entered, the losing party sought to proffer evidence that the jury forewoman had failed to disclose prodefendant bias during *voir dire*. As in *Tanner*, the Court put substantial reliance on existing safeguards for a fair trial. The Court stated: "Even if jurors lie in *voir dire* in a way that conceals bias, juror impartiality is adequately assured by the parties' ability to bring to the court's attention any evidence of bias before the verdict is rendered, and to employ nonjuror evidence even after the verdict is rendered." 574 U. S., at ___.

In *Warger*, however, the Court did reiterate that the no-impeachment rule may admit exceptions.... [T]he Court warned of "juror bias so extreme that, almost by definition, the jury trial right has been abridged." 574 U. S., at ___–___, n. 3. "If and when such a case arises," the Court indicated it would "consider whether the usual safeguards are or are not sufficient to protect the integrity of the process." *Ibid.*

The recognition in *Warger* that there may be extreme cases where the jury trial right requires an exception to the no-impeachment rule must be interpreted in context as a guarded, cautious statement. This caution is warranted to avoid formulating an exception that might undermine the jury dynamics and finality interests the no-impeachment rule seeks to protect. Today, however, the Court ... must decide whether the Constitution requires an exception to the no-impeachment rule when a juror's statements indicate that racial animus was a significant motivating factor in his or her finding of guilt....

IV

A

This case lies at the intersection of the Court's decisions endorsing the no-impeachment rule and its decisions seeking to eliminate racial bias in the jury system. The two lines of precedent, however, need not conflict.

Racial bias of the kind alleged in this case differs in critical ways from the ... drug and alcohol abuse in *Tanner*, or the pro-defendant bias in *Warger*. The behavior in those cases is troubling and unacceptable, but each involved anomalous behavior from a single jury—or juror—gone off course. Jurors are presumed to follow their oath, and neither history nor common experience show that the jury system is rife with mischief of these or similar kinds. To attempt to rid the jury of every irregularity of this sort would be to expose it to unrelenting scrutiny. "It is not at all clear ... that the jury system could survive such efforts to perfect it." *Tanner*, 483 U. S., at 120.

The same cannot be said about racial bias, a familiar and recurring evil that, if left unaddressed, would risk systemic injury to the administration of justice. This Court's decisions demonstrate that racial bias implicates unique historical, constitutional, and institutional concerns. An effort to address the most grave and serious statements of racial bias is not an effort to perfect the jury but to ensure that our legal system remains capable of coming ever closer to the promise of equal treatment under the law that is so central to a functioning democracy.

Racial bias is distinct in a pragmatic sense as well. In past cases this Court has relied on other safeguards to protect the right to an impartial jury. Some of those safeguards, to be sure, can disclose racial bias. *Voir dire* at the outset of trial, observation of juror demeanor and conduct during trial, juror reports before the verdict, and nonjuror evidence after trial are important mechanisms for discovering bias. Yet their operation may be compromised, or they may prove insufficient. For instance, this Court has noted the dilemma faced by trial court judges and counsel in deciding whether to explore potential racial bias at *voir dire*. See *Rosales-Lopez*, 451 U.S. 182 (1981); *Ristaino* v. *Ross*, 424 U. S. 589 (1976). Generic questions about juror impartiality may not expose specific attitudes or biases that can poison jury deliberations. Yet more pointed questions "could well exacerbate whatever prejudice might exist without substantially aiding in exposing it." *Rosales-Lopez, supra*, at 195 (Rehnquist, J., concurring in result).

The stigma that attends racial bias may make it difficult for a juror to report inappropriate statements during the course of juror deliberations. It is one thing to accuse a fellow juror of having a personal experience that improperly influences her consideration of the case, as would have been required in *Warger*. It is quite another to call her a bigot.

The recognition that certain of the *Tanner* safeguards may be less effective in rooting out racial bias than other kinds of bias is not dispositive. All forms of improper bias pose challenges to the trial process. But there is a sound basis to treat racial bias with added precaution. A constitutional rule that racial bias in the justice system must be addressed—including, in some instances, after the verdict has been entered—is necessary to prevent a systemic loss of confidence in jury verdicts, a confidence that is a central premise of the Sixth Amendment trial right.

B

For the reasons explained above, the Court now holds that where a juror makes a clear statement that indicates he or she relied on racial stereotypes or animus to convict a criminal defendant, the Sixth Amendment requires that the no-impeachment rule give way in order to permit the trial court to consider the evidence of the juror's statement and any resulting denial of the jury trial guarantee.

Not every offhand comment indicating racial bias or hostility will justify setting aside the no-impeachment bar to allow further judicial inquiry. For the inquiry to proceed, there must be a showing that one or more jurors made statements exhibiting overt racial bias that cast serious doubt on the fairness and impartiality of the jury's deliberations and resulting verdict. To qualify, the statement must tend to show that racial animus was a significant motivating factor in the juror's vote to convict. Whether that threshold showing has been satisfied is a matter committed to the substantial discretion of the trial court in light of all the circumstances, including the content and timing of the alleged statements and the reliability of the proffered evidence.

The practical mechanics of acquiring and presenting such evidence will no doubt be shaped and guided by state rules of professional ethics and local court rules, both of which often limit counsel's post-trial contact with jurors. These limits seek to provide jurors some protection when they return to their daily affairs after the verdict has been entered. But while a juror can always tell counsel they do not wish to discuss the case, jurors in some instances may come forward of their own accord.

That is what happened here. In this case the alleged statements by a juror were egregious and unmistakable in their reliance on racial bias. Not only did juror H. C. deploy a dangerous racial stereotype to conclude petitioner was guilty and his alibi witness should not be believed, but he also encouraged other jurors to join him in convicting on that basis....

D

It is proper to observe as well that there are standard and existing processes designed to prevent racial bias injury deliberations. The advantages of careful *voir dire* have already been noted. And other safeguards deserve mention. Trial courts, often at the outset of the case and again in their final jury instructions, explain the jurors' duty to review the evidence and reach a verdict in a fair and impartial way, free from bias of any kind. Some instructions are framed by trial judges based on their own learning and experience. Model jury instructions likely take into account these continuing developments and are common across jurisdictions. Instructions may emphasize the group dynamic of deliberations by urging jurors to share their questions and conclusions with their colleagues.

Probing and thoughtful deliberation improves the likelihood that other jurors can confront the flawed nature of reasoning that is prompted or influenced by improper biases, whether racial or otherwise. These dynamics can help ensure that the exception is limited to rare cases.

* * *

The Nation must continue to make strides to overcome race-based discrimination. The progress that has already been made underlies the Court's insistence that blatant racial prejudice is antithetical to the functioning of the jury system and must be confronted in egregious cases like this one despite the general bar of the no-impeachment rule. It is the mark of a maturing legal system that it seeks to understand and to implement the lessons of history. The Court now seeks to strengthen the broader principle that society can and must move forward by achieving the thoughtful, rational dialogue at the foundation of both the jury system and the free society that sustains our Constitution. The judgment of the Supreme Court of Colorado is reversed, and the case is remanded for further proceedings not inconsistent with this opinion.

It is so ordered

Justice ALITO, with whom Chief Justice ROBERTS and Justice THOMAS joins, dissenting.

...

II

A

... Today, for the first time, the Court creates a constitutional exception to no-impeachment rules. Specifically, the Court holds that no-impeachment rules violate the Sixth Amendment to the extent that they preclude courts from considering evidence of a juror's racially biased comments. The Court attempts to distinguish *Tanner* and *Warger*, but its efforts fail.

Tanner and *Warger* rested on two basic propositions. First, no-impeachment rules advance crucial interests. Second, the right to trial by an impartial jury is adequately protected by mechanisms other than the use of juror testimony regarding jury deliberations. The first of these propositions applies regardless of the nature of the juror misconduct, and the Court does not argue otherwise. Instead, it contends that, in cases involving racially biased jurors, the *Tanner* safeguards are less effective and the defendant's Sixth Amendment interests are more profound. Neither argument is persuasive.

B

... *Tanner* identified four "aspects of the trial process" that protect a defendant's Sixth Amendment rights: (1) *voir dire*; (2) observation by the court, counsel, and court personnel; (3) pre-verdict reports by the jurors; and (4) non-juror evidence. 483 U. S., at 127. Although the Court insists that that these mechanisms "may be compromised" in cases involving allegations of racial bias, it addresses only two of them and fails to make a sustained argument about either.

1

First, the Court contends that the effectiveness of *voir dire* is questionable in cases involving racial bias because pointed questioning about racial attitudes may highlight racial issues and thereby exacerbate prejudice. It is far from clear, however, that careful *voir dire* cannot surmount this problem. Lawyers may use questionnaires or individual questioning of prospective jurors in order to elicit frank answers that a juror might be reluctant to voice in the presence of other prospective jurors. Moreover, practice guides are replete with advice on conducting effective *voir dire* on the subject of race. They outline a variety of subtle and nuanced approaches that avoid pointed questions. And of course, if an attorney is concerned that a juror is concealing bias, a peremptory strike may be used.

The suggestion that *voir dire* is ineffective in unearthing bias runs counter to decisions of this Court holding that *voir dire* on the subject of race is constitutionally required in some cases, mandated as a matter of federal supervisory authority in others, and typically advisable in any case if a defendant requests it. *See Turner* v. *Murray*, 476 U. S. 28, 36–37 (1986). If *voir dire* were not useful in identifying racial prejudice, those decisions would be pointless. Even the majority recognizes the "advantages of careful *voir dire*" as a "proces[s] designed to prevent racial bias in jury deliberations." And reported decisions substantiate that *voir dire* can be effective in this regard. *E.g., Brewer* v. *Marshall,* 119 F. 3d 993, 995–996 (1st Cir. 1997). Thus, while *voir dire* is not a magic cure, there are good reasons to think that it is a valuable tool.

In any event, the critical point for present purposes is that the effectiveness of *voir dire* is a debatable empirical proposition. Its assessment should be addressed in the process of developing federal and state evidence rules. Federal and state rulemakers can try a variety of approaches, and they can make changes in response to the insights provided by experience and research. The approach taken by today's majority—imposing a federal constitutional rule on the entire country—prevents experimentation and makes change exceedingly hard.

2

The majority also argues—even more cursorily—that "racial bias may make it difficult for a juror to report inappropriate statements during the course of juror deliberations." This is so, we are told, because it is difficult to "call [another juror] a bigot."

Since the Court's decision mandates the admission of the testimony of one juror about a statement made by another juror during deliberations, what the Court must mean in making this argument is that jurors are less willing to report biased comments by fellow jurors prior to the beginning of deliberations (while they are still sitting with the biased juror) than they are after the verdict is announced and the jurors have gone home. But this is also a questionable empirical assessment, and the Court's seat-of-the-pants judgment is no better than that of those with the responsibility of drafting and adopting federal and state evidence rules. There is no question that jurors *do* report biased comments made by fellow jurors prior to the beginning of deliberations. *See, e.g., United States* v. *McClinton,* 135 F. 3d 1178, 1184–1185 (7th Cir. 1998). And the Court marshals no evidence that such pre-deliberation reporting is rarer than the post-verdict variety.

Even if there is something to the distinction that the Court makes between pre- and post-verdict reporting, it is debatable whether the difference is significant enough to merit different treatment. This is especially so because post-verdict reporting is both more disruptive and may be the result of extraneous influences. A juror who is initially in the minority but is ultimately persuaded by other jurors may have second thoughts after the verdict is announced and may be angry with others on the panel who pressed for unanimity. In addition, if a verdict is unpopular with a particular juror's family, friends, employer, coworkers, or neighbors, the juror may regret his or her vote and may feel pressured to rectify what the jury has done.

In short, the Court provides no good reason to depart from the calculus made in *Tanner* and *Warger*....

III
A

The real thrust of the majority opinion is that the Constitution is less tolerant of racial bias than other forms of juror misconduct, but it is hard to square this argument with the nature of the Sixth Amendment right on which petitioner's argument and the Court's holding are based. What the Sixth Amendment protects is the right to an "impartial jury." Nothing in the text or history of the Amendment or in the inherent nature of the jury trial right suggests that the extent of the protection provided by the Amendment depends on the nature of a jury's partiality or bias. As the Colorado Supreme Court aptly put it, it is hard to "discern a dividing line between different *types* of juror bias or misconduct, whereby one form of partiality would implicate a party's Sixth Amendment right while another would not." 350 P. 3d 287, 293 17 (2015).

Nor has the Court found any decision of this Court suggesting that the Sixth Amendment recognizes some sort of hierarchy of partiality or bias. The Court points to a line of cases holding that, in some narrow circumstances, the Constitution requires trial courts to conduct *voir dire* on the subject of race. Those decisions, however, were not based on a ranking of types of partiality but on the Court's conclusion that in certain cases racial bias was especially likely. See *Ristaino*, 424 U. S., at 596 (explaining that the requirement applies only if there is a "constitutionally significant likelihood that, absent questioning about racial prejudice, the jurors would not be [impartial]"). Thus, this line of cases does not advance the majority's argument.

It is undoubtedly true that "racial bias implicates unique historical, constitutional, and institutional concerns." But it is hard to see what that has to do with the scope of an *individual criminal defendant's* Sixth Amendment right to be judged impartially. The Court's efforts to reconcile its decision with ... *Tanner* and *Warger* illustrate the problem. The Court writes that the misconduct in those cases, while "troubling and unacceptable," was "anomalous." By contrast, racial bias, the Court says, is a "familiar and recurring evil" that causes "systemic injury to the administration of justice."

Imagine two cellmates serving lengthy prison terms. Both were convicted for homicides committed in unrelated barroom fights. At the trial of the first prisoner, a juror, during deliberations, expressed animosity toward the defendant because of his race. At the trial of the second prisoner, a juror, during deliberations, expressed animosity toward the defendant because he was wearing the jersey of a hated football team. In both cases, jurors come forward after the trial and reveal what the biased juror said in the jury room. The Court would say to the first prisoner: "You are entitled to introduce the jurors' testimony, because racial bias is damaging to our society." To the second, the Court would say: "Even if you did not have an impartial jury, you must stay in prison because sports rivalries are not a major societal issue."

This disparate treatment is unsupportable under the Sixth Amendment. If the Sixth Amendment requires the admission of juror testimony about statements or conduct during deliberations that show one type of juror partiality, then statements or conduct showing any type of partiality should be treated the same way....

IV

Today's decision—especially if it is expanded in the ways that seem likely—will invite the harms that no-impeachment rules were designed to prevent. First, as the Court explained in *Tanner*, "postverdict scrutiny of juror conduct" will inhibit "full and frank discussion in the jury room." 483 U. S., at 120–121....

Today's ruling will also prompt losing parties and their friends, supporters, and attorneys to contact and seek to question jurors, and this pestering may erode citizens' willingness to serve on juries.... Where post-verdict approaches are permitted or occur, there is almost certain to be an increase in harassment, arm-twisting, and outright coercion.... The majority's approach will also undermine the finality of verdicts.... And accusations of juror bias—which may be "raised for the first time days, weeks, or months after the verdict"—can "seriously disrupt the finality of the process." *Tanner, supra*, at 120..... .

In short, the majority barely bothers to engage with the policy issues implicated by no-impeachment rules. But even if it had carefully grappled with those issues, it still would have no basis for exalting its own judgment over that of the many expert policymakers who have endorsed broad no-impeachment rules.... I respectfully dissent.

[Dissenting Opinion of Thomas, J., omitted.]

V. Shortcuts to Proof

When a fact is not subject to reasonable dispute, judicial efficiency is served by entering the fact into evidence through less formal means than witness testimony, real evidence, and/or demonstrative evidence. In other words, there is no need to waste the time and resources of the court to prove the obvious. Through the actions of the court, the parties, and the law regulating the burden of proof and presumptions of the parties, the following shortcuts to proof allow the parties to establish the obvious facts and to devote their attention to the gray facts that make up a trial.

A. Stipulations

As will be discussed in *Old Chief v. United States* in Chapter 2, parties often agree to stipulate to certain facts in a dispute. Once the stipulation is written and agreed to by the parties, it is read to the jury by the judge or the proponent of the evidence. There is no standard to satisfy in a stipulation; as long as the parties agree to the facts and the language of the stipulation, it will be read to the jury. Likewise, a party may refuse an offer of stipulation, if, for example, they believe that developing the fact through other forms of evidence will assist in the narrative of their case. Thus, in a murder trial, the defendant may propose to stipulate how and when the victim died. The prosecutor may refuse this stipulation, as developing facts surrounding the murder itself may be emotionally and morally significant for a jury.

Stipulations play a role in balancing the probative value of evidence against its prejudicial effect, as stipulating to a fact may be a method that reduces the prejudice inherent in the fact. Thus, a judge may decide that stipulating that the victim in a murder trial was stabbed three times in the back may be preferable to showing gruesome autopsy photographs of the injury. The court has the power to force the parties to accept a stipulation that will diminish the prejudicial power of the evidence. As *Old Chief* will demonstrate, however, the court must take into account the fact that a piece of evidence may address numerous elements simultaneously. In our example of the victim who was stabbed in the back, the type of injury may establish not only how the victim died but also capacity, causation, motive and/or intent. It may also provide a descriptive richness to a party's narrative. Accordingly, courts have been cautious in mandating that a party (typically the government in a criminal case) accept a stipulation.

B. Judicial Notice

Relevant Rule
FRE 201

Judicial Notice of Adjudicative Facts

(a) Scope. This rule governs judicial notice of an adjudicative fact only, not a legislative fact.

(b) Kinds of Facts That May Be Judicially Noticed. The court may judicially notice a fact that is not subject to reasonable dispute because it:

(1) is generally known within the court's territorial jurisdiction; or

(2) can be accurately and readily determined from sources whose accuracy cannot reasonably be questioned.

(c) Taking Notice. At any stage of the proceeding, the court:

(1) may take judicial notice on its own; or

(2) must take judicial notice if a party requests it and the court is supplied with the necessary information.

(d) Timing. The court may take judicial notice at any stage of the proceeding.

(e) Opportunity to Be Heard. On timely request, a party is entitled to be heard on the propriety of taking judicial notice and the nature of the fact to be noticed. If the court takes judicial notice before notifying a party, the party, on request, is still entitled to be heard.

(f) Instructing the Jury. In a civil case, the court must instruct the jury to accept the noticed fact as conclusive. In a criminal case, the court must instruct the jury that it may or may not accept the noticed fact as conclusive.

The court may take notice of an undisputed fact in the name of judicial efficiency. If the fact is one that can be established conclusively by consulting reliable sources the court may take judicial notice *sua sponte* (i.e., through the court's own volition without any motion by the parties) or must take judicial notice if a party requests it, that party provides proof of its indisputability, and the opposing party is given a right to be heard. Judicial notice can be taken at any stage of a proceeding, even at the appellate level.

FRE 201(a) specifically limits its scope to judicial notice of "adjudicative fact." An adjudicative fact is one that helps prove the elements of a case. In other words, they are the facts that a jury must determine in their deliberations, such as whether a light was red or green or if a crime was committed with malice aforethought. An adjudicative fact need not be the ultimate fact that the jury needs to decide, however. It also includes any fact in the reasoning that leads to the ultimate fact that the jury needs to decide. Thus, in a car accident the ultimate fact that is necessary for the plaintiff to win may be whether the defendant driver was negligent. A link in the chain to proving negligence may be whether the defendant ran a red light. Both the ultimate fact (was he negligent?) and fact that helps prove it (did he run a red light?) are adjudicate facts.

There are two avenues available for proving that an adjudicative fact is "not subject to reasonable dispute." **First**, the fact may be "generally known within the court's territorial jurisdiction." FRE 201(b)(1). This type of adjudicative fact must be known to the general public, not specific sub-groups within the general public. Thus, the fact that Montreal is in Canada may be known to the general public, but the health care system of Canada is probably not known to the general public. Therefore, the former fact could be subject to judicial notice but the latter fact would not be under FRE 201(b)(1). Also, the facts may be specific to the jurisdiction of the court. Accordingly, under this method of judicial notice, a Connecticut court may take notice that in New Haven Elm Street and Church Street intersect, but a California court would not find this fact known within its territorial jurisdiction.

The **second** avenue concerns facts that are "accurately and readily determined from sources whose accuracy cannot reasonably be questioned." FRE 201(b)(2). This approach is significantly broader than the first approach in that, if a reliable source is found, the court may take judicial notice of an adjudicative fact that is known to sub-groups of the population or that goes beyond the boundaries of the territorial jurisdiction of the court. To use the examples from the previous paragraph, both the health care system of Canada and the intersection of streets in New Haven could be judicially noticed if accurate resources could be found. The source used need not be admissible evidence; it only must be a source whose accuracy cannot be reasonably questioned.

Judicial notice binds the jury in civil cases but not in criminal ones. In a civil case, the jury is instructed to find the judicially noticed fact to be conclusive due to the fact that it is beyond reasonable dispute. In a criminal case, however, the jury is the final arbiter of *all* facts and therefore cannot be constitutionally bound to accepting a fact as true. Therefore, while the judge may take judicial notice of a fact in a criminal case, the judge may not instruct the jury that the fact is conclusively proven.

FRE 201 does not govern judicial notice of **non-adjudicative** facts, so a judge may take judicial notice of other types of facts free from the constraints of FRE 201. For example, a judge may take judicial notice of the law ranging from local municipal ordinances to federal law or the law of other states. There has been some reluctance to take judicial notice of the law, however, due to fears that the information regarding the law may not be up to date or accurate as well as the fear that the court may not have sufficient expertise to properly gauge the law. Nonetheless, a court is free to take judicial notice of the law, unconstrained by the mandates of FRE 201.

Another area where judicial notice may be taken outside the constraints of FRE 201 is **legislative facts**. When a court is ruling on constitutional issues, statutory interpretation, and other policy issues, it must make certain assumptions about the environment the law affects. These facts are called legislative facts and are defined by the FRE Advisory Committee as facts "which have relevance to legal reasoning and the lawmaking process, whether in the formation of a legal principle or ruling by a judge or court in the enactment of a legislative body." In other words, certain historical, scientific, commercial, social, economic, and political facts influence the legal reasoning of a court. For example, in *Miranda v. Arizona,* 384 U.S. 436 (1966), the Supreme Court relied on police manuals and studies of police practices in order to determine that custodial interrogation by the police is inherently coercive. The facts from the police manuals and studies influenced the reasoning of the court in determining the scope of individual's constitutional rights. Therefore, these facts may be judicially noticed.

Thus, there exist major differences between judicial notice of adjudicative facts and legislative facts. First, legislative facts need not be indisputable. Indeed, a reasonable person looking at the police manuals mentioned in *U.S. v. Miranda* might have reached a different conclusion regarding the coerciveness of custodial interrogation. Second, the provisions of FRE 201, such as providing an opportunity to be heard, do not apply to legislative facts. Based on these differences, it is important to be able to distinguish between the two types of facts, which is not an easy task. Essentially, if the fact pertains to the what, when, where, how, and/or who that concern the specific controversy between the parties, the fact will be considered adjudicative and must satisfy FRE 201.

Problem 1-5

In 1995, Anthony Bari was convicted of bank robbery and received a prison sentence. In May, 2008, Bari was released from custody and began serving a term of supervised release. In October, 2008, the United States Probation Office submitted to the District Court an Amended Request for Court Action, alleging that Bari had violated the terms of his supervised release. The Amended Request alleged that Bari had committed bank robbery, among other things.

On November 18 and 19, 2008, the District Court held a hearing to determine whether Bari had in fact violated the terms of his supervised release. At the conclusion of the hearing, the District Court found Bari not guilty of some of the violations alleged, but guilty of the bank robbery violation and a firearms violation. With respect to the bank robbery violation, the District Court relied on evidence that the bank's surveillance footage showed that the robber wore a yellow rain hat, and that a yellow rain hat was found in the garage of Bari's landlord. The judge noted several similarities between the hat found in the landlord's garage and the hat worn by the robber. He stated that "there are clearly lots of yellow hats out there," and that "[o]ne can Google yellow rain hats and find lots of different yellow rain hats." The judge noted that his staff had in fact conducted a Google search of yellow rain hats.

Did the court err in using an independent Internet search to confirm its intuition that there are many types of yellow rain hats for sale and taking judicial notice of that fact?

Problem 1-6

Plaintiffs brought a constitutional challenge to a New York statute that restricted the sale of contraceptives to persons under the age of sixteen. The trial court took notice that persons under the age of sixteen do engage in sexual intercourse and that the result is "often venereal disease, unwanted pregnancy, or both." For support for these propositions, the court cited articles in medical journals. The court also noted that thirty of the fifty states possess similar statutes. Did the court properly take notice of this evidence?

C. Burden of Proof and Presumptions

Relevant Rules
FRE 301

Presumptions in a Civil Case Generally

In a civil case, unless a federal statute or these rules provide otherwise, the party against whom a presumption is directed has the burden of producing evidence to rebut the presumption. But this rule does not shift the burden of persuasion, which remains on the party who had it originally.

FRE 302

Effect of State Law on Presumptions in a Civil Case

In a civil case, state law governs the effect of a presumption regarding a claim or defense for which state law supplies the rule of decision.

Inferences are essential to an advocate. In order to convince a jury of your client's narrative, an advocate must be able to infer from established facts. For example, if the facts uncontrovertibly establish that the victim in a murder trial had an affair with the defendant's wife, a prosecutor will seek an inference from that fact—the motive for the murder was anger stemming from jealousy. During her closing argument, the prosecutor will undoubtedly ask the jury to adopt that inference during their deliberations.

Presumptions are a procedural device that accomplishes this same end. A presumption requires that the fact finder draw a conclusion if they find a certain fact to be true. Rather than relying on a permissive inference (the jury may or may not accept the inference), a presumption is mandatory on the fact finder. In order for a presumption to take effect, a party must establish a foundational fact or facts. After the foundational fact is proven, a presumed fact comes into existence. For example, a common presumption in many jurisdictions concerns whether a person is dead if they are missing and have not been heard from or seen for a specified number of years. Therefore, under this presumption of death, if it is established that the person has not been heard from or seen for the specified number of years (the foundational fact), the jury must assume that the person is deceased (the presumed fact).

A number of policies justify presumptions. First, presumptions allow facts that are difficult to prove but likely true to be proven in court. In our presumption of death example, it is likely that one who has gone missing without any trace for many years is deceased. If the law forced a party to prove that a missing person is deceased through concrete evidence, many parties with meritorious claims might be unable to meet that burden. Second, public policy rationales support presumptions. Without the presumption of death, a party may never be able to resolve fiscal and personal issues that resulted from the decedent's death.

Before we dive too deeply into presumptions, we need to explore the concepts of the burden of proof and the burden of producing evidence (sometimes called the burden of production). In a criminal or civil case, the plaintiff/prosecutor has a burden of proof that it must meet in order to win its case. In the civil arena, the burden of proof is typically the preponderance of the evidence (although, in a few instances, the burden of proof can be by clear and convincing evidence). That is, to satisfy the standard of preponderance of the evidence, the plaintiff must prove her case by a greater than 50% likelihood. In criminal cases, the prosecutor must prove her case beyond a reasonable doubt, which is a significantly higher standard. Similarly, if the defendant in a civil or criminal case attempts an affirmative defense, the defendant will have the burden of proof on that issue.

In addition to the burden of proof, however, a burden of producing evidence also exists for the party that possesses the burden of proof. The burden of producing evidence has little to do with convincing the jury. Rather, meeting this burden is essential to avoid a directed verdict as a matter of law. Put simply, if you have not produced sufficient evidence to prove your case (i.e., evidence sufficient to constitute a "prima facie case"), then there is no reason to submit your case to a jury, and a directed verdict is in order. For example, if the party with the burden of producing evidence offers absolutely no evidence on a required element (e.g., fails to prove "contact with the person of another" in a civil battery claim), then a directed verdict is proper. That party has failed to satisfy its burden, and the judge should direct a verdict as a matter of law.

The standard to meet the burden of producing evidence is low. For the civil party, she must produce enough evidence on each element of on which she has the burden of proof such that a reasonable jury could find in her favor. In other words, if enough facts exist such that a reasonable jury *could conceivably* find in the party's favor on each element, then the burden is met. Note that this standard is lower than proving the element by a preponderance of the evidence. The judge seeks to determine whether a directed verdict is justified. If a reasonable jury could look at the facts and conceivably reach the conclusion that plaintiff has established her case by a preponderance of the evidence, then the judge may not direct a verdict, and the burden of producing evidence has been met. In other words, the court asks if there is enough evidence to support a verdict for the party but does not ask whether the evidence *requires* a verdict in the plaintiff's favor. In a criminal case the standard is similar—the prosecutor must introduce enough evidence of guilt such that a reasonable jury could find the defendant guilty beyond a reasonable doubt. For the party with the burden of proof, producing evidence is an affirmative duty. Thus, a party with the burden of proof on an issue cannot rely solely on the theory that their opponent will introduce evidence that proves their case. Rather, the party with the burden of proof must produce the evidence in their case-in-chief.

Now that we have a better understanding of the burden of proof and the burden of producing evidence, let us explore the types of presumptions that exist. The first line of demarcation is whether the presumption is mandatory or not. In other words, if a party satisfies the requirements of a presumption, is the jury mandated to follow the presumption or not?

The weakest type of presumption is a **permissive inference**. This type of presumption merely allows the judge to instruct the jury that it may, but need not, infer one fact from another. Thus, we will see in Chapter 4 that one who flees from the police may be presumed by the jury to be conscious of their guilt. A judge could therefore instruct the jury that they may make this inference. If the jury does not believe the foundational fact (i.e., that the defendant was fleeing), it need not accept the inference (i.e., that the defendant was conscious of his guilt). Significantly, however, even if the jury does believe the foundational fact, it need not believe that the inferred fact exists. Thus, if the jury believed a defendant was fleeing, they are not mandated into accepting the premise that the defendant was fleeing due to consciousness of guilt (i.e., the defendant could have been fleeing because he feared being beaten by the police). The bottom line is that in the context of a permissive inference, the jury is not mandated to accept the inference. Instead, the jury is free to use its own reasoning process.

A "stronger" presumption is the **presumption that shifts the burden of producing evidence**. Let us re-examine the death presumption. In a civil case in a state with a five year death presumption, plaintiff offers sufficient foundational facts to prove that a person has been missing for five years and has not been heard from during that period. Because the plaintiff has offered sufficient foundational facts, they have satisfied their burden of producing evidence. The presumption now kicks in. The burden of producing evidence on the assumed fact now shifts to the defendant. If the defendant produces no evidence on this issue, then the defendant will not satisfy the burden of production that has shifted to him. The jurors will be instructed by the judge that they *must* presume that the person is dead if they find the foundational facts to be true by a preponderance of the evidence.

What if the defendant challenges the *foundational facts* established by the plaintiff by, for example, offering credible evidence that the person alleged to be dead was seen within the last five years? The issue is now one for the jury. The court must let the jury decide whether the foundational facts are true by a preponderance of the evidence, and, if the jury so finds, the judge will instruct them that they must find the presumed fact (that the missing person is dead) is true. Conversely, if the jury credits the defendant's evidence and finds that the foundational facts are not true, then the presumption will not be applicable.

What if the defendant challenges *the presumed fact*? In other words, rather than challenging whether the person had been seen in the past five years, the defendant instead offers evidence that the presumed decedent is alive. What role does the presumption possess now? Prior to the adoption of FRE 301, courts and commentators struggled with the issue. Some thought that the jury should still be instructed about the presumption and that the jury could consider the presumption in its decision making. Some thought that if a party just contested the presumed fact, it should carry the burden of proof on that issue. In the end, FRE 301 rejected these approaches and instead adopted what has been called a "bursting bubble presumption."

Under a "bursting bubble presumption," by attacking the presumed fact with credible evidence, the defendant has met its burden of producing evidence, and the presumption disappears (i.e., it dissipates like a bursting bubble). Since the purpose of the presumption was to shift the burden of production, and the defendant proceeded to meet its burden of production, there is no more need for the presumption and it should not be mentioned to the jury. All that is left is a permissible, non-mandatory inference that the jury may make if they credit one party's evidence over the other. In other words, the presumption created a bubble that forced the defendant to respond. Once the defendant did respond by attacking the presumed fact, the bubble burst, and the presumption is removed from the case. In our example, the plaintiff could still argue that the missing person is dead, but the jury would not be informed that a legal presumption exists on this issue.

Let us do a quick review on presumptions that shift the burden of producing evidence using our presumption of death hypothetical. Assume that Susan seeks to prove that her husband is dead by relying on the presumption. She offers evidence that no one has heard or seen from her husband in five years. The defendant, an insurance company, responds as follows:

- The defendant offers no evidence regarding the husband's disappearance. What result? Since Susan shifted the burden of producing evidence to the defendant through her evidence, offering no evidence means that the defendant has not met its burden of producing evidence. The judge will this instruct the jury that the husband is dead.

- The defendant offers evidence that the husband was seen alive within the last five years. What result? The defendant is now contesting the foundational fact. A judge will allow the jury to resolve the conflicting evidence. The judge will instruct the jury that if Susan has proven by a preponderance of the evidence that her husband has been missing for five years, then the jury must find that the husband is dead.

- The defendant offers evidence that the husband is alive. What result? The defendant is now contesting the presumed fact. Since the defendant has met the burden of producing evidence that had shifted to it, the bubble has burst. The jury will not be instructed as to the presumption. The jury is free to make whatever inference is best supported by the evidence.

A stronger type of presumption than the presumption that shifts the burden of producing evidence is a **presumption that shifts the burden of proof**, which are fairly common in federal and state law. In this scenario, once a party has produced sufficient facts that invoke the presumption, the opponent must carry the burden of proof in overcoming the assumed fact rather than merely meeting a burden of producing evidence. Therefore, in a civil case, the opponent must now persuade the jury that the presumed fact is false by a preponderance of the evidence. Even if the opponent offers evidence that the presumed fact is false, the jury is instructed about the presumption and informed that the opponent has the burden in rebutting it. If the opponent does not meet this burden of proof, the jury must find the presumed fact is true.

The strongest type of presumption is the **conclusive presumption.** Here, there is no shifting of the burden of producing evidence or the burden of proof. Instead, if the party invoking the presumption proves the foundational facts, the fact finder is required to draw a particular inference. One example common to many jurisdictions is the presumption that a child conceived during the time a married couple was cohabitating is conclusively presumed to be the child of the husband. Once the foundational facts are proved, the presumed fact (the paternity of the child) is irrebutable by the opposing party.

Even among the four classifications of presumptions discussed here, there are numerous variations within each classification. We will not explore each potential variation, but certain questions will guide your analysis of these presumptions. Analyze the strength of the presumption and its operation. Is it mandatory or permissive? What burden is being shifted? What foundational facts trigger the presumption? What, precisely, is the presumed fact that emerges when the foundational fact is proven?

Additionally, there are a few things to keep in mind as you analyze presumptions. First, presumptions are limited in the criminal arena. If a presumption requires a jury to reach a certain finding of fact based on the existence of another fact, then the presumption will violate a criminal defendant's Fifth and Fourteenth Amendment rights. This is so because a criminal defendant is entitled to proof beyond a reasonable doubt on every fact necessary to convict the defendant of the crime for which she is charged. If a presumption interferes with proving *every* fact beyond a reasonable doubt by allowing *some* facts to be presumed, it will violate the Constitution.

Second, you must be aware of how FRE 301 and FRE 302 operate. FRE 301, which is limited to *civil cases only*, has been interpreted to adopt "bursting bubble" presumptions, as it states that "the party against whom a presumption is directed has the burden of producing evidence to rebut the presumption. But this rule does not shift the burden of persuasion, which remains on the party who had it originally." The scope of FRE 301 is limited, however. In addition to being limited to civil cases, FRE 301 notes that Congress may give presumptions particular effect under specific federal statutes. These Congressional determinations would trump FRE 301. Additionally, under FRE 302 state law governs the effect of presumptions when state law supplies the rule of decision on a civil claim or defense, so, in diversity cases, the court will examine state law to determine the effect of a presumption. Thus, FRE 301 only applies when no other state or federal rule governs.

Problem 1-7

On March 1, 1973, the attorney for Edouard Legille and certain other inventors mailed from East Hartford, Connecticut, to the Patent Office in Washington, D.C., a package containing four patent applications. Each of the applications had previously been filed in Luxembourg, three on March 6, 1972, and the fourth on August 11, 1972. The package was marked "Airmail," bore sufficient airmail postage, and was properly addressed. Delivery of air mail from East Hartford to Washington at that time was normally two days.

The date of filing was crucial to Legille. An application for a United States patent filed within twelve months after filing of an application for a foreign patent on the same invention is statutorily accorded the filing date of the foreign application and the effect thereof. If, however, the interval between the filings exceeds twelve months, patent protection in the United States may not be available. Thus, Legille wanted to file his applications on or before March 6, 1973.

The applications were date-stamped "March 8, 1973," by the Patent Office. Each of the four applications was assigned that filing date on the ground that the stamped date was the date the Patent Office had received the applications. If March 8 was to stand as the official date of filing, then the three applications filed in Luxembourg in March, 1972 would fail in the United States as a result of the "first to file" rule (wherein the grant of a patent for a given invention lies with the first person or persons to file a patent application, regardless of the date of actual invention).

Legille petitioned the Commissioner of Patents to reassign the filing date. The petition was denied. Legille then sued in the District Court for a judgment directing the Commissioner to assign the applications a filing date not later than March 6, 1973. Both sides moved for summary judgment on the basis of their pleadings and affidavits. None of the affidavits reflected any direct evidence of the date on which the applications were actually delivered to the Patent Office.

1. What happens if Legille offers proof of the regularity of the U.S. mail, that postal employees discharge their duties in a proper manner, and that properly addressed and stamped mail, deposited in the proper receptacles, is presumed to reach the addressee in the ordinary course of mails and without unusual delay?

2. What kind of evidence would the Patent Office have to produce to rebut the presumption?

3. What happens once the Patent Office produces sufficient evidence to rebut Legille's presumption of the regularity of the mail? How should the case be resolved?

Professional Development Questions

Author's Note: At the end of each chapter, a series of questions are presented to focus on your mastery of the substantive law, to offer helpful learning strategies for the material in the chapter, and to reflect on your professional development.

*   A recent text written by a group of respected legal educators and published by the Carnegie Foundation, *Educating Lawyers: Preparation for the Profession of Law* (2007), proposes a three-part model of effective professional development, including learning to (i) think like a lawyer (knowledge); (ii) perform like a lawyer (skills); and (iii) behave like a lawyer (professional identity and professionalism). The text of this book and its case will (hopefully) impart knowledge. The problems will hone skills. Your *reaction* to some of the rules, cases, and problems help to shape your professional identity (e.g., "I would never do that if I were a lawyer …" or "I could never defend that type of client …"). As these thoughts occur to you, do not dismiss them. Discuss them with your friends and professors to better explore the parameters of your professional identity.

- You are a lawyer on trial, and you can instinctively tell that a particular jury member is siding with your narrative of a case. You also notice, however, that he smells heavily of bourbon. What do you do?

- After a criminal trial in which you were counsel, a juror approaches you. She states that, during deliberations, a fellow juror stated, "I really hate minority group X." The defendant is a member of minority group X. How do you respond? Will your argument be successful? Does it matter whether you won or lost the case?

- How comfortable are you defending an alleged murderer? How do you, personally, reconcile potential preconceived notions of guilt and instead focus on preparing the best defense for your client? Will it affect your narrative of the case?

Chapter 2

Relevance

The first threshold through which admissible evidence must pass is relevance. No matter how emotionally compelling a piece of evidence may be, and no matter how critical it is to an advocate's narrative of the case, it must be relevant to be admissible. In other words, we must ask, "What does this fact prove, and why does proving that fact matter in this case?"

Once a piece of evidence is deemed relevant, however, the inquiry is far from over. One common objection to relevant evidence is that, even if you concede that the evidence is relevant, its probative value is substantially outweighed by unfair prejudice. When this is the case, the extreme prejudicial effect of the evidence will lead to the exclusion of relevant evidence under FRE 403.

As we work through all the potential objections to relevant evidence, we need a map of the terrain. On the next two pages, you will see a flow chart that embodies the essence of the next few chapters. Rest assured, we will move through this chart box-by-box. For now, pay particular attention to the top two boxes (for FRE 401/402 and 104(b)) as well as the bottom box (for FRE 403). In essence, in the upcoming chapter we are looking at the preliminary questions when evidence is offered (is it relevant?) and the final question (even if it is relevant, should it still be inadmissible?). Future chapters will explore the middle three columns.

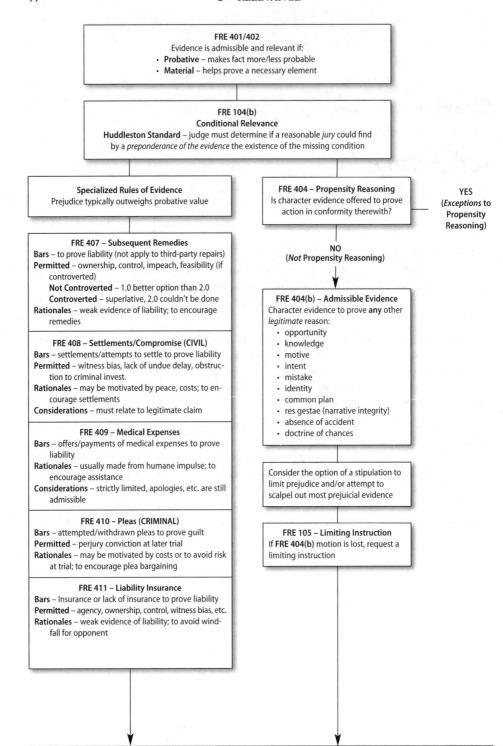

FRE 401/402
Evidence is admissible and relevant if:
- **Probative** – makes fact more/less probable
- **Material** – helps prove a necessary element

FRE 104(b)
Conditional Relevance
Huddleston Standard – judge must determine if a reasonable *jury* could find
by a *preponderance of the evidence* the existence of the missing condition

Specialized Rules of Evidence
Prejudice typically outweighs probative value

FRE 404 – Propensity Reasoning
Is character evidence offered to prove
action in conformity therewith?

YES
(*Exceptions* to
Propensity
Reasoning)

NO
(*Not* Propensity Reasoning)

FRE 407 – Subsequent Remedies
Bars – to prove liability (not apply to third-party repairs)
Permitted – ownership, control, impeach, feasibility (if controverted)
  Not Controverted – 1.0 better option than 2.0
  Controverted – superlative, 2.0 couldn't be done
Rationales – weak evidence of liability; to encourage remedies

FRE 408 – Settlements/Compromise (CIVIL)
Bars – settlements/attempts to settle to prove liability
Permitted – witness bias, lack of undue delay, obstruction to criminal invest.
Rationales – may be motivated by peace, costs; to encourage settlements
Considerations – must relate to legitimate claim

FRE 409 – Medical Expenses
Bars – offers/payments of medical expenses to prove liability
Rationales – usually made from humane impulse; to encourage assistance
Considerations – strictly limited, apologies, etc. are still admissible

FRE 410 – Pleas (CRIMINAL)
Bars – attempted/withdrawn pleas to prove guilt
Permitted – perjury conviction at later trial
Rationales – may be motivated by costs or to avoid risk at trial; to encourage plea bargaining

FRE 411 – Liability Insurance
Bars – Insurance or lack of insurance to prove liability
Permitted – agency, ownership, control, witness bias, etc.
Rationales – weak evidence of liability; to avoid windfall for opponent

FRE 404(b) – Admissible Evidence
Character evidence to prove **any** other *legitimate* reason:
- opportunity
- knowledge
- motive
- intent
- mistake
- identity
- common plan
- res gestae (narrative integrity)
- absence of accident
- doctrine of chances

Consider the option of a stipulation to limit prejudice and/or attempt to scalpel out most prejuicial evidence

FRE 105 – Limiting Instruction
If **FRE 404(b)** motion is lost, request a limiting instruction

FRE 403 – Balance Test
Relevant Evidence *may* be excluded if its probative value is *substantially* outweighed by the danger of *unfair* prejudice or delay.

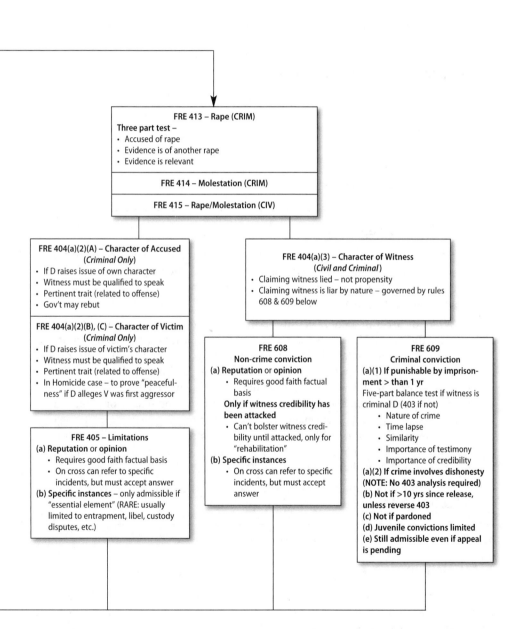

FRE 413 – Rape (CRIM)

Three part test –
- Accused of rape
- Evidence is of another rape
- Evidence is relevant

FRE 414 – Molestation (CRIM)

FRE 415 – Rape/Molestation (CIV)

FRE 404(a)(2)(A) – Character of Accused
(Criminal Only)
- If D raises issue of own character
- Witness must be qualified to speak
- Pertinent trait (related to offense)
- Gov't may rebut

FRE 404(a)(2)(B), (C) – Character of Victim
(Criminal Only)
- If D raises issue of victim's character
- Witness must be qualified to speak
- Pertinent trait (related to offense)
- In Homicide case – to prove "peaceful-ness" if D alleges V was first aggressor

FRE 405 – Limitations
(a) Reputation or **opinion**
- Requires good faith factual basis
- On cross can refer to specific incidents, but must accept answer
(b) Specific instances – only admissible if "essential element" (RARE: usually limited to entrapment, libel, custody disputes, etc.)

FRE 404(a)(3) – Character of Witness
(Civil and Criminal)
- Claiming witness lied – not propensity
- Claiming witness is liar by nature – governed by rules 608 & 609 below

FRE 608
Non-crime conviction
(a) Reputation or **opinion**
- Requires good faith factual basis
Only if witness credibility has been attacked
- Can't bolster witness credi-bility until attacked, only for "rehabilitation"
(b) Specific instances
- On cross can refer to specific incidents, but must accept answer

FRE 609
Criminal conviction
(a)(1) If punishable by imprison-ment > than 1 yr
Five-part balance test if witness is criminal D (403 if not)
- Nature of crime
- Time lapse
- Similarity
- Importance of testimony
- Importance of credibility
(a)(2) If crime involves dishonesty (NOTE: No 403 analysis required)
(b) Not if >10 yrs since release, unless reverse 403
(c) Not if pardoned
(d) Juvenile convictions limited
(e) Still admissible even if appeal is pending

I. Is It Relevant?

Relevant Rules
FRE 401

Test for Relevant Evidence

Evidence is relevant if:

> (a) it has any tendency to make a fact more or less probable than it would be without the evidence; and
>
> (b) the fact is of consequence in determining the action.

FRE Rule 402

General Admissibility of Relevant Evidence

Relevant evidence is admissible unless any of the following provides otherwise:

- the United States Constitution;
- a federal statute;
- these rules; or
- other rules prescribed by the Supreme Court.

Irrelevant evidence is not admissible.

Overview Problem

Angela Johnson was charged with aiding and abetting her boyfriend, Dustin Honken, in the execution-style slaying of two federal informants, the girlfriend of one informant, and the girlfriend's two young daughters. Honken, an alleged methamphetamine manufacturer, was arrested and charged for the five murders.

While incarcerated and awaiting trial, Angela Johnson turned to a fellow inmate, Robert McNeese, and asked him to find another inmate serving a life sentence who would take the blame for the murders. Unbeknownst to Johnson, McNeese was an informant, and he asked Johnson for information about the killings in order that whoever confessed to the crimes could have credible information. McNeese collected a series of handwritten notes and maps from Johnson that contained incriminating details of where the five missing victims were buried as well as details regarding the murders. Shortly after the bodies were found, and it became clear to Johnson that McNeese was an informant, she attempted to commit suicide by hanging herself in her cell.

The prosecution intends to offer her suicide attempt as evidence against Johnson. Is it relevant? For what, if any, purposes?

Defining Relevance

Relevancy is the primary threshold determination for each piece of evidence that is proffered. The test posed by the rule hints at its low threshold: relevant evidence possesses "*any tendency* to make a fact more or less probable than it would be without the evidence." (emphasis supplied.) "Any tendency" means just that—any opportunity to provide probative value whatsoever can satisfy the definition. Hence, a liberal standard exists that favors a policy of broad admissibility.

But what is the test for this low threshold of admissibility? The two requirements are that (1) the evidence must provide proof of the proposition it is offered to prove (i.e., the evidence is probative), and (2) the proposition to be proved must be one that is of consequence to the determination of the action (i.e., the evidence is material). Thus a **relational** concept emerges—we must weigh the evidence in light of the facts and law of consequence to the case. Does the evidence have a logical probative value toward proving some fact of legal consequence? If so, does it have "any tendency" to make a fact of consequence more likely? In other words, we must always bear in mind the relationship of the evidence to the fact that we are trying to prove by using the evidence as well as whether that fact we are trying to prove actually matters in the litigation.

Looking at our overview question, Johnson's suicide attempt is being offered because it makes some fact of consequence more likely. How would you define that fact? As we reason it out in our minds, we might think something like "Johnson tried to commit suicide after discovering the person she confessed to was a government informant and therefore … ?" To frame our answer as " … therefore she is guilty" sweeps too broadly. The inference from attempted suicide to guilt is not explicit and therefore we have taken too great a logical leap. How about framing our answer as " … therefore she is conscious of being guilty, which means she is more likely to be guilty"? Now we have an explicit connection to evidence that is probative to something material to the case. Reasonable minds might differ as to the strength of the inference of why she attempted suicide (perhaps she attempted suicide due to consciousness of guilt or perhaps it was the symptom of some deeper sadness unrelated to the case), but, under the "any tendency" standard we do not rigidly weigh the probativeness of the evidence. It need not, for example, be probative by a preponderance of the evidence. "Any tendency" will suffice.

That is not to say that the FRE 401's test is toothless. We can agree that if Johnson had tried to commit suicide three years before the murders, it would not be relevant to the prosecution's case, as it does not contribute to any inference at issue in the case. Going back to our thought exercise yields no sustainable inference: "Johnson tried to commit suicide three years before the murder, and therefore …" Therefore she is more likely to be a killer? The inference is so weak that it possesses no tendency to make a fact in consequence more likely.

Next, after determining probativeness, one must satisfy the second prong of the rule and examine if the fact is of legal consequence to the case (i.e., it is material). One can only judge this by examining the substantive law in the underlying case. For example, in a statutory rape case, where strict liability attaches and the age of the victim is not a defense, testimony that the victim looked eighteen or stated that she was eighteen has no legal consequence to the case. While it may have some probative value, it is not material and therefore not relevant. In our overview question, the fact that Johnson is conscious of guilt (if, indeed, that is why she attempted to commit suicide) is material, as it goes to the identity of the killer.

Accordingly, when you are determining relevance, you must keep in mind the relationship between the issues raised by the parties, the other evidence introduced, and the applicable substantive law. **Always** have a vision as to what this piece of evidence is relevant to in the case. Unless you can answer the question "why is this being offered?" you cannot determine relevance. One simply cannot decide whether evidence is relevant without knowing the facts or issues for which it is offered to prove.

The Judge's Role in Determining Relevance

How does a judge make a relevancy determination? The relational concept behind relevance is illustrated in the Committee notes to FRE 401. Relevance requires a "relation between an item of evidence and a matter properly provable in the case," and the existence of such a relationship is to be determined by "principles evolved by experience or science, applied logically to the situation at hand." Accordingly, a judge's life experience and common sense undoubtedly play a role in determining whether a logical relationship exists between proffered evidence and the fact to be proven.

As we have alluded to, in matters of relevancy one thing that does not concern the judge when making an admissibility determination is the weight or sufficiency of the evidence. "Weight" describes the persuasive force assigned to the evidence by the trier of fact once it has been admitted. "Sufficiency" refers to the quantum and persuasive force of evidence necessary to take an issue to the jury (e.g., to defeat a directed verdict motion). Thus, a witness who is less than credible who provides relevant testimony will be allowed to make that point to the jury—it is admissible. It is for the jury (or the judge when acting as trier of fact) to determine how much weight to give the comment, but it will not be withheld from the trier of fact based on a determination that it does not merit much weight. So, an eyewitness who makes an identification of a party but who was not wearing her glasses, was far away, and made the identification in a pitch black environment has offered relevant, admissible evidence. When it is the trier of fact's opportunity to evaluate this admissible evidence, the trier of fact may choose to give this admissible evidence limited probative weight. Likewise, whether evidence will eventually be sufficient to withstand a motion for directed verdict does not play a role in determining whether the evidence is admissible. Weighing for sufficiency will occur later, when the judge has the opportunity to weigh all admissible evidence.

Another Way of Examining Relevance: The Evidential Hypothesis

Another lens by which to view relevance is to examine precisely what the evidence is meant to prove. This can be illustrated by examining whether the evidence is direct or circumstantial. Direct evidence asserts the existence of the fact to be proven or, in the sub-category of "real evidence," embodies or represents that fact. For example, if someone had seen X hit Y with a pipe, then this would be direct evidence that X assaulted Y. Disputes about the relevance of direct evidence rarely arise due to the fact that direct evidence is probative on the point for which it is being offered (i.e., you are offering the evidence that X hit Y with a pipe to prove that, in fact, it was X who hit Y with a pipe).

However, circumstantial evidence often causes relevance concerns. Circumstantial evidence is proof that does not actually assert or represent the fact to be proven but from which a factfinder can infer an increased probability that the fact exists or does not exist (e.g., X was in debt and would profit financially from the murder of his wife—the inference is that a person in this position has a motive to kill his wife). This inference is often called an "evidential hypothesis," and the judge must analyze whether the evidential hypothesis provides a heightened probability of the fact to be proved in order to admit the circumstantial evidence. Let us take a look at how this plays out in the judge's mind:

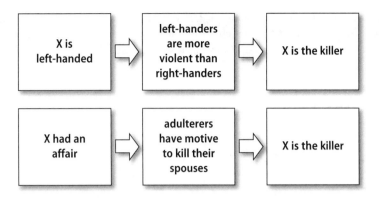

The middle "link" in the logic ("left-handers are more violent than right-handers"; "adulterers have motive to kill their spouses") is the **evidential hypothesis** the judge puts under the microscope. Lacking any basis in science or common sense, a judge is unlikely to allow the former but will likely allow the latter. As one court stated, "Common sense suggests that one measures relevance in a continuum and that at some stage evidence becomes so remote that its probative impact upon 'the existence of any fact that is of consequence' is reduced to zero. When the probative impact reaches zero, the evidence is simply not admissible under Rule 402[.]" *State v. Kotsimpulos*, 411 A.2d 79, 80 (Me. 1980).[1] Giving the judge a wide latitude as to what is a reasonable generalization allows us to conclude that the threshold for relevance is low. But, it is not without limits, as the next section will demonstrate.

Problem 2-1

Return to the facts of the overview question at the beginning of the chapter. You are the judge determining admissibility. What further facts would you need to know? Why would those facts be helpful? After thinking through those issues, assume that you will admit the evidence. Please draft an instruction to the jury informing them how they may permissibly use the evidence.

Problem 2-2

Below you will find an excerpt from the prosecution's appellate brief in the case of State v. Peterson concerning whether evidence of the decedent's financial situation was relevant in the murder trial. After you read the facts below that were introduced at trial, please craft arguments both for and against admission of the evidence. To do so, focus on determining the evidential hypothesis and

---

1. What this example demonstrates is a form of syllogistic reasoning where one moves from a major premise (the generalization) and minor premise (the evidentiary fact) to the conclusion (the inference to be drawn). Hence, adulterers have motive to kill their spouses (generalization) and X actively sought an affair (the evidentiary fact), so X is the killer (conclusion). Looking at it another way, Don has been arrested three times for fraud (evidentiary fact), and therefore Don lied in his testimony (conclusion). Can you articulate the generalization? Is that generalization reasonable? Yet another way of thinking about evidentiary hypotheses is by reasoning in an "if/then" manner regarding the evidentiary fact and the conclusion: "if convicted of fraud three times, then not likely to be telling the truth." Once again, is the unstated generalization reasonable?

evaluating its strength. In other words, fill in the missing box below and argue the relative strength of the evidential hypothesis. **After** you have done so, read an excerpt from the court's opinion on this issue that follows.

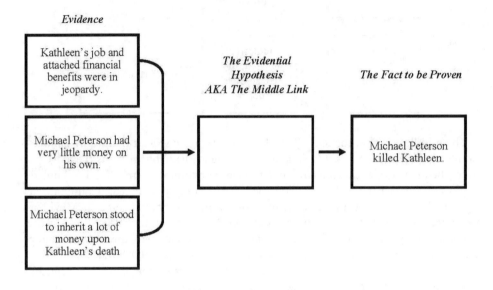

Case Excerpt: Prosecution Brief in *State v. Peterson*

Evidence Relating to Defendant's Income, Finances, and Monetary Benefits from Kathleen Peterson's Death

Katherine Kayser of Nortel's Human Resources Department provided evidence about Kathleen Peterson's salary and benefits. On 7 February 2002, defendant, as beneficiary of Kathleen's 401(k), received the proceeds of that account, amounting after taxes to $29,360.38. On 26 January 2002 defendant claimed Kathleen's Nortel pension benefits, which came to $94,455.75 after taxes, and he received that amount. Kathleen had been eligible to defer and did defer a portion of her salary each year; upon Kathleen's death defendant received her deferred compensation, which totaled $223,182.46. Thus, Nortel paid out to defendant $346,998.59.

Kathleen received "core life insurance" from Nortel ($145,000) and she had opted for "flex earnings" life insurance through Nortel amounting to four times her annual salary, or $580,000; she also had accidental death insurance in the amount of $725,000. She had filled out a Nortel form designating the defendant as her life insurance beneficiary but had not signed it. The decision regarding payment of the life insurance proceeds rested with Prudential, but the potential payout to defendant from the life insurance alone was $1,450,000. When the life insurance is added to the money defendant received from Kathleen's deferred salary and other Nortel benefits, the defendant stood to receive $1,796,998.59 from Kathleen's death.

Agent Raymond Lawrence Young, C.P.A. and certified fraud examiner, of the S.B.I.'s financial crime investigations unit prepared a cash flow analysis for the years 1999–2001 by examining the income streams flowing into and the cash flowing out of five bank accounts owned by the Petersons; he also examined the source of the funds received into those accounts. The recurrent sources consisted of Kathleen's salary, including bonuses, disability income to the defendant through the "VA and military," an IRA distribution to the defendant each year of $17,957, rental income, and interest income. In 1999 from all those sources $276,790 flowed into those accounts, and $461,400 flowed out (a net outflow of $184,610). In 2000 $203,390 was received, and $300,760 was withdrawn (a net outflow of $97,370). In 2001 $180,480 was taken in, and $288,000 was taken out (a net outflow of $107,520).

Young determined that the deficits for each year were covered by selling or otherwise cashing in assets. In 1999 defendant's sale of stock and Kathleen's net proceeds from the sale of a residence she owned totaled more than $184,610. In 2000 Kathleen cashed in a Manulife annuity and some stock options she had purchased, which were used to help cover the deficit for that year. And in 2001 Kathleen sold more stock options, the couple sold property that they owned, and in refinancing the mortgage on their home they cashed in some of the equity defendant had in it, raising a total of $110,818.

Examination of the Petersons' joint income tax returns for 1999–2001 showed that defendant's 1999 taxable income from employment was $0.00, whereas Kathleen's taxable income from salary and bonuses as a Nortel engineer and manager was $149,860. The Petersons jointly owned some rental property, but reported a loss of ($3,109) on it. The corresponding figures for 2000 were as follows: defendant—again zero; Kathleen—$120,720; rental income/loss—again a loss ($7,809). In 2001 defendant's occupation was listed as writer/author and Kathleen's was listed as engineer—deceased. Defendant's taxable income from self-employment was again zero, while Kathleen's taxable income from salary was listed as $45,151; the rental property again produced a loss ($1,706)....

Based on the 6 February 2002 Equifax credit report on the Petersons, Agent Young sought to determine the approximate amount of their "credit card and installment debt and credit line debt close to the time of Kathleen's Peterson's death." The last activity reported to Equifax from these various accounts varied from October 2001 to January 2002. The defendant was the responsible party for payment in twelve of these accounts; Kathleen was the responsible party for payment in six accounts; and two accounts were joint. The total amount of outstanding debt from those accounts was $142,728.

On cross-examination Young also testified that the "credit card companies" had been receiving the payments, at least the minimum payments, as they came due. Young was also questioned about the credit limit on certain of the credit cards, e.g., an American Express Account with a credit limit of $18,000, and he testified that the Petersons' "hadn't maxed out their credit cards." He testified, finally, that the Petersons' outstanding installment, credit line, and credit card debt in January 2001 was $163,969 and they had reduced that amount during the year by "over $20,000," i.e., to $142,728....

From 10 to 12 May 2001 Kathleen and her sister Candace were in Florida to spend "some extended time" with their mother. The two "talk[ed] for hours about [their] lives...." She told her sister that "[all I do] is lay off people," and she was afraid Nortel was going to leave North Carolina and go to Canada. She said she was working "12 to 14 hour days ... All I ever do is talk to Michael about the stresses at Nortel." When Candace suggested that Kathleen should look for another job, she replied: "No, Candace, you don't understand, I can't replace this job in the research triangle area. There is no way. There are—no one is going to pay me the salary I'm making here. I will not have the stock benefits. I won't have the same seniority."

The testimony of Kim Barker of Nortel's Human Resources department confirmed that in 2001 the corporation was laying off people in order "to survive." Nortel's somewhat Orwellian term for the process of laying off employees was "optimization," and in 2001 employees at Kathleen's level in the hierarchy were being optimized. In November 2001 Kathleen was placed on an "optimization list," and her name remained there for three days before it was removed. In all probability Kathleen never knew that she had been on that list, but the fears about her job security that she expressed to Candace were obviously well founded. At a family reunion in July 2001, Kathleen said, "I am feeling very desperate.... I go to work everyday and nothing is getting better." In mid-October 2001 she told Candace, "I am very worried that I will not have a job by the end of this year. I feel sick that nothing is turning around at work."

State v. Peterson

179 N.C.App. 437, 634 S.E.2d 594
(N.C.App. 2006)

IV. *Financial Information*

Next, defendant argues that the trial court erred in admitting irrelevant evidence of the Petersons' finances and Kathleen's job status. We disagree.

... [R]elevant evidence is defined as that having "any tendency to make the existence of any fact that is of consequence to the determination of the action more probable or less probable than it would be without the evidence." N.C. Gen.Stat. § 8C-1, Rule 401 (2005). "Evidence is relevant if it has any logical tendency, however slight, to prove a fact in issue. In criminal cases, every circumstance that is calculated to throw any light upon the supposed crime is admissible. The weight of such evidence is for the jury." The standard set by Rule 401, gives the judge great freedom to admit evidence because the rule makes evidence relevant if it has *any* logical tendency to prove any fact that is of consequence. Thus, even though a trial court's rulings on relevancy technically are not discretionary and therefore are not reviewed under the abuse of discretion standard applicable to Rule 403, such rulings are given great deference on appeal.

The State contends that evidence of the Petersons' finances and Kathleen's job status was relevant to show a possible motive or one of several motives for murder. But defendant argues that there was "no evidence establishing any link" between the Petersons' finances and Kathleen's death, and that the State relied on conjecture.

At trial the evidence presented on finances tended to show that the Petersons had some financial difficulty and defendant stood to inherit a large amount of money upon Kathleen's death. Although State's witness Kim Barker was unaware if Kathleen ever knew that she had been placed on the "optimization list," this evidence was relevant to emphasize the unstable position of employees, including Kathleen, at Nortel. The jury could infer from this evidence that defendant murdered Kathleen, at least in part, for the proceeds from her life insurance policy, which she would have lost if she was laid off, and other financial assets, which totaled approximately $1.8 million.

Defendant cites to *State v. McDowell,* 301 N.C. 279, 271 S.E.2d 286 (1980), to support his argument that the evidence related to defendant being listed as the beneficiary for Kathleen's life insurance policy and other non-probate assets was irrelevant. In *McDowell,* the defendant wanted to cross-examine a witness with respect to whether the witness was the beneficiary of the victim's life insurance policy, to show that the witness had a motive to kill the victim. *Id.* at 292, 271 S.E.2d at 295. The Supreme Court upheld the trial court's ruling that the evidence was inadmissible because "[e]vidence that a crime was committed by another must point unerringly to the guilt of another." *Id.* However, in the instant case defendant is not attempting to use the financial information to prove another person had motive to kill Kathleen. The standard of what is relevant with regard to the State showing a defendant's motive is different than for when a defendant can show motive by a third person. Therefore, *McDowell* does not support defendant's argument.

We conclude that evidence of a potential inheritance of a great deal of money combined with current financial difficulties may be evidence of a motive for murder. Accordingly, we hold that the trial court properly allowed evidence of defendant's and Kathleen's finances as well as Kathleen's job status as relevant for showing motive.

Focus Questions: *United States v. Figueroa* and *Hicks v. Commonwealth of Kentucky*

· Can these two cases be harmonized? How so?

· How do the courts differ regarding the character inferences that flow from possessing a tattoo depicting a swastika? What role should the trial judge have in determining the correctness and/or fairness of these inferences?

United States v. Figueroa
548 F.3d 222 (2nd Cir. 2008)

SACK, Circuit Judge:

Defendant Edwin Figueroa appeals from a judgment of the United States District Court for the Western District of New York, following a jury trial, convicting him of unlawful possession of a firearm. At trial, the district court ruled that the defendant's counsel could not cross-examine a government witness about his swastika tattoos. We conclude that this restriction on the scope of cross-examination was a violation of the Confrontation Clause of the Sixth Amendment. We affirm the conviction, however, because we also conclude that the error was harmless.

BACKGROUND

On January 26, 2004, Figueroa, then a New York State parolee, resided in Rochester, New York. He lived in an apartment building with two apartment units. On that date, New York State parole officers received a complaint from one Rick Kerezman, who lived in the apartment adjacent to Figueroa's, that Figueroa was drinking alcoholic beverages and using drugs in his apartment, and that he had discharged a firearm there. Because such behavior would violate Figueroa's conditions of parole, the officers decided to conduct an unannounced search of Figueroa's residence later that day.

The Search

When the parole officers arrived, Figueroa was slow to answer the door. After the parole officers knocked, they saw a shadow pass in front of a window. Some five minutes later, Figueroa opened the door and the parole officers began their search. They discovered a spent .22-caliber shell-casing on Figueroa's living-room floor. Figueroa told them that "John" had recently fired a gun in his apartment. He said he had told "John" to leave.

Continuing their search, the parole officers passed through Figueroa's apartment and into a common interior hallway that connected the building's two apartment units. There they found a sawed-off .22-caliber rifle just outside Figueroa's apartment. The officers notified the Rochester city police, who arrested Figueroa and seized the gun and shell-casing. Figueroa told the police that his fingerprints were on the gun, but that he had never fired it. He also told them that he was with a friend when the gun was purchased but that he did not know how the gun got into his house. A ballistics expert later determined that the spent shell-casing recovered from Figueroa's living room was fired from the rifle found in the hallway.

The Evidence at Trial

On June 29, 2004, Figueroa was indicted by a federal grand jury ... for unlawfully possessing the rifle. On October 3, 2005, a jury trial on the charges began.... Parole officers and police officers testified to the events described above.

In addition, Frank Keough, Figueroa's roommate, testified that Figueroa had told Keough that Figueroa wanted a weapon for personal protection. On the morning before his arrest, Keough said, Figueroa told him that he had obtained a weapon. Figueroa showed Keough the sawed-off rifle that was later recovered from the hallway. Keough acknowledged that he had a felony conviction and that he was addicted to drugs and alcohol. He testified that he had met Figueroa through their neighbor, Kerezman.

April Fouquet, Kerezman's girlfriend and the occupant of an apartment adjacent to Figueroa's, testified that she was at home when the parole officers searched Figueroa's apartment. When they knocked on his door, she ... saw Figueroa exit his apartment holding the rifle, which he placed in the hallway. Figueroa then "turned around, closed the door and proceeded to run through [his] apartment" to open the front door for the parole officers. Fouquet acknowledged that she had previously been convicted of welfare fraud. She also testified that Figueroa and Kerezman were former roommates who had had a falling out—culminating in a physical fight—a few weeks before the events that led to Figueroa's arrest.

Jonathan Wright, another acquaintance of Figueroa, testified that he purchased the rifle at issue in December 2003 while shopping at a Wal-Mart with Figueroa and Kerezman. Like Keough, Wright came to know Figueroa through Kerezman. Wright testified that he sold the rifle to Figueroa about one week before Figueroa was arrested in exchange for fifty dollars and some clothing. He asserted that at the time of the sale to Figueroa the rifle's barrel was not "sawed off."

The defense called two witnesses: Figueroa's landlord, Nicholas Petrillo, and Figueroa's sister, Marisol Figueroa. Petrillo testified that after Figueroa was arrested, Kerezman asked if he could rent Figueroa's apartment. Marisol Figueroa testified that she, with other relatives, was in her brother's apartment two days before his arrest. Wright, the initial purchaser of the rifle, was also present and behaving suspiciously: "pacing back and forth," "going in and out" of the apartment. Wright was "up to something," she said.

Figueroa did not testify in his own defense.

Swastika Tattoos

Before Jonathan Wright testified, defense counsel informed the court that Wright had swastikas tattooed on his body. Counsel said that he intended to cross-examine Wright about them. Counsel argued, among other things, that Figueroa was a member of a racial or ethnic minority; that the testimony would be used to impeach Wright as to his bias and credibility; and that Figueroa had a right to the proposed line of cross-examination under the Confrontation Clause of the Sixth Amendment. Defense counsel also argued that the tattoos could be connected to Wright's affiliation with a gang, although counsel conceded that he had no information as to whether Wright was a member of a gang.

The government objected to the proposed cross-examination, arguing that the tattoos were relevant to Wright's "belief system" but were "not in any way connected to credibility or motive to lie in this particular case."

The district court denied Figueroa's request to cross-examine Wright about the tattoos or possible gang affiliation.

> I'm not going to allow questioning of the witness about his ... tattoo swastikas.
>
> Also, there's been no proffer or anything other than a guess that he might belong to some gang or organization. I think that's an impermissible question, too, without having a better foundation.
>
> ... I don't think the fact a person has a tattooed swastika speaks to [his character for truthfulness].
>
> I mean, it just kind of attempts to attack the character of a witness....
>
> And I found no case that says because someone has a swastika tattoo, that he's more likely to be untruthful....
>
> ....
>
> So I'll deny the request to examine this witness about tattoos or gang membership based on the proffer I received so far.

Verdict and Judgment

On October 6, 2005, the jury returned a guilty verdict on all counts....

DISCUSSION I. Standard of Review

"Only when th[e] broad discretion [of the district court] is abused will we reverse [the] court's decision to restrict cross-examination." *United States v. Crowley,* 318 F.3d 401, 417 (2d Cir.), *cert. denied,* 540 U.S. 894 (2003). The district court abuses its discretion "when (1) its decision rests on an error of law (such as application of the wrong legal principle) or a clearly erroneous factual finding, or (2) its decision-though not necessarily the product of a legal error or a clearly erroneous factual finding-cannot be located within the range of permissible decisions." *Zervos v. Verizon N.Y., Inc.,* 252 F.3d 163, 169 (2d Cir. 2001).

II. Figueroa's Confrontation Clause Claim

The district court prohibited Figueroa's counsel from pursuing two lines of cross-examination of government witness Jonathan Wright: (1) Wright's possible gang affiliation, and (2) his swastika tattoos. Figueroa argues that the district court thereby violated his rights under the Confrontation Clause of the Sixth Amendment to the United States Constitution.

A. Legal Standards

The Confrontation Clause guarantees a criminal defendant the right to cross-examine government witnesses at trial. *See* U.S. Const. amend. VI ("In all criminal prosecutions, the accused shall enjoy the right ... to be confronted with the witnesses against him...."). "Cross-examination is the principal means by which the believability of a witness and the truth of his testimony are tested." *Davis v. Alaska,* 415 U.S. 308, 316 (1974).

One way of discrediting a witness is "cross-examination directed toward revealing possible biases, prejudices, or ulterior motives of the witness as they may relate directly to issues or personalities in the case at hand." *Id.* "The motivation of a witness in testifying, including her possible self-interest and any bias or prejudice against the defendant, is one of the principal subjects for cross-examination." *Henry v. Speckard,* 22 F.3d 1209, 1214 (2d Cir.), *cert. denied,* 513 U.S. 1029 (1994).

> [A] criminal defendant states a violation of the Confrontation Clause by showing that he was prohibited from engaging in otherwise appropriate cross-examination designed to show a prototypical form of bias on the part of the witness, and thereby to expose to the jury the facts from which jurors could appropriately draw inferences relating to the reliability of the witness.

Delaware v. Van Arsdall, 475 U.S. 673, 680 (1986).

"It does not follow, of course, that the Confrontation Clause of the Sixth Amendment prevents a trial judge from imposing any limits on defense counsel's inquiry into the potential bias of a prosecution witness." *Id.* at 679. District courts may "impose reasonable limits on such cross-examination based on concerns about, among other things, harassment, prejudice, confusion of the issues, the witness' safety, or interrogation that is repetitive or only marginally relevant." *Id.* "Only when this broad discretion is abused will we reverse a trial court's decision to restrict cross-examination." *Crowley,* 318 F.3d at 417.

B. Gang Affiliation

We conclude that the district court did not abuse its discretion in restricting Figueroa's cross-examination of Wright regarding his possible gang affiliation. "Although counsel may explore certain areas of inquiry in a criminal trial without full knowledge of the answer to anticipated questions, he must, when confronted with a demand for an offer of proof, provide some good faith basis for questioning that alleges adverse facts." *United States v. Katsougrakis,* 715 F.2d 769, 779 (2d Cir.1983), *cert. denied,* 464 U.S. 1040 (1984). Here, defense counsel acknowledged that he had no information as to whether Wright was affiliated with a gang. The district court therefore properly ruled that Figueroa had not laid a proper foundation to question Wright on this subject.[4]

C. Swastika Tattoos

We think that the district court abused its discretion, however, when it ruled that Figueroa could not cross-examine Wright about his tattoos. The record reflects that the defendant is a member of a racial or ethnic minority group. Wright, who testified against Figueroa, bore two tattoos depicting swastikas. Inasmuch as the tattoos suggested that

---

4. Defense counsel did not request permission to *voir dire* the witness outside the presence of the jury in an effort to establish a foundation for his proposed inquiry.

Wright harbored animus against racial or ethnic minority groups and their members, they were relevant to and probative of Wright's credibility, bias, and motive to lie when testifying against Figueroa.

The Confrontation Clause protects the right to "engag[e] in otherwise appropriate cross-examination designed to show a prototypical form of bias on the part of the witness." *Van Arsdall,* 475 U.S. at 680. As we recently stated, "It is hard to conceive of a more 'prototypical form of bias' than racial bias." *Brinson v. Walker,* 547 F.3d 387, 393 (2d Cir. 2008). And "racial bias, at least when held in extreme form, can lead people to lie or distort their testimony, and therefore might bear on the accuracy and truth of a witness' testimony, even though the bias is directed generally against a class of persons and not specifically against the accused." *Id.* at 394.

It was apparently, and understandably, assumed by the district court and the parties that the swastika is commonly associated with white supremacism and neo-Nazi groups harboring extreme forms of racial, religious and ethnic hatred and prejudice against minority groups, including that to which Figueroa assertedly belongs. The fact that a witness customarily carries or displays a swastika, as a tattoo or otherwise, therefore would tend to suggest that he or she holds racial, religious or ethnic prejudices. That in turn suggests a basis on which the jury could find the witness's testimony not credible.

"[T]he jury, as finder of fact and weigher of credibility, has historically been entitled to assess all evidence which might bear on the accuracy and truth of a witness' testimony." *United States v. Abel,* 469 U.S. 45, 52 (1984). In a criminal trial, a witness wearing or bearing a swastika should ordinarily be subject to cross-examination on credibility grounds where a jury might reasonably infer that the symbol indicated likely bias against the defendant.[6]

"[T]rial judges retain wide latitude insofar as the Confrontation Clause is concerned to impose reasonable limits on ... cross-examination based on concerns about, among other things, harassment, prejudice, confusion of the issues, the witness' safety, or interrogation that is repetitive or only marginally relevant." *Van Arsdall,* 475 U.S. at 679. The government argues that the district court did not abuse its broad discretion in this instance. We disagree....

We think the district court thereby erred as a matter of law. The Supreme Court has held that impeachment for bias is admissible under Rule 402.... *See Abel,* 469 U.S. at 51, 55-56 & n. 4. Here, as in *Abel,* the purpose of the proposed line of cross-examination ... was to impeach the witness for bias.

> Bias is a term used in the "common law of evidence" to describe the relationship between a party and a witness which might lead the witness to slant, unconsciously or otherwise, his testimony in favor of or against a party. Bias may be induced by a witness' like, dislike, or fear of a party, or by the witness' self-interest. Proof of bias is almost always relevant....

Abel, 469 U.S. at 52. Because the jury could have found that Wright's tattoos were indicative of bias, examination of him on that subject matter was relevant....

---

6. There may, of course, be occasions when it is contested whether the defendant is, or is perceived to be, a member of a racial or religious minority group targeted by white supremacist groups associated with the swastika symbol. There may also be cases in which the witness bearing the swastika is not in fact a sharer of a creed or a committed member of an organization preaching or practicing racial or religious prejudice or hatred. It may therefore be appropriate for a district court, if asked to do so, to hear evidence outside the presence of the jury before making an assessment as to the relevance of a tattoo or similar display of or association with the symbol.

We conclude that the district court's prohibition on cross-examination for bias on the grounds upon which it relied violated Figueroa's confrontation rights under the Sixth Amendment.

III. Harmless Error Analysis

It does not necessarily follow from our conclusion that Figueroa's Sixth Amendment rights were infringed that his conviction must be reversed. "[T]he constitutionally improper denial of a defendant's opportunity to impeach a witness for bias, like other Confrontation Clause errors, is subject to ... harmless-error analysis." *Van Arsdall*, 475 U.S. at 684. We will affirm the judgment of the district court if we are satisfied "beyond a reasonable doubt that the error complained of did not contribute to the verdict obtained." *Chapman v. California*, 386 U.S. 18, 24 (1967).

> Whether such an error is harmless in a particular case depends upon a host of factors.... These factors include the importance of the witness' testimony in the prosecution's case, whether the testimony was cumulative, the presence or absence of evidence corroborating or contradicting the testimony of the witness on material points, the extent of cross-examination otherwise permitted, and, of course, the overall strength of the prosecution's case.

Van Arsdall, 475 U.S. at 684. We are persuaded beyond a reasonable doubt that the Confrontation Clause error in this case did not contribute to the jury's verdict.

Wright was not the only witness who saw Figueroa in possession of the sawed-off rifle. Keough, Figueroa's roommate, testified that Figueroa had shown him "a black shotgun [that] appeared to be cut off," and that this weapon matched the weapon that the government showed him at trial. And Fouquet, Figueroa's neighbor, testified that she had seen a bullet hole in the wall of Figueroa's apartment. She also testified that she saw Figueroa put the rifle in the hallway after the parole officers knocked on his front door. The parole officers corroborated Fouquet's account, testifying that they waited several minutes before Figueroa opened the door. Any cross-examination of Wright as to his tattoos would have been unlikely to affect the credibility of Keough and Fouquet. And the physical evidence relating to the gun, too, was consistent with the testimony of Wright, Keough, and Fouquet: Officer Jenkins found a spent .22 caliber shell casing on the living room floor of Figueroa's apartment, and according to the firearms expert who testified at trial, that shell casing had been fired from the rifle that the officers discovered in the hallway. Therefore, even if Wright's credibility had been undermined by cross-examination regarding his swastika tattoos and related bias, the remainder of the government's case was overwhelming.

The district court's Confrontation Clause error contributed to the guilty verdict in this case only if the jury convicted Figueroa based substantially on Wright's unimpeached testimony while ignoring or discrediting the testimony of Keough and Fouquet, which was supported by physical evidence. Our review of the record convinces us that that is highly improbable. We therefore conclude "beyond a reasonable doubt that the error complained of," *Chapman*, 386 U.S. at 24 — the district court's refusal to permit Figueroa to impeach Wright's testimony by cross-examining him about his swastika tattoos — "did not contribute to the verdict obtained," *id.* The district court's error was therefore harmless.

CONCLUSION

For the foregoing reasons ... the judgment of the district court is affirmed.

Hicks v. Commonwealth of Kentucky

2009 WL 3526699 (Ky. 2009)

Monarch, J.

MEMORANDUM OPINION OF THE COURT

Appellant, Noah Hicks, appeals his Breckenridge Circuit Court conviction....

Facts

[Defendant Noah Hicks and three co-conspirators robbed, kidnapped, and shot Carroll Garvey. Garvey managed to escape, and he spoke to the police.] Before going to the hospital, Garvey provided the police with the names of his attackers, and specifically named [Erroll] Rogers and Appellant as responsible for his injuries. The police then executed a search warrant at Appellant's home and, although they did not find anything, Appellant confirmed that the gun was at Rogers' house. The police executed a search warrant at Rogers' home, and found the gun, a loaded 9 mm Glock 17 handgun and an extra clip, hidden in Rogers' bathroom under some laundry. They also located the crime scene on Edgar Basham Road and recovered two 9 mm shell casings on the side of the road as well as Garvey's lost tennis shoe.

Later, the Breckinridge Co. Sheriff interviewed Appellant, at which time Appellant signed a written waiver of rights. During the interrogation, Appellant admitted he picked up Garvey and took him to Appellant's home. He admitted Garvey was jumped and tied up at his house. He admitted that he grabbed a belt and extension cord to tie up Garvey. He admitted that he helped put Garvey in the trunk of his car and they drove around for one and one-half to two hours. He also admitted that he had the gun in his hand when Garvey got out of the trunk, as well as firing the gun when Garvey started running away. Appellant said that he was at the rear of the vehicle when he fired the gun and that Garvey was running last time he saw him.

Appellant, Banks, and Rogers were tried jointly. Appellant was found guilty of 1) Kidnapping (with serious physical injury); 2) Second-Degree Robbery; and 3) First-Degree Assault, enhanced by a finding of Second-Degree Persistent Felony Offender ("PFO")....

This appeal followed.... For reasons set out below, we affirm Appellant's convictions....

III. Requiring Witness to Show Tattoo

... Appellant argues that the trial court erred by requiring Appellant's witness, Ryan Spence, to take off his shirt and show an alleged swastika tattoo to the jury. We agree, but conclude that the error was harmless.

Spence was Appellant's only witness. [Despite allegations that Appellant bribed Spence for his testimony, Spence was allowed to testify.] Spence said he knew Appellant but only as an acquaintance. Spence was in jail with Rogers after Rogers' arrest for his participation in Garvey's shooting. While in jail, Rogers and Spence played basketball together and might have gone to church together.

At trial, during direct examination, Spence admitted that he was a convicted felon and testified that, while incarcerated in the Breckinridge Detention Center, he came to know Rogers and Appellant. Spence said that when other prisoners asked Rogers what he had done to be in jail, he heard Rogers say that he "shot an Asian kid and put him in the trunk."

During cross-examination, the prosecutor asked Spence to take off his shirt in order to show the jury a swastika tattoo on the back of his arm. Spence refused. A bench conference was held in chambers and the prosecutor explained that the swastika tattoo was relevant as to Spence's credibility since, in addition to the bribery allegations, his testimony might additionally be motivated by racial bias, as Rogers was African-American and Spence and Appellant were white. Appellant, on the other hand, contended that the tattoo alone did not mean that Spence actually harbored racial prejudice. Over Appellant's objections, the trial court ordered Spence to take off his shirt and show his tattoo to the jury, but cautioned that they were to view the evidence only as it bore on Spence's credibility for "testimony that appears to be non-favorable to an African-American." Notwithstanding the admonishment, Appellant now argues the trial court's decision to order Spence to show the jury his tattoo amounted to reversible error.

We begin by noting that, generally, a trial judge's ruling on an admissibility issue, if supported by substantial evidence, is dispositive of the question. Therefore, the trial court's decision to admit evidence of Spence's swastika tattoo is reviewed for an abuse of discretion. *See Commonwealth v. English,* 993 S.W.2d 941 (Ky.1999). "The test for abuse of discretion is whether the trial judge's decision was arbitrary, unreasonable, unfair, or unsupported by sound legal principles." *English,* 993 S.W.2d at 945.

Here, we hold that the trial court abused its discretion in ordering Spence to display his tattoo for the jury. While, in general, it is true that "[w]itness credibility is always at issue," *King v. Commonwealth,* 276 S.W.3d 270, 275 (Ky.2009) (*quoting Commonwealth v. Maddox,* 955 S.W.2d 718, 721 (Ky.1997)), it is equally true that evidence must be relevant, defined as "having any tendency to make the existence of any fact that is of consequence to the determination of the action more probable or less probable than it would be without the evidence." KRE 401. In this instance, the stated relevancy of Spence's swastika tattoo was that its presence on his person was tantamount to his racial bias towards African Americans. Though, by and large, that may often be the inference, we simply cannot say that it was the appropriate inference here because *no other evidence* was presented—either direct or circumstantial in character—which tended to show what Spence's swastika tattoo meant to him, why he chose to have it placed on his body, or whether he had any particular feelings, negative or positive, towards African-Americans or any ethnic group at all. In this way, the relevancy of the tattoo, defined as evidence of Spence's racial bias, depended, at least in part, "upon the fulfillment of a condition of fact," and the independent evidence presented was so patently lacking as to be insufficient to support that finding. *See* KRE 104(b).

Nevertheless, because we cannot say that " 'the error itself had substantial influence' " upon Appellant's trial such that it "substantially swayed" his conviction, we hold that the error was harmless and does not warrant a new trial. *Winstead v. Commonwealth,* 283 S.W.3d 678, 688-89 (Ky.2009) (*quoting Kotteakos v. United States,* 328 U.S. 750, 765 (1946)). In light of the fact that [another inmate] subsequently testified that Appellant offered to pay him and Spence, his cellmate, for favorable testimony, independent evidence strongly suggested that Spence's credibility was suspect for reasons other than racial bias. Moreover, the Commonwealth's evidence overwhelmingly pointed to Appellant's guilt, which evidence included not only Garvey's testimony and corroborating physical evidence, but also: Appellant's admission to picking up Garvey and taking him to his home; Appellant's admission that Garvey was attacked, bound, and placed in the truck of his car; Appellant's admission that he held the gun and shot it at Garvey as Garvey was fleeing into the woods; and, [a co-conspirator's] testimony that Appellant bound Garvey, placed him in his trunk, and shot at him as he fled.

Conclusion

For the foregoing reasons, we affirm Appellant's convictions....

Minton, C.J.; Abramson, Cunningham, Schroder, Scott, and Venters, JJ., concur. Noble, J., dissents in part by separate opinion.

NOBLE, J., DISSENTING IN PART: I concur with the majority except that I do not think admission of the tattoo was harmless.

Focus Questions: *United States v. James*

- What reasoning does the court use to determine the victim's prior actions were irrelevant to defendant's state of mind in her self-defense claim?
- How would you rule if a FRE 403 analysis was conducted on the admission of the victim's prior actions?
- Does the Court limit the scope of its holding? How so?
- Which side has the stronger reasoning—the majority or the dissent?

United States v. James

169 F.3d 1210 (9th Cir. 1999) (en banc)

NOONAN, Circuit Judge:

Ernestine Audry James appeals her conviction of aiding and abetting manslaughter within Indian country in violation of 18 U.S.C. §§ 2, 1112, 1153. Holding that the district court erred in excluding relevant evidence corroborating her testimony, we reverse the judgment of conviction.

FACTS AND PROCEEDINGS

James met her boyfriend, David Ogden (the victim), at a pow-wow in Seattle. He was nice sober, nasty drunk. Ogden had boasted to her about once killing a man and getting away with it. He told her he had sold another man a fake watch, and when the man complained, had stabbed him in the neck with a ball point pen. Ogden told James that "it was pretty funny watching a guy with a pen dangling out of his neck." He also bragged that he had once "ripped a side view mirror off the car and beat a man unconscious with it," and that, in yet another incident, he had robbed an old man by holding him down with a knife in his face and threatening to cut his eyes out.

James had seen Ogden's violence with her own eyes and suffered it. The worst was when Ogden was intoxicated and James refused to have sexual intercourse, so he threw her on the bed and raped her. On another occasion when Ogden wanted to have sexual intercourse with James and she had refused, he came into the room where she and her daughter Jaylene Jeffries were and started yelling at James and calling her names. Jaylene got up and held Ogden at knife point with a carving knife until James ordered them both to desist....

When James and Ogden would go out for dinner, a few drinks, and window shopping, he would start yelling at strangers and challenging them to fights. Sometimes he and the strangers would fight. James also testified Ogden used to take his knife out of his sock, open and close it, and switch it back and forth between hands as if he were in a fight.

Jaylene, the daughter, had beaten Ogden on three occasions. She testified that "I was the one doing something, but he wasn't." Ogden would never fight back against her. He acted scared of her, even though she was only fourteen.

Ogden hated Jaylene's boyfriend, Michas Tiatano. Ogden, James, and Jaylene were Indian, but Tiatano was part Black and Asian. Ogden hated Black people. On the day Ogden was killed, the four of them had been together at a party. At one point during the party Ogden had lifted a hammer from the carpentry tools he used at his job and said to Tiatano "I ought to hit you with this," but stopped when James told him to "knock it off." Later Ogden started pulling Tiatano around by his shirt and telling him he hated him. Jaylene told Ogden to stop, and he did.

When James decided to leave the party, her van got stuck on a fishnet lying on the ground. She and Jaylene were sitting in the van when Jaylene heard Tiatano say, "Oh man," and fall down. Ogden had just punched Tiatano in the face, possibly with some object in his hand, so hard that he broke his nose and knocked him unconscious....

James testified that after Ogden had "cold cocked" Tiatano, Jaylene chased him for awhile. According to James, the following ensued:

A. Jaylene came—excuse me. Jaylene came back to the van and she was breathing heavy, like she was running. She was very upset and she just started begging me for the gun. She said, mom, please give me the gun, give me the gun. She said it several times.

Q. And what did you do when she begged you for the gun?

A. I just grabbed for my purse and got the gun and handed it to her.

...

Q. At that moment when Jaylene asked you for the gun and you reached in and gave it to her, why did you give it to her?

A. I gave it to her to protect herself and the family members.

Q. What did you expect her to do with the gun when you gave it to her?

A. I just expected her to fend David off. I didn't want her to shoot him. It was just to scare him away from the property.

Q. Why did you want her to scare him away from the property?

A. Because I knew how violent he was and I knew that he wouldn't stop at just one punch and he wanted to continue being violent....

Defense counsel argued self-defense. He pointed out to the jury that James, his client, was charged with aiding and abetting the daughter by handing her the gun, so James had to be judged by what she knew at the moment, not by the daughter's conduct afterward in killing a man.... He argued that because the mother knew Ogden was drunk, vicious when drunk, and usually carried a knife in his sock, it was not grossly negligent to give "the gun to her daughter so that Jaylene could protect herself in that one moment when [the mother] had that decision, the split second decision to make."

The jury heard all the evidence discussed above. In the pretrial skirmishing, the court had ruled that James and Jaylene could testify about prior violent misconduct they had known about when James handed Jaylene the gun, but could not introduce extrinsic evidence of which they had no knowledge at that time. This appeal is about ... exhibits that the mother's attorney was not allowed to show the jury. He had ... court documents setting forth detailed findings on the robbery of a 58-year old man, in which Ogden sat on the man and held a knife at his throat and at his eyes while threatening to blind him....

The jury sent out a number of questions during its deliberations. One read as follows:

Dear Judge,

The jury would like to know if it is a "fact" that:
1) Ogden did stab an "old man" and was sentenced to 20 yrs & on parole
2) did he really stab someone with a pen
3) did he really murder a man and hide on an apt?
Are there police or court documents to prove this or is it "brag?"
Thanx.

Robert Reedy
Foreman

The judge declined to supplement the evidence.

The district judge further explained why he had excluded the evidence. In his ruling on defendant's motion for a new trial, he explained that "evidence of every past violent act by Ogden, known to the defendant, was placed before the jury," as was reputation and opinion evidence as to Ogden's violent character. The extrinsic evidence was not such evidence, because "the only relevant facts concerning Ogden's past were the ones defendant knew about; only to that extent could her state of mind at the time of the shooting have been affected by Ogden's past misconduct." The district judge noted that if the court records had in fact been to the contrary, and proved that Ogden had been exaggerating and was not really so violent as he claimed, the court would have sustained a defense objection, "because the court record, never seen by defendant, could not have affected her state of mind. The result should be no different when the defendant offers the extraneous record."

James was convicted and sentenced to five years probation. She appealed, and a divided panel of this court affirmed her conviction. We then took the case en banc.

ANALYSIS

A preliminary question is whether we are conducting a review of the district court's exercise of discretion or a review de novo of an error of law. If the district court's ruling is understood as a determination that any record not known to the defendant is inadmissible as part of a defense based on self-defense, its ruling was one of law, and our review is de novo. If the district court is understood to have implicitly weighed the probative force of the evidence against its prejudicial impact on the jury by making the victim seem odious, then our review is for an abuse of discretion. As both ways of interpreting the district court's action are tenable, we shall review, first, de novo as to law, and, second, review the postulated exercise of discretion.

Ernestine Audry James's only defense was that she believed that she and her daughter were in danger of grievous bodily harm or death from Ogden. Essential to that defense was her belief in Ogden's stories of previous acts of vicious violence committed by him. These stories were of such a remarkable character of atrocity that one might doubt that he had told them of himself or doubt that they had really occurred. Hence the question raised by the jurors as to Ogden's stabbing of an old man; Ogden's stabbing of another person with a pen; and Ogden's murdering a man: "Are there police or court documents to prove this or is it 'brag'?"

For the defense the records, if admitted, would have had two legitimate functions: to corroborate Ernestine James's own testimony that she had heard Ogden tell her these things and to corroborate her statement that she had reason to be afraid of Ogden in his vicious drunken mood.

The district court thought the only function of the evidence would have been to show Ernestine James's state of mind and that, since she had not seen the records, the documents proved nothing as to her state of mind. That interpretation of the proffered evidence was too narrow. It was absolutely necessary to her defense for the jury to believe (1) that she wasn't making up the stories and (2) that, when she heard them, she heard them from the man who had actually done these terrible things and who was not just spinning tales. The records proved that he had done them so that the stories of his wild exploits would have had the ring of truth to her, and the records proved that what Ernestine James testified to had actually taken place. The records corroborated her testimony, and the records corroborated her reason to fear....

Because the crux of James's defense rested on her credibility and because her credibility could be directly corroborated through the excluded documentary evidence, exclusion of the documents was prejudicial and more probably than not affected the verdict.

For the reasons stated, the judgment of the district court is **REVERSED.**

KLEINFELD, Circuit Judge, dissenting:

.... Defense counsel had to deal with a problem regarding his self defense theory. The daughter shot an unarmed man who was standing with his hands up, and she testified that she did not fear him. The mother gave her daughter a gun while the daughter was chasing the man. The mother's defense attorney dealt with the problem by reminding the jury that the mother was on trial, not the daughter, and the mother had to be judged by her state of mind, what she knew and thought, at the moment she gave her daughter the gun. The judge accordingly let in every bit of evidence with any bearing on what the mother knew at that moment. All he kept out was what the mother did not then know, that there were papers corroborating what the victim allegedly had said about the vicious things he had done. Because the mother had not known of the papers and had never seen them, the trial judge concluded that the papers could not have had any effect on her state of mind. That makes sense, and I do not think so sensible a decision can properly be characterized as an abuse of discretion.

The majority is correct, that the papers were nevertheless relevant in another sense. Evidence that the victim really had killed a man, and had stabbed another in the throat with a pen, made it more probable that the victim had told the mother that he had done these things. For that reason, it would not have been an abuse of discretion for a judge to have admitted the documents. But admissibility does not suffice to make exclusion an abuse of discretion.

There were good reasons to keep the documents out. The documents were somewhat remote corroboration, not direct evidence of anything relevant. They showed nothing directly about the mother's state of mind, because she had never seen them. And the risk of unfair prejudice to the prosecution was considerable. The victim was a bad man. Some people would say, in private and out of court, that "he deserved it," or "he needed killing." But no one says such things in a courtroom, because the law does not permit murder, even of very bad people.

The jury's questions—"did he really stab someone with a pen," "Are there police or court documents to prove this or is it 'brag?'"—may mean that the jury was asking the wrong question, whether the victim deserved to be shot. The majority says that the evidence went to the mother's credibility, not the victim's character. But the jury's questions suggest that jurors were wondering whether the victim really did what he claimed, as opposed to whether Ms. James believed him. And the trial judge who, unlike us, was there, may have seen that coming. Plenty of evidence lends itself both to permissible and impermissible uses, and trial judges have to weigh the risks as the trial proceeds....

We did not try Ms. James's case. When a trial judge makes a sensible decision to admit or exclude evidence, well within the range of what is ordinary, for a sensible reason, as the trial judge did in this case, we should let it alone. Ms. James got a fair trial.

Problem 2-3

The defendant was arrested for allegedly embezzling money from his employer, a trucking company. Embezzlement is a "wobbler," which means it can be prosecuted as a misdemeanor or a felony, at the prosecutor's discretion. The prosecutor on the case had a reputation for being especially tough. However, since this was the defendant's first brush with the law, the prosecutor offered him a plea bargain whereby the embezzlement charge would be prosecuted as a misdemeanor and he would serve only 90 days in the county jail. The county jail houses people convicted of misdemeanors such as petty larceny, DUI, and domestic violence, in addition to people who require short-term custody, such as those awaiting trial and those who cannot post bail.

Under the rules of the defendant's union (which represents the employees of all the trucking companies in the region), any employee convicted of a crime of dishonesty would lose his job and be ineligible for future union membership or employment for an employer covered by that union. (Embezzlement is considered a crime of dishonesty, and conviction includes accepting a plea bargain.) The prosecutor told the defendant that if he refused the offer, the state would prosecute it as a felony. If convicted at trial, the defendant would serve a minimum sentence of one year in a minimum to medium security state prison. State prisons house people who have been convicted of more serious crimes, from grand theft to narcotics distribution to murder, for longer stays. As a result, a complex social structure forms within prisons, often resulting in increased violence and corruption among inmates and officers. The defendant rejected the plea bargain.

At trial, the defendant offered to admit the fact that he had refused the plea bargain as evidence of his consciousness of innocence. The trial judge refused to admit this information. Was the judge correct in excluding the fact that the defendant had rejected the plea bargain?

Problem 2-4

In December 1979, the manager of Ziggy's Plant and Gift Shop in Joliet, Illinois, reported to the police that a robbery had just taken place in his shop. Officer Willie Berry heard the radio dispatch and told his partner, Richard Klepfer, that the description of the suspect matched Gary Duckworth, who was known to have been involved in robberies and purse snatchings. The two officers drove to Ziggy's to investigate.

As they approached Ziggy's, Officers Berry and Klepfer encountered two men sitting in a Cadillac in a parking lot adjacent to Ziggy's. When the Cadillac pulled out of the parking lot, the officers directed it to pull over. At that time, Officer Berry recognized the passenger as Gary Duckworth, whom he believed was the robber.

The officers exited their vehicle and approached the Cadillac with their guns aimed at the occupants of the car. Officer Berry ordered the suspects to put their hands up. Berry testified that he had to order the suspects to raise their hands three times before they complied. Berry also testified that it seemed as though Duckworth was looking at the driver, Ronald Sherrod, as if to say, "What are we going to do next?"

After making sure his partner had the suspects covered, Officer Berry raised his gun and cautiously approached the Cadillac. Berry testified that as he was looking into the vehicle and approaching the suspects, Sherrod made a quick movement with his hand into his coat, as if he was going to reach for a weapon. At that point, Officer Berry fired his revolver at Sherrod, killing him instantly.

Sherrod's father brought an action against Officer Berry and the city. Berry claimed self-defense (i.e., that he acted in reasonable fear for his life at the time he shot Sherrod and the use of deadly force was justified). At trial, the plaintiff offered evidence that a post-mortem search of Sherrod showed he was unarmed at the time Berry shot him. The defendant objected that evidence of the absence of a weapon was irrelevant to the issue of whether Berry believed that the use of deadly force was justified at the time of the shooting.

a) How should the court have ruled?

b) What if Officer Berry had testified that he saw a shiny metallic object similar to a gun in the suspect's hand?

II. Is There a Conditional Relevance Objection?

Relevant Rule
FRE 104(b)

Preliminary Questions

(b) Relevancy That Depends on a Fact. When the relevance of evidence depends on whether a fact exists, proof must be introduced sufficient to support a finding that the fact does exist. The court may admit the proposed evidence on the condition that the proof be introduced later.

Let us go back to the overview problem at the beginning of the chapter. In the prosecution of Ms. Johnson, assume that the prosecution offered evidence that the bodies of the victims were discovered at 1:00 p.m. on July 1. The prosecution then offered evidence that Ms. Johnson attempted to commit suicide in her cell at 3:00 p.m. on July 1. Is there a fact missing in the prosecution's chain of logic?

Occasionally, the relevancy of evidence depends upon proof of a *preliminary* question of fact — an earlier link in the factual chain. This is a question of conditional relevancy under FRE 104(b). In the example above, the prosecution's chain of logic would be something like: the bodies were discovered; Ms. Johnson became aware of this fact; Ms. Johnson realized that her confidant was a government informant; Ms. Johnson attempted suicide because she was aware that her guilt would be proven in court. Yet, in our hypothetical, not a single piece of evidence proves a preliminary question of fact in the chain: Did Ms. Johnson know that the bodies were found? If she did not know, the rest of the chain of logic falls apart. Indeed, if she did not know, then the chances that she attempted suicide due to consciousness of her guilt being proven fall dramatically. Without proof of this fact, the evidence is, arguably, not relevant.

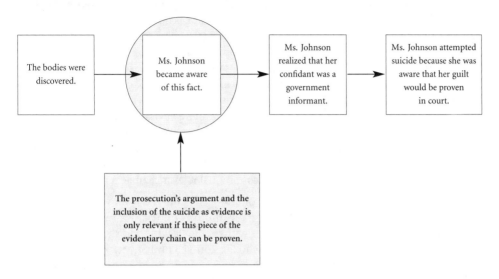

How does the court handle this situation? The judge must play a *screening* role with respect to the preliminary fact. First, the court must determine if the evidence would be relevant assuming the preliminary fact were proven. In other words, would her suicide attempt be relevant if the prosecution possessed evidence that someone told Ms. Johnson between 1:00 p.m. and 3:00 p.m. that the bodies were found? If the evidence would be relevant, the judge next must find the evidence of the preliminary fact "sufficient" to support a jury finding that the preliminary fact is true. Thus, to build on our hypothetical, assume that the prosecution offered evidence that at 2:00 p.m. on July 1, a corrections officer said to Ms. Johnson, "They just found all the bodies. Looks like you picked the wrong guy to trust." Is this evidence "sufficient" to support a finding by the jury that the preliminary fact (whether Ms. Johnson knew the bodies were found) is true? It certainly is, and the judge will admit the evidence. Significantly, once admitted, it is up to the jury to make the final determination of whether the preliminary fact is proven. If, for example, the jury doubts the credibility of the corrections officer, they may reject the evidence, as it is the jury's job to weigh the admitted evidence.

Note also how low the threshold is for the judge. The U.S. Supreme Court defined the test for conditional relevance under FRE 104(b) as whether the jury could reasonably find the fact by a preponderance of the evidence based on all the evidence of record. *Huddleston v. United States*, 485 U.S. 681 (1988). Thus, the judge merely determines whether "sufficient" support exists such that a jury could conceivably find the preliminary fact true. The judge will not ban the evidence just because she, personally, does not believe the preliminary fact was proven. If sufficient evidence exists such that reasonable people could find that the fact exists, even if the judge doubts the evidence, it will be admissible and will go to the jury. Furthermore, if a party presents the evidence out of order (e.g., offers evidence of the suicide before offering the other links of the chain), the judge is permitted to admit the evidence subject to later introduction of evidence of the preliminary fact. This is referred to as "connecting up" the proof, and it allows a party to present the evidence in a way that enhances the narrative of their case. If that party does not subsequently introduce such evidence, the initial evidence offered will be stricken and the jury will be instructed to ignore that evidence.

As you think about conditional relevance, you may have thought, "Isn't it true that most relevancy determinations depend on some factual premise?" In other words, all circumstantial evidence possesses a chain of inferences. Theoretically, then, a conditional relevance objection will very often exist. As one treatise noted, "Certainly there is no bright line.... All relevancy determinations rest on factual premises. If those factual premises can reasonably be assumed to be known by the trier of fact, the question is appropriately treated as one of 'pure' relevancy to be determined by the court without requiring proof of the underlying factual premises. However, if the factual premises are not reasonably known, the proponent is properly required to produce evidence of them as a condition of admissibility so the trier of fact can understand and determine those underlying facts that make the proffered evidence relevant." C. Mueller & L. Kirkpatrick, Evidence, Section 4.3, at 164–65 (5th ed. 2012). In short, if the factual premise cannot be reasonably understood from the context, then it is an issue of conditional relevancy. If there are unstated factual assumptions that are not reasonably determinable from the context, then you probably have a conditional relevance objection.

Let us explore the line concerning "reasonably determinable from the context" with one more hypothetical. Assume defendant Sally Smith is on trial for murder. A witness called by the prosecutor is asked whom the witness saw leaving the scene of the crime. The witness responds, "It was Sally Smith, who lives on 123 Elm Street." Are there missing links to that conclusion? How does the witness know the defendant's name and address? If the witness was, for example, Sally's son, then the missing links are explained from the context—surely a son can identify his mother and knows her address. If the witness had never met Sally Smith prior to seeing her, however, the context does not resolve the missing factual link, and a conditional relevance issue is raised.

III. Even If It Is Relevant, Is It Too Prejudicial?

Relevant Rules
FRE 403

Excluding Relevant Evidence for Prejudice, Confusion, Waste of Time, or Other Reasons

The court may exclude relevant evidence if its probative value is substantially outweighed by a danger of one or more of the following: unfair prejudice, confusing the issues, misleading the jury, undue delay, wasting time, or needlessly presenting cumulative evidence.

FRE 105

Limiting Evidence That Is Not Admissible Against Other Parties or for Other Purposes

If the court admits evidence that is admissible against a party or for a purpose — but not against another party or for another purpose — the court, on timely request, must restrict the evidence to its proper scope and instruct the jury accordingly.

FRE 403 governs the admissibility of unfairly prejudicial evidence. The idea behind FRE 403 is to counterbalance the liberal admissibility requirements of FRE 401 and FRE 402. By its very terms, FRE 403 permits the exclusion of otherwise relevant evidence. The decision-making is in the hands of the judge, who "may" exclude the evidence.

When does relevant evidence fail the FRE 403 balancing test? The two key words of the rule are "substantially" and "unfair." By authorizing exclusion only where the probative value is "substantially" outweighed by countervailing considerations, FRE 403 is designed to favor admissibility. Close calls (i.e., anything less than substantial) favor the evidence being admitted. By authorizing exclusion for "unfair" prejudice, the drafters of FRE 403 acknowledged that relevant evidence is inherently prejudicial to the opposing party. FRE 403 "expects courts to distinguish between prejudice resulting from the reasonable persuasive force of evidence and prejudice resulting from excessive emotional or irrational effects that could distort the accuracy and integrity of the factfinding process." C. Mueller & L. Kirkpatrick, Evidence, Section 4.10, at 179 (5th ed. 2012).

Preventing excessive emotion to govern the factfinding process typically concerns inflammatory, shocking and/or sensational evidence. This type of evidence could lead the jury to allow their emotions to trump the logical connections of the evidence and thereby the jury punishes or rewards regardless of guilt or responsibility. For example, a graphic picture of a murder victim may cause the jury to base their decision on the emotion they feel when viewing the picture rather than on the logical force of the evidence. In such scenarios, the court may attempt to minimize the emotional impact of the evidence by offering verbal testimony in lieu of a shocking exhibit, using stipulations (i.e., agreements between the parties as to the evidence), and other means discussed in the next section.

Another risk, preventing irrational effects, typically arises when evidence is admitted for a limited purpose. As we shall see in the chapter on impeachment, often a prior felony conviction may be used to attack the credibility of a witness. The theory behind such evidence is a prior conviction demonstrates that the witness does not respect the law and therefore may not respect the required witness oath to tell the truth. Yet, a single piece of evidence can generate numerous inferences. Let us go through an example. Assume that Peter the Plaintiff will testify in an automobile accident case that the defendant ran a red light. The defense attorney seeks to attack Peter's credibility by asking him about a prior felony conviction for child abuse. What are the possible inferences from this evidence in the eyes of the jury?

Evidence: Peter convicted of Child Abuse

- Permissible Inference: As a felon, Peter does not respect the law and should not be trusted to tell the truth in this proceeding

- Impermissible Inference: Peter is a vile human being who hurts children and therefore should not win this case

The same piece of evidence leads to both inferences, like trains running on parallel tracks. The judge will instruct the jury that they may follow the logic of the permissible track, but that they should not follow the logic of the impermissible track because the impermissible track leads to an irrational effect (i.e., Peter's conviction does not determine whether Peter was or was not hurt by a negligent driver). If the judge believes that a jury cannot differentiate between the improper and proper purpose of the evidence, then this is a factor that makes the evidence inadmissible. Likewise, evidence that would only serve to confuse (e.g., it focuses the jury's attention too closely on a factual issue that is not central to the outcome of the case), mislead (e.g., the jury will draw a mistaken inference), or waste time due to its cumulative nature may similarly be excluded.

Law students tend to over-rely on FRE 403 during their early studies of evidence law, in part because they do not give enough attention to the "probative" part of the equation. As you learned earlier in this chapter, probative value is an assessment of the weight of numerous factors, including the logical force of the evidence and its context. The greater the strength of syllogistic logic, the greater the weight of the evidence. It is this probative force that must be balanced against prejudice in a FRE 403 determination. For example, let us return to the overview problem at the beginning of the chapter. Assume all relevance and conditional relevance objections have been overcome. Should Ms. Johnson's attempted suicide be excluded under FRE 403? If you were the judge, how strong is the probative force of the evidence? Does the attempted suicide point strongly to a consciousness of guilt or is the inference rather weak? Does it strengthen the probative force if she attempted suicide within minutes of finding out McNeese was a government informant? Does it significantly weaken the probative force if we learned that Ms. Johnson has a history of repeated suicide attempts that preceded the events in question? Now, let's look at the "unfair" prejudice to Ms. Johnson. Will the jury make negative judgments on Ms. Johnson's character after hearing that she attempted to commit suicide? Will they use that evidence improperly? If so, will such dangers "substantially" outweigh the probative value?

As you can see, a judge has a great deal of discretion in making these determinations. As in FRE 401 and FRE 402, the trial judge does not weigh issues of credibility when considering the probative value of evidence. This remains the province of the jury. Instead trial judges attempt to balance "the centrality of the point to be proved, the need for the particular evidence, the availability of alternative sources of proof, and the likelihood that the jury will understand and follow a limiting instruction under [FRE 105]." C. Mueller & L. Kirkpatrick, Evidence, Section 4.9, at 175 (5th ed. 2012). Thus, prejudicial evidence on a tangential or collateral point in the trial is less likely to be admissible. The probative value increases if the proponent of the evidence has only one (or limited) avenue(s) of presenting that evidence and therefore the need for that particular evidence is greater. If fifty people witnessed defendant shoot the victim, the weight of each individual's testimony is less. But if only one person viewed the murder, then that eyewitness has much greater weight and therefore more probative value. Put simply, the more essential the evidence, the greater its probative value, and the higher its prejudicial effect must be in order for the evidence to be deemed inadmissible under FRE 403. Indeed, FRE 403's requirement that probative value be outweighed substantially requires that some risks of negative, prejudicial impacts must be tolerated.

As previously mentioned, limiting instructions to the jury also play a role in the FRE 403 balancing process. FRE 105 mandates that a court "restrict ... evidence to its proper scope and instruct the jury accordingly." Thus, the judge will instruct the jury to focus on the proper use of the evidence and warn them to avoid the minefields of impermissible inference or unfairly prejudicial effect. If a judge believes that the jury will probably follow an instruction, the judge may find the risk of unfair prejudice is lowered and will admit the item. Conversely, if a judge believes that an instruction would place the jury in a difficult position of splitting hairs, the judge may take this under consideration in her FRE 403 balancing.

Furthermore, the trial judge's determination is governed by an abuse of discretion standard that is very difficult to overrule on appeal. Why give the trial judge such great discretion? First, the judge is making a judgment call in an area without any particularized guidelines. Many unique, fact-specific scenarios are presented, often without the guidance of appellate decisions. Second, the trial judge is in a far better position to observe the level of prejudice than appellate court judges would be, as appellate court judges are limited to reviewing a trial transcript. Accordingly, a trial judge's determination of probativeness, prejudice, and the balance between the two usually survive an appeal.

Problem 2-5

In the Case Excerpt below you will find an excerpt from the prosecution's appellate brief in the case of State v. Peterson concerning whether evidence of the defendant's bisexuality was excludable under FRE 403 in the murder trial. After you read the facts below that were introduced at trial, please craft arguments both for and against admission of the evidence. **After** you have done so, read an excerpt from the court's opinion on this issue on page 63.

Case Excerpt: Prosecution Brief in *State v. Peterson*

Evidence Relating to Defendant's Interest in Male, Homosexual Pornography and Attempted Liaison With a Male Prostitute

[Officer] Daniel George testified that photographs and paperwork contained in State's Exhibit 28A were collected from defendant's den by Investigator Mike Harris, who died before trial. Investigator Anne Saccoccio also took part in this search and seizure. The material included hard copies of some of the e-mail correspondence between defendant and Brent Wolgamott; it also included reviews from Wolgamott's clients, as well as pornographic photographs of Wolgamott and others, all of which defendant had printed from the internet and placed in a manila envelope. This envelope also contained business documents and legal correspondence relating to estate planning and wills which the parties agreed to exclude. The parties entered into a stipulation that material included in State's Exhibit 28A was found in a "drawer located on the right side of the desk in the study"....

Patrick Kemmer, President of Compusleuth, testified that his company was asked to analyze data on the hard disk of defendant's computer which had been seized. A copy of that disk (State's Exhibit 162) had been made and submitted to Compusleuth. Todd Markley of Compusleuth, an expert in forensic examination of computers, performed most of the analysis on the hard disk. Defendant had two active web browsers on his computer, Internet Explorer and Netscape. Markley explained that as one browses the internet the web browser leaves information in the form of cache files. State's Exhibit 170 was an image of male, homosexual activity. Compusleuth found about 2500 photographs of homosexual pornography similar to Exhibit 170, about 2000 of these were in free space, meaning "that they were files that existed and then were deleted...."

On 23 February 2001 the defendant received an e-mail from Dirk Yates addressed to MPWriter at NC.RR.Com, which was admitted as State's Exhibit 165. "Dirk Yates," Markley testified, "runs a web service that predominantly deals in homosexual pornography." As noted below, defendant had known, or known of, Yates since the [time that the] defendant was stationed at San Diego approximately thirty years before he received this e-mail. And the defendant referred his would-be homosexual partner, Brent Wolgamott, to Yates.

As noted, on the night Kathleen Peterson died, she was expecting an e-mail from Helen Prislinger regarding a telephone conference call. The e-mail was directed to MPWriter at NC.RR.Com. The e-mail was sent to the defendant's computer from Toronto on 8 December 2001 at 11:53 p.m. Eastern Time and received at 11:55 p.m. Eastern Time; this e-mail was received into evidence as State's Exhibit 168. The e-mail had an attachment labeled Readiness.PBJ. Markley testified that Compusleuth employees tried to determine whether the attachment had been opened and were "pretty confident" that it had not been. But there was no way of determining whether the e-mail itself had been read.

In August and September 2001 Brent Wolgamott was on active duty at Fort Bragg. In his off-duty hours he worked as a male prostitute, charging fees for his sexual services, which he described as including "just about anything under the sun." Wolgamott had a web site advertised as a "male for male escort" service, listing his name as Brad, and featuring photographs of him as well as text from "various clients," who, he testified, "write in reviews of their experience with me." From information on the site new clients would contact him by phone or e-mail.

On 30 August 2002 the defendant spoke with Wolgamott by phone and followed that conversation with an e-mail message saying, "I checked out the website you gave me. You have great reviews and I would like to get together with you. I'm in Durham, just off 15/501.... Daytime is best for me, Tuesday, Wednesday, or Friday." The men exchanged numerous emails, which was a common course of dealing, Wolgamott explained, because such clients or potential clients wanted to make sure he was "not a gangster, somebody who is going to rob them."

The defendant informed Wolgamott that Dirk Yates had a studio in Palm Springs and suggested that Wolgamott audition for him:

> You really owe me for this. I should get a freebie because this could be a career change for you.
>
> Dirk Yates is one of the major figures in the male porn industry really, really big. He has been doing videos of Marines for years. He got started a long time ago in San Diego....
>
> ....
>
> If you want further info, come up Tuesday or Wednesday and I'll give you more info and some of Dirk's movies.... Or just come for straight on business, no strings attached—I'll just f____ your ... for the set price.

(mpwriter [defendant] to SoldierTop [Wolgamott], 1 September 2001; State's Exhibit 28A-4) Defendant printed a hard copy of this email, among others, which was seized. Wolgamott also sent a photograph of himself to the defendant, because, he testified "[u]sually anybody who is contacting me likes to know what they're getting."…. The defendant and Wolgamott discussed a price for his services, and Wolgamott quoted a fee of $150 per hour.

The defendant continued his solicitation writing that "[e]venings are not great for me anyway; I'm married. Very happily married with a dynamite wife.... I'm very bi.... How about this? I'll give you my cell phone number and we can try to hook up Wednesday night." ([defendant] to (Wolgamott), 2 September 2001; State's Exhibit 28A-5) The two arranged a liaison to engage in anal sex on 5 September 2001 in Durham at either the defendant's "house or another house that he had." The date was chosen on Wolgamott's part because he was flying the next morning from the Raleigh-Durham Airport to Palm Springs. The assignation was set for nine p.m., but Wolgamott decided not to meet the defendant because, he explained, "I had a very long day, and when I got up there that night, I just said ... I'll talk to him when I get back. I'm just tired, and I want to go to Palm Springs." Almost a month later Wolgamott contacted the defendant "to apologize for not showing up." The two had no further communication.

State v. Peterson

179 N.C.App. 437, 634 S.E.2d 594
(N.C.App., 2006)

...

III. *Evidence of Bi-Sexuality Under Rule 404(b)*

Defendant next argues the trial court erred, in ruling upon his motion *in limine,* to admit evidence of his bi-sexuality. Defendant contends this evidence was irrelevant and unfairly prejudicial. We disagree.

Generally, evidence is admissible at trial if it is relevant and its probative value is not substantially outweighed by, among other things, the danger of unfair prejudice. *See* N.C. Gen.Stat. §8C-1, Rules 402, 403 (2005). "Evidence is relevant if it has any logical tendency, however slight, to prove a fact in issue. In criminal cases, every circumstance that is calculated to throw any light upon the supposed crime is admissible. The weight of such evidence is for the jury." *State v. Smith,* 357 N.C. 604, 613–14, 588 S.E.2d 453, 460 (2003) (internal quotations and citations omitted); *see also* N.C. Gen.Stat. §8C-1, Rule 401 (2005) ("'Relevant evidence' means evidence having any tendency to make the existence of any fact that is of consequence to the determination of the action more probable or less probable than it would be without the evidence."). The standard set by Rule 401,

> gives the judge great freedom to admit evidence because the rule makes evidence relevant if it has *any* logical tendency to prove any fact that is of consequence. Thus, even though a trial court's rulings on relevancy technically are not discretionary and therefore are not reviewed under the abuse of discretion standard applicable to Rule 403, such rulings are given great deference on appeal.

State v. Wallace, 104 N.C.App. 498, 502, 410 S.E.2d 226, 228 (1991) (internal citations omitted).

The trial court concluded that the evidence regarding defendant's bi-sexuality was relevant for two purposes: one, it related to a possible motive; and two, it could be used "to rebut the assertions in Defendant's opening statement regarding the idyllic relationship between the Defendant and the deceased in this case." We now consider whether the evidence of defendant's bi-sexual tendencies was relevant because it rebutted defendant's opening statements of a loving relationship. Defendant argues that none of defense counsel's opening statements "opened the door" for introduction of defendant's bi-sexuality. In his opening statement, defense counsel recounted the relationship between defendant and Kathleen as follows:

> And Michael Peterson and Katherine [sic] Atwater connected. Kathleen and Michael connected in a way that a few people who are really, really lucky in life have a chance to connect. It had nothing to do with tangible things. They felt like soul mates.... And so they fell in love, and in ... 1989 they began to live together.... [W]hat kept them together, what caused them to build that, was a love that absolutely everyone who saw them or knew them understood and recognized, and envied[.]

Defense counsel also read from an essay Kathleen's daughter Caitlin had written in 1999:

> Michael Peterson stopped my mother's tears.... My father had torn her apart, crushing her shell and the illusion in which she lived, destroying her dignity and

pride. But Mike was able to restore her strength and confidence, and to show her that she could find true love.

Defense counsel also showed family pictures of defendant and Kathleen throughout his opening statement.

Our courts have previously allowed evidence in to rebut a defendant's contentions made in his opening statement. *See, e.g.,.... State v. Jones,* 342 N.C. 457, 463–64, 466 S.E.2d 696, 698–99 (testimony by the defendant's former girlfriend regarding a previous assault by the defendant and her fear of him was relevant to rebut the defendant's contentions in his opening statement that the reason the girlfriend delayed three years in reporting him was to get back at him and collect a reward), *cert. denied,* 518 U.S. 1010 (1996) ...

As defense counsel, in his opening statement, extensively discussed defendant and Kathleen's relationship and portrayed the marriage as a happy and loving one, the trial court properly found that evidence of defendant's attempts to have sexual relations with a male escort and interest in homosexual pornography were relevant to rebut defense counsel's opening statement. *See Wallace,* 104 N.C.App. at 502, 410 S.E.2d at 228 (trial court's ruling on relevancy given great deference on appeal). We need not determine whether the evidence of defendant's bi-sexuality was relevant to motive, as we conclude that the evidence was admissible as a rebuttal to defense counsel's opening statement.

Defendant also argues that the trial court erred in finding that the evidence of bi-sexuality was not unfairly prejudicial. As a general rule, relevant evidence "may be excluded if its probative value is substantially outweighed by the danger of unfair prejudice[.]" N.C. Gen.Stat. § 8C-1, Rule 403 (2005). "Evidence which is probative of the State's case necessarily will have a prejudicial effect upon the defendant; the question is one of degree." *State v. Hoffman,* 349 N.C. 167, 184, 505 S.E.2d 80, 91 (1998) (internal quotations omitted), *cert. denied,* 526 U.S. 1053 (1999). The exclusion of evidence under this rule "is within the trial court's sound discretion.... Abuse of discretion results where the court's ruling is manifestly unsupported by reason or is so arbitrary that it could not have been the result of a reasoned decision." *State v. Hennis,* 323 N.C. 279, 285, 372 S.E.2d 523, 527 (1988).

Defendant contends that the trial court abused its discretion in admitting evidence of his bi-sexuality and cites to *State v. Rinaldi,* 264 N.C. 701, 142 S.E.2d 604 (1965), in support of his argument. In *Rinaldi,* the defendant was indicted for the murder of his wife. A male witness for the State testified that the defendant solicited him to murder the defendant's wife, and for sexual relations. *Id.* at 704–05, 142 S.E.2d at 606. Our Supreme Court held that the witness's testimony regarding homosexual advances prejudiced the jury to the defendant's detriment. *Id.* at 705, 142 S.E.2d at 606–07. The Court further stated, "[t]o make such evidence competent, the State would have to show some direct connection between defendant's abnormal propensities and the charge of homicide for which he is then on trial." *Id.,* 142 S.E.2d at 607.

In the case *sub judice,* unlike in *Rinaldi,* the trial court had already specifically found that the evidence of defendant's bi-sexuality was relevant to rebut assertions made in defense counsel's opening statement. After reviewing both a written argument contained in defendant's motion *in limine* and arguments by the prosecutor and defense counsel, the trial court, in its discretion, found that the probative value of the evidence outweighed any prejudice to defendant. As the trial court's decision was not arbitrary or manifestly unsupported by reason, the trial court did not abuse its discretion.

Accordingly, the trial court did not err in admitting evidence of defendant's bi-sexuality.

Problem 2-6

John Brady was arrested during an alleged drug raid. Following his arrest, John sued the arresting officer for allegedly using excessive force and depriving him of his constitutional rights during the arrest. The arresting officer called two of his fellow officers to testify on his behalf. On cross-examination, it was revealed that the two officers had been suspended for use of excessive force. The lawyer for the arresting officer objected on the grounds of unfair prejudice under Rule 403.

How likely is the court to admit the evidence that the two officers (witnesses for the arresting officer) had been suspended for use of excessive force? How likely is it that counsel will be able to offer evidence regarding the specific facts relating to those suspensions?

Problem 2-7

After several alleged incidents of sexual harassment by a fellow employee, Janet Grogan became unable to work due to emotional distress. She eventually filed suit against the employee and her employer under a statute which prohibits employers from tolerating sexual harassment in the workplace. During trial, Janet wanted to testify that she had heard the alleged harasser had beaten his wife, to show why she feared him. She further wanted to admit evidence of a criminal conviction of the alleged harasser for "accosting" her.

The defense objects to the admission of Janet's testimony and to evidence of the criminal conviction. The defense argues that the incident with the defendant's wife is irrelevant and unfairly prejudicial. The defense also argues that the standard for accosting (a person who with offensive and disorderly acts or language accosts or annoys a person of the opposite sex) is different than the standard for sexual harassment (a person engages in unwelcome advances and/or creates a hostile work environment), and therefore the conviction is irrelevant and unfairly prejudicial. You are the judge in this case. Use Rule 403 to determine whether or not to admit the evidence and explain your reasoning. Do any potential compromises exist that will allow the use of the evidence?

IV. Can the Evidence Be Stipulated?

You have objected on relevance grounds and lost. You have objected on conditional relevance grounds and lost. You have objected under FRE 403 and lost. Do any avenues remain to limit the narrative impact of the opposing party's evidence?

One option is an offer to stipulate or admit the evidence in a less prejudicial form. (Stipulations are discussed in greater detail in Chapter 1.) Going back to the overview problem at the beginning of the chapter, let us assume that the prosecution intends to prove Ms. Johnson's attempted suicide by (i) providing testimony of the guard who discovered her hanging in her cell, (ii) introducing the sheets she used to attempt to hang herself, and (iii) offering pictures of injuries to her neck that resulted from the attempt. One way to interrupt that narrative flow, if all other attempts under FRE 401 and FRE 403 have failed, is to offer to stipulate that Ms. Johnson attempted suicide. Defense counsel would offer this stipulation to the prosecutor in an attempt to minimize the evidence and prevent the repetitive evidence relating to the attempt.

This offer to stipulate is a factor the trial judge will consider when evaluating a FRE 403 objection. If a stipulation might reduce the unfair prejudice, that is a factor in analyzing the admissibility of the evidence. The United States Supreme Court has weighed in on this practice in the following case.

Focus Questions: *Old Chief v. United States*

- Why did the prosecution refuse to stipulate in this case? What facts did the prosecution seek to emphasize?

- The Court notes that the jury might conduct bad character reasoning in this case. How so? Explain that risk in your own words.

- Are there any other types of stipulations that the prosecution could be forced to accept? What are the risks of these stipulations? How would it rob the evidence of its weight? Would that weight be a "legitimate" weight?

- Did the Court limit the scope of its holding? How so?

Old Chief v. United States
519 U.S. 172 (1997)

SOUTER, J., delivered the opinion of the Court, in which STEVENS, KENNEDY, GINS-BURG, KENNEDY, GINSBURG, and BREYER, JJ., joined. O'CONNOR, J., filed a dissenting opinion, in which REHNQUIST, C.J., and SCALIA and THOMAS, JJ., joined

Justice SOUTER delivered the opinion of the Court.

Subject to certain limitations, 18 U.S.C. § 922(g)(1) prohibits possession of a firearm by anyone with a prior felony conviction, which the Government can prove by introducing a record of judgment or similar evidence identifying the previous offense. Fearing prejudice if the jury learns the nature of the earlier crime, defendants sometimes seek to avoid such an informative disclosure by offering to concede the fact of the prior conviction. The issue here is whether a district court abuses its discretion if it spurns such an offer and admits the full record of a prior judgment, when the name or nature of the prior offense raises the risk of a verdict tainted by improper considerations, and when the purpose of the evidence is solely to prove the element of prior conviction. We hold that it does.

I

In 1993, petitioner, Old Chief, was arrested after a fracas involving at least one gunshot. The ensuing federal charges included not only assault with a dangerous weapon and using a firearm in relation to a crime of violence but violation of 18 U.S.C. §922(g)(1). This statute makes it unlawful for anyone "who has been convicted in any court of, a crime punishable by imprisonment for a term exceeding one year" to "possess in or affecting commerce, any firearm...."

The earlier crime charged in the indictment against Old Chief was assault causing serious bodily injury. Before trial, he moved for an order requiring the Government "to refrain from ... offering into evidence or soliciting any testimony from any witness regarding the prior criminal convictions of the Defendant, except to state that the Defendant has been convicted of a crime punishable by imprisonment exceeding one (1) year." He said that revealing the name and nature of his prior assault conviction would unfairly tax the jury's capacity to hold the Government to its burden of proof beyond a reasonable doubt on current charges of assault, possession, and violence with a firearm, and he offered to "solve the problem here by stipulating, agreeing and requesting the Court to instruct the jury that he has been convicted of a crime punishable by imprisonment exceeding one (1) yea[r]." He argued that the offer to stipulate to the fact of the prior conviction rendered evidence of the name and nature of the offense inadmissible under Rule 403 of the Federal Rules of Evidence, the danger being that unfair prejudice from that evidence would substantially outweigh its probative value. He also proposed this jury instruction ... :

> "[I] hereby instruct you that Defendant JOHNNY LYNN OLD CHIEF has been convicted of a crime punishable by imprisonment for a term exceeding one year."

The Assistant United States Attorney refused to join in a stipulation, insisting on his right to prove his case his own way, and the District Court agreed, ruling orally that, "If he doesn't want to stipulate, he doesn't have to." At trial, over renewed objection, the Government introduced the order of judgment and commitment for Old Chief's prior conviction. This document disclosed that on December 18, 1988, he "did knowingly and unlawfully assault Rory Dean Fenner, said assault resulting in serious bodily injury," for which Old Chief was sentenced to five years' imprisonment. The jury found Old Chief guilty on all counts, and he appealed.

The Ninth Circuit [affirmed, holding] "that the district court did not abuse its discretion by allowing the prosecution to introduce evidence of Old Chief's prior conviction to prove that element of the unlawful possession charge."

... We now reverse the judgment of the Ninth Circuit.

II

A

As a threshold matter, there is Old Chief's erroneous argument that the name of his prior offense as contained in the record of conviction is irrelevant to the prior-conviction element, and for that reason inadmissible under Rule 402 of the Federal Rules of Evidence. Rule 401 defines relevant evidence as having "any tendency to make the existence of any fact that is of consequence to the determination of the action more probable or less probable than it would be without the evidence." Fed. Rule Evid. 401. To be sure, the fact that Old Chief's prior conviction was for assault resulting in serious bodily injury rather than, say, for theft was not itself an ultimate fact, as if the statute had specifically required proof of injurious assault. But its demonstration was a step on one evidentiary route to the ultimate fact, since it served to place Old Chief within a particular sub-class of offenders for whom firearms possession is outlawed by §922(g)(1). A documentary record of the conviction for that named offense was thus relevant evidence in making Old Chief's § 922(g)(1) status more probable than it would have been without the evidence.

Nor was its evidentiary relevance under Rule 401 affected by the availability of alternative proofs of the element to which it went, such as an admission by Old Chief that he had been convicted of a crime "punishable by imprisonment for a term exceeding one year" within the meaning of the statute. The 1972 Advisory Committee Notes to Rule 401 make this point directly:

> "The fact to which the evidence is directed need not be in dispute. While situations will arise which call for the exclusion of evidence offered to prove a point conceded by the opponent, the ruling should be made on the basis of such considerations as waste of time and undue prejudice (see Rule 403), rather than under any general requirement that evidence is admissible only if directed to matters in dispute." Advisory Committee's Notes on Fed. Rule Evid. 401, 28 U.S.C.App., p. 859.

If, then, relevant evidence is inadmissible in the presence of other evidence related to it, its exclusion must rest not on the ground that the other evidence has rendered it "irrelevant," but on its character as unfairly prejudicial, cumulative or the like, its relevance notwithstanding.

B
1

The term "unfair prejudice," as to a criminal defendant, speaks to the capacity of some concededly relevant evidence to lure the factfinder into declaring guilt on a ground different from proof specific to the offense charged. So, the Committee Notes to Rule 403 explain, "'Unfair prejudice' within its context means an undue tendency to suggest decision on an improper basis, commonly, though not necessarily, an emotional one." Advisory Committee's Notes on Fed. Rule Evid. 403, 28 U.S.C.App., p. 860.

Such improper grounds certainly include the one that Old Chief points to here: generalizing a defendant's earlier bad act into bad character and taking that as raising the odds that he did the later bad act now charged (or, worse, as calling for preventive conviction even if he should happen to be innocent momentarily). As then-Judge Breyer put it, "Although … 'propensity evidence' is relevant, the risk that a jury will convict for crimes other than those charged—or that, uncertain of guilt, it will convict anyway because a bad person deserves punishment—creates a prejudicial effect that outweighs ordinary relevance." *United States v. Moccia*, 681 F.2d 61, 63 (1st Cir. 1982). Justice Jackson described how the law has handled this risk:

> "Courts that follow the common-law tradition almost unanimously have come to disallow resort by the prosecution to any kind of evidence of a defendant's evil character to establish a probability of his guilt. Not that the law invests the defendant with a presumption of good character, but it simply closes the whole matter of character, disposition and reputation on the prosecution's case-in-chief. The state may not show defendant's prior trouble with the law, specific criminal acts, or ill name among his neighbors, even though such facts might logically be persuasive that he is by propensity a probable perpetrator of the crime. The inquiry is not rejected because character is irrelevant; on the contrary, it is said to weigh too much with the jury and to so overpersuade them as to prejudge one with a bad general record and deny him a fair opportunity to defend against a particular charge. The overriding policy of excluding such evidence, despite its admitted probative value, is the practical experience that its disallowance

tends to prevent confusion of issues, unfair surprise and undue prejudice." *Michelson v. United States*, 335 U.S. 469, 475–476, (1948).

Rule of Evidence 404(b) reflects this common-law tradition by addressing propensity reasoning directly: "Evidence of other crimes, wrongs, or acts is not admissible to prove the character of a person in order to show action in conformity therewith." Fed. Rule Evid. 404(b). There is, accordingly, no question that propensity would be an "improper basis" for conviction and that evidence of a prior conviction is subject to analysis under Rule 403 for relative probative value and for prejudicial risk of misuse as propensity evidence. Cf. 1 J. Strong, McCormick on Evidence 780 (4th ed.1992) (hereinafter McCormick) (Rule 403 prejudice may occur, for example, when "evidence of convictions for prior, unrelated crimes may lead a juror to think that since the defendant already has a criminal record, an erroneous conviction would not be quite as serious as would otherwise be the case").

As for the analytical method to be used in Rule 403 balancing, two basic possibilities present themselves. An item of evidence might be viewed as an island, with estimates of its own probative value and unfairly prejudicial risk the sole reference points in deciding whether the danger substantially outweighs the value and whether the evidence ought to be excluded. Or the question of admissibility might be seen as inviting further comparisons to take account of the full evidentiary context of the case as the court understands it when the ruling must be made. This second approach would start out like the first but be ready to go further. On objection, the court would decide whether a particular item of evidence raised a danger of unfair prejudice. If it did, the judge would go on to evaluate the degrees of probative value and unfair prejudice not only for the item in question but for any actually available substitutes as well. If an alternative were found to have substantially the same or greater probative value but a lower danger of unfair prejudice, sound judicial discretion would discount the value of the item first offered and exclude it if its discounted probative value were substantially outweighed by unfairly prejudicial risk. As we will explain later on, the judge would have to make these calculations with an appreciation of the offering party's need for evidentiary richness and narrative integrity in presenting a case, and the mere fact that two pieces of evidence might go to the same point would not, of course, necessarily mean that only one of them might come in. It would only mean that a judge applying Rule 403 could reasonably apply some discount to the probative value of an item of evidence when faced with less risky alternative proof going to the same point. Even under this second approach, as we explain below, a defendant's Rule 403 objection offering to concede a point generally cannot prevail over the Government's choice to offer evidence showing guilt and all the circumstances surrounding the offense.

The first understanding of the Rule is open to a very telling objection. That reading would leave the party offering evidence with the option to structure a trial in whatever way would produce the maximum unfair prejudice consistent with relevance. He could choose the available alternative carrying the greatest threat of improper influence, despite the availability of less prejudicial but equally probative evidence. The worst he would have to fear would be a ruling sustaining a Rule 403 objection, and if that occurred, he could simply fall back to offering substitute evidence. This would be a strange rule. It would be very odd for the law of evidence to recognize the danger of unfair prejudice only to confer such a degree of autonomy on the party subject to temptation, and the Rules of Evidence are not so odd.

Rather, a reading of the companions to Rule 403, and of the commentaries that went with them to Congress, makes it clear that what counts as the Rule 403 "probative value" of an item of evidence, as distinct from its Rule 401 "relevance," may be calculated by comparing evidentiary alternatives. The Committee Notes to Rule 401 explicitly say that a party's concession is pertinent to the court's discretion to exclude evidence on the point conceded. Such a concession, according to the Notes, will sometimes "call for the exclusion of evidence offered to prove [the] point conceded by the opponent...." Advisory Committee's Notes on Fed. Rule Evid. 401, 28 U.S.C.App., p. 859. As already mentioned, the Notes make it clear that such rulings should be made not on the basis of Rule 401 relevance but on "such considerations as waste of time and undue prejudice (see Rule 403)...." *Ibid.* The Notes to Rule 403 then take up the point by stating that when a court considers "whether to exclude on grounds of unfair prejudice," the "availability of other means of proof may ... be an appropriate factor." Advisory Committee's Notes on Fed. Rule Evid. 403, 28 U.S.C.App., p. 860. The point gets a reprise in the Notes to Rule 404(b), dealing with admissibility when a given evidentiary item has the dual nature of legitimate evidence of an element and illegitimate evidence of character: "No mechanical solution is offered. The determination must be made whether the danger of undue prejudice outweighs the probative value of the evidence in view of the availability of other means of proof and other facts appropriate for making decision of this kind under 403." Advisory Committee's Notes on Fed. Rule Evid. 404, 28 U.S.C.App., p. 861. Thus the notes leave no question that when Rule 403 confers discretion by providing that evidence "may" be excluded, the discretionary judgment may be informed not only by assessing an evidentiary item's twin tendencies, but by placing the result of that assessment alongside similar assessments of evidentiary alternatives. See 1 McCormick 782, and n. 41 (suggesting that Rule 403' s "probative value" signifies the "marginal probative value" of the evidence relative to the other evidence in the case); 22 C. Wright & K. Graham, Federal Practice and Procedure § 5250, pp. 546–547 (1978) ("The probative worth of any particular bit of evidence is obviously affected by the scarcity or abundance of other evidence on the same point").

2

In dealing with the specific problem raised by § 922(g)(1) and its prior-conviction element, there can be no question that evidence of the name or nature of the prior offense generally carries a risk of unfair prejudice to the defendant. That risk will vary from case to case, for the reasons already given, but will be substantial whenever the official record offered by the Government would be arresting enough to lure a juror into a sequence of bad character reasoning. Where a prior conviction was for a gun crime or one similar to other charges in a pending case the risk of unfair prejudice would be especially obvious, and Old Chief sensibly worried that the prejudicial effect of his prior assault conviction, significant enough with respect to the current gun charges alone, would take on added weight from the related assault charge against him.

The District Court was also presented with alternative, relevant, admissible evidence of the prior conviction by Old Chief's offer to stipulate, evidence necessarily subject to the District Court's consideration on the motion to exclude the record offered by the Government. Although Old Chief's formal offer to stipulate was, strictly, to enter a formal agreement with the Government to be given to the jury, even without the Government's acceptance his proposal amounted to an offer to admit that the prior-conviction element was satisfied, and a defendant's admission is, of course, good evidence. *See* Fed. Rule Evid. 801(d)(2)(A).

Old Chief's proffered admission would, in fact, have been not merely relevant but seemingly conclusive evidence of the element. The statutory language in which the prior-conviction requirement is couched shows no congressional concern with the specific name or nature of the prior offense beyond what is necessary to place it within the broad category of qualifying felonies, and Old Chief clearly meant to admit that his felony did qualify, by stipulating "that the Government has proven one of the essential elements of the offense."

As a consequence, although the name of the prior offense may have been technically relevant, it addressed no detail in the definition of the prior-conviction element that would not have been covered by the stipulation or admission. Logic, then, seems to side with Old Chief.

3

There is, however, one more question to be considered before deciding whether Old Chief's offer was to supply evidentiary value at least equivalent to what the Government's own evidence carried. In arguing that the stipulation or admission would not have carried equivalent value, the Government invokes the familiar, standard rule that the prosecution is entitled to prove its case by evidence of its own choice, or, more exactly, that a criminal defendant may not stipulate or admit his way out of the full evidentiary force of the case as the Government chooses to present it. The authority usually cited for this rule is *Parr v. United States*, 255 F.2d 86 (5th Cir.), *cert. denied*, 358 U.S. 824 (1958), in which the Fifth Circuit explained that the "reason for the rule is to permit a party 'to present to the jury a picture of the events relied upon. To substitute for such a picture a naked admission might have the effect to rob the evidence of much of its fair and legitimate weight.'" 255 F.2d at 88.

This is unquestionably true as a general matter. The "fair and legitimate weight" of conventional evidence showing individual thoughts and acts amounting to a crime reflects the fact that making a case with testimony and tangible things not only satisfies the formal definition of an offense, but tells a colorful story with descriptive richness. Unlike an abstract premise, whose force depends on going precisely to a particular step in a course of reasoning, a piece of evidence may address any number of separate elements, striking hard just because it shows so much at once; the account of a shooting that establishes capacity and causation may tell just as much about the triggerman's motive and intent. Evidence thus has force beyond any linear scheme of reasoning, and as its pieces come together a narrative gains momentum, with power not only to support conclusions but to sustain the willingness of jurors to draw the inferences, whatever they may be, necessary to reach an honest verdict. This persuasive power of the concrete and particular is often essential to the capacity of jurors to satisfy the obligations that the law places on them. Jury duty is usually unsought and sometimes resisted, and it may be as difficult for one juror suddenly to face the findings that can send another human being to prison, as it is for another to hold out conscientiously for acquittal. When a juror's duty does seem hard, the evidentiary account of what a defendant has thought and done can accomplish what no set of abstract statements ever could, not just to prove a fact but to establish its human significance, and so to implicate the law's moral underpinnings and a juror's obligation to sit in judgment. Thus, the prosecution may fairly seek to place its evidence before the jurors, as much to tell a story of guiltiness as to support an inference of guilt, to convince the jurors that a guilty verdict would be morally reasonable as much as to point to the discrete elements of a defendant's legal fault.

But there is something even more to the prosecution's interest in resisting efforts to replace the evidence of its choice with admissions and stipulations, for beyond the power of conventional evidence to support allegations and give life to the moral underpinnings of law's claims, there lies the need for evidence in all its particularity to satisfy the jurors' expectations about what proper proof should be. Some such demands they bring with them to the courthouse, assuming, for example, that a charge of using a firearm to commit an offense will be proven by introducing a gun in evidence. A prosecutor who fails to produce one, or some good reason for his failure, has something to be concerned about. "If [jurors'] expectations are not satisfied, triers of fact may penalize the party who disappoints them by drawing a negative inference against that party." Saltzburg, A Special

Aspect of Relevance: Countering Negative Inferences Associated with the Absence of Evidence, 66 Calif. L.Rev. 1011, 1019 (1978). Expectations may also arise in jurors' minds simply from the experience of a trial itself. The use of witnesses to describe a train of events naturally related can raise the prospect of learning about every ingredient of that natural sequence the same way. If suddenly the prosecution presents some occurrence in the series differently, as by announcing a stipulation or admission, the effect may be like saying, "never mind what's behind the door," and jurors may well wonder what they are being kept from knowing. A party seemingly responsible for cloaking something has reason for apprehension, and the prosecution with its burden of proof may prudently demur at a defense request to interrupt the flow of evidence telling the story in the usual way.

In sum, the accepted rule that the prosecution is entitled to prove its case free from any defendant's option to stipulate the evidence away rests on good sense. A syllogism is not a story, and a naked proposition in a courtroom may be no match for the robust evidence that would be used to prove it. People who hear a story interrupted by gaps of abstraction may be puzzled at the missing chapters, and jurors asked to rest a momentous decision on the story's truth can feel put upon at being asked to take responsibility knowing that more could be said than they have heard. A convincing tale can be told with economy, but when economy becomes a break in the natural sequence of narrative evidence, an assurance that the missing link is really there is never more than second best.

4

This recognition that the prosecution with its burden of persuasion needs evidentiary depth to tell a continuous story has, however, virtually no application when the point at issue is a defendant's legal status, dependent on some judgment rendered wholly independently of the concrete events of later criminal behavior charged against him. As in this case, the choice of evidence for such an element is usually not between eventful narrative and abstract proposition, but between propositions of slightly varying abstraction, either a record saying that conviction for some crime occurred at a certain time or a statement admitting the same thing without naming the particular offense. The issue of substituting one statement for the other normally arises only when the record of conviction would not be admissible for any purpose beyond proving status, so that excluding it would not deprive the prosecution of evidence with multiple utility; if, indeed, there were a justification for receiving evidence of the nature of prior acts on some issue other than status (i.e., to prove "motive, opportunity, intent, preparation, plan, knowledge, identity, or absence of mistake or accident," Fed. Rule Evid. 404(b)), Rule 404(b) guarantees the opportunity to seek its admission. Nor can it be argued that the events behind the prior conviction are proper nourishment for the jurors' sense of obligation to vindicate the public interest. The issue is not whether concrete details of the prior crime should come to the jurors' attention but whether the name or general character of that crime is to be disclosed. Congress, however, has made it plain that distinctions among generic felonies do not count for this purpose; the fact of the qualifying conviction is alone what matters under the statute. "A defendant falls within the category simply by virtue of past conviction for any [qualifying] crime ranging from possession of short lobsters, *see* 16 U.S.C. § 3372, to the most aggravated murder." *Unites States v. Tavares*, 21 F.3d 1, 4 (1st Cir. 1994). The most the jury needs to know is that the conviction admitted by the defendant falls within the class of crimes that Congress thought should bar a convict from possessing a gun, and this point may be made readily in a defendant's admission and underscored in the court's jury instructions. Finally, the most obvious reason that the general presumption that the prosecution may choose its evidence is so remote from application here is that proof of the defendant's status goes to an element entirely outside the natural sequence of what the defendant is charged with thinking and doing to commit the current offense. Proving status without telling exactly why that status was imposed leaves no gap in the story of a defendant's subsequent criminality, and its demonstration by stipulation or admission neither displaces a chapter from a continuous sequence of conventional evidence nor comes across as an officious substitution, to confuse or offend or provoke reproach.

Given these peculiarities of the element of felony-convict status and of admissions and the like when used to prove it, there is no cognizable difference between the evidentiary significance of an admission and of the legitimately probative component of the official record the prosecution would prefer to place in evidence. For purposes of the Rule 403 weighing of the probative against the prejudicial, the functions of the competing evidence are distinguishable only by the risk inherent in the one and wholly absent from the other. In this case, as in any other in which the prior conviction is for an offense likely to support conviction on some improper ground, the only reasonable conclusion was that the risk of unfair prejudice did substantially outweigh the discounted probative value of the record of conviction, and it was an abuse of discretion to admit the record when an admission was available. What we have said shows why this will be the general rule when proof of convict status is at issue, just as the prosecutor's choice will generally survive a Rule 403 analysis when a defendant seeks to force the substitution of an admission for evidence creating a coherent narrative of his thoughts and actions in perpetrating the offense for which he is being tried.

The judgment is reversed, and the case is remanded to the Ninth Circuit for further proceedings consistent with this opinion.

Justice O'CONNOR, with whom THE CHIEF JUSTICE, Justice SCALIA, and Justice THOMAS join, dissenting.

The Court today announces a rule that misapplies Federal Rule of Evidence 403 and upsets, without explanation, longstanding precedent regarding criminal prosecutions. I do not agree that the Government's introduction of evidence that reveals the name and basic nature of a defendant's prior felony conviction in a prosecution brought under 18 U.S.C. §922(g)(1) "unfairly" prejudices the defendant within the meaning of Rule 403. Nor do I agree with the Court's newly minted rule that a defendant charged with violating §922(g)(1) can force the Government to accept his concession to the prior conviction element of that offense, thereby precluding the Government from offering evidence on this point. I therefore dissent.

I

Rule 403 provides that a district court may exclude relevant evidence if, among other things, "its probative value is substantially outweighed by the danger of unfair prejudice." Certainly, Rule 403 does not permit the court to exclude the Government's evidence simply because it may hurt the defendant. As a threshold matter, evidence is excludable only if it is "unfairly" prejudicial, in that it has "an undue tendency to suggest decision on an improper basis." Advisory Committee's Notes on Fed. Rule Evid. 403, 28 U.S.C.App., p. 860; *see, e.g., United States v. Munoz*, 36 F.3d 1229, 1233 (1st Cir. 1994) ("The damage done to the defense is not a basis for exclusion; the question under Rule 403 is 'one of "unfair" prejudice—not of prejudice alone'"); *Dollar v. Long Mfg., N.C., Inc.*, 561 F.2d 613, 618 (5th Cir. 1977) ("'[U]nfair prejudice' as used in Rule 403 is not to be equated with testimony simply adverse to the opposing party. Virtually all evidence is prejudicial or it isn't material. The prejudice must be 'unfair'"). The evidence tendered by the Government in this case—the order reflecting petitioner's prior conviction and sentence for assault resulting in serious bodily injury, in violation of 18 U.S.C. § 1153 and 18 U.S.C. § 113(f) (1988 ed.)—directly proved a necessary element of the § 922(g)(1) offense, that is, that petitioner had committed a crime covered by § 921(a)(20). Perhaps petitioner's case was damaged when the jury discovered that he previously had committed a felony and heard the name of his crime. But I cannot agree with the Court that it was unfairly prejudicial for the Government to establish an essential element of its case against petitioner with direct proof of his prior conviction....

Within the meaning of § 922(g)(1) ... "a crime" is not an abstract or metaphysical concept. Rather, the Government must prove that the defendant committed a particular crime. In short, under § 922(g)(1), a defendant's prior felony conviction connotes not only that he is a prior felon, but also that he has engaged in specific past criminal conduct.

Even more fundamentally, in our system of justice, a person is not simply convicted of "a crime" or "a felony." Rather, he is found guilty of a specified offense, almost always because he violated a specific statutory prohibition.... That a variety of crimes would have satisfied the prior conviction element of the § 922(g)(1) offense does not detract from the fact that petitioner committed a specific offense. The name and basic nature of petitioner's crime are inseparable from the fact of his earlier conviction and were therefore admissible to prove petitioner's guilt....

[C]onsider a murder case. Surely the Government can submit proof establishing the victim's identity, even though, strictly speaking, the jury has no "need" to know the victim's name, and even though the victim might be a particularly well loved public figure. The same logic should govern proof of the prior conviction element of the § 922(g)(1) offense. That is, the Government ought to be able to prove, with specific evidence, that petitioner committed a crime that came within § 922(g)(1)'s coverage.

The Court never explains precisely why it constitutes "unfair" prejudice for the Government to directly prove an essential element of the § 922(g)(1) offense with evidence that reveals the name or basic nature of the defendant's prior conviction. It simply notes that such evidence may lead a jury to conclude that the defendant has a propensity to commit crime, thereby raising the odds that the jury would find that he committed the crime with which he is currently charged....

Yes, to be sure, Rule 404(b) provides that "[e]vidence of other crimes, wrongs, or acts is not admissible to prove the character of a person in order to show action in conformity therewith." But Rule 404(b) does not end there. It expressly contemplates the admission of evidence of prior crimes for other purposes, "such as proof of motive, opportunity, intent, preparation, plan, knowledge, identity, or absence of mistake or accident." The list is plainly not exhaustive, and where, as here, a prior conviction is an element of the charged offense, neither Rule 404(b) nor Rule 403 can bar its admission. The reason is simple: In a prosecution brought under § 922(g)(1), the Government does not submit evidence of a past crime to prove the defendant's bad character or to "show action in conformity therewith." It tenders the evidence as direct proof of a necessary element of the offense with which it has charged the defendant. To say, as the Court does, that it "unfairly" prejudices the defendant for the Government to establish its § 922(g)(1) case with evidence showing that, in fact, the defendant did commit a prior offense misreads the Rules of Evidence and defies common sense.

Any incremental harm resulting from proving the name or basic nature of the prior felony can be properly mitigated by limiting jury instructions. Federal Rule of Evidence 105 provides that when evidence is admissible for one purpose, but not another, "the court, upon request, shall restrict the evidence to its proper scope and instruct the jury accordingly." Indeed, on petitioner's own motion in this case, the District Court instructed the jury that it was not to "'consider a prior conviction as evidence of guilt of the crime for which the defendant is now on trial.'" The jury is presumed to have followed this cautionary instruction, and the instruction offset whatever prejudice might have arisen from the introduction of petitioner's prior conviction.

II

The Court also holds that, if a defendant charged with violating § 922(g)(1) concedes his prior felony conviction, a district court abuses its discretion if it admits evidence of the defendant's prior crime that raises the risk of a verdict "tainted by improper considerations." Left unexplained is what, exactly, it was about the order introduced by the Government at trial that might cause a jury to decide the case improperly. The order offered into evidence (which the Court nowhere in its opinion sets out) stated, in relevant part:

> "And the defendant having been convicted on his plea of guilty of the offense charged in Count II of the indictment in the above-entitled cause, to-wit: That on or about the 18th day of December 1988, at Browning, in the State and District of Montana, and on and within the exterior boundaries of the Blackfeet Indian Reservation, being Indian country, JOHNNY LYNN OLD CHIEF, an Indian person, did knowingly and unlawfully assault Rory Dean Fenner, said assault resulting in serious bodily injury, in violation of Title 18 U.S.C. §§ 1153 and 113(f)."

The order went on to say that petitioner was sentenced for a term of 60 months' imprisonment, to be followed by two years of supervised release.

Why, precisely, does the Court think that this item of evidence raises the risk of a verdict "tainted by improper considerations"? Is it because the jury might learn that petitioner assaulted someone and caused serious bodily injury? If this is what the Court means, would evidence that petitioner had committed some other felony be admissible, and if so, what sort of crime might that be? Or does the Court object to the order because it gave a few specifics about the assault, such as the date, the location, and the victim's name? Or perhaps the Court finds that introducing the order risks a verdict "tainted by improper considerations" simply because the § 922(g)(1) charge was joined with counts charging petitioner with using a firearm in relation to a crime of violence, in violation of 18 U.S.C. § 924(c), and with committing an assault with a dangerous weapon, in violation of 18 U.S.C. § 1153 and 18 U.S.C. § 113(c) (1988 ed.)? Under the Court's nebulous standard for admission of prior felony evidence in a § 922(g)(1) prosecution, these are open questions.

More troubling still is the Court's retreat from the fundamental principle that in a criminal prosecution the Government may prove its case as it sees fit. The Court reasons that, in general, a defendant may not stipulate away an element of a charged offense because, in the usual case, "the prosecution with its burden of persuasion needs evidentiary depth to tell a continuous story." The rule has, however, "virtually no application when the point at issue is a defendant's legal status, dependent on some judgment rendered wholly independently of the concrete events of later criminal behavior charged against him." Thus, concludes the Court, there is no real difference between the "evidentiary significance" of a defendant's concession and that of the Government's proof of the prior felony with the order of conviction. Since the Government's method of proof was more prejudicial than petitioner's admission, it follows that the District Court should not have admitted the order reflecting his conviction when petitioner had conceded that element of the offense.

On its own terms, the argument does not hold together. A jury is as likely to be puzzled by the "missing chapter" resulting from a defendant's stipulation to his prior felony conviction as it would be by the defendant's conceding any other element of the crime. The jury may wonder why it has not been told the name of the crime, or it may question why the defendant's firearm possession was illegal, given the tradition of lawful gun ownership in this country....

Obviously, we are not dealing with a stipulation here. A stipulation is an agreement, and no agreement was reached between petitioner and the Government in this case. Does the Court think a different rule applies when the defendant attempts to stipulate, over the Government's objection, to an element of the charged offense? If so, that runs counter to the Constitution: The Government must prove every element of the offense charged beyond a reasonable doubt, and the defendant's strategic decision to "agree" that the Government need not prove an element cannot relieve the Government of its burden. Because the Government bears the burden of proof on every element of a charged offense, it must be accorded substantial leeway to submit evidence of its choosing to prove its case....

III

The Court manufactures a new rule that, in a § 922(g)(1) case, a defendant can force the Government to accept his admission to the prior felony conviction element of the offense, thereby precluding the Government from offering evidence to directly prove a necessary element of its case. I cannot agree that it "unfairly" prejudices a defendant for the Government to prove his prior conviction with evidence that reveals the name or basic nature of his past crime. Like it or not, Congress chose to make a defendant's prior criminal conviction one of the two elements of the § 922(g)(1) offense. Moreover, crimes have names; a defendant is not convicted of some indeterminate, unspecified "crime." Nor do I think that Federal Rule of Evidence 403 can be read to obviate the well accepted principle, grounded in both the Constitution and in our precedent, that the Government may not be forced to accept a defendant's concession to an element of a charged offense as proof of that element. I respectfully dissent.

Professional Development Questions

- Throughout this chapter we have seen that a relevance determination is very context-specific, and numerous potential objections to the evidence exist. Is it probative? Is it material? Is there an unproven conditional fact? Even if the evidence is relevant, does the unfair prejudice substantially outweigh the probative value? If the unfair prejudice is high, can a stipulation lessen the unfair prejudice? This is the **progression** a trial attorney evaluates when deciding whether to object and how to frame the objection. An important task for you at the end of each chapter is to think about how the rules interrelate and how you can formulate these types of progressions to evaluate the admissibility of evidence.

- Trial judges have a great deal of discretion, and the probative value and potentially unfair prejudice may fluctuate based on the facts and law of a given trial. Accordingly, bright line rules often do not exist in evidence law or, if they do exist, are riddled with exceptions. All an advocate can do is to know which tests and factors a court values and use the facts of her case as persuasively as possible. Therefore, a critical skill to emphasize at the end of each chapter is to focus more on the arguments rather than result—the goal is to use the law you have learned so far to best be able to marshal the facts.

- Educational research demonstrates that there are three key components of being an expert, self-regulated learner: (i) planning, (ii) implementing your plan with self-monitoring to ensure you stay on task, and (iii) reflecting on your learning process. *See* Schwartz, *Teaching Law Students to Be Self-Regulated Learners,* 2003 Mich.St. D.C.L. L. Rev. 447. As you go work through this textbook, how can you ensure that you use your study time as effectively as possible?

- Spend a few minutes reflecting about how well you learned the material in this chapter. Did you plan your study time effectively? Did you self-monitor to ensure your studying was effective? What will you do the same or differently to master the materials in upcoming chapters?

- The flowchart in this chapter is, by necessity, highly abbreviated. How would you adapt it to better suit your learning style? Would the "flow" of the flowchart change? The content? Try crafting a new version to help you synthesize the material. By actively engaging with the flow chart, you will increase your understanding of the material.

- When selecting the evidence to include in the narrative of your case, what role should your personal beliefs play? For example, building on the *Peterson* case, if you knew that a criminal defendant were gay, would you introduce evidence regarding his homosexuality if you were the prosecutor? What if the evidence of his sexuality was only mildly probative? What if it would be deeply embarrassing to the defendant? What if members of the jury might misuse the information? Would you still introduce the evidence and let its admission be determined by the judge? Is that the proper role of an advocate?

Overview of the Specialized Relevance Rules

FRE	Rule Prohibits	Exceptions	Probative/Prejudice Weighing	Social Policy Encouraged
Rule 407	Subsequent Remedial Measures to prove liability	May prove ownership, control, feasibility, if controverted, or to impeach	Making a change does not mean that you were negligent before	Encourage remedies that keep the population safe
Rule 408	Compromise attempts of a disputed civil claim (including statements and conduct during negotiations) to prove liability/invalidity of a claim	May use evidence to prove witness bias, lack of undue delay, or obstruction of a criminal investigation	The desire for compromise may not be an admission of weakness	Encourage compromise which satisfy parties and ease congestion of courts
Rule 409	Offers of payment of medical costs to prove liability	The scope of the rule is limited to medical costs only	If the offer springs from charitable or humane impulses, then is of limited probative value, as not an admission of fault	Encourage the offers of medical assistance
Rule 410	A criminal defendant's guilty pleas later withdrawn, nolo contendere pleas, statements in plea proceedings, and statements in plea talks	May be admissible to complete partial accounts of plea discussions and in perjury prosecutions	There are a wide range of reasons, other than guilt, explaining why someone might engage in plea discussions/ agreements	Encourage plea bargaining and thereby ease congestion of courts
Rule 411	Liability Insurance (or lack thereof) to prove negligence/wrongful action	May prove agency, ownership, control or witness bias	A jury may award plaintiff more money if defendant is insured; an insured is no less careful than an uninsured	Encourage people to obtain insurance and avoid windfalls for opponents of insured parties

Chapter 3

The Specialized Relevance Rules

Overview: Tilting the Playing Field

As we saw in the previous chapter, by authorizing exclusion only where the probative value is "substantially" outweighed by countervailing considerations, FRE 403 is designed to favor admissibility. Close calls (i.e., anything less than substantial) favor the evidence being admitted. The specialized relevance rules, FRE 407 through 411, are a form of prejudice/probative balancing for situations where the probative value is deemed low, the prejudice high, and the social implications of allowing the evidence in is extremely negative.

In other words, the drafters of the FRE crafted some rules that tilted the playing field so that certain evidence is inadmissible. The best way to think of it is that, as a matter of law, the evidence governed by FRE 407-411 has failed a FRE 403 weighing test. Each of the rules reflects a situation in which the drafters contemplated evidence that had low probative power and at least some risk of unfair prejudice. Layered in with the unfair prejudice, however, are certain public policy goals that make inadmissibility of this evidence desirable. Furthermore, there is a quest for certainty in evidence law; by establishing these rules, practitioners and judges can be more certain of what evidence will be admitted, rather than relying on ad hoc balancing tests. Accordingly, judicial discretion is limited and parties may reliably predict the admissibility of certain evidence. The table on the left presents some of the prejudice and public policy rationales behind these rules.

Thus, one can see that all the rules except FRE 410 prohibit only certain uses of the evidence but allow the evidence to come in for other purposes. Also note that just because an implicit FRE 403 balancing has occurred does not mean that FRE 403 no longer plays a role in the admissibility of this type of evidence. If a judge determines that, for example, a subsequent remedy is admissible because it goes to ownership rather than negligence, the opponent may still object under FRE 403 and argue that a FRE 105 limiting instruction would not be effective and that the jury would use the information for an improper purpose. In essence, the opponent would be arguing that the probative value of proving ownership would be substantially outweighed by the risk that the jury would use the information as proof of negligence, an act which FRE 407 expressly forbids.

Accordingly, the flowchart for the possible objections to evidence discussed in this chapter would look something like the diagram on page 80.

As we move through these rules, always keep your focus on the relevance issue for each piece of evidence. What, exactly, is the proponent of the evidence trying to prove by the

Possible Objections to Evidence

FRE 401/402
Evidence is admissible and relevant if:
- **Probative** — makes fact more/less probable
- **Material** — helps prove a necessary element

FRE 104(b)
Huddleston Standard — judge must determine if a reasonable jury could find by a preponderance of the evidence the existence of the missing condition

Specialized Rules of Evidence
Prejudice typically outweighs probative value

FRE 407 — Subsequent Remedies
Bars — to prove liability (not apply to third-party repairs)
Permitted — ownership, control, impeach, feasibility (if controverted)
 Not Controverted — 1.0 better option than 2.0
 Controverted — superlative, 2.0 couldn't be done
Rationales — weak evidence of liability; to encourage remedies

FRE 408 — Settlements/Compromise (CIVIL)
Bars — settlements/attempts to settle to prove liability
Permitted — witness bias, lack of undue delay, obstruction to criminal invest.
Rationales — may be motivated by peace, costs; to encourage settlements
Considerations — must relate to legitimate claim

FRE 409 — Medical Expenses
Bars — offers/payments of medical expenses to prove liability
Rationales — usually made from humane impulse; to encourage assistance
Considerations — strictly limited, apologies, etc. are still admissible

FRE 410 — Pleas (CRIMINAL)
Bars — attempted/withdrawn pleas to prove guilt
Permitted — perjury conviction at later trial
Rationales — may be motivated by costs or to avoid risk at trial; to encourage
 plea bargaining

FRE 411 — Liability Insurance
Bars — Insurance or lack of insurance to prove liability
Permitted — agency, ownership, control, witness bias, etc.
Rationales — weak evidence of liability; to avoid windfall for opponent

FRE 403 – Balance Test
Relevant Evidence *may* be excluded if its probative value is *substantially* outweighed by the danger of *unfair* prejudice or delay.

introduction of the evidence? How is it relevant? If the answer is an impermissible purpose, the applicable rule forbids the evidence. If the answer is both a permissible and an impermissible purpose, a FRE 403 analysis will determine its admissibility.

Finally, do not ignore the policy implications behind each rule. The encouragement of certain policy aims plays a pivotal role in making probative evidence inadmissible. Where the policy aims behind the rule are not served, the evidence will be admissible.

I. Is It a Subsequent Remedial Remedy?

Relevant Rule
FRE 407

Subsequent Remedial Measures

When measures are taken that would have made an earlier injury or harm less likely to occur, evidence of the subsequent measures is not admissible to prove:

- negligence;
- culpable conduct;
- a defect in a product or its design; or
- a need for a warning or instruction.

But the court may admit this evidence for another purpose, such as impeachment or — if disputed — proving ownership, control, or the feasibility of precautionary measures.

Overview Problem

Biff bought a new sports car from Big Auto Manufacturer ("BAM"). One week after his purchase, BAM corrected a defect with the transmission on all subsequent models of the car and fired the engineer responsible for the defective transmission. One month later, Biff's transmission falls out while he is driving on the freeway, causing him to hit a car driven by Sally. Both Biff and Sally are injured in the accident. If Biff sues BAM, is their correction of the transmission defect admissible in the case? Is the firing of the engineer admissible?

Overview

(1) Policy Underpinnings

If we know that remedial measures were taken after an injury allegedly caused by an event, and that these measures would have made the injury less likely to occur, it seems like a reasonable inference that the person who made the change thought the previous situation posed an unreasonable risk of injury. Thus, it appears that evidence of these measures is relevant in an action by someone injured by the initial condition. Yet FRE 407 expressly prohibits this type of evidence to prove "negligence, culpable conduct, a defect in a product or its design, or a need for a warning or instruction." Why?

Four reasons are most often articulated. First, the fact that a party undertook some type of remedial measure may not indicate fault. A party could have a myriad of reasons for this type of behavior; perhaps they want to make a safe situation even safer or they are extremely cautious. Thus, the probative value of the evidence is low. Second, there is a social policy that needs to be reinforced—we want to encourage people to make this type of repair. After all, if a manufacturer knew that it possessed a defective product, we do not want them to avoid remedying the situation due to a fear that the remedy might come up in a lawsuit. Third, we worry that unfairly prejudicial factors may affect the jury, such as misleading a jury by over-relying on one piece of evidence or confusing the issues for the jury. Indeed, it would seem that, in our overview problem, that a jury might jump to the conclusion that the repair must mean that the initial transmission system was faulty. Finally, it seems unfair to actually penalize someone who took socially responsible action.

Accordingly, the drafters of the FRE made a decision to reward this type of conduct and make subsequent remedial measures inadmissible, as long as all the elements of the rule are met.

(2) Elements

As with all of the Federal Rules of Evidence, you must divide the rule into elements. When, (1) subsequent to an event, (2) a remedial measure is taken, and (3) that measure is offered for a liability-based purpose ("negligence, culpable conduct, a defect in a product or its design, or a need for a warning or instruction"), then the evidence is inadmissible. **Non-liability-based purposes**, however, are admissible under FRE 407. Put simply, if the purpose of the evidence is meant to prove a **controverted** fact that does not directly establish liability (i.e., ownership, control or feasibility) or is meant to impeach a witness (i.e., call the witness' veracity into question), then it is admissible.

How does one define "**subsequent**"? "Subsequent" means after an injury or harm allegedly caused by an event. This definition has two important ramifications. First, a remedial measure undertaken after the manufacture of a product but before plaintiff's injury is not covered. Thus, in our overview problem, BAM's remedial measure was NOT subsequent to Biff's **injury**, and therefore evidence of the remedial measure is admissible (although such a remedial measure would still have to pass muster under FRE 403). Second, FRE 407 does not bar evidence of remedial measures taken after an accident similar to the one giving rise to plaintiff's claim but before plaintiff's own accident. Thus, if BAM further modified its cars' transmissions in direct response to Biff's accident and with an eye toward preventing similar incidents from occurring in the future, and Jim's unmodified car had its transmission fall out, then Jim may introduce the second modification because the modification is not subsequent to **his** injury.

How does one define "**remedial**"? The answer is, "broadly." A remedial measure, according to the language of FRE 407, is one that "would have made the earlier injury or harm less likely to occur" had the measure been made prior to the event that caused the injury or harm. Changes in design, installation of protective devices, new warnings, removal of dangerous conditions, changes in policies, and even dismissal of employees are covered. C. Mueller & L. Kirkpatrick, Sec. 4.23, at 236–37 (5th ed. 2012). Thus, in the overview problem, we can see that the firing of the engineer could be perceived as a remedial measure; the new engineer responsible for modifying the transmission system would likely, in the eyes of BAM, be a more effective and competent person to undertake that task. If the new engineer had created the initial transmission system, it conceivably would not have failed. Although courts do not tend to examine deeply the effectiveness of the remedial action, actions fitting in the above categories are almost always found to be "remedial." Accordingly, courts rarely will rarely inquire "did the alleged remedial action work?" Instead, courts focus on characterizing the action itself as "remedial" or "non-remedial." One action that is not "remedial," however, is post-event investigations, for these investigations are fact-finding events that attempt to determine whether any remedial measures should be mandated; they are not remedial measures in and of themselves.

Additionally, third-party remedial measures (those not undertaken by the defendant) are not covered by the exclusionary principle because disclosure of the remedial measure at a trial will not discourage the third party from taking remedial action — after all, the third party is not a defendant and therefore does not risk liability by making the repair. As the third party will therefore undertake the repair regardless of the existence of FRE 407, there is no reason to give a "windfall" to the manufacturer for a repair it did not undertake. For example, assume Lawnmower, Inc., manufactured a lawnmower and sold it to Laura. Laura decided of her own accord to modify the lawnmower. Then, she sold it to Kim. If Kim is injured using the lawnmower, then she can introduce Laura's modification in a suit against Lawnmower, Inc. Put simply, the defendant should not be allowed to shield itself from a repair it did not authorize.

(3) Exceptions

FRE 407 provides a **non-exclusive** list of permissible uses of subsequent remedial measures which includes ownership, control, and feasibility, if any of those three items are controverted at trial, as well as impeachment. The relevance of using a subsequent remedial measure to prove ownership and control centers on the evidentiary hypothesis that you would not fix a premises or object after an accident if you did not own or control it. For example, if someone tripped and injured herself at night in front of an apartment complex, the owner of the complex may contest that she controlled that area. However, if, after the accident, she installed a light in that area to better illuminate it, that remedial measure would be admissible for a non-liability purpose — to prove control over the area. Of course, the apartment complex could request a limiting instruction under FRE 105 to the effect of "Ladies and Gentlemen of the Jury, you may use this evidence to prove the defendant controlled the area, but you may not use it to establish that the defendant breached her duty in not lighting the area previously." How effective do you think that jury instruction would be? Would the apartment complex owner be better off conceding that she controlled the area? If she did, the issue would not be controverted, and the evidence would not be admissible under FRE 407. Its only remaining purpose would be to prove liability, which FRE 407 expressly forbids.

Using a subsequent remedial remedy to prove feasibility and impeachment has been controversial. As we shall see in the next case, a plaintiff's attempt to use a subsequent remedial measure to argue either that it impeaches the witness' credibility or that it demonstrates the feasibility of an alternate design runs the risk of creating an exception that swallows the rule.

Focus Questions: *Wood v. Morbark Indus., Inc.*

- What was defense counsel's motive in his opening statement when he discussed the subsequent use of the machine?

- It is often stated that the specialized relevance rules are a sword and not a shield. How does that maxim apply in this case?

Wood v. Morbark Industries, Inc.
70 F.3d 1201 (11th Cir. 1995)

BIRCH, Circuit Judge:

…

I. FACTS

Appellant, Ruby Wood ("Wood"), seeks recovery from Morbark Industries, Inc. ("Morbark"), for the death of her husband, Ginger Wood. On February 2, 1989, Ginger Wood and his coworker, John Infinger, were using a wood chipper known as the "Eeger Beever" to chip brush for the City of DeFuniak Springs, Florida. The "Eeger Beever" wood chipper was manufactured by appellee, Morbark, and designed by the president of Morbark, Norvel Morey. The infeed chute of the wood chipper used by Ginger Wood was seventeen inches long. Although Infinger did not see Ginger Wood when he was pulled into the wood chipper, he heard the machine make an unusual sound. When Infinger turned around, Ginger Wood's body was lying in the infeed chute of the wood chipper. Ginger Wood's head, arms, and the upper part of his torso were ablated when the knives of the wood chipper contacted his body.

Wood claims that the wood chipper was defective and unreasonably dangerous because, among other things, the infeed chute was too short to protect the operator adequately. Through an in limine motion, Morbark secured under Rule 407 the exclusion of evidence of post-accident design changes that lengthened the infeed chute of the wood chipper. Nevertheless, from the beginning of the trial, counsel for Morbark sought to imply to the jury that the seventeen-inch chute was the safest length chute available and was still in use by DeFuniak Springs as well as other government agencies.

In his opening statement to the jury, Morbark's counsel suggested that there had been no changes to the design of the wood chipper since the accident:

> COUNSEL FOR MORBARK: As a matter of fact, the evidence will indicate that after Hurricane Andrew the Army Corps of Engineers ordered thirty machines *just like the one that is involved in this case,* for disposing of the debris down there.

During his cross-examination of Infinger, Morbark's counsel once again attempted to leave the jury with the impression that there had been no subsequent change to the design of the infeed chute, and the court permitted Wood's counsel to rebut that implication:

> Q: (counsel for Morbark): Mr. Infinger, are you still actively employed by the City of DeFuniak Springs?
>
> A: Yes, I am.
>
> Q: And do you still work in the same capacity as street maintenance?
>
> A: Yes, I am.
>
> Q: And you still have that Morbark chipper machine?
>
> A: Yes, it's still there.

. . . .

Q: (counsel for Wood): Mr. Wylie [counsel for Morbark] asked you if the city was still using that machine, Mr. Infinger, and you indicated it had, is that correct?

A: That's correct.

Q: At Mr. Wylie's question you answered that. Is that exactly the same machine, Mr. Infinger?

A: It's the same machine.

Q: Is it exactly the same machine?

A: Same machine.

Q: Has there been any change to the machine?

A: The only changes within the machine is those rollers has been lifted up and there's been another chute out from the chute that's on that there.

Q: How has that chute been changed?

COUNSEL FOR MORBARK: Objection, Your Honor, beyond the scope.

THE COURT: Overruled.

Q: (Counsel for Wood): How has that chute been changed, Mr. Infinger?

A: Another chute has been, as seen on that, there has been welded another, made it that much longer.

Following the examination of Infinger, counsel engaged in the following discussion with the court outside the presence of the jury:

THE COURT: I am a little confused, Mr. Wylie [counsel for Morbark], some matters that you're object[ing] to and the court has sustained the objection at pretrial and then you go right ahead and bring them right up. I want to be sure that objection and when the court sustained that objection that's on the basis of proffers and arguments that are made and if you change that here, then don't expect those rulings to apply any longer. If you ask this man and suggest that the city is still using that chipper, it's certainly fair for the other side to point out that there have been modifications to that chipper.

COUNSEL FOR MORBARK: Well, I think the Court ruled in the pretrial subsequent remedial measures would not be admitted unless the feasibility was—

THE COURT: Well, you opened the door when you started making suggestions to the jury that the city was still using that chipper, therefore, there must not be anything wrong with this chipper if the city still continues to use it on a daily basis and that will be taking unfair advantage of the Court's ruling. So I suggest that you opened the door to the fair rebuttal that was offered. I still didn't feel it necessary to go as far into the picture and design and all of that as yet. But I just want to make you aware, rely on that ruling, if those proffers and arguments change during the trial.

Near the end of the trial, the following exchange took place during counsel for Wood's examination of Norvel Morey:

Q: (Counsel for Wood): Isn't it true that you're just precluding any possible thing that might occur in everyday life, Mr. Morey, isn't that true?

A: (Mr. Morey): That's what the control bar is for, is if there's a problem, if they get their glove caught or any of their clothes caught they can stop it instantly.

> Q: So you think that the control bar takes care of any of the problems this short chute poses as a danger to the user?
>
> A: I've said it once and a thousand times, it's the safest length chute you could possibly put on the machine.
>
> Q: Yet you're selling them to the Army Corps of Engineers longer?
>
> COUNSEL FOR MORBARK: Objection.
>
> THE COURT: Do you wish to go into it?
>
> COUNSEL FOR MORBARK: No, I thought we already ruled.
>
> THE COURT: I thought we had, too. I'm going to direct, Mr. Jennings [counsel for Wood], that you not bring this up again. It has no bearing or no relationship to this case. *And the jury is directed to disregard any comment that has been made by counsel, any question, any answer that has been elicited from any witness concerning the sale of any additional or extra length chute.* Proceed. (emphasis added.)

In a discussion outside the presence of the jury, Wood's counsel attempted to clarify the court's admonition:

> COUNSEL FOR WOOD: Your Honor, I would like to apologize to the Court. I was not intending to go against any ruling that the Court had made. I thought that you had previously made a ruling when I was asking about the Army Corps of Engineers, and he made an objection and you overruled his objection. I thought that at that point you had determined that they had opened the door completely.
>
> THE COURT: That's the same reasoning as the other, is that I did not want to leave the false impression that the machines bought by the Army Corps of Engineers was this machine. No objection to you going into and proving otherwise, but when you continue well beyond that.
>
> COUNSEL FOR WOOD: I was not intending to go beyond your ruling.

On September 14, 1993, the jury entered a verdict in favor of Morbark, finding that the "Eeger Beever" wood chipper was not unreasonably dangerous as designed and marketed. Wood moved for a new trial on the grounds that the district court committed reversible error when it admonished Wood's counsel in the jury's presence regarding counsel's attempt on cross-examination of Morey to go into the issue of subsequent remedial measures. The district court denied Wood's motion for a new trial.

In its order denying a new trial, the district court provided a detailed explanation for its pretrial and trial rulings on the evidentiary issue. The court pointed out that it granted Morbark's motion in limine to exclude any evidence of Morbark's post-accident extension of the infeed chute because Morbark did not deny feasibility. The court cautioned Morbark's attorney, however, that if feasibility ever became an issue, then the evidence of subsequent remedial measures would be allowed.

The district court's order denying the motion for a new trial discussed the direct and cross-examination of Infinger. The district court found that Morbark's counsel's cross-examination of Infinger attempted to suggest to the jury that the machine was safe because it was still being used by the City of DeFuniak Springs in an unmodified condition. The district court stated that it felt Morbark's counsel had misled the jury because the wood chipper being operated by the city had been modified by adding an extension to the infeed chute. Thus, the district court allowed Wood's counsel to elicit testimony from Infinger regarding the modification of the chute.

The district court went on to discuss its reasoning, explaining that it allowed testimony concerning design changes "solely in an effort to 'level the playing field,' if you will, because the testimony on direct undoubtedly had left the jurors with the impression that the machine was being used by both the city and the Corps of Engineers in an unmodified state, which clearly was not the case."

The district court registered surprise when "plaintiff's counsel delved further into the Corps of Engineers' use of the chipper the following day during his cross examination of Norvel Morey, the owner of Morbark Industries, Inc." Nevertheless, the district court did not find its admonition to plaintiff's counsel and its direction to the jury to be "unduly prejudicial to plaintiff's case, and the Court would have reacted in the same manner to any counsel's blatant attempt to circumvent a previous ruling by the Court."

II. ANALYSIS

... Wood ... argues that ... the district court should have applied one of the exceptions provided in the rule and allowed evidence of subsequent remedial measures to show the feasibility of precautionary measures or for impeachment. Specifically, Wood claims that Morbark's president controverted the feasibility of Wood's proposed precautionary measures and, therefore, the trial judge erred in not allowing Wood's counsel to cross-examine Morbark's president about post-accident remedial measures taken by Morbark.

The trial court was correct in granting Morbark's motion in limine to exclude the evidence of post-accident remedial changes to the design of the wood chipper. The trial court also acted properly in cautioning Morbark's attorney that, if feasibility ever became an issue, evidence of subsequent remedial measures would be allowed. In its order denying Wood's motion for a new trial, the district court describes its effort to "level the playing field" by allowing limited evidence by Wood for impeachment purposes. We agree that the admission of the testimony was necessary to prevent the jury from being misled.

In his opening statement, Morbark's counsel suggested that the wood chipper used by Ginger Wood was not defective because, after the accident, the government "ordered 30 machines just like the one that is involved in this case." Morbark's counsel later elicited testimony from Infinger that left the jury with the impression that DeFuniak Springs had made no modifications to the wood chipper. The district court correctly determined that Morbark's counsel's opening statement, particularly when combined with Morbark's counsel's cross-examination of Infinger, took unfair advantage of the court's in limine ruling and opened the door for rebuttal testimony regarding the subsequent modifications to the chute.

Wood contends that the designer of the "Eeger Beever" wood chipper, Norvel Morey, put the feasibility of using a longer infeed chute at issue when he described the seventeen-inch chute as the "safest length chute you could possibly put on the machine." While we do not find that this testimony put feasibility at issue, we do find that it opened the door to impeachment. The description of the wood chipper in superlative terms is analogous to the situation in *Muzyka v. Remington Arms Co.,* 774 F.2d 1309, 1313 (5th Cir.1985), where an allegedly defective rifle was described as "the premier rifle, the best and the safest of its kind on the market." The court in Muzyka found that the jury had been denied evidence that the design was changed within weeks of the subject accident "in impeachment of the experts who spoke in those superlatives." *Id.* By referring to the seventeen-inch chute length as the "safest" length possible, Morey opened the door for impeachment. Wood's counsel should have been allowed to ask why the supposedly safest design possible was modified after the accident involving Ginger Wood. The failure of the district court to allow impeachment of this witness is not alone enough to show an abuse of the trial court's broad discretion, but the trial court's exclusion of the evidence in conjunction with a direction to the jury substantially affected the rights of Wood....

III. CONCLUSION

... [W]e do not find that the trial court erred in its original ruling excluding evidence of Morbark's use of longer infeed chutes after the accident at issue. After a careful review of the testimony, however, we are persuaded that the posture of the defense and the manner in which the evidence developed at trial required that, under Rule 407, evidence of the design change be permitted for purposes of impeachment. We REVERSE and RE-MAND for a new trial.

Author's Note: Feasibility and Impeachment under FRE 407, continued

Let us take a closer look at the risks of using a subsequent remedial measure to prove feasibility of an alternative design or impeachment of a witness. In terms of feasibility, a "hubris" test has emerged. That is, a "defendant does not controvert feasibility merely by arguing or introducing evidence that a device, process or design is reasonably safe, but claiming that all precautions were taken or that no safer design was possible clearly does put feasibility at issue." C. Mueller & L. Kirkpatrick, Sec. 4.24, at 242 (5th ed. 2012). Once a defendant's witness begins to explore that no improvements in safety are possible, they are denying the feasibility of changes. In that situation, allowing the plaintiff to mention that changes to improve safety have indeed been made is fair. Thus, it is foolhardy for a defendant to claim that a change is not feasible if a subsequent remedial measure has been adopted; consequently, most defendants will concede feasibility in these instances and instead argue that a plaintiff's proposed design was not necessary, would have created other disadvantages to the product, or would not have prevented the plaintiff's injury.

As to impeachment, asking a defense witness if a condition was safe, receiving the inevitable "yes" answer, and then exploring the subsequent remedial measure on the grounds of impeachment runs the risk of becoming the exception that swallows the rule. "Impeachment may be allowed if the witness denies the existence of a particular hazard, testifies that the product was as safe as it could be, or characterizes an alternative design or protective measure subsequently adopted as unnecessary, ineffectual, or otherwise inadvisable." *Id.* at 239–40 (footnotes omitted). This approach is harmonious with the rule's intent. To cross-examine a witness by asking if, in fact, the situation would have been safer if a subsequent remedial remedy were done will often lead to the witness responding, "no." To then ask why the subsequent remedial remedy was done is to explore the prohibited inference; the cross-examiner is arguing the subsequent remedial remedy as proof of liability. The fact that the cross-examiner also happens to be impeaching the credibility of the witness should not allow an "end run" around the rule—the major policy implication behind the rule is violated. *Flamino v. Honda*, 733 F. 2d 463 (7th Cir. 1984); *Kelly v. Crown Equip. Co.*, 970 F.2d 1273 (3d Cir. 1992). The "hubris" test applies here as well. When a witness argues that their product was the safest it could be, and the facts demonstrate a change was made, the inference explored by mentioning the subsequent remedial measure is the witness' credibility. Thus, when the inference directly and forcefully implicates a witness' credibility through the witness' puffery, exaggeration or lying, then a subsequent remedial measure may be used to impeach the witness.

Problem 3-1

John Russell was injured in the course of his employment when he dismounted from a forklift. The forklift was constructed so that the operator could stand on a platform which could be lowered closer to the ground for a safe exit. Rather than lowering the platform and stepping off, however, John jumped off the platform from a height of two feet above the ground. His safety belt caught on a ring attached to a pole at the rear of the platform. He was jerked back onto the platform and injured his back.

John sued the manufacturer of the forklift, alleging that the forklift was defectively designed. John seeks to admit evidence that after he was injured, the manufacturer of the forklift changed the design of the forklift by removing the ring attached to the pole at the rear of the platform. He argues that he should be able to impeach the defendant's expert witness, Dr. Watkins. On cross-examination, Dr. Watkins opined that the forklift involved in the accident possessed an "excellent and proper design." Should plaintiff be allowed to impeach the witness through evidence of the subsequent remedial remedy?

Problem 3-2

One day, John Bird and Kyle McHale were splitting timber using mauls, a common tool for this purpose. John's maul got stuck, and Kyle used his maul to hit the stuck maul and hopefully loosen it from the timber. Unfortunately, a part of John's maul chipped, striking him in the eye and causing severe injury. John has filed a products liability suit against the manufacturer of the maul, claiming the maul was defective and that the manufacturer could have discovered the defect. The evidence shows that John's maul was purchased in 2004 and the injury occurred in 2006.

John seeks to admit evidence that in 2005, the manufacturer conducted tests on the 2004 model which showed that the bevel on the maul was dangerously narrow and that the steel head was not up to the uniform standard of hardness. As a result, the manufacturer corrected the problems on mauls made after 2005.

You are the judge in this case. Use FRE 407 and policy arguments to explain why you will admit or exclude the evidence.

II. Is It Evidence of a Compromise?

Relevant Rule
FRE 408

Compromise Offers and Negotiations

(a) Prohibited Uses. Evidence of the following is not admissible — on behalf of any party — either to prove or disprove the validity or amount of a disputed claim or to impeach by a prior inconsistent statement or a contradiction:

(1) furnishing, promising, or offering — or accepting, promising to accept, or offering to accept — a valuable consideration in compromising or attempting to compromise the claim; and

(2) conduct or a statement made during compromise negotiations about the claim — except when offered in a criminal case and when the negotiations related to a claim by a public office in the exercise of its regulatory, investigative, or enforcement authority.

(b) **Exceptions.** The court may admit this evidence for another purpose, such as proving a witness's bias or prejudice, negating a contention of undue delay, or proving an effort to obstruct a criminal investigation or prosecution.

Overview Problem

Sally walks into a DVD rental store and tells the cashier, "I lost my copy of *The Big Lebowski* that I rented from you. I owe you some money." The clerk responds that, yes, indeed, Sally owes $19.99 for losing the video. Sally then states, "Fine, I'm sure that's what you charge for replacement DVDs. But, are you really going to sue me over this?" The clerk responds that, yes, indeed, that is the store's policy. Sally then informs the clerk, "Fine. Here's $10. Take it or leave it." Can Sally's statements be used against her if the case goes to trial?

Overview

(1) Policy Underpinnings

FRE 408 makes settlements or offers of compromise generally inadmissible on the issues of liability or damages. The rule promotes a critical policy purpose: it encourages settlement of claims by protecting against having settlements efforts used against a party at trial should settlement fail. In an age when court dockets are heavily congested, FRE 408 serves a critical need to assist the parties in speaking freely during settlement negotiations. Furthermore, there is limited probative value in settlement statements and conduct. A defendant may choose to settle a case in which she is not liable for nuisance value, and a plaintiff may choose to settle a case in order to remove risk and get the money sooner. In neither instance is the only possible inference, "you must have a weak claim/defense." Thus, while it is relevant, its probative value pales next to its prejudicial effect.

(2) Elements

Any offer, acceptance, and/or statements made in the course of compromise negotiations are protected. Note, however, that pre-existing information cannot be "immunized" by presenting it to an adversary during compromise negotiations. Evidence will not be excluded if it is otherwise discoverable, even if that evidence was used in an attempted settlement of a claim.

Significantly, the rule only covers a claim that was disputed as to validity or amount. What is a "disputed claim"? Courts have not articulated a clear standard as to how close one must be to litigation in order to have a disputed claim, and a split of opinion has arisen over the issue. Courts largely examine the issue in a fact-intensive manner, as we shall see in *EEOC v. Gear Petroleum, Inc.* In defining this issue, courts have analyzed various factors. Was the statement intended to be part of the negotiations toward a compromise? Had a party explicitly asserted a claim against the other? Is the prospect of litigation readily apparent? Have attorneys become involved in the proceedings? Based on these factors, courts have determined that FRE 408 applies to settlement offers made in response to specific oral or written claims for relief, even if a suit has not been filed. It will not apply, however, when there is no explicit claim to compromise.

In terms of being "disputed," the validity or amount must be in dispute, or else the statement or conduct is not covered. Thus, in the overview problem, Sally concedes both liability and amount and offers to pay a lesser amount. Because the amount and liability are not in dispute, the rule does not apply and her statements may be used against her.

Finally, FRE 408 excludes evidence that a party or witness settled or offered to settle a claim with a third person if the evidence is offered to prove the validity or invalidity of the claim or its amount in the instant case. But this type of evidence may be admissible for other purposes, such as bias.

(3) Exceptions

What are the admissible purposes of settlement evidence? Yet again, the drafters put together a **non-exclusive** list of permissible purposes. These include bias or prejudice, rebuttal of a claim of undue delay, to prove breach of an agreement to settle, and to prove an effort to obstruct a criminal investigation or prosecution. Each of these admissible purposes is subject to FRE 403. One area that is not subject to any exception is when a civil defendant enters into a settlement admitting fault; that settlement is not admissible against the defendant in a subsequent criminal prosecution when offered to prove liability for a claim, invalidity of a claim or the amount of a claim.

Focus Questions: *Bradbury v. Phillips Petroleum Co.*

- Is the Court's definition of a "related case" too broad? How does that definition support the policy behind FRE 408?

- How, precisely, do the other incidents refute that this incident was a mistake or accident? Why is that not a liability-based purpose?

- How similar must the other incidents be to this incident in order to be admissible?

Bradbury v. Phillips Petroleum Co.
815 F.2d 1356 (10th Cir. 1987)

BARRETT, Circuit Judge.

* * *

This case arises out of an altercation between employees for Desert Drilling Company and landowners in southwest Colorado during a large scale uranium exploration project run by Phillips Uranium Corporation. In the summer of 1980, Phillips Uranium

Corporation was in the final stages of the three-year project in and around the town of Placerville in San Miguel County, Colorado. The operation involved drilling numerous assessment holes, five inches in diameter and as deep as five hundred feet, for the purpose of sampling and evaluating minerals in the area. Phillips retained the firm of Meuer, Serafina, and Meuer to survey the mining claims upon which the assessment drilling would take place and hired Desert Drilling Company to sink the holes.

In August, 1980, Desert Drilling personnel were in the process of drilling a hole on land they believed to be Lee Claim 74. Phillips had obtained permission to drill there from the investment company that owned the surface rights and from the United States Bureau of Land Management that owned the mineral rights. As a result of a surveying error, however, the drillers were in fact on land owned by one of the plaintiffs, Thom Panunzio, which bordered Lee Claim 74. Panunzio, who was at his home in New Jersey, had denied requests by Phillips for access to his land.

Plaintiff Alan Bradbury resided near Panunzio's property. He first noticed that the drillers were in the wrong place when he heard the noise of their machinery over the hill from his house and, thinking they were on his property, went to investigate. Bradbury, who knew that Panunzio did not want any drilling done on his land, told the Desert Drilling Company employees that they were in the wrong place. The drillers told Bradbury that they had been instructed to drill there by Cathy Suda, a geologist for Phillips Uranium Corporation, and that he should speak to her about it. Suda had been at the site earlier but had left for the day. Bradbury left a message with the drillers for Suda requesting that she stop by his house down the road so he could show her maps indicating they were on the wrong property. He also attempted to phone Suda at her room at the Telluride Lodge but was unable to reach her.

On August 19, 1985, Bradbury phoned Panunzio and apprised him of the situation. Panunzio asked Bradbury to determine for sure whether the workers were drilling on his property and reiterated that he did not want drilling on his land under any circumstances. The next day, Bradbury and Lee Proper, who held a fifty percent mineral interest in Panunzio's property, returned to the site. Proper told the drillers, "Boys, you are violating my claim." Bradbury took photographs of the drillers and their operation, then phoned Panunzio. Upon being informed that the drillers were indeed on his land, Panunzio became angry and hung up. After consulting with an attorney, Panunzio phoned Bradbury and asked him to return to the site to take more pictures.

When Bradbury returned to the drilling site on Panunzio's property he found Cathy Suda along with the drilling crew. Bradbury introduced himself to Suda and discussed the situation with her. After examining the map, Suda finally conceded that they might be on the wrong property. At that point, Bradbury asked Suda if he could take some pictures and explained that he was there on behalf of the land owner. Testimony conflicts as to whether Suda gave her approval for Bradbury to take pictures or simply said, "Don't take any pictures of me."

Bradbury then began taking photographs of the drilling operations. Bradbury testified that as he was taking a picture of the license plate of a Desert Drilling Company vehicle, one of the drillers approached him, asked what he was doing, and demanded the film from his camera. Bradbury refused, and when the drillers began advancing on him, he turned and ran.

Bradbury ran past Suda and up the road toward his property with three drillers in pursuit. Upon reaching his property line, he climbed the barbed wire fence and proceeded about fifty feet before stopping. Bradbury testified that as the drillers approached, he ordered them to stay off his property. Two of the drillers also climbed the fence, however, and demanded the film from his camera. When Bradbury again refused, a scuffle ensued in which Bradbury, who was wearing a brace to mend a broken collar bone, was pushed and jostled violently enough that his shirt was torn. Bradbury was briefly choked and strangled before the camera was wrestled away from him. The drilling company employees exposed the film and took the camera back to the drilling site. Suda asked the drillers to give her the camera and it was ultimately recovered from Suda by sheriff's officers. Suda, then eight weeks pregnant, took no part in the chase or scuffle.

As a result of these events, Bradbury brought suit against Phillips Petroleum Company and its subsidiary, Phillips Uranium Corporation, for trespass, assault and battery, and outrageous conduct. In particular, Bradbury complained that the scuffle caused him severe pain in his throat and injured shoulder as well as emotional distress. Panunzio also brought suit for trespass and outrageous conduct. A jury found in favor of both plaintiffs and awarded Bradbury $1 in actual damages for trespass, $1 in actual damages for outrageous conduct, $500 in actual damages for assault and battery, $50,000 in exemplary damages for outrageous conduct and $25,000 in exemplary damages for assault and battery. The jury awarded Panunzio $1,000 in actual damages for trespass, $10,000 in actual damages for outrageous conduct, $25,000 in exemplary damages for trespass and $50,000 in exemplary damages for outrageous conduct.

On appeal ... Phillips contends that the trial court erred in admitting exhibits and testimony regarding compromises of previous claims by landowners against Phillips. It argues that these settlements should have been excluded as compromises or offers to compromise pursuant to FRE 408....

II.

The altercation between Desert Drilling Company personnel and Bradbury in August, 1980, was not the first time landowners in the Placerville area had found reason to complain about the uranium exploration project. Before considering Phillips' objection to the admission of evidence of prior settlements or compromises between Phillips and other landowners, it will be helpful to review those incidents.

In June, 1979, Fern Foster complained that Phillips personnel had trespassed on her property and changed the lock on her gate without giving her a key. There had apparently been a mix-up between Foster and a Phillips geologist, George Vance, concerning access rights and whether or not Foster or her lessee, a Mrs. Brown, was entitled to the key to the locked gate. In the same month, Phillips paid compensation to Phillip Gibbs for surface damage to his pasture and to roads and repaired his damaged spring.

Then in July, 1979, Phillips paid for damages caused when a bulldozer operator employed by Phillips damaged a fence belonging to Louis Burkey. Following this incident, a Phillips supervisor, Robert Enz, wrote an intercompany memo indicating that a "touchy situation" existed between Phillips and the landowners in the Placerville area which would require "patience, concern, understanding and tremendous amounts of Public Relations."

In July, 1980, landowner A.M. Crews claimed that under the direction of Suda, Desert Drilling Company personnel had cut across his property to access other properties held by Phillips. Crews also complained that the drilling personnel had not yet plugged a hole they had drilled on his land the previous year.

In August, 1980, Arthur Strauss' neighbor saw a truck apparently belonging to Desert Drilling Company back into Mr. Strauss' gatepost damaging the gate and allowing two of his horses to escape. At the insistence of Phillips, which threatened to drop Desert Drilling Company from their list of eligible contractors, Desert Drilling Company paid Strauss' claim.

Also in August, 1980, Suda directed the excavation of a road to gain access to a drilling site. Due to surveying mistakes by Meuer, Serafini and Meuer, workers bulldozed a road across the property of David Greevers who had not given Phillips permission to cross his land, much less build a road. Phillips paid for the damages, admitting that it could not proceed against the surveying company since Phillips personnel were supposed to check the work of the surveyors but apparently did not discover the mistake. This incident occurred five days before the assault on Bradbury.

Finally, in September, 1980, a crew from Desert Drilling Company, apparently under the direction of Suda, veered off an existing road on William Jutten's property and drove for three-quarters mile over his meadow to the drill site. Jutten protested that this was unnecessary since the road ran so close to the drill site. In addition, the drill crew left a gate open and eighty-two head of cattle wandered off Mr. Jutten's property. It took four ranch hands and several horses two days to round up the errant cattle. The cost of the round up and reseeding the damaged land was paid by Phillips.

Phillips filed a motion in limine to exclude references to or exhibits concerning the above incidents. The district court denied the motion. Evidence relating to these incidents, in the form of correspondence and claims reports, was admitted as exhibits. These incidents were also explored at various times through the examination of witnesses at trial....

Phillips' first basis for objection is that FRE 408 forbids the admission of evidence from compromises or compromise negotiations "to prove liability for or invalidity of the claim or its amount." Phillips points out that the purpose of the rule, according to the Advisory Committee's notes, is to foster honest attempts to settle controverted claims without resorting to expensive and time consuming litigation. Phillips urges that parties will have little incentive to settle claims amicably if evidence from compromises and compromise negotiations will come back to haunt them in subsequent litigation.

In determining whether or not the disputed evidence should have been excluded under Rule 408, we must first determine whether the rule applies under the circumstances of this case. Rule 408 is limited in its application to evidence concerning the settlement or compromise of "a claim" when such evidence is offered to prove liability or validity of "*the* claim" (emphasis added) or its amount. Read literally, the rule does not appear to cover compromises and compromise offers that do not involve the dispute that is the subject of the suit, even if one of the parties to the suit was also a party to the compromise.

Phillips argues, however, that Rule 408 should not be limited to compromise evidence concerning only the claim that is being litigated. It contends that the policy concerns behind Rule 408, such as encouraging out-of-court settlement, are implicated even where, as here, the compromise evidence concerns different claims. Phillips points out that in *Scaramuzzo v. Glenmore Distilleries, Co.,* 501 F.Supp. 727 (N.D.Ill. 1980) the court excluded evidence that the employer had settled age discrimination complaints that had been filed by persons other than the plaintiff. The court in *Scaramuzzo* noted that Rule 408 did not directly apply but concluded that a settlement offer is of no legal relevance as to the offeror's liability "irrespective of whether the offer was made in the instant case or in a related case." *Id.* at 733.

The facts in *Scaramuzzo* are sketchy and the nature of the proffered settlement evidence is not explained. It is clear from the court's discussion of the matter, however, that the settlements concerned "related cases." *Id.* The *Scaramuzzo* court relied on 2 J. Weinstein, *Weinstein's Evidence,* § 408[04] at 408–27 (1986), wherein it is stated that Rule 408 excludes "attempted use of a completed compromise of a claim *arising out of the same transaction* between a third person and a party to the suit being litigated." (Emphasis added.)

In this case the settlement of the seven prior claims brought by landowners arguably involved claims that arose out of different events and transactions. Yet the stronger argument is that these claims are related inasmuch as they arose in the course of the same large scale uranium exploration project operated by Phillips, and because they are similar enough to the claim sued upon in this case to be relevant. These factors, combined with the strong policy interest in encouraging the settlement of disputes without resort to litigation, is sufficient to bring the evidence concerning the seven compromises and settlements under the umbrella of Rule 408.

Having determined that Rule 408 applies under the circumstances of this case, we must determine whether it requires exclusion of the disputed evidence. The plaintiffs point out that Rule 408 does not exclude compromise evidence in all situations, but only where the evidence is offered to prove "liability for or invalidity of the claim or its amount." The rule does not require exclusion when the evidence is offered "for another purpose...." The plaintiffs note, for example, that in *Wegerer v. First Commodity Corporation of Boston*, 744 F.2d 719 (10th Cir. 1984), evidence of prior settlements was admitted to show the defendant's intent to commit fraud and to support the issue of punitive damages. The plaintiffs argue that they offered the evidence of previous settlements in this case to demonstrate Phillips' continuous course of reckless conduct and disregard of personal and property rights, to negate the defense of mistake, to show the relationship and extent of control between Phillips and Desert Drilling Company, to prove that Phillips had noticed and was aware of Desert Drilling Company personnel's conduct, and to rebut Phillips assertion that the conduct was unintentional. For these purposes, the plaintiffs contend, the evidence was admissible.

In our view, when the issue is doubtful, the better practice is to exclude evidence of compromises or compromise offers. However, we believe that the "other purposes" described by the plaintiffs appear to represent exceptions to Rule 408....

Since the plaintiffs' allege that the actions of the Desert Drilling Company personnel amounted to extreme and outrageous conduct and Phillips responds by characterizing the conduct as accidental, the issue of mistake or accident is important in this case. Along the same lines, the court instructed the jury that one element of outrageous conduct is recklessness. The evidence that seven landowners, in addition to Bradbury and Panunzio, complained to Phillips of trespass and property damage during two summers is probative on the issue of whether the incident was simply a mistake or accident and whether or not Phillips' conduct was reckless.

The district court also instructed the jury that a "series of acts may constitute outrageous conduct even though any one of the acts might be considered only an isolated unkindness or insult...." Thus, evidence that the project created problems for local land owners on seven other occasions is probative on the issue of whether the incident involving Bradbury and Panunzio was simply an isolated mistake or, rather, part of a series of incidents that might illustrate outrageous conduct on the part of Phillips towards the rights and feelings of landowners. In an analogous situation, the court in *Dosier v. Miami Valley Broadcasting Corporation*, 656 F.2d 1295, 1300 (9th Cir. 1981), admitted evidence of past incidents of discrimination by the employer, though claims arising out of those incidents had been settled, to establish "a continuing pattern of discrimination...."

These uses, we believe, were contemplated by the district court when it ordered the admission of the evidence for the purpose of showing that Phillips "engaged in a pattern of conduct evincing conscious or reckless disregard for the rights of private property owners" and "to support the plaintiffs' claims for outrageous conduct and for punitive damages." For these purposes, the evidence legitimately fell under the "other purposes" exceptions for ... Rule 408....

Phillips also contends, however, that the evidence lacks relevancy because the incidents are not similar to the incident between Bradbury and the Desert Drilling Company personnel. Phillips points out that in *Julander v. Ford Motor Co.*, 488 F.2d 839, 847 (10th Cir. 1973), we held that evidence of other acts must "bear similarity to the circumstances surrounding the accident which is the subject of the matter on trial."

It is true that none of the incidents with other landowners involved personal injury, most appeared to be accidents, and Phillips had a lease arrangement with most of the other landowners who brought complaints. Yet the similarities are as striking as the differences. All seven of the incidents involved trespass or destruction of property, four of them involved either Suda, personnel from Desert Drilling Company, or both. Furthermore, all of the incidents occurred in the same area and all occurred in the course of two summers. The fact that the incidents did not involve personal injuries in no way detracts from the relevance of the incidents in regard to the trespass and outrageous conduct claims....

Finally, Phillips raises a heartfelt objection that the evidence of compromises and prior incidents involving other landowners lacks probative value and is highly prejudicial under FRE 403. Phillips points out that evidence of compromises is not probative on the issues involved in the compromise because there may be many reasons that a party would choose to settle rather than to dispute a claim. Indeed, the exhibits in this case reveal Phillips' concern with maintaining good relations with the local landowners....

As noted above, evidence concerning the seven other incidents involving Placerville area landowners has probative value on specific elements of the claims and defenses in this case. Further, Phillips had the opportunity to explore these incidents at trial through examination of its own witnesses and did so. Phillips was able to point out any dissimilarities for the jury and to argue any mitigating circumstances. The exhibits themselves, consisting of the contents of claims files with numerous letters and memos from Phillips personnel, do not contain inflammatory or scandalous material and generally present the incidents in light favorable to Phillips. Thus, we hold that the district court did not abuse its discretion in concluding that the probative value of the evidence outweighed the risk of prejudice. The admission of the evidence did not amount to manifest error....

AFFIRMED.

Problem 3-3

Milwaukee's sewage authority made a contract with Healy Co. for the construction of a vertical shaft to carry liquid wastes to storage and treatment facilities. Healy encountered unexpected difficulties in the construction of the shaft as a result of a heavy flow of groundwater into the underground work site. These difficulties increased the cost of construction and led Healy Co. to seek an adjustment in the contract price. The original contract had a clause which required submission to the engineer of "all claims by the Contractor arising from performance under the Contract." When Healy Co. requested an increase in the contract price, the sewage authority's engineer stated that the claim for a price adjustment, "probably has merit." However, after further review, the engineer denied the claim.

In a breach of contract case, Healy Co. seeks to admit the statement by the sewage authority's engineer. How will the court rule?

Problem 3-4

Fred Jones was fifty-two years old when he and fifteen other employees were fired from Corporation. All but two of those fired were over the age of forty. Mr. Jones met with human resources officials to discuss his severance package. He was offered a document entitled "Settlement Agreement and General Release." The document, which Mr. Jones refused to sign, offered $18,000 in exchange for Mr. Jones' release of all claims against Corporation "including, but not limited to, rights under federal, state or local laws prohibiting age or other forms of discrimination...."

a) Mr. Jones has now filed suit in federal court alleging that his termination was based on age in violation of the Age Discrimination in Employment Act and state anti-discrimination laws. He seeks to admit the "Settlement Agreement and General Release" document. How will the court rule and why?

b) Suppose Corporation does not present Mr. Jones with the "Settlement Agreement and General Release" document until three weeks after Mr. Jones is fired. In that time, Mr. Jones has retained legal counsel and informed his former employer that he has done so. He has not yet, however, filed a claim. How will the court rule and why?

Problem 3-5

The Commissioner of the Internal Revenue Service ("Commissioner") brought a deficiency suit against Tom Cramden relating to their sale of pine. Cramden and the Commissioner dispute the fair market value of the pine. Cramden claims that the fair market value of the pine is substantially higher than the Commissioner's valuation. He desires a higher valuation in order to take advantage of the more favorable capital gain tax rates.

In a similar case against a different taxpayer, the Commissioner hired Consultant to make a valuation of pine purchased from the same forest at the same time. This valuation report was used in the settlement of the previous case and showed the fair market value of pine to be higher than what the Commissioner now claims.

Cramden seeks to admit the valuation report used in the prior case in order to prove the valuation of the pine and to prove that the Commissioner is not being fair to him. How will the court rule?

III. Is It a Payment of Medical Expenses?

Relevant Rule
FRE 409

Offers to Pay Medical and Similar Expenses

Evidence of furnishing, promising to pay, or offering to pay medical, hospital, or similar expenses resulting from an injury is not admissible to prove liability for the injury.

Overview Problem

Darrel, the driver of a car, hits a pedestrian. He runs out of the car and states, "I am so sorry that I ran that red light. Let me pay for your medical expenses." Is the entire statement excluded under FRE 409?

Overview

(1) Policy Underpinnings

FRE 409 protects Good Samaritans by prohibiting the introduction of offers to pay medical expenses in order to prove liability on the part of the Good Samaritan. Yet again, we have a situation of questionable relevance (the offer may be motivated by compassion rather than acceptance of liability) that is supported by a strong public policy in that society wants to encourage humane impulses. This social policy is implemented by the fact that "similar expenses" under the rule is interpreted broadly to include expenses that are related to treatment, such as personal care.

(2) Elements

The elements of FRE 409 are simple: If a party has offered to pay the medical expenses of an injured person, that statement may not be used to prove liability or damages.

(3) Exceptions

FRE 409 is both broader and narrower than FRE 408. It is broader in that it does not require a disputed claim or that the offer be an attempt to compromise a disputed claim. Accordingly, it applies in more situations. However, it is narrower in that it does not exclude collateral admissions of liability by the offeror. Thus, in the overview problem, the second sentence would be inadmissible, but the first sentence would be admissible. The latter sentence is covered under the rule, as it specifically relates to a payment of medical expenses. The earlier statement of liability, however, has no bearing on the humanitarian impulse the rule is trying to foster, and, therefore, the first sentence is admissible. Additionally, like the other specialized relevance exceptions we have examined so far, the evidence may be admissible to prove something other than liability or damages, such as agency, control, ownership, or impeachment.

Problem 3-6

Martha Gomes slipped and fell on some grapes while doing some grocery shopping. The store manager told her to see a doctor and that the store would take care of everything. He also told Martha to have the doctor's office call him to confirm the store would pay the charges. Martha went to see a doctor the next day. The bill came to $500. The store now refuses to pay the bill. Martha claims that her conversation with store manager amounted to a promise to pay her reasonable medical bills resulting from the fall. The store objects to Martha's testimony concerning the manager's promise to pay, claiming it is inadmissible under FRE 409.

You are the judge. Use FRE 409 to decide to admit or exclude the testimony.

IV. Is It a Plea or Plea Discussions?

Relevant Rule
FRE 410

Pleas, Plea Discussions, and Related Statements

(a) Prohibited Uses. In a civil or criminal case, evidence of the following is not admissible against the defendant who made the plea or participated in the plea discussions:

(1) a guilty plea that was later withdrawn;

(2) a nolo contendere plea;

(3) a statement made during a proceeding on either of those pleas under Federal Rule of Criminal Procedure 11 or a comparable state procedure; or

(4) a statement made during plea discussions with an attorney for the prosecuting authority if the discussions did not result in a guilty plea or they resulted in a later-withdrawn guilty plea.

(b) Exceptions. The court may admit a statement described in Rule 410(a)(3) or (4):

(1) in any proceeding in which another statement made during the same plea or plea discussions has been introduced, if in fairness both statements ought to be considered together; or

(2) in a criminal proceeding for perjury or false statement, if the defendant made the statement under oath, on the record, and with counsel present.

Overview Problem

During plea negotiations with a prosecutor, Dirk admits that he ran over the victim with his car while driving drunk. He offers to plead guilty to a misdemeanor, but the prosecutor rejects the offer in order to prosecute him for a felony. At trial, Dirk is acquitted. Later, the victim's family sues Dirk in a civil action for wrongful death. Can the victim's family offer Dirk's statements during plea discussions as well as willingness to plead guilty to a misdemeanor?

Overview

(1) Policy Underpinnings

Under FRE 410, an **unwithdrawn** guilty plea may be used against the defendant in a later action (e.g., in a civil action based on the actions for which defendant was charged earlier criminally). However **withdrawn** guilty pleas and pleas of nolo contendere (i.e., a plea where the defendant does not admit guilt but does not contest the charges) cannot be used in subsequent proceedings. Why the difference? The rationale here centers on the fact that an innocent individual might accept a plea to avoid the risk of loss at trial and a potentially greater penalty, and thus this type of evidence bears minimal evidentiary weight if it is withdrawn. Should she choose to withdraw this plea, the defendant would be at an extreme disadvantage if the prosecutor could use her plea against her, as the jury will undoubtedly be influenced by the defendant's wavering. Furthermore, the exclusion of this type of evidence will promote plea bargaining, which serves an important social purpose in jurisdictions with a very busy criminal docket. Conversely, with unwithdrawn guilty pleas, the probative value is higher, as the defendant's plea is an admission of guilt. Additionally, it is thought that this will not necessarily prevent plea bargains, as the advantages to someone who plea bargains (i.e., a lighter sentence) often outweigh any subsequent use of their plea.

For these reasons, statements made during a hearing to enter a plea nolo contendere or a guilty plea that is later withdrawn cannot be used. Therefore if the court demands that the defendant admit to each element of the charge in open court, this testimony cannot be used against the defendant if she withdraws the plea of guilty or makes a nolo contendere plea.

Statements "made during plea discussions with an attorney for the prosecuting authority if the discussions did not result in a guilty plea or they resulted in a later-withdrawn guilty plea" may not be introduced. Thus both defendants and their counsel may negotiate freely without fear that their words will be used against them at trial.

(2) Elements

Most of the elements of FRE 410(a)(1)-(4) are straightforward. Whether a guilty plea was later withdrawn, whether an individual made a nolo contendere plea, or whether a statement was subject to Federal Rule of Criminal Procedure 11 is rarely disputed. Defining a "plea discussion" under FRE 410(a)(4) can be a thorny issue, however. The rule mandates that the discussion be with an attorney for the prosecuting authority. However, when prosecutors play a passive role (e.g., attend, but do not participate in, a police interrogation) or police officers play an aggressive role (e.g., allude to their ability to get the defendant a good deal with the prosecutor), the definition gets clouded. Courts have taken a two-tiered approach in these situations: statements by the accused are excludable if she exhibits a subjective expectation to negotiate a plea and that the expectation was reasonable under a totality of the circumstances. *U.S. v. Robertson*, 582 F.2d 1356, 1366 (5th Cir. 1988). In short, the accused must be attempting to strike a deal with someone reasonably presumed to possess the authority to make the deal happen. Most statements made to law enforcement personnel will not objectively meet the test unless the law enforcement personnel gave the impression of having more authority than she actually possessed.

(3) Exceptions

There are two exceptions to the inadmissibility of statements made in formal plea hearings or during plea bargaining. The first exception focuses on completeness: "in any proceeding in which another statement made during the same plea or plea discussions has been introduced, if in fairness both statements ought to be considered together," then the statement is admissible. The goal is to avoid misleading the factfinder with incomplete or misleading statements offered by one party that are taken out of context.

The second exception applies only to situations where the defendant is later prosecuted for perjury or false statement for his statements during plea bargaining. The rationale here is that the defendant must have an incentive to be truthful in negotiations and forthright in carrying out any required steps for the plea bargain, such as testifying against other parties.

Unlike the federal rules governing evidence of subsequent remedial measures, FRE 410 does not allow the use of plea evidence to impeach. Thus, even when a plea bargaining defendant admits a fact during plea discussion, if the negotiations fail and the defendant testifies inconsistently on the stand, the government may not impeach the defendant's credibility with the statement. The defendant may, however, waive their protection against the use of their plea bargaining statements to impeach. *United States v. Mezzanatto*, 513 U.S. 196, 202 (1995).

By its literal terms, FRE 410 prohibits statements only when offered against the defendant; what if the defendant wanted to offer a plea agreement that she turned down against the government? Here the literal language of the rule and its policy conflict. The rule seems to allow such a maneuver, as the evidence only may be inadmissible "against the defendant." However, it would not encourage settlements if every time the prosecutor offered a plea bargain and was turned down, those words would echo at trial. Courts are split on the issue, with some court relying on FRE 403 to exclude the evidence.

Finally, note that FRE 410 makes plea offers and collateral statements associated with plea offers inadmissible in civil proceedings. Thus, in our overview problem, Dirk's statement as well as his plea offer are inadmissible in the civil case.

Problem 3-7

Todd Rice asked Blair Lynn to loan him $50,000 because his anticipated return on an overseas investment was delayed. He agreed to pay Blair 100 percent on this amount, for a return of $100,000. Relying on what turned out to be documents falsified by Todd, Blair had the money wired from her bank account to Todd's internet bank account. When the time for repayment had passed, Blair sought to enforce the agreement by pursuing guaranteed funds Todd claimed to have with Bank. Bank informed Blair she had been defrauded, and the FBI was notified.

The government filed a lis pendens and civil complaint in forfeiture against Todd's property. Todd's attorney, Todd, and the Assistant United States Attorney ("AUSA") all met pursuant to the government investigation. During the meeting, Todd admitted to the fraud, hoping that if he cooperated, he would not be indicted at all. The government never formally made such an agreement or made a formal plea offer to Todd.

The government now seeks to admit Todd's statements made during their meeting into evidence. Todd objects claiming the statements are protected by Rule 410. How will the court Rule?

V. Is It Evidence of Insurance?

Relevant Rule
FRE 411

Liability Insurance

Evidence that a person was or was not insured against liability is not admissible to prove whether the person acted negligently or otherwise wrongfully. But the court may admit this evidence for another purpose, such as proving a witness's bias or prejudice or proving agency, ownership, or control.

Overview Problem

Defendant is on trial for hitting a pedestrian with his car. The plaintiff calls the passenger in the defendant's car as a witness. The passenger testifies that he told the defendant that she was speeding and should slow down, but the defendant responded, "Stop worrying—if I hit anything my insurance will cover it." Is that statement admissible?

Overview

(1) Policy Underpinnings

FRE 411 prohibits evidence of the presence or absence of liability insurance when offered on the issue of negligence or wrongfulness. The social policy behind the rule is clear: we want to encourage the purchase of insurance and want to prevent those who purchase it from being prejudiced at trial. A major fear is that a jury may feel that an insured will not be responsible for the verdict, as a "deep pocketed" insurance company will pay it. If a nameless company is responsible, so the theory goes, the jury may be tempted to award an excessive verdict. The lack of relevance to the evidence further buttresses the rule. The idea that someone who buys insurance will somehow be more reckless has limited probative value.

(2) Elements

FRE 411 contains a straight-forward prohibition: if the existence or non-existence of insurance is offered "to prove whether the person acted negligently or otherwise wrongfully," the evidence is inadmissible.

(3) Exceptions

As is often the case with the specialized relevance rules, uses that do not focus on liability for negligence or proof of wrongful conduct are allowed. A **non-exclusive** listing includes agency, ownership, or control as well as to show bias or prejudice of a witness. In terms of agency, ownership and control, insurance evidence helps to prove that a party denying control of a person, place or instrumentality actually did control the person, place, or instrumentality. Indeed, had they not, why did they insure it? As we shall see in the case below, the bias issue comes up often if an investigator is employed by an insurance company that insures the defendant.

The line between a liability-based purpose and a non-liability-based purpose can be a fine one. As the overview problem suggests, a statement mentioning insurance might be probative of negligence or recklessness, but it will also carry a great deal of prejudice. In such scenarios, the admissibility of the statement hinges on its probative value to something at issue in the case. Thus, it will be for the court to determine whether "Stop worrying—if I hit anything my insurance will cover it" is probative of negligence. But, if the statement is admitted, a limiting instruction alerting the jury as to the proper use of the evidence will be necessary.

Despite the prohibition against the mention of insurance, jurors bring their real world knowledge with them into deliberations, and thus they may assume parties are insured. To fight against this impermissible inference, an uninsured party can request an instruction that suggests the possibility of no insurance. One such instruction reads: "There has been no evidence in this case about whether [the party] was covered by liability insurance. The reason is that the law does not permit evidence of the absence or presence of liability insurance to be presented to you. The evidence is inadmissible because you are not supposed to consider insurance one way or the other in this case. When deciding the case, you should put out of your mind the possibility that the loss in this case was covered, or was not covered, by liability insurance." R. Park, S. Goldberg, & D. Leonard, Evidence Law, Section 5.58 at 232 (3rd ed. 2011). Do you think this instruction would work? If not, what other means would prevent a jury from speculating about insurance?

Focus Questions: *Williams v. McCoy*

- How did defense counsel hope to attack the plaintiff's credibility? Do you think this type of attack would be effective?

- To what degree do you think a jury thinks about insurance issues when it deliberates?

Williams v. McCoy

550 S.E.2d 796, 145 N.C.App. 111 (N.C. App. 2001)

TIMMONS GOODSON, Judge.

Joanne C. Williams ("plaintiff") appeals from a judgment entered pursuant to a jury's verdict finding Mia McCoy ("defendant") negligent and awarding plaintiff $3,000.00 in damages. Based upon our review of the record and arguments of counsel, we reverse the judgment and remand for a new trial on all issues.

Plaintiff filed an action against defendant claiming personal injury resulting from a 1997 automobile accident between the two litigants. Based upon a pre-trial motion by defendant, the trial court instructed plaintiff not to testify "that there was liability insurance, reference any conversations or contact with liability insurance adjusters, etcetera[,] pursuant to [North Carolina Rule of Evidence] 411." Plaintiff objected to the court's pre-trial ruling. Plaintiff informed the court that she first hired an attorney "after meeting [defendant's] claims['] adjuster." Plaintiff contended that restricting her testimony pursuant to Rule

411 was prejudicial, arguing that she would not be allowed to explain why she hired an attorney if defendant so inquired. . . .

Pertinent to the issues presented on appeal, plaintiff testified concerning the facts surrounding the alleged automobile accident. Plaintiff further testified that she visited and was subsequently released from the emergency room immediately following the accident. According to plaintiff, at the urging of her husband, she visited a chiropractor four days after being released from the emergency room. Plaintiff explained that she did not visit the doctor sooner because he was unavailable. Plaintiff further testified that in two prior work-related accidents she had injured her knee, and that following the collision with defendant, she experienced difficulty walking and a "clicking" sensation in her knee, which she had not previously noticed.

On cross-examination, defense counsel questioned plaintiff extensively concerning the timing of her visit to the chiropractor, the symptoms she related to the emergency room staff, and why she did not return to the emergency room although her condition worsened. At some point in plaintiff's testimony, defense counsel inquired, "Would you agree that you retained your attorney prior to going to the chiropractor?" Plaintiff objected to the defense's inquiry, but the court overruled the objection and ordered plaintiff to answer. Plaintiff then responded, "No." Defense counsel further inquired, "You dispute that[,]" to which plaintiff answered, "No, in fact, I was told not to talk about insurance." Again, the attorney inquired, "I asked you a question and that is did you retain your attorney prior to going to the chiropractor during which time you said your condition—," and plaintiff responded, "I don't remember."

Following the aforementioned exchange, the court excused the jury and reiterated to plaintiff that she was not to testify concerning insurance. Plaintiff's attorney requested permission to allow plaintiff to explain why she hired an attorney, arguing that defense counsel was attempting to prejudice plaintiff by suggesting that she was litigious. Plaintiff's attorney explained that defense counsel was "building his whole case" around plaintiff's alleged litigious nature. Plaintiff's attorney then quoted the following from defense counsel's opening statement: "We're going to show you that she's here for profit and that she stated it by hiring an attorney before she went to see a doctor." According to plaintiff's attorney, "that [was defendant counsel's] whole theme. He led her into that. As a matter of fact, you hired a lawyer before you went to a chiropractor."

The court subsequently allowed plaintiff to explain her answer on voir dire, outside the presence of the jury. Plaintiff offered the following explanation as to why she hired an attorney:

> [Defendant's claims' adjuster] came to my house. And he tried to persuade me to take some money. And he told me that because I had had an injury in '76 that I was wasting my time and that I needed money and let them settle with me so that I can get medical help.

The court again refused to allow plaintiff's testimony and further instructed plaintiff that if she mentioned "insurance" again, he would declare a mistrial and hold her in contempt of court.

Following the presentation of evidence, arguments from counsel, and jury instructions, the jury returned its verdict, finding defendant negligent and awarding plaintiff $3,000.00 in damages. The court denied a subsequent motion by plaintiff for a new trial and entered judgment based upon the jury's verdict, taxing the cost of the action to plaintiff. From this judgment, plaintiff appeals.

... [P]laintiff contends that the trial court erred in not permitting her to explain her answer when asked whether she hired an attorney prior to visiting the doctor. Plaintiff argues that her explanation was admissible for a purpose other than to prove the existence of liability insurance and that the court abused its discretion in not admitting it as such. With plaintiff's arguments, we agree.

Rule 411 of our Rules of Evidence provides: "Evidence that a person was or was not insured against liability is not admissible upon the issue of whether he acted negligently or otherwise wrongfully." Rule 411 represents a narrow exception providing for the exclusion of otherwise admissible and relevant evidence.... As such, the Rule does not absolutely bar the admission of evidence concerning liability when that evidence is "offered for another purpose, such as proof of agency, ownership, or control, or bias or prejudice of a witness." Id. The exceptions listed in the Rule are nonexclusive, see Commentary to N.C.R. Evid. 411, as Rule 411 only excludes insurance evidence "as an independent fact, i.e., solely on the issue of negligent or wrongful conduct" but not if it "is offered to achieve a collateral purpose," *Carrier v. Starnes*, 120 N.C.App. 513, 516, 463 S.E.2d 393, 395 (1995) (citations omitted).

In reviewing whether to admit or exclude evidence under Rule 411, the trial court must consider the mandate of North Carolina Rule of Evidence 403. Rule 403 specifies, in pertinent part, that relevant evidence "may be excluded if its probative value is substantially outweighed by the danger of unfair prejudice, confusion of the issues, or misleading the jury...." N.C. Gen.Stat. § 8C-1, Rule 403 (2000). The Rule 403 balancing test falls within the exclusive purview of the trial court, and therefore the court's decisions under Rule 403 will not be disturbed on appeal absent an abuse of discretion. An abuse of discretion occurs when the court's decision "is manifestly unsupported by reason or is so arbitrary that it could not have been the result of a reasoned decision." *State v. McDonald*, 130 N.C.App. 263, 267, 502 S.E.2d 409, 413 (1998) (citation omitted).

It is clear to this Court that Rule 411 did not bar plaintiff's explanation as to why she hired an attorney, in light of the circumstances presented by the instant case. A review of the transcript reveals that based upon pre-trial discovery, defense counsel knew plaintiff would testify that her motivation for hiring an attorney was a negative encounter with defendant's insurance adjuster. It appears that during opening statements, defense counsel then argued that plaintiff hired an attorney prior to seeing the doctor. Plaintiff's explanation as to defense counsel's subsequent question did not bear directly on defendant's liability or wrongful conduct, but, as a collateral issue, simply explained the somewhat confusing answer solicited by the defense. We therefore find that plaintiff's examination should not have been excluded per Rule 411.

Concerning Rule 403, our review of the transcript reveals that the court did not consider or balance the risk of unfair prejudice to defendant's case with the above noted probative value of plaintiff's explanation. Pursuant to a pre-trial motion, the court ruled there was to be no reference to insurance and reserved ruling on whether plaintiff's explanation was admissible. When the issue arose, the court allowed plaintiff to give voir dire testimony concerning her explanation but instructed her, without reconsidering its prior ruling, that any mention of insurance would result in a mistrial and even contempt of court.

Certainly, we recognize, as pointed out by defendant, that had plaintiff been allowed to explain why she hired an attorney, it may have had some prejudicial effect on defendant. However, this prejudice does not outweigh the probative value of plaintiff's testimony and the prejudice she suffered in not being allowed to explain her answer. This is true especially in light of the clear implication that plaintiff only visited her doctor after seeking an attorney's advice, the fact that the extent of plaintiff's injuries was a major issue at trial, and the apparent trial strategy by defendant to characterize plaintiff as blatantly seeking profit. In fact, we wholeheartedly agree with plaintiff: "Without [ ] being allowed to explain herself, the total weight of [defendant's] attack ... fell on [plaintiff] and affected the verdict. The [trial court's] denying her explanation allowed the jury to assume the worse, that she had an improper motive in hiring an attorney, was litigious, and therefore lacked credibility."

Furthermore, in assessing the prejudice to defendant which may have resulted from plaintiff's testimony, we note the realities of what the jury already assumes about defendants in motor vehicle cases. The jurors, who more than likely drive automobiles, would also more than "likely [ ] know that in all probability there is insurance, that the matter has been investigated by the insurer's claim agent or attorney, and that insurer has employed the trial counsel." [1 Kenneth S. Broun, Brandis & Broun on North Carolina Evidence, § 108, p. 333 (5th ed.1998)]. More importantly, having taken voir dire testimony of plaintiff's explanation, the court could have further limited any prejudice to defendant by restricting the import of plaintiff's testimony and giving a limiting instruction, if so requested. See N.C. Gen.Stat. § 8C-1, Rule 105 (2000) ("When evidence which is admissible as to one party or for one purpose but not admissible as to another party or for another purpose is admitted, the court, upon request, shall restrict the evidence to its proper scope and instruct the jury accordingly.") Because none of the aforementioned was considered by the trial court, we find its decision to exclude plaintiff's explanation unsupported by reason. We therefore conclude that the trial court abused its discretion in failing to admit plaintiff's explanatory testimony, and considering the obvious prejudice suffered by plaintiff, the court's abuse of discretion constituted reversible error.

As we determine plaintiff is entitled to a new trial based on the aforementioned reasoning, we find it unnecessary to address plaintiff's remaining arguments. Accordingly, the judgment of the trial court is reversed, and we remanded the case for a new trial.

Reversed and remanded.

Problem 3-8

Jack Smith sustained a permanent injury to his left hand while serving as first mate aboard the commercial fishing vessel, The Pirate, which was traveling at a high speed. Two days after the accident, an adjuster for The Pirate's insurer obtained an oral statement from Smith in Portuguese. Since Smith could speak little English and was unable to read it, the adjuster purported to translate the written English statement back to Smith in Portuguese. Unbeknownst to Smith, the statement he signed indicated that The Pirate had been traveling at a slow speed when the accident occurred, and it made no mention of other critical facts about which Smith had informed the adjuster in his interview.

Smith brought an action for negligence against the owner of The Pirate. During the trial, Smith's lawyer refers to the insurance adjuster in her direct examination as well as in her closing argument. The lawyer for The Pirate objects, stating that referring to the adjuster violates Rule 411 because it is evidence that The Pirate holds liability insurance. How will the court rule?

Professional Development Questions

- The specialized relevance rules were meant to ensure predictability by providing bright line rules that would prevent trial courts from engaging in ad hoc balancing. Nonetheless, within each of these rules some gray exists. For example, we have seen that meeting the hubris test and determining whether negotiations were effectuated over a disputed claim can be very fact-intensive. Realistically, your efforts on both your final exam and in your career will focus predominately on these gray areas. What other gray areas exist in the law in this chapter?

- Do you think a jury would award a higher or lower amount if they learned that a defendant was insured? Think about it in terms of a car accident case. On the one hand, the jury may be tempted to award higher damages because the money will not come from the defendant's pocket and juror attitudes may not be sympathetic to insurance companies. On the other hand, the jury might award a lower amount because they might reason that the plaintiff would receive a double recovery, as the plaintiff's expenses may have already been paid by an insurance company. Does either of these fears present a stronger justification for FRE 411?

- Often when multiple policy rationales support the existence of a rule of evidence, there exists a risk that the policies will conflict. For example, a piece of evidence that possesses high probative value might violate a strong social policy. For each of the rules in this chapter, try to create a hypothetical where the policy rationales for the rule conflict. As you reason through your hypotheticals, does one policy rule seem to trump the others?

- In Chapter 2, you were introduced to the three key components of being an expert learner: planning, implementing your plans with self-monitoring, and reflecting on your learning process. You were asked to craft learning goals for this chapter. Did those goals work? Why or why not?

- In the planning phase of becoming an expert learner, you should set mastery learning goals (e.g., "I will understand the policy reasons behind the specialized relevance rules") and not task-completion goals (e.g., "I will read that chapter tonight"). What were your mastery learning goals for this chapter? As you begin Chapter 4, articulate your mastery learning goals and keep them in mind as you work through the material.

Chapter 4

Character Evidence: Propensity Reasoning That Is Not Based on Character

I. FRE 404(b)

Relevant Rule
FRE 404(b)

(b) Crimes, Wrongs, or Other Acts.

(1) *Prohibited Uses.* Evidence of a crime, wrong, or other act is not admissible to prove a person's character in order to show that on a particular occasion the person acted in accordance with the character.

(2) *Permitted Uses; Notice in a Criminal Case.* This evidence may be admissible for another purpose, such as proving motive, opportunity, intent, preparation, plan, knowledge, identity, absence of mistake, or lack of accident. On request by a defendant in a criminal case, the prosecutor must:

(A) provide reasonable notice of the general nature of any such evidence that the prosecutor intends to offer at trial; and

(B) do so before trial — or during trial if the court, for good cause, excuses lack of pretrial notice.

Overview Problem

Dirk, a prison inmate, is accused of killing another inmate, Alex. Alex was found dead in the prison library at 4:00 p.m. with ligature marks around his neck and a sock stuffed in his mouth. The coroner determined that Alex was strangled to death, most likely with a wire.

Dirk never associated with Alex and denies committing the murder. The prosecution seeks to offer the following evidence:

- While in prison, Dirk recently began associating with a prison gang called the Roadrunners. The Roadrunners possessed a grudge against Alex, as they believed Alex was selling drugs on their prison "turf."

- A corrections officer will testify that Dirk falsely accused Alex of possessing drugs in his cell.

- Earlier on the day of the killing, Dirk was disciplined for not showing up for his job in the prison machine shop. It was during the time period of his missed shift that Alex was killed.

- Dirk was originally imprisoned because he strangled a stranger with wire and stuffed a sock in the victim's mouth.

- Three weeks before the killing, Dirk was disciplined for stealing wire from his job in the prison machine shop.

- Testimony from Devon, an inmate friend of Alex, that he had witnessed Dirk following Alex in the prison in the weeks before the killing and that Alex visited the prison library daily from 3:00 p.m. to 5:00 p.m.

A. Character-Propensity Reasoning

In our daily lives, we often engage in propensity reasoning. If the person who sat next to you in Evidence borrowed money from you three times but did not pay any of those loans back, you may likely reach a conclusion in your mind about whether you would give a fourth loan. You would have concluded that your fellow law student has demonstrated a propensity, a natural tendency or disposition, to avoid repaying her debts. In essence, you are using past conduct as circumstantial evidence to predict future behavior and adjusting your behavior accordingly.

The FRE often prohibits this type of reasoning, however. The prohibited inference found in FRE 404(b) is the **inference from character to conduct.** In other words, the FRE **prohibits** arguing that a person's disposition or propensity to engage in a certain conduct can be used to prove that she acted in accordance with that disposition or propensity at the time at issue in the case (henceforth we will call this "character-propensity reasoning"). In terms of the language of the rule, we cannot use an "other ... act" to "show that on a particular occasion the person acted in accordance with [their] character." To look at this reasoning linearly:

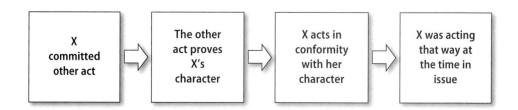

So, the fact that one has three prior speeding tickets cannot be used to prove that a person was speeding at a later time because the evidentiary hypothesis specifically attempts to "show action in conformity" with the other act(s) (i.e., the other speeding tickets):

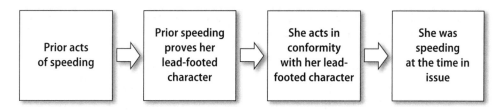

We see here that the evidentiary hypothesis for the circumstantial other act evidence is purely propensity-based—you were caught speeding before, therefore you typically drive beyond the speed limit, therefore you were speeding at the time at issue. What makes this inference so damaging that such evidence is prohibited? Two major risks arise from an inference from character to conduct. First, we worry that the inference will "over-persuade" the jury. In other words, the jury will rely on the other act evidence to the exclusion of all the other evidence presented at trial ("If she has been caught speeding so many times, then she **must** have been speeding this time"). Second, we are worried about a preventative conviction—that the jury will want to punish the person for the other acts rather than the act which must be proven at trial ("Whether she was speeding this time or not, I don't want drivers like her on the road"). Either risk brings substantial unfair prejudice in the form of confusion, distraction from the true issue being litigated, and wasting time.

Nonetheless, the risks of character-propensity reasoning are sometimes deemed acceptable under the FRE. As we shall see in Chapters 5 and 6, there are six "proper" uses of propensity reasoning that allow the argument that a party acted in conformity with her character on a given occasion. The **use** of the evidence will determine if character evidence will be allowed. Two of the uses are found in FRE 404(a)(1) and FRE 404(a)(2), where (i) a criminal defendant can prove pertinent good character traits about herself, and (ii) the criminal defendant (or, sometimes, the prosecution) can prove pertinent character traits of a victim of a crime. The third use focuses on the credibility of a witness. The credibility of a witness is always a relevant issue, and character evidence is a common method by which credibility can be assessed. FRE 404(a)(3). Additionally, policy reasons, such as fairness to parties, or the perceived logical strength of the character inference, may justify the use of character evidence. These policy reasons will be explored in greater detail when we examine the final three uses of character-propensity reasoning in the context of sexual assault and child molestation cases. FRE 413, 414, and 415. The important thing to remember, for now, is that any of the aforementioned uses will allow character-propensity evidence.

But there is yet another way "other act" evidence may be admissible: when the use of the evidence does not involve character-propensity reasoning. Think of it as the "missing word" approach. When circumstantial "other act" evidence is being introduced, what is the missing evidential hypothesis in our line of reasoning? Does that use mirror the list provided in FRE 404(b) (e.g., a **non-exclusive** list that I refer to as OKMIMIC: Opportunity, Knowledge, Motive, Intent, absence of Mistake, Identity, or Common plan or scheme)? To look at this reasoning linearly:

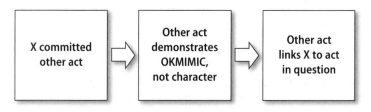

Let us look at another example: John steals his Evidence professor's car, and the prosecution offers John's prior conviction for car theft:

The proponent of the evidence seems to be making a character-propensity argument — once a car thief, always a car thief. In other words, **the probative value of the evidence depends directly on the forbidden inference** that John acted in accordance with his thieving nature. But what if John instead had previously stolen his Evidence professor's out-of-date sport coat that contained the key to his car?

Now a host of non-character traits justify the use of the evidence and serve as our evidentiary hypothesis: opportunity, intent, motive, and/or plan to name a few. This internal step is **not a character trait of John**, so the evidence is admissible. As long as the evidentiary hypothesis (the "missing word") does not require propensity reasoning based on character, it is admissible. After all, the evidence does not require propensity reasoning, as the probative value of the evidence does not depend on John's thieving nature. Rather, the probative value is that it provides John with an opportunity (or plan, or proof of intent, etc.) to steal his Evidence professor's car.

You might be thinking, "Wait a minute. There's still a potential character-propensity risk. The jury could end up thinking: John stole a jacket, he is a thief by nature, and therefore he probably stole his hard-working Evidence professor's car." That fear is absolutely correct. A **permissible**, non-character-propensity rationale for the evidence may exist side-by-side with an **impermissible** character-propensity-based rationale for the evidence. When both a permissible and impermissible use of the evidence run on parallel tracks, a FRE 403 balancing may lead to exclusion of the evidence if the judge believes a FRE 105 limiting instruction will not assist the jury in focusing on the permissible uses and ignoring the impermissible use. But, the mere existence of side-by-side permissible and impermissible inferences in and of itself does not automatically exclude the evidence; it is only when the risk exists that the impermissible use will dominate the permissible use that the evidence will be deemed inadmissible under FRE 403.

An additional aid in preventing the impermissible purpose from dominating the permissible purpose is the burden of proof under FRE 404(b). The proponent of the evidence has the burden of identifying a relevant purpose that does not involve the prohibited inference from character to conduct. Thus, the party introducing the evidence must prove the probative force of the word they choose. Furthermore, in most federal courts the proponent must articulate the specific non-propensity use(s) of the evidence. They cannot merely list all the options under FRE 404(b).

B. Evidential Hypotheses that Avoid Character-Propensity Reasoning

FRE 404(b) lists eight categories that do not require an inference from character to conduct. This is not a comprehensive list (FRE 404(b) notes that other acts "… may be admissible for another purpose, such as …"), but it is critical to understand why these categories do not implicate an inference from character to conduct. Although the cases and problems in this chapter will go into greater depth, a quick overview will be helpful. As you review this information, try to come up with other examples in your mind that might explore the gray areas of these categories.

- **Motive** is often relevant to proving a party's intent, which is often an element of a crime. Thus, in our overview problem, evidence that Dirk had begun associating with the Roadrunners and that the Roadrunners had a grudge against Alex may demonstrate Dirk's motive in killing Alex.

- As **intent** must often be proven circumstantially (i.e., there is rarely direct evidence of party's intent), other act evidence demonstrating intent often focuses on similar conduct that is committed under similar circumstances. In our overview problem, Dirk's prior attempt to falsely accuse Alex of possessing drugs may demonstrate an intent to harm Alex.

- **Opportunity** often provides proof to a location, a time, or an instrumentality necessary to commit the crime. Dirk's prior act of skipping work may demonstrate that he had an opportunity to kill Alex.

- **Identity** is revealed when an other act marks a distinctive method that sheds light on the identity in the case at issue. Evidence that Dirk committed a similar crime in a very unique manner may prove the identity of Alex's killer.

- **Preparation or plan** focuses on other acts that indicate a design by the party to accomplish an act. Dirk's attempt to obtain wire (the same type of item that was used to kill Alex) may demonstrate preparation or a plan.

- Other acts demonstrating **knowledge** are often used to rebut affirmative defenses that a party did not know a certain aspect of his actions. Dirk's attempt to stalk Alex may be perceived as an attempt to obtain knowledge of Alex's daily habits.

- **Absence of mistake or accident** other act evidence rebuts a claim of accident when the same type of event occurred previously (e.g., in an arson case, other suspicious fires of the defendant's property may rebut the defense that this particular fire was an accident).

Undoubtedly, you have noticed overlap among the categories discussed here. Courts often struggle with the proper label and often label admissible other act evidence under multiple categories, such as linking "plan" and "opportunity." Due to this cross-pollination of labels, the important skill to master is the reasoning and not the nomenclature.[1] Focus

---

1. Remember, the OKMIMIC "missing words" are not an exclusive list. One of my students added to the list by crafting the acronym "GRAND:" Consciousness of Guilt, Rebut a Defense, Absence of

your understanding on determining when character-propensity is being utilized and do not worry about labeling other acts under multiple categories.

C. The Introduction of Evidence Pursuant to FRE 404(b)

Pay particular attention to the scope of 404(b) based on its plain language. It is applicable to civil cases as well as criminal ones. The other act need not be a crime and need not even be wrongful. In fact, it need not even be a prior act—as long as a subsequent act satisfies the "other word" test, it is admissible.

The introduction of FRE 404(b) evidence is a powerful tool. In terms of the overview problem discussed above, note the flexibility in how one may prove evidence that is not based on character-propensity reasoning. A proponent of non-character-propensity evidence may use extrinsic evidence. For example, a party may offer an opinion witness, examples of specific instances of conduct, or documentary proof. Significantly, in this context, the party is **not** limited to cross-examination in proving their evidentiary hypothesis.

Another issue that arises in the FRE 404(b) context is the degree of proof required to prove that the party committed the other act. In our previous example of John stealing the evidence professor's coat, what would happen if John denied the "other act" and claimed that he never stole the coat? This is a conditional relevance issue, as a conditional fact is under dispute (i.e., without proof that John stole the coat, the inference that he had a plan or opportunity fails). Thus, pursuant to the test for conditional relevance, the judge need only find that the jury could reasonably conclude by a preponderance of the evidence that the defendant committed or is responsible for the other act. *Huddleston v. U.S.*, 485 U.S. 681, 689–90 (1988).

Finally, note that other acts "may" be admissible for other purposes. The reason that the drafters of FRE 404(b) relied on "may" rather than "shall" is due to the potential of highly prejudicial evidence that may pass the "other word" test of FRE 404(b). Thus, as previously noted, FRE 403 does apply to all evidence that is admissible under FRE 404(b). The balancing required by FRE 403 is governed by numerous factors in this context. See e.g., S. Goode and O. Wellborn, Courtroom Evidence Handbook, p. 98 (2013 ed.).

- The extent to which the point to be proved is disputed. Put simply, the more strongly an issue is contested, the more likely the evidence is necessary.
- The adequacy of proof of the other act. As previously noted, the proponent of the other act evidence must be able to prove that the party did, in fact, commit the other act.
- The probative force of the evidence.
- The proponent's need for the evidence. Thus, if other evidence in the proponent's arsenal may prove the same point, or if the point is at best marginal to the issues in the trial, its probative value is lessened.
- The availability of less prejudicial proof.
- The prejudicial effect of the other act. Here, courts analyze not only whether the evidence will inflame the jury's emotions but also examine the degree to which

---

Accident, Narrative Integrity (inextricably intertwined), Doctrine of Chances. These "missing words" will be explored in the problems in this chapter.

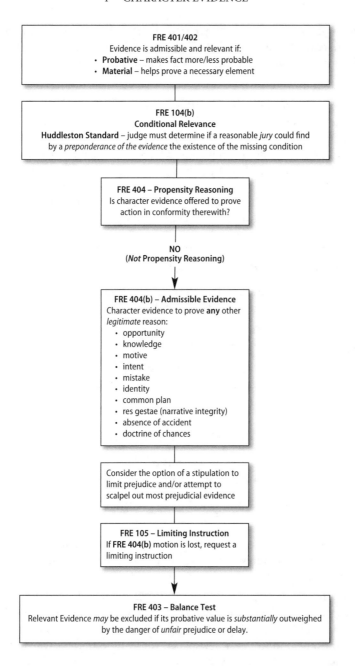

FRE 401/402
Evidence is admissible and relevant if:
- **Probative** – makes fact more/less probable
- **Material** – helps prove a necessary element

FRE 104(b)
Conditional Relevance
Huddleston Standard – judge must determine if a reasonable *jury* could find by a *preponderance of the evidence* the existence of the missing condition

FRE 404 – Propensity Reasoning
Is character evidence offered to prove action in conformity therewith?

NO
(*Not* Propensity Reasoning)

FRE 404(b) – Admissible Evidence
Character evidence to prove **any** other *legitimate* reason:
- opportunity
- knowledge
- motive
- intent
- mistake
- identity
- common plan
- res gestae (narrative integrity)
- absence of accident
- doctrine of chances

Consider the option of a stipulation to limit prejudice and/or attempt to scalpel out most prejudicial evidence

FRE 105 – Limiting Instruction
If **FRE 404(b)** motion is lost, request a limiting instruction

FRE 403 – Balance Test
Relevant Evidence *may* be excluded if its probative value is *substantially* outweighed by the danger of *unfair* prejudice or delay.

"overpersuading" the jury or a preventative conviction may occur if the evidence is introduced.

- The similarity to the charged wrongdoing. The greater the similarity of the other act to the charged wrongdoing, the more likely the evidence veers into character-propensity reasoning ("she did this before, so she must be guilty this time")

- The effectiveness of a limiting instruction. A limiting instruction that explains the use of the other act evidence to the jury (e.g., "you may use this evidence as proof of X, but you may not use this evidence as proof of Y") should **always** be requested when a party loses an objection based on FRE 404(b). If the limiting instruction will not ease jury confusion between the permissible and impermissible use of the evidence, this is a strong argument for exclusion of the evidence.

- The extent to which other act evidence prolongs proceedings.

The battle over the admissibility of FRE 404(b) evidence occurs in stages. Now would be a good time to review the relevance flowchart in Chapter 2 to see how many different ways exist to attack FRE 404(b) evidence. Is it relevant under FRE 401? If so, can you prove that the party committed the other act? If so, does the other act evidence meet the "missing word" test under FRE 404(b)? If so, is the evidence still too prejudicial under FRE 403? These are the progressions in resolving objections based on other act evidence. As you undertake the foregoing problems, keep in mind the battle lines for each of these progressions, which are illustrated in the chart on the previous page.

Focus Questions: *People v. Zackowitz*

- What narrative perspective does the majority use as compared to the dissent? Are they looking at the defendant's act differently? How so?

- Does the fact that premeditation and deliberation are difficult tests for a jury to apply influence the court? Should it?

- Were the majority's characterizations of the prosecutor's motives fair?

People v. Zackowitz

Court of Appeals of New York
254 N.Y. 192, 172 N.E. 466 (1930)

CARDOZO, C. J. (LEHMAN, KELLOGG, and O'BRIEN, JJ., concur with CARDOZO, C. J.)

On November 10, 1929, shortly after midnight, the defendant in Kings county shot Frank Coppola and killed him without justification or excuse. A crime is admitted. What is doubtful is the degree only.

Four young men, of whom Coppola was one, were at work repairing an automobile in a Brooklyn street. A woman, the defendant's wife, walked by on the opposite side. One of the men spoke to her insultingly, or so at least she understood him. The defendant, who had dropped behind to buy a newspaper, came up to find his wife in tears. He was told she had been insulted, though she did not then repeat the words. Enraged, he stepped across the street and upbraided the offenders with words of coarse profanity. He informed them, so the survivors testify, that "if they did not get out of there in five minutes, he would come back and bump them all off." Rejoining his wife, he walked with her to their apartment house located close at hand. He was heated with liquor which he had been drinking at a dance. Within the apartment he induced her to tell him what the insulting words had been. A youth had asked her to lie with him, and had offered her $2. With rage aroused again, the defendant went back to the scene of the insult and found the four young men still working at the car. In a statement to the police, he said that he had armed himself at the apartment with a .25-caliber automatic pistol. In his testimony at the trial he said that this pistol had been in his pocket all the evening. Words and blows followed, and then a shot. The defendant kicked Coppola in the stomach. There is evidence that Coppola went for him with a wrench. The pistol came from the pocket, and from the pistol a single shot, which did its deadly work. The defendant walked away and at the corner met his wife who had followed him from the home. The two took a taxicab to Manhattan, where they spent the rest of the night at the dwelling of a friend. On the way the defendant threw his pistol into the river. He was arrested on January 7, 1930, about two months following the crime.

At the trial the vital question was the defendant's state of mind at the moment of the homicide. Did he shoot with a deliberate and premeditated design to kill? Was he so inflamed by drink or by anger or by both combined that, though he knew the nature of his act, he was the prey to sudden impulse, the fury of the fleeting moment? If he went forth from his apartment with a preconceived design to kill, how is it that he failed to shoot at once? How reconcile such a design with the drawing of the pistol later in the heat and rage of an affray? These and like questions the jurors were to ask themselves and answer before measuring the defendant's guilt. Answers consistent with guilt in its highest grade can reasonably be made. Even so, the line between impulse and deliberation is too narrow and elusive to make the answers wholly clear. The sphygmograph records with graphic certainty the fluctuations of the pulse. There is no instrument yet invented that records with equal certainty the fluctuations of the mind. At least, if such an instrument exists, it was not working at midnight in the Brooklyn street when Coppola and the defendant came together in a chance affray. With only the rough and ready tests supplied by their experience of life, the jurors were to look into the workings of another's mind, and discover its capacities and disabilities, its urges and inhibitions, in moments of intense excitement. Delicate enough and subtle is the inquiry, even in the most favorable conditions, with every warping influence excluded. There must be no blurring of the issues by evidence illegally admitted and carrying with it in its admission an appeal to prejudice and passion.

Evidence charged with that appeal was, we think, admitted here. Not only was it admitted, and this under objection and exception, but the changes were rung upon it by prosecutor and judge. Almost at the opening of the trial the people began the endeavor to load the defendant down with the burden of an evil character. He was to be put before the jury as a man of murderous disposition. To that end they were allowed to prove that at the time of the encounter and at that of his arrest he had in his apartment, kept there in a radio box, three pistols and a tear-gas gun. There was no claim that he had brought these weapons out at the time of the affray, no claim that with any of them he had discharged the fatal shot. He could not have done so, for they were all of different caliber. The end to be served by laying the weapons before the jury was something very different. The end was to bring persuasion that here was a man of vicious and dangerous propensities, who because of those propensities was more likely to kill with deliberate and premeditated design than a man of irreproachable life and amiable manners. Indeed, this is the very ground on which the introduction of the evidence is now explained and defended. The district attorney tells us in his brief that the possession of the weapons characterized the defendant as "a desperate type of criminal," a "person criminally inclined." The dissenting opinion, if it puts the argument less bluntly, leaves the substance of the thought unchanged. "Defendant was presented to the jury as a man having dangerous weapons in his possession, making a selection therefrom and going forth to put into execution his threats to kill." The weapons were not brought by the defendant to the scene of the encounter. They were left in his apartment where they were incapable of harm. In such circumstances, ownership of the weapons, if it has any relevance at all, has relevance only as indicating a general disposition to make use of them thereafter, and a general disposition to make use of them thereafter is without relevance except as indicating a "desperate type of criminal," a criminal affected with a murderous propensity.

We are asked to extenuate the error by calling it an incident; what was proved may have an air of innocence if it is styled the history of the crime. The virus of the ruling is not so easily extracted. Here was no passing reference to something casually brought out in the narrative of the killing, as if an admission had been proved against the defendant that he had picked one weapon out of several. Here in the forefront of the trial, immediately following the statement of the medical examiner, testimony was admitted that weapons, not the instruments of the killing, had been discovered by the police in the apartment of the killer; and the weapons with great display were laid before the jury, marked as exhibits, and thereafter made the subject of animated argument. Room for doubt there is none that in the thought of the jury, as in that of the district attorney, the tendency of the whole performance was to characterize the defendant as a man murderously inclined. The purpose was not disguised. From the opening to the verdict, it was flaunted and avowed.

If a murderous propensity may be proved against a defendant as one of the tokens of his guilt, a rule of criminal evidence, long believed to be of fundamental importance for the protection of the innocent, must be first declared away. Fundamental hitherto has been the rule that character is never an issue in a criminal prosecution unless the defendant chooses to make it one. In a very real sense a defendant starts his life afresh when he stands before a jury, a prisoner at the bar. There has been a homicide in a public place. The killer admits the killing, but urges self-defense and sudden impulse. Inflexibly the law has set its face against the endeavor to fasten guilt upon him by proof of character or experience predisposing to an act of crime. The endeavor has been often made, but always it has failed. At times, when the issue has been self-defense, testimony has been admitted as to the murderous propensity of the deceased, the victim of the homicide, but never of such a propensity on the part of the killer. The principle back of the exclusion is one, not of logic, but of policy. There may be cogency in the argument that a quarrelsome defendant is more likely to start a quarrel than one of milder type, a man of dangerous mode of life more likely than a shy recluse. The law is not blind to this, but equally it is not blind to the peril to the innocent if character is accepted as probative of crime. "The natural and inevitable tendency of the tribunal—whether judge or jury—is to give excessive weight to the vicious record of crime thus exhibited, and either to allow it to bear too strongly on the present charge, or to take the proof of it as justifying a condemnation irrespective of guilt of the present charge." Wigmore, Evidence, vol. 1, § 194, and cases cited.

A different question would be here if the pistols had been bought in expectation of this particular encounter. They would then have been admissible as evidence of preparation and design. A different question would be here if they were so connected with the crime as to identify the perpetrator, if he had dropped them, for example, at the scene of the affray. They would then have been admissible as tending to implicate the possessor (if identity was disputed), no matter what the opprobrium attached to his possession. Different, also, would be the question if the defendant had been shown to have gone forth from the apartment with all the weapons on his person. To be armed from head to foot at the very moment of an encounter may be a circumstance worthy to be considered, like acts of preparation generally, as a proof of preconceived design. There can be no such implication from the ownership of weapons which one leaves behind at home.

The endeavor was to generate an atmosphere of professional criminality. It was an endeavor the more unfair in that, apart from the suspicion attaching to the possession of these weapons, there is nothing to mark the defendant as a man of evil life. He was not in crime as a business. He did not shoot as a bandit shoots in the hope of wrongful gain. He was engaged in a decent calling, an optician regularly employed, without criminal record, or criminal associates. If his own testimony be true, he had gathered these weapons together as curios, a collection that interested and amused him. Perhaps his explanation of their ownership is false. There is nothing stronger than mere suspicion to guide us to an answer. Whether the explanation be false or true, he should not have been driven by the people to the necessity of offering it. Brought to answer a specific charge, and to defend himself against it, he was placed in a position where he had to defend himself against another, more general and sweeping. He was made to answer to the charge, pervasive and poisonous even if insidious and covert, that he was a man of murderous heart, of criminal disposition....

The judgment of conviction should be reversed, and a new trial ordered.

POUND, J., dissents in opinion in which CRANE and HUBBS, JJ., concur.

... The people, as a part of their principal case, introduced these [weapons] in evidence over defendant's objection and exception.... The broad question is whether it had any connection with the crime charged..... .

The people may not prove against a defendant crimes not alleged in the indictment committed on other occasions than the crime charged as aiding the proofs that he is guilty of the crime charged unless such proof tends to establish (1) motive; (2) intent; (3) absence of mistake or accident; (4) a common scheme or plan embracing the commission of two or more crimes so related to each other that proof of the one tends to establish the other; (5) the identity of the person charged with the commission of the crime on trial. These exceptions are stated generally and not with categorical precision and may not be all-inclusive. None of them apply here, nor were the weapons offered under an exception to the general rule. They were offered as a part of the transaction itself. The accused was tried only for the crime charged. The real question is whether the matter relied on has such a connection with the crime charged as to be admissible on any ground. If so, the fact that it constitutes another distinct crime does not render it inadmissible.... It was "a part of the history of the case" having a distinct relation to and bearing upon the facts connected with the killing.

As the district attorney argues in his brief, if defendant had been arrested at the time of the killing, and these weapons had been found on his person, the people would not have been barred from proving the fact, and the further fact that they were near by in his apartment should not preclude the proof as bearing on the entire deed of which the act charged forms a part. Defendant was presented to the jury as a man having dangerous weapons in his possession, making a selection therefrom, and going forth to put into execution his threats to kill; not as a man of a dangerous disposition in general, but as one who, having an opportunity to select a weapon to carry out his threats, proceeded to do so....

The judgment of conviction should be affirmed.

Problem 4-1

On April 13, 1980, the remains of a human skull were found in the woods near Westport, Massachusetts. A search of the area yielded bloodied clothing, bloodied rocks, jewelry, and a clump of hair. The remains were identified as those of Karen Marsden, a woman from the nearby village who worked as a prostitute.

Carl Drew, Marsden's pimp, was tried for her murder. During the trial, the government introduced evidence that Drew was involved in a satanic cult, that he often performed and led satanic rituals, and that Marsden had joined the cult with Drew's encouragement. The government argued that during one ritual Drew murdered another prostitute, Dorothy Levesque, in the presence of Marsden. After the murder, Marsden became terrified for her life and asked to leave the cult. Consequently, the government argued it was this request that led to Marsden's subsequent murder.

To support its case the government introduced several witnesses who testified to Drew's cult practices. The testimony described cult rituals in which, among other practices, Drew chanted to conjure Satan's presence and attempted to give victims' souls to Satan. Several witnesses testified that Marsden was present for the ritual murder of Levesque and that she desired to leave the cult. Additionally, during the trial Drew was asked to remove his jacket and exhibit a tattoo on his arm; the tattoo depicted a devil's head and the inscription "Satan's Avengers." Drew was convicted of the murder.

On appeal, Drew objects to admission of the testimony describing the satanic cult rituals and to the request that he display his tattoo. He argues that neither was relevant to the issue of Marsden's murder or, even if probative, that they were unduly prejudicial. How do you rule?

Problem 4-2

Pursuant to Indiana's Safe Childhood Project, the Purdue University Police Department initiated an Internet sting operation to lure and prosecute pedophiles online. The defendant, Mark Ciesiolka, walked right into the trap. On August 2, 2006, he encountered "Ashley" (an undercover officer) in a Yahoo adults-only chat room. Ashley's Yahoo profile photo was of a woman in her 20s and her stated interests included "Purdue University" and "beer." The profile did not state her age.

Officers tracked Ciesiolka and Ashley for the next two-and-a-half weeks as they exchanged numerous, sexually explicit instant messages ("IMs"). Ciesiolka asked whether her mom and dad were home and whether she had a boyfriend. Somewhat oddly, in response to Ciesiolka's request for pictures of herself, Ashley sent a photo of the same woman in her late 20s whose picture adorned Ashley's online profile. Ciesiolka remarked that she looked 21 or so. Ashley nevertheless maintained that she was only 13, and admitted: "I lie about my age." In other conversations, when Ashley referenced her upcoming birthday, Ciesiolka asked: "You will be 15?," to which Ashley responded "14."

Following these IM conversations, the talk eventually turned to meeting up. Ciesiolka said: "I would come see you but might get in trouble." He and Ashley ultimately agreed to meet on Friday, August 18. This seemed like an opportune time, since Ashley said that her mother was leaving that Friday for the weekend to attend a wedding. Despite the arrangement and repeated encouragement from

Ashley, Ciesiolka got cold feet and never showed up on August 18. Following their last IM conversation, the authorities were able to track down and arrest Ciesiolka.

During the ensuing trial, the government introduced evidence of Ciesiolka's prior bad acts to prove Ciesiolka's knowledge and absence of mistake under Fed. R. Evid. 404(b). The evidence included other IM conversations the defendant had had with unidentified third parties containing numerous offensive sexual details. The jury was also shown approximately 100 images of child pornography that had been found on the defendant's computer. In addition, the jury heard testimony from a "Jane Doe" to the effect that the defendant had had sex with her numerous times when she was 15 years old.

In order to prevail in its case against Ciesiolka, the government had to prove that Ciesiolka believed that "Ashley" was under 18. Ciesiolka eventually was convicted of knowingly attempting to persuade, induce, entice and coerce a minor to engage in sexual activity. Ciesiolka appealed his conviction, contending that the trial court had erred in admitting evidence of his prior bad acts. How should the appellate court have ruled?

Focus Questions: *State v. Peterson*

- Should temporal proximity of the other act to the current crime be a mandatory condition for the admission of other acts or only one of many factors? Does your answer change based on the purpose of the other act evidence?

- How does the doctrine of chances differ from a showing of absence of accident?

State v. Peterson
Court of Appeals, North Carolina
179 N.C.App. 437, 634 S.E.2d 594 (2006)

Elmore, Judge

...

II. *Rule 404(b) Ratliff Evidence*

The trial court conducted an extensive *voir dire* hearing on the proposed Rule 404(b) evidence regarding Elizabeth Ratliff, an individual close to defendant who seventeen years prior to Kathleen's death was found dead at the bottom of a set of stairs.

Elizabeth Ratliff worked as a teacher with the Department of Defense Dependent School System, and her husband George was an officer in the United States Air Force. In the early 1980s the couple lived in Klein Gerau, Germany. Both were good friends with defendant and his first wife, Patty. After George's death in 1983, defendant began to help Elizabeth with funeral arrangements, financial matters, and general support. About a year after her husband's death, Elizabeth and the couple's two daughters moved to a house down the street from the Petersons in Graefenhausen, Germany. Defendant continued to help care for the Ratliff family over the next year.

Then, at around 7:15 a.m. on 25 November 1985, Barbara Malagino, permanent nanny to the Ratliff children, found Elizabeth dead at the bottom of the main staircase in her home. A friend and co-worker of Elizabeth's, Cheryl Appel-Schumacher, testified that she arrived at the house around 9:00 a.m.; she described the scene.

She stated that defendant was there, talking mainly with the police, military, and other official personnel at the house. Along with defendant and those officials, several other people were in the small foyer area: Amy Beth and Bruce Berner, neighbors of the Ratliff family; Patty Peterson [defendant's first wife]; and a taxicab driver. Elizabeth's body was at the bottom of the stairs; she was wearing a pair of yellow boots and was partially covered by a coat. There was blood sprayed down the wall of the open staircase, blood on the wall opposite the foyer area, blood on a chest and footlocker, and a pool of blood underneath Elizabeth's body. Ms. Appel-Schumacher also described a smaller pattern of blood droplets at the top of the stairs, above a light switch. It appeared to have been flicked from a brush, whereas the blood down the wall was more of a tear drop pattern which increased in size further down the stairs. Ms. Appel-Schumacher said that she, her husband, and someone else, probably defendant, helped clean up the blood after Elizabeth's body was taken away. She also testified that on the Thursday before Elizabeth died, Elizabeth complained to her about headaches and had scheduled an appointment with a doctor for the following week.

Elizabeth's sister, Margaret Blair, testified that defendant called her later in the day on 25 November 1985 and informed her of Elizabeth's death. He said she accidentally fell down the stairs and died. Sometime near the funeral, Margaret spoke with defendant regarding the events surrounding her sister's death. Defendant told her that he and his wife had the Ratliff family over for dinner and he returned with them to help get the girls to bed and take out the trash.

Margaret Blair also testified that Elizabeth had planned a trip to Copenhagen, Denmark, over the upcoming Christmas vacation. She further testified that pursuant to Elizabeth's will defendant and Patty became guardians of Martha and Margaret Ratliff. Defendant received various household goods and benefits associated with the two children.

On 27 November 1985 an autopsy performed by the United States military determined Elizabeth's cause of death to be "[i]ntracranial hemorrhage, cerebellar-brain stem secondary to Von Willebrand coagulation abnormality ... [s]calp lacerations secondary to terminal fall." The military investigation concluded there were "no indications of foul play."

On 14 April 2003 Elizabeth's body was exhumed and an autopsy performed by Dr. Deborah Radisch revealed contradictory findings. Dr. Radisch determined the cause of death to be blunt force trauma to the head. Dr. Radisch noted multiple injuries, including marks on the head, seven distinct lacerations, and injuries to the left hand, forearm, and back. Dr. Radisch opined that the "intracranial hemorrhages noted at the first autopsy were primarily the result of blunt trauma rather than any underlying natural disease process."

Defendant argues the trial court erred in admitting this evidence pursuant to Rule 404(b). Ultimately, we disagree....

First, the trial court found that evidence of Elizabeth's death was probative of defendant's intent, knowledge, and the absence of accident in Kathleen's death. Our appellate case law contains a cornucopia of comparable situations in which the courts have upheld the admission of evidence regarding prior deaths due to its probative value for these disputed elements. *See, e.g., State v. Moses,* 350 N.C. 741, 758–60, 517 S.E.2d

853, 864–65 (1999) (evidence of prior shooting death relevant to show identity of killer in similar death); *State v. Moore,* 335 N.C. 567, 594–96, 440 S.E.2d 797, 812–14 (1994) (prior poisoning deaths of males intimately associated with defendant relevant to show motive, opportunity, identity, and intent in trial for poisoning death); *State v. Stager,* 329 N.C. 278, 301–07, 406 S.E.2d 876, 888–93 (1991) (evidence of first husband's death by gunshot wound admissible in trial for second husband's shooting death to prove motive, intent, plan, preparation, knowledge, or absence of accident); *State v. Barfield,* 298 N.C. 306, 328, 259 S.E.2d 510, 529–30 (1979) (evidence of four other poisonings relevant to show intent, motive, and common plan or scheme in trial for poisoning), *overruled on other grounds by, State v. Johnson,* 317 N.C. 193, 344 S.E.2d 775 (1986); *State v. Lanier,* 165 N.C.App. 337, 346–47, 598 S.E.2d 596, 602–03 (where defendant claimed that poisoning was accidental, prior husband's drowning admissible in case against defendant for the poisoning of her husband), *disc. review denied,* 359 N.C. 195, 608 S.E.2d 59 (2004); *State v. Underwood,* 134 N.C.App. 533, 538, 518 S.E.2d 231, 236 (1999) (evidence of prior shooting death of person closely associated with defendant admissible in trial for shooting death of an individual also closely associated with defendant in order to show identity).

We can see no error in the determination that the circumstances of Elizabeth's death were admissible to, at the very least, show the absence of accident in Kathleen's death, as defendant claimed. "Where, as here, an accident is alleged, evidence of similar acts is more probative than in cases in which an accident is not alleged." *Stager,* 329 N.C. at 304, 406 S.E.2d at 891. "The doctrine of chances demonstrates that the more often a defendant performs a certain act, the less likely it is that the defendant acted innocently." *Id.* at 305, 406 S.E.2d at 891 (quoting Imwinkelried, *Uncharged Misconduct Evidence* § 5:05 (1984)).

> In isolation, it might be plausible that the defendant acted accidentally or innocently; a single act could easily be explained on that basis. However, in the context of other misdeeds, the defendant's act takes on an entirely different light. The fortuitous coincidence becomes too abnormal, bizarre, implausible, unusual, or objectively improbable to be believed. The coincidence becomes telling evidence of mens rea.

Id.; see also State v. Murillo, 349 N.C. 573, 593–94, 509 S.E.2d 752, 764 (1998) (evidence of defendant accidentally shooting his first wife ruled admissible in trial for shooting death of second wife to show the absence of accident).

Second, the trial court found the evidence to be relevant. "Evidence is admissible under Rule 404(b) only if it is relevant...." In the Rule 404(b) context, similar act evidence is relevant only if the jury can reasonably conclude that the act occurred and that the defendant was the actor." *Id.* That framework has been further refined in North Carolina such that Rule 404(b) evidence probative of a permissible purpose is admissible if it is evidence of a similar act with a certain degree of temporal proximity to the current charge.

> When the features of the earlier act are dissimilar from those of the offense with which the defendant is currently charged, such evidence lacks probative value. When otherwise similar offenses are distanced by significant stretches of time, commonalities become less striking, and the probative value of the analogy attaches less to the acts than to the character of the actor.

State v. Artis, 325 N.C. 278, 299, 384 S.E.2d 470, 481 (1989), *vacated on other grounds by,* 494 U.S. 1023 (1990), *on remand at,* 329 N.C. 679, 406 S.E.2d 827 (1991).

Here, the trial court concluded that:

> 2. Substantial evidence in the form of sufficient similar facts and circumstances exists between the two deaths so that a jury could reasonably find that the Defendant committed both acts.

> 3. The temporal proximity or remoteness in time between these two deaths does not diminish its effect of admissibility with respect to the purposes for which it is offered.

It based those conclusions on seventeen similarities between the circumstances of Elizabeth's death and that of Kathleen's, including in part:

> a. The deceased being found at the bottom of a stairway.

> b. No eyewitnesses to either alleged fall down the stairs.

> c. A large amount of blood present.

> d. Blood splatter present high and dried on the wall next to the stairway, including a bloodstain with small drops.

> e. No evidence of any forced entry or exit, or of any property being stolen.

> …

> h. Both deceased persons were females in their late 40's who had a close personal relationship with the Defendant.

> i. Both deceased persons were similar in physical characteristics so that they looked alike and reported of severe headaches in the weeks before their death.

> j. Both deceased persons were planning to go on a trip in the near future and had dinner with the Defendant on the night before their death.

> k. Both deceased persons were later determined to have died from blunt force trauma to the head, including the same number of scalp lacerations and the same general location of the scalp wounds.

> l. Both deceased persons had what could be characterized as defensive wounds on their bodies.

> …

> n. The Defendant was the last known person to see both of these persons alive.

> o. By being summoned to the scene in Germany and living at the scene in Durham, the Defendant is then present on the scene when the authorities arrive and reports that the death is the result of an accidental fall down the stairs.

> p. The Defendant is in charge of the remains, effects, and household after each death, and is potentially in charge of each estate after death.

> q. The Defendant received money or other items of value after each death.

Defendant contends that before the State could have used Elizabeth's death to show the absence of accident, it needed to establish a substantial and independent link between defendant and Elizabeth's death; otherwise the use of this evidence would potentially prejudice defendant based upon a prior act for which he had no involvement. But it is not necessary to the evidence's admissibility that the State specifically establish a direct evidentiary link between defendant and the previous crime or act. In fact, in *State v. Jeter,* 326 N.C. 457, 459, 389 S.E.2d 805, 806–07 (1990), the Supreme Court rejected that argument in favor of a more flexible test, such as that in *Huddleston* or *Stager.*

[Rule 404(b)] includes no requisite that the evidence tending to prove defendant's identity as the perpetrator of another crime be direct evidence, exclusively. Neither the rule nor its application indicates that examples of other provisions—such as admissibility of evidence of other offenses to prove motive, opportunity, intent, preparation, or plan—rest solely upon direct evidence. *E.g., State v. Price,* 326 N.C. 56, 388 S.E.2d 84 (1990) (circumstantial evidence of defendant's perpetration of "virtually identical" strangulation, proximate in time, showing preparation, plan, knowledge or identity). Under the statutory scheme of Rules 403 and 404, the concern that anything other than direct evidence of a defendant's identity in a similar offense might "mislead [the jury] and raise a legally spurious presumption of guilt" is met instead by the balancing test required by Rule 403[.]

Id., 389 S.E.2d at 806.

In *Stager,* our Supreme Court was presented with a scenario comparable to this one. There, the defendant was on trial for the first-degree murder of her husband. *Stager,* 329 N.C. at 284–85, 406 S.E.2d at 879. She claimed that she accidentally shot her husband when pulling a gun out across the bed from underneath his pillow one morning. The next day she began inquiring about death proceeds from the military, her husband being a member of the National Guard, and further inquired about life insurance proceeds. The facts, circumstances, and scientific evidence all failed to support an accidental shooting, instead suggested the possibility of foul play.

The State introduced evidence that nearly ten years prior to Mr. Stager's death, the defendant's first husband was found dead in their bedroom killed by a single gun shot. The defendant stated that her husband was upstairs cleaning the gun when it must have fired and killed him. The defendant collected nearly $86,000.00 in life insurance proceeds and estate property after her husband's death.

At her trial and on appeal, the defendant argued the evidence of her first husband's death was not relevant or admissible pursuant to Rule 404(b). Our Supreme Court disagreed and found no error in the admission of the evidence due to its probative value for intent, the absence of accident, and the fact that the deaths were sufficiently similar. Relying on *Huddleston,* the Court held:

> [I]f there is sufficient evidence to support a jury finding that the defendant committed the similar act [then] no preliminary finding by the trial court that the defendant actually committed such an act is required [;] ... evidence is admissible under Rule 404(b) of the North Carolina Rules of Evidence if it is substantial evidence tending to support a reasonable finding *by the jury* that the defendant committed a similar act or crime and its probative value is not limited *solely* to tending to establish the defendant's propensity to commit a crime such as the crime charged.

Id. at 303–04, 406 S.E.2d at 890. "Similar" acts or crimes, the Court held, means "there are 'some unusual facts present in both crimes or particularly similar acts which would indicate that the same person committed both.'" *Stager,* 329 N.C. at 304, 406 S.E.2d at 890–91.

Thus, although perhaps more persuasive, it is not necessary to the evidence's admissibility under Rule 404(b) that the State specifically connect defendant to the previous crime or act, so long as substantial evidence of the similarities of the two crimes or acts suggests that the same person committed both acts. And while defendant challenges the veracity of the trial court's findings on similarity, the numerous and unique similarities between Elizabeth's death and that of Kathleen reveal substantial circumstantial evidence that favors admissibility.

Further, we can discern little merit in defendant's argument that Elizabeth's death is too remote. It may be true that "remoteness in time tends to diminish the probative value of the evidence and enhance its tendency to prejudice," *Artis,* 325 N.C. at 300, 384 S.E.2d at 482, but "remoteness in time generally affects only the weight to be given such evidence, not its admissibility." *Stager,* 329 N.C. at 307, 406 S.E.2d at 893.

> Remoteness in time between an uncharged crime and a charged crime is more significant when the evidence of the prior crime is introduced to show that both crimes arose out of a common scheme or plan. In contrast, remoteness in time is less significant when the prior conduct is used to show intent, motive, knowledge, or lack of accident[.]

Id. (citations omitted). The striking similarities between Kathleen's death and that of Elizabeth's overshadow the seventeen-year-difference in their deaths, particular given that the State's use of the evidence was to show absence of accident, intent, or knowledge.

Third, we see no abuse of discretion in the trial court's balancing test consistent with the dictates of Rule 403.

> When prior incidents are offered for a proper purpose, the ultimate test of admissibility is whether they are sufficiently similar and not so remote as to run afoul of the balancing test between probative value and prejudicial effect set out in Rule 403. In each case, the burden is on the defendant to show that there was no proper purpose for which the evidence could be admitted. The determination of whether relevant evidence should be excluded under Rule 403 is a matter that is left in the sound discretion of the trial court, and the trial court can be reversed only upon a showing of abuse of discretion.

Lanier, 165 N.C.App. at 345, 598 S.E.2d at 602 (internal citations and quotations omitted). The trial court here conducted an extensive *voir dire,* issued numerous findings of fact, found at least seventeen similarities between the evidence proffered and the crime charged, and concluded the "probative value of this evidence outweighs any prejudicial effect on the Defendant." We have already concluded that the similarities between the two deaths were numerous and that Elizabeth's death was not too remote.

That said, "[e]vidence which is probative of the State's case necessarily will have a prejudicial effect upon the defendant; the question is one of degree." *State v. Coffey,* 326 N.C. 268, 281, 389 S.E.2d 48, 56. There is little doubt that the evidence of Elizabeth's death was useful to the State for challenging defendant's sole defense in this case, namely, that Kathleen's death was an accident. This evidence in and of itself is prejudicial to defendant, but not substantially so, considering that the balance under Rule 403 favors admissibility of probative evidence.

As such, we reject defendant's argument that evidence of Elizabeth's death was inadmissible because "[t]he two deaths would create a false image of convincing evidence, just as mirrors facing each other create the impression of a never-ending hall, while each examined in its own light would not withstand scrutiny." The evidence is admissible due to the fact it was offered for a proper purpose, and was sufficient to allow a jury to reasonably conclude that the act occurred and that the defendant was the actor.

. . . .

Wynn, Judge, Dissenting

. . . .

II.

The trial court further erred by allowing in evidence of Elizabeth Ratliff's death under North Carolina Rule of Evidence 404(b). . . .

Here, the trial court conducted a *voir dire* hearing to determine whether the evidence regarding the death of Elizabeth Ratliff was of a type made admissible under Rule 404(b) and was relevant for some purpose other than showing Mr. Peterson's propensity for the type of conduct at issue. The trial court made the required findings and conclusions in this case and ruled that the proffered evidence of the circumstances surrounding the death of Elizabeth Ratliff was admissible under Rule 404(b) as evidence of intent, knowledge, and absence of accident.

In his appeal, Mr. Peterson argues that the State did not substantially and independently link him to Elizabeth Ratliff's death and that evidence of her death was therefore inadmissible under Rule 404(b). Thus, this Court must determine, *inter alia*, whether there was substantial evidence tending to support a reasonable finding by the jury that Mr. Peterson committed the "similar act." *See Stager*, 329 N.C. at 303, 406 S.E.2d at 890.

A prior act or crime is "similar" if there are some unusual facts present indicating that the same person committed both the earlier offense and the present one. However, the similarities between the two incidents need not be "unique and bizarre." "Rather, the similarities simply must tend to support a *reasonable* inference that the same person committed both the earlier and later acts." *Id.* (emphasis in original).

Here, as outlined by the majority, the trial court specifically found seventeen similarities between Ms. Peterson's death and Elizabeth Ratliff's death, including facts related to the circumstances of the two deaths, the characteristics of the two women, and Defendant's relationships with the two women and reported discoveries of their respective bodies. Despite these findings, it would be manifestly speculative to hold that these tenuous, circumstantial similarities now link Mr. Peterson to Elizabeth Ratliff's death. . . .

. . . [T]here were not sufficient similarities between the deaths of Elizabeth Ratliff and Ms. Peterson that a jury could make a "*reasonable* inference" that Mr. Peterson committed the prior murder—or that Ms. Ratliff's death was even a murder. Here, Mr. Peterson was not intimately involved with Elizabeth Ratliff, but was simply a neighbor and friend. Also, while Mr. Peterson did receive some household goods from Elizabeth Ratliff's estate, he received the items as guardian for her daughters and in trust for them, unlike the multi-million dollar amount of money he stood to inherit individually from Ms. Peterson's estate. Moreover, at the time it occurred, Elizabeth Ratliff's death was deemed to be of natural causes by both the German and military authorities; not until her body was exhumed and re-autopsied some eighteen years later did the expert in this case opine that her death was caused by blunt trauma to the head, whereas Ms. Peterson's death was immediately determined to be a homicide. Therefore, there were not sufficient substantial similarities between the two deaths.

In addition, as noted by the majority, "Rule 404(b) evidence probative of a permissible purpose is admissible if it is evidence of a similar act with a *certain degree of temporal proximity to the current charge*" (emphasis added). This closeness in time is required because, "[w]hen otherwise similar offenses are distanced by significant stretches of time, commonalities become less striking, and the probative value of the analogy attaches less to the acts than to the character of the actor." *State v. Artis*, 325 N.C. 278, 299–300, 384 S.E.2d 470, 481 (1989), *vacated on other grounds by*, 494 U.S. 1023 (1990), *on remand at*, 329 N.C. 679, 406 S.E.2d 827 (1991). Thus, "remoteness in time tends to diminish the probative value of the evidence and enhance its tendency to prejudice." *Id.* at 300, 384 S.E.2d at 482.

Here, seventeen years passed between the deaths of Ms. Ratliff and Ms. Peterson; even if "remoteness in time generally affects only the weight to be given such evidence, not its admissibility," Stager, 329 N.C. at 307, 406 S.E.2d at 893, the passage of such a significant amount of time erodes to an even greater extent the relevance of the circumstantial similarities between the two deaths, further challenging the reasonableness of a jury's inference that Mr. Peterson was responsible for Ms. Ratliff's death.

As a jury could not make a "*reasonable inference*" that Mr. Peterson committed the prior murder, the evidence was inadmissible under Rule 404(b). Therefore, I conclude that the trial court erred in admitting evidence of the death of Elizabeth Ratliff and would grant Mr. Peterson a new trial, as the evidence was highly prejudicial.

Finally, even if evidence of Elizabeth Ratliff's death is permitted under Rule 404(b), it nonetheless should have been barred from admission in this trial under Rule 403, as the probative value of the evidence was substantially outweighed by the danger of unfair prejudice....

Following the *voir dire* hearing on the admission of evidence of Elizabeth Ratliff's death, the trial court concluded that "[t]he probative value of this evidence outweighs any prejudicial effect on the Defendant." However, the trial court set out no findings on the prejudice toward Mr. Peterson on this highly prejudicial and very circumstantial evidence. It is not evident from the record that the trial court properly balanced the two competing interests—probative value of the evidence versus prejudice to the defendant—but instead simply found that the evidence had probative value and summarily concluded that the probative value outweighed the prejudice to Mr. Peterson.

Thus, the trial court abused its discretion, as any probative value of the evidence of Elizabeth Ratliff's death was outweighed by the unfair prejudice to Mr. Peterson. As the admission of the circumstantially speculative evidence of Elizabeth Ratliff's death was highly prejudicial, a new trial should be awarded.

Problem 4-3

In 1997, officers of the U.S. Marine Corps convened a special hearing to sentence Staff Sergeant Bud Tyndale to a bad-conduct discharge. Tyndale had recently submitted a urine sample which tested positive for methamphetamine, in violation of Marine Corps conduct code. Tyndale contested the finding, and the dispute eventually reached federal court.

At trial Tyndale argued that he believed someone had slipped him the drug in a drink at a party that he was at the night before where he was a hired musician. Tyndale explained that he was an experienced musician and had played at a number of venues in the area. The party in this case was a moving-out party in which forty-five to sixty people were present. He said the crowd at the party was "pretty radical." Tyndale never got the name of the person who hired him and played halfway through the night before being paid in cash. He consumed about a case of beer over the course of the evening and hypothesized that the drug must have been slipped in one of these drinks. Since it was a moving out party, Tyndale said he had no way to locate the apartment or its occupants.

To disprove Tyndale's story, the Marine Corps seeks to offer evidence that in January, 1994, Tyndale similarly tested positive for methamphetamine during a required urine test. At that time — just as in the current case — Tyndale explained to his supervisors that the test was the result of innocent ingestion at a party frequented by various "druggies" where he was a hired musician. At both the 1994 party and the present party, Tyndale's brother was the only available witness to testify about the events alleged, Tyndale could not remember the location of the party, and Tyndale had not notified police of the alleged involuntary drugging.

Tyndale objects to the admission of the 1994 incident as improper character evidence under 404(b). He states that as a musician for hire at parties in which drugs are sometimes present, he runs the risk of innocent ingestion more frequently than others. The issue is now before you. How do you rule on the admission of this evidence?

Problem 4-4

Mr. Lord has two daughters, Vicki and Tina. Vicki is his daughter from his first marriage to Jean while Tina is his daughter from his second marriage to Dorian. He is now divorced from a third wife and retains visitation rights to his two daughters. One day, his first wife, Jean, called his second wife, Dorian, telling her that she feared that the young girls were being sexually molested by their father. Dorian became further alarmed when signs of physical abuse became apparent on Tina.

After consulting specialists in the field of child sexual abuse, Dorian became convinced that Tina was being abused during the visitation periods with her father. Dorian quickly filed suit to revoke visitation rights and for damages on behalf of Tina.

Mr. Lord maintains that he did not abuse Tina and that the injuries were self-inflicted. Plaintiffs want to introduce out-of-court evidence showing that Tina's sister, Vicki, displayed similar signs of sexual abuse. Will the court admit the evidence?

Problem 4-5

In 2001, Gwenda Lewis and Kathleen Corke informed their employer, the Triborough Bridge and Tunnel Authority ("TBTA"), that they were experiencing sexual harassment and gender discrimination at their branch, the Whitestone Bridge Facility. They complained, in part, that their supervisors Michael Chin and Peter Senesi knew about but had failed to acknowledge the hostile work environment toward women at the Whitestone Facility.

Shortly after the complaint was filed, TBTA charged Senesi with investigating Lewis and Corke's allegations. As a result of TBTA giving Senesi this responsibility, Lewis and Corke claimed they experienced retaliation and further harassment.

They then filed suit against TBTA in federal court, alleging sexual harassment based on a hostile work environment.

To rebut plaintiffs' claims at trial, TBTA must prove that it took immediate and appropriate corrective action once it became aware of plaintiffs' complaints. As part of their case, plaintiffs argue that TBTA inappropriately charged Senesi with the sexual harassment investigation. Specifically, the plaintiffs seek to introduce testimony that Senesi viewed pornography at work and that he was widely known among all the employees as "the porno king of the Whitestone Bridge."

TBTA has filed a motion in limine objecting to the admission. It argues that such evidence is too attenuated from plaintiffs' claims and thus lacks sufficient probative value. Additionally, it argues that the evidence must be excluded pursuant to 404(b). The motion is now before you. How do you rule?

Problem 4-6

Brian Serrano and Robert Martinez were charged with various crimes arising from the smuggling of methamphetamine from San Francisco into Hawaii. Their courier, Crystal York, who was Serrano's girlfriend, got caught in the airport with five pounds of methamphetamine taped to her body under her loosely fitting dress. She agreed to help the police catch Serrano and Martinez, the person to whom Serrano was to deliver the methamphetamine.

Crystal then called Serrano on the telephone, with the police taping the call. He was angry that she had been in Hawaii for five hours without calling him and complained about all the effort and money he had spent trying to find out if she got in all right. Crystal said, "I was going to surprise you," "I love you," and explained that the reason for the delay was that "one of the pac—the things, you know.... was jabbing me in the back, so I was messing with it. And the package broke. And then this stuff coming out, so I been ... sitting here in the bathroom trying to do it." Crystal never said in so many words what, exactly, was jabbing her in the back or coming out. The closest she came was "I'm ... scared, dude, I've been ... carrying this [stuff].... []."

Serrano did not have a car, only a motorcycle, so he got a ride to the airport from Martinez, to whom the government alleged Serrano was to transfer the methamphetamine. Serrano went inside the terminal and was arrested. Martinez was detained and was arrested as well when Crystal identified him to police as a man to whom Serrano had previously delivered drugs. Martinez and Serrano were charged with conspiracy and aiding and abetting the importation of methamphetamine into the United States.

At trial, Martinez claimed that he had not overheard Serrano's phone call, that he thought he was simply giving Serrano a ride, and that he did not know that he was driving Serrano to the airport for a drug handoff. The government sought to admit his prior conviction for heroin importation. Should the court have admitted Martinez's prior conviction for importing heroin under Rule 404(b)?

- How closely related must an other act be to satisfy modus operandi?

- Is evidence that is "inextricably intertwined" with a charged offense, standing alone, a permissible use of other act evidence?

United States v. Robinson

161 F.3d 463 (7th Cir. 1998)

KANNE, Circuit Judge.

Richard Robinson was convicted of armed bank robbery and of use of a firearm in relation to the commission of the armed bank robbery. The District Court sentenced Robinson to 35 years in prison and ordered him to pay $5,134 in restitution. On appeal, Robinson raises two issues: (1) whether the trial court erred in admitting evidence pertaining to another later bank robbery to which Robinson pleaded guilty and (2) whether the evidence was insufficient to convict him of the charges alleged in the indictment. We reject the arguments presented by Robinson and affirm his conviction.

I. History

A federal grand jury returned a four-count indictment against Richard Robinson on charges stemming from two armed bank robberies. Counts one and two of the indictment alleged that on April 8, 1997, Robinson robbed the Americana Bank in Anderson, Indiana, and that he used a firearm during the commission of this offense. Counts three and four of this same indictment alleged that ten days later, on April 18, 1997, Robinson committed another armed robbery with a firearm, this time robbing Harrington Bank in Fishers, Indiana. The cities of Anderson and Fishers are separated by approximately twenty-five miles. Robinson pleaded guilty to the later armed robbery of Harrington Bank and went to trial on the charges stemming from the earlier Americana Bank robbery. Because the government offered evidence of the April 18 Fishers robbery at Robinson's trial, it is necessary to review the facts of both robberies when considering the issues before us.

On the afternoon of Tuesday, April 8, 1997, Robinson set out from his home in his wife's blue Chevrolet Cavalier to commit the first of the two bank robberies. Upon arriving at Americana Bank in Anderson at approximately 3:40 p.m., he donned an orange ski mask with a single oval opening and proceeded into the bank brandishing his mother's handgun in one hand and carrying a large and distinctive "Louis Vuitton"-brand duffle bag in the other. In addition to the orange ski mask, Robinson wore a pair of brown work coveralls. Once inside the bank, Robinson sprinted to the teller counter and vaulted over the counter as he demanded money. He personally gathered money from the two teller stations after placing the handgun on an adding machine, vaulted back over the counter, and exited the bank. Robinson then made his getaway in the Cavalier while being observed by an off-duty police officer.

Robinson robbed Harrington Bank in Fishers ten days later, on April 18, at approximately 12:00 p.m., in a manner mirroring the heist that occurred in Anderson. Robinson drove to the bank in his wife's Cavalier and pulled on the orange ski mask prior to entering the bank. After leaping over the teller counter, he placed his handgun down and personally removed money from the teller drawers. Robinson once again departed in the Cavalier.

While Robinson's technique remained the same, the results did not, and his career as a bank robber was brought to a hasty conclusion. [Police officers observed Robinson's car and saw him reach for his handgun. A high speed pursuit followed, often reaching over 100 miles per hour. Once police were able to stop the vehicle, a prolonged struggle occurred, and the officers finally subdued Robinson.]....

... Upon inspection of Robinson's vehicle, the officers recovered the orange ski mask, the "Louis Vuitton"-brand duffle bag containing money from the most recent robbery, including several "bait bills" taken from the three teller stations at Harrington Bank, and a .38 caliber handgun loaded with four live rounds....

II. Analysis
A. Admission of Evidence of the Harrington Bank Robbery and the Subsequent Chase

Robinson contends that the District Court abused its discretion by allowing the government to admit evidence of his plea of guilty to the charges stemming from the April 18 armed bank robbery at his trial for the April 8 armed bank robbery. The evidence of the April 18 armed bank robbery included evidence tending to demonstrate the similarities between the two robberies, evidence of the high speed chase and Robinson's struggle with police subsequent to the chase, and the materials recovered from Robinson's vehicle following his apprehension, including the orange ski mask, the distinctive duffle bag containing money from the April 18 armed bank robbery, and the handgun used in both robberies. Prior to trial, the District Court conducted an evidentiary hearing on the admissibility of this evidence and, over Robinson's objections, ruled that the admission of this evidence was not prohibited by Rule 404(b) of the Federal Rules of Evidence. The admission of evidence under Rule 404(b) by a district court is reviewed only for an abuse of discretion.

Rule 404(b) specifically prohibits the introduction of evidence of other crimes, wrongs, or acts when such evidence is offered to prove the character of a person in order to show conduct in conformity therewith on a particular occasion. As we have explained, "[a]lthough a defendant's past criminality may well have some probative worth concerning whether the defendant acted criminally at a later date, the probative value of this evidence will be relatively small and the risk of its misuse by the factfinder will be great." *United States v. Smith*, 103 F.3d 600, 602 (7th Cir.1996). However, Rule 404(b) expressly permits evidence of other crimes, wrongs, or acts to be introduced for purposes other than to establish a defendant's criminal propensity, including proof of "motive, opportunity, intent, preparation, plan, knowledge, identity, or absence of mistake or accident." At the evidentiary hearing conducted by the District Court, the government submitted that the evidence at issue would be offered primarily to establish identity and consciousness of guilt with respect to the April 8 bank robbery.

The categories that appear in the text of Rule 404(b) are not exclusive. Indeed, Rule 404(b) does not require the party offering the evidence to force the evidence into a particular listed category, but simply to show any relevant purpose other than proving conduct by means of a general propensity inference. We have held that evidence may be admissible under Rule 404(b) to demonstrate modus operandi. Evidence of modus operandi is evidence that shows a defendant's distinctive method of operation. Such evidence may be properly admitted pursuant to Rule 404(b) to prove identity. In addition, some courts have interpreted the admission of evidence establishing consciousness of guilt as coming within the identity exception to Rule 404(b). *See, e.g., United States v. Sims*, 617 F.2d 1371,

1378 (9th Cir.1980) ("Flight immediately after the commission of a crime, especially where the person learns that he may be a suspect ... supports an inference of guilt.... It was therefore relevant under the identity exception to Rule 404(b)."). Irrespective of whether such evidence may be admitted specifically to show identity, we have held that evidence demonstrating consciousness of guilt may be properly admitted under Rule 404(b).

We have fashioned a four-prong test to determine the appropriateness of admitting evidence of other crimes, wrongs, or acts. Under this test, the admissibility of the evidence is dependant upon whether: (1) the evidence is directed toward establishing a matter in issue other than the defendant's propensity to commit the crime charged; (2) the evidence shows that the other act is similar enough and close enough in time to be relevant to the matter in issue; (3) the evidence is sufficient to support a jury finding that the defendant committed the similar act; and (4) the evidence has probative value that is not substantially outweighed by the danger of unfair prejudice. The fourth prong of this test incorporates Rule 403, which provides for the exclusion of relevant evidence on grounds of prejudice, confusion, or waste of time. Though not specifically stated as such, the primary thrust of Robinson's argument, both before the District Court during the evidentiary hearing and before this Court on appeal, is that the second and fourth prongs of this test were not met with respect to the District Court's admission of evidence relating to the April 18 armed bank robbery.

We are able to dispense quickly with consideration of the first and third prongs. With respect to the first prong, the government offered evidence demonstrating the similarities between the two robberies and the evidence of flight and Robinson's struggle with police after the April 18 robbery to show identity and consciousness of guilt with respect to the April 8 robbery. Evidence demonstrating the similarities between the manner in which the two armed bank robberies were carried out goes toward proving identity by establishing the perpetrator's modus operandi. Evidence of flight is admissible under Rule 404(b) to show consciousness of guilt, as well as guilt itself. By offering this evidence to establish identity and consciousness of guilt rather than to show a general bad character or a propensity to commit criminal acts, it is clear that the government met the requirements contemplated by the first prong. The third prong also need not detain us long, as Robinson's plea of guilty to the April 18 robbery satisfies its requirements.

When considering the second and fourth prongs—whether the evidence shows that the other act is similar enough and close enough in time to be relevant to the matter in issue and whether the evidence has a probative value that is not substantially outweighed by the danger of unfair prejudice—it is helpful to consider the evidence of the similarities between the two armed bank robberies first and then to turn our attention to the evidence of flight and Robinson's struggle with the police.

As stated, the evidence demonstrating the similarities between the two crimes amounts, in essence, to evidence demonstrating modus operandi. We have cautioned that "[i]f defined broadly enough, modus operandi evidence can easily become nothing more than the character evidence that Rule 404(b) prohibits." *Smith*, 103 F.3d at 603. To ensure that the evidence at issue is not merely offered to establish the defendant's propensity to commit certain conduct, we require that modus operandi evidence bear "a singular strong resemblance to the pattern of the offense charged," *United States v. Shackleford*, 738 F.2d 776, 783 (7th Cir.1984) (quoting *United States v. Jones*, 438 F.2d 461, 466 (7th Cir.1971)), and that the similarities between the crimes be "sufficiently idiosyncratic to permit an inference of pattern for purposes of truth." *United States v. Hudson*, 884 F.2d 1016, 1021 (7th Cir.1989) (quoting *Shackleford*, 738 F.2d at 783 (citations omitted)). "Thus, we must first determine whether there are sufficient similarities between the other crime evidence and the charged crime that clearly distinguish the defendant from other criminals committing bank robberies." [*United States v. Moore*, 115 F.3d 1348, 1355 (7th Cir.1997)].

There are numerous similarities between the armed bank robberies of April 8 and April 18 that make them "clearly distinctive from the thousands of other bank robberies committed each year." Moore, 115 F.3d at 1355 (quoting Smith, 103 F.3d at 603). In both cases, the robber donned an orange ski mask prior to entering the bank, and he entered the bank carrying a distinctive duffle bag in one hand and brandishing a handgun in the other. Once inside the banks, the robber vaulted over the teller counter and demanded money. The robber emptied the teller drawers at each bank by himself, but only after placing the handgun down. The getaway vehicle in both cases was identified as a blue Chevrolet Cavalier. Furthermore, the robberies occurred within ten days and twenty-five miles of each other. This proximity in both time and location has significant bearing on the determination of whether the robberies are sufficiently idiosyncratic so as to permit an inference of pattern when considered in conjunction with the distinctive characteristics of each robbery. *See Smith*, 103 F.3d at 603 (noting the one month interval and 40 mile distance between two bank robberies when viewed in light of the rural locations of the banks in Wisconsin was relevant to demonstrating modus operandi). It is clear that sufficient similarities exist with respect to the April 8 and the April 18 robberies to identify Robinson as the individual responsible for committing these robberies.

Given the similarities between the two robberies, it cannot be said that the probative value of evidence demonstrating these similarities is substantially outweighed by the danger of unfair prejudice. Moreover, any risk of unfair prejudice was lessened by the jury instruction given by the District Court that the evidence offered by the government relating to the April 18 bank robbery was relevant only to the purposes contemplated by Rule 404(b).

The government's theory for the admission of evidence of the chase and Robinson's struggle with the police following the April 18 armed bank robbery, however, is somewhat more troublesome. During the evidentiary hearing before the District Court, the government argued that the evidence of the chase and subsequent struggle demonstrated Robinson's consciousness of guilt with respect to the April 8 armed bank robbery. The government explained that the motivation prompting flight and struggle on April 18 was twofold—Robinson was fleeing from the most recent armed bank robbery and he also knew that he possessed evidence connecting him to the April 8 armed bank robbery. Thus, he had a dual purpose in fleeing from law enforcement after the April 18 armed bank robbery. The government argued that the fervor with which he attempted to escape from the police was proportional to Robinson's consciousness of guilt, and, therefore, the magnitude of Robinson's resistance was directly related to Robinson's consciousness that he possessed evidence connecting him with not one, but two armed bank robberies. In short, the government asserted that Robinson was fleeing, in effect, from both armed bank robberies.

We have long adhered to the Supreme Court's cautionary language urging courts to be wary of the probative value of flight evidence. *See Wong Sun v. United States*, 371 U.S. 471, 483 n. 10, (1963) ("[W]e have consistently doubted the probative value in criminal trials of evidence that the accused fled the scene of an actual or supposed crime."). While we allow evidence of flight to be presented, courts must engage in careful deliberation when considering its admission. Determination of the probative value of flight as evidence of a defendant's guilt depends on the degree of confidence with which four inferences can be drawn: (1) from behavior to flight; (2) from flight to consciousness of guilt; (3) from consciousness of guilt to consciousness of guilt concerning the crime charged; and

(4) from consciousness of guilt concerning the crime charged to actual guilt of the crime charged.

In the instant case, Robinson's conduct in attempting to elude police after the April 18 armed bank robbery certainly constituted flight. It cannot be seriously disputed that this flight was the result of consciousness of guilt. The degree of confidence with which the jury could reasonably draw inferences from Robinson's flight to an ultimate finding of his guilt with respect to the April 8 armed bank robbery is also substantial. The relative proximity in time between the crime charged and Robinson's flight and the fact that at the time he fled from police he possessed considerable evidence linking him to the April 8 armed bank robbery are sufficient to establish a reasonable inference that he fled because of consciousness of guilt stemming from both the April 8 and the April 18 armed bank robberies.

Despite Robinson's arguments to the contrary, evidence of flight from the April 18 bank robbery is not merely generalized evidence offered to establish Robinson's character or his propensity to commit criminal acts. By establishing that Robinson fled from the April 18 armed bank robbery and struggled with police while in possession of evidence linking him to both that robbery and an armed bank robbery occurring a mere ten days before that date, the government was able to offer proof that Robinson possessed a culpable state of mind. As we have explained, "[t]his is a legitimate use of such evidence, whether one conceives of it as outside the scope of Rule 404(b) because of the evidence's 'intrinsic' value deriving from its specific relationship to the facts of the offense or as countenanced by Rule 404(b) because of its relevance in proving a non-character-related consequential fact-consciousness of guilt." [*United States v. Acevedo*, 28 F.3d 686, 688 (7th Cir.1994).] Under either theory, the evidence is probative of Robinson's state of mind in a manner entirely separate from how it reflects upon his character.

While it may be tempting to conclude Robinson's flight from the April 18 armed bank robbery has no bearing on his consciousness of guilt with respect to the April 8 armed bank robbery, and, indeed, Robinson argues as much, this position can be dispensed with if one considers two scenarios not far removed from the instant case. Under Rule 404(b), evidence of flight certainly would be admissible to show consciousness of guilt of a defendant who knew he was in possession of evidence demonstrating his involvement in an armed bank robbery if that defendant fled from or struggled with police even if the police were attempting to stop him for a mere routine traffic violation, such as a broken taillight, shortly after the commission of the bank robbery. *Cf. United States v. Dierling*, 131 F.3d 722, 731 (8th Cir.1997) (concluding that evidence of a defendant's flight and struggle with a police officer attempting to arrest the defendant for violation of a domestic protection order was admissible as evidence of consciousness of guilt with respect to a conviction for conspiracy to distribute narcotics and stating that "[t]he intended purpose of the attempted stop need not be related to the conspiracy.... The real question is what is in the mind of the person who flees and whether there is sufficient evidence to allow the inference that the flight was prompted by consciousness of guilt."), *cert. denied*, 523 U.S. 1054 (1998). Similarly, if a defendant committed a string of five armed bank robberies and was pursued by police after robbing a sixth, it can hardly be said that evidence of flight could not be admitted to show consciousness of guilt with respect to the other five robberies based on the contention that he was merely fleeing from his latest endeavor to plunder a bank. *Cf. United States v. Clark*, 45 F.3d 1247, 1251 (8th Cir.1995) ("The existence of other possible reasons for flight does not render the inference [of guilt] impermissible or irrational."). And so it is with this case. Robinson had knowledge that he committed acts proscribed by law on both April 8 and April 18. This knowledge was manifested in his efforts to evade police after the robbery on

April 18. In such a case, it is not the role of the District Court to parse the mind of a defendant to determine which act may have created a higher consciousness of guilt on a given occasion when the defendant is in possession of evidence linking him to both robberies and when the underlying crimes are virtually identical and separated by a mere ten days.

To the extent that the evidence at issue falls outside the scope of Rule 404(b), we will not deprive a party from presenting evidence when its exclusion leaves a conceptual or chronological void. *See United States v. Lahey*, 55 F.3d 1289, 1295–96 (7th Cir.1995); *see also United States v. King*, 126 F.3d 987, 995 (7th Cir.1997) ("[A] court may admit evidence of other criminal conduct that is inextricably intertwined with a charged offense or that completes the story of the charged offense."). The government needed the evidence of the chase and Robinson's struggle to present a complete picture of the events transpiring between the short time separating the April 8 armed bank robbery and Robinson's capture on April 18. Beyond merely establishing consciousness of guilt, this evidence explains the circumstances surrounding Robinson's arrest and how the government came into possession of the orange ski mask, the distinctive duffle bag, and the handgun—three pieces of evidence of paramount importance to the government's case. "While prosecutorial need alone does not mean probative value outweighs prejudice, the more essential the evidence, the greater its probative value, and the less likely that a trial court should order the evidence excluded." [*United States v. Jackson*, 886 F.2d 838, 847 (7th Cir.1989)].

Robinson contends that the District Court failed to balance the probative value of the evidence against its potential for undue prejudice as dictated by Rule 403. This contention is simply belied by the record in this case. After identifying the probative worth of the evidence of the similarities between the two armed bank robberies and of the evidence of flight, the District Court expressly concluded that this worth was not substantially outweighed by the danger of undue prejudice. Although the danger of unfair prejudice to Robinson existed with respect to the evidence of the chase and struggle, the District Court took careful steps to insure that the jury viewed this evidence in the proper light by specifically instructing the jury as to the limited use to which it could be put, and we presume the jury obeyed the court's instruction. The potential for prejudice was further reduced by the fact that the government called only one witness, Officer Craig, to testify regarding the chase and Robinson's struggle with police. Accordingly, we conclude that the District Court properly employed a careful and well-reasoned analysis before determining that the probative worth of the evidence at issue was not substantially outweighed by the risk of undue prejudice and did not abuse its discretion by admitting this evidence....

AFFIRMED.

Problem 4-7

On February 21, 1992, police were chasing two robbers who were presumed to be armed, Anthony Casella and Tammy Obloy. Eventually Casella and Obloy hid behind a garage in the backyard of a nearby house, in an extremely narrow passage between the wall of the garage and the yard fence. One end of the passage was obstructed by a post and the other by a woodpile. Police Officer Joseph Wing soon arrived with his dog, "Iron," and eventually located the hiding place. Wing then released Iron into the hiding place and followed the dog with his flashlight. Officer Wing saw Iron attack Obloy and yelled for Obloy and Casella to raise their hands. When they did not, Wing permitted the dog to begin biting Casella. Two other officers soon arrived at the scene, and the dog biting continued as Casella screamed and flailed his arms.

By this time, Wing knew that Casella was unarmed. Still, he did not order Iron to release Casella. Iron then began biting Casella in the thigh and groin, as Casella continued to flail at the dog. At some point, Wing began to strike Casella, yelling angrily, "Don't touch my dog." Casella was eventually knocked unconscious due to the beating and taken to the hospital, where he was treated for head lacerations, a fractured skull, an epidural hematoma, and dog-bites on his lip, right arm, chest, knee, thigh, and scrotum.

Casella spent five months in a brain rehabilitation program but never fully recovered cognitively. He later pled guilty to armed robbery and was sentenced to state prison. Later that year, he was attacked in prison and killed.

Casella's mother, Ada Kopf, brought a § 1983 action against the police officers involved in the dog-mauling. (Section 1983 claims provide equitable relief to a person deprived of his or her constitutional rights by any actor acting under State or Federal authority). The issue at trial was whether Wing hit Casella intentionally or by mistake. Kopf argues that the blows to the head were intentional, intended specifically as retribution for Casella's kicking of Iron.

To support her case, Kopf seeks to introduce evidence of a 1982 incident in which a burglar that Officer Wing was chasing stabbed Wing's dog, "Rebel," to death. Wing shot and killed the suspect and was seen carrying Rebel from the building in tears. He later gave the dog a full funeral. Wing was quoted in the local newspaper as stating "any time hereafter that a dog enters a building, the incident will not be forgotten." An officer in Wing's department, Officer Bancroft, was prepared to testify that it was common knowledge that Wing did not like anyone to touch his dog because of the loss of Rebel.

Obloy will testify that Wing had angrily shouted "don't touch my dog" just before he struck Casella in the head. Additionally, a paramedic that arrived at the scene will testify that while Casella was being carted away in a stretcher, Wing called him a "son of a bitch" because he "kicked my dog."

The officers oppose admission into evidence of the 1982 incident as improper character evidence under 404(b). How do you rule?

Problem 4-8

On September 30th, while New York state inmate George Eng was being transferred from one correctional facility to another, he alleges that officers began hitting him and yelling profanities and racial epithets at him. Eng spat on the officers in response. What happened next became the subject of litigation: Eng claims that officers responded by beating him with excessive force after he was subdued; the officers deny the allegation. Instead, the officers argue that Eng's behavior was unprovoked and calculated to induce a response from the officers so that Eng could file a § 1983 action.

Eng did file a § 1983 action. The issue at trial was whether officers used excessive force—more specifically, whether the officers used force simply to restore order or whether they used force maliciously and intentionally to cause harm to Eng.

As part of their defense, the officers seek to introduce Eng's disciplinary records as an inmate. The records show a history of ongoing confrontations with supervisory officers, all of which Eng initiated. The defendants argue that this evidences Eng's intent to evoke a response from the officers and precipitate the alleged September assault. In the alternative, they argue that the evidence rebuts Eng's argument that the spitting was provoked.

As part of his case, Eng seeks to introduce several "unusual incidents reports" which Eng had previously filed with the correctional facility. In the reports, Eng claimed that the same officers involved in the September incident had used excessive force against him at various other times in the years prior. The reports are complaints made by Eng and were never substantiated or investigated by authorities.

Both sides have filed motions opposing the other side's proffered evidence pursuant to 404(b). The motions are now before you. How do you rule?

Focus Questions: *United States v. Hernandez*

- When does a defendant put intent at issue?
- Why does the Court consider the jury instruction "exemplary"?

United States v. Hernandez

975 F.2d 1035 (4th Cir. 1992)

BUTZNER, Senior Circuit Judge:

Xiomaro E. Hernandez appeals a judgment entered on the verdict of a jury convicting her of conspiracy to distribute and to possess with intent to distribute cocaine. She alleges that the district court abused its discretion by admitting extraneous evidence of bad acts or crimes under Federal Rule of Evidence 404(b). We hold that the district court erred in admitting the challenged evidence over her lawyer's objection. Because we cannot conclude that the error was harmless, we vacate the judgment and remand the case for a new trial.

I

Xiomaro Hernandez, a native of the Dominican Republic, came to the United States in 1976 and is now a naturalized citizen. She lived at first in Puerto Rico and Miami, then moved to New York City where she worked in a travel agency owned by her family. She then moved with Rodolfo Fernandez to the District of Columbia where they shared an apartment. She testified that she supported herself during this time by traveling to New York, buying clothes, and bringing them back to Washington for resale.

The charges against Hernandez arose out of an undercover operation run by a joint task force set up by the Drug Enforcement Agency (DEA) and local police in northern Virginia. A DEA Special Agent, Frank Shroyer, obtained an introduction to a suspected drug dealer named Naikin DeLaCruz Duran (DeLaCruz). On August 23, 1990, Shroyer arranged to purchase powder cocaine and a sample of cocaine base, or crack cocaine, from DeLaCruz. One week later, Shroyer solicited DeLaCruz to sell him crack. After this conversation, task force officers observed DeLaCruz entering the apartment building where Hernandez lived with Fernandez. After DeLaCruz left the building, he met Shroyer at a metro station and gave him the promised crack. On September 10, 1990, Shroyer sought to purchase a substantial amount of crack from DeLaCruz. DeLaCruz stated that he would go to the District, get the drug, and return to Virginia to sell it to Shroyer. A surveillance team saw DeLaCruz enter the same building, then exit in the company of Fernandez. DeLaCruz delivered the drug to Shroyer in the parking lot outside DeLaCruz's apartment building. Federal agents and police immediately arrested DeLaCruz and then entered his apartment, where they found and arrested Fernandez.

DeLaCruz negotiated a plea agreement requiring him to cooperate with the government in its prosecution of Fernandez, Hernandez, and a third person, Victor "Shorty" Liriano....

Romulo DeLeon, who was testifying pursuant to a plea agreement in an unrelated drug case, related that he had met Hernandez at the clothing store where he worked. The meeting occurred more than six months before the acts alleged in the indictment. He testified that Hernandez had told him that she knew a special recipe for cooking crack "to make more quantity while you are cooking it." He said she had told him that she knew the recipe because "she used to do that, sell that in New York."

The government offered DeLeon's testimony as part of the government's case in chief, not in rebuttal to Hernandez's defense. Counsel for Hernandez objected to the testimony. The district court admitted it under Rule 404(b) and instructed the jury that they were not to "consider[ ] that these defendants are guilty of the crimes for which they are on trial here today merely because they are bad people, or that they have a propensity for crime." The court cautioned the jury that they were to consider the evidence only if they found that Hernandez had committed the acts charged in the indictment and, if so, to consider it only as evidence of the intent with which she did those acts.

Hernandez testified that she was out of town during the first two drug transactions and that she had left Hotke, an acquaintance whom she had met in Puerto Rico, in charge of her apartment during her absence. She stated that she had never had more than minimal contact with DeLaCruz and that she had "[n]ever in my life" sold him crack or drugs. She did not testify that she had no knowledge of crack or that she had never been exposed to or involved with drugs in general but only that, on the occasions alleged in the indictment, she was not involved in or aware of the drug transactions at issue....

II

... "This court has held that Rule 404(b) is an inclusive rule that allows admission of evidence of other acts relevant to an issue at trial except that which proves only criminal disposition." *United States v. Watford*, 894 F.2d 665, 571 (4th Cir.1990). The decision to admit evidence of other acts under Rule 404(b) is within the discretion of the trial court. *United States v. Mark*, 943 F.2d 444, 447 (4th Cir.1991).

Some trouble and confusion in applying this rule are only to be expected, for it is designed to exclude evidence that many both within and without the legal system intuitively find powerful and useful. The Supreme Court has noted:

> The inquiry is not rejected because character is irrelevant; on the contrary, it is said to weigh too much with the jury and to so overpersuade them as to prejudge one with a bad general record and deny him a fair opportunity to defend against a particular charge. The overriding policy of excluding such evidence, despite

its admitted probative value, is the practical experience that its disallowance tends to prevent confusion of issues, unfair surprise and undue prejudice.

Michelson v. United States, 335 U.S. 469, 475–76, (1948) (footnotes omitted).

In *Huddleston v. United States*, 485 U.S. 681, 691–92 (1988), the Court expressed its concern about the possibility of undue prejudice that might result from the introduction of evidence under Rule 404(b) and stipulated the measures a district court must take to protect against prejudice:

> We share petitioner's concern that unduly prejudicial evidence might be introduced under Rule 404(b). We think, however, that the protection against such unfair prejudice emanates not from a requirement of a preliminary finding by the trial court, but rather from four other sources: first, from the requirement of Rule 404(b) that the evidence be offered for a proper purpose; second, from the relevancy requirement of Rule 402—as enforced through Rule 104(b); third, from the assessment the trial court must make under Rule 403 to determine whether the probative value of the similar acts evidence is substantially outweighed by its potential for unfair prejudice; and fourth, from Federal Rule of Evidence 105, which provides that the trial court shall, upon request, instruct the jury that the similar acts evidence is to be considered only for the proper purpose for which it was admitted.

In this circuit, we have evolved a test for evidence proffered pursuant to Rule 404(b). "Under Rule 404(b) … prior bad acts are admissible if they are (1) relevant to an issue other than character; (2) necessary, and (3) reliable." *United States v. Rawle*, 845 F.2d 1244, 1247 (4th Cir.1988) (footnotes omitted). Evidence that passes this test is not automatically admissible, however. Rule 403 requires the trial judge to determine that its probative value outweighs the danger of undue prejudice to the defendant. In this circuit, unlike others, the trial court is not required to make an explicit statement of the purpose for which the evidence is admitted. The use of limiting instructions setting out the purpose for which the evidence is admitted and admonishing the jury against considering it as improper evidence of guilt will do much to alleviate difficulties raised by its admission. The district court offered an exemplary limiting instruction.

III

Under the doctrine of *Rawle*, we must begin by considering what, if any, relevance the challenged testimony bears to the issue for which it was offered. Evidence is relevant if it has "any tendency to make the existence of any fact that is of consequence to the determination of the action more probable or less probable than it would be without the evidence." Fed.R.Evid. 401. "In order for evidence to be relevant, it must be sufficiently related to the charged offense." *Rawle*, 845 F.2d at 1247 n. 3.

Judged by this standard, the relevance of DeLeon's testimony was at best small. It was offered as evidence of the intent with which Hernandez engaged in the charged conspiracy. The testimony did not establish anything about her conduct or mental state during the course of the conspiracy alleged in the indictment. Hernandez offered as her defense the contention that she had not sold the crack in question to DeLaCruz. She did not testify that she had in some way sold or handled the crack but without the requisite knowledge or intent; nor did she testify that she had never touched crack or did not know what it was. The DeLeon testimony showed that, before her move from New York to Washington, Hernandez had learned a special recipe for making crack and that she had made and apparently sold it in New York at that time. The testimony did not show that she intended to engage in crack distribution in Washington or that she had continued to deal in crack after leaving New York. Nor did it show that she intended to engage in crack distribution with Fernandez, or even that she intended to engage in future crack dealing at all.

It is a truism that a plea of "not guilty" to a charge requiring intent places that mental state in issue and that the state may offer evidence of other bad acts to address that issue. This principle, however, does not permit any sort of uncharged bad act to be brought to bear against defendants charged with intentional crimes. Most crimes involve some level of intent, but all evidence of other intentional acts or crimes does not for this reason become relevant. Evidence to show intent is not admissible when the unrelated bad act is "tenuous and remote in time from the charges in the indictment." *United States v. Cole*, 491 F.2d 1276, 1279 (4th Cir.1974). For example, evidence of a prior stabbing by the defendant is not relevant to show intent in a later encounter with a different victim when the defendant admitted stabbing the victim but pleaded self-defense. *United States v. Sanders*, 964 F.2d 295, 298–99 (4th Cir.1992).

A plausible interpretation of the rule holds that evidence of other crimes may not be offered when the defendant unequivocally denies committing the acts charged in the indictment. This circuit has no similar precept. Our cases examine the use for which intent evidence is offered in each instance, following the admonition that "the rule and the exceptions should be considered with meticulous regard to the facts of each case." *United States v. Baldivid*, 465 F.2d 1277, 1290 (4th Cir.1972) (Soboleff, J., concurring in part and dissenting in part). We have admitted evidence of other acts on the issue of intent, for example, where the defendant claimed that "he was present but innocent" during the sale of the drugs, and he elicited false testimony that he had no prior involvement in any cocaine transaction; where the defendant contended he had merely obtained a truck for friends without knowing it would be used to transport stolen property; where intent was a "key issue" because the defendant was "sharply contesting the sufficiency of the government's proof of lascivious intent" in a child-molestation case; and where the defendant has sought "to depict herself as one whose essential philosophy and habitual conduct in life is completely at odds with the possession of a state of mind requisite to guilt of the offense charged...."

The government insists that because intent and knowledge are essential elements of the charge against Hernandez, which were placed in issue by her plea of not guilty, the DeLeon testimony about prior bad acts is admissible. For this proposition it relies on *Mark*, 943 F.2d at 448. But reliance on *Mark* for this sweeping ground for admission is unwarranted. The evidence must still be relevant. In *Mark* the trial court pointed out that the evidence of prior bad acts disclosed how the defendant got the drugs that he was charged with selling. Consequently, *Mark* is well within the mainstream of our cases that have admitted evidence of prior similar acts to show intent and knowledge. Because *Mark* differs significantly from the case before us, it does not support the government's contention that DeLeon's evidence was relevant.

Necessity is the second part of the *Rawle* test. In some sense all evidence that tends to make conviction more likely is necessary, particularly in a case like this one where the other evidence of guilt is tenuous. Our cases dictate a more sophisticated inquiry: "The evidence is necessary and admissible where it is an essential part of the crimes on trial [citation omitted] or where it 'furnishes part of the context of the crime.'" *Rawle*, 845 F.2d at 1247 n. 4, quoting *United States v. Smith*, 446 F.2d 200, 204 (4th Cir.1971). DeLeon's testimony serves no such purpose. It bears at best a slight relationship to the acts charged in the indictment. Indeed, its principal value relates not to the crime but to the alleged criminal. The charged acts become more plausible when the defendant has admitted involvement with crack on other occasions. But this, once again, is precisely the criminal propensity inference Rule 404(b) is designed to forbid.

As for the third part of the test, reliability, *see Rawle*, 845 F.2d at 1247, this evidence barely passes muster. Admissible prior acts testimony is sometimes corroborated by a judgment of conviction; by other testimony as to the time and place at which the prior acts allegedly occurred; or by audio- or videotaped evidence. Such corroboration, however, is not required; the weight and credibility of uncorroborated testimony of defendants testifying pursuant to plea agreements is largely for the jury. However, "the convincingness of the evidence that other crimes were committed is a factor that should be weighed in the decision to admit such evidence." *Cole*, 491 F.2d at 1279. In this case, careful consideration of reliability might not in itself require barring the testimony, but it surely does not generate a compelling argument for its admission.

IV

Even assuming the DeLeon testimony did not fail the *Rawle* test, it still was inadmissible unless it could be held more probative than prejudicial....

"The prejudice which the rule is designed to prevent is jury emotionalism or irrationality." *United States v. Greenwood*, 796 F.2d 49, 53 (4th Cir.1986). A court should exclude evidence when "there is a genuine risk that the emotions of the jury will be excited to irrational behavior, and that this risk is disproportionate to the probative value of the offered evidence." [*United States v. Masters*, 622 F.2d 83, 87 (4th Cir.1980) (citation omitted)]. In this case, the trial record does not reflect that the district court engaged in an explicit balancing of the probative value of the evidence against prejudice. However, "[a]s long as the record as a whole indicates appropriate judicial weighing, we will not reverse for a failure to recite mechanically the appropriate balancing test." *United States v. Lewis*, 780 F.2d 1140, 1142 (4th Cir.1986).

In *Lewis* the record disclosed that the attorneys presented lengthy arguments on the balancing test and that the probative value of the evidence was high. Based on these factors the court was able to conclude on appeal that the trial court had complied with the admonition to balance the probative value of prior extraneous culpability with its prejudicial effect. But in Hernandez's case the record is silent about the balancing test, and there is no mention of Rule 403. Perhaps balancing was accomplished at an unreported bench conference. Here—unlike *Lewis*—the probative value of the evidence is slight. Hernandez's "cooking" recipe and her sale of crack in New York at some indefinite time are in no way connected to the cocaine she is charged with conspiring to sell in this case. The evident effect, if not the purpose, of DeLeon's testimony relating Hernandez's statement about her activities in New York was to bolster DeLaCruz's testimony about her acts in Washington by depicting her as an experienced crack dealer. But this is precisely the effect Rules 403 and 404(b) seek to avoid. Upon consideration of all the circumstances, we think the balance so one-sided that admission of the evidence was error....

The judgment is vacated, and the case is remanded for retrial consistent with this opinion.

VACATED AND REMANDED.

Problem 4-9

In 1982, Andrew Wilson allegedly shot and killed two Chicago policemen. He confessed during interrogation and his confession was used against him at trial. He was later convicted and sentenced to life in prison; however, the Supreme Court of Illinois reversed the conviction on grounds that Wilson's confession was coerced. Wilson later brought a § 1983 action against the interrogating officers and the city of Chicago based on the coercion during interrogation.

At trial Wilson testified that on the day of his arrest he was punched, kicked, smothered with a plastic bag, electronically shocked, and forced against a hot radiator until he gave a confession. His testimony was corroborated by contemporaneous medical and photographic evidence.

To make his case Wilson also sought to introduce the testimony of Melvin Jones and Donald White. Jones was prepared to testify that he was interrogated about a crime and subjected to electroshock nine days before Wilson's interrogation, by the same officers involved in Wilson's interrogation. White was arrested the same day as Wilson for an alleged murder and was prepared to testify that he was beaten by several of the same police officers for hours during interrogation.

The city opposed the introduction of Jones and White's testimony as improper propensity evidence pursuant to 404(b), and the district court excluded the evidence. The issue is now before you on appeal. How do you rule?

Problem 4-10

On a sunny afternoon, two Sea-Doos collided in a lake in North Carolina. The collision resulted in the death of one of the parties; the other party survived but sustained substantial injuries. The surviving party is now suing the manufacturer of the Sea-Doo, alleging that the collision occurred because of a defective stop switch.

The manufacturer denies responsibility and claims that the collision was caused by the Plaintiff's own recklessness. Specifically, the manufacturer argues that the Plaintiff was known for engaging in dangerous and potentially life-threatening 180 and 360-degree tricks on his Sea-Doo, that he was engaged in such tricks at the time of the collision, and that such behavior eradicated the effectiveness of the stop-switch.

To support its case, the manufacturer seeks to admit testimony that it elicited during an investigation at the time of the collision. Several witnesses present at the date and time of the collision testified that the Plaintiff was engaged in 180 and 360-degree maneuvers in the area of the collision, right before the collision occurred. In addition, several people testified that they had witnessed the Plaintiff performing these maneuvers prior to the date of the collision.

The Plaintiff has moved to exclude this evidence pursuant to Rule 404(b). How do you rule?

Problem 4-11

Herbert McGill was an inmate at Indiana State Prison when he was placed in "protective custody" in an "IDU," which is generally known as a unit assigned to prisoners for disciplinary purposes. While there, McGill was sodomized by another male prisoner at knifepoint. McGill subsequently brought § 1983 charges against several prison guards and officials, alleging they had deprived him of his due process rights by placing him in the disciplinary unit. As part of his claim for damages, he argued emotional anguish brought on by the experience.

At trial, the defendants argue that the encounter was consensual and that McGill did not experience the emotional anguish alleged. To prove their case, they seek to introduce evidence that McGill had engaged in consensual homosexual activity both before and during his incarceration. In particular, they seek to introduce McGill's own testimony—given during the trial for manslaughter for which he was serving time—in which he admitted that his male victim was a former love interest with whom he had had oral sex.

McGill has filed a motion in limine to exclude the evidence pursuant to 404(b). The motion is now before you. How do you rule?

II. Habit Evidence

Relevant Rules
FRE 406

Habit; Routine Practice

Evidence of a person's habit or an organization's routine practice may be admitted to prove that on a particular occasion the person or organization acted in accordance with the habit or routine practice. The court may admit this evidence regardless of whether it is corroborated or whether there was an eyewitness.

Overview

As we have seen, evidence that relies on character-propensity reasoning is inadmissible unless one of the six exceptions exists. However, evidence of a person's habit or an organization's routine practice is admissible to prove a seemingly forbidden propensity inference: the evidence may be used to demonstrate that a person or organization acted in conformity with its habit on a particular occasion. Why this difference?

The answer lies in the fact that, under the FRE, habit is perceived as different from character. While character evidence focuses on a person's disposition (e.g., one chooses to exceed the speed limit when driving a car, so it is volitional behavior, not automatic behavior), habit is perceived as a uniform or semi-automatic response to a repeated situation (e.g., one often puts on seat belts in a car without even thinking about it, making it a semi-automatic response to getting into a car). Because habit is not volitional, it is not equated to character under the FRE. Similarly, because habit is perceived semi-automatic, its probative value is considered very strong. If a person always puts a seat belt on when entering a car, then it is very likely that she used a seat belt on a particular occasion.

How does one determine whether a behavior qualifies as a habit? Certainly the more specific the behavior, the more likely it qualifies as a habit. "Victor is a careful driver" expresses a very general trait that may not present itself in all situations. "Victor always wears his seat belt" expresses a very narrow trait that relies less on Victor's perceived character. Another factor is regularity. To be a habit, it cannot be a behavior that possesses numerous exceptions. "Victor often stops by a bar on his way home from work" likely does not indicate the required regularity. Finally, it must be non-volitional, automatic behavior. The more thought that goes into whether or not to exhibit a behavior, the less likely it is a habit.

A proponent of habit evidence may use extrinsic evidence. For example, a party may offer an opinion witness, examples of specific instances of conduct, or documentary proof. The proponent must also prove a large enough sample to convince the court that the behavior is automatic. Engaging in a pattern of behavior only two or three times will likely not a habit make.

Accordingly, qualifying a behavior as a habit is a powerful tool for an advocate. No exception to the character-propensity ban is required. No "missing word" needs to be argued under FRE 404(b). Extrinsic evidence is allowed to prove the evidential hypothesis, giving that party maximum flexibility. The major battle, therefore, centers on the fact-intensive inquiry as to whether a behavior can be fairly called a habit or if it is more accurately an attempt to gauge a party's character.

Focus Questions: *Reyes v. Missouri Pacific R.R.*

- What controlling considerations does the court use to distinguish between habit and character?
- Could frequent prior intoxication ever rise to the level of habit? If so, how?

Reyes v. Missouri Pacific R.R. Co.
589 F.2d 791 (5th Cir. 1979)

JAMES C. HILL, Circuit Judge:

In this diversity case plaintiff-appellant challenges the admission into evidence of his four prior misdemeanor convictions for public intoxication, introduced for the purpose of showing that he was intoxicated on the night that he was run over by defendant-appellee's train. We agree with appellant, finding the evidence of his prior convictions to be inadmissible under Rule 404(a) of the Federal Rules of Evidence; therefore, we reverse and remand the case for a new trial.

I.

Shortly after midnight on June 17, 1974, appellant Reyes was run over by appellee-railroad's train as he lay on the railroad tracks near a crossing in Brownsville, Texas. Reyes brought this diversity suit against the railroad, alleging negligence on the part of the railroad's employees in failing to discover plaintiff as he lay on the tracks and stop the train in time to avoid the accident. The railroad answered by claiming that Reyes, dressed in dark clothing that night, was not visible from the approaching train until it was too late for its employees to avert the accident. Moreover, the railroad alleged that Reyes was contributorily negligent because he was intoxicated on the night of the accident and passed out on the tracks before the train arrived. Reyes explained his presence on the railroad tracks by claiming that he was knocked unconscious by an unknown assailant as he walked along the tracks.

Reyes made a motion *in limine* to exclude the evidence relating to his prior misdemeanor convictions for public intoxication. The railroad opposed this motion, arguing that the convictions were admissible to show that Reyes was intoxicated on the night of the accident. The district court agreed and refused to grant Reyes' motion.

In an attempt to minimize the damaging effects of his prior convictions, Reyes brought them out on direct examination. In answering a special interrogatory submitted to them, the jury found the plaintiff more negligent than the defendant; under Texas law, this finding precluded Reyes from recovering against the railroad.

II.

Rule 404 of the Federal Rules of Evidence embodies the well-settled principle that evidence of a person's character is usually not admissible for the purpose of proving that the person acted in conformity with his character on a particular occasion. Fed.R.Evid. 404, 28 U.S.C.A. This general rule of exclusion, applicable to both civil and criminal proceedings, is based upon the assumption that such evidence is of slight probative value yet very prejudicial.

An analysis of the admissibility of character evidence necessarily begins, then, with an examination of the purposes for which the evidence is proffered. If the evidence is introduced for the purpose of showing that a person acted in accordance with his character on a given occasion, then the evidence is inadmissible unless it falls within one of the exceptions noted in Rule 404.

The record in this case makes clear that the railroad intended for Reyes' prior convictions to show that he was intoxicated on the night of the accident. Indeed, that purpose was the only possible one for which the evidence could be offered. Moreover, the trial judge specifically noted in the motion in limine hearing that evidence of the prior convictions would be relevant to the issue of whether Reyes was intoxicated on the night of the accident. Because the evidence of Reyes' prior convictions was admitted for the sole purpose of showing that he had a character trait of drinking to excess and that he acted in conformity with his character on the night of the accident by becoming intoxicated, we conclude that the prior convictions were inadmissible character evidence under Rule 404.

III.

The suggestion that the prior convictions constituted evidence of Reyes' "habit" of excessive drinking is equally unpersuasive. Rule 406 allows the introduction of evidence of the habit of a person for the purpose of proving that the person acted in conformity with his habit on a particular occasion. Fed.R.Evid. 406. Habit evidence is considered to be highly probative and therefore superior to character evidence because "the uniformity of one's response to habit is far greater than the consistency with which one's conduct conforms to character or disposition." McCormick on Evidence s 195 at 463 (2d ed. 1972).

Perhaps the chief difficulty in deciding questions of admissibility under Rule 406 arises in trying to draw the line between inadmissible character evidence and admissible habit evidence. Quite often the line between the two may become blurred.

Character and habit are close akin. Character is a generalized description of one's disposition, or one's disposition in respect to a general trait, such as honesty, temperance, or peacefulness. "Habit," in modern usage, both lay and psychological, is more specific. It describes one's regular response to a repeated specific situation. If we speak of character for care, we think of the person's tendency to act prudently in all the varying situations of life, in business, family life, in handling automobiles and in walking across the street. A habit, on the other hand, is the person's regular practice of meeting a particular kind of situation with a specific type of conduct, such as the habit of going down a particular stairway two stairs at a time, or of giving the hand-signal for a left turn, or of alighting from railway cars while they are moving. The doing of the habitual acts may become semi-automatic. Although a precise formula cannot be proposed for determining when the behavior may become so consistent as to rise to the level of habit, "adequacy of sampling and uniformity of response" are controlling considerations. Notes of Advisory Committee on Proposed Rules, Fed.R.Evid. 406, 28 U.S.C.A. at p. 153. Thus, the probative force of habit evidence to prove intoxication on a given occasion depends on the "degree of regularity of the practice and its coincidence with the occasion." McCormick on Evidence s 195 n. 16 (2d ed. 1972).

We do not undertake here to prescribe the precise quantum of proof necessary to transform a general disposition for excessive drinking into a "habit" of intemperance; we simply find that four prior convictions for public intoxication spanning a three and one-half year period are of insufficient regularity to rise to the level of "habit" evidence. Consequently, we hold the evidence to be inadmissible under Rule 406 as well.

IV.

A principle purpose behind the exclusion of character evidence, as we have said, is the prejudicial effect that it can have on the trier of fact. This concern is especially compelling here where the character evidence relates to one of the critical issues in the case, i.e., the contributory negligence of Reyes. Finding the introduction of the prior convictions to be extremely prejudicial, we feel that the error affected the substantial rights of Reyes, thus requiring a new trial.

REVERSED and REMANDED.

Problem 4-12

Milton Levin was on trial for an alleged larceny that took place in Washington, D.C., at 5:00 p.m. on Friday, February 13, 1959. Both he and his wife claimed he was in his New York home at the time. Indeed, Mr. Levin testified that "Friday afternoon was the Sabbath, which we observe quite diligently, and I never go away from home and my family on the Sabbath." His wife also testified that her husband was always with her on Friday nights. To further support his testimony, the defendant called Rabbi Irwin Isaacson to testify as to defendant's habit of staying home on the Sabbath. Is the testimony of Rabbi Isaacson admissible?

Professional Development Questions

- Let us continue the discussion of how to become an expert learner by exploring the implementation phase. In order to master material you must maintain focused attention and monitoring of your comprehension and learning pace. For example, regularly ask yourself whether you understand what you are learning and whether your learning strategies are working. You may benefit by taking a learning self-assessment to ensure you are using learning strategies that are a good fit for you. One helpful learning assessment is found at vark-learn.com.

- Should you always object to character-propensity evidence? Occasionally, the other act evidence may cast your client in a positive light (e.g., Problem 3-7, when an officer's dog was killed in the line of duty). Just because evidence is objectionable does not always mean you should object. Especially in the context of FRE 404(b), the other act evidence may be more helpful than hurtful to your narrative. Do any of the other cases or problems illustrate this principle?

- Many evidentiary arguments in a trial invites a counterargument. For example, the prosecution's reliance on motive may open the door for a conditional relevance objection (did the defendant know of the facts that would have arguably created a motive?). The conditional relevance argument may decrease the probative weight of the other act such that the unfair prejudice may substantially outweigh the probative value. The analysis of FRE 404(b) contains perhaps the greatest number of moves and countermoves that can open the door to other types of objections. Therefore, try to create a list of counterarguments to the OKMIMIC "missing words." Add arguments to this list as we learn more objections in the upcoming chapters.

- Can an attorney commit an ethical violation by introducing other act evidence that is highly prejudicial and possesses very little chance of being admissible? Under what circumstances would an ethical violation exist?

- One helpful technique for learning the FRE is to see if you can change the result of a case by changing one or more facts. By understanding what facts are outcome-determinative, you better understand the parameter of the rules. For example, what factual change would have made the evidence in *People v. Zackowitz* admissible?

Chapter 5

Exceptions to the Character-Propensity Ban

When is one allowed to prove that a person acted in accordance with his character propensities on a given occasion? In other words, when can one explicitly argue that "she did X because that is the type of person she is; she has done X in the past"? Or, conversely, when can one argue, "She would never do X; I have known her all my life, and she has never done X"?

We shall explore six exceptions to the ban on character-propensity evidence (noted in the chart below). The first category is proving character under FRE 404(a)(1) and 404(a)(2) for (or against) a criminal defendant. Next, FRE 413, 414, and 415 focuses on sexual assault and child molestation in both the criminal and civil arenas. Finally, in the next chapter, we shall explore character for truthfulness under FRE 404(a)(3).

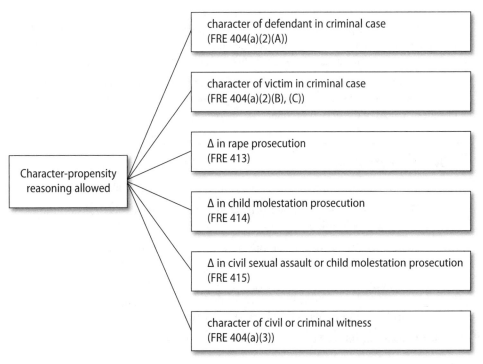

159

I. "Opening the Door" to Character in Criminal Cases

Relevant Rules
FRE 404(a)(1) and (2)

Character Evidence; Crimes or Other Acts

(a) Character Evidence.

(1) *Prohibited Uses.* Evidence of a person's character or character trait is not admissible to prove that on a particular occasion the person acted in accordance with the character or trait.

(2) *Exceptions for a Defendant or Victim in a Criminal Case.* The following exceptions apply in a criminal case:

(A) a defendant may offer evidence of the defendant's pertinent trait, and if the evidence is admitted, the prosecutor may offer evidence to rebut it;

(B) subject to the limitations in Rule 412, a defendant may offer evidence of an alleged victim's pertinent trait, and if the evidence is admitted, the prosecutor may:

(i) offer evidence to rebut it; and

(ii) offer evidence of the defendant's same trait; and

(C) in a homicide case, the prosecutor may offer evidence of the alleged victim's trait of peacefulness to rebut evidence that the victim was the first aggressor.

FRE 405

Methods of Proving Character

(a) By Reputation or Opinion. When evidence of a person's character or character trait is admissible, it may be proved by testimony about the person's reputation or by testimony in the form of an opinion. On cross-examination of the character witness, the court may allow an inquiry into relevant specific instances of the person's conduct.

(b) By Specific Instances of Conduct. When a person's character or character trait is an essential element of a charge, claim, or defense, the character or trait may also be proved by relevant specific instances of the person's conduct.

Overview Problem

Dirk is on trial for the murder of Victor. He intends to offer the following evidence:

(a) Dirk's first witness will be his reverend who will testify as to his opinion of Dirk's peacefulness.

(b) Dirk's second witness is Victor's parole officer who will testify that, in his opinion, Victor was a "born liar."

(c) Dirk's third witness will testify that he witnessed the altercation between Victor and Dirk and that Victor pulled a knife on Dirk and threatened Dirk's life moments before Dirk shot Victor.

The prosecution intends to offer the following evidence:

(d) On cross-examination of Dirk's reverend, the prosecution will ask the reverend if she knew that Dirk had previously been convicted of aggravated assault.

(e) The prosecution will offer the testimony of Victor's mother, who will testify that Victor belonged to "Pacifists for Peace," a group that espoused non-violence.

Which testimony is admissible? Which is inadmissible?

A. Proving Character Under FRE 404(a)(1) and 404(a)(2)

These two exceptions are limited to a criminal defendant, the most vulnerable litigant in the system whose freedom is at stake and who must defeat the vast resources of the government. The three questions that are central to a FRE 404(a)(1) and FRE 404(a)(2) analysis are (i) **what type** of evidence is admissible, (ii) **who may introduce** this evidence and how may it be rebutted, and (iii) **what process** governs its admission?

1. What Type of Evidence?

A criminal defendant may only offer evidence of a character trait that is **pertinent** to the underlying crime charged under FRE 404(a)(1) or may offer (subject to exceptions under FRE 412) **pertinent** character traits of an alleged crime victim. Thus, evidence of veracity would not be pertinent to a crime of violence and peacefulness would not be pertinent if the defendant were charged with a nonviolent crime. However, certain general character traits, such as a character for lawfulness, are considered pertinent no matter what the crime charged. Put simply, a trait is pertinent if its existence is relevant to the outcome of the case.

The limitation to pertinent traits is a matter of relevance. A defendant charged with tax fraud would be wasting the court's time if she offered three character witnesses who testified as to her peacefulness. Peacefulness has nothing to do with tax fraud and is thus irrelevant. Similarly, if the defendant offers non-pertinent character traits of the victim, unfair prejudice may arise, as the jury will be weighing irrelevant character traits.

2. Who May Introduce and How May It Be Rebutted?

First, the **defendant** must initiate the process or, as it is commonly referred, "open the door," by offering a pertinent trait of character of herself or the alleged victim. Typically, a defendant can open the door three ways: she can offer this evidence (i) through a character witness who testifies as to the defendant or victim's character, (ii) through the defendant's own testimony as to her character or the character of the victim (e.g., the defendant becomes her own character witness by describing her character or that of the victim), or even (iii) through cross-examination of a government witness that involves asking the witness about the witness's perception of defendant's or the victim's character. Thus, the defendant (with one exception described below) controls the potential introduction of character evidence in a trial. It is her door to open, but if she opens it, ramifications of that decision quickly flow.

In response to the defendant's opening of the door, the prosecution can rebut that evidence based on how the defendant opened the door. FRE 404(a)(2) nicely illustrates the options.

If the defendant offers character evidence about herself (e.g., "I am peaceful"), then the prosecutor may rebut by proving that the defendant lacks that trait or holds the opposite one (e.g., "The defendant is violent"). FRE 404(a)(2)(A). If the defendant attacks the victim's character (e.g., "The victim was violent"), then, subject to the limits of FRE 412 (the Rape Shield Law) discussed in the next chapter, the prosecutor has two options. First, the prosecutor may rebut the evidence by attempting to show that the **victim** lacked that trait or held the opposite trait (e.g., "The victim was peaceful"). Second, the prosecutor may also attempt to demonstrate that the **defendant** has the exact same trait that the defendant attributed to the victim (e.g., "The defendant is violent"). FRE 404(a)(2)(B). Thus, by opening the door, the defendant faces rebuttal character evidence that may cast the defendant in a bad light or the victim in a very positive light. Due to a fear of rebuttal evidence, a defendant with skeletons in his closet on a pertinent trait typically will not open the door to the trait. Indeed, by opening the door to character, a defendant may make a once irrelevant piece of evidence relevant to character. For example, a previous arrest for a violent crime would not be pertinent to a charge of criminal fraud, but if the defendant claimed that he possessed a law-abiding character, the arrest for violence may rebut defendant's claim that he is law-abiding.

Finally, we come to the only exception to the criminal defendant controlling the introduction of character evidence. In the limited circumstance of a homicide case, the defendant can open the door by claiming the victim was the first aggressor. In essence, this strategy by the defendant would be a quasi-character attack, as the defendant would be claiming that the victim had a violent character that was exemplified by the victim's attack on the defendant. As a victim in a homicide case is deceased and cannot take the stand, the prosecutor may introduce evidence of the victim's peaceable character. FRE 404(a)(2)(C).

3. What Process Must Be Followed?

When either the prosecution or the defendant offers a character witness, the mandates of FRE 405(a) must be followed. The party is limited pursuant to FRE 405(a) to reputation or opinion evidence as to character on direct examination. Thus, the character witness may only testify to such things as "Defendant's reputation in his community for honesty is quite good" or "In my opinion, the defendant is honest." In other words, the character witness cannot base her opinion on specific incidents by, for example, offering an example of when defendant exhibited honest behavior. A natural question to ask is, "But that makes no sense—don't we learn more from a person's actions than from self-serving comments about a defendant's character by a witness the defendant chose?" The answer is "yes," and even the drafters of the Federal Rules of Evidence believed that to be the case. As they noted in their comments to FRE 405, of "the three methods of proving character provided by the rule [reputation, opinion and specific acts], evidence of specific instances of conduct is the most convincing." Advisory Committee Notes for FRE 405. Nonetheless, this type of evidence is inadmissible on direct examination of a character witness, as it has historically been perceived as both confusing to the jury and a potential waste of time.

Imagine, for instance, a witness who testifies, "D is very honest. I remember that once he found an expensive watch on the street and turned it in to the police." The prosecutor might then feel obligated to put forth a witness to testify that perhaps the incident did not occur as described or that it was in fact a cheap watch. The defendant may then feel obligated to call another witness to appraise the value of the watch. This tangential foray into the mysterious lost watch episode is of limited probative import in the grander scheme of a criminal trial and diverts the trial into an unwanted direction that leads to confusion and wasted time.

Thus, on direct examination, the character witness for either the defense or prosecution is limited to reputation or opinion evidence. A reputation character witness ("I think the defendant's reputation in the community for honesty is very good") must first set forth a foundation that they are familiar with the defendant's reputation in a relevant community (e.g., neighborhood, workplace, etc.) during the relevant time period. Similarly, an opinion character witness ("In my opinion, the defendant is a truthful person") must also lay a foundation that the witness has sufficient knowledge to offer the opinion (e.g., "I have known the defendant for ten years and am aware of his character for truthfulness").

Next, a character witness may be cross-examined on her testimony. This cross-examination may include an exploration of specific instances. You might think, "That's odd — you can prove a character trait with specific instances on cross but not direct — what about the concerns of confusion and waste of time?" The response is that using specific instances on cross-examination is **not a method of proving a character trait**. Rather, it is a **method of testing the character witness' testimony**, either through testing the character witness' credibility or by testing the character witness' knowledge. In other words, the prosecutor is not using the specific acts to prove the existence of a trait but rather to prove that this particular character witness does not know or cannot judge the defendant as well as she claims.

Take, for example, a witness who testifies that "D is a very honest person." On cross-examination, the prosecutor asks, "Did you know that D was once convicted of perjury?" If the character witness responds, "No, I didn't know that," then the character witness's **knowledge** of the subject on which she is testifying (D's veracity) is called into question. Why should we trust this witness if she did not even know that D had a perjury conviction? If, instead, the witness replies, "Yes, I did know that," then the character witness's **judgment** is called into question. After all, she just testified that a person convicted of perjury is a "very honest person." Thus, whether a witness answers "yes" or "no," her credibility **as a witness** is called into question. That is the purpose of allowing specific instances on cross-examination. The fact that defendant's reputation is damaged because the jury learned that he was convicted of perjury is perceived as collateral damage. The prosecutor is entitled to probe the credibility of the witness, and the defendant can request a jury instruction as to the proper use of the evidence.

Also, note that "specific instances of conduct" may refer to any type of conduct that calls the witness' testimony into question. So, arrests or uncharged misconduct that reflects on the pertinent character trait is fair game. As long as (i) the specific instance is relevant, (ii) the cross-examiner possesses a good faith basis for the question, and (iii) it can survive a FRE 403 analysis, it may be inquired into on cross-examination. In terms of the relevance of specific instances, the witness must likely have been able to obtain knowledge of the specific incident for it to be relevant. Thus, if a witness testifies that she knew the defendant for ten years, the prosecutor may not refer to specific incidents from thirty years ago. If the witness does not know about them, it does not reflect on her credibility, as she testified that she did not know the defendant at the time the specific instances occurred. The specific incidents are simply irrelevant as a source of impeachment.

Furthermore, because the purpose of the specific instance evidence is to test the credibility of the character witness, the questioner cannot prove the incident occurred if the witness claims no knowledge of the incident. In other words, the cross-examiner must accept the answer of the witness, and no extrinsic evidence is allowed. By demonstrating a lack of any knowledge of the incident, the cross-examiner has sufficiently attacked the credibility of the witness.

Once the defendant has presented character evidence, the prosecutor has an additional option other than cross-examination of a character witness. The prosecutor may call a character witness to disprove that the defendant possesses an alleged character trait. This rebuttal character witness is limited to reputation or opinion on her direct, however. If the prosecutor wants to explore specific instances of conduct, she must rely on the cross-examination of the defendant's character witness.

In summary, the interplay between the defense and prosecution under 404(a)(2) can be viewed as follows:

What Type of Evidence	Who Opens Door	How	Prosecutorial Response
Pertinent trait of accused	Δ	Reputation or opinion	Δ has bad character for same trait
Pertinent trait of alleged victim	Δ	Reputation or opinion	Alleged victim has good character and/or Δ had bad character for same trait
Exception: Peacefulness of alleged victim	Prosecution, if Δ alleges that alleged victim was first aggressor	Reputation or opinion	N/A

B. The Role of FRE 405(b)

One narrow exception requires further analysis. Note that FRE 405(b) allows specific instances of character on direct in cases in which "a person's character or character trait is an essential element of a charge, claim, or defense[.]" Instances where the existence of a character trait **is the thing to be proved** (as opposed to conduct done in conformity of a character trait) are rare. Thus a prosecution for seduction (where "chastity of the victim" may need to be proven) or a defense to entrapment (where the question may be whether the defendant was "predisposed" to committing a crime) are two criminal examples of where the thing that must be proved is a character trait (i.e., a person's propensity to engage or not engage in certain forms of behavior must be proved). In the civil arena, negligent entrustment or hiring, parental custody disputes, libel, slander, and defamation are examples where character may be an essential element of a claim or defense. Think of it this way: if a party with the initial burden of producing evidence will need to introduce character evidence in order to avoid a directed verdict, then character is essential to the charge, claim, or defense.

Be careful not to confuse **character** with **reputation** in the context of FRE 405(b). In each of the aforementioned examples, **character** is "essential" to the charge, claim, or defense, not **reputation**. As we have seen, "character" refers to a person's propensity to engage or not engage in certain forms of behavior. Reputation is a means to prove character. In cases where a person's reputation may be relevant, as in, for example, a self-defense claim, character is usually not an essential element to the charge, claim, or defense. In the self-defense situation, a defendant may argue that the alleged victim's violent reputation made the defendant reasonably respond to a situation with force. Thus, the reasonableness of response is the essential element of the defense. Whether or not the character of the alleged victim was truly violent is not essential to proving a reasonable reaction of force, and therefore FRE 405(b) will not apply.

C. Conclusion

Let us now return to the overview problem to further hone our knowledge of all the permutations of FRE 404(a)(1) and (2). Go back and review the question before proceeding to the next paragraph.

The evidence in (a) is admissible, as Dirk has the right to open the door to exploring a pertinent trait of his character. The evidence in (b), however, is likely not pertinent. In the context of a non-testifying victim of a violent crime, the truthfulness of the victim is probably not a pertinent character trait. The evidence in (c) is admissible, as it technically is not character evidence. This evidence merely describes the fight that led to Victor's death. However, context is everything. This is a homicide case, and by painting Victor as the first aggressor, the prosecution may now offer evidence as to Victor's peacefulness.

The evidence in (d) is admissible, as exploring the character witness' credibility is a price Dirk must pay for opening the door to the inquiry into character. This evidence tests the character witness's knowledge and judgment by exploring what she knows about Dirk. The evidence in (e) is not admissible. Even though Dirk painted Victor as the first aggressor, a prosecution's rebuttal character witness may only testify as to reputation or opinion on direct. By offering a specific instance of peacefulness, she violated this rule.

Remember that in the realm of FRE 404(a)(1) and (2), **context is everything.** Is the trait pertinent to the particular charge? Did the proper party open the door? Is the scope of the rebuttal proper? Was appropriate evidence offered on direct and cross-examination of the witness? You need to pay attention to each variable in order to determine the correct result.

FRE 404(a)(2): Opening the Door to a Pertinent Character Trait

Elements	Satisfied? ☑ ☒
Criminal Case	
Evidence of Defendant or Victim's Character	
Character trait is pertinent to the underlying crime	
Introduced by the defendant	
If Direct Examination, Evidence is in the form of Reputation or Opinion	
If Cross-Examination, Evidence can refer to a specific relevant instance	

FRE 404(a)(2): Opening the Door to Proof of Peacefulness

Elements	Satisfied? ☑ ☒
Criminal Case	
Defendant Alleged that Victim was the instigator	
Evidence is in the form of Reputation or Opinion	

Focus Questions: *Broyles v. Commonwealth*

- How is the other act evidence different from the other act evidence in *Smith* and *Albertson*?

- Is it always within the discretion of the court to allow trait specific incidents or are there some clear distinctions for certain kinds of evidence that can always be admitted?

Broyles v. Commonwealth

Court of Appeals of Kentucky
267 S.W.2d 73 (1954)

COMBS, Justice.

George Richard Broyles appeals from a sentence of life imprisonment imposed after a jury found him guilty of the murder of Billy D. Smithers....

The appellant introduced several witnesses who testified that his reputation for peace and quietude was good. These witnesses were asked on cross-examination if they knew appellant had been arrested and convicted on separate occasions for drunken driving, for reckless driving, and for disorderly conduct. One witness admitted to having knowledge of these convictions; the others disavowed such knowledge. Appellant contends the questions were improper because they related to a trait of charact[e]r not involved in the crime with which he was charged.

Broadly speaking, it is the rule in this state that where the defendant introduces evidence of his good reputation, the witness so testifying may be asked on cross-examination whether he has heard reports of particular acts of misconduct by the defendant. But the rule is not absolute. When there is an objection to such evidence or a motion to limit its effect, the court is required to admonish the jury that it is admitted only for the purpose of testing the accuracy and credibility of the witness' testimony and not as substantive evidence of defendant's guilt. Moreover, inquiry may be made only about those acts of misconduct having some relation to the particular trait of character which the defendant has put in issue.

Another limitation to the rule, but one with which we are not here concerned, is that the attorney for the Commonwealth may not deliberately inject into the case the issue of previous acts of misconduct by the defendant without some basis for his questions.

The question here is whether one who is guilty of drunken driving, reckless driving, and disorderly conduct thereby evinces a trait of character inconsistent with a good reputation for peace and quietude. Courts in other jurisdictions have answered the question in the affirmative and have permitted questions designed to test the witness' knowledge of the other offenses.

We find no Kentucky case directly in point, but an examination of related cases reveals that this court has taken a cautious attitude toward the introduction of such testimony. In *Smith v. Commonwealth*, 206 Ky. 728, 268 S.W. 328 (1925), the defendant, being tried for murder, introduced witnesses who testified that his reputation for peace and quietude was good. The witnesses were asked on cross-examination if they had heard that defendant had an illegitimate child by his sister-in-law; that he had taken another man's wife to Tennessee and lived with her, and that he had been convicted for the illegal sale of whisky. It was held that the questions should not have been permitted because responsive answers would have thrown no light on defendant's reputation for peace and quietude.

In *Albertson v. Commonwealth*, 312 Ky. 68, 226 S.W.2d 523 (1950), the defendant, under charge of murder, introduced witnesses who testified to his good reputation for peace and quietude. The witnesses were asked on cross-examination if they knew the defendant had engaged in the illegal traffic of whisky. This was held to be reversible error on the ground that a responsive answer to the question would have had no bearing on defendant's reputation for peace and quietude.

Although we are of the opinion the practice should be indulged in cautiously and that the rule should be kept within strict limitations, it seems to us that a conviction for drunken driving, or reckless driving, or disorderly conduct has some reasonable connection with a man's reputation for peace and quietude. In the legal sense, peace and quietude signify obedience to law, public quiet, good order and tranquility. A jury might reasonably infer that a propensity to drunken driving, reckless driving, or disorderly conduct is evidence of an attitude of disrespect for the law inconsistent with a good reputation for peace and quietude. It should be kept in mind that such evidence is never competent unless the defendant himself puts his reputation in issue; and even then it is competent only for the purpose of testing the witness' credibility, and not as substantive evidence. It is noted that proper admonition to this effect was given by the trial judge in this case. We conclude that the court properly permitted the attorney for the state to ask the defendant's character witnesses whether they had heard reports of his previous conviction for drunken driving, reckless driving, or disorderly conduct....

[The Court reversed the judgment on other grounds.]

Problem 5-1

After a tax rebate check was stolen from a post office, suspicion turned to postal employee Erica Hill. Hill was aware that she was under investigation but was allowed to keep her job until the investigation was completed. In order to determine if she was the thief, postal inspectors placed three "test letters" containing money in a bin of letters that Hill was processing. Hill properly processed each test letter and did not steal them.

At her trial, Hill sought to prove her law-abidingness by offering proof that she did not steal any of the test letters. Is this evidence admissible?

Problem 5-2

Two young men entered a bar shortly before midnight. Soon thereafter, one of the young men got in a heated argument with two older men at the bar and was forced to leave by the bar's owner. His friend left with him, and the two young men waited outside in the darkness for the two older men. About forty-five minutes later, the two older men left the bar and proceeded to a waiting car. Immediately thereafter, the bar proprietor, still inside, heard two shots. He rushed to the door and witnessed a young man firing a third shot into the back of the car. The two older men were later found dead in the front seats of the vehicle.

Defendant Allan Peterson was identified as the shooter and charged with homicide. At his trial, Peterson presented an alibi witness, Rios, who claimed that he was with Peterson on the night of the murders. Rios said that he and Allan had baked bread together that night and then gone to bed early. Rios testified that they were baking special Rastafarian bread and that in fact he and Allan knew each other because they were both Rastafarians. In response to questioning, Rios also explained that the Rastafarian religion was peaceful and rejected violence.

The prosecution objected to the testimony and the judge struck it from the record. Peterson was convicted and now appeals. He argues that Rios' testimony was wrongfully excluded, and that it should have been admitted as evidence of his peaceful character under Rule 404(a). The issue is now before you. How do you rule?

Problem 5-3

In 2004, the Washington D.C. police became aware of a peculiar example of urban entrepreneurship—the drive by drug bazaar. Something like a drug drive-through, the enterprise functioned through use of a wholesaler (the "bagman"), one or more retail clerks who handle individual transactions ("runners"), and numerous customers who wait in vehicles, engines running, while their drugs are delivered. One evening shortly after discovering the existence of the drug enterprise, police apprehended Antonio Roundtree—one of the alleged "runners"—as he left the hub of the operation. Although Roundtree did not have drugs on him when arrested, officers found drugs hidden behind a tree behind which he had been hiding.

At trial, Roundtree argued that he had no drugs on him the night of his arrest and no plans to distribute drugs later that evening. To prove his case he introduced the testimony of his girlfriend, who was also the mother of his son. She testified generally about what Roundtree had done the day he was arrested, explaining that Roundtree had dropped off their son at her house because "Antonio keeps our child, he always keeps him during the day, and then he drops him off and we all have dinner together in the evenings." The drop off of his son would have occurred right before the arrest, and Roundtree argues that his girlfriend's testimony supports his contention that he had no drugs at the time nor intent to possess them later.

The prosecution has moved to exclude the testimony pursuant to 404(a). Roundtree reiterates that the testimony 1) establishes that he did not have drugs that night nor did he have the demeanor of a drug dealer and 2) establishes his character for "law abidingness" because it shows him to be a committed family man and father.

The issue is now before you. How do you rule?

Focus Questions: *United States v. Gilliland*

- When does one become a character witness? What form must a witness' testimony about the defendant take for it to be considered affirmative character evidence testimony?

United States v. Gilliland

586 F.2d 1384 (10th Cir. 1978)

LOGAN, Circuit Judge.

This is an appeal from a jury conviction of Roy Valentine Gilliland for transportation of a stolen automobile across state lines in violation of the Dyer Act, 18 U.S.C. s 2312.

The issues upon appeal relate to the propriety of certain questions asked of Gilliland's stepson, Billy Tull, who appeared as a defense witness, concerning criminal convictions of Gilliland 14 to 34 years prior to the offense involved in this trial.

The federal prosecutors presented their case based principally upon stopping defendant near Guymon, Oklahoma while he was driving a vehicle stolen a few hours earlier in Dumas, Texas. The totality of the government's evidence was ample to support the jury conviction, in the absence of the error discussed herein. The defense was that Gilliland did not steal the car, but bought it on approval from a purported car salesman in a bar in Oklahoma, with a portion of the consideration being repayment of a gambling debt owed by the salesman to Gilliland. Defendant's stepson Billy Tull was a defense witness presented as one who had been present at the transfer and who had personally observed much of the paper work in the exchange of title. After Tull had so testified the government attorney initiated his cross-examination as follows:

Q How long have you known this Defendant, your step father?

A Approximately 11 years.

Q As I understand it, you are telling the ladies and gentlemen of the Jury, he is just the kind of man that would not do this thing; is that right?

A Yes, sir.

Q He is the kind of man who would not steal a car and take it across the state line; it is that correct?

A Yes, sir.

Q And he is certainly the kind of man who would not forge items like you have in front of you there; is that correct?

A Yes, sir.

Q He just wouldn't do that?

A No, sir.

MR. MILLER: May I approach the bench if the Court please?

FOLLOWING PROCEEDINGS HELD AT BENCH OUT OF THE HEARING OF THE JURY:

MR. MILLER: I have got two things to advise the Court. I am going to ask this man about his step father's criminal record because he has been convicted twice of the Dyer Act. He has been convicted twice of Forgery. He has been convicted more times of that. I want to ask him about those particular convictions. Some of these convictions are more than ten years old.... I wanted to clear it with the Court.

THE COURT: You may do so over the objection of the Defendant.

(Following proceedings held in Open Court)

THE COURT: Go ahead, Mr. Miller.

Q (By Mr. Miller) Mr. Tull, did you know that your step father in 1942 in Del Rio, Texas, in the Federal Court there was convicted of the Dyer Act, which is transporting motor vehicles across the state line, and was sentenced to two years in the Federal Reformatory?

A I knew he had been in prison, but I did not know why.

Q Mr. Tull, did you know that your step father in October of 1961 was convicted of Dyer Act, which is transporting a motor vehicle across the state line in Los Angeles, California, and was sentenced to five years in the Federal Penitentiary?

A No, sir, I did not know about that.

Q Mr. Tull, did you know that your step father was convicted in November of 1950 in Sacramento, California, of two separate counts of Forgery and was convicted and sentenced to a term of 1 to 14 years on each one of those counts?

A No, sir.

Q Mr. Tull, did you know that your step father was convicted in February of 1962 of Interstate Transportation of Forged Securities in Federal Court in Fort Worth, Texas that is wrong. It would have been in California that he was convicted, but he was sentenced at that time to another five years in the Federal Reformatory and he was in a Reformatory in Fort Worth, Texas. Did you know that?

A No, sir.

Q Now let me ask you this: Do you think your step father is capable of stealing cars and taking them across the state line?

A Sir, for the 11 years that I have known him, I would say no.

Q Do you think your step father is capable of forging documents like you have got right there in front of you?

A I would say no....

I

The government attempts to justify its inquiry into the criminal convictions on grounds that Tull was testifying as to the character of the defendant. The general rule is, "Evidence of other crimes, wrongs, or acts is not admissible to prove the character of a person in order to show that he acted in conformity therewith." Fed.R.Evid. 404(b). The rationale for this exclusionary rule is well-stated by Mr. Justice Jackson in *Michelson v. United States*, 335 U.S. 469, 475–476 (1948):

> Courts that follow the common-law tradition almost unanimously have come to disallow resort by the prosecution to any kind of evidence of a defendant's evil character to establish a probability of his guilt. Not that the law invests the defendant with a presumption of good character, but it simply closes the whole matter of character, disposition and reputation on the prosecution's case-in-chief. The state may not show defendant's prior trouble with the law, specific criminal acts, or ill name among his neighbors, even though such facts might logically be persuasive that he is by propensity a probable perpetrator of the crime. The inquiry is not rejected because character is irrelevant; on the contrary, it is said to weigh too much with the jury and to so overpersuade them as to prejudge one with a bad general record and deny him a fair opportunity to defend against a particular charge. The overriding policy is excluding such evidence, despite its admitted probative value, is the practical experience that its disallowance tends to prevent confusion of issues, unfair surprise and undue prejudice.

The accused defendant may make character an issue, however, for the reasons also outlined in the *Michelson* case:

> But this line of inquiry firmly denied to the State is opened to the defendant because character is relevant in resolving probabilities of guilt. He may introduce affirmative testimony that the general estimate of his character is so favorable that the jury may infer that he would not be likely to commit the offense charged. This privilege is sometimes valuable to a defendant for this Court has held that such testimony alone, in some circumstances, may be enough to raise a reasonable doubt of guilt and that in the federal courts a jury in a proper case should be so instructed.

335 U.S. at 476.

If the defendant utilizes a character witness then the government may cross-examine or introduce evidence of prior convictions to rebut the defense evidence of good character. Fed.R.Evid. 404(a)(1), 405(a). The judge, of course, has a duty of continuing surveillance as to whether the evidence's prejudicial effect outweighs its probative value [pursuant to Rule 403]. We do not need to discuss application of Rule 403 here, however, because Billy Tull was not a character witness. His entire testimony on direct examination was as purported eyewitness to the purchase of the automobile. The government may not turn him into a character witness by asking him what kind of a man defendant was, and then use those questions to bootstrap into the case evidence of defendant's prior convictions which it was prohibited from using in its case-in-chief....

The judgment of the district court is reversed, and the cause is remanded for a new trial.

Problem 5-4

Frank McLister and three co-defendants were charged with selling a pound of cocaine to an undercover police officer. McLister did not deny his participation or his knowledge that the sale involved cocaine. Rather, he contended that he lacked the requisite criminal intent. More specifically, McLister testified that he thought two of his co-defendants were acting as undercover agents for the Denver Police and that he reluctantly agreed to assist them in arranging for the arrest of a narcotics trafficker. McLister testified further that the cocaine belonged to one of his co-defendants.

In his opening statement, McLister's counsel told the jury that McLister was engaged in the antique business, had purchased property in Colorado and intended to go into the hydroponics business, and came from "what may be called a relatively privileged background" with no need to get into any illegal business. McLister testified regarding his property interests and his intention of going into the hydroponics business.

Based on the testimony and counsel's opening statement, the prosecutor argued that the defendant had opened the door to his character by characterizing himself as someone who would not use drugs. The prosecutor then sought to introduce evidence of a prior misdemeanor conviction for possession of marijuana on the cross-examination of the defendant. Is the conviction admissible?

Problem 5-5

Thomas Silverstein, an inmate in Illinois, was on trial for killing a corrections officer. On his direct examination, he testified that he killed the corrections officer because that officer was planning to let other inmates out of their cells to kill Silverstein. He also testified that he had previously been convicted of two murders. On cross-examination, he stated that he had not been "out to hurt anybody or anything." During cross-examination, the prosecutor went into greater detail about his prior convictions: "March 3rd, 1980, United States Penitentiary at Leavenworth, you killed an inmate, didn't you? . . . . You are a peaceable man?" Silverstein answered, "I like to think so."

The prosecutor claims that the defendant opened the door to his character and that his line of inquiry on cross-examination was proper. Was this line of inquiry on cross-examination proper?

Problem 5-6

Oscar Saenz invited two friends to his home. While there they drank heavily and took extensive prescription pain medication. Under the influence of drugs and alcohol, Saenz and one of his friends erupted in several confrontations throughout the day, one of which culminated in a physical fight at Saenz's house. After the men struggled for some time, Saenz eventually chased his friend from his house, hitting him continuously. At some point — though Saenz cannot recall this — Saenz apparently hit his friend with a rock, seriously wounding him. Saenz's friend sustained considerable injuries, and the government eventually filed charges against Saenz for assault with a deadly weapon.

At trial Saenz argued self-defense. To prove his case, he sought to demonstrate reasonable fear of his friend by introducing evidence that he knew the victim had been carrying brass knuckles earlier that day and that the victim had recently attempted to inflict severe physical injury on a relative who had slighted him. Saenz emphasized that he knew this information due to their friendship and time spent together leading up to the unfortunate encounter.

The prosecution has moved to exclude the evidence under 404(a). The issue is now before you. How do you rule?

II. FRE 413–415: Sexual Assault and Child Molestation

Relevant Rules
FRE 413

Similar Crimes in Sexual-Assault Cases

(a) Permitted Uses. In a criminal case in which a defendant is accused of a sexual assault, the court may admit evidence that the defendant committed any other sexual assault. The evidence may be considered on any matter to which it is relevant.

(b) Disclosure to the Defendant. If the prosecutor intends to offer this evidence, the prosecutor must disclose it to the defendant, including witnesses' statements or a summary of the expected testimony. The prosecutor must do so at least 15 days before trial or at a later time that the court allows for good cause.

(c) Effect on Other Rules. This rule does not limit the admission or consideration of evidence under any other rule.

(d) Definition of "Sexual Assault." In this rule and Rule 415, "sexual assault" means a crime under federal law or under state law (as "state" is defined in 18 U.S.C. § 513) involving:

> **(1)** any conduct prohibited by 18 U.S.C. chapter 109A;

> **(2)** contact, without consent, between any part of the defendant's body — or an object — and another person's genitals or anus;

> **(3)** contact, without consent, between the defendant's genitals or anus and any part of another person's body;

> **(4)** deriving sexual pleasure or gratification from inflicting death, bodily injury, or physical pain on another person; or

> **(5)** an attempt or conspiracy to engage in conduct described in paragraphs (1)–(4).

FRE 414

Similar Crimes in Child-Molestation Cases

(a) Permitted Uses. In a criminal case in which a defendant is accused of child molestation, the court may admit evidence that the defendant committed any other child molestation. The evidence may be considered on any matter to which it is relevant.

(b) Disclosure to the Defendant. If the prosecutor intends to offer this evidence, the prosecutor must disclose it to the defendant, including witnesses' statements or a summary of the expected testimony. The prosecutor must do so at least 15 days before trial or at a later time that the court allows for good cause.

(c) Effect on Other Rules. This rule does not limit the admission or consideration of evidence under any other rule.

(d) Definition of "Child" and "Child Molestation."

In this rule and Rule 415:

> **(1)** "child" means a person below the age of 14; and

> **(2)** "child molestation" means a crime under federal law or under state law (as "state" is defined in 18 U.S.C. § 513) involving:

(A) any conduct prohibited by 18 U.S.C. chapter 109A and committed with a child;

(B) any conduct prohibited by 18 U.S.C. chapter 110;

(C) contact between any part of the defendant's body — or an object — and a child's genitals or anus;

(D) contact between the defendant's genitals or anus and any part of a child's body;

(E) deriving sexual pleasure or gratification from inflicting death, bodily injury, or physical pain on a child; or

(F) an attempt or conspiracy to engage in conduct described in paragraphs (A)–(E).

FRE 415

Similar Acts in Civil Cases Involving Sexual Assault or Child Molestation

(a) Permitted Uses. In a civil case involving a claim for relief based on a party's alleged sexual assault or child molestation, the court may admit evidence that the party committed any other sexual assault or child molestation. The evidence may be considered as provided in Rules 413 and 414.

(b) Disclosure to the Opponent. If a party intends to offer this evidence, the party must disclose it to the party against whom it will be offered, including witnesses' statements or a summary of the expected testimony. The party must do so at least 15 days before trial or at a later time that the court allows for good cause.

(c) Effect on Other Rules. This rule does not limit the admission or consideration of evidence under any other rule.

Overview Problem

Dirk is currently facing charges for raping Johanna. It is alleged that Dirk stopped his car next to Johanna's car after her car broke down. Dirk had never met Johanna before, but he offered her a ride to a gas station to find a mechanic. Once Johanna was in the car, he took her to a deserted field, bound her with rope, and raped her. The prosecution seeks to offer the testimony of Belinda at Dirk's trial. Belinda will testify that she was raped by Dirk fifteen years ago. Belinda had known Dirk for over ten years when the incident occurred. She will testify that Dirk dropped by her house on a social visit, drugged her drink, and proceeded to rape her. She never reported the incident to the police.

Would Belinda's testimony be admissible under FRE 404(b) and/or FRE 413?

Overview: Sexual Offenses and Character-Propensity Evidence

FRE 413, 414, and 415 are "pure" exceptions to the ban on admitting character evidence to prove the propensity of the defendant. Regardless of whether a prior sexual offense was even reported to authorities, specific details of that prior sexual offense are admissible based on purely propensity-based logic — you may use a fact that a defendant once committed a sexual offense to prove that he committed the sexual offense for which he is on trial. The evidence is admissible "on any matter to which it is relevant," and the presumption is in favor of admission. The prosecution is also afforded a great deal of freedom in presenting this evidence: they may open the door to the proof and may offer specific instances of sexual assault on direct examination of a witness. In terms of the other sexual assault, there is no requirement that a criminal charge was ever filed, and whether the other sexual assault occurred is a conditional relevance question governed by the relatively lenient *Huddleston* standard (i.e., could a reasonable jury find by a preponderance of the evidence that the prior sexual assault occurred?).

These rules were controversial when passed and remain controversial today. The Judicial Conference, the American Bar Association, and many academics strongly opposed these rules when they were before Congress. Many objected on the grounds previously discussed when we reviewed FRE 404(b). Certainly a high risk of "overpersuading" the jury exists when they are informed that the defendant on trial for a sexual offense had previously committed a sexual offense. Likewise, the risk of a preventative conviction exists—perhaps members of the jury will want to punish the defendant for the previous sexual offense no matter how the evidence presented in the current case unfolds.

Other concerns about the rules emerged as well. Are these rules truly necessary when FRE 404(b) exists? After all, if the prior rape or child molestation helped to prove identity, motive or knowledge, why not rely on the existing rule rather than fashion a broader rule? One response to this argument is that FRE 404(b) will not allow evidence of a prior sexual offense in many cases. For example, in the overview problem, the alleged incidents are not similar; Johanna was a stranger forcibly bound and raped while Belinda is an acquaintance who was drugged. Does the prior incident prove identity, modus operandi, or plan? It is unlikely it would be allowed on these grounds, and, therefore, a court will likely find it to be inadmissible character-propensity evidence under FRE 404(b).

Furthermore, if FRE 413, 414, and 415 were necessary precisely because the drafters of those rules wanted broader admissibility for sexual crimes, is the probative value of the evidence sufficiently compelling to justify this exception? Does empirical evidence sufficiently justify a recidivism rate for sexual crimes that makes it more predictive of future behavior than other crimes, such as drug possession crimes? Studies have demonstrated that the propensity of sex offenders to commit another sex offense is high. When one factors in the fact that many sexual offenses go unreported, the likely recidivism rate is probably even higher.

In the end, Congress passed the rules based on the belief that prior sexual crime evidence is exceptionally probative. Furthermore, the difficulty of proving sexual assault cases adds another rationale: the victim's testimony may need bolstering. A sexual assault trial often boils down to a battle of credibility between the defendant and alleged victim with little physical corroborative evidence (especially in cases where the defendant claims consent on the part of the alleged victim). This is especially the case in child molestation prosecutions, as a child witness may face numerous attacks on his or her credibility due to the child's age. Additionally, jurors may hold stereotypes that may lead them to discount a victim's story, and these rules allow a direct challenge to those stereotypes.

Returning to the overview problem, we see that the evidence will likely be admissible under FRE 413. Belinda's evidence likely meets the *Huddleston* test, and it does not matter that Dirk was never charged for the crime. But what about the unfair prejudice to Dirk? Should FRE 403 keep out this evidence that occurred fifteen years ago, was not brought to police attention, and was dissimilar to the sexual assault on Johanna? Should FRE 403 even apply? Should specialized factors govern its application in this context? The next two cases will explore these issues.

Focus Questions: *United States v. LeCompte*

- Does the court use a strict or lenient gauge in deciding whether prejudice to the defendant is "substantial" enough for inadmissibility?
- What factors does the court use in its FRE 403 analysis? To which does the court give the most weight?

United States v. LeCompte
131 F.3d 767 (8th Cir. 1997)

RICHARD S. ARNOLD, Chief Judge.

Before the trial of Leo LeCompte for the alleged sexual abuse of his wife's 11-year-old niece, "C.D.," under 18 U.S.C. §§ 2244(a)(1) and 2246(3) (1994), the defendant moved in limine to exclude evidence of prior uncharged sex offenses against another niece by marriage, "T.T." The government argued that the evidence was admissible under Federal Rule of Evidence 414 (Evidence of Similar Crimes in Child Molestation Cases). The District Court excluded the evidence under Rule 403. The government appeals this evidentiary ruling.... We reverse and hold that the motion in limine should not have been granted. We do so in order to give effect to the decision of Congress, expressed in recently enacted Rule 414, to loosen to a substantial degree the restrictions of prior law on the admissibility of such evidence.

I.

LeCompte is charged with child sex offenses allegedly committed in January 1995. According to the victim C.D., prior to January 1995, LeCompte had played games with her at her aunt's trailer and had exposed himself to her on at least one occasion. The actual incidents of molestation allegedly occurred while she was lying on a couch at her aunt's, with her siblings sleeping on the floor next to her. LeCompte allegedly joined her on the couch, forced her to touch his penis, and touched her breasts.

The government offered evidence of sex offenses committed by LeCompte against a niece of his first wife during that marriage, between 1985 and 1987. This niece, T.T., would testify that LeCompte had played games with her at her aunt's house, had exposed himself to her, had forced her to touch his penis, and had touched her private parts.

The admissibility of T.T.'s testimony has been considered by this Court once before. In LeCompte's first trial, the government offered the evidence under Rule 404(b). It was not then able to offer the evidence under Rule 414 because of its failure to provide timely notice of the offer, as required by Rule 414. The District Court admitted the evidence, and the jury convicted LeCompte. On appeal, this Court held that the District Court's admission of the evidence under Rule 404(b) was improper, and reversed LeCompte's conviction. We now consider the admissibility of T.T.'s testimony in LeCompte's retrial, under Rule 414, the government having given timely notice the second time around.

II.

On remand, LeCompte moved in limine to exclude the evidence. The District Court ruled that T.T.'s testimony was potentially admissible under Rule 414, but excluded by Rule 403. It noted that although the evidence's only relevance was as to LeCompte's propensity to commit child sexual abuse, Rule 414 expressly allowed its use on that basis. The Court then turned to a Rule 403 analysis of the evidence. As to the evidence's probative value, the Court recognized the similarities between C.D.'s and T.T.'s accounts: they were both young nieces of LeCompte at the time he molested them, he forced them both to touch him, he touched them both in similar places, and he exposed himself to both of them. The Court found that the evidence's probative value was limited, however, by several differences. First, the acts allegedly committed against C.D. occurred with her siblings present, while the acts against T.T. occurred in isolation. Second, LeCompte had not played games with C.D. immediately before molesting her, as he had with T.T. Finally, the acts against C.D. and T.T. were separated by a period of eight years. The District Court concluded that the probative value of T.T.'s testimony was limited.

On the other hand, it found that the risk of unfair prejudice was high, reasoning that "T.T.'s testimony is obviously highly prejudicial evidence against defendant.... 'child sexual abuse deservedly carries a unique stigma in our society; such highly prejudicial evidence should therefore carry a very high degree of probative value if it is to be admitted.'" The Court therefore excluded the evidence under Rule 403.

III.

.... Rule 414 and its companion rules—Rule 413 (Evidence of Similar Crimes in Sexual Assault Cases), and Rule 415 (Evidence of Similar Acts in Civil Cases Concerning Sexual Assault or Molestation)—are "general rules of admissibility in sexual assault and child molestation cases for evidence that the defendant has committed offenses of the same type on other occasions.... The new rules will supersede in sex offense cases the restrictive aspects of Federal Rule of Evidence 404(b)." 140 Cong. Rec. H8992 (daily ed. Aug. 21, 1994) (statement of Rep. Molinari).

Evidence offered under Rule 414 is still subject to the requirements of Rule 403. This Court has recognized that evidence otherwise admissible under Rule 414 may be excluded under Rule 403's balancing test. However, Rule 403 must be applied to allow Rule 414 its intended effect.

We review the District Court's application of Rule 403 for abuse of discretion. In light of the strong legislative judgment that evidence of prior sexual offenses should ordinarily be admissible, we think the District Court erred in its assessment that the probative value of T.T.'s testimony was substantially outweighed by the danger of unfair prejudice. The sexual offenses committed against T.T. were substantially similar to those allegedly committed against C.D. By comparison, the differences were small. In particular, the District Court itself acknowledged that the time lapse between incidents "may not be as significant as it appears at first glance, because defendant was imprisoned for a portion of the time between 1987 and 1995, which deprived defendant of the opportunity to abuse any children."

Moreover, the danger of unfair prejudice noted by the District Court was that presented by the "unique stigma" of child sexual abuse, on account of which LeCompte might be convicted not for the charged offense, but for his sexual abuse of T.T. This danger is one that all propensity evidence in such trials presents. It is for this reason that the evidence was previously excluded, and it is precisely such holdings that Congress intended to overrule. Compare *United States v. Fawbush*, 900 F.2d 150 (8th Cir.1990) (prior acts of child sexual abuse inadmissible to show propensity under Rule 404(b)). On balance, then, we hold that the motion in limine should not have been granted.

The order of the District Court is reversed, and the cause remanded for further proceedings not inconsistent with this opinion.

Focus Questions: *United States v. Guardia*

- What, if any, common techniques of analysis are shared by both the court in *Guardia* and the court in *LeCompte*?

- In the *Guardia* jurisdiction, is the court stricter or more lenient in balancing the prejudice of evidence?

- What factors does the court use in its FRE 403 analysis? To which factors does the court give more weight?

- How strongly does the court weigh jury confusion? Can jury confusion be mitigated?

United States v. Guardia
135 F.3d 1326 (10th Cir. 1998)

TACHA, Circuit Judge.

On September 5, 1996, a federal grand jury in New Mexico returned an indictment charging defendant David Guardia with two counts of sexual abuse.... In addition, the grand jury charged the defendant under the Assimilative Crimes Statute with two counts of criminal sexual penetration ... and two counts of battery.... These charges arose from the defendant's allegedly improper behavior during gynecological exams he performed at Kirtland Air Force Base in October and November of 1995. Dr. Guardia moved *in limine* to exclude evidence proffered by the United States under Federal Rule of Evidence 413. The district court granted Dr. Guardia's motion, finding under Federal Rule of Evidence 403 that the risk of jury confusion substantially outweighed the probative value of the Rule 413 evidence....

BACKGROUND

The indictment is based upon the complaints of two alleged victims who contend that Dr. Guardia sexually abused them in the course of gynecological procedures that he conducted at Kirtland. Both complainants, Carla G. and Francesca L., allege that during an examination Dr. Guardia engaged in direct clitoral contact that exceeded the bounds of medically appropriate examination techniques and constituted sexual abuse. Francesca L. alleges that Dr. Guardia demonstrated the sexual nature of his conduct by stating "I love my job" during the examination. In addition, Carla G. alleges that Dr. Guardia called her at home and performed other acts suggesting his sexual interest in her. Neither of the examinations occurred in the presence of a chaperon.

In addition to offering the testimony of Carla G. and Francesca L., the government moved to introduce, under Rule 413, the testimony of four women who allege that Dr. Guardia abused them during gynecological examinations in a manner similar to the alleged abuse of Carla G. and Francesca L. For example, two of the four additional witnesses also complained of excessive, direct clitoral contact, and one complained of similarly suggestive comments. On the other hand, the testimony of Carla G. and Francesca L. differs significantly in some respects from the testimony of the Rule 413 witnesses. For instance, one of the witnesses complains that Dr. Guardia improperly touched her breasts, not her pelvic area. Another complains of the defendant's use of a medical instrument, not his hands. Chaperons were present during the examination of two of the four Rule 413 witnesses. All six women had extraordinary gynecological problems that appeared to require different courses of treatment and examination....

DISCUSSION

Congress recently enacted Federal Rule of Evidence 413, along with Rules 414 and 415, as part of the Violent Crime Control and Law Enforcement Act of 1994, Pub.L. No. 103-322, tit. XXXII, § 320935(a), 108 Stat. 1796, 2136 (1994). This case presents important questions regarding the way in which Rule 413 interacts with Rule 403....

I. Requirements of Rule 413

... [E]vidence offered under Rule 413 must meet three threshold requirements before a district court can admit it. A district court must first determine that "the defendant is accused of an offense of sexual assault." Second, the court must find that the evidence proffered is "evidence of the defendant's commission of another offense of ... sexual assault." Fed.R.Evid. 413(a). The district court implicitly recognized these requirements in its hearing on the motion *in limine* and in its written opinion.

The third requirement, applicable to all evidence, is that the evidence be relevant. *See* Fed.R.Evid. 402 ("Evidence which is not relevant is not admissible."). The rules define relevant evidence as evidence that "ha[s] any tendency to make the existence of any fact that is of consequence to the determination of the action more probable or less probable than it would be without the evidence." Fed.R.Evid. 401. A defendant with a propensity to commit acts similar to the charged crime is more likely to have committed the charged crime than another. Evidence of such a propensity is therefore relevant. *See Old Chief v. United States,* 519 U.S. 172, 181 ("Propensity evidence is relevant...."); *Michelson v. United States,* 335 U.S. 469, 475–76 (1948) (noting the "admitted probative value" of propensity evidence).

In most cases, though not in Rule 413 cases, the court must exclude propensity evidence despite its acknowledged relevance. Rule 404(b) prohibits the use of prior acts of a person "to prove the character of a person in order to show action in conformity therewith." Fed.R.Evid. 404(b). Under Rule 413, however, evidence of a defendant's other sexual assaults may be admitted "for its bearing on *any* matter to which it is relevant." Fed.R.Evid. 413 (emphasis added). Thus, Rule 413 supersedes Rule 404(b)'s restriction and allows the government to offer evidence of a defendant's prior conduct for the purpose of demonstrating a defendant's propensity to commit the charged offense....

... If believed, the Rule 413 evidence in this case would demonstrate that the defendant has a propensity to take advantage of female patients by touching them in a salacious manner and making comments while doing so. Because the defendant's propensity is to engage in conduct which closely matches that alleged in this case, the evidence is probative of his guilt.... The evidence proffered in this case, therefore, satisfies Rule 413's three threshold requirements.

II. The Applicability of Rule 403

... Rule 403 applies to all evidence admitted in federal court, except in those rare instances when other rules make an exception to it. *See, e.g.,* Fed.R.Evid. 609(a)(2) (mandating that prior conviction of a witness be admitted for impeachment purposes if prior crime involved dishonesty).

The wording of Rule 413 has led some commentators to infer that it creates an exception for itself to the Rule 403 balancing test. Rule 413 states that evidence meeting its criteria "is admissible." Fed.R.Evid. 413. Rule 412, on the other hand, which also allows evidence of prior sexual behavior, states that certain evidence "is admissible, *if otherwise admissible under these rules.*" Fed.R.Evid. 412(b) (emphasis added). One could assume from this fact that because the emphasized clause does not appear in Rule 413, Congress intended to make the introduction of Rule 413 evidence mandatory rather than subject to the discretion of the trial judge under Rule 403. *See* Judicial Conference of the United States, *Report of the Judicial Conference on the Admission of Character Evidence in Certain Sexual Misconduct Cases,* 159 F.R.D. 51, 53 (1995) (noting that the advisory committee believed the above position to be "arguable").

The other rules, however, demonstrate that the difference between Rule 412 and Rule 413 is not significant. Most importantly, Rule 402, the rule allowing admission of all relevant evidence and a rule to which the 403 balancing test undoubtedly applies, contains language no more explicit than that in Rule 413. The rule states simply that "[a]ll relevant evidence *is admissible.*" Fed.R.Evid. 402 (emphasis added). Furthermore, when the drafters of the federal rules of evidence alter the 403 balancing test or make it inapplicable to certain evidence, they use language much more explicit than that found in Rule 413. *See, e.g.,* Fed.R.Evid. 609(a)(2) (stating that convictions involving dishonesty "shall be admitted" for impeachment purposes); Fed.R.Evid. 609(a)(1) (requiring court to find that the probative value of a prior conviction outweighs its prejudicial effect on the accused).

Thus, in *United States v. Meacham,* 115 F.3d 1488, 1495 (10th Cir.1997), we found that evidence proffered under Rule 414, which concerns prior acts of child molestation and uses language identical to Rule 413, is subject to Rule 403 balancing. Following *Meacham,* and for the above reasons, we hold that the 403 balancing test applies to Rule 413 evidence.

III. The 403 Balancing Test and Rule 413

In accordance with the above, after the district court resolves the three threshold issues, including a finding that the proffered evidence is relevant, it must proceed to balance the probative weight of the Rule 413 evidence against "the danger of unfair prejudice, confusion of the issues, or misleading the jury, or ... considerations of undue delay, waste of time, or needless presentation of cumulative evidence." Fed.R.Evid. 403. We hold that a court must perform the same 403 analysis that it does in any other context, but with careful attention to both the significant probative value and the strong prejudicial qualities inherent in all evidence submitted under 413.

A. Legal Principles

Rule 413 marks a sea change in the federal rules' approach to character evidence, a fact which could lead to at least two different misapplications of the 403 balancing test. First, a court could be tempted to exclude the Rule 413 evidence simply because character evidence traditionally has been considered too prejudicial for admission. Second, a court could perform a restrained 403 analysis because of the belief that Rule 413 embodies a legislative judgment that propensity evidence regarding sexual assaults is never too prejudicial or confusing and generally should be admitted. *See United States v. LeCompte,* 131 F.3d 767, 769–70 (8th Cir.1997).

We find both interpretations illogical. With regard to the first position, we note that this court refrains from construing the words and phrases of a statute—or entire statutory provisions—in a way that renders them superfluous. Rule 413 allows for evidence that otherwise would be excluded to be admitted. If Rule 413 evidence were always too prejudicial under 403, Rule 413 would never lead to the introduction of evidence. Therefore, Rule 413 only has effect if we interpret it in a way that leaves open the possibility of admission.

This interpretation harmonizes with the Supreme Court's comment in *Old Chief* and similar statements in the advisory committee's notes to Rules 401 and 403 that the ban on character evidence is merely an application of Rule 403 to a recurring issue. *See Old Chief,* 519 U.S. at 182. All of the rules in Article IV of the Federal Rules of Evidence, not just Rule 404, are "concrete applications [of rules 402 and 403] evolved for particular situations." Fed.R.Evid. 403 advisory committee's note. The fact that Congress created Rule 413 can only mean that Congress intended to partially repeal the "concrete application" found in 404(b) for a subset of cases in which Congress found 404(b)'s rigid rule to be inappropriate. That conclusion is not surprising, given the fact that propensity evidence has a unique probative value in sexual assault trials and that such trials often suffer from a lack of any relevant evidence beyond the testimony of the alleged victim and the defendant. Rule 413 is a refinement, and it exemplifies the type of evolution of Rules 402 and 403 that one can expect to find in Article IV.

While Rule 413 removes the per se exclusion of character evidence, courts should continue to consider the traditional reasons for the prohibition of character evidence as "risks of prejudice" weighing against admission. For example, a court should, in each 413 case, take into account the chance that "a jury will convict for crimes other than those charged—or that, uncertain of guilt, it will convict anyway because a bad person deserves punishment." *Old Chief,* 519 U.S. at 181. A court should also be aware that evidence of prior acts can have the effect of confusing the issues in a case. These risks will be present every time evidence is admitted under Rule 413. The size of the risk, of course, will depend on the individual case.

With regard to the second potential misapplication of Rule 413, the government urges us to approve a lenient 403 balancing test. We agree that Rule 413, like all other rules of admissibility, favors the introduction of evidence. *See* 140 Cong. Rec. H8968-01, H8991 (Aug. 21, 1994) (statement of S. Molinari) ("The presumption is in favor of admission."). Rule 413, however, contains no language that supports an especially lenient application of Rule 403. Furthermore, courts apply Rule 403 in undiluted form to Rules 404(a)(1)–(3), the other exceptions to the ban on propensity evidence. Those rules allow a criminal defendant to use character evidence of himself, his victim, or in limited circumstances, of other witnesses, in order to "prov[e] action in conformity therewith." Fed.R.Evid. 404(a)(1–3). Like Rule 413, these rules carve out exceptions to Rule 404(a) and reflect a legislative judgment that certain types of propensity evidence should be admitted. Courts have never found, however, that because the drafters made exceptions to the general rule of 404(a), they tempered 403 as well.

Similarly, under Rule 404(b), evidence of a person's prior acts can be used for other purposes other than proving character. Despite Rule 404(b)'s legislative judgment in favor of admission, Rule 403 applies with all its vigor to Rule 404(b) evidence.

When balancing Rule 413 evidence under 403, then, the district court should not alter its normal process of weighing the probative value of the evidence against the danger of unfair prejudice. In Rule 413 cases, the risk of prejudice will be present to varying degrees. Propensity evidence, however, has indisputable probative value. That value in a given case will depend on innumerable considerations, including the similarity of the prior acts to the acts charged, the closeness in time of the prior acts to the charged acts, the frequency of the prior acts, the presence or lack of intervening events, and the need for evidence beyond the testimony of the defendant and alleged victim. Because of the sensitive nature of the balancing test in these cases, it will be particularly important for a district court to fully evaluate the proffered Rule 413 evidence and make a clear record of the reasoning behind its findings.

B. Balancing in the Present Case

The decision to exclude evidence under Rule 403 is within the sound discretion of the trial court, and will be reversed only upon a showing of a clear abuse of that discretion. During the motion hearing and in its written decision, the district court made clear that its overriding, if not exclusive, concern was the danger that the proffered testimony would confuse the issues in the case, thereby misleading the jury. The district court properly exercised its discretion in determining that the potential for confusion of the issues substantially outweighed the probative value of the proffered testimony.

We must consider the trial court's ruling in light of the unusual nature of this case. This trial undoubtedly will focus upon whether the manner in which Dr. Guardia examined the complaining patients was medically appropriate. Unlike other sexual assault cases, resolution of credibility issues alone will not enable the jury to decide whether Dr. Guardia's act was proper. Rather, the jury will be required to evaluate expert testimony regarding the medical propriety of each examination to determine whether Dr. Guardia acted within the scope of his patients' consent.

Because so much depends upon the medical propriety of Dr. Guardia's conduct towards Carla G. and Francesca L., the fact that Dr. Guardia treated the four additional witnesses under similar but distinct circumstances creates a substantial risk of jury confusion. Admission of the testimony would transform the trial of two incidents into the trial of six incidents, each requiring description by lay witnesses and explanation by expert witnesses. The subtle factual distinctions among these incidents would make it difficult for the jury to separate the evidence of the uncharged conduct from the charged conduct.

Expert testimony explaining the propriety of Dr. Guardia's conduct as to each witness would exacerbate the risk of confusion by multiplying conflicting and overlapping testimony. Although the evidence proffered under Rule 413 is probative of Dr. Guardia's disposition and supports the testimony of the complaining witnesses, we cannot conclude that the district court exceeded the bounds of permissible choice by excluding the evidence under the circumstances of this case.

Finally, we reject the government's contention that the district court erred by failing to engineer a method of presenting the evidence to minimize the risk of jury confusion. In *Hill v. Bache Halsey Stuart Shields Inc.*, 790 F.2d 817, 826–27 (10th Cir.1986), we held that the district court abused its discretion under Rule 403 because it excluded evidence that had a high probative value even though its prejudicial effect could have been minimized through a "less elaborate" method of presentation. In this case, however, the evidence that the district court excluded is not realistically susceptible to any less elaborate presentation than that proposed by the government. Thus, the district court did not abuse its discretion by failing to require such a presentation.

CONCLUSION

… Given the deference due district courts in making Rule 403 determinations, we find that the district court did not abuse its discretion in concluding under Rule 403 that the risk of jury confusion substantially outweighed the probative value of the Rule 413 evidence proffered by the government. Therefore, the decision of the district court is AFFIRMED.

Problem 5-7

Jan was at a graduation party on May 8th. She was drinking alcohol and at some point passed out. She awoke to find Larry holding her down and having sexual intercourse with her. She attempted to stop him but was unsuccessful. The next day, she reported the incident to her school counselor, and Larry was arrested. The government planned to introduce testimonial evidence regarding a similar sexual assault committed by Larry against Shannon approximately three months after he had assaulted Jan.

Should this evidence be admitted?

Problem 5-8

Bob is facing criminal charges for molesting his ten year-old niece, Maya, at a slumber party, while she was sleeping on a couch. Maya's mother, Lana (who is Bob's sister), would like to testify that Bob raped her eleven years ago at a New Year's Eve party, after she had passed out, when Lana was 20 years old. Lana had reported the rape but dropped the charges due to family pressure. Bob objects to the admission of Lana's testimony.

How should the court rule? What are the best arguments for both sides?

Problem 5-9

Ken has been arrested for possession of child pornography and is soon going to trial. The government seeks to introduce evidence of Ken's two year-old conviction for selling child pornography under Chapter 110 of Title 18 of the U.S. Code. Ken files a motion *in limine*, hoping to prevent the prior conviction's admission in court. Ken asserts that prior possession of child pornography cannot constitute evidence of child molestation because there was no actual contact with a child. He also argues that the prior conviction is not relevant.

How should the court rule?

Problem 5-10

Mrs. Martinez was rushed to Mass General Hospital due to a sudden pain she was feeling in her abdomen after her car was rear ended. When she arrived at the hospital she was taken to the Emergency Department and was first seen by Dr. Hongyi Cui. Martinez has alleged that during her medical examination Dr. Cui digitally penetrated her, both vaginally and rectally, against her will. There was no medical reason for the defendant to probe either of these parts of Mrs. Martinez's body. Dr. Cui has denied all of these assertions.

Mrs. Martinez is currently suing Dr. Cui, and defense counsel has impeached Martinez on a number of material inconsistencies within her deposition on cross-examination. Moreover, witnesses to the defendant's treatment of Martinez and the medical forms which Martinez signed corroborate the defendant's story and contradict Martinez's allegations. In an effort to persuade the jury, Mrs. Martinez's lawyers want to introduce a prior civil complaint issued to the appropriate medical board by another woman who six years earlier claimed that Dr. Cui inserted his finger into her vagina during a postoperative exam. The woman who issued the prior civil complaint had surgery for Crohn's disease which had led to medical complications in her vagina and rectum. At the time of this alleged occurrence the woman was heavily sedated and claims to only have felt vaginal penetration. All charges against Dr. Cui as a result of this prior civil complaint were dropped.

How should the court rule?

Professional Development Questions

- Let us conclude our discussion of how to become an expert learner by focusing on reflection. In essence, expert learners evaluate how well they have learned the rules, identify any deficiencies in their studying and plan how they will study more effectively in the future. By doing so, you learn where you may have gone astray and learn how to correct your studying approach.

- One of the difficulties in learning evidence law from a law student's perspective is their unfamiliarity with a trial. It is hard to understand a motive for cross-examination when you have never conducted a cross-examination. As you think about the rules in this chapter and the next one, it will be helpful to try to conduct some mock cross-examinations of witnesses. Your form does not need to perfect. Rather, the act of simulating a trial will help you understand how these rules apply at trial.

- FRE 413–415 remain controversial to this day. Some argue that an exception for sexual offenses goes too far by allowing preventative convictions. After all, once a jury finds out that the defendant committed a sexual offense before, they may be inclined to punish the defendant for that offense. Where do you think the line should be drawn in sexual offense cases? Do FRE 413–415 go too far?

Chapter 6

Impeachment

Overview

Impeachment, simply defined, means to call into question the veracity of a witness. The goal is to show the witness is unworthy of belief. There are two major strategies one may take in impeaching a witness, and within each strategy runs different avenues. The strategy you choose, and the avenue within that strategy that you travel, call different rules and procedures into play. We will begin by outlining those routes and then examine them in depth.

Initially, pay particular attention to the fact that impeachment is always relevant. Anyone who steps onto the witness stand and testifies is open to attack for their truthfulness. Thus, a criminal defendant can be impeached on her truthfulness, as can a character witness.

We will use one broad overview problem throughout this chapter. Let us say you represent the defendant in a car accident case in which the plaintiff claims that your client ran a red light and hit the plaintiff as he was walking across the street. The plaintiff offers a witness, Winnie, who will testify that she saw the entire episode and that your client ran a red light. You now must cross-examine that witness. How will you impeach her?

The first threshold question is whether you aim to cast doubt on her **specific testimony** in the case or whether you aim to cast doubt on **general trustworthiness**. If you take the former track, you are essentially positing that Winnie lied or was mistaken about something specific in her testimony. You are not attacking her truthful character generally, but instead focusing on the specific words she chose and questioning their veracity. If you take the latter track by focusing on general trustworthiness, you are essentially positing that Winnie is a liar by nature, that her ability to tell the truth in general is questionable, and/or that she should not be believed in this instance. In other words, the attack centers not on specific testimony but on her ability to tell the truth. C. Mueller and L. Kirpatrick, Evidence, Section 6.18 at p. 483 (5th ed. 2012).

To cast doubt on the **general trustworthiness** of the witness, you have three options. First, you can argue that she is biased. Second, you can argue that she has a defect in her mental or sensory capacity that would lead her testimony to be false. Finally, you can argue that her very character demonstrates that she is a liar by nature. Under all three avenues, you are arguing that this witness is a person not to be believed.

To cast doubt on her **specific testimony**, you have two options. First, you can point to a prior statement that she made which is inconsistent with her testimony. Second, you can offer proof, through either cross-examination or through other extrinsic evidence (i.e., evidence brought out other than by the witness testifying), that something she testified to was wrong and can be contradicted by other evidence. Under either avenue, you are proving the witness's testimony is inaccurate.

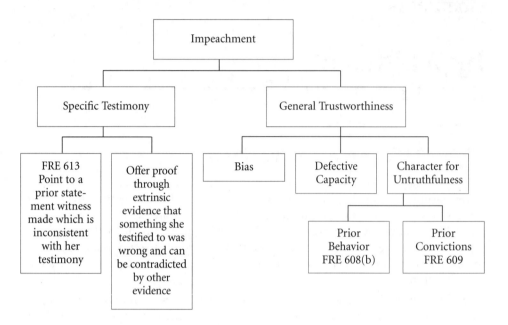

So, now it is time to impeach Winnie and to see how the method we choose affects the evidence we can present.

I. Impeachment by Attacking General Trustworthiness

A. Bias

Overview Problem

Defense Counsel: I'd like to show you exhibit #3. Is this your handwriting?

Winnie: Yes, I wrote this document.

Defense Counsel: Would you read it please?

Winnie: It says: "Dear Plaintiff, I sit behind you in Evidence. I saw your accident and will be willing to testify **very** favorably if you would give me your Evidence outline."

Overview

Bias is a very broad term that reflects an attitude of a witness that might cause her to be more or less favorable to a party for a reason other than the merits. Almost anything that might so sway a party may be introduced as evidence of bias: personal relationships, business relationships, bribes, a financial stake in the outcome of the suit, etc. Although the Federal Rules of Evidence do not expressly provide for impeachment through evidence of bias, it has a long common law history that was reinforced in *U.S. v. Abel*, which we will read shortly. Bias is not considered collateral to the issues at trial and is therefore always relevant. Significantly, you may prove bias through the use of extrinsic evidence. In other words, you are not limited to proving bias through the cross-examination of the witness. You may call another witness, introduce a document that demonstrates bias, or use other extrinsic options to prove the witness is biased.

Thus, in the example above, defense counsel is **not limited to cross-examination** in proving bias. This is an incredibly valuable tool, because if the witness denies being biased, the attorney has options to prove her bias and does not have to accept her word. Defense counsel could therefore introduce into evidence the letter that purports to show bias or could offer other proof of the witness's bias.

There are limits to impeaching through evidence of bias. First, FRE 403 applies to any impeachment via evidence of bias, and therefore any attack with a low probative value will not be allowed. Second, remember that bias is an attack on **general trustworthiness**. Some circumstance is impairing the witness's impartiality. As the Supreme Court stated in *Abel*, bias may cause a witness "to slant, unconsciously or otherwise, his testimony in favor or against a party." 469 U.S. 45, 51 (1984). Thus, introducing evidence of bias is not a character attack in an important sense: you are not claiming that the witness is a liar by their very nature. Instead, you are exploring the circumstances that have the potential to cause this witness to slant their testimony, even if it is unconscious. While the line between acts that indicate bias and acts that indicate a poor character for truthfulness is a blurry one, it is a critical distinction. Attacks based purely on character are more limited in terms of the use of extrinsic evidence, as we shall see in section I.C below. Therefore, focus on specific acts or relationships that **impair impartiality** in order to determine if bias exists.

Focus Questions: *United States v. Abel*

- How does the Court define "bias" and why do they believe it is relevant?

- If a fact does not rise to the level of bias, are there other grounds on which the evidence can be used to impeach?

- In the context of this case, what techniques were available to the Court to prevent undue prejudicial affects on the jury? Do you believe they were effective?

United States v. Abel
469 U.S. 45 (1984)

Justice REHNQUIST delivered the opinion of the Court.

… Respondent John Abel and two cohorts were indicted for robbing a savings and loan in Bellflower, Cal., in violation of 18 U.S.C. §§ 2113(a) and (d). The cohorts elected to plead guilty, but respondent went to trial. One of the cohorts, Kurt Ehle, agreed to testify against respondent and identify him as a participant in the robbery.

Respondent informed the District Court at a pretrial conference that he would seek to counter Ehle's testimony with that of Robert Mills. Mills was not a participant in the robbery but was friendly with respondent and with Ehle, and had spent time with both in prison. Mills planned to testify that after the robbery Ehle had admitted to Mills that Ehle intended to implicate respondent falsely, in order to receive favorable treatment from the Government. The prosecutor in turn disclosed that he intended to discredit Mills' testimony by calling Ehle back to the stand and eliciting from Ehle the fact that respondent, Mills, and Ehle were all members of the "Aryan Brotherhood," a secret prison gang that required its members always to deny the existence of the organization and to commit perjury, theft, and murder on each member's behalf.

Defense counsel objected to Ehle's proffered rebuttal testimony as too prejudicial to respondent. After a lengthy discussion in chambers the District Court decided to permit the prosecutor to cross-examine Mills about the gang, and if Mills denied knowledge of the gang, to introduce Ehle's rebuttal testimony concerning the tenets of the gang and Mills' and respondent's membership in it. The District Court held that the probative value of Ehle's rebuttal testimony outweighed its prejudicial effect, but that respondent might be entitled to a limiting instruction if his counsel would submit one to the court.

At trial Ehle implicated respondent as a participant in the robbery. Mills, called by respondent, testified that Ehle told him in prison that Ehle planned to implicate respondent falsely. When the prosecutor sought to cross-examine Mills concerning membership in the prison gang, the District Court conferred again with counsel outside of the jury's presence, and ordered the prosecutor not to use the term "Aryan Brotherhood" because it was unduly prejudicial. Accordingly, the prosecutor asked Mills if he and respondent were members of a "secret type of prison organization" which had a creed requiring members to deny its existence and lie for each other. When Mills denied knowledge of such an organization the prosecutor recalled Ehle.

Ehle testified that respondent, Mills, and he were indeed members of a secret prison organization whose tenets required its members to deny its existence and "lie, cheat, steal [and] kill" to protect each other. The District Court sustained a defense objection to a question concerning the punishment for violating the organization's rules. Ehle then further described the organization and testified that "in view of the fact of how close Abel and Mills were" it would have been "suicide" for Ehle to have told Mills what Mills attributed to him. Respondent's counsel did not request a limiting instruction and none was given.

The jury convicted respondent. On his appeal a divided panel of the Court of Appeals reversed....

We hold that the evidence showing Mills' and respondent's membership in the prison gang was sufficiently probative of Mills' possible bias towards respondent to warrant its admission into evidence. Thus it was within the District Court's discretion to admit Ehle's testimony, and the Court of Appeals was wrong in concluding otherwise.

Both parties correctly assume, as did the District Court and the Court of Appeals, that the question is governed by the Federal Rules of Evidence. But the Rules do not by their terms deal with impeachment for "bias," although they do expressly treat impeachment by character evidence and conduct, Rule 608, by evidence of conviction of a crime, Rule 609, and by showing of religious beliefs or opinion, Rule 610. Neither party has suggested what significance we should attribute to this fact. Although we are nominally the promulgators of the Rules, and should in theory need only to consult our collective memories to analyze the situation properly, we are in truth merely a conduit when we deal with an undertaking as substantial as the preparation of the Federal Rules of Evidence. In the case of these Rules, too, it must be remembered that Congress extensively reviewed our submission, and considerably revised it.

Before the present Rules were promulgated, the admissibility of evidence in the federal courts was governed in part by statutes or Rules, and in part by case law. This Court had held in *Alford v. United States,* 282 U.S. 687 (1931) that a trial court must allow some cross-examination of a witness to show bias. This holding was in accord with the overwhelming weight of authority in the state courts as reflected in Wigmore's classic treatise on the law of evidence. See *id.* at 691, citing 3 J. Wigmore, Evidence § 1368 (2d ed. 1923)....

With this state of unanimity confronting the drafters of the Federal Rules of Evidence, we think it unlikely that they intended to scuttle entirely the evidentiary availability of cross-examination for bias. One commentator, recognizing the omission of any express treatment of impeachment for bias, prejudice, or corruption, observes that the Rules "clearly contemplate the use of the above-mentioned grounds of impeachment." E. Cleary, McCormick on Evidence § 40, p. 85 (3d ed. 1984). Other commentators, without mentioning the omission, treat bias as a permissible and established basis of impeachment under the Rules. 3 D. Louisell & C. Mueller, Federal Evidence § 341, p. 470 (1979); 3 J. Weinstein & M. Berger, Weinstein's Evidence ¶ 607[03] (1981).

We think this conclusion is obviously correct. Rule 401 defines as "relevant evidence" evidence having any tendency to make the existence of any fact that is of consequence to the determination of the action more probable or less probable than it would be without the evidence. Rule 402 provides that all relevant evidence is admissible, except as otherwise provided by the United States Constitution, by Act of Congress, or by applicable rule. A successful showing of bias on the part of a witness would have a tendency to make the facts to which he testified less probable in the eyes of the jury than it would be without such testimony.

The correctness of the conclusion that the Rules contemplate impeachment by showing of bias is confirmed by the references to bias in the Advisory Committee Notes to Rules 608 and 610, and by the provisions allowing any party to attack credibility in Rule 607, and allowing cross-examination on "matters affecting the credibility of the witness" in Rule 611(b). The Courts of Appeals have upheld use of extrinsic evidence to show bias both before and after the adoption of the Federal Rules of Evidence.

We think the lesson to be drawn from all of this is that it is permissible to impeach a witness by showing his bias under the Federal Rules of Evidence just as it was permissible to do so before their adoption....

Ehle's testimony about the prison gang certainly made the existence of Mills' bias towards respondent more probable. Thus it was relevant to support that inference. Bias is a term used in the "common law of evidence" to describe the relationship between a party and a witness which might lead the witness to slant, unconsciously or otherwise, his testimony in favor of or against a party. Bias may be induced by a witness's like, dislike, or fear of a party, or by the witness's self-interest. Proof of bias is almost always relevant because the jury, as finder of fact and weigher of credibility, has historically been entitled to assess all evidence which might bear on the accuracy and truth of a witness's testimony. The "common law of evidence" allowed the showing of bias by extrinsic evidence, while requiring the cross-examiner to "take the answer of the witness" with respect to less favored forms of impeachment....

Respondent argues that even if the evidence of membership in the prison gang were relevant to show bias, the District Court erred in permitting a full description of the gang and its odious tenets. Respondent contends that the District Court abused its discretion under Federal Rule of Evidence 403, because the prejudicial effect of the contested evidence outweighed its probative value. In other words, testimony about the gang inflamed the jury against respondent, and the chance that he would be convicted by his mere association with the organization outweighed any probative value the testimony may have had on Mills' bias.

Respondent specifically contends that the District Court should not have permitted Ehle's precise description of the gang as a lying and murderous group. Respondent suggests that the District Court should have cut off the testimony after the prosecutor had elicited that Mills knew respondent and both may have belonged to an organization together. This argument ignores the fact that the *type* of organization in which a witness and a party share membership may be relevant to show bias. If the organization is a loosely knit group having nothing to do with the subject matter of the litigation, the inference of bias arising from common membership may be small or nonexistent. If the prosecutor had elicited that both respondent and Mills belonged to the Book of the Month Club, the jury probably would not have inferred bias even if the District Court had admitted the testimony. The attributes of the Aryan Brotherhood—a secret prison sect sworn to perjury and self-protection—bore directly not only on the *fact* of bias but also on the *source* and *strength* of Mills' bias. The tenets of this group showed that Mills had a powerful motive to slant his testimony towards respondent, or even commit perjury outright.

A district court is accorded a wide discretion in determining the admissibility of evidence under the Federal Rules. Assessing the probative value of common membership in any particular group, and weighing any factors counseling against admissibility is a matter first for the district court's sound judgment under Rules 401 and 403 and ultimately, if the evidence is admitted, for the trier of fact.

Before admitting Ehle's rebuttal testimony, the District Court gave heed to the extensive arguments of counsel, both in chambers and at the bench. In an attempt to avoid undue prejudice to respondent the court ordered that the name "Aryan Brotherhood" not be used. The court also offered to give a limiting instruction concerning the testimony, and it sustained defense objections to the prosecutor's questions concerning the punishment meted out to unfaithful members. These precautions did not prevent *all* prejudice to respondent from Ehle's testimony, but they did, in our opinion, ensure that the admission of this highly probative evidence did not *unduly* prejudice respondent. We hold there was no abuse of discretion under Rule 403 in admitting Ehle's testimony as to membership and tenets.

Respondent makes an additional argument based on Rule 608(b). That Rule allows a cross-examiner to impeach a witness by asking him about specific instances of past conduct, other than crimes covered by Rule 609, which are probative of his veracity or "character for truthfulness or untruthfulness." The Rule limits the inquiry to cross-examination of the witness, however, and prohibits the cross-examiner from introducing extrinsic evidence of the witness's past conduct.

Respondent claims that the prosecutor cross-examined Mills about the gang not to show bias but to offer Mills' membership in the gang as past conduct bearing on his veracity. This was error under Rule 608(b), respondent contends, because the mere fact of Mills' membership, without more, was not sufficiently probative of Mills' character for truthfulness. Respondent cites a second error under the same Rule, contending that Ehle's rebuttal testimony concerning the gang was extrinsic evidence offered to impugn Mills' veracity, and extrinsic evidence is barred by Rule 608(b).

The Court of Appeals appears to have accepted respondent's argument to this effect, at least in part. It said:

> "Ehle's testimony was not simply a matter of showing that Abel's and Mills' membership in the same organization might 'cause [Mills], consciously or otherwise, to color his testimony.'... Rather it was to show as well that because Mills and Abel were members of a gang whose members 'will lie to protect the members,' Mills must be lying on the stand."

It seems clear to us that the proffered testimony with respect to Mills' membership in the Aryan Brotherhood sufficed to show potential bias in favor of respondent; because of the tenets of the organization described, it might also impeach his veracity directly. But there is no rule of evidence which provides that testimony admissible for one purpose and inadmissible for another purpose is thereby rendered inadmissible; quite the contrary is the case. It would be a strange rule of law which held that relevant, competent evidence which tended to show bias on the part of a witness was nonetheless inadmissible because it also tended to show that the witness was a liar.

We intimate no view as to whether the evidence of Mills' membership in an organization having the tenets ascribed to the Aryan Brotherhood would be a specific instance of Mills' conduct which could not be proved against him by extrinsic evidence except as otherwise provided in Rule 608(b). It was enough that such evidence could properly be found admissible to show bias.

The judgment of the Court of Appeals is

Reversed.

B. Defect in Capacity

Overview Problem

Defense Counsel: Were you wearing your prescription glasses on the day you observed the light?

Winnie: No.

Defense Counsel: How far can you see without your prescription glasses?

Winnie: Maybe one hundred yards.

Defense Counsel: And how far away was the light?

Winnie: Three hundred yards.

Overview

When you attack a defect in a witness's capacity, you are arguing that the witness could not accurately perceive, remember, or narrate an event and therefore her description should be given little or no weight. Like bias, it is not considered collateral to the issues at trial and is relevant. Nonetheless, a party must have a reasonable basis for this avenue of impeachment; fishing expeditions are not allowed. Significantly, you may prove a defect in capacity through the use of extrinsic evidence.

Anything that may affect a witness's ability to accurately perceive, remember, or narrate is fair game for this avenue of impeachment. For example, intoxication at the time of the event would be relevant. The farther away we move temporally from the event, the higher the burden of introducing the evidence, however. Thus, for example, a history of alcoholism would not be relevant unless it influenced the witness's capacity to observe or communicate on the date in question.

Focus Questions: *Henderson v. DeTella*

- How much weight does the court give to the time frame of the alleged narcotics use? Is this the only factor it weighs in its analysis?

Henderson v. DeTella

97 F.3d 942 (7th Cir. 1996)

ILANA DIAMOND ROVNER, Circuit Judge.

An Illinois jury convicted Ladell Henderson of murder and attempted murder, for which he was sentenced to respective prison terms of life and thirty years. [The prosecution contended at trial that Henderson killed Mona Chavez's uncle and proceeded to shoot Chavez in the head three times. Chavez survived and testified against Henderson at his trial.] ...

... Chavez ... identified Henderson as the assailant. On cross-examination, the defense inquired into her relationship with one Quintin Jones and asked Chavez whether she had used "speed" in the presence of Henderson and Jones. Chavez acknowledged knowing Jones but denied that she had been involved with him romantically and denied having ever used speed. When the defense later attempted to have Jones testify that he had seen Chavez use drugs on numerous occasions, the trial court sustained the state's objection, noting that "the only reason [you're] doing it is to dirty up the witness...."

Chavez's testimony was crucial to the state's case against Henderson. The use of narcotics can, obviously, affect the ability of a witness to perceive, to recall, and to recount the events she has observed. Whether Chavez may have been under the influence of narcotics at the time of the offense (or at some other pertinent time) was thus an appropriate subject of inquiry and impeachment.

But we agree that Henderson was not deprived of his right to confront the witnesses against him when the trial court barred the testimony of Quintin Jones. Had the proffer of Jones' testimony established that Chavez was using narcotics within the time frame of the events to which she testified, it might have been improper and prejudicial to Henderson to exclude the testimony. Instead, however, Jones was held up as a witness who would testify simply that he had known Chavez to use drugs on many occasions; we do not know when those occasions were in reference to the murder of Leonard and the attempted murder of Chavez. It is thus not at all clear that the testimony was probative of Chavez's ability to recognize and identify the individual who committed the offense. *See United*

States v. Robinson, 956 F.2d 1388, 1398 (7th Cir.), *cert. denied*, 506 U.S. 1020 (1992) (testimony as to witness's drug use properly excluded where voir dire did not establish that it affected the witness's memory of relevant events). Absent a connection to Chavez's cognitive abilities, Jones' testimony would have served only to impeach her character, a purpose we have repeatedly deemed improper. Under these circumstances, we see no error, and certainly none rising to the level of a constitutional deprivation, in the decision to bar Jones from testifying on this topic.

[The Court affirmed the conviction.]

C. Character for Untruthfulness

In exploring the general character for untruthfulness of a witness, you are making a character-propensity argument. Essentially, you are claiming, "once a liar, always a liar," and trying to discredit the testimony based upon the witness failure to tell the truth in the past. Pursuant to FRE 404(a)(3), this tactic is allowed, as long as the methodologies of FRE 608 and 609 are followed (while FRE 405 governs the methodology for FRE 404(a)(1) and (2), it plays no role in FRE 404(a)(3)). This, then, is the sixth and final exception under the FRE for the admission of character-propensity evidence.

There are more requirements for this type of evidence, but, as you can imagine, the effect is powerful: you will be able to (i) call a witness to testify as to their opinion of the witness's honesty, (ii) explore past examples of dishonest behavior by the witness, and/or (iii) introduce the witness's prior convictions. Each of these avenues will be explored in turn.

1. Calling a Character Witness

Relevant Rules
FRE 404(a)(3)

Character Evidence; Crimes or Other Acts

(a) Character Evidence.

(1) *Prohibited Uses.* Evidence of a person's character or character trait is not admissible to prove that on a particular occasion the person acted in accordance with the character or trait....

(3) *Exceptions for a Witness.* Evidence of a witness's character may be admitted under Rules 607, 608, and 609.

FRE 607

Who May Impeach a Witness

Any party, including the party that called the witness, may attack the witness's credibility.

FRE 608

A Witness's Character for Truthfulness or Untruthfulness

(a) Reputation or Opinion Evidence. A witness's credibility may be attacked or supported by testimony about the witness's reputation for having a character for truthfulness or untruthfulness, or by testimony in the form of an opinion about that character. But evidence of truthful character is admissible only after the witness's character for truthfulness has been attacked.

(b) Specific Instances of Conduct. Except for a criminal conviction under Rule 609, extrinsic evidence is not admissible to prove specific instances of a witness's conduct in order to attack or support the witness's character for truthfulness. But the court may, on cross-examination, allow them to be inquired into if they are probative of the character for truthfulness or untruthfulness of:

> **(1)** the witness; or

> **(2)** another witness whose character the witness being cross-examined has testified about.

By testifying on another matter, a witness does not waive any privilege against self-incrimination for testimony that relates only to the witness's character for truthfulness.

Overview Problem

Defense Counsel: Do you know Winnie's reputation in the community for truthfulness?

Character Witness: I do. I've known her for three years, and we attend law school together.

Defense Counsel: What is her reputation in that community for truthfulness?

Character Witness: Winnie's reputation for truthfulness is horrible. She is a liar, plain and simple.

Overview

FRE 608(a) allows the "credibility" of any witness to be attacked via opinion or reputation of a character witness. Thus, in our automobile accident example, after witness Winnie has testified and been excused from the stand, the defendant can later call a witness to testify as to Winnie's "character for truthfulness." This witness is often referred to as a character witness, because his sole role is to testify on the credibility of the earlier witness (whom we shall call "the target witness").

There are many procedural prerequisites with the character witness. While he may testify as to either opinion or reputation of the target witness, a proper foundation must be laid. For reputation, the character witness must testify to familiarity with the relevant community (broadly defined) of the target witness. For opinion, the character witness must testify as to his knowledge of the target witness, whether it be personal or professional. Significantly, the character witness is limited to opinion and reputation evidence on the truthfulness of the target witness and may not rely on specific instances to demonstrate the validity of his testimony. Thus, unlike bias or defect in capacity, the character witness is limited to his conclusory statements regarding character for truthfulness. The reasoning for this limitation is similar to the reasons articulated in our discussion of FRE 405 — the fear of tangential evidence and the risk of confusion, prejudice or wasted time.

Like FRE 405, the cross-examination of the character witness may explore specific acts of the target witness as long as those specific acts relate to the target witness's truthfulness. Thus, in the example at the beginning of this section, on cross-examination of the character witness, the plaintiff's attorney can ask, "Did you know that Winnie [the target witness] won the professional ethics award at her law school?" If the character witness answers "yes," then **his** credibility is diminished ("how could he hold that opinion if she won that award?"). If he answers "no," the jury is left to wonder how well the character witness knows the target witness. In essence, the purpose of this cross-examination is **not to bolster** the target witness. Instead, the purpose is to **test the knowledge and/or judgment** of the character witness, similar to the process under FRE 405.

But this cross-examination dance is far from over. The character witness is a testifying witness, and he may thus be impeached regarding **his** truthfulness. FRE 608(b)(2). Thus, every avenue we have been exploring is available to plaintiff's counsel to impeach this character witness. To give one example, the plaintiff could produce another character witness who will testify about the initial character witness's truthfulness. Likewise, if the character witness is biased, that bias can be explored by extrinsic evidence. The bottom line is that any witness's character for truthfulness may be attacked, subject to the limits of FRE 403.

2. Cross-Examining a Witness Regarding Non-Conviction Misconduct

Overview Problem

Defense Counsel: You attend law school, right?

Winnie: Yes.

Defense Counsel: Isn't it true that you lied on your law school application?

Winnie: I did not.

Defense Counsel: Isn't it true that you falsely listed that you graduated with honors from your undergraduate college on your law school application?

Winnie: I most certainly did not.

Overview

Under FRE 608(b), one may cross-examine a witness regarding specific instances of conduct **that relate to truthfulness only**. Once again, the rationale is that anyone who testifies (e.g., a fact witness, a character witness, a criminal defendant, etc.) has put their personal veracity at issue. Demonstrating their inability to be honest is highly relevant.

The question of what types of acts bear on truthfulness is not an easy one to answer. Certainly the conduct must reflect adversely on honesty, but where does one draw the line? Violent behavior and drug use have been found to be too weak a link to veracity, as the actions of violence and drug use bear little relationship to dishonesty. Theft by stealth has been linked to veracity, but more "straightforward" types of theft, such as armed robbery, have not been linked to veracity. All told, the core component of the non-conviction misconduct must involve dishonesty, but courts have sent mixed signals as to what crimes qualify. C. Mueller and L. Kirpatrick, Evidence, Section 6.25 at p. 500 (5th ed. 2012). The decision ultimately rests on a fact-intensive inquiry regarding the degree to which dishonesty was linked to the underlying conduct.

FRE 608(b) contains other explicit limitations. First, the misconduct must not lead to a conviction. For convictions, one can impeach with FRE 609, as discussed in the next section. Second, extrinsic evidence is not allowed to prove character for truthfulness. In the example at the beginning of the section, the attorney must accept the answer of the witness regarding her lie on her law school application. This is true even if defense counsel has her application to law school in his hand, and it does in fact falsely state that she graduated with honors from her undergraduate college. He nonetheless cannot introduce it as an exhibit or call another witness to testify about it. Why is this so? In large part, this requirement is in place to prevent a trial from becoming sidetracked on collateral matters. We do not want extensive testimony (e.g., from the Registrar of Winnie's undergraduate college defining what "honors" means) to cloud the real issue of the trial (e.g., was the light red or green? Who was at fault for the accident?). Additionally, accepting the answer of the witness reduces surprise and prejudice at trial.

A clever attorney may, however, try to introduce extrinsic evidence by arguing that she is conducting a different type of impeachment. As we have seen, if the attorney is arguing that the witness is biased or lacks sensory capacity, then extrinsic evidence is allowed. As we shall soon see, if the impeachment concerns contradicting prior statements, FRE 608(b) does not apply. In each of these instances, the key to removing the impeachment from the realm of FRE 608(b) is to argue that the focus of the impeachment is not focused on the untruthful **character traits** of the witness (i.e., you are not relying on the "she lied about things in the past, so she is a liar by nature" type of argument). Rather, in order to gain the benefit of the use of extrinsic evidence, one should argue that the focus of the impeachment is to demonstrate a reason that the testimony is slanted in particular direction (e.g., the witness is related to a party, the witness could not see that far without her glasses, etc.). When you are not relying on the character inference, extrinsic evidence is allowed.

Also note that safeguards are in place to prevent the harassment of a witness on a FRE 608(b) cross-examination. The questioner must have a reasonable basis for her inquiry, and courts have discretion under FRE 403 to block overly prejudicial impeachment attempts.

Focus Questions: *State v. Morgan*

- Why is this not a FRE 404(a)(2) case, whereby the defendant opened the door to the inquiry by attacking the alleged victim's character?
- Do you agree that the error here was harmless?

State v. Morgan

340 S.E. 2d 84, 315 N.C. 626 (1986)
Supreme Court of North Carolina

MEYER, Justice.

... [D]efendant contends that the trial court committed reversible error in allowing the prosecutor, over objection, to cross-examine the defendant concerning a specific instance of prior assaultive conduct that was not probative of truthfulness or veracity.

The State's evidence tended to show that in the fall of 1983, defendant and the deceased, Austin Yates Harrell, entered into a partnership agreement for the operation of a produce business and "flea market" in Alexander, North Carolina. [The prosecution contended that the defendant shot the unarmed victim. The defendant contended that prior to the shooting the victim first attacked him by throwing a hatchet at him and then chasing him with a butcher knife.]....

Defendant's theory of the case was that he had shot Harrell in self-defense; that he reasonably felt it necessary to shoot Harrell in order to protect himself from Mr. Harrell, a 6'-3", 280-pound manic depressive who was coming at him through the doorway of his home and business threatening to kill him. Defendant admitted on cross-examination, however, that at the time he shot Harrell, Harrell did not have a weapon in his hand.

I.

During recross-examination of the defendant at trial, the following exchange took place:

Q. Mr. Morgan, do you recall that on April 26th, 1984, less than three months before this incident, that you assaulted Mike Hall with a deadly weapon, a shotgun, by pointing it at Mr. Hall and stating that you would cut him in two with the shotgun there at this same place of business, did you not do that did you not do that [sic] with Mike Hall?

MR. MITCHELL: Objection.

THE COURT: Objection Overruled.

A. Mike Hall followed me from the station and come into my sotre [sic], yes sir, I remember that.

Q. And then when Roger Poteat, the CHief [sic] of Police of Alexander Mills, came to serve the Warrant, did you not point the shotgun at Roger Poteat?

A. No sir, I did not. I showed Roger the gun and it wouldn't [sic] even loaded.

The trial judge thus allowed the prosecutor to question defendant on cross-examination about a prior act of assaultive conduct not charged in the indictment upon which he was being tried. Also referred to as "uncharged misconduct evidence," "prior bad acts," or "extrinsic conduct evidence," introduction of this type of evidence has the potential of raising problems under two sections of the Evidence Code, N.C.G.S. § 8C-1, Rules 404(b) and 608(b) (Cum.Supp.1985). Before analyzing the propriety of the trial judge's ruling here, we must be clear about what the transcript reveals.

This colloquy took place on recross-examination of the defendant by the prosecutor. The defendant had just testified on his own behalf and had admitted shooting Mr. Harrell but claimed he had done so in self-defense. Defendant testified that he would not have shot Mr. Harrell if he had not been afraid of him. During direct and redirect examination, defendant had testified as to Mr. Harrell's often violent behavior and his drinking during the days preceding his death. Apparently without having requested a ruling on admissibility prior to trial, the prosecutor on recross-examination then inquired of defendant whether he had engaged in a specific act of misconduct, which involved the same type of conduct (use of a shotgun at defendant's place of business) as that resulting in the charges for which defendant was being tried, but directed toward unrelated third parties at a time three months prior to the Harrell incident. Defendant admitted pointing the shotgun at Mike Hall but denied pointing the shotgun at Police Chief Poteat. The prosecutor did not then seek to further prove this conduct by extrinsic evidence; thus the record does not reveal the specific circumstances surrounding the 26 April 1984 incident. In the record before us, there is no indication why defendant pointed a gun at Mr. Hall, whether Chief Poteat ever served the warrant or even what or for whom the warrant was issued, or whether defendant was ever charged and convicted of pointing a gun at either man. For purposes of this discussion, we shall assume that defendant was not convicted of either alleged previous assault. Thus, this exchange informed the jury that defendant, at his place of business, may have pointed a shotgun at two men other than Mr. Harrell within three months of the 4 July tragedy when similar conduct resulted in Mr. Harrell's death and defendant's arrest therefor.

The trial judge's ruling allowing this information to be heard by the jury raises important evidentiary questions to be answered in accordance with the North Carolina Evidence Code. The briefs on appeal of this matter argue for and against admissibility of evidence of defendant's character traits through questions regarding his alleged prior act of misconduct pursuant to two sections of the Evidence Code. Defendant argues that the prosecutor's questions were improper under N.C.G.S. § 8C-1, Rule 608(b) (evidence of specific instances of conduct for the purpose of proving credibility of witness or lack thereof). The State contends that the evidence was properly admitted pursuant to Rule 404(b) (evidence of specific instances of a party's conduct for the purpose of proving motive, opportunity, etc.) as well as Rule 608(b).

Although both rules concern the use of specific instances of a person's conduct, the two rules have very different purposes and are intended to govern entirely different uses of extrinsic conduct evidence. *See* Commentary, N.C.G.S. § 8C-1, Rule 608(b) ("Evidence of wrongful acts admissible under Rule 404(b) is not within this rule...."). Our task on appellate review is complicated by the fact that there is nothing in the record indicating under which rule the prosecutor was proceeding or under which rule the trial judge overruled the objection. We must therefore consider the admissibility of the evidence under both Rule 404(b) and Rule 608(b).

A.

Defendant correctly argues that the evidence of his alleged prior act of misconduct was inadmissible pursuant to Rule 608(b) (evidence of specific instances of conduct for the purpose of proving credibility of a witness or lack thereof)....

Rule 608(b) addresses the admissibility of specific instances of conduct (as opposed to opinion or reputation evidence) only in the very narrow instance where (1) the *purpose* of producing the evidence is to impeach or enhance credibility by proving that the witness's conduct indicates his character for truthfulness or untruthfulness; and (2) the conduct in question *is in fact probative* of truthfulness or untruthfulness and is not too remote in time; and (3) the conduct in question did *not result in a conviction;* and (4) the inquiry into the conduct *takes place during cross-examination.* If the proffered evidence meets these four enumerated prerequisites, before admitting the evidence the trial judge must determine, in his discretion, pursuant to Rule 403, that the probative value of the evidence is not outweighed by the risk of unfair prejudice, confusion of issues or misleading the jury, and that the questioning will not harass or unduly embarrass the witness. Even if the trial judge allows the inquiry on cross-examination, extrinsic evidence of the conduct is not admissible.

Because the only purpose for which this evidence is sought to be admitted is to impeach or to bolster the credibility of a witness, the only character trait relevant to the issue of credibility is veracity or the lack of it. The focus, then, is upon whether the conduct sought to be inquired into is of the type which is indicative of the actor's character for truthfulness or untruthfulness. Among the types of conduct most widely accepted as falling into this category are "use of false identity, making false statements on affidavits, applications or government forms (including tax returns), giving false testimony, attempting to corrupt or cheat others, and attempting to deceive or defraud others." 3 D. Louisell & C. Mueller, Federal Evidence § 305 (1979) (footnotes omitted). On the other hand, evidence routinely disapproved as irrelevant to the question of a witness's general veracity (credibility) includes specific instances of conduct relating to "sexual relationships or proclivities, the bearing of illigitimate [sic] children, the use of drugs or alcohol, ... *or violence against other persons.*" *Id.* (footnotes omitted) (emphasis added). *See also* 3 J. Weinstein & M. Berger, Weinstein's Evidence ¶ 608[05] (1985) ("crimes primarily of force or intimidation ... or crimes based on malum prohibitum are not included."). For example, in *United States v. Alberti*, 470 F.2d 878 (2d Cir.1972), *cert. denied*, 411 U.S. 919 (1973), cross-examination of a witness regarding a prior assault was properly disallowed because "the conduct involved does not relate to truthfulness or untruthfulness." *Id.* at 882. *See also United State v. Hill*, 550 F.Supp. 983 (E.D.Pa.1982), *aff'd*, 716 F.2d 893 (3d Cir.1983), *cert. denied*, 464 U.S. 1039 (1984) ("acts of assault, force, or intimidation do not directly indicate an impairment of a witness' character for veracity." *Id.* at 990.); *United States v. Kelley*, 545 F.2d 619 (8th Cir.1976), *cert. denied*, 430 U.S. 933 (1977) (evidence tending to show defendant had directed threats and violence toward these victims in the past properly excluded under Rules 607, 608, 609; court intimates that had defendant asserted self-defense at trial, the evidence might have been admissible under Rule 404(b)).

We conclude that the prosecutor's cross-examination of defendant in this case concerning an alleged specific instance of misconduct, i.e., two assaults by pointing a gun at two people during the same incident, was improper under Rule 608(b) because extrinsic instances of assaultive behavior, standing alone, are not in any way probative of the witness' character for truthfulness or untruthfulness.

B.

Our inquiry does not end here, however, because the State contends that the prosecutor's cross-examination was proper under Rule 404(b)....

The State here contends that the evidence brought out during defendant's cross-examination was admissible under Rule 404(b) because it was relevant to the issue of whether defendant was the aggressor in the altercation he described during direct examination. Since defendant claimed he shot Mr. Harrell in self-defense and since the aggressor in an affray cannot claim the benefit of self-defense unless he has abandoned the fight and has withdrawn by giving notice to his adversary, whether the defendant was the aggressor was a contested element of defendant's self-defense claim.... The State's rationale here is precisely what is prohibited by Rule 404(b). In order to reach its conclusion, the State is arguing that, because defendant pointed a shotgun at Mr. Hill three months earlier, he has a propensity for violence and therefore he must have been the aggressor in the alleged altercation with Mr. Harrell and, thus, could not have been acting in self-defense....

Although we find that it was error to admit the extrinsic conduct evidence pursuant to Rule 404(b) *on the theory presented by the State on this appeal*, we hold that there is no "reasonable possibility that, had the error in question not been committed, a different result would have been reached at trial." The error was, therefore, harmless in light of the other evidence properly admitted at trial.

The State presented eyewitness testimony tending to negate defendant's self-defense claim, as well as extensive physical evidence regarding the path of the fatal shotgun slug and the position of decedent's body. We also note that the objected-to exchange, although improper, was quite brief, and the prosecutor did not belabor his point.

[A dissenting opinion is omitted.]

Problem 6-1

Gerald Whitmore was standing on the street in Washington, D.C., when he was approached by a police officer. Whitmore began to run away, and the police officer gave chase, but Whitmore eluded him. Police Officer Efrain Soto was patrolling the neighborhood in his police cruiser, saw Whitmore, and also gave chase, first by car and then by foot. Officer Soto saw Whitmore throw a gun towards an apartment building next to the alley Whitmore ran into. Shortly thereafter, Soto apprehended Whitmore. He then returned to the apartment building and found the gun. Whitmore was charged with illegal possession of a firearm.

At trial, Officer Soto was the sole eyewitness to support the firearm conviction. No fingerprints were found on the gun. Whitmore defended on the ground that Officer Soto manufactured the story about the gun and had planted the gun near the apartment building. He attempted to impeach Officer Soto in two ways.

First, he offered the testimony of Bruce Cooper, a local criminal defense counsel who, Whitmore claimed, would testify regarding Officer Soto's reputation for untruthfulness within what he called the "court community." Cooper would also testify as to his opinion that Officer Soto was untruthful. Whitmore proffered that Cooper would testify that several defense counsel thought Soto was a liar and that Cooper had the same opinion based on having tried many cases in which Officer Soto was a government witness.

Second, Whitmore sought to cross-examine Officer Soto regarding the recent suspension of Officer Soto's driver's license and his failure to report the suspension to his supervisors at the police department.

You are the trial judge. Should these methods of impeachment be allowed?

3. Cross-Examining a Witness Regarding the Witness's Convictions

Relevant Rule
FRE 609

Impeachment by Evidence of a Criminal Conviction

(a) In General. The following rules apply to attacking a witness's character for truthfulness by evidence of a criminal conviction:

> **(1)** for a crime that, in the convicting jurisdiction, was punishable by death or by imprisonment for more than one year, the evidence:
>
>> **(A)** must be admitted, subject to Rule 403, in a civil case or in a criminal case in which the witness is not a defendant; and
>>
>> **(B)** must be admitted in a criminal case in which the witness is a defendant, if the probative value of the evidence outweighs its prejudicial effect to that defendant; and
>
> **(2)** for any crime regardless of the punishment, the evidence must be admitted if the court can readily determine that establishing the elements of the crime required proving — or the witness's admitting — a dishonest act or false statement.

(b) Limit on Using the Evidence After 10 Years. This subdivision (b) applies if more than 10 years have passed since the witness's conviction or release from confinement for it, whichever is later. Evidence of the conviction is admissible only if:

(1) its probative value, supported by specific facts and circumstances, substantially outweighs its prejudicial effect; and

(2) the proponent gives an adverse party reasonable written notice of the intent to use it so that the party has a fair opportunity to contest its use.

(c) Effect of a Pardon, Annulment, or Certificate of Rehabilitation. Evidence of a conviction is not admissible if:

(1) the conviction has been the subject of a pardon, annulment, certificate of rehabilitation, or other equivalent procedure based on a finding that the person has been rehabilitated, and the person has not been convicted of a later crime punishable by death or by imprisonment for more than one year; or

(2) the conviction has been the subject of a pardon, annulment, or other equivalent procedure based on a finding of innocence.

(d) Juvenile Adjudications. Evidence of a juvenile adjudication is admissible under this rule only if:

(1) it is offered in a criminal case;

(2) the adjudication was of a witness other than the defendant;

(3) an adult's conviction for that offense would be admissible to attack the adult's credibility; and

(4) admitting the evidence is necessary to fairly determine guilt or innocence.

(e) Pendency of an Appeal. A conviction that satisfies this rule is admissible even if an appeal is pending. Evidence of the pendency is also admissible.

Overview Problem

Defense Counsel: You've been convicted of a crime, have you not?

Winnie: Well, that was a long time ago.

Defense Counsel: Well, not that long ago. According to this court document I hold in my hand, you were convicted of felony car theft three years ago in this jurisdiction, correct?

Winnie: Well, it was more of a joyride than a theft …

Defense Counsel: Did you plead guilty to second degree car theft, yes or no?

Winnie: Yes.

Overview

Another way to attack the veracity of a witness is to cross-examine her on prior convictions. Yet again, this is a character-based attack: due to your conviction of a crime you have demonstrated a disregard for social obligations, and therefore you are more likely not to follow an oath to tell the truth. The major issue that emerges is what types of crimes will be sufficiently probative to justify the character inference? While a perjury conviction is clearly probative, a jaywalking misdemeanor would not be. Where does one draw the line?

The drafters of the FRE chose to place the line in different places depending on how probative the crime is on the issue of truthfulness. Thus, the more serious the crime, the more probative it is toward truthfulness. Likewise, if the crime involves dishonesty, it is perceived as very probative, even if it is a misdemeanor. If the crime occurred recently, it is considered more probative, as it reflects on the witness's present character. If the crime occurred when the witness was a minor, it is perceived as less probative because the witness's behavior may have improved in adulthood. Let us examine each rule to see where the specific line is drawn.

FRE **609(a)(1)** deals with felony convictions ("punishable by death or by imprisonment for more than one year"). While it may appear the connection between many felonies and a character for untruthfulness is somewhat attenuated, the drafters of the FRE believed that it is the seriousness of the crime that supports the idea that one convicted of a felony is less likely to follow societal rules by telling the truth under oath. Under FRE 609(a)(1) it is the possible punishment for the crime rather than the punishment actually imposed that counts. If one **could** have received a sentence in excess of one year, the rule applies even if the defendant was sentenced to less.

Note also that FRE 609(a)(1) is essentially two different rules — one that applies if the witness is a criminal defendant (FRE 609(a)(1)(B)), and one that applies if she is not (FRE 609(a)(1)(A)). For non-criminal defendants, the conviction(s) is to be admitted subject to the balancing test of FRE 403. As you may recall from our earlier exploration of FRE 403, it is a rule that favors admission and puts the burden on the objecting party. Thus, it is much easier to admit prior felony convictions against witnesses who are not the criminal defendant.

The criminal defendant receives a more lenient test — the evidence is admitted only if its probative value outweighs its potential to cause unfair prejudice to the defendant. As we have encountered elsewhere, the perception that the criminal defendant is the most vulnerable litigant — her freedom is at stake and she faces the investigatory and prosecutorial resources of the government — results in a test that changes the balance of FRE 403 and thereby favors excluding rather than admitting evidence. After all, the burden is on the proponent to show probative value, and this test does not require that prejudice "substantially outweigh" the probative value. Even though this evidence is offered toward credibility only, the fear exists that a jury may not so confine the evidence. If this fear is true, a risk of "over-persuading" the jury and preventative conviction emerge here as well, thereby justifying a more protective rule. For example, a previous conviction for the exact same crime for which defendant is on trial may be probative of honesty, but it carries a great risk of unfair prejudice (e.g., "If he did it once, he probably did it again"). But, how protective should this rule be and what factors should govern its analysis? This issue will be explored in *U.S. v. Brewer*, below.

In FRE **609(a)(2)**, the drafters created the clearest rule for the most probative type of evidence — crimes of dishonesty and false statement. This classification of conviction is automatically admissible to impeach unless one of the exceptions found in FRE 609(b)–(e) applies. Evidence admitted under FRE 609(a)(2) is not balanced under FRE 403, and the rule covers misdemeanors as well as felonies.

FRE 609(a)(2) applies only "if the court can readily determine that establishing the elements of the crime required proving — or the witness's admitting — a dishonest act or false statement." How does this determination occur? The drafters of the rule focused on the idea of *crimen falsi*, crimes that require proof of some element of deceit, untruthfulness, or falsification. Committing such a crime would be a strong indication that the witness would not testify truthfully. But the same criminal offense may be committed differently. A theft may be committed through outright deceit (e.g., by impersonating someone) or by mere stealth (e.g., shoplifting). In order to readily determine the degree of deceit involved in the offense, one may look to the statutory elements of the charged crime, the face of the trial court's judgment, the indictment, a statement of admitted facts, and/or jury instructions. But do not forget that deceit, untruthfulness, or falsification must be an **element** of the crime in order to qualify under FRE 609(a)(2). Committing, for example, a violent crime in a deceitful manner does not qualify, as deceit, untruthfulness, and/or falsification are not elements of most violent crimes.

Another variable to consider in the context of both FRE 609(a)(1) and (a)(2) is the depth of detail that may be inquired into by the impeaching attorney. Is she limited to the date of conviction, the name and elements of the offense, and the punishment? One could argue that if prior behavior correlates directly with truthfulness, then an impeaching attorney should be able to offer details of the offense, such as the underlying circumstances that led to the conviction. On the other hand, allowing a detailed exploration of a crime that is collateral to the issues at trial could inflame juror passions and waste the court's time. Largely due to concerns of excessive prejudice, most courts limit the scope of prior conviction impeachment to the bare facts concerning what the witness was convicted of and when.

This type of prejudice is illustrated in the overview problem at the beginning of the section. Defense counsel is using a prior felony conviction to cast doubt on Winnie's truthfulness. The fact that she committed a felony and did not respect the law, so the argument goes, indicates a greater likelihood that she will be dishonest. Thus, our concern is whether Winnie is credible, and her status as a felon demonstrates that. To explore the degree to which she is an expert car thief or foolish joyrider is beside the point, as her expertise as a car thief is not at issue.

FRE **609(b)–(e)** represent further line drawing on the issue of probativeness. As noted earlier, each of these rules apply to FRE 609(a)(1) and (2). FRE 609(b) sets a ten-year limit to all convictions found in FRE 609(a). The drafters of the rule found very little probative value in older convictions, as the evidence must clear a "reverse 403" test in that the probative value of the conviction must substantially outweigh its prejudicial effect. Very few convictions will meet this test, and the drafters intended older convictions to rarely be used to impeach a witness. In deciding admissibility, the judge typically weighs similar factors to the FRE 609(a)(1) balancing, such as the nature of the crime, remoteness, and similarity to the charged crime.

U.S. v. Brewer will explore what constitutes the beginning of the ten year point. In terms of the end point of the ten year point, some courts have relied on the date of indictment on the current charges, and others have relied on date of the trial.

The strictest test in FRE 609 applies to using juvenile adjudications to demonstrate untruthful disposition. FRE 609(d). The evidence is generally not admissible unless, in a criminal case for witnesses other than the defendant, the admission "is necessary to fairly determine guilt or innocence." Thus, it is not admissible in civil cases or to impeach a criminal defendant.

Based on the foregoing, we can see that the more probative the conviction is toward establishing dishonesty, the more likely it will be admitted (see chart below). Accordingly, calling a witness with a criminal conviction can be a risky maneuver for a party. An impeachment of witness under FRE 609, which can be conducted on cross-examination of the witness and/or through documentary evidence of the conviction, can have a devastating effect on the witness's credibility. The usual practice is that this issue is often raised on a motion *in limine* prior to trial. If the judge refuses to rule on the motion prior to trial, or if the witness is essential the party's case, counsel will typically mention the witness's conviction on direct in order to remove some of the sting of the impeachment.

Hierarchy of Probative Weight under 609

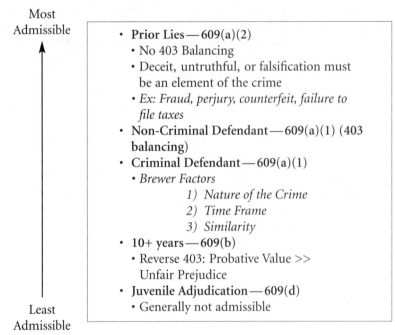

Most Admissible

Least Admissible

- **Prior Lies** — 609(a)(2)
  - No 403 Balancing
  - Deceit, untruthful, or falsification must be an element of the crime
  - *Ex: Fraud, perjury, counterfeit, failure to file taxes*
- **Non-Criminal Defendant** — 609(a)(1) (403 balancing)
- **Criminal Defendant** — 609(a)(1)
  - *Brewer Factors*
    1) *Nature of the Crime*
    2) *Time Frame*
    3) *Similarity*
- **10+ years** — 609(b)
  - Reverse 403: Probative Value >> Unfair Prejudice
- **Juvenile Adjudication** — 609(d)
  - Generally not admissible

Focus Questions: *United States v. Brewer*

- For each factor considered by the court in its determination of admitting prior convictions as impeachment evidence, which favor admission and which disfavor admission?

- What guidance does the court offer to assist other judges when they are reviewing evidence of convictions that are of the same or substantially the same conduct as the crime being charged?

- Why do the fourth and fifth factors counterbalance each other?

United States v. Brewer

451 F.Supp. 50 (E.D.Tenn.1978)

ROBERT L. TAYLOR, District Judge.

....

[Defendant was charged with one count of kidnapping and one count of transporting a stolen motor vehicle.]

Motion

... The defendant has moved to suppress the Government's proposed introduction of certain past convictions as impeachment evidence if the defendant takes the stand. While the defendant filed the motion, Rule 609 places upon the Government the burden of persuading the Court that the convictions are admissible....

The four convictions which the Government wants to introduce to impeach the defendant's testimony, should he take the stand, all ... meet the first requirement under FRE 609(a)(1), i.e., they were punishable by death or imprisonment in excess of one year. Thus, the only requirement to be met before these convictions are admissible for impeachment, is the requirement that the Court determine that the probative value of admitting the evidence of these convictions outweighs the prejudicial effect to the defendant.

Before discussing the standards used by the courts in determining whether the probative value outweighs the prejudicial effect, it must be noted that defendant's attorney argues that the special provisions of 609(b), dealing with convictions over ten years old (computed under the standard provided by 609(b)) should apply to all four convictions. For the reasons stated below, the special provisions of subpart (b) of Rule 609 do not appear to apply to any of the convictions.

Time Limit in 609(b)

Under subpart (b) of Rule 609, when a conviction is offered as impeachment evidence and it is over ten years old, it is not admissible unless:

> The Court determines, in the interests of justice, that the probative value of the conviction supported by specific facts and circumstances substantially outweighs its prejudicial effect.

609(b) also requires the Government to give advance notice of its intention to use such evidence.

The Government argues that the more stringent test of 609(b) does not apply to these convictions because, under the formula provided in the Rule for determining how old a conviction is, none of these convictions is over ten years old.

Rule 609(b) states that it shall apply when "more than ten years has elapsed since the date of the conviction or of the release of the witness from the confinement imposed for that conviction, whichever is the later date...."

The convictions in question are as follows:

Date of Conviction			
10-20-60	Kidnapping	E. D. Kentucky	10 years
1-6-68	Rape	Greene County, Ohio (State Court)	3–20 years
1-6-68	Aggravated Assault	"	1–5 years
1-6-68	Assault with a deadly weapon	"	1–15 years (the three Ohio convictions were consecutive)

The relevant date obviously is the date the defendant was released from the confinement imposed for each conviction. While the three 1968 Ohio state convictions were rendered slightly over 10 years ago, the minimum sentence of one year on each conviction means that whichever he served first, the one year minimum set his release date for that conviction within the last ten years. Defendant was not actually sentenced until March 22, 1968, less than ten years ago. Therefore, March 22, 1969 would have been the earliest release date on either the 1–3 years or 1–15 years sentences, and that release date is unquestionably within the last ten years.

As to the federal kidnapping charge, although the conviction occurred over seventeen years ago, the release date is the determinative date. Defendant was first released from federal custody on June 27, 1967, and placed on parole. If this were the only release date, it would have occurred over ten years ago, and the special provisions of 609(b) would apply. However, while on federal parole, defendant was convicted of the above mentioned state crimes on January 6, 1968. After serving time on the state convictions, defendant was recommitted to federal confinement for violation of parole on the kidnapping conviction. He was released on February 9, 1976, and again placed on parole. This second release date is well within the last ten years, and thus 609(b) does not apply.

Defendant argues that release from "confinement imposed for that conviction" means the initial release and not subsequent releases following reconfinement for parole violations. While no case addressing this issue has been cited by either side, and the Court has found none, the Court is of the opinion that reconfinement pursuant to parole violation is "confinement imposed for (the original) conviction," and therefore the release date from that second confinement is the one used in computing time under Rule 609(b).

It should be noted that, even without the intervening 5½ years state incarceration, i.e., had defendant immediately been returned to federal confinement upon conviction of the state crimes, his release date (assuming an identical period of federal incarceration of over two years) would have been in April 1970, also well within the last ten years. Having ruled that none of these convictions requires the application of the stringent standards of 609(b), the Court must now determine if the Government has met the standard applicable under 609(a).

Balancing Tests Under 609(a)

Application by the Courts of the 609(a) requirement that a determination be made that the probative value of admitting the evidence outweighs its prejudicial effect has generally followed the formula developed in the D.C. Circuit in a string of cases starting with Judge McGowan's opinion in *Luck v. United States*, 348 F.2d 763 (D.C.Cir.1965), and including an often quoted opinion by then Judge Burger in *Gordon v. United States*, 383 F.2d 936 (1967), *cert. denied*, 390 U.S. 1029 (1968)....

The five factors discussed by Judge Burger in *Gordon* are:

(1) the nature of the crime;

(2) the time of conviction and the witness' subsequent history;

(3) similarity between the past crime and the charged crime;

(4) importance of defendant's testimony; and

(5) the centrality of the credibility issue.

(1) The Nature of the Crimes

The nature of these crimes is that of violent action against individuals. In *Gordon*, Judge Burger noted, "Acts of violence on the other hand, which may result from a short temper, a combative nature, extreme provocation, or other causes, generally have little or no direct bearing on honesty and veracity." *Id.*, 383 F.2d at 940. Thus, the nature of these four convictions is a factor against admitting them for impeachment purposes.

(2) The Time of Conviction and the Witness' Subsequent History

While the time elapsed since the actual convictions at issue here range from ten to seventeen years, the defendant's conduct following release from custody has been less than would be expected of a rehabilitated individual. Not only did the defendant commit the three, previously mentioned, serious state crimes while on federal parole in 1968, after his release on parole from federal custody in February 1976, he was convicted of another crime in Ohio and was reconfined again for violation of his federal parole. The Court is of the opinion that the defendant's continued conflict with the law, even while on parole, is a factor supporting admission of the convictions for impeachment purposes.

(3) The Similarity Between the Past Crime and the Charged Crime

The principle involved here was explained by Judge Burger in *Gordon:*

> A special and even more difficult problem arises when the prior conviction is for the same or substantially the same conduct for which the accused is on trial. Where multiple convictions of various kinds can be shown, strong reasons arise for excluding those which are for the same crime because of the inevitable pressure on lay jurors to believe that 'if he did it before he probably did so this time.' As a general guide, those convictions which are for the same crime should be admitted sparingly; one solution might well be that discretion be exercised to limit the impeachment by way of a similar crime to a single conviction and then only when the circumstances indicate strong reasons for disclosure, and where the conviction directly relates to veracity. 383 F.2d at 940.

This principle would apply only to the prior kidnapping conviction. If the Court should admit any of the four convictions, a limiting instruction would be given to the jury emphasizing that they are admitted only to impeach the credibility of the defendant as a witness. The question is whether, even with a limiting instruction, the evidence of a prior conviction for the same crime might, nevertheless, allow the jury to engage in the impermissible assumption that "if he did it before he probably did so this time...."

Based on the principle stated in *Gordon*, the Court is of the opinion that there is a strong argument to keep the prior kidnapping conviction from the jury's knowledge.

(4) & (5) Final Factors

Factors four and five seem to counterbalance each other in this case. While defendant's testimony may be of some importance, a factor favoring nonadmission, at the same time his credibility may be a central issue in the case, a factor favoring admission.

Conclusion

Although the Court, at the hearing on this motion, initially ruled that all four convictions were admissible, further consideration has convinced the Court that the probative value of the prior kidnapping conviction on the issue of defendant's truthfulness, should he take the stand, does not outweigh the prejudicial effect knowledge of such conviction could have on the jury. Admission of the other three convictions, all involving serious crimes, should sufficiently serve the purpose of impeaching the defendant's credibility. The addition of one more conviction would seem to add little to the Government's attempt to impeach the defendant's credibility. However, the fact that the additional conviction was for the same crime as one of those for which the defendant is presently charged, would substantially increase the possible prejudicial effect such testimony might have on the jury, in spite of any limiting instruction the Court would give contemporaneously with the admission. Rather than allow this "overkill" at the risk of prejudicial error, the Court is of the opinion, and holds, that the prior kidnapping conviction is inadmissible under Rule 609(a). As for the three other convictions, the Court holds that the Government has established that the probative value of these three convictions for impeachment purposes outweighs the prejudicial effect that admission of such evidence would have on the jury.

Order Accordingly.

Problem 6-2

Defendant Yvonne Gross was once a drug user and a drug dealer. She no longer is involved in these kinds of illegal activities. Though she turned this part of her life around, her husband, Warren Gross, continues to be involved in the drug trade. On February 2, 1974, DEA Agent Hu arranged for Bogan, an undercover DEA agent, to purchase some cocaine from Warren Gross. Once that transaction was successfully completed, DEA agents Hu, McKinnon and Bogan went to the defendant's home to arrest Warren Gross. When the agents arrived, Warren Gross answered the door, and the agents asked permission to come into the apartment. Mr. Gross declined their request. Agent McKinnon and Mr. Gross started to shove each other. Agent Hu jumped into the fray to help Agent McKinnon. Defendant Yvonne Gross then joined the fight and grabbed Agent Hu by his hair. Eventually the three agents were able to subdue both Mr. and Mrs. Gross. The prosecution is now trying Mrs. Gross for assaulting a federal officer. Mrs. Gross is arguing that she was acting in self-defense on behalf of her husband. When Mrs. Gross testified, she did not represent herself as a person who lacked knowledge of drugs or drug trafficking.

To aid their case, the prosecution wants to admit Mrs. Gross' prior convictions for possession of narcotics on their cross-examination of her. How do you rule?

Problem 6-3

Defendant Christopher Miller was a bank teller at Sovereign Bank. He was steadily employed there for a period of ten years. On sixteen separate occasions he allegedly made unauthorized withdrawals from different bank accounts and kept the money for himself. As such, defendant has been charged with sixteen counts of embezzlement.

Miller has a prior car theft conviction (a felony) from two years ago. He is worried that if he decides to take the case to trial, the prosecution will introduce his prior conviction into evidence if he decides to testify or if any witnesses on his behalf are called to testify to a pertinent trait of his character. His defense in the case is one of misidentification; he asserts that another teller at the bank stole the money.

You are Mr. Miller's attorney. What arguments would you make in a motion in limine to prevent the introduction of the prior conviction?

II. Impeachment to Cast Doubt on Specific Testimony

As we explored in the opening of this chapter, there is a difference between a general attack on a witness's character (i.e., this person is not to be believed due to bias, sensory perception, or they are a liar by nature) and a specific attack on their testimony to show it was either a lie or a mistake. To cast doubt on **specific testimony**, you have two options. First, you can point to a prior inconsistent statement that the witness made which contradicts her testimony. Second, you can offer proof, through either cross-examination or through other extrinsic evidence (i.e., evidence brought out other than by the witness testifying), that something she testified to was wrong. We will explore each in order.

A. Demonstrating Prior Inconsistent Statements

Relevant Rule
FRE 613

Witness's Prior Statement

(a) Showing or Disclosing the Statement During Examination. When examining a witness about the witness's prior statement, a party need not show it or disclose its contents to the witness. But the party must, on request, show it or disclose its contents to an adverse party's attorney.

(b) Extrinsic Evidence of a Prior Inconsistent Statement. Extrinsic evidence of a witness's prior inconsistent statement is admissible only if the witness is given an opportunity to explain or deny the statement and an adverse party is given an opportunity to examine the witness about it, or if justice so requires. This subdivision (b) does not apply to an opposing party's statement under Rule 801(d)(2).

Overview Problem

Defense Counsel: You testified that my client ran through a red light, correct?

Winnie: Yes.

Defense Counsel: You spoke to an officer at the scene of the accident?

Winnie: Yes.

Defense Counsel: And that conversation occurred fifteen minutes after the accident?

Winnie: Yes.

Defense Counsel: And the events were fresh in your mind when you spoke to the officer, correct?

Winnie: Yes.

Defense Counsel: And did you tell that officer, "That car went through a green light and hit that jaywalker?"

Winnie: Yes.

Overview

As the example above indicates, a prior inconsistent statement is meant to combat specific testimony in a case by creating a "were you lying then or are you lying now?" moment. Was Winnie lying to the police officer or is she lying now? While inconsistent statements combat specific testimony at trial, they also plant a seed in the jury's mind that the witness may have been untruthful about other matters she testified to as well. As we explore this type of statement, we will ignore its hearsay implications for now. For our present purposes, suffice it to say that if you are offering a prior inconsistent statement solely for the purpose of impeaching a witness, the statement is not hearsay.

An important issue surrounding prior inconsistent statements is whether, in fact, the statement is inconsistent. Again, this is often a fact-intensive issue. Certain statements, such as the example at the beginning of this section are diametrically opposite. The light was either red or green. But what if a witness testified at trial that the defendant was driving "recklessly" but had previously told an officer at the scene that the defendant had been driving "a bit fast"? What if a witness testified at trial that she did not remember how fast the defendant was driving but had previously told an officer at the scene that he had been driving "five miles an hour under the speed limit"? Are these statements inconsistent?

The most common test for inconsistency is when the witness's statement is "irreconcilably at odds" with a prior statement.

> [T]he trial court has broad discretion in determining whether a prior statement is inconsistent with the witness's testimony, and it need not be squarely at odds with the testimony. For example, a witness's prior statement that omits details included in the trial testimony is inconsistent with the testimony only if it would have been natural for the witness to have included the details in the prior testimony.

J. Weinstein & M. Berger, Weinstein's Evidence Manual, Sec. 12-61 (9th ed., 2011) (footnotes omitted). The goal of introducing the previous statement is to impeach, so the allegedly inconsistent statement must cast doubt on the witness's credibility. In the example in the previous paragraph, there does appear to be a difference between a "reckless" driver and one who drove "a bit fast." This change in testimony casts doubt on the believability of the witness — why did she re-characterize the driving when she testified at trial? Likewise, a lack of memory at trial may cast doubt on a witness's credibility if she once had knowledge — is she feigning lack of memory? Whether these inferences are correct are for the jury to weigh, but both examples cast doubt on the witness's credibility and therefore should be admissible as inconsistent statements.

FRE 613 provides two procedural hurdles. First, FRE 613(a) requires that, on request, the statement must be shown or disclosed to an adverse party's attorney. Second, FRE 613(b) provides that when extrinsic evidence of prior inconsistent statement is introduced, the witness must, either before or after the contents of the statement are made known to the jury, be afforded a chance to explain or deny the statement, and an adverse party is afforded an opportunity to interrogate the witness regarding the prior inconsistent statement. Thus, if the lawyer introduces the prior inconsistent statement while cross-examining the witness, the witness will have an opportunity to explain or deny the statement on cross or on his attorney's re-direct examination. FRE 613(b) allows the attorney to introduce evidence of the witness's prior inconsistent statement **after** the witness has left the stand, but only if the opposing attorney can recall the witness to the stand to give the witness an opportunity to explain or deny the statement.

Focus Questions: *United States v. Winchenbach*

- What distinction does the court make between FRE 613(b) and FRE 608(b)?
- Based on your reading of this case, how would you frame an argument that certain evidence falls under FRE 613(b) rather than FRE 608(b)? Try creating hypotheticals that includes evidence that falls on both sides of the rule.

United States v. Winchenbach
197 F.3d 548 (1st Cir. 1999)

SELYA, Circuit Judge.

This appeal ... requires us to plot the line of demarcation between two closely related but poorly understood rules of evidence, Fed.R.Evid. 608(b) and Fed.R.Evid. 613(b). Concluding, as we do, that ... the trial court's admission of the challenged extrinsic evidence passes muster, we affirm the judgment of conviction....

[The Maine Drug Enforcement Agency ("MDEA") used a confidential informant to purchase cocaine. On numerous occasions, the informant gave Wendy Spinney money and asked her to obtain cocaine for him. On September 3, 1997, the MDEA arrested Spinney outside the trailer of the defendant and his girlfriend, Arlene Jones, shortly after Spinney purchased cocaine.]

III. THE EVIDENTIARY QUESTION

At trial, the appellant called Arlene Jones's son, Robbie Flint, as an alibi witness. Flint testified, *inter alia*, that the appellant was not in the trailer when Spinney arrived on September 3. On cross-examination, the following exchange took place:

Q: Do you have any knowledge of [the appellant's] selling drugs or being involved in drugs on September 3rd 1997?

A: No.

Q: None at all?

A: No.

Q: As far as you know he was not involved in anything?

A: Right.

Q: ... [I]n that interview with [agent] Dan Bradford, you did talk about [the appellant's] drug activity that night, didn't you?

A: No.

Q: You didn't? Well, isn't it true that what you told Dan Bradford was that the night that MDEA searched the house ... they missed several ounces of cocaine that were buried in jars outside the residence?

A: No.

Q: You did not tell that to Dan Bradford?

A: No I didn't.

On redirect examination, defense counsel ignored this testimony. In rebuttal, however, the prosecutor called Bradford and sought to interrogate him about the conversation. The court overruled the appellant's objections, and Bradford testified that he spoke with Flint some months after the fact and that Flint, in an effort "to redeem himself" for assisting in a jailbreak, told him that the agents overlooked a quantity of buried cocaine during the search of Winchenbach's trailer. The judge then instructed the jury to consider Bradford's testimony only as it related to Flint's credibility and not for the truth of the matter asserted.

We review the district court's admission of this evidence for abuse of discretion. The appellant maintains that such an abuse occurred because the court should have excluded Bradford's testimony under either Fed.R.Evid. 608(b) or Fed.R.Evid. 403. We address both objections.

A. Rule 608(b).

In this court, as below, the government parries the appellant's Rule 608(b) objection by claiming that Rule 613(b), not Rule 608(b), controls. On a superficial level at least, an apparent tension exists between these two rules. Rule 608(b) bars the credibility-related use of some extrinsic evidence, while Rule 613(b), albeit by negative implication, permits the credibility-related use of some extrinsic evidence if the proponent satisfies certain enumerated conditions. In this instance, the appellant characterizes Bradford's testimony as extrinsic evidence relating to a specific instance of Flint's misconduct, offered by the prosecutor to attack Flint's credibility (and thus prohibited by Rule 608(b)). The government demurs, characterizing the testimony as extrinsic evidence of a prior inconsistent statement made by Flint, offered after Flint had been afforded an opportunity to explain or deny the remark and in circumstances wherein the appellant had a full opportunity to interrogate both Flint and Bradford on the matter (and thus admissible under Rule 613(b)).

At first blush, neither of these characterizations seems implausible—but they cannot both be right. There are, moreover, two wrinkles. In the first place, the district court, though deeming the evidence admissible, mistakenly relied on Rule 608(b). This bevue need not detain us, for the trial court's use of an improper ground for admission of evidence is harmless if the evidence was admissible for the same purpose on some other ground. Thus, this wrinkle irons itself out.

In the second place, each party presses a theory that fails to fit. The appellant seems to say that the evidence should be excluded under Rule 608(b) simply because it was offered to impugn Flint's credibility. This is an overbroad generalization which, among its other vices, contradicts the time-honored tenet that prior inconsistent statements ordinarily may be used to impeach a witness's credibility. In the bargain, this interpretation of Rule 608(b) leaves no room at all for the admission of extrinsic impeachment evidence under the auspices of Rule 613(b). Thus, we reject it.

For its part, the government urges us to hold that a strict statement/conduct dichotomy triggers the choice of rule. Under this dichotomy, Rule 613(b) always would apply to statements and Rule 608(b) always would apply to conduct. A glance at the case law unmasks this gross oversimplification. Cases invoking Rule 608(b) in respect to statements, as opposed to conduct, are not uncommon.... We, too, reject it.

Although we cannot accept either of the parties' self-serving taxonomies, we think that there is a principled distinction between the types of evidence covered by the two rules. In our view, Rule 613(b) applies when two statements, one made at trial and one made previously, are irreconcilably at odds. In such an event, the cross-examiner is permitted to show the discrepancy by extrinsic evidence if necessary—not to demonstrate which of the two is true but, rather, to show that the two do not jibe (thus calling the declarant's credibility into question). In short, comparison and contradiction are the hallmarks of Rule 613(b). As one treatise puts it:

> The theory of attack by prior inconsistent statements is not based on the assumption that the present testimony is false and the former statement true but rather upon the notion that talking one way on the stand and another way previously is blowing hot and cold, and raises a doubt as to the truthfulness of both statements.

McCormick on Evidence, supra, § 34, at 114.

In contrast, Rule 608(b) addresses situations in which a witness's prior activity, whether exemplified by conduct or by a statement, in and of itself casts significant doubt upon his veracity. Thus, Rule 608(b) applies to, and bars the introduction of, extrinsic evidence of specific instances of a witness's *misconduct* if offered to impugn his credibility. So viewed, Rule 608(b) applies to a statement, as long as the statement in and of itself stands as an independent means of impeachment without any need to compare it to contradictory trial testimony.

Applying this analysis to the case at hand, Bradford's testimony falls within the compass of Rule 613(b). At trial, Flint denied any knowledge of drug dealing at the premises, of the appellant's involvement with drugs, or of having told the agent about jars of cocaine buried in the yard. Bradford's testimony—that Flint had told him that the MDEA, in searching the premises, had overlooked several ounces of buried cocaine—directly contradicted Flint's trial testimony in all three respects and therefore constituted extrinsic evidence of a prior inconsistent statement.

The appellant's contrary argument will not work unless the statement attributed to Flint by Bradford, standing alone and without any reference to Flint's trial testimony, somehow calls into question Flint's credibility. The testimony fails this test: the appellant does not squarely argue that the mere assertion that the officers missed some buried jars of cocaine during their search of the premises, offered in an effort to cooperate with law enforcement, sinks to the level of an affirmative example of *Flint's* misconduct such as would significantly affect Flint's credibility, and such an argument, if made, would be unconvincing. It is only the comparison of the earlier statement with Flint's trial testimony that imbues the evidence with probative value for impeachment purposes.

That ends the matter. Inasmuch as Flint was afforded an opportunity to explain or deny the prior inconsistent statement and the appellant had a chance to interrogate him about it, the conditions for the operation of Rule 613(b) were fully satisfied. Unless some other ground of objection looms—a matter to which we now turn—Bradford's testimony was admissible under that rule....

[The court next concluded that the trial court did not abuse its discretion under FRE 403 by admitting the evidence.]

Affirmed.

B. Contradicting a Witness on Cross or Through Extrinsic Evidence

Overview Problem

Defense Counsel: You were outside when you witnessed the accident?

Winnie: Yes.

Defense Counsel: And you testified earlier that it was a warm day?

Winnie: Yes.

Defense Counsel: But it wasn't a warm day, was it?

Winnie: Excuse me?

Defense Counsel: According to the meteorological data I'm holding in my hands, it was 32 degrees at the time of the accident. That could hardly be considered warm, could it?

Winnie: Um, I guess not.

Overview

Impeaching a witness through contradiction of their testimony simply means to offer counterproof to a proposition on which the witness has testified. This can be done by cross-examining the witness and noting facts which indicate the witness may have lied or been mistaken (e.g., "You testified that the defendant speeding, but you do not know the speed limit on that road, correct?"). It can also occur through the use of extrinsic evidence, such as calling another witness to contradict the target witness or by introducing a document that contradicts the target witness (e.g., an expert witness who can testify as to the speed of a car at impact). The difference between this type of impeachment and the use of prior inconsistent statements is that you are now using underlying facts, not statements, to impeach.

FRE 608(b), and its ban on extrinsic evidence, plays no role in this type of impeachment. FRE 608(b) is a character attack, implying that the witness is a liar by nature and using prior acts of the witness to demonstrate their character. Contradicting a witness's testimony, on the other hand, contains no character inference. We are not arguing that the witness has lied about things in the past and therefore cannot be trusted about what they say in the courtroom. Instead, we are arguing that **the testimony given in this courtroom** was wrong or mistaken, without drawing an inference about the witness's character.

One major limitation to contradicting a witness is that the contradiction cannot concern a "collateral" matter. In other words, the issue which you are impeaching must concern the merits of the claim (i.e., substantive issues) or credibility issues other than contradiction, such as bias, lack of capacity, and untruthfulness. Thus, it is not enough that the evidence conflicts with the witness testimony; instead, it must conflict about a point that matters in the litigation or that matters in determining the credibility of the witness. As one court stated, evidence is not collateral if "the fact, as to which error is predicated, [could] have been shown independently of the contradiction." *State v. Oswalt,* 381 P.2d 617, 619 (Wash.1963). In other words, it is not collateral if, **ignoring the contradiction**, it is still independently relevant to the issues at stake in the case.

Let us take a look at the example at the beginning of the section. Defense counsel did catch the witness in a contradiction. In most places, thirty-two degrees does not qualify as a warm day. But, **other than contradicting the witness**, what does this line of evidence prove? It does not go to any substantive matter in the litigation involving the alleged running of a red light. It does not demonstrate a lack of credibility on the party of the witness, as it does not show bias, a diminished relevant sensory capacity, or a character for untruthfulness. All it does is contradict the witness on a point which does not affect the litigation or the credibility of the witness. Now, imagine that the witness denied it was thirty-two degrees. Should the defense attorney be allowed to enter the meteorological data? Should the defense attorney be allowed to introduce a witness from the National Weather Service? Of course not. This collateral issue is rapidly turning into a mini-trial which bears no relevance to any issue at stake in the case. Under FRE 403, this line of questioning, or extrinsic proof relating to it, will be excluded, as it will be perceived as confusing, prejudicial, or a waste of the court's time.

Focus Questions: *United States v. Opager*

- What was the main characteristic about the contradicting evidence that caused the court to deem it admissible?

- What fact material to the defendant's defense does the evidence disprove? Why is this fact material?

United States v. Opager

589 F.2d 799 (5th Cir. 1979)

JOHN R. BROWN, Chief Judge:

On February 23, 1977, appellant Patricia Lynn Opager made the regrettable mistake of selling a pound of 90.4% Pure cocaine to three buyers, two of whom happened to be law enforcement officers, and the third a government informant and acquaintance of Opager. As a result of this incident, Opager was convicted by a jury of knowingly and intentionally possessing cocaine with the intent to distribute and knowingly and intentionally distributing cocaine in violation of 21 U.S.C.A. s 841(a)(1). She was sentenced to serve two concurrent sentences of fifty-four months imprisonment, with a three year special parole term....

At her trial, Opager attempted to establish an entrapment defense. Opager took the stand, testifying that she had never sold cocaine before and that she was pressured into this sale by the informant, Phillip Posner, and the two police officers. In turn, Posner testified to show Opager's "predisposition" to sell cocaine. He stated that he had observed her engage in cocaine transactions in the past. On cross-examination, Posner explained that he had worked at a beauty salon (the Clipper) with defendant in 1974 and again in 1976 and that during both times he had seen her use and sell cocaine. To impeach Posner's testimony, Opager presented five witnesses to attack Posner's character. By questioning witnesses and by attempting to offer into evidence business records from the beauty salon, she also sought to prove that she and Posner had not worked together in 1974. The District Court ruled that the records were inadmissible under F.R.Evid. 608(b) as extrinsic evidence of a specific instance of conduct introduced to discredit the witness's testimony.

Applicability of F.R.Evid. 608(b)

The District Court erred in applying F.R.Evid. 608(b) to determine the admissibility of the business records. The application of Rule 608(b) to exclude extrinsic evidence of a witness's conduct is limited to instances where the evidence is introduced to show a witness's general character for truthfulness. The purpose of such evidence is to show that if a person possesses "certain inadequate character traits as evidenced in a variety of ways including that he has acted in a particular way he is more prone than a person whose character, in these respects, is good, to testify untruthfully." 3 Weinstein, Evidence P 608(01).

In this case, we are convinced that the records were not offered for such a purpose. The documents show and would permit the jury to find that, contrary to Posner's testimony, Posner and Opager did not work together in 1974 and that therefore Posner did not witness any of the drug transactions he described as occurring at that time. Thus, the records do more than indicate Posner's capacity to lie, about which five witnesses had testified. Instead, as Opager's counsel strenuously argued at trial, [t]he records were introduced to disprove a specific fact material to Opager's defense. The District Court's finding that such evidence merely went to the witness's character for truthfulness is unsupported by the trial record.

We consider Rule 608(b) to be inapplicable in determining the admissibility of relevant evidence introduced to contradict a witness's testimony as to a material issue. So long as otherwise competent, such evidence is admissible. This was long the rule in this Circuit prior to the enactment of the Federal Rules of Evidence.

In making this determination, we find helpful the Ninth Circuit's opinion in *United States v. Batts*, 558 F.2d 513 (9th Cir. 1977). In that case, the defendant on cross-examination testified that he had no knowledge of cocaine or its uses. To rebut this testimony, the trial court allowed the government to introduce evidence showing that the defendant had in fact recently sold a large amount of cocaine to an undercover agent. The Court observed that the case presented a "confrontation" between Rule 608(b) and the basic purpose of the federal rules as evidenced by F.R.Evid. 102. Balancing these two interests, the Court held that in this case Rule 608(b) did not bar the admission of such evidence:

> We believe that the ultimate purpose of the rules of evidence should not be lost by a rigid, blind application of a single rule of evidence. Individual rules of evidence, in this instance Rule 608(b), should not be read in isolation, when to

do so destroys the purpose of ascertaining the truth. This is especially so when a witness directly contradicts the relevant evidence which Rule 608(b) seeks to exclude.

By admitting the rebuttal evidence, the trial court merely completed the picture as to appellant's true involvement and knowledge in the drug world and thereby corrected a distorted view of appellant's testimony.

Id. at 517, 518. Similarly, we believe that Rule 608(b) should not stand as a bar to the admission of evidence introduced to contradict, and which the jury might find disproves, a witness's testimony as to a material issue of the case.

The fact that the business records might have the incidental effect of proving Posner a liar does not affect their admissibility as relevant evidence. In countless cases where facts are in dispute, one party may be able overwhelmingly to disprove the testimony of a prior witness. To exclude under Rule 608(b) the latter otherwise relevant evidence, as the government would have us do today, would completely divorce legal proceedings from the truth seeking process.

That the payroll records are relevant evidence is unmistakable. The Federal Rules of Evidence define relevant evidence as "evidence having any tendency to make the existence of any fact that is of consequence to the determination of the action more probable or less probable than it would be without the evidence." F.R.Evid. 401. Posner's testimony that he saw Opager deal in cocaine in 1974 was a factor in establishing Opager's criminal "predisposition," itself a matter clearly of consequence to her case. Hence, the payroll records, "as indicative that a fact in issue did or did not exist," were clearly relevant....

The District Court's exclusion of the records is itself reversible error....

III. Final Thoughts on Impeachment

Now that we have travelled the avenues of impeachment, two questions remain. First, can the party who sponsors a witness impeach her? Second, once a witness has been impeached, is there any way the party that called her to the stand can rehabilitate her?

In response to the first question, FRE 607 allows the party that called the witness to impeach her. Let us use our overview question as an example. Assume that the plaintiff's attorney called Winnie to the stand and expected her to testify that defendant ran a red light. Once Winnie is on the stand, however, she surprises the attorney by testifying that the light was green. It is only fair that every mode of impeachment should be available to plaintiff's counsel in this situation.

Now, let us change the hypothetical. Suppose that plaintiff's counsel knows before he calls Winnie to the stand that she will recant her testimony; he knows that she told a police officer at the scene that the light was red, but she now will testify that the light was green. Let us further assume that the statement to the police officer is inadmissible substantively (i.e., that it is not admissible for its truth). Can plaintiff's counsel call Winnie to the stand *solely* to impeach her (e.g., to get her earlier statement to the police officer into evidence for the purpose of impeachment)? Plaintiff's counsel would argue that she can do this, as the judge will undoubtedly offer a jury instruction to explain the use of the evidence (e.g., "You may use her earlier statement for impeachment purposes, but you may not use that statement to prove the truth of what she said to the police officer.")

Nonetheless, the answer, according to many courts, is that this maneuver is not allowed. To hold otherwise would allow parties to offer evidence solely in the hope that a jury would not follow (or be confused by) the jury instruction.

Now let us move to the second question: What principles apply to the rehabilitation of an impeached witness? The primary principle is that a witness who has not been attacked cannot be vouched for or bolstered. The rationale for this principle is to save time and prevent confusion. There is no need to vouch for a witness who has not been attacked, and engaging in long bolstering sessions on direct would waste the court's time, especially if no attack on character was forthcoming on cross-examination.

When a witness has been attacked and can be bolstered, a party usually offers a direct rebuttal to the attack. Thus, depending on how the witness was attacked, they will offer evidence that shows good character or limits the scope of the alleged bad character of the witness. Similarly, on re-direct, a witness may attempt to explain, deny, or mitigate the damage caused by impeachment.

While direct rebuttal is a forceful means to bolster a witness, when can a party call a character witness to support her character for truthfulness? Recall that FRE 608(a) mandates that "evidence of truthful character is admissible only after the witness's character for truthfulness has been attacked." Thus, if a witness's character for truthfulness has been attacked by (i) opinion or reputation evidence under FRE 608(a), (ii) cross-examination using specific incidents under FRE 608(b), or (iii) conviction evidence under FRE 609, then the party that called that witness may call a character witness to bolster her reputation for truthfulness. The usual limits apply to this bolstering character witness. The character witness can only testify regarding the truthfulness of the witness who was impeached (the target witness), can only rely on reputation and opinion evidence on direct, and, significantly, can be cross-examined using specific incidents relating to the target witness.

When the attack on the veracity of the party has taken non-character forms, such as a prior inconsistent statement, courts have struggled with the issue of whether to allow the target witness to bolster herself through a character witness. On the one hand, these types of attack are not technically character-based attacks. They imply that the witness may be mistaken, but they do not necessarily rely on propensity-based reasoning (e.g., "you are a liar by nature"). On the other hand, depending on how the attack is conducted, impeachment of this kind may seem like a direct attack on character, as they imply the witness is lying or corrupt. In the end, whether to allow bolstering of a witness after a non-character attack has been a fact-intensive endeavor centering on the degree to which it may be fairly assumed that the witness's direct character has been attacked.

IV. Rape Shield Law

Relevant Rule
FRE 412

Sex-Offense Cases: The Victim's Sexual Behavior or Predisposition

(a) Prohibited Uses. The following evidence is not admissible in a civil or criminal proceeding involving alleged sexual misconduct:

   (1) evidence offered to prove that a victim engaged in other sexual behavior; or

   (2) evidence offered to prove a victim's sexual predisposition.

(b) Exceptions.

(1) *Criminal Cases.* The court may admit the following evidence in a criminal case:

(A) evidence of specific instances of a victim's sexual behavior, if offered to prove that someone other than the defendant was the source of semen, injury, or other physical evidence;

(B) evidence of specific instances of a victim's sexual behavior with respect to the person accused of the sexual misconduct, if offered by the defendant to prove consent or if offered by the prosecutor; and

(C) evidence whose exclusion would violate the defendant's constitutional rights.

(2) *Civil Cases.* In a civil case, the court may admit evidence offered to prove a victim's sexual behavior or sexual predisposition if its probative value substantially outweighs the danger of harm to any victim and of unfair prejudice to any party. The court may admit evidence of a victim's reputation only if the victim has placed it in controversy.

(c) Procedure to Determine Admissibility.

(1) *Motion.* If a party intends to offer evidence under Rule 412(b), the party must:

(A) file a motion that specifically describes the evidence and states the purpose for which it is to be offered;

(B) do so at least 14 days before trial unless the court, for good cause, sets a different time;

(C) serve the motion on all parties; and

(D) notify the victim or, when appropriate, the victim's guardian or representative.

(2) *Hearing.* Before admitting evidence under this rule, the court must conduct an in camera hearing and give the victim and parties a right to attend and be heard. Unless the court orders otherwise, the motion, related materials, and the record of the hearing must be and remain sealed.

(d) Definition of "Victim." In this rule, "victim" includes an alleged victim.

Overview Problem

Defendant is charged with raping complainant in her car. Defendant denies that the rape took place, and the prosecution offers evidence that defendant's fingerprints were found in complainant's car. Defendant seeks to offer evidence that three days before the alleged rape took place he had consensual sex with the complainant in her car. Is the defendant's evidence admissible?

Overview: Impeachment of the Alleged Victim of a Sexual Offense

FRE 412 limits the impeachment of alleged victims of sexual offenses. Unless one of the exceptions apply, evidence of reputation (e.g., under FRE 404(a)(2)) and/or sexual behavior (e.g., under FRE 404(b)) is not admissible for the inference that the complainant consented to sex on the occasion in question at trial. The probative value of this type of evidence is limited: that a person has engaged in a particular sexual activity before does not mean she consented to a certain sexual activity with a certain person on a certain later occasion. A strong policy reason for the rule exists as well: often, evidence of a sexual history is used at trial more as a harassment technique against the complainant rather than as a method to obtain probative evidence.

Based on these underpinnings, FRE 412 was meant to be read broadly so as to exclude harassing, prejudicial information with limited probative value. Accordingly, it applies to a broad range of cases. On the civil side, it covers any matter alleging sexual misconduct, including sexual harassment. On the criminal side, it applies to sexual misconduct evidence even when a sex crime is not charged (e.g., an attempted murder or kidnapping case in which the complainant is alleged to be sexually assaulted).

Additionally, the prohibitions of FRE 412 apply to a broad range of behaviors. "Sexual behavior" not only includes physical conduct but also applies to behaviors that imply sexual contact, such as the use of contraceptives. "Behavior" also includes "activities of the mind," such as fantasies and dreams. FRE 412 also bars evidence of "sexual predisposition," which includes evidence that may have a sexual connotation to the jury, including dress, speech, or lifestyle. Additionally, both past behavior and behavior subsequent to the alleged incident are covered under the rule. Finally, the coverage of the rule is also broad in terms of the type of evidence prohibited; neither specific acts nor reputation evidence is allowed under the rule.

Exceptions to the rule do exist in order to protect the rights of defendants. Three exceptions apply to criminal cases. First, the complainant's prior sexual conduct is admissible when the evidence suggests that someone other than the defendant was responsible for semen or other physical evidence. This exception would not be available if the defendant admits the sexual act occurred but claims the complainant consented, as the source of the semen or injury would thereby be irrelevant. Second, the defendant may offer evidence of prior sexual encounters between the complainant and the defendant in order to prove consent. A prosecutor, however, may offer this evidence for any purpose, including any relevant purpose under FRE 404(b), such as intent or motive. Finally, an exception exists where the exclusion of the evidence "would violate the defendant's constitutional rights" such as a defendant's guaranteed rights of confrontation, compulsory process, and due process.

In the civil arena, evidence of sexual acts or sexual predisposition faces a "reverse 403" test: the evidence is admissible only if its probative value substantially outweighs the danger of harm to any victim or substantially outweighs the unfair prejudice to any party. This test favors the inadmissibility of the evidence. Thus, evidence of a sexual assault of a non-party in a sexual harassment case would not be admissible if *either* the probative value does not substantially outweigh the harm to the non-party victim *or* the probative value does not substantially outweigh the unfair prejudice to any party in the litigation. The burden is on the proponent of the evidence.

Also note that each criminal and civil exception is subject to the other Federal Rules of Evidence. Thus, even though an exception exists under FRE 412, if the evidence violates any other rule, such as FRE 404 or FRE 403, the evidence is inadmissible.

Now, let us explore the overview problem. The defendant may first rely on FRE 412(b)(1)(A) and argue that this evidence explains the source of the physical evidence. FRE 412(b)(1)(A) is unlikely to apply, however, as it mandates that "someone other than the defendant" is the source of the physical evidence. Defendant is claiming that he is the source, so this provision will not work. Next, defendant may try FRE 412(b)(1)(B) and offer the evidence on the theory that her prior consent is relevant. But, again, this factual application does not fit the rule, as defendant is not arguing that the complainant consented on the night of the alleged rape. Rather, he is claiming no sex occurred on the night of the alleged rape. Is this result satisfactory? Could FRE 412(b)(1)(C) offer support to the defendant?

Focus Questions: *Doe v. United States*

- Should the court consider a jury instruction as a condition of admitting the evidence? How effective do you think a jury instruction would be in this instance?

- Is evidence of a victim's prior behavior admissible if it corroborates otherwise admissible evidence?

Doe v. United States

666 F.2d 43 (4th Cir. 1981)

BUTZNER, Circuit Judge:

These appeals concern the district court's evidentiary ruling in a pre-trial proceeding held pursuant to rule 412 of the Federal Rules of Evidence. The court held that evidence concerning the past sexual behavior and habits of the prosecutrix was admissible in the rape trial of Donald Robert Black. We ... affirm in part and reverse in part the order of the district court.

I

The appellant is the alleged victim and chief government witness in the impending rape trial of Black. Pursuant to rule 412 of the Federal Rules of Evidence, Black made a pre-trial motion to admit evidence and permit cross-examination concerning the victim's past sexual behavior. After a hearing, the district court ruled that Black could introduce the evidence which he proffered.

Several days later, the district court granted Black's motion for the issuance of subpoenas for individuals who were to testify about the victim's sexual history. These included the victim's former landlord, a social worker who had previously investigated the victim, a sexual partner of the victim, and two people who claimed to be aware of the victim's reputation for promiscuity.

Thereafter, the victim instituted a civil action seeking the permanent sealing of the record of the rule 412 proceedings and other relief. During the course of this civil action, the court learned that the rape victim had not received notice of the earlier proceeding as mandated by subsection (c)(1) of rule 412. Consequently, it reopened the rule 412 hearing. The court then reaffirmed its prior ruling in the criminal case and entered summary judgment in favor of the defendants in the civil action. The victim appeals from the orders in both the civil and criminal actions....

III

At the pre-trial rule 412 evidentiary hearing, Black presented several witnesses who told about the victim's past sexual behavior and reputation. Black testified that although he had talked on the phone with the victim several times, he did not meet her until the night of the alleged crime. Several men previously had told him the victim was promiscuous, and he had read a love letter she had written to another man.

At the conclusion of the hearing, the district court ruled that the following evidence was admissible:

> (1) evidence of the victim's "general reputation in and around the Army post ... where Mr. Black resided;"

> (2) evidence of the victim's "habit of calling out to the barracks to speak to various and sundry soldiers;"

> (3) evidence of the victim's "habit of coming to the post to meet people and of her habit of being at the barracks at the snack bar;"

> (4) evidence from the victim's former landlord regarding "his experience with her" alleged promiscuous behavior;

> (5) evidence of what a social worker learned of the victim;

> (6) telephone conversations that Black had with the victim;

> (7) evidence of the defendant's "state of mind as a result of what he knew of her reputation ... and what she had said to him."

Black argues that all of the evidence delineated in items 1–7 is admissible to support his claim that the victim consented, to show the reasonableness of his belief that she consented, and to corroborate his testimony. He relies on the rule's provision for the admission of constitutionally required evidence. Exclusion of the evidence, he maintains, will deprive him of the rights secured by the due process clause of the fifth amendment and the right of confrontation and compulsory process guaranteed by the sixth amendment.

Rule 412 restricts the admission of evidence in several respects. Subsection (a) excludes reputation or opinion evidence of the past sexual behavior of the victim. Subsection (b) provides that evidence of past sexual behavior, other than reputation and opinion, is only admissible in three circumstances: first, the defendant may introduce this evidence when it is constitutionally required, 412(b)(1); second, when the defendant claims that he was not the source of semen or injury, he may introduce evidence of the victim's relations with other men, 412(b)(2)(A); and third, when the defendant claims the victim consented, he may testify about his prior relations with the victim, 412(b)(2)(B).

The evidence delineated in items 1–5 of the district court's order clearly falls within the proscription of subsection (a) of the rule. Though sometimes couched in terms of habit, this evidence is essentially opinion or reputation evidence. Consequently, the exceptions set forth in subsection (b) do not render it admissible.

The constitutional justification for excluding reputation and opinion evidence rests on a dual premise. First, an accused is not constitutionally entitled to present irrelevant evidence. Second, reputation and opinion concerning a victim's past sexual behavior are not relevant indicators of the likelihood of her consent to a specific sexual act or of her veracity. Privacy of Rape Victims: Hearings on H.R. 14666 and Other Bills Before the Subcomm. on Criminal Justice of the Committee on the Judiciary, 94th Cong., 2d Sess. 14–15 (1976). Indeed, even before Congress enacted rule 412, the leading federal case on the subject, *United States v. Kasto*, 584 F.2d 268, 271–72 (8th Cir. 1978), stated that in the absence of extraordinary circumstances:

> evidence of a rape victim's unchastity, whether in the form of testimony concerning her general reputation or direct or cross-examination testimony concerning specific acts with persons other than the defendant, is ordinarily insufficiently probative either of her general credibility as a witness or of her consent to

intercourse with the defendant on the particular occasion … to outweigh its highly prejudicial effect.

State legislatures and courts have generally reached the same conclusion. We are not prepared to state that extraordinary circumstances will never justify admission of such evidence to preserve a defendant's constitutional rights. The record of the rule 412 hearing in this case, however, discloses no circumstances for deeming that the rule's exclusion of the evidence classified in items 1–5 is unconstitutional.

The evidence described in items 6 and 7 of the district court's ruling is admissible. Certainly, the victim's conversations with Black are relevant, and they are not the type of evidence that the rule excludes. Black's knowledge, acquired before the alleged crime, of the victim's past sexual behavior is relevant on the issue of Black's intent. Moreover, the rule does not exclude the production of the victim's letter or testimony of the men with whom Black talked if this evidence is introduced to corroborate the existence of the conversations and the letter.

The legislative history discloses that reputation and opinion evidence of the past sexual behavior of an alleged victim was excluded because Congress considered that this evidence was not relevant to the issues of the victim's consent or her veracity. Privacy of Rape Victims: Hearings on H.R. 14666 and Other Bills Before the Subcomm. on Criminal Justice of the Committee on the Judiciary, 94th Cong., 2d Sess. 14–15, 45 (1976). There is no indication, however, that this evidence was intended to be excluded when offered solely to show the accused's state of mind. Therefore, its admission is governed by the Rules of Evidence dealing with relevancy in general. Knowledge that Black acquired after the incident is irrelevant to this issue….

[The court affirmed in part and reversed in part, and the case was remanded.]

Focus Questions: *Stephens v. Miller*

- Did the trial court have any other options to reduce the prejudice of the defendant's proposed testimony?

- How does the concept of res gestae utilized in this case compare to how the issue was analyzed in the materials you have read for FRE 404(b)?

- What considerations does the dissent in this case articulate that the majority opinion dismissed? Were these considerations not relevant to the majority decision or were they simple not strong enough arguments to change the result?

- Does the exception created by the dissent ignore the policy considerations behind the Rape Shield Law? If not, could the exception still "swallow" the rule?

Stephens v. Miller

13 F.3d 998 (7th Cir. 1994), *cert. denied*, 513 U.S. 808 (1994)

En Banc. Before POSNER, Chief Judge, CUMMINGS, BAUER, CUDAHY, COFFEY, FLAUM, EASTERBROOK, RIPPLE, MANION, KANNE, and ROVNER, Circuit Judges.

BAUER, Circuit Judge.

. . . .

I.

On the night of March 17, 1987, Lonnie Stephens went to Melissa Wilburn's trailer. At trial, Stephens and Wilburn told vastly different stories about what happened after Stephens arrived. The events of that evening began after Stephens and David Stone finished drinking. Stone drove Stephens to Wilburn's trailer and dropped him off. Stephens and Wilburn knew each other as casual acquaintances. Wilburn was asleep on the couch when Stephens arrived, and her sister and brother-in-law were asleep in the guest room. Wilburn's son and nephew were asleep in another bedroom.

According to Wilburn, she did not lock the door before she fell asleep. She awoke and found Stephens standing in front of the door inside the trailer. Stephens sat down next to Wilburn and attempted to kiss her. Wilburn told Stephens of the others who were asleep in the trailer and called out for her sister. Stephens hesitated but, after a moment, continued his advances. Wilburn yelled one more time for her sister, but her sister again did not respond. Stephens went to the bathroom and, when he returned, angrily told Wilburn that she lied to him about the others being in the trailer. He threw her down on the couch and covered her mouth with his hand to prevent her from screaming. Stephens pressed his body against Wilburn's, undid her bra, and tore a button from her shirt. Next, Stephens reached down to undo his pants. Wilburn pushed Stephens off of her and ran screaming into the bedroom occupied by her sister and brother-in-law.

Stephens ran out the door to the nearby home of his friends, Jeff and Lisa Strait. Stephens told the Straits that he had been at a local Pic a Pac Store. Later, Stephens told that same story to the police officer who investigated the incident. Stephens directed Stone to say, if he were asked, that Stone dropped him off at the Pic a Pac. At trial, Stone first repeated the Pic a Pac story, then admitted on cross-examination that he dropped Stephens off at Wilburn's trailer. Stone also admitted that he told the Pic a Pac story pursuant to directions from Stephens.

Stephens testified at trial and painted a quite different picture of the evening's events. He claimed that Wilburn invited him into her trailer after Stone dropped him off. Stephens stated that when he entered the trailer, Wilburn's son was asleep on the couch. Stephens carried him to one of the bedrooms and Wilburn explained that her sister, brother-in-law, and their child were also asleep in the bedroom. All three slept through Stephens' visit to the trailer. Stephens and Wilburn talked in the living room, and Wilburn told Stephens he could kiss her. One thing led to another, according to Stephens, until the two of them ended up on the floor as two consenting adults engaged in sexual intercourse.

Stephens stated in an offer of proof that the two of them were "doing it doggy fashion" when he said to her "[d]on't you like it like this? ... Tim Hall said you did." Stephens also asserted that he said something to Wilburn about "switching partners." The trial court excluded these statements pursuant to the Indiana Rape Shield Statute. The court did, however, allow Stephens to testify that he said something to Wilburn that angered her and led her to fabricate the attempted rape charge. Stephens testified that after he made these statements, Wilburn ordered him to stop and leave. Stephens claimed that he did as she asked, got dressed, and left.

The jury returned a guilty verdict against Stephens on the attempted rape charge. The Indiana Supreme Court affirmed his conviction and the district court denied his petition for writ of habeas corpus.

II.

Stephens ... claims that the court's application of the Indiana Rape Shield Statute violated his constitutional right to testify in his own defense.... [Additionally], Stephens argues that the excluded testimony should be admissible as the *res gestae* of the attempted rape.

B. Constitutionality of the Indiana Rape Shield Statute as Applied Here

... Stephens claims that Indiana unconstitutionally applied its Rape Shield Statute in this case. His primary argument is that Indiana denied him his constitutional right to testify in his own defense when it did not allow him to tell his version of the events, in their entirety and in his own words, about what happened on March 17, 1987 at Melissa Wilburn's trailer. Stephens argues that the Indiana court violated the federal constitution when it excluded his statements about "doggy fashion" sexual intercourse and partner switching.

The Supreme Court has interpreted the Constitution to provide a criminal defendant, like Stephens, with an implicit right to testify in his or her own defense ...

A criminal defendant's right to testify, however, is not unlimited and may bow to accommodate other legitimate interests in the criminal trial process. There is, for example, no constitutional right to commit perjury. Furthermore, numerous procedural and state evidentiary rules control the presentation of evidence and do not offend a criminal defendant's right to testify.

... Rape shield statutes, like Indiana's, represent the valid legislative determination that victims of rape and, as here, attempted rape deserve heightened protection against surprise, harassment, and unnecessary invasions of privacy. These statutes also protect against surprise to the prosecution. Restrictions imposed by rape shield statutes, especially as they relate to a criminal defendant's right to testify, may not, however, be arbitrary or disproportionate to the purposes they are designed to serve. Rather, the state is required to evaluate whether the interests served by the rule justify the limitation imposed on the criminal defendant's right to testify.

In this case, Stephens was allowed to give his entire version of the facts, except for the excluded evidence. The Indiana court allowed Stephens to testify in front of the jury that he said something to Wilburn that angered her and caused her to fabricate the attempted rape charge. The court did nothing arbitrary or disproportionate to the purposes the Indiana Rape Shield Statute was designed to serve when it excluded the "doggy fashion" and "partner switching" statements. The Indiana Rape Shield Statute was enacted to prevent just this kind of generalized inquiry into the reputation or past sexual conduct of the victim in order to avoid embarrassing her and subjecting her to possible public denigration. Its application to exclude references here to "doggy fashion" sexual intercourse and partner switching effectuate its purpose. The Indiana trial court properly balanced Stephens' right to testify with Indiana's interests because it allowed him to testify about what happened and that he said something that upset Wilburn. The Constitution requires no more than this. The interests served by the Indiana Rape Shield Statute justify this very minor imposition on Stephens' right to testify.

We note also that Stephens and Wilburn told drastically different stories of what happened and that Stephens directed David Stone to commit perjury. The jury was entitled to credit Wilburn's story, discount Stephens' account, and return a guilty verdict. Testimony about Wilburn's alleged sexual preferences would have served no other purpose than to embarrass and humiliate her. Accordingly, the Indiana trial court properly balanced the state's interests with Stephens' right to testify when it excluded the testimony at issue here.

Stephens was not deprived of his constitutional right to testify.

C. Res Gestae

Stephens raises one other argument: that the excluded testimony was evidence concerning the *res gestae* of the offense and therefore should have been admitted. Literally "the thing done," the *res gestae* of a particular offense under Indiana law is admissible and is defined as evidence of happenings near in time and place which complete the story of a crime. There are two problems with Stephens' *res gestae* argument.

First, we do not accept Stephens' *res gestae* argument because to do so would effectively gut rape shield statutes.... If Stephens' *res gestae* argument were correct, as a matter of constitutional law, criminal defendants could always circumvent rape shield statutes by claiming that they said something near in time and place to the alleged rape or attempted rape about the victim's past sexual history or reputation.

Second, Stephens offers nothing, probably because nothing exists, to support his *res gestae* argument as a constitutional violation. In fact, the use of the term *res gestae*, for purposes of federal law, is essentially obsolete. The Federal Rules of Evidence, adopted in 1976, govern evidentiary questions in federal court, and, more significantly given the issue here, no court has ever held that *res gestae* is a concept with any constitutional significance. Other federal courts have described the phrase *res gestae* as useless, harmful, and almost inescapable of a definition. Simply put, as a federal matter, "[t]he old catchall, '*res gestae*,' is no longer part of the law of evidence." *Miller v. Keating*, 754 F.2d 507, 509 (3d Cir.1985).

We observe only that for purposes of the Constitution and federal law, the term *res gestae* is without significance. Indiana and the other states are, of course, free to keep the *res gestae* concept as part of their law of evidence. But here, as we have said, we ask only whether the Indiana court denied Stephens any right guaranteed to him by the Constitution. It did not.

III.

Nothing in the Constitution prohibited the exclusion of the testimony at issue in this case. The district court's decision to deny Stephens' petition for writ of habeas corpus is therefore

Affirmed.

[Concurring opinions of Flaum, J., and Diamond Rovner, J., omitted.]

CUMMINGS, Circuit Judge, joined by CUDAHY and MANION, Circuit Judges, dissenting.

Lonnie Stephens claims that on the night of March 17, 1987, he made comments to the complainant that caused her to end their consensual sexual encounter, send Stephens immediately from her home, wake her sister, and the next day to file a groundless charge of attempted rape. The content of the offending statement—a cornerstone of Stephens' case—was never presented to the jury, the trial judge having ruled that the proposed testimony was barred by the Indiana Rape Shield Statute. The exclusion of this evidence indisputably gives rise to a colorable claim that the application of an evidentiary rule, the rape shield statute, has interfered with the defendant's right to present his defense. When a defendant presents such a colorable claim, the task of the court is to balance the exculpatory import of the excluded evidence against the interest of the state manifested in the rule at issue.

The interests served by the Indiana [Rape Shield Statute] are obvious—and substantial. The Indiana Rape Shield Statute furthers laudable and pragmatic goals.

It protects victims from needless exposure of their past sexual conduct; ensures that the focus of rape trials remains the guilt or innocence of the accused rather than the sexual history of the complainant; and, by reducing the embarrassment and anguish of trial, encourages victims to report rapes. Without the protection provided by rape shield statutes, victims may find trial an ordeal not worth enduring. Moreover, Indiana has the power to pursue these goals through evidentiary rules—it is each state's "sovereign prerogative" to regulate the presentation of evidence in its courts. Indiana's rape shield statute is a valid legislative determination that rape victims deserve heightened protection from harassment and unnecessary explorations into their personal life, and exceptions to it should not be carved out liberally. Nonetheless, the desire to shield rape victims from harassment must yield in certain cases to another vital goal, the accused's right to present his defense. Sending the innocent to jail, or depriving the guilty of due process, is not a price our Constitution allows us to pay for the legitimate and worthy ambition to protect those already victimized from additional suffering. Though relevant and competent evidence may properly be excluded to accommodate other legitimate interests, *Chambers v. Mississippi,* 410 U.S. 284, 295 (1973), evidence with genuine exculpatory potential must be admitted. In the end then, what matters here—and what must be weighed against Indiana's policy choice—is the significance of the contested evidence to Lonnie Stephens' case.

The jury in this case heard conflicting accounts of the events that occurred at the complainant's house trailer: she testified that Lonnie Stephens was an unwelcome guest who attempted to rape her; Stephens testified that he and the complainant were engaging in consensual sex, but that in response to statements he made during intercourse she became angry, ended the encounter, ordered him to leave and fabricated a rape allegation in retaliation. The prosecution offered physical and testimonial evidence tending to corroborate complainant's version. Stephens' account consisted primarily of his own testimony. The plausibility of Stephens' defense turned in substantial part on whether the jury could be persuaded that something Stephens had said to the complainant could have so enraged her that she would have responded in the manner he alleged. Central to Stephens' case then are the words he claims to have said that night, words the jury never heard. Stephens proposed to testify that while he and the complainant were engaged in intercourse "doggy fashion," he said to her "Don't you like it like this?.... Tom Hall said you did." Stephens instead was permitted only to testify without elaboration that he had said *something* that angered the complainant. The judge required Stephens to convince the jury of the truth of his story without allowing him to reveal the fragments on which its plausibility turned. He was asked to counter the detailed and vivid depiction offered by the prosecution with a version whose essential elements had been expunged. The jury might well have disbelieved Stephens' testimony even if he had testified fully; however, it is hard to imagine his story being believed absent this evidence.

The majority is dismissive of the significance of Stephens' statements to his defense— the exclusion is but a "very minor burden" on Stephens. Stephens, according to the majority, is not harmed by the exclusion because he "was allowed to give [the rest of] his [ ] version of the facts" and little was expunged. That Stephens was allowed to present the rest of his defense, however, is irrelevant to the question of whether the excluded evidence was in itself important. At issue is not whether Stephens was allowed to present *some* defense, but whether the Sixth Amendment requires that he be allowed to present the specific evidence excluded. Since the majority has failed to explore the exculpatory significance of the excluded evidence, it is not surprising that it concludes that the exclusion of Stephens' testimony is not "disproportionate to the purposes [of] the Indiana Rape Shield Statute"—the majority has weighed only one of the issues to be balanced.

Moreover, I do not believe that allowing the evidence at issue would undermine the operation of the Indiana Rape Shield Statute. The statute may, consistent with the Sixth Amendment, operate to exclude a significant body of evidence—likely the type of evidence with which the drafters of the legislation were most concerned. Prohibited still is evidence suggesting that because of an alleged victim's past sexual conduct she probably consented this time or "asked" to have intercourse or other argument that seeks to explain or excuse a rape based on the victim's past behavior.... Admittedly, allowing Stephens' testimony would create an exception to the statute, but the exception is a narrow one. That Stephens allegedly uttered these comments during the evening in question is not alone sufficient to compel admission. The Sixth Amendment does not create a broad *res gestae* exception to rape shield statutes. Neither does the Sixth Amendment require that the statements be admitted because they have some tendency to aid Stephens' defense. *Chambers,* 410 U.S. at 295 (relevant and competent evidence may be excluded). Rather, Stephens' statements must be admitted here because they are central to his defense.

This is not to say that the purpose of the rape shield statute would not be frustrated at all by the admission of Stephens' offered testimony. Although admitting Stephens' statement is unlikely to transform the trial into an inquiry into the complainant's private life, she would undoubtedly suffer some anguish and embarrassment—anguish and embarrassment from which Indiana, in the cause of encouraging victims to report assaults, has an interest in protecting her. However, the state's interest in allowing rape victims to testify "free of embarrassment and with [their] reputation unblemished must fall before the right of [the defendant] to seek out the truth in the process of defending himself.... [T]he State cannot ... require [the defendant] to bear the full burden of vindicating the State's interest[s]...." *Davis v. Alaska,* 415 U.S. 308, 320 (1974).

Allowing Stephens' testimony acknowledges that because the protection of defendants' rights is fundamental to our system, at times other interest may be impaired. Given the significance of the excised testimony to his case, Indiana's interests must yield to Stephens' fundamental constitutional right to present his defense. I, therefore, respectfully dissent.

[Dissenting opinions of Cudahy, J., Coffey, J., and Ripple, J., omitted.]

Problem 6-4

Defendant Anthony Damian Azure was convicted of carnal knowledge of a female under the age of sixteen. He allegedly had sex with Wendy, the ten-year-old daughter of his common law wife. Azure sought to introduce evidence of past sexual relations between Wendy and a boy named David Malterre under FRE 412. More specifically, Azure claims that Malterre was the source of a three centimeter laceration on Wendy's vaginal wall.

At an evidentiary hearing, Malterre was a vague and contradictory witness. He stated he had had consensual sexual intercourse with Wendy, but could not remember how many times. He also could not remember any specific dates; he could only recall that the first was when he was thirteen years old. Moreover, Malterre was unable to testify that his contact with Wendy occurred during the time the laceration was received. He also testified that he never forced or hurt

Wendy, and she never cried during their sexual relations. Two expert witnesses testified that the laceration on Wendy's vaginal wall would have been very painful and would be something that a child would not have submitted to voluntarily.

The issue is before you. Is Malterre's testimony admissible?

Problem 6-5

Jessie Redmond, a counselor at an institution for drug and alcohol-abusing minors, is on trial for the statutory rape of Heather, a fifteen-year-old resident of the institution. The prosecution's principal evidence was Heather's testimony.

Redmond sought to introduce evidence of an unrelated event that concerned Heather. Eleven months before the alleged offense, Heather had told her mother that she had been forcibly raped, and she had offered her torn clothes as evidence. She had repeated the story of the rape, with many circumstantial details, to a hospital nurse and to a police officer investigating the incident, but later had admitted making up the story (and ripping her clothes herself) in order to get her mother's attention. Her new story was that she had had sex with the man she had accused of forcible rape, but that it had been with her consent. Since she was underage, the police continued to investigate the incident as a crime. The man was never found, and there is no evidence other than Heather's say-so that the incident actually occurred. There is no serious doubt that her recantation of the forcible-rape story was truthful. Redmond offered more than thirty police reports of the investigation of Heather's claim that she had been forcibly raped, convincingly demonstrating its falsity. In addition, the district attorney had instituted contempt charges against Heather concerning her allegations.

Redmond wanted to bring out her lie on cross-examination in order to show that Heather would lie about a sexual assault in order to get attention and thus had a motive to accuse him falsely. The issue is before you. How do you rule?

Professional Development Questions

- Is it ethical to discredit a witness when the attorney believes the witness is telling the truth? Why or why not?

- A lawyer should have a good faith belief in evidence that is used to impeach. How high a standard is a good faith belief? How certain must the lawyer be?

- In the next chapter we will explore hearsay, which is a transition point in this book. Now is an excellent time to craft a one-page substantive law summary of the material learned to date. By doing this synthesis now, you will develop a solid foundation of the first part of this course.

- If you began this semester with a strong interest in being a trial attorney, how has learning the rules of evidence influenced your desire? If you had limited or no interest in trial work as the semester began, has that interest changed or stayed the same?

Chapter 7

Hearsay

I. Unraveling Hearsay

Relevant Rule
FRE 801(a)–(c)

Definitions That Apply to This Article; Exclusions from Hearsay

(a) Statement. "Statement" means a person's oral assertion, written assertion, or nonverbal conduct, if the person intended it as an assertion.

(b) Declarant. "Declarant" means the person who made the statement.

(c) Hearsay. "Hearsay" means a prior statement that:

   (1) the declarant does not make while testifying at the current trial or hearing; and

   (2) a party offers in evidence to prove the truth of the matter asserted in the statement.

Overview Problem

Scene: Evidence Professor is in his office, furiously preparing for class. Student knocks on door, opens door, and enters the office.

Student (nervously): Professor, do you have a moment to talk?

Professor (angrily): How many times have I told you not to walk in unless I say, "Come in"?

Student (beginning to hyperventilate and staring at his shoes): I, I, I . . .

Professor (with saint-like patience): Never mind. Of course I have time for you, student-whose-name-I-can-never-remember. What can I do for you?

Student (gaining more confidence): Mike Tyson is after you, he is in the law school lobby with a knife, and he is angry.

Professor (flabbergasted): Mike Tyson? Former heavyweight boxing champion Mike Tyson? Is after me? Are you serious?

Student (suddenly worrying that this might affect his grade): Yes. Remember Neil, your student from last semester? Mike Tyson is his uncle.

Professor (with dawning realization): And I gave Neil a "D" for misspelling my last name on the final exam. So now Mike Tyson is here to gain vengeance for Neil?

231

Student (suddenly enjoying the conversation): Does the sun rise in the east?

Professor (sweating): Don't be cleverly rhetorical at a time like this. What, exactly, did Mr. Tyson say?

Student (dramatically): He said, "I'm going to see Neil's evidence professor and when I do …"

Professor (annoyed): What? What did he say next?

Student (now thoroughly enjoying himself): He didn't say anything. He just began to shadow box. By the way, his jab is still lethal.

Professor (sweating profusely): Well, that's wonderful to know. Okay, please leave now. I need to prepare for class.

Student: Oh, professor? Could you not call on me today? I'm shook up over this Mike Tyson thing.

Professor: Are you enjoying my class?

Student: Yes.

Professor: Then I suggest you start studying for it.[1]

Hearsay: The Quest for Reliable, Accurate Information

The concept of hearsay raises the blood pressure of law students and lawyers throughout the country. Certainly, some parts of hearsay analysis are tricky. But, by going through the definition of hearsay step-by-step, we will be able to simplify the puzzle.

First of all, the policy behind prohibiting hearsay is straightforward: we want reliable evidence in front of the jury, and hearsay ("I heard someone say …") can be wildly unreliable. To understand why this is so, let us examine a nonhearsay situation from the overview problem and watch it unfold into a hearsay situation. First, the nonhearsay situation: Student testifies that he saw Mike Tyson in his law school. With every witness, we are concerned with unreliability stemming from four testimonial capacities:

- Perception: was Student correct in how he perceived the situation? Did Student think he saw Mike Tyson, but, in actuality, that person was not Mike Tyson?

- Memory: when Student encoded this information in his mind, did he encode it accurately? For example, Student saw someone who might vaguely resemble Mike Tyson, but now Student thinks he actually saw Mike Tyson.

- Narration: when it comes time to narrate an event from memory, is the narration precisely what happened? Did Student mean to say "Mike Johnson" but instead mistakenly say "Mike Tyson"?

- Sincerity: did Student intend to lie? Was this all a ruse so Student could get the professor to agree not to call on him?

---

1. This is entirely a work of fiction. I am sure Mike Tyson would never behave this way, and I once gave a student a D+, not a D, for misspelling "Wonsowicz."

Thus, we can see that accuracy depends on all four testimonial capacities being sound; if even one is incorrect, the entire testimony may be inaccurate.

Fortunately, in this instance, we have a way of testing Student's testimonial capacity. As he will be testifying in the courtroom, Student must give an **oath** affirming that he will tell the truth. The jury may be able to observe his **demeanor** to see if he is telling the truth, if he is precise in his testimony and/or if he is trustworthy. Furthermore, during **cross-examination** of Student, opposing counsel will be able to attack each of his testimonial capacities. Each of these devices allows the jury to assess the truthfulness of Student's testimony.

You can predict what will happen if Professor gets on the stand to explain what Student explained to him. We now have a hearsay situation ("I heard him say …"). The truth of Professor's testimony (e.g., "Student told me that he saw Mike Tyson in the law school") depends on all four of Professor's testimonial capacities. Did Professor perceive Student correctly? Did Professor remember Student's words accurately? Did Professor narrate the story precisely? Was Professor sincere? The jury will be able to assess his testimonial capacities, as he is testifying in the courtroom, so oath, demeanor, and cross-examination will aid the fact finder. But, the accuracy of Professor's testimony **still depends on the testimonial capacities of Student**. As we outlined on the previous page, Student's perception, memory, narration, and sincerity are still part of the accuracy equation when Professor states, "Student told me that he saw Mike Tyson in the law school." **Yet there is no way to check Student's accuracy**. He will not appear in the courtroom, and a failure in any of his testimonial capacities will go unchecked. Thus, even if the jury absolutely believes that Professor is being accurate, the story may still not be true because Student was inaccurate in one or more of his testimonial capacities.

Thus, we can think about the rule prohibiting hearsay as a rule that seeks firsthand reports rather than secondhand reports. By relying on firsthand reports (e.g., Student), we only have to worry about the testimonial capacities of one witness who is in the courtroom. By relying on secondhand reports (e.g., Professor telling us what Student said), we double the amount of testimonial capacities upon which the accuracy of the statement is dependent upon, which thereby increases the risk that it is inaccurate. Furthermore, while doubling the risk of inaccuracy, we also have no means of detecting inaccuracies with secondhand reports, as one party is not observable in the courtroom. So, one way of thinking about hearsay is to ask if you are relying on the testimonial capacities of a non-cross-examined witness.

Now that we see the reasoning behind the rule, let us return to its definition under FRE 801(a)–(c).

Hearsay: Rule Deconstruction

Through the cryptic styling of FRE 801(a)–(c), we learn that we need a "declarant." What's a declarant? It is one who makes a "statement." What's a statement? It is an oral assertion, a written assertion, or nonverbal conduct of a person, if the nonverbal conduct is intended by the person as an assertion. So what is hearsay? Once a declarant makes a statement, other than one made by the declarant "while testifying at the current trial or hearing," we must determine whether that statement was offered "in evidence to prove the truth of the matter asserted in the statement." If yes, then it is hearsay. If no, it is not hearsay.

Fairly simple, right? Of course not. The circular reasoning and vague, undefined terms make the rule practically incomprehensible. Let us break it down piece by piece.

A. The Hearsay Declarant

A declarant is more than just a "person who made the statement." Because FRE 602 requires that a witness have "personal knowledge on the matter" to which she testifies, a declarant is a person who makes a statement based on personal knowledge. So, in our overview problem, who has personal knowledge of what Mike Tyson said? Student does, as he heard Mike Tyson speak. Professor does not; his only personal knowledge relates to what Student said, not to what Mike Tyson said.

In fact, only Student has knowledge that Mike Tyson was in the lobby; if Professor wanted to testify to that fact, he would have to depend on the statement of Student. To understand why this matters, let us imagine both witnesses testifying at trial. If Student testifies, "I saw Mike Tyson in the lobby of the law school and had a conversation with him," then this is not hearsay. Student is testifying to a matter for which he has personal knowledge and, most importantly, hearsay is a statement "other than one made by the declarant while testifying at the trial or hearing." So, since Student is testifying at the trial, his statement while testifying would not be hearsay.

Is the same true for Professor? Professor, in order to testify from personal knowledge regarding Mike Tyson's location, would have to testify, "Student told me that Mike Tyson was in the lobby." Certainly the assertion that Professor and Student actually had a conversation is not hearsay; it is reporting a fact rather than actual statements from the conversation. But revealing **the content of the conversation** creates a hearsay problem. Now we have Professor referring to a statement made out of court by a declarant (Student) who will not take an oath, have his demeanor scrutinized, or be cross-examined. Thus, in this scenario, Student, not Professor, is the declarant to whom the hearsay rule applies. If the declarant makes a statement outside the courtroom and someone brings that statement into the courtroom by repeating it at trial, it is hearsay if it is offered to prove the truth of the matter asserted in the statement.

B. For the Truth of the Matter Asserted

In order to understand what it means to offer a statement for the truth of the matter asserted, we must go back to the idea of evidential hypothesis from Chapter 2. If you are offering an out of court statement at trial, what is the evidential hypothesis that makes the evidence relevant? In other words, **for what purpose is the evidence offered?** If the matter asserted in the statement **must be true for that purpose to be effectuated**, then the statement is offered for the truth of the matter and is hearsay.

But, there is a potentially easier way to look at the issue. Ask yourself: If the statement were a lie, would it still be relevant to the jury? In other words, would the jury care whether the statement was true or not? If the statement would still be relevant, then it was not offered by the proponent for its truth and is not hearsay. To understand this test, let us look again at the overview problem and add some facts to it. Mike Tyson was shot by Professor, and Professor pleads self-defense. Student is a defense witness at Professor's trial:

Defense Counsel: And what did you tell the professor about Mike Tyson?

Student: I told him, "Mike Tyson is after you, he is in the law school lobby with a knife, and he is angry."

Defense Counsel: But you were lying, weren't you?

Student: Yes.

Defense Counsel: And Professor did not know you were lying, correct?

Student: That's correct.

Here, Student has confessed that he made the statement, so that is not in dispute. Let us imagine that the defendant is offering this evidence to prove the reasonableness of his actions. Professor will argue that the ex-heavyweight champion of the world was after him, seeking vengeance and possessing a knife and a lethal jab. He thus will claim he acted reasonably when he shot Mike Tyson, as he was basing his reaction on the statement of Student. In other words, Professor is offering the statement for its effect on him. **For this purpose**, it does not matter whether the statement was true or not. All that matters is that it was said, Professor heard it, and Professor believed it. Whether it was true or not, it would still be relevant to the fact finder, who will use the information to judge the reasonableness of the defendant's actions. In short, in this context the statement is offered for the effect on the listener.

Let us look at a second example: take the same statement ("Mike Tyson is after you, he is in the law school lobby with a knife, and he is angry"), in the same setting (Student talking to Professor), but for a different purpose. Suppose the Professor shot Mike Tyson with a gun when he saw Mr. Tyson with a knife in his hands. Further assume that when police arrived at the scene, they saw an injured Mike Tyson, Professor with a gun, but no knife. Professor offers Student's statement to prove Mr. Tyson was armed. Is it now offered for its truth? Yes, it is. If Student were lying, then Mr. Tyson did not have a knife, and Professor's defense fails. If Student was telling the truth, it helps prove Professor's theory of self-defense. The jury absolutely cares whether the statement is true or not. In fact, its value **depends** on its truth.

Now let us explore a third example by examining the statement in the same setting but for yet another purpose. Assume that at Professor's murder trial Student testifies that he has never heard of Mike Tyson, does not know who he is, and does not know what he looks like. Professor then testifies as to Student's statement ("Mike Tyson is after you, he is in the law school lobby with a knife, and he is angry") in Professor's office. Professor is now offering the statement to show that Student knew who Mike Tyson is. **For this purpose**, it does not matter whether the statement is true or not. All that matters is that it demonstrates the declarant's knowledge and thereby impeaches his previous testimony. Even if what is in quotation marks is a lie, the fact that Student uttered Mike Tyson's name demonstrates, at minimum, that he has knowledge of who Mike Tyson is, and that casts doubt on Student's earlier testimony.

Accordingly, we see that a statement can be hearsay if offered for one purpose, and it is not hearsay if offered for another purpose. It all depends on the evidential hypothesis. Just as in other situations of parallel permissible and impermissible uses, a statement will be admitted if a nonhearsay purpose is demonstrated and that nonhearsay purpose satisfies a FRE 403 test (e.g., a jury instruction will minimize the risk of the impermissible use).

Many different evidential hypotheses can indicate a situation where the truth of the matter does not matter. For example:

- Where proving the state of mind of either the declarant (as in the third example above) or listener (as in the first example above) is the purpose of the evidence. Often, in proving someone possessed knowledge, belief, or intent, what matters is not the truth of a statement but rather that someone uttered it or someone heard it.

- Where impeachment is the purpose of the evidence. Here, the fact that two statements are in conflict is what matters, not whether one statement is the truth.

- Where a "verbal act" is the purpose of the evidence. A verbal act takes two forms. First, a verbal act can be a statement of operative fact which gives rise to legal consequences. It is the words themselves that carry a legal consequence, because they represent, for example, an offer, a defamatory statement, or an illegal threat. These statements are not offered for their truth; they are offered because they were said by someone and/or someone heard the declarant. Another use of the term "verbal act" is a verbal part of a physical act. When a physical act is ambiguous, sometimes the words that accompany it resolve the ambiguity. For example, if I give you a pen, you might ask yourself if it is a loan or a gift. My stating, "I expect that back" when I am handing you the pen resolves the ambiguity.

This is not an exclusive list of nonhearsay purposes. Just as FRE 404(b) allows evidence to be offered as long as it is not introduced for a forbidden purpose, evidence will be admitted **as long as the articulated purpose does not require that the declarant's statement is offered to prove the truth of the matter asserted in the statement.**

Now that we have a better understanding of a declarant and the phrase "truth of the matter asserted," it is time to examine the final part of equation: what is a statement?

C. The Hearsay Statement

Because statements include oral or written communication and assertive conduct, we will divide our analysis of statements accordingly. But one common thread unites the two: whether we are analyzing an oral statement, written statement, or physical conduct, the conduct must be assertive to qualify as a statement. An "assertion," according to FRE 801, means any action undertaken by the declarant that is intended to communicate a fact.

1. Assertive Conduct as a "Statement"

Oftentimes, physical conduct, such as a gesture of nodding, is used to communicate with others. When is conduct both assertive and hearsay? Apply the following test:

(i) For what purpose is the proponent of the evidence offering it?

(ii) Did the declarant intend to communicate that purpose to an audience?

In other words, **if there was an intent** to assert something, and the conduct **is offered for the purpose that matches the intent,** then we have hearsay. To understand why, think back to the four testimonial capacities. If I respond to your question with an affirmative nod rather than the word "yes," then perception, memory, narration, and sincerity are all in play when evaluating my nod. Particularly, whenever someone is trying to communicate to an audience, their sincerity may be called into question, and the hearsay rules are **very** reluctant to rely on a declarant's sincerity without cross-examination. Let us look to two examples from the overview problem.

First, at one point in the overview problem, Mike Tyson completes a thought ("when I do …") with a physical action (shadow boxing). Is this conduct assertive? We cannot answer that question unless we know the purpose for which it is offered. Let us assume that Mike Tyson is on trial for assault of Professor and claims that he did not intend to assault. The prosecutor offers his action of shadow boxing as evidence of his intent to assault. Is it hearsay? In other words, did Mike Tyson intend to communicate the intent to assault Professor to an audience through his actions? It seems so, as he appeared to be demonstrating to an audience what he intended to do to Professor. The party claiming the conduct is an assertion possesses the burden under FRE 104(a) to prove that the actor intended his conduct to be assertive, but here it seems likely that the burden will be met. Thus, because we are relying on Mr. Tyson's sincerity without the benefit of cross-examination, we are concerned about the reliability of the statement.

Second, at another point in the overview problem Student responds to Professor's question by staring at his shoes and hyperventilating. If this is offered to prove Student was nervous, is it hearsay? Probably not. It is unlikely that Student intended to assert his nervousness to an audience; instead, his hyperventilating was a natural, unintended response. Therefore, **we are not worried about the actor's sincerity when he did not mean to express something.** The lack of cross-examination of the witness would be tolerable, because his testimonial capacities are not being implicated.

The previous two examples, where we explored what the declarant intended to say and what the proponent is offering this evidence to prove, are illustrated below:

Action	Actor's Intent	Proponent's Purpose	Result (if offered for truth)
Shadow boxing	I will hit him	He intends to hit him	Hearsay (sincerity concern)
Hyperventilating	None (natural reaction)	He was nervous	Not hearsay (no sincerity concern)

We see that when the actor's intent matches the proponent's purpose, we have a significant concern regarding sincerity, which raises hearsay concerns. If, as in the case of hyperventilating, the actor did not mean to express his nervousness, we are not worried about his sincerity, and no hearsay concerns exist.

2. Oral and Written Communication as a Statement

Most oral and written assertions are clearly meant to assert a message to an audience. Conversely, some words are clearly nonassertive, such as involuntarily screaming "OW!" when a hammer comes into forceful contact with your thumb. In this scenario, it is unlikely that the declarant wanted to assert her pain to an audience.

But some oral or written assertions walk a very fine line. Called "implied assertions," these statements possess an underlying, implied message. For example, if you see someone accidently hit his thumb with a hammer and ask him if his thumb hurts, a response of "What do you think?" carries an implied message. True, it is possible the injured party may be very concerned about what you think, but it is more likely "What do you think" equates to "Yes, you fool, I am enveloped in pain." The statement carries an implied message.

If the evidence is offered for its implied message, then the statement may be an assertion and may be hearsay. Framing it as a two-part test:

(i) For what purpose is the proponent of the evidence offering it?

(ii) Does the proponent's purpose in introducing the evidence match the declarant's intent?

If the answer to part (ii) is "yes", the statement is an assertion, and it may be hearsay if it is offered for the truth of the matter asserted in the statement. Again, the declarant's underlying testimonial capacities come into play in an implied assertion. If someone wanted to assert something, then sincerity issues arise regarding that assertion, and therefore we do not want to enter the statement into evidence without cross-examination of the declarant.

Let us return to the overview problem for some examples of implied assertions. The first words spoken by Professor to Student are "How many times have I told you not to walk in unless I say, 'Come in'?" Is there an implied assertion here? Theoretically, Professor could be literal here: he is genuinely curious as to how many times he has uttered this statement to this particular person. But, more likely, Professor meant to communicate to his audience (Student) an implied message: please stop walking into my office without my express consent. The reason it is essential to determine the implied meaning is because our hearsay determination depends on whether the implied meaning and the purpose for which the evidence is offered match. If the prosecutor wants to prove that Student barged into Professor's office without knocking, then the purpose matches the intent, which calls into question the declarant's sincerity, which makes the statement an assertion that is hearsay if it is offered for the truth of the matter asserted. (Please see the chart below for an illustration of this scenario.)

What about Student uttering "Does the sun rise in the east?" in response to Professor's question? On the one hand, Student could suddenly be very curious about astronomy issues. More likely, however, Student was merely responding affirmatively to Professor's question. Therefore, if the statement is being offered to prove that, indeed, Mike Tyson was seeking vengeance, then the declarant's intent and proponent's purpose match. It will be hearsay if it is offered for the truth of the matter asserted.

Now, let us explore a tougher example. Near the end of the overview problem, Professor asks Student if Student is enjoying the class. Is there any implied assertion here? Perhaps Professor is genuinely curious or perhaps he is trying to imply that the class will require a great deal of work. What if, during Professor's criminal trial, someone offered the statement, "Are you enjoying my class?" as proof that Student was enrolled in the class? It is unlikely that Professor meant to assert "You are a student in my class" when Professor asked "Are you enjoying my class?" After all, Professor knows Student is in the class and would have no reason to assert a fact known to both of them. Thus, the declarant's intent does not match the proponent's purpose. **The proponent is offering it for a reason the declarant did not intend to assert.** If the declarant did not mean to assert this meaning, then we have no sincerity concerns. The declarant could not be lying if he never meant to assert that point. Accordingly, the statement is not hearsay.

Here is a review of the last three examples, where we explored what the declarant intended to say and what the proponent is offering this evidence to prove:

Statement	Declarant's Intent	Proponent's Purpose	Result (if offered for truth)
How many times have I told you … ?	You keep barging in	The student barged in	Hearsay (sincerity concern)
Does the sun rise in the east?	Tyson wants vengeance	Tyson wants vengeance	Hearsay (sincerity concern)
Are you enjoying class?	Are you enjoying class?	Person addressed is a student in the class	Not Hearsay (no sincerity concern)

Thus we can see the illustration of the implied assertion doctrine. If the declarant's intent matches the proponent's purpose, then issues regarding testimonial capacities (especially sincerity) arise, and the statement is considered hearsay if it is offered for its truth. If the declarant's intent does not match the proponent's purpose, we are not concerned with the declarant's sincerity, and the statement is not hearsay.

D. Mini-Review

It is the interrelationship of the terms that makes hearsay so difficult. Just establishing something is a "statement" does not end the matter. You still must demonstrate whether it is offered to prove what it asserts. But understanding whether it is offered to prove what it asserts requires one to understand proponent's purpose and/or the speaker's intent. What we have done in this chapter so far is to define each of these variables. There is much more nuance to explore, but, for now, a visual approximation of the hearsay rule would look something like this:

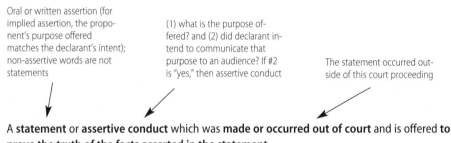

Oral or written assertion (for implied assertion, the proponent's purpose offered matches the declarant's intent); non-assertive words are not statements

(1) what is the purpose offered? and (2) did declarant intend to communicate that purpose to an audience? If #2 is "yes," then assertive conduct

The statement occurred outside of this court proceeding

A **statement** or **assertive conduct** which was **made or occurred out of court** and is offered **to prove the truth of the facts asserted in the statement**.

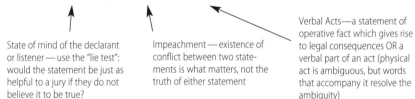

State of mind of the declarant or listener — use the "lie test": would the statement be just as helpful to a jury if they do not believe it to be true?

Impeachment — existence of conflict between two statements is what matters, not the truth of either statement

Verbal Acts — a statement of operative fact which gives rise to legal consequences OR a verbal part of an act (physical act is ambiguous, but words that accompany it resolve the ambiguity)

The above chart outlines the nonhearsay arguments the proponent of evidence possesses when faced with a hearsay objection. Thus, the proponent of the evidence can argue it is not hearsay because:

Proponent: Your Honor, **this statement is not assertive.** The declarant did not mean to assert anything when she uttered these non-assertive words (e.g., "Ouch," etc.)

Proponent: Your Honor, **this statement is not assertive.** I am offering these words for a purpose that does not match the declarant's intent when she uttered the words (e.g., implied assertions). As it was never the declarant's goal to articulate the purpose for which I am offering this evidence, no sincerity issues arise.

Proponent: Your Honor, **this conduct is not assertive.** The declarant did not intend to communicate the purpose for which I am offering this evidence to an audience.

Proponent: Your Honor, **this statement was not made out of court.** The declarant is not attempting to recite any statement made outside of this proceeding.

Proponent: Your Honor, **this statement is not offered for its truth.** I am offering it to demonstrate the state of mind of the declarant (or the listener). This statement would be just as helpful to the jury if they did not believe it to be true, because it only demonstrates what the declarant (or listener) knew (or felt, believed, etc.).

Proponent: Your Honor, **this statement is not offered for its truth.** I am offering it to impeach, and therefore I am attempting to prove the conflict between this statement and another statement, not the truth of either statement.

Proponent: Your Honor, **this statement is not offered for its truth.** It is a verbal act which gives rise to legal consequences (e.g., a defamatory statement in a defamation action; an offer in a contract action, etc.).

Proponent: Your Honor, **this statement is not offered for its truth.** It is a verbal part of an act which seeks to explain the ambiguity behind a physical act (e.g., "you may borrow this pen, but please give it back").

If the proponent of the evidence is successful on any of these arguments, the evidence will be deemed nonhearsay and will be admissible as long as it clears any other hurdles under the FRE.[1] If the proponent is not successful, then the proponent must find a hearsay exception or exemption in order to make the hearsay evidence admissible. A simplified version of this path looks like this:

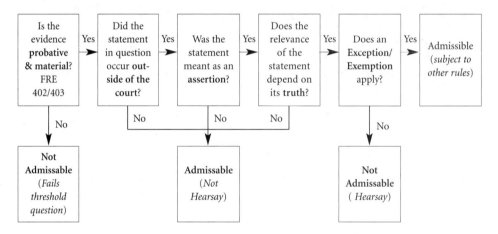

Now, let us examine some cases that explore the gray areas of hearsay.

Focus Questions: *United States v. Parry*

- For what purpose is the declarant's statement being offered? Is it the only purpose for which it could be offered?

- Does it matter that the statement adds only to circumstantial evidence and is not direct evidence? Can that distinction affect its admissibility?

---

1. One such hurdle, which we will discuss later in this chapter, is hearsay within hearsay. When a statement in court encompasses two hearsay statements (e.g., "Dick told me (hearsay statement #1) that Sally said (hearsay statement #2) …") then the hearsay analysis applies to both statements.

United States v. Parry

649 F.2d 292 (5th Cir. 1981)

LEWIS R. MORGAN, Circuit Judge.

The question in this case is whether the district court erred in excluding certain testimony by the appellant's mother as inadmissible hearsay. We conclude that the evidence should have been admitted and therefore reverse appellant's convictions and remand for a new trial.

Scott Parry was tried before a jury and convicted in consolidated cases of conspiring to distribute phenycyclidine hydrochloride (PCP) and of possessing with intent to distribute PCP and dl-methamphetamine hydrochloride. At trial the government presented its case primarily through the testimony of two undercover agents with the Drug Enforcement Administration, Robert Starratt and Douglas Driver. Essentially, these agents testified that Parry had acted as a middleman or intermediary in arranging three separate drug transactions between the agents and certain individuals who had drugs for sale.

In his defense to these charges, Parry did not deny that he had participated in the drug transactions described by the DEA agents but argued that, during each of these transactions, he had proceeded upon the good faith belief that he was working for the agents, assisting them in locating drug dealers. As proof of the purity of his intentions, Parry testified that he had learned that Starratt was an undercover agent several days before he had met the agent or engaged in any of the activities alleged in the indictment. Although Parry conceded that he never entered into any formal agreement to cooperate with the agents, he argued that, at least from his perspective, there was an implied understanding that he would lead the agents to drug sources.

In support of his position that he had known from the outset of the agents' identities, Parry related a conversation he had had with his mother shortly after he met Agent Starratt in October 1974 and well in advance of his arrest in January 1975. Parry testified that, in response to his mother's inquiry, he had stated that the person who had frequently telephoned her home asking to speak to Parry was a narcotics agent with whom he was then working. In an effort to corroborate his story, Parry called his mother as a witness. Outside the presence of the jury his mother testified that

> Scott received several phone calls and I would tell Scott that Bob called and I questioned Scott on who he was because I thought at first it was a painting job and Scott had said told me that his name was Bob Starratt, he was working with him, he was a narcotics agent, he was working with and not to worry.

Although the government voiced no objection to the proffered testimony, the court ruled that Parry's mother could not testify to "any conversations that she had with her son or that her son had with her." Parry's objection that his mother's testimony was not hearsay and therefore should not be excluded was overruled by the district court.

It is our judgment that the court erred in excluding the proffered testimony. First, we find that Parry's out-of-court statement to his mother is simply outside the scope of the hearsay prohibition. Rule 801(c) of the Federal Rules of Evidence defines hearsay as "a statement, other than one made by the declarant while testifying at the trial or hearing, offered in evidence to prove the truth of the matter asserted." The reasons for excluding hearsay are clear: when an out-of-court statement is offered as a testimonial assertion of the truth of the matter stated, we are vitally interested in the credibility of the out-of-court declarant. Because a statement made out of court is not exposed to the normal credibility safeguards of oath, presence at trial, and cross-examination, the jury has no basis for evaluating the declarant's trustworthiness and thus his statement is considered unreliable. Implicit in both the definition and justification for the rule, however, is the recognition that whenever an out-of-court statement is offered for some purpose other than to prove the truth of the matter asserted, the value of the statement does not rest upon the declarant's credibility and, therefore, is not subject to attack as hearsay.

Parry contends, and we agree, that in this case the excluded testimony was not offered to evidence the truth of the matter asserted in the out-of-court statement. Parry's mother sought to testify that her son had stated that the person who had been telephoning her home was a narcotics agent and that he, Parry, was working with the agent. As Parry explained to the district court, this statement was not offered to prove that the caller was a narcotics agent or that Parry was working with the agent, but to establish that Parry had knowledge of the agent's identity when he spoke. In other words, Parry offered the statement as the basis for a circumstantial inference by the jury that, if this statement was in fact made a question which the in-court witness could testify to while under oath, before the jury, and subject to cross-examination then Parry probably knew of the agent's identity. Using an out-of-court utterance as circumstantial evidence of the declarant's knowledge of the existence of some fact, rather than as testimonial evidence of the truth of the matter asserted, does not offend the hearsay rule. Contrary to the government's position, the danger that the jury could improperly use the out-of-court statement as an assertion to be believed does not render the statement inadmissible. Where evidence is admissible for one purpose but not for another, the accepted practice is to admit the evidence with instructions that the jury consider the evidence only for the permissible purpose. A different rule applies only where the probative value of the evidence when used for its allowable purpose is outweighed by the prejudice that would result if the evidence were used for its improper purpose. In this case the dangers associated with the jury's possible misuse of the out-of-court statement are not sufficient to require that the evidence be excluded. The court should admit the statement and give a limiting instruction that the statement is admissible only as circumstantial evidence of Parry's knowledge and not as evidence of the truth of the matter asserted....

Finally, the government argues that even if the district court erred in excluding the proffered testimony of Parry's mother, the error was harmless because her narration of the alleged out-of-court conversation was merely cumulative of evidence already testified to by Parry. We reject this characterization of the proffered testimony. Rather than being merely cumulative, the excluded testimony was the only available evidence that could corroborate Parry's story that he had known of the agents' identities, a story the jury may have found self-serving if not farfetched. Parry's defense, discounted by the jury when standing alone, may have been believed when bolstered by his mother's testimony. Moreover, the jury may well have assumed that because Parry did not ask his mother to confirm the existence of the critical conversation, the conversation probably never occurred. Because we are unable to say with fair assurance that the jury was not substantially influenced by the error, we must reverse Parry's conviction and remand for a new trial.

REVERSED and REMANDED.

Focus Questions: *State v. Galvan*

- If the girl's statement in this case is found to be assertive conduct, what assertion does the court believe is being communicated? To whom is it being asserted? Would it matter if the little girl did not know whether someone was observing her actions?

- Why does the court dismiss the contention that the little girl's conduct is offered to show knowledge and not being offered for the truth of the matter asserted?

- Does the court use the term "verbal act" correctly?

State v. Galvan

297 N.W.2d 344 (Iowa 1980)

HARRIS, Justice.

This appeal, following defendant's conviction of first-degree murder ... challenges the sufficiency of evidence and the admissibility of certain evidence. We reverse the trial court....

Taking the evidence offered in this case in the light most consistent with the verdict the following facts appear. Sometime during the night of October 5, 1977, William Turk died of multiple skull fractures. These fractures were inflicted by a blunt instrument. Turk's hands and feet had been bound with electrical cord. Turk had also been repeatedly stabbed.

Galvan's former wife, Mrs. Jenny Perez, testified that on October 5, 1977, she, Galvan, and their two daughters were residing together at 605 Maple Street, West Des Moines, Iowa. At about 10:00 p.m. that evening all four were at home. Galvan received a telephone call from Phillip Cuevas. Upon receiving the call Galvan told Mrs. Perez he was going to pick up Phillip Cuevas and Cuevas' wife Mary at Galvan's other house in Des Moines. So saying he left at approximately 10:15, taking with him his youngest daughter, then age two.

Mrs. Perez said that Galvan returned at approximately 11:00 p.m. Mrs. Perez had tried without success to phone defendant at the other house during the 45 minutes he had been absent. When he returned Galvan told Mrs. Perez the Cuevases were getting out of the car. When they did so and came into the house they proceeded directly to the bathroom. While the Cuevases were in the bathroom, Galvan asked Mrs. Perez if she had an extra pair of pants that Mary might use. Mrs. Perez provided a pair of green slacks for Mary. After the Cuevases finished in the bathroom, they asked Mrs. Perez for a paper sack. When it was provided they filled it with clothing and placed it outside and placed lighter fluid on it. Later, as Mrs. Perez was preparing for bed, she noticed blood spots inside the lavatory in the bathroom used by the Cuevases. There had been no blood spots on the lavatory before the time the Cuevases were there.

At about midnight the Cuevases left. Galvan remained. Mrs. Perez noticed that the Cuevases left in a red and white car. Later it was determined this car was owned by the victim, William Turk.

Over defense counsel's objections, Mrs. Perez testified that two days after these events she observed her two-year-old daughter, the one who had accompanied the defendant, behaving in a way that was, for the child, unique. The child had taken a belt from her mother's robe and bound her own hands with it. Then she made several gestures as if beating her own chest.

Also over objections, Mrs. Perez was allowed to testify that, on the day before she testified, some five months after the October events, the same daughter had an adverse reaction to a television cartoon. In the cartoon a mouse was shown tied up and this caused the daughter to cry.

We shall consider the assignments in reverse order.

I. Mrs. Perez's testimony of her daughter's conduct was objected to as irrelevant, immaterial, and incompetent hearsay and unduly prejudicial. On appeal defendant argues most strongly that it is prejudicial hearsay. The State first defends against the objection by asserting the testimony is not hearsay....

In former times it was sometimes argued that only oral or written statements could constitute hearsay. Assertive conduct, such as Mrs. Perez described, was thought by many authorities to fall outside hearsay's definition. In our view, however, assertive conduct, as well as oral or written statements, can be hearsay. In *State v. Miller*, 204 N.W.2d 834, 840 (Iowa 1973), we quoted with approval what is now Federal Rule of Evidence 801(a): "A 'statement' is (1) an oral or written assertion or (2) nonverbal conduct of a person, if it is intended by him as an assertion." The evidence of the child here was offered in the belief that the child intended to assert what she had seen. Accordingly, it makes no difference in our determinations that the assertion offered was of the child's conduct, rather than her statement.

We look to a statement's purpose in deciding whether it is hearsay. The State then argues:

> The testimony of Jenny Perez concerning her daughter's conduct was offered to prove that the child had knowledge of the fact that someone had been bound and stabbed, not to prove that the victim was bound and stabbed. As such, the Perez testimony is part of the State's circumstantial evidence, from which a reasonable juror could infer from the fact of the young child's conduct that she had seen the stabbing of someone who was tied up....

The State cites [McCormick's Handbook of the Law of Evidence, § 249 at 591–92 (2d ed. E. Cleary (1972)], and the case of *Bridges v. State*, 247 Wis. 350, 19 N.W.2d 529 (1945), in support of its position. Under these authorities "circumstantial nonassertive use of utterances to show a state of mind," rather than to prove the truth of the matter asserted often falls outside the definition of hearsay. McCormick, supra. We subscribe to the principle but think it does not apply in this situation.

We think the little girl's verbal act was in fact being offered to prove the truth of the matter asserted, that is, that someone was stabbed who was tied up. The little girl's knowledge of that fact could have no other relevance or significance in the case. The child's mother could not testify over a hearsay objection that her daughter had told of seeing such a stabbing. It does not change the hearsay characteristic of such testimony to change it into the child's knowledge of having seen it.

McCormick's treatise, in the section cited by the State, goes on to point out the danger of this very same misapplication. *Id.* at 592. It cites the Wisconsin case relied on by the State, *Bridges v. State, supra,* as an example: "However, statements of memory or belief are not generally allowed as proof of the happening of the event remembered or believed, since allowing the evidence would destroy the hearsay rule. For this purpose, knowledge would seem to be indistinguishable from memory and belief, save under unusual circumstances." We therefore conclude the two incidents related by the child's mother were hearsay. It is accordingly necessary to determine whether they were admissible under an exception to the hearsay rule....

[The court examined applicable hearsay exceptions and determined only one of the statements was admissible.]

REVERSED AND REMANDED.

All Justices concur, except REYNOLDSON, C. J., who concurs in the result.

Focus Questions: *United States v. Long*

- What reasoning does the court use to distinguish between the admissibility of express and implied assertions? What deems one more reliable than the other?

- What risks exist when dismissing the existence of implied assertions?

United States v. Long
905 F.2d 1572 (D.C. Cir. 1990)

CLARENCE THOMAS, Circuit Judge:

[Keith Long was charged with possessing in excess of five grams of cocaine base with intent to distribute and other charges.]

… During the search of Mayfield's apartment, the telephone rang, and a police officer answered it. An unidentified female voice asked to speak with "Keith." The officer replied that Keith was busy. The caller then asked if Keith "still had any stuff." The officer asked the caller what she meant, and the caller responded "a fifty" [i.e., a bag of crack worth fifty dollars.] The officer said "yeah." The caller then asked whether "Mike" could come around to pick up the "fifty." Again, the officer answered yes.

Before trial, Long's counsel moved in limine to exclude evidence of this telephone conversation as inadmissible hearsay. The trial judge denied the motion. At trial, the police officer who had taken the call testified about the conversation. In this appeal, Long renews his hearsay challenge to the introduction of the officer's testimony.

Although Long concedes that the caller did not expressly assert that he was involved in drug distribution, he argues that her questions contain *implicit* assertions about his involvement. Long contends that it is irrelevant that these alleged assertions were couched in question form, since the questions plainly revealed assumptions that are the functional equivalent of direct assertions. Long maintains that the caller, through her questions, in effect asserted that "Keith has crack and sells it out of Mayfield's apartment." He argues that the government introduced this testimony to prove the truth of precisely these assertions, and that the testimony, thus, should have been excluded as hearsay.

Hearsay is an out-of-court statement offered to prove the truth of the matter asserted in the statement. Fed.R.Evid. 801(c). As a threshold matter, then, Long must show that the evidence he seeks to exclude as hearsay is a "statement," which the rule defines as "an oral or written assertion." Fed.R.Evid. 801(a)(1). Although the rule does not define "assertion," the accompanying advisory committee note stresses that "nothing is an assertion unless *intended* to be one." Fed.R.Evid. 801 advisory committee note (emphasis added).

The caller's words, thus, cannot be characterized as an "assertion," even an implied one, unless the caller intended to make such an assertion. While Long's criticism of a rigid dichotomy between express and implied assertions is not without merit, it misses the point that the crucial distinction under rule 801 is between intentional and unintentional messages, regardless of whether they are express or implied. It is difficult to imagine any question, or for that matter any act, that does not in some way convey an implicit message. One of the principal goals of the hearsay rule is to exclude declarations when their veracity cannot be tested through cross-examination. When a declarant does not intend to communicate anything, however, his sincerity is not in question and the need for cross-examination is sharply diminished. Thus, an unintentional message is presumptively more reliable. Evidence of unintended implicit assertions is "[a]dmittedly ... untested with respect to the perception, memory, and narration (or their equivalents) of the actor," but "these dangers are minimal in the absence of an intent to assert and do not justify the loss of the evidence on hearsay grounds." Fed.R.Evid. 801 advisory committee note.

With our inquiry focused on the *intent* of the caller, we have little trouble disposing of Long's theory about implied assertions. Long has not provided any evidence to suggest that the caller, through her questions, intended to assert that he was involved in drug dealing. The caller may indeed have conveyed messages about Long through her questions, but any such messages were merely incidental and not intentional. *See United States v. Zenni*, 492 F.Supp. 464, 469 (E.D.Ky.1980) (phone calls from bettors, answered by police during raid of illegal gambling establishment, were not assertions and therefore were outside scope of hearsay rule). Long thus fails to satisfy the intent component of rule 801, which "place[s] the burden upon the party claiming that the intention existed." Fed.R.Evid. 801 advisory committee note[.] Because the caller's questions were nonassertive, they fall outside the scope of the hearsay rule, and the trial judge did not err in admitting the testimony concerning the questions....

It is so ordered.

[concurring opinion omitted.]

Focus Questions: *State v. Dullard*

- How does this Court's treatment of the distinction between express and implied assertions differ from the court in *United States v. Long*? What dangers does the court articulate as the justification for the exclusion of out of court statements? What dangers exist in this case?

- Under what circumstances does the Court suggest that implied assertions are no more reliable than express assertions?

State v. Dullard

668 N.W.2d 585 (Iowa 2003)

CADY, Justice.

... [A major question on appeal is] whether the district court erred in admitting a note written by an unknown person as evidence in a trial involving the crime of possession with intent to manufacture a controlled substance....

I. Background Facts and Proceedings.

Police officers from the city of Des Moines police department went to a home in a residential neighborhood of Des Moines in response to a report of a methamphetamine lab located at the house.... The search of the garage revealed potential methamphetamine precursors and numerous materials commonly used to manufacture methamphetamine, including six cans of starting fluid, a sack containing a white granular substance, two metal cylinders with brass fittings, a one-gallon glass jar, plastic pitchers, a container of acetone, a container of Coleman camping fluid, and three unopened boxes of Benadryl. The brass fittings on the metal cylinders were corroded with a blue substance, indicating the cylinders once contained anhydrous ammonia.

The police also found a small spiral notebook in a wooden desk located in the garage. It contained a handwritten note from an unidentified person. The note read as follows:

> B—
> I had to go inside to pee + calm my nerves somewhat down.
> When I came out to go get Brian I looked over to the street North of here + there sat a black + white w/the dude out of his car facing our own direction—no one else was with him

... The handwritten note was also introduced into evidence over Dullard's hearsay objection. The State argued the note was not offered to prove the truth of the matters it asserted but to connect Dullard to the items in the garage used to manufacture methamphetamine and the Benadryl. The State argued the note was written to Dullard based on the first letter of his first name....

III. Hearsay.

Hearsay "is a statement, other than one made by the declarant while testifying at the trial ... offered in evidence to prove the truth of the matter asserted." Iowa R. Evid. 5.801(c). Hearsay is not admissible unless it is exempt from the rule or falls within one of the exceptions.

Before considering the exemptions and exceptions to the rule against hearsay, an inquiry must first be made to determine if the evidence under consideration is "a statement ... offered in evidence to prove the truth of the matter asserted." Id. 5.801(c). If not, it is not hearsay and is excluded from the rule by definition. Thus, a declaration is excluded from the definition of hearsay when it is not a statement or is not offered to prove the truth of the matter asserted. See 4 Clifford S. Fishman, Jones on Evidence § 24:10, at 218 (7th ed.1992) [hereinafter Jones] ("categorizing a person's words as an assertion ... does not answer the question" of whether the evidence is hearsay without also determining if "the statement is being offered to prove the truth of the matter asserted").

A statement is defined under our rules of evidence as "(1) an oral or written assertion or (2) nonverbal conduct of a person, if it is intended by the person as an assertion." Iowa R. Evid. 5.801(a). The term assertion is not similarly defined in the Iowa or federal rules of evidence. Nevertheless, it is generally recognized to be a statement of fact or belief.

Under the State's argument in this case, the author of the note asserts he or she is nervous and that the police are watching the house. The State acknowledges this note constitutes a written assertion under the rule, but claims it was not hearsay because it was not offered to prove the truth of the assertion, but a different proposition inferred from the words of warning. The State maintains it was offered to show the declarant's belief that the recipient of the note needed to be told of the events because he was involved in the drug activity in the garage and was in possession of the drug lab materials.

The court of appeals considered the note in a different light. It found the relevant assertion made in the note was not the expressed assertion that the police are watching or that the author of the note is worried and upset. Instead, it found the note contained an implied proposition by the writer that Dullard possessed the methamphetamine materials. Under this approach, the court of appeals determined the note was hearsay because it was offered to show the declarant's belief in this implied proposition, and the declarant was not available at trial to be cross-examined about the proposition. Thus, the resolution of this issue requires us to examine the concept of implied assertions and the extent to which they constitute statements under our definition of hearsay within rule 5.801(c).

The issue we confront has been imbedded in debate and controversy throughout the development of the common law, and has continued to be debated to a large degree following the adoption of the federal rules of evidence. Despite the wealth of legal commentary and some scholarly court decisions on the subject, no clear answer or approach has emerged. In truth, many courts have not engaged in a serious examination of the subject of implied assertions as hearsay, while those who have follow divergent paths. Legal scholars advocate a variety of positions, with a slight preference, perhaps, to favor an approach that would include most implied assertions within the definition of hearsay, at least where the declarant intended to some degree to assert the proposition. The United States Supreme Court has never squarely addressed the issue, but has previously endorsed the concept of implied assertions as hearsay. The federal circuit courts of appeals are fairly evenly divided on the issue.

The implied assertion issue arises in this case because the words written by the out-of-court declarant are not offered to prove the truth of the words. In fact, the words themselves have no real relevance to the case. Instead, the handwritten note is offered solely to show the declarant's belief, implied from the words and the message conveyed, in a fact the State seeks to prove—Dullard's knowledge and possession of drug lab materials. Thus, the question is whether this implied belief of the declarant is a statement under our definition of hearsay under rule of evidence 5.801(c).

The starting point for the common law approach to implied assertions inevitably begins with the celebrated and durable case of *Wright v. Tatham,* 112 Eng. Rep. 488 (Ex. Ch. 1837). The case involved an action to set aside a will based on the incompetency of the testator. *Id.* at 489. At trial, the proponents of the will offered several letters written to the testator by various individuals concerning a variety of business and social subjects. *Id.* at 489–92. The purpose of the letters was to show the absent declarants must have believed the testator was able to engage in intelligent discourse on the various topics discussed in the letters. *Id.* at 515. This belief, therefore, constituted evidence of the testator's competency.

In the course of holding that the statements contained in the letters were hearsay, the court in *Wright,* through the scholarship of Baron Parke's opinion, utilized the now-famous example of a sea captain, who, after carefully inspecting his ship, embarked on an ocean voyage with his family, an action offered as proof of the seaworthiness of the ship. *See id.* at 516. Baron Parke used the illustration to show that such nonverbal conduct would nevertheless constitute hearsay because its value as evidence depended on the belief of the actor. *See id.* at 516–17. This illustration was important in the court's analysis because the main problem sought to be avoided by the rule against hearsay—an inability to cross-examine the declarant—is the same whether or not the assertion is implied from a verbal statement or implied from nonverbal conduct. Thus, assertions that are relevant only as implying a statement or opinion of the absent declarant on the matter at issue constitute hearsay in the same way the actual statement or opinion of the absent declarant would be inadmissible hearsay.

This approach became the prevailing common law view, but did not escape criticism and debate over the years from legal scholars and some courts. Two central arguments surfaced to support a competing approach that advocated a separation between implied assertions and expressed assertions so that implied assertions would be removed from the rule against hearsay. One legal scholar summarized these arguments:

First, when a person acts in a way consistent with a belief but without intending by his act to communicate that belief, one of the principal reasons for the hearsay rule—to exclude declarations whose veracity cannot be tested by cross-examination—does not apply, because the declarant's sincerity is not then involved. In the second place, the underlying belief is in some cases self-verifying:

> There is frequently a guarantee of the trustworthiness of the inference to be drawn ... because the actor has based his actions on the correctness of his belief, i.e., his actions speak louder than words.

4 Jack B. Weinstein et al., *Weinstein's Evidence* ¶ 801(a)[01], at 801–61 to 801–62 (1st ed.1990) (citation omitted)[.]

Once the proposition is accepted that the lack of intent to assert frees conduct from the hearsay rule, the opponents of the common law rule concluded that an unintended implication of a verbal assertion should similarly fall outside the hearsay rule. As with conduct, the opponents argue, the lack of intent to assert an implied assertion from speech also makes unintended implied assertions much less vulnerable than expressed assertions to the problem sought to be avoided by the hearsay rule. In particular, the opponents point out that there is a reduced risk of mendacity in implied assertions when the declarant has no real intention of asserting a fact sought to be proved. Consequently, the critics of the common law approach claim implied assertions should not be treated as express assertions because of lack of opportunity for cross-examination to test the veracity of the implied assertion would have no significant impact.

Federal rule of evidence 801(a) appears to support the departure from the common law, evidenced more by the advisory committee note accompanying the rule than the language of the rule itself.... The thrust of the advisory committee note is that the same considerations that justify the specific exclusion of nonverbal conduct not intended as an assertion from the definition of a statement under rule 801(a)—the minimal dangers resulting from the inability to cross-examine the declarant—support, by analogy, the similar exclusion of nonassertive verbal conduct, as well as assertive verbal conduct offered as a basis for inferring something other than the asserted matter....

Generally, a position taken by the advisory committee on federal rules is persuasive authority for determining the meaning of our Iowa rules of evidence.... On the other hand, the persuasiveness of the committee notes on implied assertions is undermined by the clear split of authority among the federal circuit courts, as well as many legal scholars. The criticism of the advisory committee notes is capsulized by one leading scholar as follows:

> The Advisory Committee's apparent attempted rejection of Wright v. Doe d. Tatham is as unfortunate as it is incorrect. When a statement is offered to infer the declarant's state of mind from which a given fact is inferred in the form of an opinion or otherwise, since the truth of the matter asserted must be assumed in order for the nonasserted inference to be drawn, the statement is properly classified as hearsay under the language of Rule 801(c). Since the matter asserted in the statement must be true, a reduction in the risk of sincerity is not present. The Advisory Committee's reliance on the analogy to nonverbal nonassertive conduct where a reduction in the risk of fabrication is caused by a lack of intent to assert anything is thus clearly misconceived. It is further suggested that the fact that the practical importance of the concept (even if assumed theoretically sound) is so small in relation to the confusion in analysis the concept causes in the minds of those attempting to apply the hearsay rule argues strongly in favor

of rejection of the concept that statements should be found to be non-hearsay solely on the basis of being offered for the truth of a different inference. With respect to those statements possessing sufficient guarantees of trustworthiness, resort to the residual hearsay exception of Rule 807 is clearly preferable.

3 Michael H. Graham, *Handbook of Federal Evidence* § 801.7, at 73–77 (5th ed. 2001) (footnotes omitted).

The circumstances of this case, as well as other cases, can make it tempting to minimize hearsay dangers when a declaration is assertive but offered as a basis for inferring a belief of the declarant that most likely was not a significant aspect of the communication process at the time the declaration was made. Absent unusual circumstances, the unknown declarant likely would not have thought about communicating the implied belief at issue, and this lack of intent arguably justifies excluding the assertion from the hearsay rule. Nevertheless, we are not convinced that the absence of intent necessarily makes the underlying belief more reliable, especially when the belief is derived from verbal conduct as opposed to nonverbal conduct.

Four dangers are generally identified to justify the exclusion of out-of-court statements under the hearsay rule: erroneous memory, faulty perception, ambiguity, and insincerity or misrepresentation. Yet, the distinction drawn between intended and unintended conduct or speech only implicates the danger of insincerity, based on the assumption that a person who lacks an intent to assert something also lacks an intent to misrepresent. The other "hearsay dangers," however, remain viable, giving rise to the need for cross-examination. Moreover, even the danger of insincerity may continue to be present in those instances where the reliability of the direct assertion may be questioned. If the expressed assertion is insincere, such as a fabricated story, the implied assertion derived from the expressed assertion will similarly be unreliable. Implied assertions can be no more reliable than the predicate expressed assertion.

The consequence of the committee's approach is to admit into evidence a declarant's belief in the existence of a fact the evidence is offered to prove, without cross-examination, just as if the declarant had explicitly stated the belief. Yet, if the declarant of the written note in this case had intended to declare his or her belief that Dullard had knowledge and possession of drug lab materials, the note would unquestionably constitute hearsay. Implied assertions from speech intended as communication clearly come within the definition of a statement under rule 5.801(a)(1). Unlike the committee, however, we do not believe indirect or unintentional assertions in speech are reliable enough to avoid the hearsay rule. We think the best approach is to evaluate the relevant assertion in the context of the purpose for which the evidence is offered.

We recognize this approach will have a tendency to make most implied assertions hearsay. However, we view this in a favorable manner because it means the evidence will be judged for its admission at trial based on accepted exceptions or exclusions to the hearsay rule. It also establishes a better, more straightforward rule for litigants and trial courts to understand and apply.

Additionally, we interpret legislative enactments consistent with common law principles when the language used by the legislature does not specifically negate the common law. Clearly, there is no explicit language in our definition of hearsay under rule 5.801(a) and (c), as with the federal rule, that categorizes implied assertions from oral or written words as nonhearsay. The rule only expressly excludes unintended conduct. The characterization arrived at by the committee is achieved by analogy to nonverbal conduct. Yet, the specific exclusion under the rule of nonverbal conduct as nonhearsay, in the absence of the specific exclusion of nonassertive verbal conduct or assertive verbal conduct offered to infer something other than the matter asserted from the definition of a statement, tends to indicate that the legislature may not have intended to exclude such implied assertions from the hearsay rule. Thus, the rule should be read to incorporate our common law approach....

[The court found no exemption or exception to the hearsay rule applicable to the note.] [Dissenting opinion omitted.]

Hearsay Quiz

Dirk owns a number of legal businesses, and the government believes he runs some illegal businesses as well, including gambling, loansharking and money laundering operations, with his second in command, Edgar. The FBI has tapped the phones of and placed a tail on Dirk and Edgar to monitor their day-to-day activities. The following statements have been heard on the wiretap or by the agents that have been following Dirk and/or Edgar. Before the U.S. Attorney (USA) gives the FBI the permission to arrest Dirk, she wants to make sure there is sufficient evidence to prosecute Dirk for his illicit financial dealings. The USA has asked you to determine if the following pieces of evidence are hearsay **per FRE 801(c) only** (in other words, just determine whether it is or is not hearsay—do not worry about possible exceptions to the hearsay rule). You may assume each piece of evidence is relevant. You may also assume each of the foregoing actions or statements were either overheard by an FBI agent or taped on a wiretap. Please consider each piece of evidence separately when analyzing the facts of each question.

1. Edgar approached Dirk and asked what he should do about a "client" named Daniel Sheriff who was behind in his gambling repayments. Dirk picked up a pencil, broke it in half, and threw it in the trash. On the issue of whether Dirk ordered an assault on Daniel Sheriff, is this evidence hearsay?

2. Edgar sees Daniel Sheriff on the street and begins to run after him. On the issue of proving that Edgar killed Sheriff, is this evidence hearsay?

3. After learning that Daniel Sheriff was shot and killed under mysterious circumstances, Dirk went to see Edgar. When Dirk asked Edgar what happened to Daniel Sheriff, Edgar began to sing Bob Marley's song "I Shot the Sheriff." In order to prove Edgar killed Daniel Sheriff, is this evidence hearsay?

4. The FBI followed Edgar to a crowded street where he was traveling west by foot. Edgar opened and closed an umbrella, even though it was a sunny day. After Edgar closed the umbrella, a man started walking toward him. As the two men passed each other, they exchanged briefcases. They did not say anything to each other or make eye contact when they exchanged briefcases. To prove a drug deal occurred, is this exchange hearsay?

5. After the briefcases were exchanged, Edgar made a phone call and in Turkish said, "It's all taken care of." To prove that a drug transaction occurred, is this hearsay?

6. At the trial for the briefcase drug transaction, Dirk claims he cannot speak Turkish. To prove that he speaks Turkish, the prosecution wants to introduce a number of recordings where Dirk is fluently conversing in Turkish concerning the state of Turkish soccer. Are these conversations hearsay?

7. During one of the Turkish conversations, the person alleged to be Dirk boasts, "I sell more cocaine than anyone in this town." The prosecution also wants to admit this conversation to prove that Dirk controls a large drug enterprise and to prove he speaks Turkish. For these purposes, are these conversations hearsay?

8. Dirk had a conversation with his father on a street corner. The FBI could not overhear this conversation. After Dirk walked away, the father began to cry. In order to prove that Dirk confessed to a crime to his father, is this evidence hearsay?

9. Dirk met with a local businesswoman, who stated that she needed money to keep running her business. The defendant responded by saying, "Granting you a loan at our normal interest rate will not be a problem, consider it done." To prove he made an illegal loan, is this statement by Dirk hearsay?

10. When Edgar was arrested, he told the police his name was John Doe. In order to prove consciousness of guilt, the government offers the statement. Is it hearsay?

11. When Edgar was arrested, he told the police his name was Napoleon Bonaparte. In order to prove that Edgar is insane, is the statement hearsay?

12. When Dirk learned that Edgar was under arrest, he sent Edgar a note in jail that read: "I know that you know that I know that your mother lives on 1212 Main Street and has a frail heart." In order to prove that Dirk illegally threatened Edgar, is the message hearsay?

13. When Dirk learned that Edgar was under arrest, he sent Edgar a note in jail that read: "I know that you know that I know that your mother lives on 1212 Main Street and has a frail heart." In order to prove that Edgar's mother lives on 1212 Main Street, is the message hearsay?

14. In order to prove that Edgar's mother has a frail heart, the government offers the testimony of Edgar's mother's nurse. The nurse will testify that the doctor told her to put Edgar's mother on the standard treatment plan for someone with a frail heart. Is this hearsay?

15. In order to prove that his import/export business is legitimate, Dirk offers proof that no one had ever complained on Yelp about his business. Is this hearsay?

16. Fearing a biased jury due to prejudicial publicity in the media, Dirk wants to remove the trial to a less biased venue. As proof of bias, Dirk wants to introduce newspaper headlines regarding his trial into evidence. Is the introduction of these headlines hearsay?

17. Dirk, while on the stand, testifies that he did not write the note threatening Edgar and that he did not order anyone to do so. On cross-examination the prosecution wants to show the jury a videotape of Dirk writing the note to prove that the he wrote it. Is the videotape hearsay?

18. Dirk, while on the stand, testifies that he did not write the note threatening Edgar and that he did not order anyone to do so. On cross-examination the prosecution plays an audiotape where Dirk states, "I just wrote a note telling Edgar to do the right thing." Is the audiotape hearsay?

19. On direct examination of Dirk at his trial for threatening Edgar, Dirk states, "I once told Edgar, 'I love you like a brother.'" Is this statement hearsay if it is offered to demonstrate Dirk's feelings for Edgar?

20. A car salesman will testify that Edgar walked into his showroom and stated, "My boss, Dirk, wants to buy your most expensive Rolls Royce." If this is offered by the prosecutor to prove that Dirk has substantial assets, is this hearsay?

21. An FBI agent will testify that Edgar asked Dirk, "I have some Rolls Royce hub caps. You want them, don't you?" If this is offered to prove Dirk owned a Rolls Royce, is this hearsay?

22. An FBI agent will testify that he overheard Edgar tell Dirk, "Our entire cocaine shipment was captured by the Coast Guard—we are out $2 million." If offered to prove Dirk had a financial motive to commit a crime, is this hearsay?

23. Dirk wants to introduce a character witness who will testify that he has lived in Dirk's neighborhood for the last 10 years and that Dirk has a reputation as a peaceful person in the neighborhood. If offered to prove his reputation, is this hearsay?

II. The Hearsay Exemptions

Relevant Rule
FRE 802

The Rule Against Hearsay

Hearsay is not admissible unless any of the following provides otherwise:
- a federal statute;
- these rules; or
- other rules prescribed by the Supreme Court.

Introduction

If the proponent's evidence has been deemed hearsay, the battle is far from over. As we shall see, FRE 802 mandates that hearsay is inadmissible except as provided by the FRE, a federal statute, or other rules prescribed by the Supreme Court. The drafters of the FRE crafted thirty-seven exemptions or exceptions to the rule prohibiting hearsay. We will not review all thirty-seven (much to your chagrin, I am sure) but you will see some commonality to these exceptions and exemptions.

First, a quick word on nomenclature. Technically, all the admissible prior statements by witnesses and admissions by party-opponents under FRE 801(d) are not considered hearsay that is excepted from the ban on hearsay evidence; instead, they are considered "not hearsay." In other words, they are expressly exempted from being considered hearsay. Because of this label, the items listed in FRE 801(d) are not hearsay, while the items listed in FRE 803, 804, and 807 are hearsay that are excepted from the hearsay rule. For our current purposes, this is a difference without any substance, as both exemptions and exceptions are admissible.

As we examine these exemptions/exceptions, we shall take an approach that is similar to how we approached the specialized relevance rules in Chapter 3. Namely, we shall first explore the underpinnings of why this evidence is admissible. Usually, hearsay will be admissible due to its reliability (we trust it due to its context) and/or its necessity (this type of hearsay is the only source we have to this proof because the declarant is unavailable).

Secondly, we shall explore the foundation for these exceptions/exemptions. Think of the foundational requirements for a hearsay exception/exemption as similar to the prima facie elements of a tort: The proponent of the hearsay must establish each foundational element in order to gain the benefit of exception/exemption. Thinking through the foundational requirement will not only hone your statutory interpretation skills, but it will also give you a better vision of how these exceptions/exemptions will be used at trial.

A. Prior Statements of Testifying Witnesses

1. Prior Inconsistent Statements

Relevant Rule
FRE 801(d)(1)(A)

(d) Statements That Are Not Hearsay. A statement that meets the following conditions is not hearsay:

(1) *A Declarant-Witness's Prior Statement.*

The declarant testifies and is subject to cross-examination about a prior statement, and the statement:

(A) is inconsistent with the declarant's testimony and was given under penalty of perjury at a trial, hearing, or other proceeding or in a deposition;

FRE 801(d)(1)(A) is interconnected with a number of rules and doctrines we have already explored. First among them is the idea that a testifying witness's prior statement is still hearsay, even if the declarant is on the stand and subject to oath/demeanor evaluation/cross-examination. If the foundation is established, FRE 801(d)(1) classifies certain hearsay statements as non-hearsay.

The second interconnected idea is the scope of impeachment. When we reviewed FRE 613 we saw that prior inconsistent statements under that rule were (i) nonhearsay and (ii) not offered substantively. Now we can understand why a prior inconsistent statement could be nonhearsay—it is not being offered for its truth but rather to show conflicting narratives have been offered by this witness. The price the proponent pays for not offering the evidence for its truth under FRE 613 is that the proponent cannot use the information in the statement substantively (i.e., for its truth). Thus, the evidence cannot be offered to prove a light was green; it can only be offered to show that previously the witness said the light was green and now she states it was red.

FRE 801(d)(1)(A) allows a declarant-witness's prior inconsistent statement to be used substantively in narrow circumstances. In other words, to bring back our impeachment example, if the witness testified at trial (today) that a traffic light was red, but in the past, in a deposition, she testified that the light was green, then under FRE 801(d)(1)(A) the prior inconsistent statement could be used by opposing counsel substantively to prove that the light was green.

Now, take a look at this rule, and try to craft the foundation that one must establish in order to meet this rule. Try to craft that foundation before you read on.

In the context of FRE 801(d)(1)(A), that foundation is:

- the prior statement must be inconsistent with the trial testimony that comes after it,
- the prior statement must be made in a proceeding or deposition where the witness was under oath, and

- the speaker must be subject to cross-examination at the current proceeding regarding her earlier statement.

So, in reviewing that foundation, where are the gray areas? The first is to define "inconsistent." Certainly, a diametrically opposed statement will work, but courts have allowed lesser inconsistencies to qualify. If the more recent statement is indicative of a change of view or mistake, then it possesses impeachment value. Thus, as we discussed previously in the impeachment chapter, going from specific to general, or from certain to uncertain, may satisfy the inconsistency requirement if an impeachment value exists in pointing out the differing statements.

The next gray area is to explore what types of "proceedings" qualify under the rule. In crafting the rule in the manner they did, the drafters of the FRE clearly wanted certainty surrounding the prior statement—we want to be sure the witness actually said it. Thus, the more formal the setting, the more likely the statement was captured accurately. Similarly, the drafters of this rule wanted the prior statement to be under oath to increase the likelihood of honest responses. Accordingly, grand jury testimony has been found to fit under "proceedings," as have preliminary hearings and prior trials.

Finally, we come to the "subject to cross-examination" requirement. This foundational element requires that witnesses be tested on the statement. But just how "tested" must the witness-declarant be? What happens if the witness possesses a total memory lapse? As we shall see in a future case, *United States v. Owens*, this is not a simple question to answer.

Keep in mind as we undertake our review that many hearsay exceptions/exemptions can be conceptualized quite well with a flow chart. For example, one way of viewing FRE 801(d)(1)(A) is:

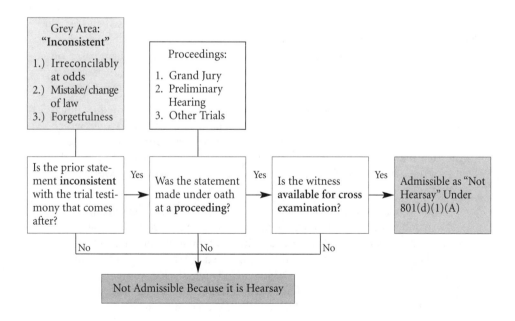

If this method of synthesizing the material works well for you, consider applying it to the remaining exceptions/exemptions.

Problem 7-1

In February of 1982, a burglar stole 72 postal money orders from the Oxley, Missouri U.S. post office. A month later, police apprehended Kenneth Polin who had cashed five of the stolen money orders in Poplar Bluff, Missouri. Polin testified before a federal grand jury, stating that the defendant, Richard Russell, had asked him to cash the money orders in return for half of the money. Polin also testified that Russell prepared the money orders, drove him to the stores where they were cashed, and gave him a fake ID to use when cashing them. Polin plead guilty to passing forged money orders and agreed to cooperate with the government's case against Russell in exchange for leniency in sentencing.

Russell was charged with aiding and abetting the passing of forged United States postal money orders. When Polin was called as a witness at Russell's trial, he stated that he could not remember if he had any contact with Russell in February or March of 1982. The trial court allowed the government to introduce Polin's prior statements to the federal grand jury into evidence. Russell was convicted. On appeal he challenges the admission of Polin's grand jury testimony as hearsay. What result?

Problem 7-2

On March 5, 1980 two men robbed the Brookland Station Post Office in Washington, D. C. John T. Livingston and David Coyle were arrested for the crime. While investigating the crime, the postal inspector interviewed Yvonne Hester, who claimed that she had accompanied Livingston and Coyle on a trip to Trenton and Philadelphia where they attempted to cash postal money orders stolen from the post office. Hester claimed that Livingston and Coyle openly discussed and joked about the robbery on this trip. This interview took place at Hester's home, where the postal inspector asked her questions, took notes, wrote a statement based on her responses, asked her to read a typewritten copy and to make any necessary changes, and then obtained her signature swearing to the accuracy of the statement.

At Livingston and Coyle's trial for armed robbery, Hester denied or failed to recall the incriminating statements made by Livingston and Coyle which she had sworn to in her statement to the postal inspector. The court then admitted Hester's statement to the postal inspector into evidence to prove the guilt of the defendants. The statement included the following portion that was read at trial:

> They were … laughing and talking. David said John had the gun and they were laughing about how scared the man in the post office was. David said that besides the money orders … he and John took out a machine to make the money orders on and that they used the machine to make up the money orders later. I saw David with a whole stack of postal money orders.… John asked David if he made sure he wiped off their fingerprints and David said "yeah, man, I'm sure that I didn't leave any."

On appeal, Livingston and Coyle challenge the admission of Hester's prior statement as inadmissible hearsay. How would you rule?

2. Prior Consistent Statements

Relevant Rule
FRE 801(d)(1)(B)

(d) Statements That Are Not Hearsay. A statement that meets the following conditions is not hearsay:

(1) *A Declarant-Witness's Prior Statement.* The declarant testifies and is subject to cross-examination about a prior statement, and the statement ...

(B) is consistent with the declarant's testimony and is offered:

(i) to rebut an express or implied charge that the declarant recently fabricated it or acted from a recent improper influence or motive in so testifying; or

(ii) to rehabilitate the declarant's credibility as a witness when attacked on another ground;

FRE 801(d)(1)(B) allows a witness to rebut an impeaching attack by offering consistent statements. Thus, if a witness is accused of lying, she may point to a prior statement that is consistent with her testimony to rebut the attack. By doing so, a witness rebuts the implication that she lied because her earlier statements are consistent with her current testimony. As in the previous section, please try to craft the foundation for yourself before moving on to the next paragraph.

The foundation for the rule is:

- the statement offered must be consistent with the present testimony by the witness,

- it must be admissible either to rehabilitate the witness's credibility or to rebut a charge of recent fabrication or recent improper influence or motive, and

- the witness must be subject to cross-examination at the current proceeding.

In terms of the first element, note that there are fewer requirements for consistent statements than inconsistent ones under FRE 801(d)(1)(A). In a FRE 801(d)(1)(B) situation, the prior consistent statement need not be sworn to and need not be part of a formal "proceeding." It must, however, be "consistent." On the one hand, small variations in phrasing would not necessarily prevent an earlier statement from being "consistent" with a statement made at trial. To argue that small variations make the two statements "inconsistent" would be unfair and unrealistic.

On the other hand, the allegedly "consistent" statement cannot be read too broadly—it must relate to the testimony at trial and should not introduce new points not covered in the witness's testimony. In other words, the "consistent" words must be consistent with matters on which the witness was actually impeached.

The second element explores the degree to which the consistent statement is effective for rehabilitation. For FRE 801(d)(1)(b)(i), a consistent statement rehabilitates when it rebuts a charge of recent fabrication or improper influence/motive. For FRE 801(d)(1)(b)(ii), a consistent statement rehabilitates when it invalidates attack on a witness such as inconsistency or faulty memory. The effectiveness of the consistent statement for rehabilitation will be explored in the *Tome v. United States* case, which applies to both (b)(i) and (b)(ii). The third element, like the third element of FRE 801(d)(1)(A), will be explored in greater depth later.

Focus Questions: *Tome v. United States*

- Should corroborating statements that are made after a motive to fabricate arises still be admissible so that the jury can weigh its applicability in rebutting that motive instead of the court? Why would the court take this determination out of the jury's control?

- Why does the dissent advocate for a more flexible application of FRE 801(d)(1)(B)?

Tome v. United States
513 U.S. 150 (1995)

KENNEDY, J., announced the judgment of the Court and delivered the opinion of the Court with respect to Parts I, II-A, II-C, and III, in which STEVENS, SCALIA, SOUTER, and GINSBURG, JJ., joined, and an opinion with respect to Part II-B, in which STEVENS, SOUTER, and GINSBURG, JJ., joined. SCALIA, J., filed an opinion concurring in part and concurring in the judgment. BREYER, J., filed a dissenting opinion, in which REHNQUIST, C.J., and O'CONNOR and THOMAS, JJ., joined.

Various Federal Courts of Appeals are divided over the evidence question presented by this case. At issue is the interpretation of a provision in the Federal Rules of Evidence bearing upon the admissibility of statements, made by a declarant who testifies as a witness, that are consistent with the testimony and are offered to rebut a charge of a "recent fabrication or improper influence or motive." Fed.Rule Evid. 801(d)(1)(B). The question is whether out-of-court consistent statements made after the alleged fabrication, or after the alleged improper influence or motive arose, are admissible under the Rule.

I

Petitioner Tome was charged in a one-count indictment with the felony of sexual abuse of a child, his own daughter, aged four at the time of the alleged crime. The case having arisen on the Navajo Indian Reservation, Tome was tried by a jury in the United States District Court for the District of New Mexico....

Tome and the child's mother had been divorced in 1988. A tribal court awarded joint custody of the daughter, A.T., to both parents, but Tome had primary physical custody. In 1989 the mother was unsuccessful in petitioning the tribal court for primary custody of A.T., but was awarded custody for the summer of 1990.... On August 27, 1990, the mother contacted Colorado authorities with allegations that Tome had committed sexual abuse against A.T.

The prosecution's theory was that Tome committed sexual assaults upon the child while she was in his custody and that the crime was disclosed when the child was spending vacation time with her mother. The defense argued that the allegations were concocted so the child would not be returned to her father. At trial A.T., then 6½ years old, was the Government's first witness. For the most part, her direct testimony consisted of one- and two-word answers to a series of leading questions. Cross-examination took place over two trial days. The defense asked A.T. 348 questions. On the first day A.T. answered all the questions posed to her on general, background subjects.

The next day there was no testimony, and the prosecutor met with A.T. When cross-examination of A.T. resumed, she was questioned about those conversations but was reluctant to discuss them. Defense counsel then began questioning her about the allegations of abuse, and it appears she was reluctant at many points to answer. As the trial judge noted, however, some of the defense questions were imprecise or unclear. The judge expressed his concerns with the examination of A.T., observing there were lapses of as much as 40–55 seconds between some questions and the answers and that on the second day of examination the witness seemed to be losing concentration. The trial judge stated, "We have a very difficult situation here."

After A.T. testified, the Government produced six witnesses who testified about a total of seven statements made by A.T. describing the alleged sexual assaults: A.T.'s babysitter recited A.T.'s statement to her on August 22, 1990, that she did not want to return to her father because he "gets drunk and he thinks I'm his wife"; the babysitter related further details given by A.T. on August 27, 1990, while A.T.'s mother stood outside the room and listened after the mother had been unsuccessful in questioning A.T. herself; the mother recounted what she had heard A.T. tell the babysitter; a social worker recounted details A.T. told her on August 29, 1990, about the assaults; and three pediatricians, Drs. Kuper, Reich, and Spiegel, related A.T.'s statements to them describing how and where she had been touched by Tome. All but A.T.'s statement to Dr. Spiegel implicated Tome....

A.T.'s out-of-court statements, recounted by the six witnesses, were offered by the Government under Rule 801(d)(1)(B). The trial court admitted all of the statements over defense counsel's objection, accepting the Government's argument that they rebutted the implicit charge that A.T.'s testimony was motivated by a desire to live with her mother.... Following trial, Tome was convicted and sentenced to 12 years' imprisonment.

On appeal, the Court of Appeals for the Tenth Circuit affirmed, adopting the Government's argument that all of A.T.'s out-of-court statements were admissible under Rule 801(d)(1)(B) even though they had been made after A.T.'s alleged motive to fabricate arose.... We granted certiorari ... and now reverse.

II

The prevailing common-law rule for more than a century before adoption of the Federal Rules of Evidence was that a prior consistent statement introduced to rebut a charge of recent fabrication or improper influence or motive was admissible if the statement had been made before the alleged fabrication, influence, or motive came into being, but it was inadmissible if made afterwards. As Justice Story explained: "[W]here the testimony is assailed as a fabrication of a recent date, ... in order to repel such imputation, proof of the *antecedent* declaration of the party may be admitted." *Ellicott v. Pearl,* 35 U.S. (10 Pet.) 412, 439, 9 L.Ed. 475 (1836) (emphasis added).

McCormick and Wigmore stated the rule in a more categorical manner: "[T]he applicable principle is that the prior consistent statement has no relevancy to refute the charge unless the consistent statement was made before the source of the bias, interest, influence or incapacity originated." E. Cleary, McCormick on Evidence § 49, p. 105 (2d ed. 1972) (hereafter McCormick). See also 4 J. Wigmore, Evidence § 1128, p. 268 (J. Chadbourn rev. 1972) (hereafter Wigmore) ("A consistent statement, at a *time prior* to the existence of a fact said to indicate bias ... will effectively explain away the force of the impeaching evidence" (emphasis in original)). The question is whether Rule 801(d)(1)(B) embodies this temporal requirement. We hold that it does.

A

... Rule 801 defines prior consistent statements as nonhearsay only if they are offered to rebut a charge of "recent fabrication or improper influence or motive." Fed.Rule Evid. 801(d)(1)(B). Noting the "troublesome" logic of treating a witness' prior consistent statements as hearsay at all (because the declarant is present in court and subject to cross-examination), the Advisory Committee decided to treat those consistent statements, once the preconditions of the Rule were satisfied, as nonhearsay and admissible as substantive evidence, not just to rebut an attack on the witness' credibility. See Advisory Committee's Notes on Fed.Rule Evid. 801(d)(1) ... A consistent statement meeting the requirements of the Rule is thus placed in the same category as a declarant's inconsistent statement made under oath in another proceeding, or prior identification testimony, or admissions by a party opponent. See Fed.Rule Evid. 801.

The Rules do not accord this weighty, nonhearsay status to all prior consistent statements. To the contrary, admissibility under the Rules is confined to those statements offered to rebut a charge of "recent fabrication or improper influence or motive," the same phrase used by the Advisory Committee in its description of the "traditiona[l]" common law of evidence, which was the background against which the Rules were drafted. See Advisory Committee's Notes, *supra*. Prior consistent statements may not be admitted to counter all forms of impeachment or to bolster the witness merely because she has been discredited. In the present context, the question is whether A.T.'s out-of-court statements rebutted the alleged link between her desire to be with her mother and her testimony, not whether they suggested that A.T.'s in-court testimony was true. The Rule speaks of a party rebutting an alleged motive, not bolstering the veracity of the story told.

This limitation is instructive, not only to establish the preconditions of admissibility but also to reinforce the significance of the requirement that the consistent statements must have been made before the alleged influence, or motive to fabricate, arose. That is to say, the forms of impeachment within the Rule's coverage are the ones in which the temporal requirement makes the most sense. Impeachment by charging that the testimony is a recent fabrication or results from an improper influence or motive is, as a general matter, capable of direct and forceful refutation through introduction of out-of-court consistent statements that predate the alleged fabrication, influence, or motive. A consistent statement that predates the motive is a square rebuttal of the charge that the testimony was contrived as a consequence of that motive. By contrast, prior consistent statements carry little rebuttal force when most other types of impeachment are involved. McCormick § 49, p. 105 ("When the attack takes the form of impeachment of character, by showing misconduct, convictions or bad reputation, it is generally agreed that there is no color for sustaining by consistent statements. The defense does not meet the assault" (footnote omitted)); see also 4 Wigmore § 1131, p. 293 ("The broad rule obtains in a few courts that consistent statements may be admitted *after* impeachment of any sort—in particular after any impeachment by *cross-examination*. But there is no reason for such a loose rule" (footnote omitted)).

There may arise instances when out-of-court statements that postdate the alleged fabrication have some probative force in rebutting a charge of fabrication or improper influence or motive, but those statements refute the charged fabrication in a less direct and forceful way. Evidence that a witness made consistent statements after the alleged motive to fabricate arose may suggest in some degree that the in-court testimony is truthful, and thus suggest in some degree that that testimony did not result from some improper influence; but if the drafters of Rule 801(d)(1)(B) intended to countenance rebuttal along that indirect inferential chain, the purpose of confining the types of impeachment that open the door to rebuttal by introducing consistent statements becomes unclear. If consistent statements are admissible without reference to the timeframe we find imbedded in the Rule, there appears no sound reason not to admit consistent statements to rebut other forms of impeachment as well. . . .

The underlying theory of the Government's position is that an out-of-court consistent statement, whenever it was made, tends to bolster the testimony of a witness and so tends also to rebut an express or implied charge that the testimony has been the product of an improper influence. Congress could have adopted that rule with ease, providing, for instance, that "a witness' prior consistent statements are admissible whenever relevant to assess the witness' truthfulness or accuracy." The theory would be that, in a broad sense, any prior statement by a witness concerning the disputed issues at trial would have some relevance in assessing the accuracy or truthfulness of the witness' in-court testimony on the same subject. The narrow Rule enacted by Congress, however, cannot be understood to incorporate the Government's theory.

Our analysis is strengthened by the observation that the somewhat peculiar language of the Rule bears close similarity to the language used in many of the common-law cases that describe the premotive requirement. "Rule 801(d)(1)(B) employs the precise language — 'rebut[ting] . . . charge[s] . . . of recent fabrication or improper influence or motive' — consistently used in the panoply of pre-1975 decisions." Ohlbaum, The Hobgoblin of the Federal Rules of Evidence: An Analysis of Rule 801(d)(1)(B), Prior Consistent Statements and a New Proposal, 1987 B.Y.U.L.Rev. 231, 245.

The language of the Rule, in its concentration on rebutting charges of recent fabrication or improper influence or motive to the exclusion of other forms of impeachment, as well as in its use of wording that follows the language of the common-law cases, suggests that it was intended to carry over the common-law premotive rule.

B

Our conclusion that Rule 801(d)(1)(B) embodies the common-law premotive requirement is confirmed by an examination of the Advisory Committee's Notes to the Federal Rules of Evidence. We have relied on those well-considered Notes as a useful guide in ascertaining the meaning of the Rules. Where, as with Rule 801(d)(1)(B), "Congress did not amend the Advisory Committee's draft in any way . . . the Committee's commentary is particularly relevant in determining the meaning of the document Congress enacted." *Beech Aircraft Corp. v. Rainey,* 488 U.S. 153, 165–166, n. 9 (1988). The Notes are also a respected source of scholarly commentary. Professor Cleary was a distinguished commentator on the law of evidence, and he and members of the Committee consulted and considered the views, criticisms, and suggestions of the academic community in preparing the Notes.

The Notes disclose a purpose to adhere to the common law in the application of evidentiary principles, absent express provisions to the contrary. Where the Rules did depart from their common-law antecedents, in general the Committee said so. The Notes give no indication, however, that Rule 801(d)(1)(B) abandoned the premotive requirement. The entire discussion of Rule 801(d)(1)(B) is limited to the following comment:

> "Prior consistent statements traditionally have been admissible to rebut charges of recent fabrication or improper influence or motive but not as substantive evidence. Under the rule they are substantive evidence. The prior statement is consistent with the testimony given on the stand, and, if the opposite party

wishes to open the door for its admission in evidence, no sound reason is apparent why it should not be received generally." Notes on Rule 801(d)(1)(B).

Throughout their discussion of the Rules, the Advisory Committee's Notes rely on Wigmore and McCormick as authority for the common-law approach. In light of the categorical manner in which those authors state the premotive requirement, it is difficult to imagine that the drafters, who noted the new substantive use of prior consistent statements, would have remained silent if they intended to modify the premotive requirement.... Here, we do not think the drafters of the Rule intended to scuttle the whole premotive requirement and rationale without so much as a whisper of explanation....

D

The case before us illustrates some of the important considerations supporting the Rule as we interpret it, especially in criminal cases. If the Rule were to permit the introduction of prior statements as substantive evidence to rebut every implicit charge that a witness' in-court testimony results from recent fabrication or improper influence or motive, the whole emphasis of the trial could shift to the out-of-court statements, not the in-court ones. The present case illustrates the point. In response to a rather weak charge that A.T.'s testimony was a fabrication created so the child could remain with her mother, the Government was permitted to present a parade of sympathetic and credible witnesses who did no more than recount A.T.'s detailed out-of-court statements to them. Although those statements might have been probative on the question whether the alleged conduct had occurred, they shed but minimal light on whether A.T. had the charged motive to fabricate. At closing argument before the jury, the Government placed great reliance on the prior statements for substantive purposes but did not once seek to use them to rebut the impact of the alleged motive.

We are aware that in some cases it may be difficult to ascertain when a particular fabrication, influence, or motive arose. Yet, as the Government concedes, a majority of common-law courts were performing this task for well over a century, and the Government has presented us with no evidence that those courts, or the judicial circuits that adhere to the rule today, have been unable to make the determination. Even under the Government's hypothesis, moreover, the thing to be rebutted must be identified, so the date of its origin cannot be that much more difficult to ascertain. By contrast, as the Advisory Committee commented, the Government's approach, which would require the trial court to weigh all of the circumstances surrounding a statement that suggest its probativeness against the court's assessment of the strength of the alleged motive, would entail more of a burden, with no guidance to attorneys in preparing a case or to appellate courts in reviewing a judgment.

III

... Our holding is confined to the requirements for admission under Rule 801(d)(1)(B). The Rule permits the introduction of a declarant's consistent out-of-court statements to rebut a charge of recent fabrication or improper influence or motive only when those statements were made before the charged recent fabrication or improper influence or motive. These conditions of admissibility were not established here.

The judgment of the Court of Appeals for the Tenth Circuit is reversed, and the case is remanded for further proceedings consistent with this opinion.

It is so ordered.

Justice SCALIA, concurring in part and concurring in the judgment.

I concur in the judgment of the Court, and join its opinion except for Part II-B. That Part, which is devoted entirely to a discussion of the Advisory Committee's Notes pertinent to Rule 801(d)(1)(B), gives effect to those Notes not only because they are "a respected source of scholarly commentary," but also because they display the "purpose," or "inten[t]," of the draftsmen.

I have previously acquiesced in, *see, e.g., Beech Aircraft Corp. v. Rainey*, 488 U.S. 153, (1988), and indeed myself engaged in, *see United States v. Owens*, 484 U.S. 554, 562 (1988), similar use of the Advisory Committee Notes. More mature consideration has persuaded me that is wrong. Having been prepared by a body of experts, the Notes are assuredly persuasive scholarly commentaries — ordinarily *the* most persuasive — concerning the meaning of the Rules. But they bear no special authoritativeness as the work of the draftsmen, any more than the views of Alexander Hamilton (a draftsman) bear more authority than the views of Thomas Jefferson (not a draftsman) with regard to the meaning of the Constitution. It is the words of the Rules that have been authoritatively adopted — by this Court, or by Congress if it makes a statutory change. In my view even the adopting Justices' thoughts, unpromulgated as Rules, have no authoritative (as opposed to persuasive) effect, any more than their thoughts regarding an opinion (reflected in exchanges of memoranda before the opinion issues) authoritatively demonstrate the meaning of that opinion. And the same for the thoughts of congressional draftsmen who prepare statutory amendments to the Rules. Like a judicial opinion and like a statute, the promulgated Rule says what it says, regardless of the intent of its drafters....

Justice BREYER, with whom THE CHIEF JUSTICE, Justice O'CONNOR, and Justice THOMAS join, dissenting.

... [T]he common-law premotive rule was not as uniform as the majority suggests. A minority of courts recognized that postmotive statements could be relevant to rebut a charge of recent fabrication or improper influence or motive under the right circumstances. I concede that the majority of courts took the rule of thumb as absolute. But, I have searched the cases (and the commentators) in vain for an explanation of why that should be so.

One can imagine a possible explanation: Trial judges may find it easier to administer an absolute rule. Yet, there is no indication in any of the cases that trial judges would, or do, find it particularly difficult to administer a more flexible rule in this context. And, there is something to be said for the greater authority that flexibility grants the trial judge to tie rulings on the admissibility of rehabilitative evidence more closely to the needs and circumstances of the particular case. 1 J. Weinstein & M. Berger, Weinstein's Evidence ¶ 401[01], pp. 401–8 to 401–9 (1994) ("A flexible approach ... is more apt to yield a sensible result than the application of a mechanical rule"). Furthermore, the majority concedes that the premotive rule, while seemingly bright line, poses its own administrative difficulties....

In this case, the Court of Appeals, applying an approach consistent with what I have described above, decided that A.T.'s prior consistent statements were probative on the question of whether her story as a witness reflected a motive to lie. There is no reason to reevaluate this factbound conclusion. Accordingly, I would affirm the judgment of the Court of Appeals.

Problem 7-3

On Christmas Eve 1992, Vincent Price was eating dinner in a restaurant when he heard what sounded like a car crash outside. He got up to investigate and just as he approached the front parking lot of the restaurant he heard what sounded like a gunshot. A few seconds later, he saw Shannon Wilson, another restaurant patron who had just left, lying on the ground in the parking lot with an armed man standing over him. Wilson yelled, "He shot me!" The gunman then drove away in Wilson's car. Wilson later died from a gunshot wound to the chest.

Bruce Reliford was arrested that night and identified in a line-up as the assailant by Price and several other witnesses. At Reliford's trial for car-jacking, Price testified that Reliford had looked him full in the face twice during the car-jacking. Specifically he said that Reliford looked at him as he got into Wilson's car, and again as he backed up the car before driving away. On cross-examination of Price, Reliford's attorney sarcastically asked: "Mr. Price, your memory gets better with time, doesn't it?" On redirect, the court granted the government's motion to admit written statements Price had given to police on the day of the crime where he recounted the events he had witnessed. Those prior written statements were consistent with Price's testimony in court. Reliford was convicted of car-jacking. On appeal he contests admission of Price's prior written statement as hearsay. How do you rule?

Problem 7-4

Eric Conroy was accused of sexually assaulting three women in South Dakota. The victims did not report these assaults right away because, they claim, Conroy's father is a powerful local police officer and they feared retribution for reporting Conroy's crimes.

One of the alleged victims, Raelene Tail, provided a detailed written statement to the police at the time of Conroy's arrest. At Conroy's trial, the defense impeached Tail on cross-examination pointing out several inconsistencies between her testimony at trial and her prior written statement. Specifically, her statements were inconsistent in regard to whether the porch light was on, the number of adults at home, her missing clothes, and an earlier encounter with Conroy at a mutual friend's home. On redirect, the government attempted to rehabilitate Tail by pointing out several consistencies between her prior statement and her testimony that did not specifically relate to the subject matter of the statements impeached by Conroy. These included her stated desire to end her relationship with Conroy. Conroy was convicted and now appeals. Conroy argues that the use of Tail's prior statement by the government on redirect was inadmissible hearsay. How do you rule?

Problem 7-5

Al-Moayad and Zayed were accused of attempting to provide material support to the terrorist organizations Hamas and Al-Qaeda. Two paid government informants, Al-Anss and Saeed, met with the defendants in Yemen while posing as wealthy patrons seeking to support terrorist groups. At these meetings, they discussed to which groups the money would go. In one meeting, Saeed asked "whether his money would go to Hamas, Al-Qaeda, or other groups." Defendant Al-Moayad answered, "Hamas, Al-Qaeda, Massajins [prisoners], Mujahidins, and such. Anyone who we know of, who is in the Jihad field." Informant Al-Anss kept detailed notes on what they learned at these meetings. Prior to these meetings, Al-Anss had asked the U.S. government for millions of dollars for his help, but was only paid $100,000.

At trial, the government did not call the informants as witnesses but the defense called Al-Anss as a witness, alleging that Al-Anss had entrapped them. More specifically, the defendants alleged that Al-Anss's lies and trickery induced their actions. On cross-examination of Al-Anss, the government introduced some of Al-Anss's notes from the meetings to rebut the allegation that his actions induced the defendants' alleged crimes. The notes contained the following:

> "[Defendant] Al-Moayad was 'the right hand' to Sheikh Abdul Majid Al-Zindani; at some point in the past, Al-Moayad was 'the main person choosing the volunteers' to send to fight in the conflicts in Chechnya, Afghanistan, and Bosnia; ... Al-Moayad visited and supported Bin Laden in Afghanistan; he knew young volunteers who were ready for training in jihad; and he gave $3.5 million to Palestine and $20 million to Al-Qaeda 'during last few years and before ... Sept. 11th 2001.'"

Al-Moayad and Zayed were convicted. On appeal, they challenge the admission of these notes. How do you rule?

3. Statements of Identification

Relevant Rule
FRE 801(d)(1)(C)

(d) Statements That Are Not Hearsay. A statement that meets the following conditions is not hearsay:

(1) *A Declarant-Witness's Prior Statement.* The declarant testifies and is subject to cross-examination about a prior statement, and the statement ...

(C) identifies a person as someone the declarant perceived earlier.

FRE 801(d)(1)(C) possesses a simple foundation:

- The statement must be one of identification after having "perceived" the identified person and
- The speaker must be subject to cross-examination on the statement.

The underlying rationale for the rule is that pretrial identifications often prove more reliable than those made in court because they occurred at a time closer to the time of the offense. In order to make the statement admissible in a broad range of situations, the rule does not link the statement to impeachment or rehabilitation in any way. Even if the declarant-witness is supremely confident of her identification at trial, and even if opposing counsel does not attempt to impeach her on that identification, her prior identification is admissible as a crucial component of many criminal trials—the identification of the defendant.

Focus Questions: *United States v. Owens*

- If opposing counsel is unsuccessful in obtaining information from a witness on cross-examination due to the witness's inability to recall details, are FRE 801(d)(1)(C)'s requirements still fulfilled? If so, could a witness's inability to recall ever rise to the level of non-compliance?

United States v. Owens

484 U.S. 554 (1988)

SCALIA, J., delivered the opinion of the Court, in which REHNQUIST, C.J., and WHITE, BLACKMUN, STEVENS, and O'CONNOR, JJ., joined. BRENNAN, J., filed a dissenting opinion, in which MARSHALL, J., joined. KENNEDY, J., took no part in the consideration or decision of the case.

This case requires us to determine whether … Rule 802 of the Federal Rules of Evidence bars testimony concerning a prior, out-of-court identification when the identifying witness is unable, because of memory loss, to explain the basis for the identification.

I

On April 12, 1982, John Foster, a correctional counselor at the federal prison in Lompoc, California, was attacked and brutally beaten with a metal pipe. His skull was fractured, and he remained hospitalized for almost a month. As a result of his injuries, Foster's memory was severely impaired. When Thomas Mansfield, an FBI agent investigating the assault, first attempted to interview Foster, on April 19, he found Foster lethargic and unable to remember his attacker's name. On May 5, Mansfield again spoke to Foster, who was much improved and able to describe the attack. Foster named respondent as his attacker and identified respondent from an array of photographs.

Respondent was tried in Federal District Court for assault with intent to commit murder … At trial, Foster recounted his activities just before the attack, and described feeling the blows to his head and seeing blood on the floor. He testified that he clearly remembered identifying respondent as his assailant during his May 5th interview with Mansfield. On cross-examination, he admitted that he could not remember seeing his assailant. He also admitted that, although there was evidence that he had received numerous visitors in the hospital, he was unable to remember any of them except Mansfield, and could not remember whether any of these visitors had suggested that respondent was the assailant. Defense counsel unsuccessfully sought to refresh his recollection with hospital records, including one indicating that Foster had attributed the assault to someone other than respondent. Respondent was convicted and sentenced to 20 years' imprisonment to be served consecutively to a previous sentence.…

III

… Rule 801(d)(1)(C) defines as not hearsay a prior statement "of identification of a person made after perceiving the person," if the declarant "testifies at the trial or hearing and is subject to cross-examination concerning the statement." The Court of Appeals found that Foster's identification statement did not come within this exclusion because his memory loss prevented his being "subject to cross-examination concerning the statement".…

It seems to us that the more natural reading of "subject to cross-examination concerning the statement" includes what was available here. Ordinarily a witness is regarded as "subject to cross-examination" when he is placed on the stand, under oath, and responds willingly to questions.… [L]imitations on the scope of examination by the trial court or assertions of privilege by the witness may undermine the process to such a degree that meaningful cross-examination within the intent of the Rule no longer exists. But that effect is not produced by the witness' assertion of memory loss—which … is often the very result sought to be produced by cross-examination, and can be effective in destroying the force of the prior statement. Rule 801(d)(1)(C), which specifies that the cross-examination need only "concer[n] the statement," does not on its face require more.…

… The premise for Rule 801(d)(1)(C) was that, given adequate safeguards against suggestiveness, out-of-court identifications were generally preferable to courtroom identifications. Advisory Committee's Notes on Rule 801. Thus, despite the traditional view that such statements were hearsay, the Advisory Committee believed that their use was to be fostered rather than discouraged. Similarly, the House Report on the Rule noted that since, "[a]s time goes by, a witness' memory will fade and his identification will become less reliable," minimizing the barriers to admission of more contemporaneous identification is fairer to defendants and prevents "cases falling through because the witness can no longer recall the identity of the person he saw commit the crime." H.R.Rep. No. 94-355, p. 3 (1975). To judge from the House and Senate Reports, Rule 801(d)(1)(C) was in part directed to the very problem here at issue: a memory loss that makes it impossible for the witness to provide an in-court identification or testify about details of the events underlying an earlier identification.…

So ordered.

Justice KENNEDY took no part in the consideration or decision of this case.

[A dissenting opinion by Justice Brennan, joined by Justice Marshall, is omitted.]

B. Admissions by Opposing Parties

1. Individual Admissions

Relevant Rule
FRE 801(d)(2)(A)

(d) **Statements That Are Not Hearsay.** A statement that meets the following conditions is not hearsay: …

(2) *An Opposing Party's Statement.* The statement is offered against an opposing party and:

(A) was made by the party in an individual or representative capacity …

FRE 801(d)(2)(A) typifies the adversary system: your words can be used against you, and, if they are offered against you at trial, your words will be deemed non-hearsay. The scope of this exemption is extremely broad. The statement need not be against the party's interest, and there is no requirement that the declarant have personal knowledge regarding the topic of the statement (in fact, each of the FRE 801(d)(2) exemptions do not require personal knowledge of the declarant). If a party is speaking in a representative capacity (e.g., as a corporate agent), the statement can be used against the party as an individual. Even if a party claims to have not uttered the words, the relatively lenient *Huddleston* test will govern and will allow admissibility if a reasonable jury could find that the party uttered the statement.

This, then, is a rule that favors inclusion. As long as it is offered against the party, and not by the party, the statement will not face a hearsay obstacle. The other rules of evidence may make the evidence inadmissible, however. Thus, FRE 403, FRE 404 or any other federal rule can prohibit the admission of this nonhearsay.

Problem 7-6

On April 27, 1995, William Belew was driving a truck through Kentucky on behalf of Three Rivers Trucking Co. Belew picked up a stranded motorist, Myra

Stalbosky, at an interstate rest area. He later raped and murdered her in the cab of his truck. Michael Stalbosky, the administrator of Myra Stalbosky's estate, brought suit against both Belew and Three Rivers. He alleged that Three Rivers should be held liable for negligently hiring and retaining Belew because the company knew or should have known that Belew posed an unreasonable risk to members of the general public such as Myra Stalbosky.

Prior to hiring Belew as a driver, Three Rivers checked with his previous employer, obtained a copy of his driving record, and performed a drug screen. According to Three Rivers, none of these inquiries indicated that Belew was unfit for a position as a truck driver. On his application form, Belew denied that he had ever been convicted of a felony, despite a prior conviction for arson in 1991.

In order to establish Three Rivers's knowledge of Belew's prior criminal history, the plaintiff offered an affidavit by a private investigator who interviewed Belew on April 10, 1997. In that affidavit, the private investigator related Belew's statement that managers at Three Rivers were aware of his criminal history but told him not to worry about it and not to list it on his application.

Are Belew's statements admissible against Three Rivers?

2. Adoptive Admissions

Relevant Rule
FRE 801(d)(2)(B)

(d) Statements That Are Not Hearsay. A statement that meets the following conditions is not hearsay: ...

   (2) *An Opposing Party's Statement.* The statement is offered against an opposing party and: ...

      (B) is one the party manifested that it adopted or believed to be true ...

Continuing the philosophy embodied in FRE 801(d)(2)(A)'s exemption from hearsay of an opposing party's statement, FRE 801(d)(2)(B) exempts from the definition of hearsay any statement to which a party has manifested an adoption or belief in its truth. Thus any express agreement to a statement by a party, ranging from a verbal declaration to a nod and numerous scenarios in between, will allow the statement to come in against that party. Personal knowledge of the declarant is not required.

A trickier situation involves adoption by inaction or silence. These "tacit admissions" have been admitted against a party when the following foundation has been laid:

- The party heard and understood a statement made in his or her presence,
- The circumstances naturally called for a reply (i.e., under similar circumstances, a reasonable innocent person would have immediately denied the accusation),
- The party had the opportunity to deny the statement, and
- The party either remained silent or made an evasive or equivocal reply.

The second element is usually the most hotly contested, as what circumstances mandate an immediate denial are open to debate, as we shall see in the problems in this section. On the one hand, someone walking up to Gus and stating, "I was in the bank that was robbed yesterday, and I know you did it," is a situation where we would expect a reasonable innocent person to deny the accusation. On the other hand, a stranger stating to Gus,

"You have the face of a bank robber," may be too vague a comment from an unknown accuser to merit a response. The issue is a fact-intensive one, and the specificity and context of the accusation are important variables.

Another tricky application of tacit admissions concerns silence by the accused and the degree to which use of a defendant's silence can violate a defendant's rights under *Miranda v. Arizona*, 384 U.S. 436 (1966) (defendant cannot be penalized for exercising their right to remain silent under the 5th Amendment during custodial interrogation). The debate centers on whether a defendant's silence in response to a police questioning can be used to impeach (i.e., not for its truth but to show inconsistency) and/or whether it can be used substantively (i.e., the silence can be offered for its truth). If, for example, a defendant claims self-defense at his murder trial, can his silence to a police officer's question at the scene (e.g., "You killed him in cold blood didn't you?") be used to show his current testimony is inconsistent with his silence? Can his silence be used substantively as an adoptive admission?

Certainly, if a defendant is in custody and has been Mirandized, silence cannot be used to impeach and cannot be used substantively as an adoption under FRE 801(d)(2)(B). Conversely, prearrest silence that is not induced by government action (e.g., the government has not given the defendant his *Miranda* warnings but he chooses to remain silent) can be used to impeach and used substantively as an adoption. The middle ground, where defendant is in custody but has not been Mirandized, allows for prearrest silence to be used to impeach, but the Circuit courts are split as to whether the statements can be used substantively as an adoption.

Problem 7-7

Hugh Pilgrim was employed as a research analyst for Tufts University. On September 24, 1990, Pilgrim initiated an internal grievance procedure alleging discrimination by his immediate supervisor, Kurt Fisher. Pilgrim accused Fisher (who is white) of treating him differently because he is black and from Barbados. Pilgrim complained that Fisher had given him poor job performance reviews and subjected him to disciplinary measures without explanation or the required opportunity to discuss job performance problems with the head of their department. Pilgrim further claimed that Fisher called him "space pilgrim," "lazy" and accused him of "shifting positions all the time." Pilgrim took these comments as racial slurs.

The grievance committee investigated Pilgrim's claims and issued a report. The report concluded that the disciplinary restrictions Fisher placed on Pilgrim resulted in Pilgrim being treated differently from the rest of the department staff and recommended that Fisher be relieved of supervisory duties over Pilgrim. The report further recommended that Pilgrim be assigned to a different supervisor, and that an independent overseer be appointed to monitor this new relationship. Finally, the report concluded that there was no substantive evidence that Fisher intended to discriminate against Pilgrim because of his race, color, or national origin and that it was plausible that Fisher's actions were motivated by other factors, such as personality conflict.

University President Jean Mayer received the committee's report and implemented all of its recommendations. Pilgrim continued receiving poor performance reviews under his new supervisor and was eventually terminated in October of 1991. He filed suit against Tufts claiming racial harassment, failure to promote, and wrongful termination. The cornerstone of Pilgrim's case is the grievance committee report which corroborates his claim of unequal treatment under Fisher. The district court, in the process of granting a summary judgment in favor of Tufts, declared this report inadmissible as a "collection of multi-level hearsay statements." Pilgrim appealed the suppression of the committee report. How do you rule?

Problem 7-8

Chad Henke, a former Chief Financial Officer of Cal Micro Systems, was indicted on charges of conspiracy, making false statements, securities fraud, and insider trading. In the mid-90's, Cal Micro Systems took a major financial hit when its biggest customer, Apple Computers, ceased purchasing from them. Rather than allow the company's downturn to come to light and see their stock prices plummet, Henke allegedly conspired with other top executives to "cook the books" to make the company look more financially sound than it really was.

At Henke's trial, the government introduced an out of court statement made at a press conference by a co-defendant who was one of Henke's coconspirators, former CEO Chan M. Desaigoudar. In response to an accusation made at the press conference that they were "cooking the books," Desaigoudar replied, "Next question."

Henke was convicted and appealed. He challenges the admission of Desaigoudar's statement as hearsay. How do you rule?

Problem 7-9

Gail Collins was shot dead in her own apartment with no signs of forced entry. The government arrested Joseph Williams, a crack cocaine addict who lived in Collins's apartment building and had been seen out with Collins socially several times in the months before she was killed. During this period it seems Williams's drug addiction was spiraling out of control. He stopped making payments on his car, stopped paying his rent, and just a few weeks before Collins's death, stopped going to work. He began borrowing money from everyone he knew including Collins. Just a week before her death, Collins told her mother that she was not going to give Williams any more money. This, the state believed, was the motive for her murder. Collins had refused to give Williams any more money, and Williams then allegedly killed her and took her car and ATM card. Someone withdrew all the money in Collins's checking account using her ATM card the morning she was killed. Kathleen Simmons, an admitted drug addict and prostitute, claimed that she spent that morning with Williams, who withdrew all the money from Collins's account and used it to buy crack which she and Williams then smoked. Simmons also claimed that she saw Williams hide a pistol in an air-conditioning duct in his apartment building that morning. The murder weapon used to kill Collins was never found.

Williams was not charged with murder, but rather was charged with being a felon in possession of a firearm. At trial, the government wanted to introduce the testimony of Williams's friend and drug dealer, Keith Bartee. Bartee would testify that after Collins's death, Williams's behavior became very strange and paranoid. On one occasion, Bartee asked Williams if he had killed someone. Williams did not answer. Williams objects to the admission of Bartee's testimony about his silence as inadmissible hearsay. How do you rule?

Problem 7-10

Hugh Robinson was fined $250 in the Brooklyn, New York, Criminal Court for an unspecified infraction. He wanted to pay the fine immediately, and Bailiff Paul Moriarty was assigned to accompany him down to the cashier's office, deliver the court papers there and see that Robinson actually paid the fine.

As appellant stood at the cashier's cage, Moriarty stood approximately two feet behind him. He observed the cashier review the papers and ask Robinson for $250. Appellant took his wallet from his pocket and opened it. Moriarty noticed that the wallet contained three separate "packets" of currency, each folded over with the ends facing downward into the wallet. Appellant selected $250 in bills and gave them to the cashier, who placed them under a counterfeit currency detector light. Moriarty's testimony was as follows:

> "A.... I seen (sic) that all the bills were not of the same quality as the rest of the bills. She gave him back the four bills and said now give me real money.
>
> Q: What did Mr. Robinson do at that point?
>
> A: At that point he went back into his wallet and produced another $80.
>
> Q: Were you able to see where Mr. Robinson took that from his wallet? Was it any one particular packet?
>
> A: I really couldn't say.
>
> Q: Did Mr. Robinson say anything?
>
> A: No.
>
> Q: You were unable to see the expression on his face at that time?
>
> A: No.
>
> Q: Continue with your description of what happened after that. Mr. Robinson went back into his wallet, paid the money. Was there any further problem with the production of counterfeit notes?
>
> A: No. There were no further problems. It was genuine cash."

The cashier then gave Robinson a receipt and told Moriarty he could leave. Mr. Moriarty then escorted Robinson to his captain's office, where Robinson turned over his wallet without objection. In Robinson's wallet, they found eleven counterfeit $20 bills.

Robinson was convicted of "knowingly offering, exposing and keeping with intent to furnish counterfeit United States currency." Robinson appealed. In his defense, Robinson claimed he did not know that the bills were fake. How do you rule?

3. Statements of Agents

Relevant Rules
FRE 801(d)(2)(C) and (D)

(d) Statements That Are Not Hearsay. A statement that meets the following conditions is not hearsay: ...

> **(2)** *An Opposing Party's Statement.* The statement is offered against an opposing party and: ...
>
> > **(C)** was made by a person whom the party authorized to make a statement on the subject;
> >
> > **(D)** was made by the party's agent or employee on a matter within the scope of that relationship and while it existed; ...
>
> The statement must be considered but does not by itself establish the declarant's authority under (C); [or] the existence or scope of the relationship under (D); ...

The agency exemptions under FRE 801(d)(2)(C) and (D) further exemplify the needs of the adversary system: not only may your words be used against you, but the words of your agents may be used against you as well. The difference between FRE 801(d)(2)(C) and (D) is essentially the difference between an express agent and an implied agent. FRE 801(d)(2)(C) covers the express agent, someone who the party authorized to speak for her. The existence and limits of the authority of an express agent are governed under agency law which seeks to determine the scope of the authority by focusing on the conduct of the parties and the surrounding circumstances. Essentially, the totality of circumstances must indicate that the principal gave the agent the authority to make statements on behalf of the principal.

There are times, however, when an agency situation may be implied. For example, an employee in charge of purchasing raw materials for a manufacturer may conduct numerous conversations with suppliers. If the subject of those statements were within the scope of her employment and occurred while she was employed, then her statements may be attributable to her employer even though the employee had no express authority to speak for the principal. She would not, however, be considered an agent on matters outside the scope of her employment, such as the future of the company's pension plan.

Like all of the other FRE 801(d)(2) exemptions, personal knowledge is not required on the part of the express or implied declarant-agent; the party will still be bound even if the declarant-agent has no actual knowledge and is merely relaying what she was told. FRE 801(d)(2)(C) and (D) also contain a provision addressing whether the offered statement can be used to help establish the foundation for the exemption. In other words, the statement offered as an express or implied admission may be considered when determining whether that person is truly an express or implied agent, but that statement itself does not establish the predicate facts of agency and scope. Accordingly, the statement, "I'm speaking for my boss right now, and she'll offer you $500 for the merchandise," may be used to establish whether the declarant was an agent, but standing alone it is not sufficient to establish a foundation. More proof of agency would be required. The trial judge determines whether the foundation has been established under FRE 104(a), and the offering party has the burden of proof.

Focus Questions: *Mahlandt v. Wild Canid Survival & Research Center, Inc.*

- Why does the court's treatment of the witness's note and the company's meeting notes differ?

- How reliable are the statements at issue in this case?

Mahlandt v. Wild Canid Survival & Research Center, Inc.

588 F.2d 626 (8th Cir. 1978)

VAN SICKLE, District Judge.

This is a civil action for damages arising out of an alleged attack by a wolf on a child. The sole issues on appeal are as to the correctness of three rulings which excluded conclusionary statements against interest. Two of them were made by a defendant, who was also an employee of the corporate defendant; and the third was in the form of a statement appearing in the records of a board meeting of the corporate defendant.

On March 23, 1973, Daniel Mahlandt, then 3 years, 10 months, and 8 days old, was sent by his mother to a neighbor's home on an adjoining street to get his older brother, Donald. Daniel's mother watched him cross the street, and then turned into the house to get her car keys. Daniel's path took him along a walkway adjacent to the Poos' residence. Next to the walkway was a five foot chain link fence to which Sophie had been chained with a six foot chain. In other words, Sophie was free to move in a half circle having a six foot radius on the side of the fence opposite from Daniel.

Sophie was a bitch wolf, 11 months and 28 days old, who had been born at the St. Louis Zoo, and kept there until she reached 6 months of age, at which time she was given to the Wild Canid Survival and Research Center, Inc. It was the policy of the Zoo to remove wolves from the Children's Zoo after they reached the age of 5 or 6 months. Sophie was supposed to be kept at the Tyson Research Center, but Kenneth Poos, as Director of Education for the Wild Canid Survival and Research Center, Inc., had been keeping her at his home because he was taking Sophie to schools and institutions where he showed films and gave programs with respect to the nature of wolves. Sophie was known as a very gentle wolf who had proved herself to be good natured and stable during her contacts with thousands of children, while she was in the St. Louis Children's Zoo.

Sophie was chained because the evening before she had jumped the fence and attacked a beagle who was running along the fence and yapping at her.

A neighbor who was ill in bed in the second floor of his home heard a child's screams and went to his window, where he saw a boy lying on his back within the enclosure, with a wolf straddling him. The wolf's face was near Daniel's face, but the distance was so great that he could not see what the wolf was doing, and did not see any biting. Within about 15 seconds the neighbor saw Clarke Poos, about seventeen, run around the house, get the wolf off of the boy, and disappear with the child in his arms to the back of the house. Clarke took the boy in and laid him on the kitchen floor.

Clarke had been returning from his friend's home immediately west when he heard a child's cries and ran around to the enclosure. He found Daniel lying within the enclosure, about three feet from the fence, and Sophie standing back from the boy the length of her chain, and wailing. An expert in the behavior of wolves stated that when a wolf licks a child's face that it is a sign of care, and not a sign of attack; that a wolf's wail is a sign of compassion, and an effort to get attention, not a sign of attack. No witness saw or knew how Daniel was injured. Clarke and his sister ran over to get Daniel's mother. She says that Clarke told her, "a wolf got Danny and he is dying." Clarke denies that statement.

The defendant, Mr. Poos, arrived home while Daniel and his mother were in the kitchen. After Daniel was taken in an ambulance, Mr. Poos talked to everyone present, including a neighbor who came in. Within an hour after he arrived home, Mr. Poos went to Washington University to inform Owen Sexton, President of Wild Canid Survival and Research Center, Inc., of the incident. Mr. Sexton was not in his office so Mr. Poos left the following note on his door:

> Owen, would call me at home, 727-5080? Sophie bit a child that came in our back yard. All has been taken care of. I need to convey what happened to you.

Denial of admission of this note is one of the issues on appeal.

Later that day, Mr. Poos found Mr. Sexton at the Tyson Research Center and told him what had happened. Denial of plaintiff's offer to prove that Mr. Poos told Mr. Sexton that, "Sophie had bit a child that day," is the second issue on appeal.

A meeting of the Directors of the Wild Canid Survival and Research Center, Inc., was held on April 4, 1973. Mr. Poos was not present at that meeting. The minutes of that meeting reflect that there was a "great deal of discussion … about the legal aspects of the incident of Sophie biting the child." Plaintiff offered an abstract of the minutes containing that reference. Denial of the offer of that abstract is the third issue on appeal.

Daniel had lacerations of the face, left thigh, left calf, and right thigh, and abrasions and bruises of the abdomen and chest. Mr. Mahlandt was permitted to state that Daniel had indicated that he had gone under the fence. Mr. Mahlandt and Mr. Poos, about a month after the incident, examined the fence to determine what caused Daniel's lacerations. Mr. Mahlandt felt that they did not look like animal bites. The parallel scars on Daniel's thigh appeared to match the configuration of the barbs or tines on the fence. The expert as to the behavior of wolves opined that the lacerations were not wolf bites or wounds caused by wolf claws. Wolves have powerful jaws and a wolf bite will result in massive crushing or severing of a limb. He stated that if Sophie had bitten Daniel there would have been clear apposition of teeth and massive crushing of Daniel's hands and arms which were not injured. Also, if Sophie had pulled Daniel under the fence, tooth marks on the foot or leg would have been present, although Sophie possessed enough strength to pull the boy under the fence.

The jury brought in a verdict for the defense.

The trial judge's rationale for excluding the note, the statement, and the corporate minutes, was the same in each case. He reasoned that Mr. Poos did not have any personal knowledge of the facts, and accordingly, the first two admissions were based on hearsay; and the third admission contained in the minutes of the board meeting was subject to the same objection of hearsay, and unreliability because of lack of personal knowledge....

… [T]he statement in the note pinned on the door is not hearsay, and is admissible against Mr. Poos. It was his own statement, and as such was clearly different from the reported statement of another.... It was also a statement of which he had manifested his adoption or belief in its truth. And the same observations may be made of the statement made later in the day to Mr. Sexton that, "Sophie had bit a child...."

Are these statements admissible against Wild Canid Survival and Research Center, Inc.? They were made by Mr. Poos when he was an agent or servant of the Wild Canid Survival and Research Center, Inc., and they concerned a matter within the scope of his agency, or employment, i. e., his custody of Sophie, and were made during the existence of that relationship.

Defendant argues that Rule 801(d)(2) does not provide for the admission of "in house" statements; that is, it allows only admissions made to third parties.

The notes of the Advisory Committee on the Proposed Rules discuss the problem of "in house" admissions with reference to Rule 801(d)(2)(C) situations. This is not a (C) situation because Mr. Poos was not authorized or directed to make a statement on the matter by anyone. But the rationale developed in that comment does apply to this (D) situation. Mr. Poos had actual physical custody of Sophie. His conclusions, his opinions, were obviously accepted as a basis for action by his principal. See minutes of corporate meeting. As the Advisory Committee points out in its note on (C) situations.

> ... communication to an outsider has not generally been thought to be an essential characteristic of an admission. Thus a party's books or records are usable against him, without regard to any intent to disclose to third persons. V Wigmore on Evidence s 1557.

Weinstein's discussion of Rule 801(d)(2)(D) (Weinstein's Evidence s 801(d)(2)(D)(01), p. 801-137), states that:

> Rule 801(d)(2)(D) adopts the approach ... which, as a general proposition, makes statement made by agents within the scope of their employment admissible.... Once agency, and the making of the statement while the relationship continues, are established, the statement is exempt from the hearsay rule so long as it relates to a matter within the scope of the agency.

After reciting a lengthy quotation which justifies the rule as necessary, and suggests that such admissions are trustworthy and reliable, Weinstein states categorically that although an express requirement of personal knowledge on the part of the declarant of the facts underlying his statement is not written into the rule, it should be. He feels that is mandated by Rules 805 and 403....

... [N]either rule mandates the introduction into Rule 801(d)(2)(D) of an implied requirement that the declarant have personal knowledge of the facts underlying his statement. So we conclude that the two statements made by Mr. Poos were admissible against Wild Canid Survival and Research Center, Inc.

As to the entry in the records of a corporate meeting, the directors as primary officers of the corporation had the authority to include their conclusions in the record of the meeting. So the evidence would fall within 801(d)(2)(C) as to Wild Canid Survival and Research Center, Inc., and be admissible. The "in house" aspect of this admission has already been discussed....

But there was no servant, or agency, relationship which justified admitting the evidence of the board minutes as against Mr. Poos.

None of the conditions of 801(d)(2) cover the claim that minutes of a corporate board meeting can be used against a non-attending, non-participating employee of that corporation. The evidence was not admissible as against Mr. Poos.

There is left only the question of whether the trial court's rulings which excluded all three items of evidence are justified under Rule 403. He clearly found that the evidence was not reliable, pointing out that none of the statements were based on the personal knowledge of the declarant.

Again, that problem was faced by the Advisory Committee on Proposed Rules. In its discussion of 801(d)(2) exceptions to the hearsay rule, the Committee said:

> The freedom which admissions have enjoyed from technical demands of searching for an assurance of trustworthiness in some against-interest circumstances, and from the restrictive influences of the opinion rule and the rule requiring first

hand knowledge, when taken with the apparently prevalent satisfaction with the results, calls for generous treatment of this avenue to admissibility.

So here, remembering that relevant evidence is usually prejudicial to the cause of the side against which it is presented, and that the prejudice which concerns us is unreasonable prejudice; and applying the spirit of Rule 801(d) (2), we hold that Rule 403 does not warrant the exclusion of the evidence of Mr. Poos' statements as against himself or Wild Canid Survival and Research Center, Inc.

But the limited admissibility of the corporate minutes, coupled with the repetitive nature of the evidence and the low probative value of the minute record, all justify supporting the judgment of the trial court under Rule 403.

The judgment of the District Court is reversed and the matter remanded to the District Court for a new trial consistent with this opinion.

Problem 7-11

The Grace Methodist Church in Cheyenne, Wyoming wanted to open a church-run child day-care center in a residential area. The proposed facility would provide care for children newly born to age thirteen, would be open to the public regardless of religious affiliation, and would operate eighteen hours a day, seven days a week. The church would hire care providers to work at the day care center also without regard to their religious affiliation.

Running a day-care business in such a location violated the city's zoning laws, and so Cheyenne denied the church a permit to build the day care center. The church filed suit against the city, arguing that the city's refusal to grant a permit violated the Religious Land Use and Institutionalized Persons Act ("RLUIPA") which mandates that a land use regulation cannot "substantially burden" the exercise of religion unless the government can show the regulation furthers a compelling governmental interest and is the least restrictive means of furthering that interest.

Cheyenne argued that the proposed day-care center did not "substantially burden" the church under the RLUIPA because the day-care center was a largely secular commercial business and not a fundamental part of the church members' religious practice. In support of this, the city proffered a letter written by Bishop Warner Brown. Bishop Brown, who presided over the Rocky Mountain and Yellowstone Conferences of the United Methodist Church, was directly responsible for the ordination and appointment of all clergy in the region, including those at Grace church. The Bishop's letter was part of a correspondence between the bishop and the pastor of Grace church, John McLaughlin. In the letter, the Bishop said that the Church's proposed daycare center "seems to look more like a commercial venture and less like a religious function." The church objected to admission of this letter as hearsay. How do you rule?

Problem 7-12

Two African-American maintenance workers, Mays and Young, brought suit against their former employer, James Green Management ("JGM"), alleging that they were fired from their jobs at a Chateaux Town Home Complex—a JGM-owned apartment building—because of their race. JGM claims both men were fired for poor job performance. In an effort to prove JGM's discriminatory motives, Mays and Young offered into evidence a resignation letter written by their former supervisor, Gary Olsen, who is white. The letter was addressed and sent to JGM's owner, James Green, and reads as follows:

> I hereby tender my resignation from your company effective immediately. My resignation is based on the following events that transpired during my employment.
>
> Approximately 1 1/2–2 weeks ago, I was informed by your supervisor to "hide out" a minority worker for the next week and "get rid of him" on the first opportunity. I questioned your supervisor for the reasoning behind this thought process. He informed me "James Green doesn't like blacks working for him. We already have Lee and that is one too many." He continued stating, "Lee would never be maintenance supervisor because of his skin color and that Mr. Green would not approve of a black supervisor at the Chateau Town Home complex." I find this repugnant and a gross violation of State and Federal laws. I refuse to act upon the supervisor's demands and will leave that decision to one of your other managers. I find it very disturbing that all of the minority workers I hired are only granted an $8.00 per hour wage while our only Caucasian worker be paid $8.50 per hour whom has less experience and is being trained by Lee to do the electrical work. The pay inequities and rent concessions and other benefits given to certain property managers and ordinary maintenance workers reinforce my belief that a serious reevaluation of your management staff is in order.
>
> My resignation is due to the illegal acts that have been asked of me to perform ...

This letter was written and sent less than two months before Mays and Young, the only African-American employees at Chateaux Town Home Complex, were fired. JGM objects that this resignation letter is inadmissible hearsay. How do you rule?

Problem 7-13

Jose Sanchez-Godinez was pulled over for speeding by Missouri State troopers on Interstate 44 outside Kansas City, MO. He was driving a UHaul truck, which he gave the troopers permission to search. Inside the truck they found 542 kilograms of marijuana. Sanchez-Godinez was arrested and interrogated by DEA Agent Mark Wooten. Although Sanchez-Godinez could speak English, he preferred to answer questions in Spanish. Therefore, Special Agent Joel Jauregui of the Bureau of Alcohol, Tobacco, and Firearms (ATF) served as an interpreter between Sanchez-Godinez and the DEA agent who was questioning him. In addition to interpreting, Jauregui Mirandized Sanchez-Godinez in Spanish and asked him some additional questions that had not been asked by Wooten. At Sanchez-Godinez's trial for possession of marijuana with intent to distribute, Jauregui testified to the following: 1) that he often serves as an interpreter for the ATF and other agencies; 2) that during this interview he acted as both a translator and as a federal law enforcement officer; 3) that during the interview, Sanchez-

Godinez admitted to knowing about the marijuana in the truck; and 4) that Sanchez-Godinez told him where he had picked up the marijuana and where it was going.

Agent Wooten then testified as to what Sanchez-Godinez had told him (through Jauregui) during this interrogation. His testimony of what Sanchez-Godinez said was substantially the same as that of Jauregui. All parties concede that, at times during the interrogation, Sanchez-Godinez clarified Jauregui's English translations of what he was saying (meaning the defendant corrected his own interpreter's English interpretation of what he was saying in Spanish).

Sanchez-Godinez was convicted and sentenced to 70 months in federal prison. On appeal, he challenges the admission of Wooten's testimony under the rule against hearsay. How do you rule?

---

4. Coconspirator Statements

Relevant Rules
FRE 801(d)(2)(E)

(d) Statements That Are Not Hearsay. A statement that meets the following conditions is not hearsay: …

   (2) *An Opposing Party's Statement.* The statement is offered against an opposing party and: …

      (E) was made by the party's coconspirator during and in furtherance of the conspiracy.

   The statement must be considered but does not by itself establish … the existence of the conspiracy or participation in it under (E).

The rationale for the coconspirator exemption relies more on necessity than trustworthiness. Indeed, those engaged in an illegal enterprise are seeking to avoid liability at all costs, making their statements' veracity highly questionable. Nonetheless, using coconspirators' statements against their fellow conspirator fits the "litigation is war" rationale.

FRE 801(d)(2)(E) requires the following foundation:

- A conspiracy existed,
- The conspiracy was in progress when the declarant made the statement,
- The declarant was a coconspirator,
- The declarant made the statement in furtherance of the conspiracy, and
- The party against whom the statement is offered was a member of the conspiracy.

The term "conspiracy" does not depend on the substantive definition of a crime or civil wrong, for this exemption can apply anytime people act together by mutual understanding in pursuit of a common purpose. As such, it is practically synonymous with "joint venture." Thus, one need not be charged with the crime of conspiracy in order for this exemption to apply. This exemption applies in civil cases as well as criminal ones.

Determining whether a conspiracy was still in progress is not an easy task. Statements made after the main objectives of a conspiracy have been accomplished or thwarted by law enforcement do not fit the exemption. Typically, courts seek to determine whether the statements occurred before or after the last overt act necessary for the conspiracy. Statements made during the concealment phase (i.e., after the last overt act) do not satisfy the exemption unless the proponent can demonstrate that the conspirators agreed at the outset to the concealment.

The "in furtherance" requirement is a mechanism to ensure that the statements are reliable. Any statement that is meant to advance the ball on a conspiracy by promoting the conspiratorial objectives may carry some trustworthiness, as the coconspirators are trying to accomplish a joint goal. Therefore, statements that can reasonably be interpreted as encouraging an advancement of the conspiracy, such as initiating the conspiracy, mapping out of strategy, keeping coconspirators apprised of the progress of the conspiracy, and encouraging further cooperation among the coconspirators would be "in furtherance" of the conspiracy. Other types of statements, such as bragging about a concluded conspiracy, would not further the objectives of the conspiracy and would not fit under the exemption.

Focus Questions: *Bourjaily v. United States*

- How reliable were the contested statements in this case? What role should their reliability play?

- How does the Court rebut petitioner's "bootstrapping" argument?

Bourjaily v. United States
483 U.S. 171 (1987)

REHNQUIST, C.J., delivered the opinion of the Court, in which WHITE, POWELL, STEVENS, O'CONNOR, and SCALIA, JJ., joined. STEVENS, J., filed a concurring opinion. BLACKMUN, J., filed a dissenting opinion, in which BRENNAN and MARSHALL, JJ., joined.

Federal Rule of Evidence 801(d)(2)(E) provides: "A statement is not hearsay if ... [t]he statement is offered against a party and is ... a statement by a coconspirator of a party during the course and in furtherance of the conspiracy." We granted certiorari to answer three questions regarding the admission of statements under Rule 801(d)(2)(E): (1) whether the court must determine by independent evidence that the conspiracy existed and that the defendant and the declarant were members of this conspiracy; (2) the quantum of proof on which such determinations must be based; and (3) whether a court must in each case examine the circumstances of such a statement to determine its reliability.…

In May 1984, Clarence Greathouse, an informant working for the Federal Bureau of Investigation (FBI), arranged to sell a kilogram of cocaine to Angelo Lonardo. Lonardo agreed that he would find individuals to distribute the drug. When the sale became imminent, Lonardo stated in a tape-recorded telephone conversation that he had a "gentleman friend" who had some questions to ask about the cocaine. In a subsequent telephone call, Greathouse spoke to the "friend" about the quality of the drug and the price. Greathouse then spoke again with Lonardo, and the two arranged the details of the purchase. They agreed that the sale would take place in a designated hotel parking lot, and Lonardo would transfer the drug from Greathouse's car to the "friend," who would be waiting in the parking lot in his own car. Greathouse proceeded with the transaction as planned, and FBI agents arrested Lonardo and petitioner immediately after Lonardo placed a kilogram of cocaine into petitioner's car in the hotel parking lot. In petitioner's car, the agents found over $20,000 in cash.

Petitioner was charged with conspiring to distribute cocaine ... and possession of cocaine with intent to distribute.... The Government introduced, over petitioner's objection, Angelo Lonardo's telephone statements regarding the participation of the "friend" in the transaction. The District Court found that, considering the events in the parking lot and Lonardo's statements over the telephone, the Government had established by a preponderance of the evidence that a conspiracy involving Lonardo and petitioner existed, and that Lonardo's statements over the telephone had been made in the course of and in furtherance of the conspiracy. Accordingly, the trial court held that Lonardo's out-of-court statements satisfied Rule 801(d)(2)(E) and were not hearsay. Petitioner was convicted on both counts and sentenced to 15 years. The United States Court of Appeals for the Sixth Circuit affirmed.... We affirm.

Before admitting a co-conspirator's statement over an objection that it does not qualify under Rule 801(d)(2)(E), a court must be satisfied that the statement actually falls within the definition of the Rule. There must be evidence that there was a conspiracy involving the declarant and the nonoffering party, and that the statement was made "during the course and in furtherance of the conspiracy." Federal Rule of Evidence 104(a) provides: "Preliminary questions concerning ... the admissibility of evidence shall be determined by the court." Petitioner and the Government agree that the existence of a conspiracy and petitioner's involvement in it are preliminary questions of fact that, under Rule 104, must be resolved by the court. The Federal Rules, however, nowhere define the standard of proof the court must observe in resolving these questions.

We are therefore guided by our prior decisions regarding admissibility determinations that hinge on preliminary factual questions. We have traditionally required that these matters be established by a preponderance of proof. Evidence is placed before the jury when it satisfies the technical requirements of the evidentiary Rules, which embody certain legal and policy determinations. The inquiry made by a court concerned with these matters is not whether the proponent of the evidence wins or loses his case on the merits, but whether the evidentiary Rules have been satisfied. Thus, the evidentiary standard is unrelated to the burden of proof on the substantive issues, be it a criminal case or a civil case. The preponderance standard ensures that before admitting evidence, the court will have found it more likely than not that the technical issues and policy concerns addressed by the Federal Rules of Evidence have been afforded due consideration. As in *Lego v. Twomey*, 404 U.S. 477, 488 (1972), we find "nothing to suggest that admissibility rulings have been unreliable or otherwise wanting in quality because not based on some higher standard." We think that our previous decisions in this area resolve the matter. Therefore, we hold that when the preliminary facts relevant to Rule 801(d)(2)(E) are disputed, the offering party must prove them by a preponderance of the evidence.[1]

Even though petitioner agrees that the courts below applied the proper standard of proof with regard to the preliminary facts relevant to Rule 801(d)(2)(E), he nevertheless

---

1. We intimate no view on the proper standard of proof for questions falling under Federal Rule of Evidence 104(b) (conditional relevancy). We also decline to address the circumstances in which the burden of coming forward to show that the proffered evidence is inadmissible is appropriately placed on the nonoffering party. Finally, we do not express an opinion on the proper order of proof that trial courts should follow in concluding that the preponderance standard has been satisfied in an ongoing trial.

challenges the admission of Lonardo's statements. Petitioner argues that in determining whether a conspiracy exists and whether the defendant was a member of it, the court must look only to independent evidence—that is, evidence other than the statements sought to be admitted. Petitioner relies on *Glasser v. United States,* 315 U.S. 60 (1942), in which this Court first mentioned the so-called "bootstrapping rule....":

> "[Co-Conspirator statements] are admissible over the objection of an alleged co-conspirator, who was not present when they were made, only if there is proof *aliunde* that he is connected with the conspiracy.... Otherwise, hearsay would lift itself by its own bootstraps to the level of competent evidence." *Id.,* at 74–75.

... Read in the light most favorable to petitioner, *Glasser* could mean that a court should not consider hearsay statements at all in determining preliminary facts under Rule 801(d)(2)(E). Petitioner, of course, adopts this view of the bootstrapping rule. *Glasser,* however, could also mean that a court must have *some* proof *aliunde,* but may look at the hearsay statements themselves in light of this independent evidence to determine whether a conspiracy has been shown by a preponderance of the evidence. The Courts of Appeals have widely adopted the former view and held that in determining the preliminary facts relevant to co-conspirators' out-of-court statements, a court may not look at the hearsay statements themselves for their evidentiary value.

... [*Glasser,* however, was] decided before Congress enacted the Federal Rules of Evidence in 1975. These Rules now govern the treatment of evidentiary questions in federal courts. Rule 104(a) provides: "Preliminary questions concerning ... the admissibility of evidence shall be determined by the court.... In making its determination it is not bound by the rules of evidence except those with respect to privileges." Similarly, Rule 1101(d)(1) states that the Rules of Evidence (other than with respect to privileges) shall not apply to "[t]he determination of questions of fact preliminary to admissibility of evidence when the issue is to be determined by the court under rule 104." The question thus presented is whether any aspect of *Glasser*'s bootstrapping rule remains viable after the enactment of the Federal Rules of Evidence.

Petitioner concedes that Rule 104, on its face, appears to allow the court to make the preliminary factual determinations relevant to Rule 801(d)(2)(E) by considering any evidence it wishes, unhindered by considerations of admissibility. That would seem to many to be the end of the matter. Congress has decided that courts may consider hearsay in making these factual determinations. Out-of-court statements made by anyone, including putative co-conspirators, are often hearsay. Even if they are, they may be considered, *Glasser* and the bootstrapping rule notwithstanding. But petitioner nevertheless argues that the bootstrapping rule, as most Courts of Appeals have construed it, survived this apparently unequivocal change in the law unscathed and that Rule 104, as applied to the admission of co-conspirator's statements, does not mean what it says. We disagree.

Petitioner claims that Congress evidenced no intent to disturb the bootstrapping rule, which was embedded in the previous approach, and we should not find that Congress altered the rule without affirmative evidence so indicating. It would be extraordinary to require legislative history to *confirm* the plain meaning of Rule 104. The Rule on its face allows the trial judge to consider any evidence whatsoever, bound only by the rules of privilege. We think that the Rule is sufficiently clear that to the extent that it is inconsistent with petitioner's interpretation of *Glasser*..., the Rule prevails.[2]

---

2. The Advisory Committee Notes show that the Rule was not adopted in a fit of absentmindedness. The Note to Rule 104 specifically addresses the process by which a federal court should make the factual determinations requisite to a finding of admissibility:

Nor do we agree with petitioner that this construction of Rule 104(a) will allow courts to admit hearsay statements without any credible proof of the conspiracy, thus fundamentally changing the nature of the co-conspirator exception. Petitioner starts with the proposition that co-conspirators' out-of-court statements are deemed unreliable and are inadmissible, at least until a conspiracy is shown. Since these statements are unreliable, petitioner contends that they should not form any part of the basis for establishing a conspiracy, the very antecedent that renders them admissible.

Petitioner's theory ignores two simple facts of evidentiary life. First, out-of-court statements are only *presumed* unreliable. The presumption may be rebutted by appropriate proof. Second, individual pieces of evidence, insufficient in themselves to prove a point, may in cumulation prove it. The sum of an evidentiary presentation may well be greater than its constituent parts. Taken together, these two propositions demonstrate that a piece of evidence, unreliable in isolation, may become quite probative when corroborated by other evidence. A *per se* rule barring consideration of these hearsay statements during preliminary factfinding is not therefore required. Even if out-of-court declarations by co-conspirators are presumptively unreliable, trial courts must be permitted to evaluate these statements for their evidentiary worth as revealed by the particular circumstances of the case. Courts often act as factfinders, and there is no reason to believe that courts are any less able to properly recognize the probative value of evidence in this particular area. The party opposing admission has an adequate incentive to point out the shortcomings in such evidence before the trial court finds the preliminary facts. If the opposing party is unsuccessful in keeping the evidence from the factfinder, he still has the opportunity to attack the probative value of the evidence as it relates to the substantive issue in the case. See, *e.g.,* Fed.Rule Evid. 806 (allowing attack on credibility of out-of-court declarant).

We think that there is little doubt that a co-conspirator's statements could themselves be probative of the existence of a conspiracy and the participation of both the defendant and the declarant in the conspiracy. Petitioner's case presents a paradigm. The out-of-court statements of Lonardo indicated that Lonardo was involved in a conspiracy with a "friend." The statements indicated that the friend had agreed with Lonardo to buy a kilogram of cocaine and to distribute it. The statements also revealed that the friend would be at the hotel parking lot, in his car, and would accept the cocaine from Greathouse's car after Greathouse gave Lonardo the keys. Each one of Lonardo's statements may itself be unreliable, but taken as a whole, the entire conversation between Lonardo and Greathouse was corroborated by independent evidence. The friend, who turned out to be petitioner, showed up at the prearranged spot at the prearranged time. He picked up the cocaine, and a significant sum of money was found in his car. On these facts, the trial court

---

"If the question is factual in nature, the judge will of necessity receive evidence pro and con on the issue. The rule provides that the rules of evidence in general do not apply to this process. McCormick § 53, p. 123, n. 8, points out that the authorities are 'scattered and inconclusive,' and observes:

'Should the exclusionary law of evidence, "the child of the jury system" in Thayer's phrase, be applied to this hearing before the judge? Sound sense backs the view that it should not, and that the judge should be empowered to hear *any relevant evidence,* such as affidavits *or other reliable hearsay.*'" 28 U.S.C.App., p. 681 (emphasis added).

The Advisory Committee further noted: "An item, offered and objected to, *may itself be considered in ruling on admissibility,* though not yet admitted in evidence." *Ibid.* (emphasis added). We think this language makes plain the drafters' intent to abolish any kind of bootstrapping rule. Silence is at best ambiguous, and we decline the invitation to rely on speculation to import ambiguity into what is otherwise a clear rule.

concluded, in our view correctly, that the Government had established the existence of a conspiracy and petitioner's participation in it.

We need not decide in this case whether the courts below could have relied solely upon Lonardo's hearsay statements to determine that a conspiracy had been established by a preponderance of the evidence. To the extent that *Glasser* meant that courts could not look to the hearsay statements themselves for any purpose, it has clearly been superseded by Rule 104(a). It is sufficient for today to hold that a court, in making a preliminary factual determination under Rule 801(d)(2)(E), may examine the hearsay statements sought to be admitted.... The courts below properly considered the statements of Lonardo and the subsequent events in finding that the Government had established by a preponderance of the evidence that Lonardo was involved in a conspiracy with petitioner. We have no reason to believe that the District Court's factfinding of this point was clearly erroneous. We hold that Lonardo's out-of-court statements were properly admitted against petitioner....

The judgment of the Court of Appeals is

Affirmed.

[Justice Stevens' concurrence is omitted; Justice Blackmun's dissent, with whom Justice Brennan and Justice Marshall join, is omitted.]

Problem 7-14

Eric Goins is accused of distributing cocaine from his Atlanta home to Greensboro, North Carolina. Prosecutors allege that Goins sells cocaine to William Wadelington who then sells the drugs to William Peoples and Antonio Capel. In order to prove that Goins is the main supplier, the prosecution offers the testimony of Capel, who will testify that Peoples asked Capel to talk to Goins about selling cocaine directly to them and bypassing Wadelington in the chain of distribution.

As Peoples and Capel are distributors of Goins's drugs, the prosecution argues that this statement fits under the co-conspirator exemption to hearsay. Goins argues that the statement between Peoples and Capel was made in furtherance of an independent conspiracy in which he never participated. Specifically, he claims that this statement was made as part of a separate conspiracy between Peoples and Capel to create their own cocaine distribution scheme and eliminate the middle man, Wadelington. Is the statement admissible?

Problem 7-15

Recall the facts of the Overview Problem in Chapter 2:

Angela Johnson was charged with aiding and abetting her boyfriend, Dustin Honken, in the execution-style slaying of two federal informants, the girlfriend of one informant, and the girlfriend's two young daughters. Honken, an alleged methamphetamine manufacturer, was arrested and charged for the five murders.

While incarcerated and awaiting trial, Angela Johnson turned to a fellow inmate, Robert McNeese, and asked him to find another inmate serving a life sentence who would take the blame for the murders. Unbeknownst to Johnson, McNeese was an informant, and he asked Johnson for information about the killings in order that whoever confessed to the crimes could have credible information. McNeese collected a series of handwritten notes and maps from Johnson as well as details regarding the murders. He then provided all the documents to the police. Are these documents admissible under the co-conspirator exemption?

Author's Note: Opposing Party Statements in Multiparty Cases

Another complication when dealing with opposing party statements is to determine whether they should be admissible when two or more defendants are tried together. Often, a hearsay statement, such as a confession by Defendant X, may be admissible against one defendant as an opposing party statement. But, to be admissible against Defendant Y another hearsay exception is needed, as Defendant X's confession is not an opposing party statement of Defendant Y. If no exception can be found to admit the statement against Defendant Y, what should be done? Should the court admit the statement by providing a limiting instruction that the confession can only be used against Defendant X but should not be used against Defendant Y? Or, should the court, fearing that the jury will not follow this instruction, rule that the confession is inadmissible?

This scenario invokes what has been called the *Bruton* doctrine, named after the case of *Bruton v. United States*, 391 U.S. 123 (1968). In *Bruton*, one of the defendants, Evans, confessed during an interrogation by authorities that he and an accomplice had committed armed robbery. During the joint trial of co-defendants Evans and Bruton, the trial court admitted testimony describing Evans's confession. Evans did not testify at trial. You can see the dilemma that resulted. In terms of hearsay, while the Evans' statement is admissible against him as a statement of an opposing party, there is no applicable hearsay exception to allow the statement to be admissible against Bruton (e.g., it was not in furtherance of a conspiracy, as Evans was confessing to the authorities). Furthermore, Bruton possessed a Sixth Amendment Confrontation Clause objection: he could not cross-examine the declarant of a testimonial statement offered against him. (We will explore the Confrontation Clause in more detail in Chapter 8).

The trial court attempted to use a jury instruction to resolve the dilemma: it cautioned the jury that Evans's admission was inadmissible hearsay as applied to Bruton and should not be considered in determining Bruton's guilt or innocence. *Id.* at 125. The Supreme Court reversed Bruton's conviction, holding that the admission at a joint trial of a nontestifying defendant's statement inculpating a co-defendant violates the co-defendant's Confrontation Clause rights, notwithstanding a curative instruction. The Supreme Court concluded that "the introduction of Evans' confession posed a substantial threat to petitioner's right to confront the witnesses against him, and this is a hazard we cannot ignore. Despite the concededly clear instructions to the jury to disregard Evans' inadmissible hearsay evidence inculpating petitioner, in the context of a joint trial we cannot accept limiting instructions as an adequate substitute for petitioner's constitutional right of cross-examination." *Id.* at 137

Remedies exist to the *Bruton* problem, however. The court could order that the trials be severed so that the defendants are tried separately or that separate juries be empanelled for each defendant, so that one jury would decide Defendant X's guilt or innocence while another decides Defendant Y's guilt or innocence. Additionally, references to the codefendant can be redacted from the declarant-defendant's statement in order to bypass the

Confrontation Clause and hearsay problems. *See Richardson v. Marsh*, 481 U.S. 200 (1987) (*Bruton* rule not implicated where declarant-defendant's confession omitted references to the codefendant, and the jury was instructed not to use the confession in deciding the codefendant's guilt); *Gray v. Maryland*, 523 U.S. 185 (1998) (*Bruton* rule prohibits a redacted confession of declarant-defendant that replaces the name of a codefendant with black space, the word "deleted," or similar symbols).

III. The FRE 803 Exceptions

The FRE 803 exceptions are presumed to be highly reliable. They are so reliable, in fact, that the hearsay is admissible "regardless of whether the declarant is available as a witness." Thus, even though we could have a witness on the stand, which would afford oath/demeanor/cross-examination, the secondhand hearsay is deemed equally preferable. As we review the major FRE 803 exceptions, it is fair to ask whether each of these exceptions is sufficiently reliable to merit an exception to FRE 802.

A. Present Sense Impressions and Excited Utterances

Relevant Rules
FRE 803(1)

The following are not excluded by the rule against hearsay, regardless of whether the declarant is available as a witness:

(1) Present Sense Impression. A statement describing or explaining an event or condition, made while or immediately after the declarant perceived it.

FRE 803(2)

The following are not excluded by the rule against hearsay, regardless of whether the declarant is available as a witness: …

(2) Excited Utterance. A statement relating to a startling event or condition, made while the declarant was under the stress of excitement that it caused.

Overview

The core rationale behind FRE 803(1) and FRE 803(2) focuses on the idea of immediacy or contemporaneousness. Under the present sense impression exception, spontaneity between the observance of the event and the utterance would prevent the type of reflection that may lead to insincerity. Thus, if declarant saw a car traveling at a high rate of speed down the street and immediately stated, "Wow, that car sure is speeding," the immediacy of the utterance makes it unlikely the declarant observed the event, decided to craft a lie, crafted a lie, and then uttered the lie. Additionally, the immediacy of the statement makes errors of memory less likely. Similarly, under the excited utterance exception, the idea that the witness is under the influence of an excited state while spontaneously uttering a statement makes it less likely that the witness would break away from that excited state and craft a lie. The startling event also makes it less likely that the statement was a product of faulty memory.

One cannot argue that these statements are 100% accurate, however. Especially in the context of an excited utterance, the risks of misstatement or misperception are arguably enhanced. If one observes a car crash, it is easy to imagine that one might lose track of details due to the startling nature of the event and thereby diminish the accuracy of a statement. These risks go largely to weight and will typically not affect admissibility decisions.

The evidentiary foundations for these rules are not difficult to craft. For a **present sense impression:**

- The declarant made the statement during or very shortly after the event (usually classified as within minutes of the event), and
- The statement describes or explains the event or condition.

The evidentiary foundation for an **excited utterance** is:

- The event was startling or stressful,
- Declarant made a statement relating to the event or condition, and
- Declarant made the statement while she was in a state of nervous excitement.

So, how do the foundations differ? First, the present sense impression possesses a much shorter temporal leash. As we are not relying on nervous excitement in the present sense impression, the statement must be made within minutes (usually under fifteen minutes, according to some courts) in order to qualify. The temporal leash is longer for an excited utterance; as long as the nervous excitement continues to exist, the statement is deemed reliable. Second, the event in a present sense impression need not be startling. Any event, even one that happens daily (e.g., "there goes the postman") can qualify. For an excited utterance, the event must be startling enough to cause nervous excitement on the part of the declarant. It is precisely due to this excitement that we presume that the declarant did not have time to reflect on her statement. Third, present sense impressions must actually describe or explain an event or condition observed. An excited utterance can be broader in scope, as it only needs to "relate" to a startling event or condition. Any subject matter that would likely be evoked by the event would be covered as long as it is not too analytical or does not recount distant, past events. For example, "Dirk has a knife, and he is going to stab Charlie" would likely "relate" to the startling event of seeing Dirk with a knife; even though the declarant did not witness Dirk stab Charlie, seeing Dirk with a knife could evoke the subject matter of who was going to be stabbed. A statement like, "Dirk has a knife, and he is going to stab Charlie, whom Dirk has hated since high school" is more problematic; recounting the history between Dirk and Charlie no longer "relates" to the startling event, and that portion of the statement should not be admissible.

Before we dive into some problems to explore these foundational elements, let us explore the idea of "excitement" under FRE 803(2) in a bit more depth. That the event was startling or stressful carries with it an objective component. The nature of the event must be likely to inspire nervous excitement in order for us to believe that it is trustworthy. Whether, in fact, the declarant was in a state of nervous excitement is a more subjective inquiry. The exception does not apply if the declarant was not excited even though most people would be; after all, the state of the excitement is central to believing the statement is trustworthy. Thus, the nature of the event, the behavior of the declarant, and the contents of the statement are central factors to determining whether this element is met. It is a context-dependent inquiry, and, as the problems below illustrate, numerous other factors may come into play (e.g., the age of the declarant, any lapse of time, etc.).

Problem 7-16

On April 29, 1989, Ronald Bemis and James Kates were arguing at a park when Bemis pulled a gun on Kates. Kates immediately grabbed the gun and broke it against a tree. Bemis ran to his nearby home to retrieve another gun, only to discover he had forgotten his keys and was forced to break in. City police officers soon arrived at the scene and apprehended Bemis and Kates.

Officers later testified that they believed Bemis to be an armed burglar and that Bemis had pointed a rifle at them and resisted arrest. Bemis claims that he dropped the gun upon the officers' orders and was severely beaten even though he offered no resistance.

When Bemis emerged from the house with a gun, his neighbor, Gary Estep, called 911 to report what he believed to be an armed burglary. As Estep spoke to the 911 operator, others at his home gathered around the window, describing the scene unfold. Estep could be heard repeating some of the statements in the background, stating to the 911 operator:

"Now there's a cop beating the … out of the guy …" and "There's five units … but it's kind of getting ridiculous guys. I mean, the cop's beating the … out of the guy right now. The guy's got a gun, though. I guess it's legal." At some point the 911 operator also told Estep "apparently he must have thrown the gun down."

Estep is not a testifying witness. Are his statements to the 911 operator admissible? Is the 911 operator's statement to him admissible?

Problem 7-17

Gail Duncan, acting as a confidential informant for the Drug Enforcement Agency ("DEA"), purchased four ounces of cocaine from Deron Cole and another individual on the night of January 31, 1995. Approximately ten minutes after the transaction, Duncan met with DEA Agent Schrempt and Detective Warman for a debriefing. She told them that although she recognized Cole, she did not recognize the individual who had accompanied him. The agents then showed her 20 to 30 photographs of suspected co-conspirators. Warman testified that Duncan picked out the picture of Cornelius Anderson immediately, identifying him as the man who had accompanied Cole. Agent Schrempt recorded the debriefing with Duncan, and Duncan verified it. However, Schrempt had failed to include Duncan's identification of Anderson in the record.

Is Duncan's identification admissible?

Problem 7-18

Thomas Jones is charged with the involuntary murder of his 9-month-old son, Christopher, by shaking him to death. As part of their case against Jones the government seeks to admit the testimony of Sergeant Andrews, who lived next door to Jones and whose wife often baby-sat for Christopher.

Mr. Andrews will testify that in January, around eight months before the homicide, Mrs. Jones came to pick up Christopher after Andrews's wife had baby-sat him since that morning for about twelve hours. Mrs. Jones was "crying" and appeared "very nervous," and Mr. Andrews offered to assist Mrs. Jones carry her things back to her home. When they arrived, Mrs. Jones burst into tears. Mr. Andrews asked her "what was wrong," and she responded that her husband "got mad this morning and tried to destroy everything of Christopher's because he was jealous." She also said that her husband had "grown to be very jealous of Christopher during the month of January."

Is Andrews's testimony admissible? Would your answer change if Mrs. Jones made the comment when she dropped Christopher off in the morning?

Problem 7-19

Mrs. Caruso, a resident of Portland, Oregon, was found unconscious and with severe head injuries just outside of Vancouver, Washington. Fingerprints from a nearby rifle, gun, and from elsewhere in her car suggested that Jimmy Lee Napier had kidnapped her and driven her out of state. This was further corroborated by a finding of Napier's personal effects inside Caruso's car.

After the accident, Caruso underwent two brain operations and was hospitalized for seven weeks. Although she suffered brain damage, her memory was intact. She only communicated following situations of stress or strain, and even then her communication was limited to isolated words and phrases.

One week after Caruso returned from the hospital, her sister, Eileen Moore, showed her a news article with Napier's photograph. Moore says that Caruso looked at the photograph and immediately became distressed, then pointed to the picture and "said very clearly, 'He killed me, he killed me.'" Moore also claims that no one in the family had yet discussed the incident with Caruso.

Caruso cannot understand the significance of an oath and thus cannot testify at trial. Is her statement to Moore admissible against Napier?

Problem 7-20

The defendant is charged with the battery of Joshua, his girlfriend's 19-month-old son. The prosecution seeks to admit the testimony of Mrs. Susan Charles, a baby-sitter who frequently watched Joshua at her quarters at the Naval Air Station family housing unit, where both parties lived.

Mrs. Charles says Joshua had bruises and face injuries when he was brought to her on Tuesday, July 30th, and that he appeared to be "in a daze." When the defendant later arrived to "spend quality time with Joshua," Joshua put his arms around Mrs. Charles's neck and attempted to pull himself away from the defendant.

On July 31st, Joshua was again brought to Mrs. Charles's home for the day. His mother had taken him to see a doctor earlier that morning. Mrs. Charles noticed new injuries on the child and said that the entire right side of his face was swollen and bruised. She testified:

> "[H]e climbed up on my couch, and he just kind of sat there, like in a daze ... He was a very playful kid. He would go with me, follow me around the house, and jabber and—but he didn't that morning. He just sat on the couch like he was in a daze, like he wasn't even there."

Troubled, Mrs. Charles summoned her friend, another day-care provider. When they asked Joshua what happened, he took his right hand, balled it into a fist, placed it against his right cheek, "and started rambling on."

The defendant says that he accidentally dropped Joshua from a playground slide. On appeal, he objects to Mrs. Charles's testimony describing Joshua's demonstration of a fist. Is the testimony admissible?

B. Then-Existing Mental, Emotional, or Physical Condition

Relevant Rule
FRE 803(3)

The following are not excluded by the rule against hearsay, regardless of whether the declarant is available as a witness: ...

(3) *Then-Existing Mental, Emotional, or Physical Condition.* A statement of the declarant's then-existing state of mind (such as motive, intent, or plan) or emotional, sensory, or physical condition (such as mental feeling, pain, or bodily health), but not including a statement of memory or belief to prove the fact remembered or believed unless it relates to the validity or terms of the declarant's will.

Overview

FRE 803(3) crafts an exception for then-existing mental, emotional, or physical conditions. In large part, then-existing state of mind statements are considered trustworthy because there is little risk of misperception—you are the best judge as to your state of mind. Similarly, because the statement is focused on the **present,** there is no risk of faulty memory. A risk of fabrication is certainly present in these statements, as is a risk of ambiguity, but the longstanding common law tradition of trusting these statements was embodied in FRE 803(3).

Four categories of statements are covered under FRE 803(3). First, the rule covers statements of **present** bodily condition (e.g., "My elbow is really hurting me right now"), regardless of whether it is made to a medical professional or to a lay person. The statement does **not** cover past conditions (although, as we will see, FRE 803(4) covers certain past conditions for medical diagnosis or treatment).

Second, the rule crafts an exception for statements of present state of mind or emotion when offered to prove a state of mind or emotion of a declarant that is in issue. In other words, if the state of mind or emotion is a material proposition (or is used to imply the existence or non-existence of a material proposition) of a crime, cause of action, or defense, then the statement is admissible substantively. For example, in a suit for race discrimination, racist comments by management personnel are arguably not offered for the truth of the matter asserted (i.e., what matters is that they stated the words, not that they were true). Yet some courts have ruled that these statements are offered for the truth of the matter asserted but are admissible under FRE 803(3) because they capture the state of mind of the employer that must be proved by the plaintiff. Other examples where the rules of substantive law treat the state of mind or emotion as material include motive to prove guilt, damages in a personal injury case, and fear in an extortion case.

The third category, which will be the subject of most of the cases and problems in this section, involves allowing statements of the declarant's state of mind in order to show subsequent conduct of the declarant. Thus the statement, "I am going to the library" can be offered to prove the intent or plan of the declarant to go to the library if that is relevant to the dispute. From this straightforward rule comes two troubling applications. First, can these statements cover joint conduct? In other words, can the statement "I am going to the library with Lucinda" be offered to prove Lucinda, the non-declarant, was at the library? Second, can the forward-looking statement include backward-looking aspects? For example, can the statement "I am going to the library because I got a C on my Evidence midterm" be offered not only to prove the declarant went to the library but also to prove that declarant received a C on her midterm? The famous case of *Mutual Life Ins. Co. v. Hillmon* will explore precisely these issues.

Finally, a very narrow use of FRE 803(3) is a testator's statements that relate to the "execution, revocation, identification, or terms" of a will. In this context, backward-looking statements of memory or belief that are offered to prove the fact remembered or believed are absolutely allowed. Thus, the testator's statement that she tore up her will is admissible to prove that she tore up her will. Note, however, that statements concerning the conduct of others are not admissible to prove the fact remembered or believed. One therefore cannot offer the statement that "Dirk forced me to name him in my will" to prove that Dirk in fact forced the testator to name him in her will.

Focus Questions: *Mutual Life Ins. Co. v. Hillmon*

- Can the jury easily make the distinction between evidence that is being offered as a narrative of facts versus evidence that is offered to show someone's intention? Does the court address the jury's ability to understand how to use the evidence appropriately? If not, how could it be addressed by the court?

- How reliable is the hearsay evidence to demonstrate Walters's intent? How reliable is the hearsay evidence to prove Hillmon's intent? Should any difference in reliability be an issue for the court or for the jury?

Mutual Life Ins. Co. v. Hillmon

145 U.S. 285 (1892)

STATEMENT BY MR. JUSTICE GRAY.

On July 13, 1880, Sallie E. Hillmon, a citizen of Kansas, brought an action against the Mutual Life Insurance Company, a corporation of New York, on a policy of insurance, dated December 10, 1878, on the life of her husband, John W. Hillmon, in the sum of $10,000, payable to her within 60 days after notice and proof of his death. On the same day the plaintiff brought two other actions,—the one against the New York Life Insurance Company, a corporation of New York, on two similar policies of life insurance, dated, respectively, November 30, 1878, and December 10, 1878, for the sum of $5,000 each; and the other against the Connecticut Mutual Life Insurance Company, a corporation of Connecticut, on a similar policy, dated March 4, 1879, for the sum of $5,000.

In each case the declaration alleged that Hillmon died on March 17, 1879, during the continuance of the policy, but that the defendant, though duly notified of the fact, had refused to pay the amount of the policy, or any part thereof; and the answer denied the death of Hillmon, and alleged that he, together with John H. Brown and diverse other persons, on or before November 30, 1878, conspiring to defraud the defendant, procured the issue of all the policies, and afterwards, in March and April, 1879, falsely pretended and represented that Hillmon was dead, and that a dead body which they had procured was his, whereas in reality he was alive and in hiding....

On February 29, 1888, after two trials at which the jury had disagreed, the three cases came on for trial.... At the trial plaintiff introduced evidence tending to show that on or about March 5, 1879, Hillmon and Brown left Wichita, in the state of Kansas, and traveled together through southern Kansas in search of a site for a cattle ranch; that on the night of March 18th, while they were in camp at a place called "Crooked Creek," Hillmon was killed by the accidental discharge of a gun; that Brown at once notified persons living in the neighborhood, and that the body was thereupon taken to a neighboring town, where, after an inquest, it was buried. The defendants introduced evidence tending to show that the body found in the camp at Crooked Creek on the night of March 18th was not the body of Hillmon, but was the body of one Frederick Adolph Walters. Upon the question whose body this was there was much conflicting evidence, including photographs and descriptions of the corpse, and of the marks and scars upon it, and testimony to its likeness to Hillmon and to Walters.

The defendants introduced testimony that Walters left his home at Ft. Madison, in the state of Iowa, in March, 1878, and was afterwards in Kansas in 1878, and in January and February, 1879; that during that time his family frequently received letters from him, the last of which was written from Wichita; and that he had not been heard from since March, 1879. The defendants also offered the following evidence:

Elizabeth Rieffenach testified that she was a sister of Frederick Adolph Walters, and lived at Ft. Madison; and thereupon, as shown by the bill of exceptions, the following proceedings took place:

> "Witness further testified that she had received a letter written from Wichita, Kansas, about the 4th or 5th day of March, 1879, by her brother Frederick Adolph; that the letter was dated at Wichita, and was in the handwriting of her brother; that she had searched for the letter, but could not find the same, it being lost; that she remembered and could state the contents of the letter.

> "Thereupon the defendants' counsel asked the question, 'State the contents of that letter;'" to which the plaintiff objected, on the ground that the same is incompetent, irrelevant, and hearsay. The objection was sustained, and the defendants duly excepted. The following is the letter as stated by witness:

> 'Wichita, Kansas, March 4th or 5th or 3d or 4th,—I don't know,—1879. Dear Sister and All: I now in my usual style drop you a few lines to let you know that I expect to leave Wichita on or about March the 5th with a certain Mr. Hillmon, a sheep trader, for Colorado, or parts unknown to me. I expect to see the country now. News are of no interest to you, as you are not acquainted here. I will close with compliments to all inquiring friends. Love to all. I am truly your brother, FRED. ADOLPH WALTERS.'

Alvina D. Kasten testified that she was 21 years of age, and resided in Ft. Madison; that she was engaged to be married to Frederick Adolph Walters; that she last saw him on March 24, 1878, at Ft. Madison; that he left there at that time, and had not returned; that she corresponded regularly with him, and received a letter about every two weeks until March 3, 1879, which was the last time she received a letter from him; that this letter was dated at Wichita, March 1, 1879, and was addressed to her at Ft. Madison, and the envelope was postmarked "Wichita, Kansas, March 2, 1879;" and that she had never heard from or seen him since that time.

The defendants put in evidence the envelope with the postmark and address, and thereupon offered to read the letter in evidence. The plaintiff objected to the reading of the letter. The court sustained the objection, and the defendants excepted.

This letter was dated "Wichita, March 1, 1879," was signed by Walters, and began as follows:

> "Dearest Alvina: Your kind and ever welcome letter was received yesterday afternoon about an hour before I left Emporia. I will stay here until the fore part of next week, and then will leave here to see a part of the country that I never expected to see when I left home, as I am going with a man by the name of Hillmon, who intends, to start a sheep ranch, and, as he promised me more wages than I could make at anything else, I concluded to take it, for a while at least, until I strike something better. There is so many folks in this country that have got the Leadville fever, and if I could not of got the situation that I have now I would have went there myself; but as it is at present I get to see the best portion of Kansas, Indian Territory, Colorado, and Mexico. The route that we intend to take would cost a man to travel from $150 to $200, but it will not cost me a cent; besides, I get good wages. I will drop you a letter occasionally until I get settled down. Then I want you to answer it."

… The jury, being instructed by the court to return a separate verdict in each case, returned verdicts for the plaintiff against the three defendants respectively for the amounts of their policies and interest, upon which separate judgments were rendered. The defendants sued out four writs of error, one jointly in the three cases as consolidated, and one in each case separately.

Mr. Justice GRAY, after stating the case as above, delivered the opinion of the court.

… The matter chiefly contested at the trial was the death of John W. Hillmon, the insured; and that depended upon the question whether the body found at Crooked Creek on the night of March 18, 1879, was his body or the body of one Walters....

The evidence that Walters was at Wichita on or before March 5th, and had not been heard from since, together with the evidence to identify as his the body found at Crooked Creek on March 18th, tended to show that he went from Wichita to Crooked Creek between those dates. Evidence that just before March 5th he had the intention of leaving Wichita with Hillmon would tend to corroborate the evidence already admitted, and to show that he went from Wichita to Crooked Creek with Hillmon. Letters from him to his family and his betrothed were the natural, if not the only attainable, evidence of his intention.

The position taken at the bar that the letters were competent evidence … as memoranda made in the ordinary course of business, cannot be maintained, for they were clearly not such.

But upon another ground suggested they should have been admitted.... The existence of a particular intention in a certain person at a certain time being a material fact to be proved, evidence that he expressed that intention at that time is as direct evidence of the fact as his own testimony that he then had that intention would be. After his death these can hardly be any other way of proving it, and while he is still alive his own memory of his state of mind at a former time is no more likely to be clear and true than a bystander's recollection of what he then said, and is less trustworthy than letters written by him at the very time and under circumstances precluding a suspicion of misrepresentation.

The letters in question were competent not as narratives of facts communicated to the writer by others, nor yet as proof that he actually went away from Wichita, but as evidence that, shortly before the time when other evidence tended to show that he went away, he had the intention of going, and of going with Hillmon, which made it more probable both that he did go and that he went with Hillmon than if there had been no proof of such intention. In view of the mass of conflicting testimony introduced upon the question whether it was the body of Walters that was found in Hillmon's camp, this evidence might properly influence the jury in determining that question....

Upon principle and authority, therefore, we are of opinion that the two letters were competent evidence of the intention of Walters at the time of writing them, which was a material fact bearing upon the question in controversy; and that for the exclusion of these letters, as well as for the undue restriction of the defendants' challenges, the verdicts must be set aside, and a new trial had....

Judgment reversed, and case remanded to the circuit court, with directions to set aside the verdict and to order a new trial.

Focus Questions: *United States v. Houlihan*

- Why do some jurisdictions mandate independent corroborating evidence connecting the declarent's intent with the non-declarant's conduct? Why does this Court reject that view? Which argument is more persuasive?

United States v. Houlihan

871 F.Supp. 1495 (D.Mass. 1994)

YOUNG, District Judge.

I. BACKGROUND

In the early morning hours of Monday, March 2, 1992, James Boyden Jr. was found dead in the vicinity of Spice Street, Charlestown. He had been shot in the back of the head.... Prior to his death, James Boyden Jr. allegedly told his sister, Marie Boyden Connors, that he had had a loud argument with the defendant Jennierose Lynch ("Lynch") in which she warned him that if he did not stop selling cocaine from her corner, she would have the defendant Michael Fitzgerald ("Fitzgerald") "blow [his] head off." James Boyden Jr. allegedly related similar accounts of this event to his mother, Veronica Boyden; his father, James Boyden Sr.; and another witness. His sister and mother each reported seeing him afterwards with a bandage on his face. Both women reported that James Boyden Jr. told them that Fitzgerald had beaten him up. The senior Mr. Boyden and another witness also reported that James Boyden Jr. had told them that he had been hit by Fitzgerald. On the evening before he was found dead, James Boyden Jr. was hanging out in his sister's Charlestown apartment drinking beer, departing at about 8:00 PM. As he was leaving, he allegedly told his sister that he was going out "to meet Billy Herd." William "Billy" Herd ("Herd") is a co-defendant in this case.

As the trial unfolded, the government ... [sought] to admit the statement of James Boyden Jr. to his sister that he intended to meet Herd as relevant circumstantial evidence that it was Herd who killed him later that evening. The government argued that this statement is admissible because it constitutes a statement of a then existing mental or emotional condition under Federal Rule of Evidence 803(3) ("Rule 803(3)"). Over objection, the Court admitted the statement and Marie Boyden Connors was allowed so to testify. This memorandum explains the Court's reasoning.

II. ANALYSIS

This case presents an issue of first impression in the First Circuit, namely, whether the out-of-court statement of a victim-declarant of an intention to meet with a defendant on the evening of the victim's murder can be admitted at trial as circumstantial evidence of the meeting. Rule 803(3), commonly referred to as the "state of mind exception," excludes from the hearsay rule statements of "the declarant's then existing state of mind, emotion, sensation, or physical condition (such as intent, plan, motive, design, mental feeling, pain, and bodily health)...." Thus, although the statement of James Boyden Jr. that he was going to meet Herd would clearly be admissible, if relevant, as a statement of James Boyden Jr.'s **own** intention, it is unclear whether it can be admitted against others—the defendants here—as evidence that the meeting **actually** took place.

A. The Common Law Prior to Rule 803(3)

Prior to the adoption of the Federal Rules of Evidence, the Supreme Court addressed this issue in the famous case of *Mutual Life Insurance Co. of New York v. Hillmon,* 145 U.S. 285 (1892). In *Hillmon,* an insurance company sought to introduce out-of-court statements by a declarant, Walters, that he intended to travel with the insured, Hillmon. The hearsay statement was used as the principal proof that Hillmon had actually traveled with Walters.... Thus, under *Hillmon,* out-of-court statements of a declarant are admissible to prove the subsequent conduct of others.

The analysis, however, does not end here. In 1973, Congress codified *Hillmon* in Federal Rule of Evidence 803(3). The question for this Court, then, is whether in enacting Rule 803(3) Congress codified in full the reasoning of *Hillmon,* or whether it sought to limit the case's application.

B. Rule 803(3) and its Legislative History

Rule 803(3) states that a declarant's out-of-court statement of intent is admissible at trial as an exception to the rule against hearsay. The text of the rule is silent as to whether such statements are admissible against third parties.

Unfortunately, the legislative history of Rule 803(3) only serves to obfuscate the analysis. While the Advisory Committee's Note to Rule 803(3) states that "the rule of *Mutual Life Insurance Co. v. Hillmon,* allowing evidence of intention as tending to prove the doing of the act intended, is, of course, left undisturbed," Fed.R.Evid. 803(3) advisory committee's note, the Report of the House Judiciary Committee states that "the committee intends that the rule be construed to limit the doctrine of *Mutual Life Insurance Co. v. Hillmon,* so as to render statements of intent by a declarant admissible only to prove his future conduct, not the future conduct of another person." The Senate Report and the Conference Report are silent on this point.

C. Circuit Split

Courts that have had the opportunity to consider the application of Rule 803(3) are divided.... Some courts have held that a declarant's statement of intent may be admitted against a non-declarant only when there is independent evidence connecting the declarant's statement with the non-declarant's conduct. *See United States v. Jenkins,* 579 F.2d 840, 842–43 (4th Cir.), *cert. denied,* 439 U.S. 967 (1978) (declarant's statement of intent is not admissible to prove subsequent conduct of third party, but is admissible to prove **why** third party acted as he did where there exists independent evidence that third party did in fact engage in the alleged conduct).

Similarly, the Second Circuit has held that "declarations of intentions or future plans are admissible against a nondeclarant when they are linked with independent evidence that corroborates the declaration." *United States v. Nersesian,* 824 F.2d 1294, 1325 (2d Cir.), *cert. denied,* 484 U.S. 958 (1987); *see also United States v. Cicale,* 691 F.2d 95, 103–104 (2d Cir.1982), *cert. denied,* 460 U.S. 1082 (1983) (where defendant's participation in drug transaction was proven by eyewitness testimony, statements by co-conspirator that he was going to meet the defendant for purposes of engaging in drug transaction were admissible)....

To the contrary, the Ninth Circuit has held that statements of a declarant's intent are admissible under Rule 803(3) to prove subsequent conduct of a person other than the declarant without corroborating evidence. *See United States v. Pheaster,* 544 F.2d 353, 374–80 (9th Cir.1976), *cert. denied sub nom. Inciso v. United States,* 429 U.S. 1099 (1977) (in kidnapping prosecution, trial court did not err in admitting testimony of a friend of the victim that shortly before the victim disappeared he told his friend that he was going to meet a person with the same name as the defendant). In holding statements of intent admissible against third parties, the *Pheaster* court recognized that such testimony could be unreliable, but rejected this as grounds for its exclusion. The Ninth Circuit explained that

> [t]he inference from a statement of present intention that the act intended was in fact performed is nothing more than an inference.... The possible unreliability of the inference to be drawn from the present intention [of the declarant] is a matter going to the weight of the evidence which might be argued to the trier of fact, but it should not be a ground for completely excluding the admittedly relevant evidence.

Id. at 376 n. 14. The court also acknowledged the "theoretical awkwardness" of applying a state of mind exception to prove conduct, but dismissed this objection because of the impressive array of authority favoring such application. *Id.* at 377....

III. GROUND OF DECISION

... The language of Rule 803(3) clearly says that statements of intent are admissible. Thus, because it does not **by its terms** limit the class of persons against whom such statements of intent may be admitted, this Court rules that Rule 803(3) codifies *Hillmon* as written and does not disturb its conclusion or its reasoning.

The Court's holding is supported by examining Rule 803(3) in the context of the rest of the Federal Rules of Evidence. The Rules are replete with examples of Congress' familiarity with the concept of limited admissibility. *Compare* Fed.R.Evid. 803(3) *with* Fed.R.Evid. 404(a) (limiting circumstances in which character evidence may be admitted); Fed.R.Evid. 404(b) (limiting purposes for which evidence of other crimes, wrongs, or acts may be admitted); Fed.R.Evid. 407 (limiting purposes for which subsequent remedial measures may be admitted); Fed.R.Evid. 408 (limiting purposes for which compromises and offers to compromise may be admitted); and Fed.R.Evid. 411 (limiting purposes for which evidence of liability insurance may be admitted). Thus, had Congress intended to limit the admissibility of such statements, it presumably would have done so. This Court will not venture to graft a limitation where none exists.

As Rule 803(3) is unambiguous, this Court is unpersuaded by appeals to legislative history. Even if the Court were properly to engage in an examination of Rule 803(3)'s legislative history, the conflicting nature of that evidence would nevertheless lead us right back to the text.

Likewise, this Court is not persuaded by the decisions of the Fourth and Second Circuits requiring independent evidence before such testimony can be admitted. Indeed, this requirement is without foundation in either the text or the legislative history of Rule 803(3). Thus, while the approach adopted by the Second and Fourth Circuits may seem practical and fair, it is really little more than judicial policymaking.

This Court finds the decisions of the Ninth Circuit, with their emphasis on text and Supreme Court precedent, more persuasive.... Thus, James Boyden Jr.'s statement that he was going out "to meet Billy Herd" is admissible against Herd under Fed.R.Evid. 803(3). Although it is true that James Boyden Jr.'s statement of intent is only circumstantial evidence that he actually met Herd, this statement will be allowed to function as part of the larger array of evidence before the jury so that they may decide for themselves what weight—if any—to give Ms. Connors' testimony. *See Pheaster,* 544 F.2d at 376 n. 14 (juries should be able to decide what weight to give a victim-declarant's assertion of intent to meet with defendant); *see also Cicale,* 691 F.2d at 104 n. 4 (articulating, but not adopting, the position that statements of intent should be allowed to function as part of a "larger matrix of circumstantial evidence").

Problem 7-21

On Friday, February 20th, Leonard DiMaria was arrested by FBI Agents near a truckload of hijacked cigarettes. Months later, at his trial for unlawful possession of stolen contraband cigarettes and conspiracy, DiMaria seeks to elicit testimony from an FBI agent witness stating that as the agents approached him to arrest him in front of the truck, DiMaria exclaimed:

"I thought you guys were just investigating white collar crime; what are you doing here? I only came to get some cigarettes real cheap."

DiMaria argues that the term "real cheap" refers to bootleg cigarettes rather than stolen cigarettes. Bootleg cigarettes are non-stolen cigarettes illegally brought from low-tax states for sale in high-tax states. If his argument convinces the jury, it will disprove the state of mind required for conviction for possession of stolen contraband cigarettes.

Are DiMaria's statements admissible? What if DiMaria made the statement to a police officer one week after he was arrested?

Problem 7-22

Eric Vogel, who had a long history of mental illness which included delusions, was arrested in Arizona for assaulting a police officer. A psychological counselor at the jail found him "disoriented, paranoid, and psychotic" and ordered that he continue to be confined in the jail. The administrators at the jail ordered Vogel to change from civilian clothes into prison garb. Vogel refused, and five officers subdued him and changed his clothes forcibly. Throughout this process, Vogel yelled that he was being raped by the officers.

Vogel was eventually bailed out of prison, but died within weeks of leaving prison. His family brought a Section 1983 claim alleging that the state acted with deliberate indifference to his serious medical needs. They claim that his treatment in prison, including forcibly changing his clothes, caused Vogel anguish that led to his death.

At trial, Vogel's sister wants to testify about a conversation she had with Vogel one week after he was released from prison. In that conversation, Vogel stated the he "believed he was being raped" while in prison, relayed the details of his alleged rape, and described the emotional impact it had on him. The plaintiffs claim they are offering Vogel's words to show his state of mind at the time of the conversation with his sister.

Is the testimony hearsay? If so, is it admissible under FRE 803(3)?

C. Statements for Medical Diagnosis or Treatment

Relevant Rule
FRE 803(4)

The following are not excluded by the rule against hearsay, regardless of whether the declarant is available as a witness: …

(4) *Statement Made for Medical Diagnosis or Treatment.* A statement that:

(A) is made for — and is reasonably pertinent to — medical diagnosis or treatment; and

(B) describes medical history; past or present symptoms or sensations; their inception; or their general cause.

Overview

FRE 803(4) allows the introduction of statements regarding past bodily condition. The statements are considered trustworthy because, at least in the situation of a patient seeking treatment from a physician, the patient will speak sincerely and accurately in order that she can receive the best care possible. The risk of misperception and faulty memory are minimal when the declarant herself has perceived the bodily condition.

The foundational elements of FRE 803(4) are thus:

- The declarant made a statement to a proper addressee,
- The declarant made the statement for a medical motive, and
- The subject matter of the statement is reasonably pertinent to diagnosis or treatment.

Although typically the declarant is the patient and the listener is the doctor, FRE 803(4) does not mandate this cast of characters. Thus, if the patient spoke to a family member or Good Samaritan in the hopes that they would convey the information to a doctor, then the statement is covered. Likewise, if the declarant speaks to a nurse or hospital intake assistant, the statement is covered if the goal is to get diagnosis or treatment. Most courts have held that statements from doctor to patient are not covered, however.

In terms of medical motive, the statement must focus on diagnosis or treatment. Thus, even an expert retained for litigation purposes can use FRE 803(4) at trial to demonstrate a diagnosis. The subject matter of the declarant's statement must be reasonably pertinent to treatment or diagnosis. Accordingly, the Advisory Committee's Note stated that "ordinarily" statements as to fault would not be covered, as those statements are rarely necessary for diagnosis. We can see why this would be so: ordinarily, a doctor would want to know that the patient was struck by a car going thirty miles per hour. Most likely, however, it is not reasonably pertinent to diagnosis that the speed limit was twenty miles per hour and that the driver ran a red light. In this case, statements attributing fault would not be admissible under the exception.

Focus Questions: *United States v. Iron Shell*

- What factors might the court consider in determining whether the patient's motive in making statements to a doctor was that of a patient seeking treatment or, in the alternative, seeking something other than treatment?

- How much weight does the court give to the fact that the doctor's exam would have been significantly similar even without the patient's statements? Why?

- According to FRE 803(4), in which category does the patient's statements fall? Are these fluid categories or distinct categories?

United States v. Iron Shell

633 F.2d 77 (8th Cir. 1980)

STEPHENSON, Circuit Judge.

Defendant, John Louis Iron Shell, appeals from a jury conviction of assault with intent to commit rape....

The indictment in this case arose out of the defendant's acts on July 24, 1979, in the community of Antelope, which is within the Rosebud Indian Reservation and near Mission, South Dakota. The defense conceded at trial that Iron Shell had assaulted Lucy, a nine-year-old Indian girl. The key questions at trial concerned the nature of the assault and the defendant's intent....

Dr. Mark Hopkins, a physician with the Indian Health Service, examined Lucy at about 8:20 p.m. on the night of the assault. During his examination the doctor elicited a series of statements from Lucy concerning the cause of her injuries. Dr. Hopkins was only aware that Lucy was allegedly a rape victim and was not told of the details surrounding the assault. During the examination, in response to questions posed by the doctor, Lucy told Dr. Hopkins she had been drug into the bushes, that her clothes, jeans and underwear, were removed and that the man had tried to force something into her vagina which hurt. She said she tried to scream but was unable because the man put his hand over her mouth and neck.[6] The doctor, over objection, repeated Lucy's statement at trial.

---

6. Out of the presence of the jury, the doctor testified that he first asked Lucy "what happened" and she didn't answer. He asked whether she was in any pain and she pointed to her vaginal area. He asked if she hurt anywhere else and she didn't answer. Dr. Hopkins again asked "what happened" and Lucy said she had been drug into the bushes. The doctor then asked if the man "had taken her clothes

Dr. Hopkins' examination also revealed that there was a small amount of sand and grass in the perineal area but not in the vagina. He also found superficial abrasions on both sides of Lucy's neck and testified that they were consistent with someone grabbing her but qualified his statement by adding that he could not absolutely determine that they were so caused. Dr. Hopkins also testified that there was no physical evidence of penetration, the hymen was intact and no sperm was located.

Lucy was able to add little and could only partially confirm the above record at trial. Lucy, a nine-year-old, was able to answer a number of preliminary questions demonstrating her ability to understand and respond to counsel but was unable to detail what happened after she was assaulted by the defendant. She did testify that she remembered something happening near the bushes and that a man had pushed her down. Lucy also said at trial that the man told her if she "didn't shut up he would choke me." In response to a series of leading questions she confirmed that the man had put his hand over her neck, hit her on the side of the face, held her down, taken her clothes off and that [a neighbor] had scared the man, making him leave.[7] On cross-examination defense counsel did not explore any of the substantive issues, nor did he examine Lucy concerning the statement she made to Dr. Hopkins and Officer Marshall, although he had the opportunity.

A. Dr. Hopkins' Testimony

... Defendant challenges the admission of statements made by Lucy to Dr. Hopkins during his examination. The prosecution offered this testimony admittedly as hearsay but within the exception expressed in Rule 803(4).... The defendant argues that the questions asked by Dr. Hopkins and the information received in response to those

---

off." She said yes, and then related the facts set out above. Dr. Hopkins testified that he was not "badgering" the patient, nor "dragging information out," but was asking "simple questions."

7. The following is a representative sample of the prosecutor's direct examination of Lucy:

Q What did the man do when he pushed you down, Lucy?
A (Long hesitation)
Q What did he do?
A (Long hesitation)
Q Did he hurt you any place?
A (Long hesitation)
Q Do you remember that?
A (Long hesitation)
Q Where did he put his hand, did he put his hand on your neck?
A Yes
Q Did you get hit on the side of the face?
A Yes.
Q When he pushed you down, did he hold you down?
A Yes.
Q Did you start crying?
A Yes.
THE COURT: As much as you can, phrase your questions in a way to avoid any unnecessary leading.
Q What else happened when he had you down, Lucy; did he say anything to you, do you remember?
A (Long hesitation)
Q What did he say to you, can you tell me? Tell me what he said?
A (Long hesitation)
Q Could you do that for me?
A Yes.
Q Okay, tell me what he said?
A If I didn't shut up he would choke me.

questions were not "reasonably pertinent" to diagnosis or treatment. The defense stresses Dr. Hopkins' question in which he asked Lucy whether the man had taken her clothes off and suggests that this was asked by one in the role of an investigator, seeking to solve the crime, rather than a doctor treating or diagnosing a patient. The defendant also asserts that the doctor's examination would have been the same whether or not this extra information had been received. The defense argues that this point supports his claim that the questions were not pertinent to treatment or diagnosis because they had no affect on the doctor's examination. Lastly, the defendant urges that the doctor was employed for the specific purpose of qualifying as an expert witness and as such his testimony should be more suspect.

It is clear that Rule 803(4) significantly liberalized prior practice concerning admissibility of statements made for purposes of medical diagnosis or treatment. See Notes of Advisory Committee on Proposed Rules, Rule 803. Rule 803(4) admits three types of statements: (1) medical history, (2) past or present sensations, and (3) inception or general cause of the disease or injury. All three types are admissible where they are "reasonably pertinent to diagnosis or treatment." The rule changed prior law in two main points. First, the rule adopted an expansive approach by allowing statements concerning past symptoms and those which related to the cause of the injury. Second, the rule abolished the distinction between the doctor who is consulted for the purpose of treatment and an examination for the purpose of diagnosis only; the latter usually refers to a doctor who is consulted only in order to testify as a witness.[8]

Lucy's statements fall primarily within the third category listed by 803(4).[9] The key question is whether these statements were reasonably pertinent to diagnosis or treatment. The rationale behind the rule has often been stated. It focuses upon the patient and relies upon the patient's strong motive to tell the truth because diagnosis or treatment will depend in part upon what the patient says. It is thought that the declarant's motive guarantees trustworthiness sufficiently to allow an exception to the hearsay rule. Judge Weinstein, in his treatise, suggests another policy ground. He writes that "a fact reliable enough to serve as the basis for a diagnosis is also reliable enough to escape hearsay proscription." [4 Weinstein & Berger, Weinstein's Evidence 803-129 (1979)]. This principle recognizes that life and death decisions are made by physicians in reliance on such facts and as such should have sufficient trustworthiness to be admissible in a court of law. This rationale closely parallels that underlying rule 703 and suggests a similar test should apply, namely—is this fact of a type reasonably relied upon by experts in a particular field in forming opinions. See Fed.R.Evid.

---

8. This is the first Eighth Circuit opinion to consider the effect of 803(4) on its pre-1975 case law. This circuit had followed the majority rule which prevented admission of testimony concerning the cause of the injury as not connected with treatment and excluded statements made to a physician who examined the patient solely for the purpose of testifying. These cases are no longer controlling but they may provide persuasive authority within the boundaries of 803(4) when analyzing whether statements are reasonably pertinent to diagnosis or treatment. Some courts had also held that a physician could repeat a patient's statement regarding medical history or past symptoms for the limited purpose of explaining the basis of an opinion and not in order to prove the truth of the out-of-court declarations. This distinction was likewise rejected by the federal rules. Notes of Advisory Committee on Proposed Rules, Rule 803.

9. Dr. Hopkins testified that Lucy said she was experiencing pain in her vaginal area. This expression of a present symptom falls within the second category of 803(4) and would also be excepted from the hearsay rule under rule 803(3) covering a then existing physical condition. Fed.R.Evid. 803(3). The remainder of Lucy's statement concerns the general character and nature of the cause of the injury. Because of the result we reach in this case, it is not necessary to discuss this distinction at length.

703 (Basis of Opinion Testimony by Experts). Thus, two independent rationales support the rule and are helpful in its application. A two-part test flows naturally from this dual rationale: first, is the declarant's motive consistent with the purpose of the rule; and second, is it reasonable for the physician to rely on the information in diagnosis or treatment.

We find no facts in the record to indicate that Lucy's motive in making these statements was other than as a patient seeking treatment. Dr. Hopkins testified that the purpose of his examination was two-fold. He was to treat Lucy and to preserve any evidence that was available. There is nothing in the content of the statements to suggest that Lucy was responding to the doctor's questions for any reason other than promoting treatment. It is important to note that the statements concern what happened rather than who assaulted her. The former in most cases is pertinent to diagnosis and treatment while the latter would seldom, if ever, be sufficiently related.[10] All of Lucy's statements were within the scope of the rule because they were related to her physical condition and were consistent with a motive to promote treatment. The age of the patient also mitigates against a finding that Lucy's statements were not within the traditional rationale of the rule. The trial court placed special emphasis on this factor and we likewise find that it is important to our holding.

During an extensive examination outside the presence of the jury, Dr. Hopkins explained in detail the relevancy of his questions to the task of diagnosis and treatment. He testified that a discussion of the cause of the injury was important to provide guidelines for his examination by pinpointing areas of the body to be examined more closely and by narrowing his examination by eliminating other areas. It is not dispositive that Dr. Hopkins' examination would have been identical to the one he performed if Lucy had been unable to utter a word. The doctor testified that his examination would have been more lengthy had he been unable to elicit a description of the general cause, although he stated the exam would have been basically the same. The fact that in this case the discussion of the cause of the injury did not lead to a fundamentally different exam does not mean that the discussion was not pertinent to diagnosis. It is enough that the information eliminated potential physical problems from the doctor's examination in order to meet the test of 803(4). Discovering what is not injured is equally as pertinent to treatment and diagnosis as finding what is injured. Dr. Hopkins also testified, in response to specific questions from the court, that most doctors would have sought such a history and that he relied upon Lucy's statements in deciding upon a course of treatment.[11]

---

10. The advisory committee notes on 803(4) provide that statements as to fault would not ordinarily qualify. The notes use this example: "a patient's statement that he was struck by an automobile would qualify but not his statement that the car was driven through a red light." Advisory Committee Notes, supra, at 585. Another example concludes that a statement by a patient that he was shot would be admissible but a statement that he was shot by a white man would not. And the fact that a patient strained himself while operating a machine may be significant to treatment but the fact that the patient said the machine was defective may not.

11. Judge Weinstein approached the problem as follows:

Much depends on the doctor's analysis. The doctor may or may not need to know that his patient was struck by a train and what caused him to fall under the train since dizziness before the accident may bear on diagnosis. A doctor consulted after the patient was involved in an automobile accident may need to know that the accident was precipitated when the patient fainted while driving. Since doctors may be assumed not to want to waste their time with unnecessary history, the fact that a doctor took the information is prima facie evidence that it was pertinent. Courtroom practice has tended to let in medical records and statements to nurses and doctors fairly freely, leaving it to the jury to decide probative force.

Weinstein & Berger, supra, at 803–130 (footnotes omitted). It is not necessary to find, and we do not hold in this case, that the fact that the doctor took the information is prima facie evidence that it was

In light of this analysis we hold that it was not an abuse of discretion to admit the doctor's testimony....

Affirmed.

[Concurrence by Heaney, J., and Dissent by Bright, J., omitted.]

Problem 7-23

To secure FDA approval of its drug Halcion, drug manufacturer Upjohn Company conducted a series of tests at the Jackson State Prison in Michigan. Called "Protocol 321," the tests exposed prisoners afflicted with insomnia to varying dosages of the drug. The prisoners filled out report forms that physicians then used to assess the drug's impact on human subjects. An institutional researcher oversaw the testing.

Product liability plaintiffs are in the early phases of suing Upjohn for issues related to Halcion. They have secured a subpoena for the reports submitted during Protocol 321, to which Defendant Upjohn objects. How do you rule?

Problem 7-24

Melvin and Julia Joe filed for divorce and separated in August 1991. After a day of drinking on February 23, 1992, Melvin drove to Julia's home, where he proceeded to fight with Julia and become physically abusive. Melvin eventually returned to his car and began circling Julia's home. As Julia and a neighbor attempted to flee, Melvin accelerated his vehicle directly into them, killing both women upon impact.

At trial Melvin sought to negate the intent needed for first degree murder, stating he was enraged over the pending divorce. The prosecution offered the testimony of family physician Dr. Brett Smoker. Dr. Smoker stated that he treated Julia for an alleged rape eight days before she was killed. At that time she identified Melvin as her assailant. She further stated that she was afraid because Melvin suspected her of having an extramarital affair and that he had threatened to kill her.

Are Julia's statements to Dr. Smoker regarding the rape admissible? What about the statements regarding Melvin's threats? Do any other objections exist?

Problem 7-25

On the night of December 22–23, 2000, Benjamin Bucci was waiting in line at a nightclub when he was hit in the back of the head by an unknown assailant. After the first blow, he lost consciousness and does not remember what happened until the time he awoke at the hospital.

---

pertinent. Rather, we conclude that a close examination of the facts and circumstances in each case is required.

Bucci eventually sued the nightclub. The issue at trial is whether Bucci's injuries were intentionally caused. If they were, they are excluded from the nightclub's commercial general liability policy, and Bucci cannot recover.

At trial, Bucci objected to the admission of three forms of medical records. The first, completed by the ambulance crew, was made minutes after a bystander called for help:

> "Patient complained of [neck] pain after struck once in face [by] a fist. Witness [said] patient [suffered] loss of consciousness [for] approximately 1 minute. Patient denies spine pain, denies shortness of breath."

The second was the emergency physician record for Bucci. Under the heading "context," the word "direct blow" was circled and the statement "hit & kicked [in the] face" was written underneath. The third was the triage report filled out by the triage nurse at 2:00 a.m. on December 23, 2000. There, the following statement appeared under the heading of "primary assessment": "Punched in [left] side of head."

How do you rule on Bucci's objection?

D. Writing to Refresh Memory/Recorded Recollection

Relevant Rules
FRE 803(5)

The following are not excluded by the rule against hearsay, regardless of whether the declarant is available as a witness: …

(5) *Recorded Recollection.* A record that:

(A) is on a matter the witness once knew about but now cannot recall well enough to testify fully and accurately;

(B) was made or adopted by the witness when the matter was fresh in the witness's memory; and

(C) accurately reflects the witness's knowledge.

If admitted, the record may be read into evidence but may be received as an exhibit only if offered by an adverse party.

FRE 612

Writing Used to Refresh a Witness's Memory

(a) Scope. This rule gives an adverse party certain options when a witness uses a writing to refresh memory:

(1) while testifying; or

(2) before testifying, if the court decides that justice requires a party to have those options.

(b) Adverse Party's Options; Deleting Unrelated Matter. Unless 18 U.S.C. §3500 provides otherwise in a criminal case, an adverse party is entitled to have the writing produced at the hearing, to inspect it, to cross-examine the witness about it, and to introduce in evidence any portion that relates to the witness's testimony. If the producing party claims that the writing includes unrelated matter, the court must examine the writing in camera, delete any unrelated portion, and order that the rest be delivered to the adverse party. Any portion deleted over objection must be preserved for the record.

(c) Failure to Produce or Deliver the Writing. If a writing is not produced or is not delivered as ordered, the court may issue any appropriate order. But if the prosecution does not comply in a criminal case, the court must strike the witness's testimony or — if justice so requires — declare a mistrial.

Overview

You have prepped your witness for trial. As your brilliant direct examination unfolds, the witness does not keep her end of the bargain. She begins to forget crucial facts. What are you to do?

Your first option is to use FRE 612 to refresh the witness's memory. You provide the witness with any document or object you feel will aid her memory. There are no foundational requirements for this document or object; it need not be crafted by the witness and need not have anything to do with the litigation. You ask the witness to silently read the writing or study the object. After she is done, you ask the witness if viewing the document or object has refreshed her memory. If the witness answers "yes," then her memory is refreshed, and she may continue with the direct examination. Opposing counsel has the right to review the document or object and may even introduce it as an exhibit at trial.

What if the witness's memory is not refreshed? What if, when she hands the document or object back to you, she states that she still cannot testify from memory? Now you may want to rely on a document in lieu of testimony. But this document is being offered for its truth, and is therefore hearsay. FRE 803(5) allows a party to introduce a document in lieu of testimony if the following foundation is established:

- The witness previously possessed personal knowledge of the facts recorded,
- The witness subsequently prepared or adopted a record of those facts,
- The witness prepared or adopted the record while the events were still fresh in her memory,
- The witness can vouch that when she prepared the record or adopted the record, the record was accurate, and
- At trial, the witness cannot completely and accurately recall the facts even after reviewing the document.

You now have established the foundation for the document and may read the document to the jury. Only opposing counsel may offer it as an exhibit, which would allow the jury to view it.

Focus Questions: *Baker v. State*

- The court articulates several qualities that a present recollection refreshed writing can possess which do not affect its admissibility. What are these qualities, and what is the court's reasoning for deeming them immaterial to an admissibility determination?

- How will the reliability of the testimony in this case be tested if it is admitted as a present recollection refreshed? How is it tested if it is admitted as a past recollection recorded?

Baker v. State

35 Md.App. 593, 371 A.2d 699 (1977)

MOYLAN, Judge.

This appeal addresses the intriguing question of what latitude a judge should permit counsel when a witness takes the stand and says, "I don't remember." What are the available keys that may unlock the testimonial treasure vaults of the subconscious? What are the brush strokes that may be employed "to retouch the fading daguerreotype of memory?" The subject is that of Present Recollection Revived.[2]

The appellant, Teretha McNeil Baker, was convicted by a Baltimore City jury of both murder in the first degree and robbery. Although she raises two appellate contentions, the only one which we find it necessary to consider is her claim that the trial judge erroneously refused her the opportunity to refresh the present recollection of a police witness by showing him a report written by a fellow officer.

The ultimate source of most of the evidence implicating the appellant was the robbery and murder victim himself, Gaither Martin, a now-dead declarant who spoke to the jury through the hearsay conduit of Officer Bolton. When Officer Bolton arrived at the crime scene, the victim told him that he had "picked these three ladies up ... at the New Deal Bar"; that when he took them to their stated destination, a man walked up to the car and pulled him out; that "the other three got out and proceeded to kick him and beat him." It was the assertion made by the victim to the officer that established that his money, wallet and keys had been taken. The critical impasse, for present purposes, occurred when the officer was questioned, on cross-examination, about what happened en route to the hospital. The officer had received a call from Officer Hucke, of the Western District, apparently to the effect that a suspect had been picked up. Before proceeding to the hospital, Officer Bolton took the victim to the place where Officer Hucke was holding the appellant. The appellant, as part of this cross-examination, sought to elicit from the officer the fact that the crime victim confronted the appellant and stated that the appellant was not one of those persons who had attacked and robbed him. To stimulate the present memory of Officer Bolton, appellant's counsel attempted to show him the police report relating to that confrontation and prepared by Officer Hucke.

The record establishes loudly and clearly that appellant's counsel sought to use the report primarily to refresh the recollection of Officer Bolton and that he was consistently and effectively thwarted in that attempt:

"BY MR. HARLAN:

Q. Do you have the report filed by Officer Hucke and Officer Saclolo or Saclolo?

A. Right, I have copies.

Q. Okay.

MR. DOORY: I would object to that, Your Honor.

THE COURT: I will sustain the objection. This is not his report.

BY MR. HARLAN:

Q. Can you look at this report and refresh your recollection as to whether or not you ever had the victim in a confrontation with Mrs. Baker?

---

2. Frequently and alternatively referred to as Present Recollection Refreshed.

MR. DOORY: Objection, Your Honor.

MR. HARLAN: He can refresh—

THE COURT: Well, he can refresh his recollection as to his personal knowledge. That's all right.

A. That is what I am saying, I don't know who it was that we confronted really.

BY MR. HARLAN:

Q. All right. Would you consult your report and maybe it will refresh your recollection.

THE COURT: I think the response is he doesn't know who—

MR. HARLAN: He can refresh his recollection if he looks at the report.

THE COURT: He can't refresh his recollection from someone else's report, Mr. Harlan.

MR. HARLAN: I would object, Your Honor. Absolutely he can.

THE COURT: You might object, but—

MR. HARLAN: You are not going to permit the officer to refresh his recollection from the police report?

THE COURT: No. It is not his report.

MR. HARLAN: Your Honor, I think I am absolutely within my rights to have a police officer read a report which mentions his name in it to see if it refreshes his recollection. If it doesn't refresh his recollection, then fine.

THE COURT: Well, he did that.

MR. HARLAN: You have not afforded him the opportunity to do that yet, Your Honor.

THE COURT: He says he does not know who it was before. So, he can't refresh his recollection if he does not know simply because someone else put some name in there.

MR. HARLAN: He has to read it to see if it refreshes his recollection, Your Honor.

THE COURT: We are reading from a report made by two other officers which is not the personal knowledge of this officer.

MR. HARLAN: I don't want him to read from that report. I want him to read it and see if it refreshes his recollection."

On so critical an issue as possible exculpation from the very lips of the crime victim, appellant was entitled to try to refresh the memory of the key police witness. She was erroneously and prejudicially denied that opportunity. The reason for the error is transparent. Because they both arise from the common seedbed of failed memory and because of their hauntingly parallel verbal rhythms and grammatical structures, there is a beguiling temptation to overanalogize Present Recollection Revived and Past Recollection Recorded. It is a temptation, however, that must be resisted. The trial judge in this case erroneously measured the legitimacy of the effort to revive present recollection against the more rigorous standards for the admissibility of a recordation of past memory.

It is, of course, hornbook law that when a party seeks to introduce a record of past recollection, he must establish 1) that the record was made by or adopted by the witness at a time when the witness did have a recollection of the event and 2) that the witness can presently vouch for the fact that when the record was made or adopted by him, he knew that it was accurate. McCormick, *Law of Evidence* (1st Ed., 1954), describes the criteria, at 15:

> "Appropriate safeguarding rules have been developed for this latter kind of mem-oranda, requiring that they must have been written by the witness or examined and found correct by him, and that they must have been prepared so promptly after the events recorded that these must have been fresh in the mind of the witness when the record was made or examined and verified by him. We have treated such memoranda separately, as an exception to the hearsay rule."

Had the appellant herein sought to offer the police report as a record of past recollection on the part of Officer Bolton, it is elementary that she would have had to show, inter alia, that the report had either been prepared by Officer Bolton himself or had been read by him and that he can now say that at that time he knew it was correct. Absent such a showing, the trial judge would have been correct in declining to receive it in evidence.

When dealing with an instance of Past Recollection Recorded, the reason for the rigorous standards of admissibility is quite clear. Those standards exist to test the competence of the report or document in question. Since the piece of paper itself, in effect, speaks to the jury, the piece of paper must pass muster in terms of its evidentiary competence.

Not so with Present Recollection Revived! By marked contrast to Past Recollection Recorded, no such testimonial competence is demanded of a mere stimulus to present recollection, for the stimulus itself is never evidence. Notwithstanding the surface similarity between the two phenomena, the difference between them could not be more basic. It is the difference between evidence and non-evidence. Of such mere stimuli or memory-prods, McCormick says, at 18, "(T)he cardinal rule is that they are not evidence, but only aids in the giving of evidence." When we are dealing with an instance of Present Recollection Revived, the only source of evidence is the testimony of the witness himself. The stimulus may have jogged the witness's dormant memory, but the stimulus itself is not received in evidence. Dean McCormick makes it clear that even when the stimulus is a writing, when the witness "speaks from a memory thus revived, his testimony is what he says, not the writing." *Id.*, at 15....

The catalytic agent or memory stimulator is put aside, once it has worked its psychological magic, and the witness then testifies on the basis of the now-refreshed memory. The opposing party, of course, has the right to inspect the memory aid, be it a writing or otherwise, and even to show it to the jury. This examination, however, is not for the purpose of testing the competence of the memory aid (for competence is immaterial where the thing in question is not evidence) but only to test whether the witness's memory has in truth been refreshed. As McCormick warns, "But the witness must swear that he is genuinely refreshed.... And he cannot be allowed to read the writing in the guise of refreshment, as a cloak for getting in evidence an inadmissible document." One of the most thorough reviews of this aspect of evidence law is found in *United States v. Riccardi*, 174 F.2d 883 (3rd Cir., 1949), where the court said at 888:

> "In the case of present recollection revived, the witness, by hypothesis, relates his present recollection, and under oath and subject to cross-examination asserts that it is true; his capacities for memory and perception may be attacked and tested; his determination to tell the truth investigated and revealed; protestations of lack of memory, which escape criticism and indeed constitute a refuge in the situation of past recollection recorded, merely undermine the probative worth of his testimony."

In solid accord with both the psychological sciences and the general common law of evidence, Maryland has long established it that even when a writing of some sort is the implement used to stir the embers of cooling memory, the writing need not be that of the forgetful witness himself, need not have been adopted by him, need not have been made contemporaneously with or shortly after the incident in question, and need not even be necessarily accurate. The competence of the writing is not in issue for the writing is not offered as evidence but is only used as a memory aid.…

When the writing in question is to be utilized simply "to awaken a slumbering recollection of an event" in the mind of the witness, the writing may be a memorandum made by the witness himself, 1) even if it was not made immediately after the event, 2) even if it was not made of firsthand knowledge and 3) even if the witness cannot now vouch for the fact that it was accurate when made. It may be a memorandum made by one other than the witness, even if never before read by the witness or vouched for by him.… All that is required is that it ignite the flash of accurate recall—that it accomplish the revival which is sought.…

… [T]he process might proceed, "Your Honor, I am about to show the witness a written report, ask him to read it and then inquire if he can now testify from his own memory thus refreshed." In a far less conventional mode, the process could just as well proceed, "Your Honor, I am pleased to present to the court Miss Rosa Ponselle who will now sing 'Celeste Aida' for the witness, for that is what was playing on the night the burglar came through the window." Whether by conventional or unconventional means, precisely the same end is sought. One is looking for the effective elixir to revitalize dimming memory and make it live again in the service of the search for truth.

Even in the more conventional mode, it is quite clear that in this case the appropriate effort of the appellant to jog the arguably dormant memory of the key police witness on a vital issue was unduly and prejudicially restricted.

JUDGMENTS REVERSED; CASE REMANDED FOR A NEW TRIAL; COSTS TO BE PAID BY MAYOR AND CITY COUNCIL OF BALTIMORE.

Problem 7-26

On the night of December 16, 1991, federal inmate Sheldon Schoenborn entered the prison gym and struck fellow inmate Gordon Roy several times on the head with a metal object. He was convicted of assault with a dangerous weapon and intent to do bodily harm.

On appeal, Schoenborn objects to the trial court's admission of a report by FBI Special Agent Richard Staedtler. On December 31, Staedtler conducted an interview with Todd Coleman, an inmate who was in the gym on the night of the assault. Staedtler transcribed the interview into a report and returned to the prison four months later to review it with Coleman. Coleman refused to sign it. The report read:

> A couple of weeks ago, in the evening, [Coleman] was in the gymnasium, sitting on the steps between the pool room and the basketball court. He saw a Native American inmate doing sit-ups on the floor of the stage and another Native American punching the heavy bag. The inmate who had been punching the heavy bag then picked up a piece of pipe about two feet long from the weight bench and went over to the inmate doing sit-ups and hit him in the head with the pipe.

At trial Coleman was uneasy. He said he thought there had been a fight that night, and when asked if he had witnessed it, he said "to a point." He testified that he did not see Schoenborn strike Roy, only that he saw one Native American jump off the gym stage and run in one direction, and another Native American jump off the stage and head in the opposite direction. Coleman said he had responded truthfully to Staedtler's questions, but that he did not sign the statement because he did not think it was accurate. Staedtler said the interview was accurately transcribed, and that when he reviewed the notes with Coleman, Coleman had confirmed their accuracy.

How do you rule on Schoenborn's appeal?

E. Business Records

Relevant Rules
FRE 803(6)

The following are not excluded by the rule against hearsay, regardless of whether the declarant is available as a witness: …

(6) *Records of a Regularly Conducted Activity.* A record of an act, event, condition, opinion, or diagnosis if:

(A) the record was made at or near the time by — or from information transmitted by — someone with knowledge;

(B) the record was kept in the course of a regularly conducted activity of a business, organization, occupation, or calling, whether or not for profit;

(C) making the record was a regular practice of that activity;

(D) all these conditions are shown by the testimony of the custodian or another qualified witness, or by a certification that complies with Rule 902(11) or (12) or with a statute permitting certification; and

(E) the opponent does not show that the source of information or the method or circumstances of preparation indicate a lack of trustworthiness.

FRE 803(7)

The following are not excluded by the rule against hearsay, regardless of whether the declarant is available as a witness: …

(7) *Absence of a Record of a Regularly Conducted Activity.* Evidence that a matter is not included in a record described in paragraph (6) if:

(A) the evidence is admitted to prove that the matter did not occur or exist;

(B) a record was regularly kept for a matter of that kind; and

(C) the opponent does not show that the possible source of the information or other circumstances indicate a lack of trustworthiness.

Overview

Business records are deemed trustworthy due to the fact that they are kept routinely. A business must be precise and accurate in its recordkeeping in order to avoid conflicts with its customers. Thus, there is no intent to lie in noting these transactions. Rather, an employee keeping business records possesses an incentive to be accurate in order to keep from getting fired. There also exists a great deal of necessity in relying on business records. An employee, such as a clerk at a bank, will undertake perhaps hundreds of mundane transactions in a business day. Few of them will likely be memorable the very next day, and far fewer would be memorable one or two years after the transactions. Thus, calling the teller at a trial to confirm a two-year-old deposit will result in the teller honestly testifying that she does not remember the transaction. By relying on a business record, this potentially vital evidence can be introduced even if the maker of the record cannot fully remember the transaction.

The foundational elements of a business record mandates:

- The record was made and kept in the course of regularly conducted business activity,
- It was a routine practice of the business to make the record,
- The record was made at or near the time of the transaction it records, and
- The record was made by, or from information transmitted by, a person with knowledge who acted in the regular course of business.

This foundation need not be established by the person who crafted the business record; the rule allows an "other qualified witness," such as a business' custodian of records, to testify as to the foundation. Thus, the custodian of records for a bank could testify that a record of a customer's deposit met the foundation because the bank always makes and keeps such records in the regular course of business, that it was routine practice to do so, that, based on the record itself, it was made within minutes of the deposit, and that the teller who made the record would have had first-hand knowledge of the business transaction. Even though this witness does not have personal knowledge that customer X deposited $100 in the bank, the witness can testify as to the routine business practice of the organization and meet the foundational requirements of the rule.

In terms of the specific elements of the foundation, the terms within each element are typically defined broadly. Thus, a "business activity" includes any regular organized activity, including criminal enterprises. The level to which the practice was routine means that the organization regularly conducted that practice. Just because a business crafts a record does not necessarily mean it was routine to do so, however. So, while a bank keeps detailed records of deposits that usually are considered business records, if the bank created an unusual record about a customer it may not qualify, as *United States v. Kim*, below, will suggest. The timing element of the foundation is usually satisfied if the record was created within a reasonable time after the transaction.

The final element raises a host of hearsay within hearsay concerns (i.e., a hearsay statement incorporates another hearsay statement — in this situation, an exception is needed for each layer of hearsay, as will be discussed later in the chapter). Often a business record may incorporate a statement of someone outside the business, such as a customer. That person has no business duty to report information, and therefore their hearsay is considered unreliable. Accordingly, if a statement from someone outside the business is incorporated within the business record, another hearsay exception is needed with regard to the "outsider's" statement if it is offered for its truth. So, if a bank's deposit record included a statement from the customer (e.g., "This is the fifth check that I've received for my birthday!"), another hearsay exception is needed if the record is offered to prove that the customer received five birthday checks. *Scheerer v. Hardee's Food Systems, Inc.* and the problems in this section will explore this issue in greater detail.

Finally, note well that a court does not have to admit the document if some aspect of the business record makes it seem untrustworthy. If a motive to misrepresent is apparent, such as if the document was made solely for litigation purposes, a court may rule that the document is inadmissible. The burden is on the opponent to show a lack of trustworthiness.

FRE 803(7) governs proof the of the nonoccurrence or nonexistence of a matter by showing that no record of it is found in regularly kept records that would have recorded it if it did occur or exist. The foundation mandates that all the elements of FRE 803(6) be met and that a qualified witness must testify that a diligent search revealed no record. Thus, if someone claimed they deposited one million dollars in a bank on April 1, 2009, we would expect some record exists of the deposit. A qualified witness from the bank would articulate their recordkeeping procedure pursuant to the foundation of FRE 803(6) and then would add that no record was found. Perhaps the bank's witness might offer a document of all the transactions at the bank on that date to prove plaintiff's alleged deposit was not recorded. This absence of entry would be excepted from the hearsay rule under FRE 803(7).

Focus Questions: *United States v. Kim*

- How does the Court determine that the document in question is hearsay within hearsay? Define each of the two levels of hearsay in your own words.

- What does the court consider in its determination of whether the circumstances of the document's preparation indicate a lack of trustworthiness?

- If a document is produced by a business for something other than a regular business purpose, will it invariably be determined as inadmissible by the court? What would the decision hinge upon?

United States v. Kim

595 F.2d 755 (D.C.Cir. 1979)

MacKINNON, Circuit Judge:

Defendant Hancho C. Kim was convicted of conspiracy to defraud the United States and of making false declarations before a grand jury. Allegedly, Kim received money from the Korean Central Intelligence Agency (hereinafter KCIA) for the purpose of bribing United States Congressmen (conspiracy) and lied to the grand jury when he denied receiving the money (false declaration). Kim was sentenced to three years imprisonment on each count, to be served concurrently. All but six months of his sentence was suspended and supplanted by a period of probation.

Kim appeals asserting that ... the trial court erroneously excluded as inadmissible hearsay an exculpatory telex despite its admissibility under ... the business records exception ...

I

The government's evidence indicated that money was delivered to Kim by Sang Keun Kim (hereinafter S. K. Kim) for the purpose of bribing Congressmen. The government acknowledges that defendant Kim never bribed or approached any Congressmen. It contends that after taking the money, the defendant converted it to his own use.

S. K. Kim, who was a KCIA agent stationed at the Korean Embassy in Washington, was the government's principal witness. He testified that on the orders of General Yang Doo Wan, his superior at the KCIA, he delivered a total of $600,000 to defendant Kim. The money was delivered in two installments: $300,000 on September 12, 1974, and $300,000 on June 6, 1975.

S. K. Kim was not a completely credible witness. He admitted that he had been a KCIA spy, and that when he first learned of the Justice Department's investigation he forged documents and fabricated a cover story in order to impede the investigation. Some of his trial testimony was inconsistent with statements he made to the Federal Bureau of Investigation immediately after he defected. He admitted that he stood to gain from his cooperation with the Government.

The Government buttressed S. K. Kim's testimony with certain corroborating evidence. First, it presented evidence of clandestine meetings between S. K. Kim and the defendant. Second, a government handwriting expert testified that a receipt for the 1974 installment of $300,000, which was in S. K. Kim's possession, was written by the defendant. Third, the government introduced evidence that over one-hundred telex messages [a precursor to the fax] were sent from a telex machine in the defendant's house to General Yang's telex number in Seoul. This corroborated S. K. Kim's claim that he sent reports about the defendant's activities to General Yang at KCIA headquarters in Seoul from the defendant's telex machine.

Finally, the government introduced evidence that beginning in 1972 the defendant had serious financial problems. He began to borrow heavily on his life insurance, on his property, and from finance companies. He was tardy in paying his bills, building up large balances with a number of retail stores. The checks drawn to pay for his children's private school tuition bounced. In July of 1974 he tried to borrow from a finance company that had earlier extended him a loan, but he was turned down because of his slow payment on his previous loan and because he had no sources of income in the United States.

The defendant's financial troubles apparently ended abruptly, on September 13, 1974, the day after S. K. Kim allegedly delivered the first installment of $300,000 in $100 bills. Within weeks, defendant Kim paid all of his bills, many of them with $100 bills, and in the next fifteen months spent close to $200,000 on personal expenditures. The defendant's sudden access to large amounts of money, after a prolonged period of financial difficulty, strongly corroborates S. K. Kim's testimony that he delivered $300,000 to the defendant.

The defendant did not testify at trial. His counsel argued that "Hancho Kim was the innocent scapegoat of a private scheme of S. K. Kim and co-conspirator Yang Doo Wan to enrich themselves by siphoning KCIA funds. The defense also sought to show that Hancho Kim had abundant sources of money in Korea to account for his expenditures." The jury was not persuaded by this defense. Hancho Kim was convicted.

II

To bolster its assertion that Hancho Kim had "abundant sources of money," the defense sought to introduce a telex from the Korean Exchange Bank in Seoul, Korea. The telex was sent instead of the defendant's bank records which were sought by a government subpoena. It stated that on January 13, 1977 the defendant personally withdrew $400,000 which had been deposited in U.S. dollars to his account on three separate days in 1975. Defense counsel contends that the telex proves "that Hancho Kim must have had other substantial sources of funds. Those funds were as likely a source for his expenditures in the United States as for the deposits in Korea." But counsel's argument is flawed by its complete failure to explain the source of his funds in 1974 or the $200,000 of expenditures beginning at that time, and by the incompetence of the evidence upon which it relies. The trial court refused to admit the telex into evidence, holding it to be inadmissible hearsay.

The defendant maintains that the court erred when it excluded the telex because it falls within ... the business records exception....

A

The telex was offered to prove that during 1975 Hancho Kim deposited $400,000 in the Korean Exchange bank in three installments. It contains two hearsay links. The bank's record of deposits made by the defendant is the first hearsay link. The second hearsay link is the telex itself, which contains another bank employee's statement as to what the bank's records show. In each case, the out-of-court statement of the declarant was offered to prove the "truth of the matter asserted" that the defendant deposited the money (link 1) and that those deposits are reflected in bank records (link 2)....

B

The defendant maintains that the telex is admissible under the business records exception to the hearsay rule. Essentially, that exception provides that records made and kept in the ordinary course of business may be introduced into evidence despite their hearsay nature. The business records exception is codified in Federal Rule of Evidence 803(6)....

The telex fails to meet the business records exception for three reasons. First, Rule 803(6) states that a business record will only be admissible if it is made "at or near the time" of the events that it reports. The telex does not meet this requirement. It reports deposits that took place in 1975. Yet it was not prepared until April of 1977, over two years after the first deposit was allegedly made.

The defendant acknowledges this shortcoming. He argues, however, that the timeliness requirement should be waived in this case. The gist of his argument is that the timeliness requirement is designed to ensure that the declarant's memory is accurate. Here, the argument goes, there is no doubt about memory because the telex merely summarizes bank records that were made contemporaneously with the deposits.

Assuming, *arguendo*, that there is no question about the accuracy of the declarant's memory in this case, we still reject defendant's argument. He cites no authority for waiving the timeliness requirement.... There is no place in the scheme of the Rules of Evidence for selective waiver of the requirements of particular exceptions. If the requirements of an exception are not met, then the evidence must be excluded unless it falls within the residual exception....

The second reason that the telex does not fall within the business records exception is that it was not made for a regular business purpose. In order for a document to qualify as a business record, it must have been the "regular practice of that business activity to make the memorandum...." Fed.R.Evid. 803(6). The Advisory Committee on Proposed Rules explained the reason for this requirement:

> The element of unusual reliability of business records is said variously to be supplied ... by actual experience of business in relying upon them, or by a duty to make an accurate record as part of a continuing job or occupation.

Similarly, the First Circuit explained in *Hiram Ricker & Sons v. Students International Meditation Society*, 501 F.2d 550, 554 (1st Cir. 1974): "A crucial aspect of the business-records exception is that entries be prepared as a Regular part of the business.... Otherwise, there is no basis for the presumption of reliability which is at the heart of the exception." Thus, when a document is made for something other than a regular business purpose, it does not fall within the business records exception.

The telex was sent in response to a government subpoena for the defendant's bank records. The defendant's account at the bank was closed. The telex was not relied on by the bank. And "(a)lthough the method by which the information supplied in (the telex) was retrieved is a method commonly used by the bank, the transaction which gave rise to the Telex message was, according to the manager of the New York branch, the first one of its kind in the bank's history." Thus, the telex was not made for a regular business purpose and it was not "a part of a Series of entries or Reports...."

The defendant's attempts to meet this objection are unpersuasive. He argues that the New York branch of the Korean Exchange Bank frequently relies on telex messages from Seoul in making loans and carrying on its business. While that is undoubtedly true, it does not make this telex a business record. The defendant wrongly focuses on the means by which the message was transmitted. The critical factor in determining whether the document satisfied the "business purpose" requirement lies in the reason that the message was prepared and sent, not the means by which it was transmitted. In this case a regular business means of communication was used, but the message did not serve a regular business purpose. Hence, the telex is not a business record.

The defendant also states that the "Federal Rules of Evidence do not Per se prohibit the admissibility of records prepared in response to judicial process." While this may be true, neither does subpoenaing a record guarantee its admissibility, and the argument does not support defendant's claim that the telex should be admitted as a business record. In fact, the case cited for this proposition involves not the business record exception, but the residual exception. In summary, on the second point, the telex is not admissible under the business records exception because it was not prepared for a regular business purpose.

Finally, it was within the trial court's discretion to refuse to admit the telex under the business records exception because the "circumstances of preparation indicate lack of trustworthiness." Fed.R.Evid. 803(6). In *United States v. Reese*, 561 F.2d 894, 903 n. 18 (D.C.Cir. 1977) we stated that "the trial court has broad discretion in determining whether documents otherwise admissible as business records are sufficiently trustworthy." Here the trustworthiness of the document was in question because (1) the telex was not entirely consistent with a letter sent by the bank to the appellant, and (2) there was no testimony as to the circumstances surrounding its preparation in Korea. It was not an abuse of discretion for the court to conclude that the telex was not trustworthy in light of these considerations.

In summary, we hold that the telex is not admissible under the business records exception to the hearsay rule for three reasons. First, the telex was not prepared at or near the time of the acts reported. Second, the telex was not sent in the regular course of business. Finally, it was not an abuse of discretion for the trial court to doubt the trust-worthiness of the telex....

Since we find no reversible error in the trial court's handling of this case, we affirm defendant Hancho Kim's convictions.

Judgment accordingly.

Focus Questions: *Scheerer v. Hardee's*

- What is it about the circumstances surrounding the incident report and the report itself that renders it unreliable or untrustworthy by the court?

- What leads the court to believe that the report was created with the knowledge that the incident would result in litigation?

- Could documents prepared in response to an event that could result in litigation still be prepared for an ordinary business purpose and be sufficiently reliable and trustworthy? Why or why not?

Scheerer v. Hardee's Food Systems, Inc.

92 F.3d 702 (8th Cir. 1996)

McMILLIAN, Circuit Judge.

Cheryle Ann Scheerer and her husband John Scheerer appeal from a final judgment entered in the United States District Court for the Western District of Missouri in favor of Hardee's Food Systems, Inc. (Hardee's), a North Carolina corporation, in their action to recover damages for personal injuries sustained when Mrs. Scheerer slipped and fell in the parking lot of a Hardee's restaurant....

On the evening of June 28, 1989, the Scheerers visited the Hardee's restaurant. A Hardee's employee had watered the plants around the restaurant shortly before the accident. Mrs. Scheerer had exited the restaurant and was walking across the parking lot when she slipped and fell behind a parked car. The Scheerers' theory of the case was that the surface of the parking lot was slippery due to a combination of water over oil and grease deposits and that Hardee's failed to warn its customers about the dangerous condition. Hardee's defended on several alternative theories: the surface of the parking lot was dry, not wet, and Mrs. Scheerer's hard-soled shoes caused her to slip and fall; if there was any dangerous condition on the parking lot due to oil or grease or water on its surface, Hardee's did not cause such a dangerous condition and had no notice of it; the dangerous condition on the parking lot was open and obvious as a matter of law; or Mrs. Scheerer had failed to keep a proper lookout.

... The district court admitted into evidence, over objection, an "incident report" prepared by a Hardee's employee that described the surface of the parking lot as dry, not wet or oily, and included the statement that "a friend explained [Mrs. Scheerer's] shoes were slick...." The jury found no liability on the part of Hardee's....

First, we consider the Scheerers' contention that the district court abused its discretion in admitting into evidence the "incident report" as a business record under Fed.R.Evid. 803(6).... The incident report was prepared by a non-witness Hardee's employee and contained not only a description of the condition of the surface of the parking lot as dry, not wet or oily, but also a statement attributed to a "friend" of Mrs. Scheerer that the cause of the accident was Mrs. Scheerer's "slick shoes." Although the "friend" was not identified at trial, there was an inference that the friend was a Mrs. Fran, who was a trial witness. (The Scheerers describe Mrs. Fran as a neighbor and acquaintance rather than a friend.) The author who prepared the incident report did not testify. The Scheerers argue that even if the incident report was admissible as a business record, the statement in the incident report about the shoes should have been excluded as untrustworthy. The Scheerers also argue that the incident report was not admissible as a business record because it was prepared in anticipation of litigation.

Hardee's argues the incident report was admissible as a business record and was trustworthy because such reports are routinely made at or close to the time of an incident whenever a customer is injured or claims to have been injured. Hardee's argues that it is "perfectly clear" that the friend, that is, the source of the information in the incident report, was Mrs. Fran, who, Hardee's notes, was a trial witness. Mrs. Fran testified that she could not remember stating that the cause of the accident was Mrs. Scheerer's shoes. Hardee's also argues that the incident report rebutted the Scheerers' claim that the surface of the parking lot was wet at the time of the accident.

We hold the incident report was not admissible as a business record under Fed.R.Evid. 803(6) because the source of the information contained therein was never identified at trial. In particular, although we agree that Mrs. Fran was probably the "friend," it is unclear whether she was the source of the information about Mrs. Scheerer's shoes. In the absence of any evidence about the source of that information, we cannot test its reliability or trustworthiness. *E.g., Meder v. Everest & Jennings, Inc.*, 637 F.2d 1182, 1187 & n. 6 (8th Cir.1981) (reference in police report about cause of accident should have been excluded because the author was not on the scene at the time of the accident, did not remember whether victim-plaintiff made a statement and did not recall with whom he spoke at the scene).

In addition, the incident report was inadmissible as a business record under Fed.R.Evid. 803(6) because it had been prepared in anticipation of litigation. Even if we assume that Mrs. Fran was the source of the information about Mrs. Scheerer's shoes, the incident report lacks reliability or trustworthiness because it was not made in the ordinary course of business but instead with the knowledge that the incident could result in litigation. *E.g., United States v. Blackburn*, 992 F.2d 666, 670 (7th Cir.) (lensometer report prepared at behest of FBI and with knowledge that any information it supplied would be used in ongoing criminal investigation was not prepared and kept in ordinary course of eyeglasses business), *cert. denied*, 510 U.S. 949 (1993); *Picker X-Ray Corp. v. Frerker*, 405 F.2d 916, 922–23 (8th Cir.1969) (hospital report made by business manager after accident which he knew could result in litigation was not used for treatment or any other ordinary business purpose but instead with knowledge that incident could result in litigation). Here, the incident report shows on its face that it was prepared in anticipation of litigation and not in the ordinary course of Hardee's usual restaurant business operations. The directions on the incident report form instructed the person completing the form to "[g]et COMPLETE information," "[p]hone report within 30 minutes of incident, if serious," and "[f]orward written report same day." Other directions on the form noted that "[t]his form is to be used for reporting all types of incidents—Premises or Product Liability, Fire, Theft and Property Damage" and specifically instructed the person completing the form to distribute the white copy "[t]o your local claims office," the pink copy to the "Risk Management Dept.," and the yellow copy to the "Area Director of Operations."

In light of the importance of the incident report and the information contained therein about the condition of the surface of the parking lot and Mrs. Scheerer's shoes, the incident report was extremely prejudicial and therefore its admission was reversible error ...

Accordingly, the judgment of the district court is reversed and the case is remanded to the district court for further proceedings consistent with this opinion.

Problem 7-27

Jose Reyes was convicted of multiple counts of conspiracy to commit murder based on the testimony of Raul Vargas, who claimed that Reyes (as the head of a large criminal gang) ordered him to kill several people. Vargas claimed he was given these orders on three separate visits he made to Reyes in prison. To corroborate Vargas's testimony, the state introduced the prison visitor log book into evidence. A prison guard with eight years of experience in the administration of prison visits testified that the prison requires visitors to enter their name and address in the prison visitor log book, and then a guard verifies that information by checking the visitors' identification. On appeal, Reyes challenges the admission of this log book as hearsay within hearsay. How do you rule?

Problem 7-28

Thomas Sinkovich was out on his yacht when it struck some rocks and sank. His hull was insured by Lloyd's. Lloyd's hired Ed Geary as an independent contractor to investigate the incident. Geary was a professional investigator who specialized in incidents such as this. Geary wrote, and Lloyd's submitted as evidence, a report detailing the results of Geary's investigation which included findings that Sinkovich had breached his insurance agreement with Lloyd's in a number of ways including "the failure of the insured to avert the grounding, failure to attempt to mitigate the damages after the grounding, failure to act as a prudent uninsured, and failure to advise Underwriters as soon as possible of the loss are considered to be a clear breach and violation of the terms and conditions of the policy as specified under 11. Your Duties in the Event of a Loss." For these and other reasons Lloyd's refused to honor the policy.

Mr. Sinkovich disputed the admission of Geary's report as inadmissible hearsay. How do you rule?

Problem 7-29

On the morning of September 13, 2005, the First Source Bank in Fort Wayne, Indiana, was robbed. The police arrested James Leshore for the crime, in part because some bait money from the bank was found on Leshore when he was apprehended a short time after the robbery. Bait money is pre-selected cash that banks intentionally surrender in the event of a robbery. The serial numbers of the bait money are pre-recorded on a list so that the police might later match the numbers, thereby helping to establish the identity of the culprits. This bait money list is made by bank employees but does not change unless there is a robbery in which case a new list is made with new bait money. The bait money list is verified three times a year when a bank employee checks the serial numbers on the list against those on the actual bait money.

The prosecution submitted the bait money list into evidence to prove that the money Leshore was carrying was in fact the bait from the robbery. Leshore argued that the list was inadmissible hearsay. How do you rule?

Author's Note: Hearsay within Hearsay

Relevant Rule
FRE 805

Hearsay Within Hearsay

Hearsay within hearsay is not excluded by the rule against hearsay if each part of the combined statements conforms with an exception to the rule.

Hearsay can exist on multiple layers. The problem of hearsay within hearsay has shown up in some of our cases and problems. One example was in *United States v. Kim*, where the bank's telex had two levels of hearsay: "In each case, the out-of-court statement of the declarant was offered to prove the 'truth of the matter asserted' that the defendant deposited the money (link 1) and that those deposits are reflected in bank records (link 2)." We also saw the issue arise in *Scheerer v. Hardee's Food Systems, Inc.*, where the witness made a statement to defendant's employee (link 1), and the employee put that statement into a business document which the defendant attempted to introduce at trial (link 2). In order for both of these statements to be admissible, each link must fit an exemption or exception. Sometimes the same exception could satisfy both links (in *Kim* the defendant argued that both links were business records), and sometimes you need to reach for different exceptions or exemptions (could link #1 in *Scheerer* be a present sense impression? Could the second link be a business record?). Either way, you must be able to analyze **how many** out of court statements are being offered for their truth in order to understand how many levels of hearsay exist in a piece of evidence.

F. Public Records

Relevant Rules
FRE 803(8)

(8) *Public Records.* A record or statement of a public office if:

    (A) it sets out:

        (i) the office's activities;

        (ii) a matter observed while under a legal duty to report, but not including, in a criminal case, a matter observed by law-enforcement personnel; or

        (iii) in a civil case or against the government in a criminal case, factual findings from a legally authorized investigation; and

    (B) the opponent does not show that the source of information or other circumstances indicate a lack of trustworthiness.

FRE 803(10)

(10) *Absence of a Public Record.* Testimony — or a certification under Rule 902 — that a diligent search failed to disclose a public record or statement if:

    (A) the testimony or certification is admitted to prove that

        (i) the record or statement does not exist; or

        (ii) a matter did not occur or exist, if a public office regularly kept a record or statement for a matter of that kind; and

(B) in a criminal case, a prosecutor who intends to offer a certification provides written notice of that intent at least 14 days before trial, and the defendant does not object in writing within 7 days of receiving the notice — unless the court sets a different time for the notice or the objection.

Overview

FRE 803(8) admits a record of a public office if it sets out that office's activities, a matter observed while under a legal duty to report, or factual findings from a legally authorized investigation. The trustworthiness of the record stems from the belief that public servants will perform their duties accurately and carefully. The foundation is straightforward: the proponent must prove that the document is an authentic public record and that it contains any of the three types of information articulated in the rule. As we shall see in *Beech Aircraft Corp. v. Rainey*, below, factual findings from a legally authorized investigation are admissible if "neither the source of information nor other circumstances indicate a lack of trustworthiness." The party that argues lack of trustworthiness carries the burden on the issue.

FRE 803(8)(A)(ii) and (iii) both limit the application of the rule in criminal cases. The limitation of FRE 803(8)(A)(ii) does not allow a party in a criminal case to use "a matter observed by law-enforcement personnel[.]" The limitation of FRE 803(8)(A)(iii) prohibits investigative findings from being offered against the accused. The rationale behind these limitations centers on the fact that the purpose of a police report or other criminal investigative report in the criminal arena is to help prepare the government's case. As such, the reports may contain a pro-government bias and often contain secondhand and thirdhand outsider statements that are unreliable. Furthermore, the term "law-enforcement personnel" has been read broadly to include scientists, criminologists and forensic specialists. *See e.g., United States v. Oates,* 560 F.2d 45, 68 (2nd Cir. 1977). However, courts have allowed routine, nonadversarial reports to be admitted against against a criminal defendant, as there is a lesser risk of bias. *See e.g., United States v. Dancy,* 861 F.2d 77, 79–80 (5th Cir. 1988) (allowing admission of a fingerprint card). Government laboratory reports occupy a middle ground. On the one hand, they are the product of science. On the other hand, they are compiled as part of the adversarial process. We will explore the issue of government laboratory reports in greater detail in Chapter 8, where we discuss the Confrontation Clause.

Similar to FRE 803(7), the absence of entries in public records is admissible under FRE 803(10). This exception allows the proponent to offer a certificate by a recordkeeper indicating that a diligent search failed to turn up a record where one would expect it to be found.

Focus Questions: *Beech Aircraft Corp. v. Rainey*

- The Advisory Committee outlined several factors in determining the trustworthiness of a public office record. How are they applied in this case? Does the court apply all of the factors?

- What other safeguards exist in the FRE that favor the introduction of the evidence at issue in this case? Do those safeguards cut in favor of or against admission of the evidence in this case?

Beech Aircraft Corp. v. Rainey

488 U.S. 153

BRENNAN, J., delivered the opinion of the Court, in which WHITE, MARSHALL, BLACKMUN, STEVENS, SCALIA, and KENNEDY, JJ., joined, and in Parts I and II of which REHNQUIST, C.J., and O'CONNOR, J., joined. REHNQUIST, C.J., filed an opinion concurring in part and dissenting in part, in which O'CONNOR, J., joined.

In this action we address a longstanding conflict among the Federal Courts of Appeals over whether Federal Rule of Evidence 803(8)(C), which provides an exception to the hearsay rule for public investigatory reports containing "factual findings," extends to conclusions and opinions contained in such reports.…

I

This litigation stems from the crash of a Navy training aircraft at Middleton Field, Alabama, on July 13, 1982, which took the lives of both pilots on board, Lieutenant Commander Barbara Ann Rainey and Ensign Donald Bruce Knowlton. The accident took place while Rainey, a Navy flight instructor, and Knowlton, her student, were flying "touch-and-go" exercises in a T-34C Turbo-Mentor aircraft, number 3E955. Their aircraft and several others flew in an oval pattern, each plane making successive landing/takeoff maneuvers on the runway. Following its fourth pass at the runway, 3E955 appeared to make a left turn prematurely, cutting out the aircraft ahead of it in the pattern and threatening a collision. After radio warnings from two other pilots, the plane banked sharply to the right in order to avoid the other aircraft. At that point it lost altitude rapidly, crashed, and burned.

Because of the damage to the plane and the lack of any survivors, the cause of the accident could not be determined with certainty. The two pilots' surviving spouses brought a product liability suit against petitioners Beech Aircraft Corporation, the plane's manufacturer, and Beech Aerospace Services, which serviced the plane under contract with the Navy. The plaintiffs alleged that the crash had been caused by a loss of engine power, known as "rollback," due to some defect in the aircraft's fuel control system. The defendants, on the other hand, advanced the theory of pilot error, suggesting that the plane had stalled during the abrupt avoidance maneuver.

At trial, the only seriously disputed question was whether pilot error or equipment malfunction had caused the crash. Both sides relied primarily on expert testimony. One piece of evidence presented by the defense was an investigative report prepared by Lieutenant Commander William Morgan on order of the training squadron's commanding officer and pursuant to authority granted in the Manual of the Judge Advocate General. This "JAG Report," completed during the six weeks following the accident, was organized into sections labeled "finding of fact," "opinions," and "recommendations," and was supported by some 60 attachments. The "finding of fact" included statements like the following:

> "13. At approximately 1020, while turning crosswind without proper interval, 3E955 crashed, immediately caught fire and burned.

> "27. At the time of impact, the engine of 3E955 was operating but was operating at reduced power."

Among his "opinions" Lieutenant Commander Morgan stated, in paragraph 5, that due to the deaths of the two pilots and the destruction of the aircraft "it is almost impossible to determine exactly what happened to Navy 3E955 from the time it left the runway on its last touch and go until it impacted the ground." He nonetheless continued with a detailed reconstruction of a possible set of events, based on pilot error, that could have caused the accident.[2] The next two paragraphs stated a caveat and a conclusion:

"6. Although the above sequence of events is the most likely to have occurred, it does not change the possibility that a 'rollback' did occur.

"7. The most probable cause of the accident was the pilots [sic] failure to maintain proper interval."

The trial judge initially determined, at a pretrial conference, that the JAG Report was sufficiently trustworthy to be admissible, but that it "would be admissible only on its factual findings and would not be admissible insofar as any opinions or conclusions are concerned." The day before trial, however, the court reversed itself and ruled, over the plaintiffs' objection, that certain of the conclusions would be admitted. Accordingly, the court admitted most of the report's "opinions," including the first sentence of paragraph 5 about the impossibility of determining exactly what happened, and paragraph 7, which opined about failure to maintain proper interval as "[t]he most probable cause of the accident." *Id.*, at 97. On the other hand, the remainder of paragraph 5 was barred as "nothing but a possible scenario," *id.*, at 40, and paragraph 6, in which investigator Morgan refused to rule out rollback, was deleted as well....[3]

---

2. Paragraph 5 reads in its entirety as follows:

"Because both pilots were killed in the crash and because of the nearly total destruction of the aircraft by fire, it is almost impossible to determine exactly what happened to Navy 3E955 from the time it left the runway on its last touch and go until it impacted the ground. However, from evidence available and the information gained from eyewitnesses, a possible scenario can be constructed as follows:

"a. 3E955 entered the Middleton pattern with ENS Knowlton at the controls attempting to make normal landings.

"b. After two unsuccessful attempts, LCDR Rainey took the aircraft and demonstrated two landings 'on the numbers.' After getting the aircraft safely airborne from the touch and go, LCDR Rainey transferred control to ENS Knowlton.

"c. Due to his physical strength, ENS Knowlton did not trim down elevator as the aircraft accelerated toward 100 knots; in fact, due to his inexperience, he may have trimmed incorrectly, putting in more up elevator.

"d. As ENS Knowlton was climbing to pattern altitude, he did not see the aircraft established on downwind so he began his crosswind turn. Due to ENS Knowlton's large size, LCDR Rainey was unable to see the conflicting traffic.

"e. Hearing the first call, LCDR Rainey probably cautioned ENS Knowlton to check for traffic. Hearing the second call, she took immediate action and told ENS Knowlton she had the aircraft as she initiated a turn toward an upwind heading.

"f. As the aircraft was rolling from a climbing left turn to a climbing right turn, ENS Knowlton released the stick letting the up elevator trim take effect causing the nose of the aircraft to pitch abruptly up.

"g. The large angle of bank used trying to maneuver for aircraft separation coupled with the abrupt pitch up caused the aircraft to stall. As the aircraft stalled and went into a nose low attitude, LCDR Rainey reduced the PCL (power control lever) toward idle. As she was rolling toward wings level, she advanced the PCL to maximum to stop the loss of altitude but due to the 2 to 4 second lag in engine response, the aircraft impacted the ground before power was available."

3. The record gives no indication why paragraph 6 was deleted. See, *e.g.*, *id.*, at 40 (striking most of paragraph 5, as well as paragraphs 8 and 9, but silent on paragraph 6). Neither at trial nor on appeal have respondents raised any objection to the deletion of paragraph 6.

Following a 2-week trial, the jury returned a verdict for petitioners. A panel of the Eleventh Circuit reversed and remanded for a new trial.... [T]he panel agreed with Rainey's argument that Federal Rule of Evidence 803(8)(C), which excepts investigatory reports from the hearsay rule, did not encompass evaluative conclusions or opinions. Therefore, it held, the "conclusions" contained in the JAG Report should have been excluded....

II

... Because the Federal Rules of Evidence are a legislative enactment, we turn to the "traditional tools of statutory construction," *INS v. Cardoza-Fonseca,* 480 U.S. 421, 446 (1987), in order to construe their provisions. We begin with the language of the Rule itself. Proponents of the narrow view have generally relied heavily on a perceived dichotomy between "fact" and "opinion" in arguing for the limited scope of the phrase "factual findings." *Smith v. Ithaca Corp.,* 612 F.2d 215 (5th Cir. 1980) contrasted the term "factual findings" in Rule 803(8)(C) with the language of Rule 803(6) (records of regularly conducted activity), which expressly refers to "opinions" and "diagnoses." "Factual findings," the court opined, must be something other than opinions. 612 F.2d, at 221–222.[8]

For several reasons, we do not agree. In the first place, it is not apparent that the term "factual findings" should be read to mean simply "facts" (as opposed to "opinions" or "conclusions"). A common definition of "finding of fact" is, for example, "[a] conclusion by way of reasonable inference from the evidence." Black's Law Dictionary 569 (5th ed. 1979). To say the least, the language of the Rule does not compel us to reject the interpretation that "factual findings" includes conclusions or opinions that flow from a factual investigation. Second, we note that, contrary to what is often assumed, the language of the Rule does not state that "factual findings" are admissible, but that "*reports ...* setting forth ... factual findings" (emphasis added) are admissible. On this reading, the language of the Rule does not create a distinction between "fact" and "opinion" contained in such reports.

Turning next to the legislative history of Rule 803(8)(C), we find no clear answer to the question of how the Rule's language should be interpreted. Indeed, in this litigation the legislative history may well be at the origin of the dispute. Rather than the more usual situation where a court must attempt to glean meaning from ambiguous comments of legislators who did not focus directly on the problem at hand, here the Committees in both Houses of Congress clearly recognized and expressed their opinions on the

---

8. The court in *Smith* found it significant that different language was used in Rules 803(6) and 803(8)(C): "Since these terms are used in similar context within the same Rule, it is logical to assume that Congress intended that the terms have different and distinct meanings." 612 F.2d, at 222. The Advisory Committee Notes to Rule 803(6) make clear, however, that the Committee was motivated by a particular concern in drafting the language of that Rule. While opinions were rarely found in traditional "business records," the expansion of that category to encompass documents such as medical diagnoses and test results brought with it some uncertainty in earlier versions of the Rule as to whether diagnoses and the like were admissible. "In order to make clear its adherence to the [position favoring admissibility]," the Committee stated, "the rule specifically includes both diagnoses and opinions, in addition to acts, events, and conditions, as proper subjects of admissible entries." Advisory Committee's Notes on Fed.Rule Evid. 803(6), 28 U.S.C.App., p. 723. Since that specific concern was not present in the context of Rule 803(8)(C), the absence of identical language should not be accorded much significance. See 827 F.2d 1498, 1511–1512 (11th Cir. 1987) (en banc) (Tjoflat, J., concurring). What is more, the Committee's report on Rule 803(8)(C) strongly suggests that that Rule has the same scope of admissibility as does Rule 803(6): "Hence the rule, *as in Exception [paragraph] (6),* assumes admissibility in the first instance but with ample provision for escape if sufficient negative factors are present." Advisory Committee's Notes on Fed.Rule Evid. 803(8), 28 U.S.C.App., p. 725 (emphasis added).

precise question at issue. Unfortunately, however, they took diametrically opposite positions. Moreover, the two Houses made no effort to reconcile their views, either through changes in the Rule's language or through a statement in the Report of the Conference Committee.

The House Judiciary Committee, which dealt first with the proposed rules after they had been transmitted to Congress by this Court, included in its Report but one brief paragraph on Rule 803(8):

> "The Committee approved Rule 803(8) without substantive change from the form in which it was submitted by the Court. The Committee intends that the phrase 'factual findings' be strictly construed and that evaluations or opinions contained in public reports shall not be admissible under this Rule."

The Senate Committee responded at somewhat greater length, but equally emphatically:

> "The House Judiciary Committee report contained a statement of intent that 'the phrase "factual findings" in subdivision (c) be strictly construed and that evaluations or opinions contained in public reports shall not be admissible under this rule.' The committee takes strong exception to this limiting understanding of the application of the rule. We do not think it reflects an understanding of the intended operation of the rule as explained in the Advisory Committee notes to this subsection.... We think the restrictive interpretation of the House overlooks the fact that while the Advisory Committee assumes admissibility in the first instance of evaluative reports, they are not admissible if, as the rule states, 'the sources of information or other circumstances indicate lack of trustworthiness....'"

Clearly this legislative history reveals a difference of view between the Senate and the House that affords no definitive guide to the congressional understanding. It seems clear however that the Senate understanding is more in accord with the wording of the Rule and with the comments of the Advisory Committee.

The Advisory Committee's comments are notable, first, in that they contain no mention of any dichotomy between statements of "fact" and "opinions" or "conclusions." What was on the Committee's mind was simply whether what it called "evaluative reports" should be admissible. Illustrating the previous division among the courts on this subject, the Committee cited numerous cases in which the admissibility of such reports had been both sustained and denied. It also took note of various federal statutes that made certain kinds of evaluative reports admissible in evidence. What is striking about all of these examples is that these were *reports that stated conclusions. E.g., Moran v. Pittsburgh-Des Moines Steel Co.*, 183 F.2d 467, 472–473 (3rd Cir. 1950) (report of Bureau of Mines concerning the cause of a gas tank explosion admissible); *Franklin v. Skelly Oil Co.*, 141 F.2d 568, 571–572 (CA10 1944) (report of state fire marshal on the cause of a gas explosion inadmissible). The Committee's concern was clearly whether reports of this kind should be admissible. Nowhere in its comments is there the slightest indication that it even considered the solution of admitting only "factual" statements from such reports. Rather, the Committee referred throughout to "reports," without any such differentiation regarding the statements they contained. What the Committee referred to in the Rule's language as "reports ... setting forth ... factual findings" is surely nothing more or less than what in its commentary it called "evaluative reports." Its solution as to their admissibility is clearly stated in the final paragraph of its report on this Rule. That solution consists of two principles: First, "the rule ... assumes admissibility in the first instance...." Second, it provides "ample provision for escape if sufficient negative factors are present."

That "provision for escape" is contained in the final clause of the Rule: evaluative reports are admissible "unless the sources of information or other circumstances indicate lack of trustworthiness." This trustworthiness inquiry—and not an arbitrary distinction between "fact" and "opinion"—was the Committee's primary safeguard against the admission of unreliable evidence, and it is important to note that it applies to all elements of the report. Thus, a trial judge has the discretion, and indeed the obligation, to exclude an entire report or portions thereof—whether narrow "factual" statements or broader "conclusions"—that she determines to be untrustworthy.[11] Moreover, safeguards built into other portions of the Federal Rules, such as those dealing with relevance and prejudice, provide the court with additional means of scrutinizing and, where appropriate, excluding evaluative reports or portions of them. And of course it goes without saying that the admission of a report containing "conclusions" is subject to the ultimate safeguard—the opponent's right to present evidence tending to contradict or diminish the weight of those conclusions.

Our conclusion that neither the language of the Rule nor the intent of its framers calls for a distinction between "fact" and "opinion" is strengthened by the analytical difficulty of drawing such a line. It has frequently been remarked that the distinction between statements of fact and opinion is, at best, one of degree:

> "All statements in language are statements of opinion, i.e., statements of mental processes or perceptions. So-called 'statements of fact' are only more specific statements of opinion. What the judge means to say, when he asks the witness to state the facts, is: 'The nature of this case requires that you be more specific, if you can, in your description of what you saw.'" W. King & D. Pillinger, Opinion Evidence in Illinois 4 (1942) (footnote omitted), quoted in 3 J. Weinstein & M. Berger, Weinstein's Evidence ¶ 701[01], p. 701–6 (1988).

See also E. Cleary, McCormick on Evidence 27 (3d ed. 1984) ("There is no conceivable statement however specific, detailed and 'factual,' that is not in some measure the product of inference and reflection as well as observation and memory")....

In the present action, the trial court had no difficulty in admitting as a factual finding the statement in the JAG Report that "[a]t the time of impact, the engine of 3E955 was operating but was operating at reduced power." Surely this "factual finding" could also be characterized as an opinion, which the investigator presumably arrived at on the basis of clues contained in the airplane wreckage. Rather than requiring that we draw some inevitably arbitrary line between the various shades of fact/opinion that invariably will be present in investigatory reports, we believe the Rule instructs us—as its plain language states—to admit "reports ... setting forth ... factual findings." The Rule's limitations and safeguards lie elsewhere: First, the requirement that reports contain factual findings bars the admission of statements not based on factual investigation. Second, the trustworthiness provision requires the court to make a determination as to whether the report, or any portion thereof, is sufficiently trustworthy to be admitted.

A broad approach to admissibility under Rule 803(8)(C), as we have outlined it, is also consistent with the Federal Rules' general approach of relaxing the traditional barriers to "opinion" testimony. Rules 702–705 permit experts to testify in the form of an opinion,

---

11. The Advisory Committee proposed a nonexclusive list of four factors it thought would be helpful in passing on this question: (1) the timeliness of the investigation; (2) the investigator's skill or experience; (3) whether a hearing was held; and (4) possible bias when reports are prepared with a view to possible litigation (citing *Palmer v. Hoffman,* 318 U.S. 109 (1943)). Advisory Committee's Notes on Fed.Rule Evid. 803(8) ...

and without any exclusion of opinions on "ultimate issues." And Rule 701 permits even a lay witness to testify in the form of opinions or inferences drawn from her observations when testimony in that form will be helpful to the trier of fact. We see no reason to strain to reach an interpretation of Rule 803(8)(C) that is contrary to the liberal thrust of the Federal Rules.

We hold, therefore, that portions of investigatory reports otherwise admissible under Rule 803(8)(C) are not inadmissible merely because they state a conclusion or opinion. As long as the conclusion is based on a factual investigation and satisfies the Rule's trustworthiness requirement, it should be admissible along with other portions of the report. As the trial judge in this action determined that certain of the JAG Report's conclusions were trustworthy, he rightly allowed them to be admitted into evidence. We therefore reverse the judgment of the Court of Appeals in respect of the Rule 803(8)(C) issue....

It is so ordered.

[Concurring and dissenting opinion by Rehnquist, C.J., omitted.]

Problem 7-30

Ms. Estelle Sopp suffered catastrophic injuries after she was negligently given contaminated diagnostic test fluid at the University of Pennsylvania Hospital. The hospital made a settlement with Ms. Sopp. The hospital's excess insurer, Lexington Insurance, initially refused to pay for their share of the settlement made between the hospital and Ms. Sopp. The hospital sued Lexington. At trial, the jury found in favor of the hospital and against Lexington, awarding the hospital $4.8 million in compensatory damages as well as punitive damages, legal fees, and pre-judgment interest.

Lexington appealed on the ground that the hospital's settlement with Ms. Sopp had been unreasonably excessive. The hospital countered by offering into evidence the transcript of the trial court proceeding which included a statement made by the trial court judge that he believed the settlement between the hospital and Ms. Sopp had been "fair and reasonable." Lexington objects that this statement in the transcript is inadmissible hearsay. How do you rule?

Problem 7-31

Rafeal Pagan allegedly assisted his friend Dr. Yamil Kouri in covering up the theft of over a million dollars which Dr. Kouri had embezzled from his employer, the San Juan AIDS Institute in Puerto Rico. Pagan allegedly helped Kouri make phony receipts accounting for the stolen money and then lied about it as a defense witness at Kouri's trial for embezzlement.

At Pagan's trial for perjury, conspiracy, and obstruction of justice, he wanted to introduce self-exculpatory statements he made in a telephone conversation with a government informant. The government had taped the conversation without Pagan's knowledge, and Pagan now wanted to play the tape for the jury. The Government objected that such statements were inadmissible hearsay. How do you rule?

IV. The FRE 804 Exceptions

While the FRE 803 exceptions were based on reliability, the FRE 804 exceptions are based on necessity. The FRE 804 exceptions are only available if the declarant is unavailable to be a witness pursuant to the mandates of FRE 804(a), and the underlying assumption is that the absolute necessity of the evidence counterbalances some of the reliability concerns. Furthermore, unavailability is a necessary but not sufficient condition for the FRE 804(b) exceptions. That is, unavailability alone will not make the hearsay admissible; the foundational requirements of each of the exceptions **plus** unavailability must be demonstrated.

A. Unavailability

Relevant Rule
FRE 804(a)

Exceptions to the Rule Against Hearsay — When the Declarant Is Unavailable as a Witness

(a) Criteria for Being Unavailable. A declarant is considered to be unavailable as a witness if the declarant:

(1) is exempted from testifying about the subject matter of the declarant's statement because the court rules that a privilege applies;

(2) refuses to testify about the subject matter despite a court order to do so;

(3) testifies to not remembering the subject matter;

(4) cannot be present or testify at the trial or hearing because of death or a then-existing infirmity, physical illness, or mental illness; or

(5) is absent from the trial or hearing and the statement's proponent has not been able, by process or other reasonable means, to procure:

(A) the declarant's attendance, in the case of a hearsay exception under Rule 804(b)(1) or (6); or

(B) the declarant's attendance or testimony, in the case of a hearsay exception under Rule 804(b)(2), (3), or (4).

But this subdivision (a) does not apply if the statement's proponent procured or wrongfully caused the declarant's unavailability as a witness in order to prevent the declarant from attending or testifying.

Overview

FRE 804(a) defines the grounds of unavailability. The listed grounds are illustrative, not exclusive, and the burden of showing unavailability of the declarant is on the proponent of the hearsay evidence. The five listed grounds of unavailability are largely self-explanatory. Claiming a privilege will equate to unavailability, but a defendant cannot invoke his Fifth Amendment privilege and then claim that he is therefore an unavailable hearsay declarant. Absence equates to unavailability under FRE 804(a)(5) as long as sufficient efforts to obtain attendance or testimony of the declarant have been undertaken. In general, all good faith efforts must be undertaken to procure the declarant.

Problem 7-32

John McGuire was a member of an anti-government group called the "Montana Freemen." He allegedly robbed sound recording equipment from a three-person ABC news television crew that had come to the Freemen's rural Montana property, "Justus Township," to interview the Freemen. At McGuire's first trial, which resulted in a hung jury, one of the TV crew-members testified that she had witnessed the robbery. At his second trial, which resulted in a conviction for robbery, this witness did not testify. The witness's doctor submitted an opinion that the witness's pregnancy made her unable to undergo the stresses of testifying. The witness was twenty-eight weeks pregnant, and the trial court had to accommodate the schedules of scores of witnesses, ten defense attorneys, and a judge from another judicial district. The judge permitted the prosecution to play a videotape of the witness's testimony from the first trial. On appeal, McGuire challenges the admission of this earlier testimony as hearsay. Is she unavailable pursuant to FRE 804(a)?

Problem 7-33

In an antitrust action, the plaintiffs offered the testimony of Ron Moody. Moody intended to testify regarding a statement made by Steve Ballard, but Moody stated on the witness stand that "the specific dialogue of this conversation has faded with the years." Moody recalled the general subject matter of the conversation, but he lacked memory of the details of the conversation.

The plaintiffs argue that the gaps in his knowledge made Moody "partially unavailable" under FRE 804(a). How do you rule?

B. Former Testimony

Relevant Rule
FRE 804(b)(1)

(b) The Exceptions. The following are not excluded by the rule against hearsay if the declarant is unavailable as a witness:

   (1) *Former Testimony.* Testimony that:

   (A) was given as a witness at a trial, hearing, or lawful deposition, whether given during the current proceeding or a different one; and

   (B) is now offered against a party who had — or, in a civil case, whose predecessor in interest had — an opportunity and similar motive to develop it by direct, cross-, or redirect examination.

Overview

We have now seen numerous ways that the past statements of witnesses and past testimony may be admissible. FRE 801(d)(1) allows for past inconsistent statements, past consistent statements, and past statements of identification, as long as the witness is on the stand. FRE 613 allows past inconsistent statements offered to impeach as long as the declarant testified at the trial. Thus, in both instances, the fact finder has the benefit of oath/cross-examination/demeanor. With FRE 804(b)(1), prior statements of an **absent** witness are allowed. Certainly such testimony is necessary, as the witness is absent and there is no other option to obtain this evidence. But how is it trustworthy? FRE 804(b)(1) enhances reliability by mandating that the **past statement** was (i) testimony, (ii) at a proceeding, and (iii) subject to examination by a party against whom it is now offered (or, in a civil case, by a "predecessor in interest"), (iv) who then had similar motive. Thus, this prior testimony was previously tested, or at least the opportunity existed to test it, through examination under oath in the earlier proceeding. Although this does not allow the fact finder at the second proceeding to see the demeanor of the witness, it at least establishes a baseline of trustworthiness.

"Testimony" covers sworn statements made in response to questions on the record. "Proceeding" carries a very broad meaning, including not only judicial inquiry but also administrative or legislative inquiries. One inquiry that is not covered under "proceeding," however, is statements to law enforcement officers during investigations.

The party against whom the testimony was offered at the second trial (or its predecessor in interest) must have had an opportunity to develop the testimony at the first proceeding through direct or cross-examination. All that is required is an opportunity—the party or its "predecessor in interest" did not need to conduct a direct or cross-examination, it just needed to have been given the opportunity to do so.

The next question is whether the parties in the two proceedings have to be identical. If the second proceeding is a **criminal** trial, the prior testimony is only admissible against a party if that party was a party to first proceeding. Let us make that previous sentence more concrete: In the case of United States v. Dirk, a federal criminal proceeding against defendant Dirk, the government seeks to offer prior testimony of witness Winnie. Winnie testified at the earlier trial of Commonwealth v. Dirk, a state court criminal proceeding against defendant Dirk. Since Dirk was a party at proceeding #1 and #2, the testimony can be offered against Dirk as long as the other elements of FRE 804(b)(1) are met. Note that it does not matter that the prosecuting authority changed in the two cases from a state to the federal government. The only common party must be the party *against whom* the testimony is offered.

What if the second proceeding is a civil trial? In that case, courts are forced to examine the words "predecessor in interest" to determine whether the term should be used narrowly (i.e., a predecessor in interest must be in privity with the current party) or broadly (i.e., any party with a similar interest and motive is a predecessor in interest). *Clay v. Johns-Manville Sales Corp.,* below, addresses that question.

The final question is whether the party or predecessor in interest possessed a similar motive to develop the witness's testimony at proceeding #1 and proceeding #2. Typically, as discussed in *United States v. Feldman,* below, if the issue to which the testimony related at the former proceeding is substantially identical to the issue in the present proceeding, then a similar motive to develop the testimony is likely to exist.

At the end of the day, our hope is that the party against whom the previous testimony was offered had an opportunity to develop the previous testimony in a manner consistent with his interests. Whether that entails a blistering cross-examination of a hostile witness or developing the narrative through the direct examination of a friendly witness, we want to believe the party who will not get a chance to examine this witness now had a full and fair opportunity to do so in the past.

Focus Questions: *United States v. Feldman*

- How does the Court define "opportunity" in this case? How does the court apply the test?

- How does the Court define "similar motive" in this case? How does the court apply the test?

United States v. Feldman

761 F.2d 380 (7th Cir. 1985)

WISDOM, Senior Circuit Judge.

This case presents the question whether a deposition taken in an earlier civil proceeding is admissible in a later criminal prosecution. The defendants were found guilty of several counts of wire fraud from practices in connection with the sale of precious metal futures. The government's case relied heavily on the deposition of a former business associate taken without any cross-examination in an earlier civil proceeding. On appeal, the defendants argue that the admission of this deposition violated [the hearsay rule].... We agree and accordingly reverse.

I. FACTS AND PROCEEDINGS BELOW

... The company filed for bankruptcy on January 29, 1980. On January 30, 1980, FBI agents searched FGM's offices under a warrant. The same day, the Commodity Futures Trading Commission ("CFTC") filed a complaint against FGM alleging that the company defrauded customers by its salesmen's misrepresentations.... CFTC sought to freeze the assets of FGM and to obtain its profits.

As part of this "disgorgement" action, CFTC sought the deposition of the three defendants in its case: Sanburg, Feldman, and Martenson. Each party received notice of the depositions through counsel. Neither Feldman nor Martenson attended the Sanburg deposition, nor did their attorneys represent them at the deposition. Sanburg, however, had agreed with the government the day before his deposition to testify against Feldman and Martenson in return for a promise that Sanburg himself would not be a target of any later legal proceedings. This agreement between Sanburg and the government was not disclosed for almost a year, until just a short time before Feldman's and Martenson's criminal trial. At the time of Sanburg's deposition, the government had not returned a criminal indictment against any party in connection with FGM. Sanburg, whom the government knew to be terminally ill, died less than a month after his deposition.

On December 17, 1981, ten months after Sanburg gave his deposition, the U.S. Attorney in Chicago returned an indictment charging Richard Feldman and Richard Martenson with mail fraud, ... wire fraud, ... and fraudulent bullion transactions. In an order and memorandum of May 28, 1981, the district court ruled that it would admit the Sanburg deposition if the government could establish that Sanburg and the present defendants were parties in the civil case in which the deposition was taken; that the defendants were represented by counsel at that time; and that the defendants received notice of the deposition and were afforded an opportunity to be present. On November 1, 1981, the district court conducted a hearing on the admissibility of the deposition. The court admitted the deposition on the grounds that the defendants had an adequate opportunity to appear at the Sanburg deposition, that the defendants knew what Sanburg would say, and that the defendants were represented by counsel and were parties to the civil litigation for which the deposition was taken. The deposition became the centerpiece of the government's prosecution....

[Defendants were found guilty.] Both defendants appeal, arguing that the introduction of the deposition violated their right to cross examination....

1. Inadmissibility Under Fed.R.Evid. 804(b)(1)

Under Fed.R.Evid. 804(b)(1), the testimony or deposition of a witness taken in another proceeding is admissible if the party against whom the testimony is now offered had "an opportunity and similar motive" to examine the witness.

Fed.R.Evid. 804(b)(1) requires that a defendant have sufficient notice and opportunity for cross examination. Putting aside the question of notice, Feldman and Martenson did not have the opportunity to cross-examine Sanburg. Mere "naked opportunity" to cross-examine is not enough; there must also be a perceived "real need or incentive to thoroughly cross-examine" at the time of the deposition. *United States v. Franklin*, 235 F.Supp. 338, 341 (D.C. Cir. 1964). At the time of Sanburg's deposition, the defendants Feldman and Martenson were not adverse parties to Sanburg. There was no reason for Feldman or Martenson to believe that Sanburg, who was a co-defendant in the CFTC action, would testify against them on criminal charges. Both Feldman and Martenson had chosen not to defend in the CFTC's civil suit, and they could reasonably expect that Sanburg, who had left the company well before its demise, would chose to do the same. It is undisputed that not until after the deposition were Feldman and Martenson informed of the non-subject agreement between Sanburg and the government. The defendants therefore did not make a meaningful waiver of their right to cross-examination.

Fed.R.Evid. 804(b)(1) also requires that even if Feldman and Martenson had sufficient notice and opportunity to cross-examine Sanburg, they must have had a "similar motive to develop the testimony by direct, cross, or redirect examination". In determining whether a party had such a motive, a court must evaluate not only the similarity of the issues, but also the purpose for which the testimony is given. *Zenith Corp. v. Matsushita Electric Industrial Co.*, 505 F.Supp. 1190, 1251, *aff'd in part, rev'd in part*, 723 F.2d 319 (3d Cir. 1983). Circumstances or factors which influence motive to develop testimony include "(1) the type of proceeding in which the testimony is given, (2) trial strategy, (3) the potential penalties or financial stakes, and (4) the number of issues and parties". *Id.* at 1252 (footnotes omitted). Consideration of the second and third criteria persuades us that under Fed.R.Evid. 804(b)(1)'s "similarity of motive" test, Sanburg's deposition was inadmissible in the criminal trial.

Sanburg's deposition was taken in a civil proceeding and ultimately used in criminal prosecution. It is well-settled that strategies for civil and criminal trials may differ greatly. As one court has observed, in antitrust litigation where the defendants faced criminal prosecution and later civil proceedings and the plaintiffs sought to admit into the civil proceeding a witness's cross-examined deposition taken in the criminal suit:

"[S]uccessive defendants do not always share the same interests when defending against claims which arise out of the same circumstances. For instance, in the antitrust field, a defendant in a criminal trial may be motivated in its defense to protect itself against liability by implicating other defendants—perhaps defendants who have pled *nolo contendere* to the same criminal charges."

In re Screws Antitrust Litigation, 526 F.Supp. 1316, 1319 (D.Mass. 1981). The court therefore ruled that the deposition failed to qualify for admission under Fed.R.Evid. 804(b)(1).

Here Feldman and Martenson pursued opposite strategies in the civil and criminal trial. Neither of the defendants contested CFTC's motion for a permanent injunction or ancillary relief. Their strategy was not to contest any CFTC's claims. In the criminal case, by contrast, the defendants vigorously sought to prove their innocence.

The admission of Sanburg's deposition also fails under the third criterion enunciated in *Zenith,* that is, whether the "potential penalties or financial stakes" are similar. In the civil proceeding, neither Feldman nor Martenson had any exposure to personal liability. Martenson had severed his ties with FGM before its demise. Feldman, who was still associated with FGM upon its bankruptcy, nevertheless was willing to let the government obtain the declaratory and injunctive relief it sought, and his attorney allegedly offered to enter a consent judgment on behalf of Feldman several months before the deposition. It appears from the record that both Feldman and Martenson had little personal or financial stake in CFTC's litigation. It is understandable that neither party attended Sanburg's deposition in that case. In the subsequent criminal proceeding, however, the defendants faced, and received, fines and imprisonment.... The stakes at the time of the Sanburg deposition—disgorgement of a trading company's profits—were quantitatively less and qualitatively different from the stakes in the criminal trial....

Finally, the government has argued that the Trustee's questions to Sanburg count as cross-examination. The Trustee, however, seemed more interested in the movement of FGM's assets than in fraudulent sales practices. He was uninterested in discrediting Sanburg, which would have been of utmost importance to the co-defendants. In any event, the Trustee's questions cannot be deemed to have the same measure of scrutiny or the same focus as questions that would have come from a criminal defendant. In short, no one at the Sanburg deposition had the requisite stake in the proceeding that would be necessary for them to be deemed a predecessor in interest to the criminal de-fendants, and those who did have the requisite stake had no reason to suspect that they should be there. We hold that the deposition fails to pass the test of Fed.R.Evid. 804(b)(1) and that Sanburg's deposition from the civil suit was not admissible under Fed.R.Evid. 804(b)(1)....

The convictions of the co-defendants are therefore REVERSED and the cause REMANDED for a new trial consistent with this opinion.

Focus Questions: *Clay v. Johns-Manville Sales Corp.*

- How does the Court expand the interpretation of "predecessor in interest"?

- Why does the Court prefer an interpretation that is "realistically generous" over that which is "formalistically grudging"?

- How does the legislative history assist the court in determining the scope of FRE 804(b)(1)?

Clay v. Johns-Manville Sales Corp.

722 F.2d 1289 (6th Cir. 1983)

GEORGE CLIFTON EDWARDS, Jr., Circuit Judge.

In these two cases plaintiffs John Ed Clay and Curtis Bailey, each joined by his wife, brought actions for damages against defendants Johns-Manville Sales Corporation and Raybestos-Manhattan, Inc., on the basis of products liability claims resulting from plaintiffs' exposure to asbestos containing products manufactured by the defendants. The cases were tried in the United States District Court for the Eastern District of Tennessee and ended in jury verdicts for the defendants....

II.

We turn now to ... whether the District Judge erred in excluding a deposition taken from a witness, Dr. Kenneth Wallace Smith, in *DeRocco v. Forty-eight Installation, Inc.,* No. 7880 (W.D.Pa.1974). At the time of the *DeRocco* proceeding, Dr. Smith was 63 years of age and had acquired his knowledge about asbestos disease in the employment of the Johns-Manville Corporation, the largest asbestos manufacturer in the field. Serving Johns-Manville during a good portion of his 22 years of employment as the only full-time physician in the organization, Dr. Smith's deposition is peculiarly relevant to the extent of the knowledge possessed by manufacturers of the hazards of asbestos containing products during the years when appellants Clay and Bailey allege they were exposed to asbestos.

Dr. Smith had died before the trial of this case. The key question in relation to the admissibility of this evidence is posed by the language of Rule 804(b)(1) of the Federal Rules of Evidence [and, more specifically, the meaning of "predecessor in interest"]....

To ascertain the meaning of "predecessor in interest," an examination of legislative history is necessary. As originally proposed by the Supreme Court, Rule 804(b)(1) would have admitted prior testimony of an unavailable witness if the party against whom it is offered or a person "with a motive and interest" similar to him had an opportunity to examine that witness. H.R.Rep. No. 650, 93d Cong., 1st Sess. 15 (1973), *reprinted in* 1974 U.S.Code Cong. & Ad.News 7051, 7088. The House of Representatives substituted the current "predecessor in interest" language. The House Committee on the Judiciary offered the following explanation for the alteration:

> The Committee considered that it is generally unfair to impose upon the party against whom the hearsay evidence is being offered responsibility for the manner in which the witness was previously handled by another party. The sole exception to this, in the Committee's view, is when a party's predecessor in interest in a civil action or proceeding had an opportunity and similar motive to examine the witness. The Committee amended the Rule to reflect these policy determinations.

H.R.Rep. No. 650, U.S.Code Cong. & Admin.News 1974, p. 7088, *supra.*

> ... The House amended the rule to apply only to a party's predecessor in interest. Although the committee recognizes considerable merit to the rule submitted by the Supreme Court, a position which has been advocated by many scholars and judges, we have concluded that the difference between the two versions is not great and we accept the House amendment.

S.Rep. No. 1277, 93d Cong., 2d Sess. 28 (1974), *reprinted in* 1974 U.S.Code Cong. & Ad.News 7051, 7074.

We join the Third Circuit in agreeing with the Senate Committee that the difference between the ultimate revision and the Rule, as originally proposed, is "not great." *Lloyd v. American Export Lines, Inc.*, 580 F.2d 1179, 1185 (3d Cir.), *cert. denied,* 439 U.S. 969 (1978). Accordingly, we adopt the position taken by the *Lloyd* court which it expressed in the following language:

> While we do not endorse an extravagant interpretation of who or what constitutes a "predecessor in interest," we prefer one that is realistically generous over one that is formalistically grudging. We believe that what has been described as "the practical and expedient view" expresses the congressional intention: "if it appears that in the former suit a party having a like motive to cross-examine about the same matters as the present party would have, was accorded an adequate opportunity for such examination, the testimony may be received against the present party." Under these circumstances, the previous party having like motive to develop the testimony about the same material facts is, in the final analysis, a predecessor in interest to the present party.

Id. at 1187. *See also Weinstein & Berger, Evidence* §804(b)(1) [04] at 804–67 (1969) ("[C]ases decided since the enactment of Rule 804(b)(1) for the most part indicate a reluctance to interpret 'predecessor in interest' in its old, narrow, and substantive law sense, of privity").

Our examination of the record submitted in this case satisfies us that defendants in the *DeRocco* case had a similar motive in confronting Dr. Smith's testimony, both in terms of appropriate objections and searching cross-examination, to that which Raybestos has in the current litigation. We therefore hold that the purposes of Rule 804(b)(1) will be fulfilled by the admission of Dr. Smith's deposition on retrial....

The judgments entered below against plaintiffs are vacated and the cases are remanded for retrial against defendant Raybestos in accordance with this opinion.

Problem 7-34

Monte McFall was accused of extortion and mail fraud. It was alleged that he and several co-defendants exerted their private economic interest through a county supervisor. McFall subpoenaed Neat Sawyer, one of his alleged co-conspirators, to testify on his behalf, but Sawyer invoked the Fifth Amendment and refused to testify. McFall then attempted to use Sawyer's earlier grand jury testimony to rebut a particular accusation made by a prosecution witness that McFall had made extortionate threats on a specific occasion. A grand jury determines whether there is probable cause to indict a criminal defendant, and only the prosecution presents a case (i.e., there is no cross-examination of witnesses by the defense). In Sawyer's grand jury testimony, he testified that the idea that these threats were made was "ridiculous." The prosecution objected to this admission on hearsay grounds. How do you rule?

Problem 7-35

Seventeen African-American iron workers filed a lawsuit alleging discriminatory employment practices on the part of their local labor union, their national labor union, and the labor union's apprenticeship committee. The plaintiffs claimed that these organizations had deliberately discriminated against African-Americans both by failing to admit qualified African-American ironworkers into the union and by withholding promotion from those who were admitted. The plaintiffs attempted to introduce into evidence depositions given by officers and officials of the local labor union to the government in a separate investigation into discriminatory practices against African-Americans by the local labor union that was conducted by the federal government.

The defense claims that these depositions were inadmissible hearsay and that FRE 804(b)(1) does not apply because the parties are not the same. In particular, they point out that the national union was not a party in the government's case, which proceeded only against the local union and the apprenticeship committee. The plaintiffs respond that the national union is represented by the same attorney who represented the local union and the apprenticeship committee in the Government's case and who was present at the taking of most of the depositions sought to be admitted. How do you rule?

C. Dying Declarations

Relevant Rule
FRE 804(b)(2)

(b) The Exceptions. The following are not excluded by the rule against hearsay if the declarant is unavailable as a witness: …

(2) *Statement Under the Belief of Imminent Death.* In a prosecution for homicide or in a civil case, a statement that the declarant, while believing the declarant's death to be imminent, made about its cause or circumstances.

Overview

The trustworthiness behind a statement under belief of impending death is based on the belief that we do not want to waste our dying breath with lies; furthermore, at the moment that one believes he is dying, a truthful impulse relating to the cause of death is arguably strong. Certainly necessity plays a role here as well — to lose these words to hearsay would mean that they would never be uttered in the courtroom. FRE 804(b)(2) does not mandate that the declarant die; instead, he must only be unavailable pursuant to FRE 804(a). Additionally, FRE 804(b)(2) expanded the common law roots of the exception to include civil actions as well as homicide prosecutions.

The foundational elements for FRE 804(b)(2) mandates that:

- The statement relate to the cause or circumstances of impending death,
- The declarant had personal knowledge of the matter asserted, and
- The declarant believed that death was imminent.

If the speaker is explaining the circumstances that lead him to his situation, the statement will "relate" to the circumstances of his impending death. Broad backward-looking statements qualify. Thus, a statement like "Dirk never liked me" would likely qualify. The personal knowledge requirement mandates that the declarant must do more than guess; he must be speaking about matters of which he personally knows. Accordingly, a statement such as "Dirk must have poisoned me" would likely not qualify unless the declarant possessed some personal knowledge of being poisoned by Dirk specifically. The imminence of death requirement mandates that the declarant had a settled hopeless expectation that death is imminent. Anything less would make the statement less reliable.

Focus Questions: *State v. Adamson*

- What facts does the court look at to determine whether the declarant had a sense of impeding death? How does this translate into factors that can be applied to other cases and sets of facts?

- Why is personal knowledge by the declarant required for FRE 804(b)(2)? How does the court determine whether the declarant had personal knowledge? What should other courts be looking for to make this determination?

State v. Adamson

665 P.2d 972 (Ariz. 1983)

GORDON, Vice Chief Justice:

On October 17, 1980, a jury found appellant guilty of first degree murder for the bombing death of newspaper reporter Donald Bolles. Following an aggravation-mitigation hearing on November 14, 1980, the defendant was sentenced to death. Appellant now challenges the conviction on the basis of several allegations of error.... We affirm.

Adamson was charged with the June 2, 1976, bombing murder of Donald Bolles. The evidence at trial showed that Bolles, an investigative reporter for the Arizona Republic newspaper, had arranged to meet the defendant at a Phoenix hotel in order to gather information for a potential news story. Two notes concerning the meeting were found after the bombing at Bolles' office. Bolles went to the hotel at the designated time and waited for Adamson in the lobby. While Bolles was waiting, he received a telephone call from an individual he later identified as the defendant. Bolles later stated that Adamson wanted to change the place of the meeting and asked Bolles for directions to his office. Bolles then went to his car and began backing out of the parking space in route to the newly-arranged meeting. As he was backing out a bomb exploded sending pieces of Bolles' car throughout the parking lot and into a neighboring construction site. Witnesses testified that the force of the explosion shook neighboring buildings.

Several rescuers administered first aid to the victim who was still conscious although critically injured. Both of his legs and one arm were severely mutilated. Bolles made statements to the rescuers which implicated the defendant and asked one witness to call his wife. He mentioned the defendant's name several times and stated that "Adamson [set or sent] me." He also told the individuals rendering first aid, "You better hurry up, boys. I feel like I'm going."

The next day the victim responded to questions from the Phoenix Police by means of finger and hand signals. Bolles indicated that he had gone to the hotel the day before to meet Adamson and had received a call from him while waiting for his arrival. Bolles identified a driver's license photograph of the defendant and indicated that he was the man Bolles had met four days earlier while investigating the same story. After having both legs and one arm amputated, Bolles died June 13, 1976.

Intensive police investigations in the days immediately following the bombing revealed the structure of the bomb and that it was a radio-controlled device. The police also established that the defendant was involved in the incident and a warrant was issued to search his apartment. In searching Adamson's residence the police found materials similar to those used to construct the bomb which was attached by magnets to the underside of Bolles' automobile. Literature which contained information concerning the making of explosive devices was also seized. Further investigations revealed that Adamson had purchased remote control equipment two months earlier at a hobby shop in San Diego, California which could have been used to trigger the explosive device. Furthermore, in May, 1976, Adamson had gone to the Arizona Republic parking lot and asked the guard where "Don-So-and-so['s]" car was, saying he had some papers to drop off in the car. Adamson and his companion then went to an automobile dealership and inspected the underside of several cars similar to that owned by Bolles. In route to the dealership the defendant told the individual riding in his car that "he was going to blow up a car" and when asked why, Adamson responded because "this guy was giving people a lot of hard times and stepping on people's toes." At trial testimony was given to establish that Adamson was paid $10,000 to kill Donald Bolles....

Statements and Notes of Victim

A. Hospital Statements

The day after the bombing three detectives went to the hospital to question Bolles about the bombing. In response to their questions Bolles indicated that he had gone to the hotel to meet the defendant and that while at the hotel he received a call from Adamson. Bolles also identified a photograph of Adamson and indicated that the defendant was the person he had intended to meet on the morning of June 2nd. Appellant contends that the trial court erred in denying his motion to suppress the hospital statements on the grounds that they were inadmissible hearsay.

... The trial court ruled that the statements were admissible as dying declarations under Ariz.R.Evid. 804(b)(2). That rule requires the following: (1) that the statements in this case are being used in a homicide prosecution; (2) the statements were made by a declarant while believing his death was imminent; and (3) that the statement concerned the cause or circumstances of what he believed to be his impending death. Defendant objects to the admission of the statements under this rule because there is no evidence that the victim believed death was imminent at the time the statements were made. We disagree. The law does not require that there be a direct assertion by the declarant that he is dying at the time the statements were made. The party offering dying declarations may show that the victim was under a sense of impending death either by express language of the deceased or by the indubitable circumstances. In this case the state has shown both. Witnesses who were at the scene of the bombing described Bolles' legs as having the consistency of hamburger. One witness testified that he had seen a piece of flesh the size of a softball on the pavement as he was rushing across the hotel parking lot towards Bolles' car. At the scene of the bombing the victim made the following statement to rescuers: "You better hurry up, boys. I feel like I'm going." Several hours after the bombing the victim's right leg was amputated. The hospital statements were made one day after the bombing. At the time of the statements Bolles was in grave condition in the intensive care unit. Under these conditions it is reasonable to conclude that when the statements were made Bolles was under a sense of impending death. There was no error in admitting the hospital statements.

B. Statements at the Scene

Immediately after the bombing Bolles made several statements to the individuals who were rendering emergency care. These statements indicated that in some manner the defendant was involved in the bombing. The victim further stated that a mafia-related organization could have played a role in the bombing. The trial court denied the defendant's motion to suppress these statements allowing them to come in as evidence by applying both the excited utterance and dying declaration exceptions to the hearsay rule. On appeal appellant contends that the statements should not have been admitted at trial since they were not based on the personal knowledge of the victim. . . .

There is . . . a general requirement imposed on declarations coming in under all exceptions to the hearsay rule that the declarant, like witnesses, must have had an opportunity to observe or personal knowledge of the fact declared. Bolles, an investigative reporter, told rescuers that he was investigating "a mafia called Emprise . . ." and " . . . the mafia was responsible." The victim also stated that "Adamson did it . . ." and "Adamson [set or sent] me." We believe that Bolles' statements regarding the mafia and Emprise, as well as his statement that "Adamson did it . . .", were not within his personal knowledge since they were mere suspicions. The statements were not "based on events perceived by [Bolles] through one of the physical senses." [3 J. Weinstein & M. Berger, Weinstein's Evidence § 602[01] at 602–2 (1981).] Therefore, the trial court erred in allowing these statements to be admitted.

Error does not require reversal if it can be said beyond a reasonable doubt that it had no influence on the verdict of the jury. . . . In this case we believe that this question can be answered affirmatively.

Robert Lettiere testified that he went to the Arizona Republic parking lot with Adamson and overheard him ask the guard where "Don so-and-so's car was." Adamson told Lettiere that he "was looking for a certain white car." (Bolles' car was white.) He also told Lettiere that he was going to blow a car up because this guy was stepping on people's toes and that he was being paid $10,000 for the job. After leaving the Arizona Republic parking lot the defendant and Lettiere went to a Datsun dealership where Adamson examined the underside of several cars similar to that owned by Bolles. The day after the bombing Adamson and his wife visited Lettiere where the defendant told Lettiere "You didn't believe I could do something like that . . . and you got to believe it now." Adamson also said that if he ever bought a car himself he "would have to get a Datsun because it sure as hell took a jolt." He also said "He could be in the same boat that Don Bolles was in because he had botched the job." Evidence was introduced which established that Adamson purchased a device at a San Diego hobby shop which could have been used to trigger the bomb. A battery, tape, and magnets similar to that used to construct the actual bomb were found in Adamson's apartment. The Anarchist Cookbook which contained information that would be helpful in constructing the type of bomb used in this case was also found in the apartment. Statements made by Bolles at the hospital and notes that he had written indicated that Bolles went to the hotel to meet Adamson. Bolles' on-the-scene statement "Adamson [set or sent] me" was also properly available for the jury's consideration. Finally, Gail Owens, an acquaintance of Adamson, testified that the day of the bombing the defendant called her and said that something had happened and that he would not see her for awhile. In light of this evidence we can say beyond a reasonable doubt that without the improperly admitted on-the-scene statements the jury would have found the defendant guilty....

The judgment of conviction of first degree murder and the sentence of death are affirmed.

Problem 7-36

At 2:00 a.m. on October 10, 2004, John Duich was awakened by his domestic partner, James Garrison, who was badly hurt and screaming for help. Garrison told Duich that he had been doused with gasoline and set on fire. According to Duich, when he asked Garrison who set him on fire, Garrison told him it was Joey Ragusa and a large black man.

Duich called 911, and when police and paramedics arrived they discovered Garrison was critically burned. Detective Redden, the first on the scene, had seen many burn victims but later testified that he had never seen anyone so badly burned that was still alive. Garrison had in fact suffered 3rd degree burns (the most severe burns one can have) on 77% of his body. Though he was in terrible agony (repeatedly screaming "God help me"), Garrison was surprisingly responsive and lucid (this despite the fact that he was later found to have both crack cocaine and alcohol in his system). After arrival at the hospital a nurse told Duich that Garrison would most likely die within 72 hours. A doctor at the hospital's burn center told Duich that Garrison had a 10% chance of surviving his burns. At no time was Garrison told the chances of his survival.

Two days after the attack, Garrison was questioned by police from his hospital bed. He was only able to respond to questions by nodding or shaking his head. When the police asked him if it was Joey Ragusa who set him on fire, he nodded yes. When asked if he knew the identity of the black man who was with Ragusa, he shook his head no. Remarkably, Garrison lived for seven and a half months before succumbing to his injuries.

Joey Ragusa and Benjamin Stiff will stand trial for first degree murder. The state appeals a pre-trial order denying admission of Garrison's statements to either Duich or the police identifying his attackers. How do you rule?

Problem 7-37

Michael Stamper lived with his girlfriend, Gloria Logan, and her two children. During the late afternoon or evening of September 8, 2004, Stamper was supervising Gloria's four-year-old son, Jake. Later that evening, Stamper informed Gloria that Jake was "passing out." Gloria found her son lying on the bed eyes closed. When Gloria asked him to open his eyes, he responded, "Mom, I can't, I'm dead." After a similar request from his older sister, Jake responded once again "don't bother me, I'm already dead." Gloria eventually called 911, and Jake was taken to a hospital.

At the hospital it was discovered that Jake had bruises on his neck, arms, chest, abdomen, groin, testicles, and legs. The nurse asked Jake how he got his bruises, and he responded, "from 'Mike.'" The nurse asked Jake who Mike was, and the victim responded, "Mom's wife." The victim died shortly thereafter.

According to the forensic pathologist who examined the victim, there were 88 bruises on his body as well as signs of sexual abuse. The primary cause of death was judged to be multiple blows to the abdomen with a blunt object such as a man's fist. The doctor also found that all the injuries had been caused within 24 hours of the victim's admission to the hospital, some as recent as 4–6 hours before.

At Stamper's trial for Jake's murder, the trial court admitted the victim's statements. Stamper challenges them as hearsay on appeal. How do you rule?

D. Statements Against Interest

Relevant Rule
FRE 804(b)(3)

(b) Hearsay exceptions. The following are not excluded by the hearsay rule if the declarant is unavailable as a witness: ...

(3) Statement against interest. A statement that:

(A) a reasonable person in the declarant's position would have made only if the person believed it to be true because, when made, it was so contrary to the declarant's proprietary or pecuniary interest or had so great a tendency to invalidate the declarant's claim against someone else or to expose the declarant to civil or criminal liability; and

(B) is supported by corroborating circumstances that clearly indicate its trustworthiness, if it is offered in a criminal case as one that tends to expose the declarant to criminal liability.

Overview

As we explore FRE 804(b)(3), it is important not to confuse it with statements of party opponents. FRE 804(b)(3) differs from the party opponent exemption under FRE 801(d)(2)(A) in multiple ways. FRE 801(d)(2)(A) need not be against a party's interest, but it must be statement by a party opponent offered against the party opponent. FRE 804(b)(3) need not be a party (even a witness's statement can qualify), but it must be against the declarant's interest when uttered. The trustworthiness component to FRE 804(b)(3) stems from the idea that one does not usually make false statements that go against one's interest.

The declarant must be aware that the statement is against her interest. This subjective component is often proved through an objective test ("a reasonable person in the declarant's position would not have made the statement unless believing it to be true"). Accordingly, a very fact-intensive analysis unfolds—under the circumstances known to the declarant, would a reasonable person utter the statement? For example, a man walks out of bar and states, "I am far too drunk to drive." Is this against self-interest? If he intended to walk home, then it is unlikely to be so. If he utters the statement as he is walking to his car, it may be. If he utters the statements moments after hitting a pedestrian, it definitely would be.

In deciding what is "against interest" it is critical to note whether the statement is against a proprietary, pecuniary, or penal interest. Statements against a penal interest will cause criminal liability to attach to the declarant, but it need not be an outright confession. If the statement may conceivably cause criminal liability to attach, it will be against the declarant's penal interest. Thus, declarant stating, "I gave Dirk a ride on Wednesday morning" may cause criminal liability to attach to the declarant if Dirk robbed a bank on Wednesday morning. The statement is not a confession to bank robbery, but it does indicate that the declarant is an accomplice and therefore subjects her to potential criminal liability.

Whether statements are against pecuniary interest (e.g., "I owe Sally $10,000") or proprietary interest (e.g., "I do not own Blackacre; I sold it three weeks ago") depend on context. If the surrounding facts indicate that the statement would hurt the declarant's financial or ownership interest, it will be against self-interest. Likewise, a statement that either subjects someone to civil liability (e.g., "I sideswiped my neighbor's car and drove away") or destroys declarant's civil claim (e.g., "I drove my car into a tree, but I told the insurance company someone sideswiped my car") would also qualify. Note that statements that go against a speaker's societal interest, such that it would potentially open the declarant to public disgrace (e.g., "I know she is married, but I am the father of her baby"), are not covered under the federal version of the rule.

FRE 804(b)(3)(B) mandates that, in a criminal case, corroborating evidence is needed for a statement that exposes the declarant to criminal liability. Thus, if defendant Jones puts witness X on the stand to state, "Smith said to me, 'I committed the crime for which Jones is charged,'" then the statement is not admissible unless corroborating circumstances make the statement trustworthy. In essence, having a witness declare that an unavailable witness is taking full blame is a little too convenient; the court wants greater trustworthiness in this context. To find that trustworthiness, courts will examine numerous factors, including the relationship between the declarant and the accused, whether other people heard the statement, the motive of the declarant, and whether the statement was made spontaneously.

FRE 804(b)(3) requires corroboration for all statements against penal interest in criminal cases regardless of whether the prosecution or defense offers the evidence. Thus whether the statement is offered by the defendant to exculpate him (e.g., "I did it; defendant did not do it") or by the prosecution to inculpate the defendant (e.g., "Defendant did it, and I helped him") the statement must be corroborated.

One thorny issue remains. How does the court handle statements that appear to be both self-serving **and** against interest? In other words, is a statement like, "Dirk robbed the bank, but I did drive him there" purely against self-interest or does it also encompass some self-serving motive (e.g., "I was a small part of this, but Dirk is the real bad guy in this situation"). The Supreme Court tackled this issue in *Williamson v. U.S.*

Focus Questions: *Williamson v. United States*

- The Court adopts a fact-intensive inquiry to determine whether a statement is self-inculpatory. Upon what factors do they rely? What other factors might be helpful?

- What are the advantages of the Court's suggested approach?

Williamson v. United States
512 U.S. 594 (1994)

O'CONNOR, J., announced the judgment of the Court and delivered the opinion of the Court with respect to Parts I, II–A, and II–B, in which BLACKMUN, STEVENS, SCALIA,

SOUTER, and GINSBURG, JJ., joined, and an opinion with respect to Part II–C, in which SCALIA, J., joined. SCALIA, J., filed a concurring opinion. GINSBURG, J., filed an opinion concurring in part and concurring in the judgment, in which BLACKMUN, STEVENS, and SOUTER, JJ., joined. KENNEDY, J., filed an opinion concurring in the judgment, in which REHNQUIST, C.J., and THOMAS, J., joined..

In this case we clarify the scope of the hearsay exception for statements against penal interest. Fed.Rule Evid. 804(b)(3).

I

A deputy sheriff stopped the rental car driven by Reginald Harris for weaving on the highway. Harris consented to a search of the car, which revealed 19 kilograms of cocaine in two suitcases in the trunk. Harris was promptly arrested.

Shortly after Harris' arrest, Special Agent Donald Walton of the Drug Enforcement Administration (DEA) interviewed him by telephone. During that conversation, Harris said that he got the cocaine from an unidentified Cuban in Fort Lauderdale; that the cocaine belonged to petitioner Williamson; and that it was to be delivered that night to a particular dumpster. Williamson was also connected to Harris by physical evidence: The luggage bore the initials of Williamson's sister, Williamson was listed as an additional driver on the car rental agreement, and an envelope addressed to Williamson and a receipt with Williamson's girlfriend's address were found in the glove compartment.

Several hours later, Agent Walton spoke to Harris in person. During that interview, Harris said he had rented the car a few days earlier and had driven it to Fort Lauderdale to meet Williamson. According to Harris, he had gotten the cocaine from a Cuban who was Williamson's acquaintance, and the Cuban had put the cocaine in the car with a note telling Harris how to deliver the drugs. Harris repeated that he had been instructed to leave the drugs in a certain dumpster, to return to his car, and to leave without waiting for anyone to pick up the drugs.

Agent Walton then took steps to arrange a controlled delivery of the cocaine. But as Walton was preparing to leave the interview room, Harris "got out of [his] chair ... and ... took a half step toward [Walton] ... and ... said, ... 'I can't let you do that,' threw his hands up and said 'that's not true, I can't let you go up there for no reason.'" Harris told Walton he had lied about the Cuban, the note, and the dumpster. The real story, Harris said, was that he was transporting the cocaine to Atlanta for Williamson, and that Williamson was traveling in front of him in another rental car. Harris added that after his car was stopped, Williamson turned around and drove past the location of the stop, where he could see Harris' car with its trunk open. Because Williamson had apparently seen the police searching the car, Harris explained that it would be impossible to make a controlled delivery.

Harris told Walton that he had lied about the source of the drugs because he was afraid of Williamson. Though Harris freely implicated himself, he did not want his story to be recorded, and he refused to sign a written version of the statement. Walton testified that he had promised to report any cooperation by Harris to the Assistant United States Attorney. Walton said Harris was not promised any reward or other benefit for cooperating.

Williamson was eventually convicted of possessing cocaine with intent to distribute, conspiring to possess cocaine with intent to distribute, and traveling interstate to promote the distribution of cocaine. When called to testify at Williamson's trial, Harris refused, even though the prosecution gave him use immunity and the court ordered him to testify and eventually held him in contempt. The District Court then ruled that, under Rule

804(b)(3), Agent Walton could relate what Harris had said to him … Williamson appealed his conviction, claiming that the admission of Harris' statements violated Rule 804(b)(3).…

II
A

The hearsay rule, Fed.Rule Evid. 802, is premised on the theory that out-of-court statements are subject to particular hazards. The declarant might be lying; he might have misperceived the events which he relates; he might have faulty memory; his words might be misunderstood or taken out of context by the listener. And the ways in which these dangers are minimized for in-court statements—the oath, the witness' awareness of the gravity of the proceedings, the jury's ability to observe the witness' demeanor, and, most importantly, the right of the opponent to cross-examine—are generally absent for things said out of court.

Nonetheless, the Federal Rules of Evidence also recognize that some kinds of out-of-court statements are less subject to these hearsay dangers, and therefore except them from the general rule that hearsay is inadmissible. One such category covers statements that are against the declarant's interest.…

To decide whether Harris' confession is made admissible by Rule 804(b)(3), we must first determine what the Rule means by "statement," which Federal Rule of Evidence 801(a)(1) defines as "an oral or written assertion." One possible meaning, "a report or narrative," Webster's Third New International Dictionary 2229, defn. 2(a) (1961), connotes an extended declaration. Under this reading, Harris' entire confession—even if it contains both self-inculpatory and non-self-inculpatory parts—would be admissible so long as in the aggregate the confession sufficiently inculpates him. Another meaning of "statement," "a single declaration or remark," *ibid.,* defn. 2(b), would make Rule 804(b)(3) cover only those declarations or remarks within the confession that are individually self-inculpatory.

Although the text of the Rule does not directly resolve the matter, the principle behind the Rule, so far as it is discernible from the text, points clearly to the narrower reading. Rule 804(b)(3) is founded on the commonsense notion that reasonable people, even reasonable people who are not especially honest, tend not to make self-inculpatory statements unless they believe them to be true. This notion simply does not extend to the broader definition of "statement." The fact that a person is making a broadly self-inculpatory confession does not make more credible the confession's non-self-inculpatory parts. One of the most effective ways to lie is to mix falsehood with truth, especially truth that seems particularly persuasive because of its self-inculpatory nature.

In this respect, it is telling that the non-self-inculpatory things Harris said in his first statement actually proved to be false, as Harris himself admitted during the second interrogation. And when part of the confession is actually self-exculpatory, the generalization on which Rule 804(b)(3) is founded becomes even less applicable. Self-exculpatory statements are exactly the ones which people are most likely to make even when they are false; and mere proximity to other, self-inculpatory, statements does not increase the plausibility of the self-exculpatory statements.

We therefore cannot agree with Justice KENNEDY's suggestion that the Rule can be read as expressing a policy that collateral statements—even ones that are not in any way against the declarant's interest—are admissible. Nothing in the text of Rule 804(b)(3) or the general theory of the hearsay Rules suggests that admissibility should turn on whether a statement is collateral to a self-inculpatory statement. The fact that a statement is self-inculpatory does make it more reliable; but the fact that a statement is collateral to a self-inculpatory statement says nothing at all about the collateral statement's reliability. We see no reason why collateral statements, even ones that are neutral as to interest, should be treated any differently from other hearsay statements that are generally excluded.

Congress certainly could, subject to the constraints of the Confrontation Clause, make statements admissible based on their proximity to self-inculpatory statements. But we will not lightly assume that the ambiguous language means anything so inconsistent with the Rule's underlying theory. In our view, the most faithful reading of Rule 804(b)(3) is that it does not allow admission of non-self-inculpatory statements, even if they are made within a broader narrative that is generally self-inculpatory. The district court may not just assume for purposes of Rule 804(b)(3) that a statement is self-inculpatory because it is part of a fuller confession, and this is especially true when the statement implicates someone else. "[T]he arrest statements of a codefendant have traditionally been viewed with special suspicion. Due to his strong motivation to implicate the defendant and to exonerate himself, a codefendant's statements about what the defendant said or did are less credible than ordinary hearsay evidence." *Lee v. Illinois,* 476 U.S. 530, 541 (1986) (internal quotation marks omitted).

Justice KENNEDY suggests that the Advisory Committee's Notes to Rule 804(b)(3) should be read as endorsing the position we reject—that an entire narrative, including non-self-inculpatory parts (but excluding the clearly self-serving parts), may be admissible if it is in the aggregate self-inculpatory. The Notes read, in relevant part:

> "[T]he third-party confession ... may include statements implicating [the accused], and under the general theory of declarations against interest they would be admissible as related statements.... [*Douglas v. Alabama,* 380 U.S. 415 (1965), and *Bruton v. United States,* 391 U.S. 123 (1968),] ... by no means require that all statements implicating another person be excluded from the category of declarations against interest. Whether a statement is in fact against interest must be determined from the circumstances of each case. Thus a statement admitting guilt and implicating another person, made while in custody, may well be motivated by a desire to curry favor with the authorities and hence fail to qualify as against interest.... On the other hand, the same words spoken under different circumstances, *e.g.,* to an acquaintance, would have no difficulty in qualifying....
>
> "The balancing of self-serving against dissenting *[sic]* aspects of a declaration is discussed in McCormick § 256." 28 U.S.C.App., p. 790.

This language, however, is not particularly clear, and some of it—especially the Advisory Committee's endorsement of the position taken by Dean McCormick's treatise—points the other way:

> "A certain latitude as to contextual statements, neutral as to interest, giving meaning to the declaration against interest seems defensible, but bringing in self-serving statements contextually seems questionable..... .
>
> "... [A]dmit[ting] the disserving parts of the declaration, and exclud[ing] the self-serving parts ... seems the most realistic method of adjusting admissibility to trustworthiness, where the serving and disserving parts can be severed." See C. McCormick, Law of Evidence § 256, pp. 552–553 (1954) (footnotes omitted).

Without deciding exactly how much weight to give the Notes in this particular situation, we conclude that the policy expressed in the Rule's text points clearly enough in one direction that it outweighs whatever force the Notes may have. And though Justice KENNEDY believes that the text can fairly be read as expressing a policy of admitting collateral statements, for the reasons given above we disagree.

B

We also do not share Justice Kennedy's fears that our reading of the Rule "eviscerate[s] the against penal interest exception," or makes it lack "meaningful effect[.]" There are many circumstances in which Rule 804(b)(3) does allow the admission of statements that inculpate a criminal defendant. Even the confessions of arrested accomplices may be admissible if they are truly self-inculpatory, rather than merely attempts to shift blame or curry favor.

For instance, a declarant's squarely self-inculpatory confession—"yes, I killed X"—will likely be admissible under Rule 804(b)(3) against accomplices of his who are being tried under a co-conspirator liability theory. Likewise, by showing that the declarant knew something, a self-inculpatory statement can in some situations help the jury infer that his confederates knew it as well. And when seen with other evidence, an accomplice's self-inculpatory statement can inculpate the defendant directly: "I was robbing the bank on Friday morning," coupled with someone's testimony that the declarant and the defendant drove off together Friday morning, is evidence that the defendant also participated in the robbery.

Moreover, whether a statement is self-inculpatory or not can only be determined by viewing it in context. Even statements that are on their face neutral may actually be against the declarant's interest. "I hid the gun in Joe's apartment" may not be a confession of a crime; but if it is likely to help the police find the murder weapon, then it is certainly self-inculpatory. "Sam and I went to Joe's house" might be against the declarant's interest if a reasonable person in the declarant's shoes would realize that being linked to Joe and Sam would implicate the declarant in Joe and Sam's conspiracy. And other statements that give the police significant details about the crime may also, depending on the situation, be against the declarant's interest. The question under Rule 804(b)(3) is always whether the statement was sufficiently against the declarant's penal interest "that a reasonable person in the declarant's position would not have made the statement unless believing it to be true," and this question can only be answered in light of all the surrounding circumstances.

C

In this case, however, we cannot conclude that all that Harris said was properly admitted. Some of Harris' confession would clearly have been admissible under Rule 804(b)(3); for instance, when he said he knew there was cocaine in the suitcase, he essentially forfeited his only possible defense to a charge of cocaine possession, lack of knowledge. But other parts of his confession, especially the parts that implicated Williamson, did little to subject Harris himself to criminal liability. A reasonable person in Harris' position might even think that implicating someone else would decrease his practical exposure to criminal liability, at least so far as sentencing goes. Small fish in a big conspiracy often get shorter sentences than people who are running the whole show, especially if the small fish are willing to help the authorities catch the big ones.

Nothing in the record shows that the District Court or the Court of Appeals inquired whether each of the statements in Harris' confession was truly self-inculpatory. As we explained above, this can be a fact-intensive inquiry, which would require careful examination of all the circumstances surrounding the criminal activity involved; we therefore remand to the Court of Appeals to conduct this inquiry in the first instance....

So ordered.

[Concurrences by Scalia, J., Ginsburg, J., and Kennedy, J., omitted.]

Problem 7-38

At about 6:00 p.m. on August 23, 2004, Mike Chase and several of his family members and friends gathered at Chase's mother's home in the Eastridge housing development on the Pine Ridge Indian Reservation in South Dakota. At this gathering, Chase argued with Clay Gibbons, who proceeded to threaten Chase with a knife. Chase disarmed Gibbons and ejected him from the party.

Gibbons returned a short time later with 15–20 friends armed with pipes, boards, and rocks. Chase met the crowd outside his mother's home accompanied by four armed friends. The two groups began yelling and throwing things at one another. One of Chase's friends was injured when struck in the head by a thrown crowbar. Chase then scuffled with an unarmed member of the crowd, Winston Bad Bear, and stabbed Bad Bear several times with the knife he had taken off Gibbons. Bad Bear died from his injuries.

At his trial for second degree murder, Chase claimed the killing of Bad Bear had been self-defense. As part of his defense, Chase wanted Dana Fast Horse to testify. During the altercation, Fast Horse had driven her car into the crowd resulting in an injury to a member of the group, for which Fast Horse was later indicted. Fast Horse exercised her Fifth Amendment right against self-incrimination and refused to testify at Chase's trial. Chase then sought to offer into evidence Fast Horse's written statement to the police. In that statement, she stated that she had driven her car into the rival group and was thereupon attacked by the mob. Through this statement, Chase intended to demonstrate the violent and threatening nature of the mob. The prosecution raises a hearsay objection. How do you rule?

Problem 7-39

Jack Love allegedly violated the Mann Act when he transported three female dancers from St. Paul, Minnesota, to Fargo, North Dakota, for the purpose of engaging in prostitution. One of the girls, Mary Jo Arm, was arrested for prostitution in Fargo. Arm, a minor, was allowed to post bond in Fargo and forfeit it, thereby ending her prosecution in North Dakota. She returned to St. Paul in the custody of Minnesota juvenile authorities.

Upon her return to Minnesota, Arm gave the following statement to the police:

On Wednesday or Thursday afternoon, March 9, 1978, Jack Love in his automobile drove me, Rhonda Holmes, and a girl named Red ... from St. Paul, Minnesota to Fargo, North Dakota, arriving at approximately 7:00 P.M. Rhonda, Red and me checked into the Travel Inn Motel in Fargo. Jack had previously told me I had to earn $1500 prostituting myself and that I was to turn over all of the money I made to him. All three girls worked as prostitutes for four days and I made approximately $900. Jack Love had dropped us off in Fargo and then drove back to St. Paul. He was scheduled to pick us up in Fargo on March 20, 1978 after we had completed our dancing engagement at the Flame bar in Fargo, North Dakota.

At Love's trial for violation of the Mann Act, Arm is unavailable to testify. The prosecution wishes to call the Minnesota detective who took Arm's statement as a witness and have him read the contents of the statement he took from Arm. The statement was not made under oath. It was written in the detective's own handwriting and signed by Arm. The defense objects on hearsay grounds. How do you rule?

E. Forfeiture by Wrongdoing

Relevant Rule
FRE 804(b)(6)

(b) The Exceptions. The following are not excluded by the rule against hearsay if the declarant is unavailable as a witness: …

(6) *Statement Offered Against a Party That Wrongfully Caused the Declarant's Unavailability.* A statement offered against a party that wrongfully caused — or acquiesced in wrongfully causing — the declarant's unavailability as a witness, and did so intending that result.

Overview

The underlying rationale behind FRE 804(b)(6) is one of fairness. A party who wrongfully caused a declarant's unavailability in order to prevent the declarant from testifying should not be allowed to profit from her misconduct. Certainly the evidence is necessary as well, because the declarant is now unavailable. Additionally, the evidence may be considered reliable, as the party's intent to silence the declarant means the party feared the declarant's testimony, most likely because it was truthful and convincing.

Therefore, the party who undertakes the wrongdoing forfeits her hearsay exception to the words of the silenced declarant. That party retains all her other objections under the Federal Rules of Evidence, however. Thus, for example, the party that silenced the declarant could still object that the hearsay was irrelevant, improper character evidence, or substantially more prejudicial than probative.

The foundational elements of FRE 804(b)(6) are as follows:

- The opposing party engaged or acquiesced in wrongdoing,
- The intent of the wrongdoing was to procure the unavailability of the declarant as a witness, and
- The wrongdoing did, in fact, cause the unavailability of the declarant as a witness.

The wrongdoing mentioned in FRE 804(b)(6) need not be a crime, but it must be an improper, significant interference with the declarant's appearance as a witness, such as the use of force or threats on the declarant. Furthermore, the opposing party need not personally commit or actively participate in the wrongdoing; even tacitly assenting to someone else committing the wrongdoing will be enough to qualify under the rule. Accordingly, if X silences a witness, the rule applies to others who conspired or tacitly agreed with X's plan.

The opposing party must undertake the wrongdoing with the intent to silence the declarant. However, the intent to silence the declarant **need not be the only intent of the opposing party.** Imagine a criminal defendant orders others to kill the prosecutor's star witness. The criminal defendant (i) hates the star witness because the star witness had an affair with defendant's wife and (ii) realizes that the prosecution's case will fall apart without the star witness. The fact that the first motive exists does not diminish the second motive; because the defendant intended to procure the unavailability of the declarant, the intent element is satisfied.

The preponderance of the evidence standard applies to the foundational elements of FRE 804(b)(6). Interestingly, in the trial of X for killing Y, the prosecution must prove by a preponderance of the evidence that X killed Y in order to be able to use Y's hearsay under FRE 804(b)(6). Thus, in a trial where the prosecution must prove that X killed Y beyond a reasonable doubt in order to convict, a lower standard (prove X is the murderer by a preponderance of the evidence) applies in order to make the decedent's words admissible. It is precisely for this reason that the resolution of a FRE 804(b)(6) objection should be conducted outside the hearing of a jury.

Finally, many courts have held that that a party who procures a witness's absence waives the right of confrontation for all purposes with regard to that witness under the Sixth Amendment's Confrontation Clause. This forfeiture of a constitutional right will be discussed in Chapter 8.

Problem 7-40

Former Enron CEO Jeffrey K. Skilling was indicted with conspiracy, securities fraud, making false representations to auditors, and insider trading offenses. In preparing his defense, Skilling contacted nearly 300 former Enron employees as potential witnesses, but only four were even willing to talk with Skilling and his lawyers. Skilling argued that this reluctance to speak with him was the result of intimidation by the United States government. According to Skilling, the heavily publicized prosecution of himself and several other former Enron employees left all of his potential witnesses too frightened to testify on his behalf lest they become the targets of prosecutorial retaliation. He argued that since no one was willing to testify, then he should be allowed to testify as to statements made to him by his reticent former co-workers.

The government responded to this concern by sending out letters to all Skilling's potential witnesses promising that there would be no prosecutorial retaliation toward anyone who met with or testified on behalf of Skilling. The prosecution did, however, object on hearsay grounds to the admission of any statements made by Skilling's non-testifying co-workers. How do you rule?

Problem 7-41

In late August 1990, Robert Gray brought criminal charges against his wife, Josephine Gray, alleging that Josephine had assaulted him at his workplace by swinging at him with a club and lunging at him with a knife. Robert Gray also brought charges against his wife's paramour, Clarence Goode, alleging that Goode had threatened him with a 9-millimeter handgun. Robert Gray appeared in court on October 5, 1990, but the case against Josephine and Clarence was continued. Later that same day, Robert Gray was driving home when he noticed his wife's car behind him. She was flashing her lights and signaling her husband to pull over. When Robert Gray did not pull over, Josephine drove her car alongside her husband's car. As Robert Gray turned to look toward his wife, Clarence sat up (from a reclined position) in the front passenger seat and pointed a gun at him.

Robert Gray reported this incident to police, and a warrant was issued for the arrests of Josephine and Clarence. One week before the November 16, 1990 trial date, Robert Gray was discovered dead in his new apartment, shot once in the chest and once in the neck with a .45 caliber handgun.

Josephine is now charged with wire fraud and mail fraud relating to her receipt of insurance proceeds after the death of Robert. The prosecution offers hearsay testimony of Robert pursuant to FRE 804(b)(6). She argues that FRE 804(b)(6) should not apply in this case because she did not intend to procure Robert Gray's unavailability as a witness at this trial. Rather, if the alleged charges are true, she sought to procure his unavailability in the trial regarding the earlier criminal charge brought by her husband. How do you rule?

V. The Residual Hearsay Exception

Relevant Rule
FRE 807

Residual Exception

(a) In General. Under the following circumstances, a hearsay statement is not excluded by the rule against hearsay even if the statement is not specifically covered by a hearsay exception in Rule 803 or 804:

   (1) the statement has equivalent circumstantial guarantees of trustworthiness;

   (2) it is offered as evidence of a material fact;

   (3) it is more probative on the point for which it is offered than any other evidence that the proponent can obtain through reasonable efforts; and

   (4) admitting it will best serve the purposes of these rules and the interests of justice.

(b) Notice. The statement is admissible only if, before the trial or hearing, the proponent gives an adverse party reasonable notice of the intent to offer the statement and its particulars, including the declarant's name and address, so that the party has a fair opportunity to meet it.

Overview

The residual or "catchall" exception to the hearsay rule exists to allow particularly trustworthy and necessary hearsay to be admitted. While a trial judge has a great deal of discretion in applying FRE 807, the Congressional intent behind the rule indicated that it should be used very rarely and only in exceptional circumstances. Loosely framed, the foundational elements of FRE 807 are:

   • The proponent of the evidence has given proper notice pursuant to the rule,
   • The statement possesses circumstantial guarantees of trustworthiness equivalent to the exceptions found in FRE 803 and FRE 804, and
   • The statement must be more probative on the point for which it is offered than any other evidence the proponent can procure through reasonable efforts.

The *Dallas County v. Commercial Union Assurance Co.* opinion, below, will further illuminate some of these elements. But, this is a very good moment for you to test your understanding of hearsay. What factors should prove "circumstantial guarantees of trustworthiness"? How necessary must an item be to satisfy the third element?

One philosophical debate concerning the residual exception concerns what the phrase "not specifically covered by Rule 803 or 804" means in the opening sentence. One meaning, as a majority of circuits hold, is that if the evidence fits under a FRE 803 or 804 exception, the court should rely on that exception rather than FRE 807. But another interpretation exists: if a piece of evidence came close to qualifying under FRE 803 or 804 but did not meet the exception (i.e., it was a "near miss"), then you should **not** admit it under FRE 807; otherwise, you are weakening the prerequisites required by Congress if every time a near miss occurs it is admitted under FRE 807. Under this interpretation, which is the minority position, FRE 807 should only apply to situations not contemplated by Congress.

To better understand the near miss theory, let us examine one common battleground under FRE 807: the attempts by the prosecution to admit grand jury testimony by a witness who was unavailable for trial. As we know, this evidence would not qualify under FRE 804(b)(1), as there was no previous cross-examination by the defendant at the grand jury. We know it will not fit under FRE 801(d)(1)(A), as the witness must be subject to cross-examination at trial under that exemption. Two options yield two near misses. Should the evidence still be admitted under FRE 807 if circumstantial indicia of trustworthiness can be found? If so, have we diluted the requirements of FRE 804(b)(1) (mandating a prior examination of the witness by the party against whom it is offered) and FRE 801(d)(1)(A) (mandating that the witness be on the stand, subject to cross-examination) when we admit this evidence under FRE 807?

In fact, many cases have allowed grand jury testimony under FRE 807. It has been found in many instances to be trustworthy even though the testimony cannot be tested by the defense and the witnesses may be under pressure from the government. Some cases ruled grand jury testimony inadmissible where the facts indicated it was particularly untrustworthy. So, the key inquiry for this fact-intensive rule is how high is the standard for trustworthiness under FRE 807 and what factors help us determine that it is met.

Focus Questions: *Dallas County v. Commercial Union Assurance Co.*

- Do any other hearsay exceptions or exemptions apply to the evidence of this case? Why or why not?

- How does the Court define "necessity" and "trustworthiness"? Are these definitions too narrow or too broad?

- Does the test adopted by this Court favor admissibility or inadmissibility?

Dallas County v. Commercial Union Assurance Co.
286 F.2d 388 (5th Cir. 1961)

WISDOM, Circuit Judge.

This appeal presents a single question—the admissibility in evidence of a newspaper to show that the Dallas County Courthouse in Selma, Alabama, was damaged by fire in 1901. We hold that the newspaper was admissible, and affirm the judgment below.

On a bright, sunny morning, July 7, 1957, the clock tower of the Dallas County Courthouse at Selma, Alabama, commenced to lean, made loud cracking and popping noises, then fell, and telescoped into the courtroom. Fortunately, the collapse of the tower took place on a Sunday morning; no one was injured, but damage to the courthouse exceeded $100,000. An examination of the tower debris showed the presence of charcoal and charred timbers. The State Toxicologist, called in by Dallas County, reported the char was evidence that lightning struck the courthouse. Later, several residents of Selma reported that a bolt of lightning struck the courthouse July 2, 1957. On this information, Dallas County concluded that a lightning bolt had hit the building causing the collapse of the clock tower five days later. Dallas County carried insurance for loss to its courthouse caused by fire or lightning. The insurers' engineers and investigators found that the courthouse collapsed of its own weight. They reported that the courthouse had not been struck by lightning; that lightning could not have caused the collapse of the tower; that the collapse of the tower was caused by structural weaknesses attributable to a faulty design, poor construction, gradual deterioration of the structure, and overloading brought about by remodeling and the recent installation of an air-conditioning system, part of which was constructed over the courtroom trusses. In their opinion, the char was the result of a fire in the courthouse tower and roof that must have occurred many, many years before July 2, 1957. The insurers denied liability.

The County sued its insurers in the Circuit Court of Dallas County. As many of the suits as could be removed, seven, were removed to the United States District Court for the Southern District of Alabama, and were consolidated for trial. The case went to the jury on one issue: did lightning cause the collapse of the clock tower?

The record contains ample evidence to support a jury verdict either way. The County produced witnesses who testified they saw lighting strike the clock tower; the insurers produced witnesses who testified an examination of the debris showed that lightning did not strike the clock tower. Some witnesses said the char was fresh and smelled smoky; other witnesses said it was obviously old and had no fresh smoky smell at all. Both sides presented a great mass of engineering testimony bearing on the design, construction, overload or lack of overload. All of this was for the jury to evaluate. The jury chose to believe the insurers' witnesses and brought in a verdict for the defendants.

During the trial the defendants introduced a copy of the Morning Times of Selma for June 9, 1901. This issue carried an unsigned article describing a fire that occurred at two in the morning of June 9, 1901, while the courthouse was still under construction. The article stated, in part: "The unfinished dome of the County's new courthouse was in flames at the top, and ... soon fell in. The fire was soon under control and the main building was saved." The insurers do not contend that the collapse of the tower resulted from unsound charred timbers used in the repair of the building after the fire; they offered the newspaper account to show there had been a fire long before 1957 that would account for charred timber in the clock tower.

As a predicate for introducing the newspaper in evidence, the defendants called to the stand the editor of the Selma Times-Journal who testified that his publishing company maintains archives of the published issues of the Times-Journal and of the Morning Times, its predecessor, and that the archives contain the issue of the Morning Times of Selma for June 9, 1901, offered in evidence. The plaintiff objected that the newspaper article was hearsay; that it was not a business record nor an ancient document, nor was it admissible under any recognized exception to the hearsay doctrine. The trial judge admitted the newspaper as part of the records of the Selma Times-Journal. The sole error Dallas County specifies on appeal is the admission of the newspaper in evidence.

In the Anglo-American adversary system of law, courts usually will not admit evidence unless its accuracy and trustworthiness may be tested by cross-examination. Here, therefore, the plaintiff argues that the newspaper should not be admitted: "You cannot cross-examine a newspaper." Of course, a newspaper article is hearsay, and in almost all circumstances is inadmissible. However, the law governing hearsay is somewhat less than pellucid. And, as with most rules, the hearsay rule is not absolute; it is replete with exceptions. Witnesses die, documents are lost, deeds are destroyed, memories fade. All too often, primary evidence is not available and courts and lawyers must rely on secondary evidence....

We turn now to a case, decided long before the Federal Rules were adopted, in which the court used an approach we consider appropriate for the solution of the problem before us. *G. & C. Merriam Co. v. Syndicate Pub. Co.*, 207 F. 515, 518 (2nd Cir. 1913), concerned a controversy between dictionary publishers over the use of the title "Webster's Dictionary" when the defendant's dictionary allegedly was not based upon Webster's dictionary at all. The bone of contention was whether a statement in the preface to the dictionary was admissible as evidence of the facts it recited. Ogilvie, the compiler of the dictionary, stated in his preface that he used Webster's Dictionary as the basis for his own publication. The dictionary, with its preface, was published in 1850, sixty-three years before the trial of the case. Ogilvie's published statement was challenged as hearsay. Judge Learned Hand, then a district judge, unable, as we are here, to find a case in point, for authority relied solely on Wigmore on Evidence (then a recent publication), particularly on Wigmore's analysis that "the requisites of an exception to the hearsay rule are necessity and circumstantial guaranty of trustworthiness". Wigmore on Evidence, §§ 1421, 1422, 1690 (1st ed. 1913). Applying these criteria, Judge Hand held that the statement was admissible as an exception to the hearsay rule:

> "Ogilvie's preface is of course an unsworn statement and as such only hearsay testimony, which may be admitted only as an exception to the general rule. The question is whether there is such an exception. I have been unable to find any express authority in point and must decide the question upon principle. In the first place, I think it fair to insist that to reject such a statement is to refuse evidence about the truth of which no reasonable person should have any doubt whatever, because it fulfills both the requisites of an exception to the hearsay rule, necessity and circumstantial guaranty of trustworthiness. Wigmore, §§ 1421, 1422, 1690, ... Besides Ogilvie, everyone else is dead who ever knew anything about the matter and could intelligently tell us what the fact is.... As to the trustworthiness of the testimony, it has the guaranty of the occasion, at which there was no motive for fabrication." 207 F. 515, 518.

The Court of Appeals adopted the district court's opinion in its entirety.

The first of the two requisites is necessity. As to necessity, Wigmore points out this requisite means that unless the hearsay statement is admitted, the facts it brings out may otherwise be lost, either because the person whose assertion is offered may be dead or unavailable, or because the assertion is of such a nature that one could not expect to obtain evidence of the same value from the same person or from other sources. Wigmore, § 1421 (3rd ed.). "In effect, Wigmore says that, as the word necessity is here used, it is not to be interpreted as uniformly demanding a showing of total inaccessibility of firsthand evidence as a condition precedent to the acceptance of a particular piece of hearsay, but that necessity exists where otherwise great practical inconvenience would be experienced in making the desired proof. (Wigmore, 3rd Ed., Vol. V, sec. 1421; Vol. VI, sec. 1702).... If it were otherwise, the result would be that the exception created to the hearsay rule would thereby be mostly, if not completely, destroyed." *United States v. Aluminum Co. of America*, 35 F.Supp. 820, 823 (D.C.Cir. 1940).

The fire referred to in the newspaper account occurred fifty-eight years before the trial of this case. Any witness who saw that fire with sufficient understanding to observe it and describe it accurately, would have been older than a young child at the time of the fire. We may reasonably assume that at the time of the trial he was either dead or his faculties were dimmed by the passage of fifty-eight years. It would have been burdensome, but not impossible, for the defendant to have discovered the name of the author of the article (although it had no by-line) and, perhaps, to have found an eye-witness to the fire. But it is improbable—so it seems to us—that any witness could have been found whose recollection would have been accurate at the time of the trial of this case. And it seems impossible that the testimony of any witness would have been as accurate and as reliable as the statement of facts in the contemporary newspaper article.

The rationale behind the "ancient documents" exception is applicable here: after a long lapse of time, ordinary evidence regarding signatures or handwriting is virtually unavailable, and it is therefore permissible to resort to circumstantial evidence. Thus, in *Trustees of German Township, Montgomery County v. Farmers & Citizens Savings Bank Co.*, 113 N.E.2d 409, 412, aff'd Ohio App., 115 N.E.2d 690 (Ohio Com.Pl.1953), the court admitted as ancient documents newspapers eighty years old containing notices of advertisements for bids relating to the town hall: "Such exhibits, by reason of age, alone, and unquestioned authenticity, qualify as ancient documents." The ancient documents rule applies to documents a generation or more in age. Here, the Selma Times-Journal article is almost two generations old. The principle of necessity, not requiring absolute impossibility or total inaccessibility of first-hand knowledge, is satisfied by the practicalities of the situation before us.

The second requisite for admission of hearsay evidence is trustworthiness. According to Wigmore, there are three sets of circumstances when hearsay is trustworthy enough to serve as a practicable substitute for the ordinary test of cross-examination: "Where the circumstances are such that a sincere and accurate statement would naturally be uttered, and no plan of falsification be formed; where, even though a desire to falsify might present itself, other considerations, such as the danger of easy detection on the fear of punishment, would probably counteract its force; where the statement was made under such conditions of publicity that an error, if it had occurred, would probably have been detected and corrected." 5 Wigmore, Evidence, § 1422 (3rd ed.) These circumstances fit the instant case.

There is no procedural canon against the exercise of common sense in deciding the admissibility of hearsay evidence. In 1901 Selma, Alabama, was a small town. Taking a common sense view of this case, it is inconceivable to us that a newspaper reporter in a small town would report there was a fire in the dome of the new courthouse—if there had been no fire. He is without motive to falsify, and a false report would have subjected the newspaper and him to embarrassment in the community. The usual dangers inherent in hearsay evidence, such as lack of memory, faulty narration, intent to influence the court proceedings, and plain lack of truthfulness are not present here. To our minds, the article published in the Selma Morning-Times on the day of the fire is more reliable, more trustworthy, more competent evidence than the testimony of a witness called to the stand fifty-eight years later.

We hold, that in matters of local interest, when the fact in question is of such a public nature it would be generally known throughout the community, and when the questioned fact occurred so long ago that the testimony of an eye-witness would probably be less trustworthy than a contemporary newspaper account, a federal court, under Rule 43(a), may relax the exclusionary rules to the extent of admitting the newspaper article in evidence. We do not characterize this newspaper as a "business record", nor as an "ancient document", nor as any other readily identifiable and happily tagged species of hearsay exception. It is admissible because it is necessary and trustworthy, relevant and material, and its admission is within the trial judge's exercise of discretion in holding the hearing within reasonable bounds.

Judgment is affirmed.

Problem 7-42

Let us revisit Problem 7-17:

Gail Duncan, acting as a confidential informant for the Drug Enforcement Agency, purchased four ounces of cocaine from Deron Cole and another individual on the night of January 31, 1995. Approximately ten minutes after the transaction, Duncan met with DEA Agent Schrempt and Detective Warman for a debriefing. She told them that although she recognized Cole, she did not recognize the individual who had accompanied him. The agents then showed her 20 to 30 photographs of suspected co-conspirators. Warman testified that Duncan picked out the picture of Cornelius Anderson immediately, identifying him as the man who had accompanied Cole. Agent Schrempt recorded the debriefing with Duncan, and Duncan verified it. However, Schrempt had failed to include Duncan's identification of Anderson in the record.

We have discussed earlier that the court decided that this was not a present sense impression. Is Duncan's identification admissible under FRE 807?

Problem 7-43

Mechelle, who was 17 years old, deaf, mute, and severely mentally challenged, was the victim of an assault by her neighbor. She could function in her daily activities on the level of a normal 7-year-old and could communicate with others on the level of a normal 3-year-old. She could use sign language, but her signing vocabulary was limited to about 200 words. Accordingly, getting her to respond to questions was a long process that required expert assistance to ask the questions and to help understand her answers—whenever she, in fact, did answer at all.

Mechelle informed her mother that she was assaulted by her neighbor, Rickey Lyons. With the help of her mother and one of her teachers, she repeated her story to the police. Three days after the incident, the police (again with the help of one Mechelle's teachers) videotaped Mechelle reenacting the assault at Lyons's house. In the video, the police officer was more of an observer than an interviewer, and the questions that were asked of Mechelle were not leading. They did not rehearse the reenactment prior to taping it.

At trial, Mechelle testified, but her responses were largely substantively unintelligible. The trial court admitted the video reenactment over the defendant's hearsay objection. The trial judge found the tape admissible under FRE 807, allowed it to be shown at the conclusion of Mechelle's direct testimony, and ruled that the defense could cross-examine her on the tape's contents if he wished.

The judge also allowed one of her teachers to testify that, based on her mental challenges, it "would be almost impossible for her to fabricate an entire incident of such complexity" as the one described on the video.

The defendant appeals the admission of the reenactment video. How do you rule?

VI. Final Thoughts on Hearsay

Relevant Rules
FRE 806

Attacking and Supporting the Declarant's Credibility

When a hearsay statement — or a statement described in Rule 801(d)(2)(C), (D), or (E) — has been admitted in evidence, the declarant's credibility may be attacked, and then supported, by any evidence that would be admissible for those purposes if the declarant had testified as a witness. The court may admit evidence of the declarant's inconsistent statement or conduct, regardless of when it occurred or whether the declarant had an opportunity to explain or deny it. If the party against whom the statement was admitted calls the declarant as a witness, the party may examine the declarant on the statement as if on cross-examination.

Congratulations! You have come to the end of the hearsay chapter. Undoubtedly, along the way confusion has occasionally triumphed over comprehension. This is a tricky topic, and it does take some practice to learn. With all the micropropositions that inhabit the world of hearsay, it is important that you do not lose sight of some of the macropropositions that govern how the hearsay rules works. Namely:

The hearsay declarant is a witness who can be impeached. Like any other witness, the hearsay declarant's words enter the courtroom, even if she is not physically present. Therefore FRE 806 permits impeachment and rehabilitation as if "the declarant has testified as a witness." FRE 806 applies to all statements admitted under 801(d)(2)(C), (D), or (E) as well as FRE 803, FRE 804, and FRE 807. The reason the FRE 801(d)(1) exemptions are not included is because the witness is already on the stand for those exemptions, so impeachment clearly applies. The reason FRE 801(d)(2)(A) and (B) are excluded is because the opposing party is present at trial, and her veracity is obviously fair game.

Thus, one can impeach a hearsay declarant under the five modes we have discussed in Chapter 6. However, an open question exists as to whether specific instances of non-conviction misconduct that demonstrates dishonesty can be used under FRE 608(b). On the one hand, FRE 608(b) mandates that such evidence can only be admitted on cross-examination, and there is no cross-examination of an out of court witness. On the other hand, this powerful method of impeaching a witness should not be denied because the delcarant is not in the courtroom. Courts have split over the issue.

Be aware of other objections after the battle over hearsay concludes. Just because the proponent of evidence may win the hearsay round does not mean an opponent is finished objecting to the evidence. As we have seen in the problems in this chapter, hearsay evidence may raise character, impeachment, and unfair prejudice issues. Any other appropriate objection is still a fair method to attack admissible hearsay. Perhaps the most powerful method of attacking admissible hearsay will be discussed in the next chapter on the Confrontation Clause.

A pattern emerges in hearsay objections. Do not forget the big picture with hearsay objections. The proponent tries to introduce a hearsay statement. The opponent objects on hearsay grounds. The proponent may argue that this statement is not hearsay because it is (i) not an out of court statement, (ii) not an assertion or assertive conduct, and/or (iii) not offered for its truth. If it fails one element, it is **not** hearsay and is therefore admissible subject to other rules. If it does satisfy the definition of hearsay, the proponent will then reach for a hearsay exemption or exception. There are now numerous tools in your toolbox, and you can reach for multiple exemptions/exceptions in attempting to convince the judge as to the admissibility of the statement. Can you think of a way to organize the hearsay exemptions and exceptions into broader categories that cover multiple exemptions and exceptions? For example, which exceptions and exemptions often focus on documents? Which focus on statements? What other categories can you develop to enhance your understanding and memory of the hearsay rules?

Professional Development Questions

- Hearsay is one of the toughest concepts to master in evidence law. Try to re-write the rules governing when an out of court statement if offered for the truth of the matter asserted in your own words. By undertaking this exercise, you will make the knowledge your own and gain a deeper understanding of hearsay, rather than trying to repeat a test you may not fully comprehend.

- At this stage in your knowledge of evidence rules, you should be aware of how critical it is to prepare your witnesses. Is there a way to phrase a question that will avoid having your witness offer an out of court statement? Would asking a witness, "What did you learn during your conversation with X?" necessarily involve an out of court statement? Are there any other ways to phrase a question to avoid reliance on hearsay?

- Experienced attorneys are experts at understanding the elasticity of case holdings. If a court opinion hurts their case, they will try to contract the holding by limiting it to the facts of that opinion. If a court opinion helps their case, they will try to expand the holding by arguing that similar facts, precedent, and/or policies apply in their case. As you review the material in this chapter, try to craft hypotheticals that expand and contract the holdings in the cases you have read. Through this exercise, you will better master the material by understanding its elasticity.

Chapter 8

The Confrontation Clause
and Due Process

I. The Confrontation Clause

A. Overview to the Confrontation Clause

The Sixth Amendment mandates that "in all criminal prosecutions, the accused shall enjoy the right ... to be confronted with the witnesses against him[.]" Does the Confrontation Clause therefore forbid a prosecutor's use of all hearsay when the declarant does not testify at trial? In this situation, the defendant would not be able to "be confronted with the witnesses against him." If banning all hearsay is too draconian, then where do we draw the line? Should hearsay be admitted only if it meets certain hearsay exceptions or exemptions? Which ones? Should hearsay be admitted if it is first found to be reliable? How do we make that determination? Should hearsay be admitted only when hearsay testimony harmonizes with the framer's intent behind the 6th Amendment? If so, what is that intent?

Before we dive into the evolution of Confrontation Clause jurisprudence, let us note its limitations. It does not apply in civil cases and does not apply to hearsay offered **against** the government in a criminal case. As both the hearsay rule and the Confrontation Clause are exclusionary rules, evidence must survive scrutiny under **both** principles in order to be admissible. Furthermore, the linking of hearsay and the Confrontation makes sense because both focus on the same core concern—the lack of cross-examination. We have seen under the hearsay rule that a lack of cross-examination means that we cannot test the testimonial capacities of the witness at trial. Likewise, under the Confrontation Clause, the inability to cross-examine a witness against you means that you cannot confront your accusers— faceless accusers, and very possibly very unreliable ones, are substituted for live witnesses.

Early Confrontation Clause cases, typified by *Mattox v. U.S.*, 156 U.S. 237 (1895), relied on public policy and the necessities of the case to allow hearsay against a criminal defendant. In *Mattox*, the defendant was convicted, had the conviction overturned on appeal, and then was re-tried. Two witnesses against him at the first trial died before the second trial. Noting that the witnesses had previously been cross-examined at the defendant's previous trial, the Supreme Court ruled that the "incidental benefit" to the accused of confrontation was not justified in this case: "A technical adherence to the letter of a constitutional provision may occasionally be carried farther than is necessary to the just protection of the accused, and farther than the safety of the public would warrant." *Id.* at 243. While this is a defensible conclusion, the Court made no attempt to draw a bright line rule for future Confrontation Clause cases.

In *Ohio v. Roberts*, 448 U.S. 56 (1980), the Supreme Court attempted to draw a clearer, predictive line. In order for hearsay to be admitted against a criminal defendant, it must be both necessary (i.e., the witness was unavailable) and reliable. Indicia of reliability included hearsay exceptions that were "firmly rooted" in the common law, an earlier chance to examine the declarant, and/or "particularized guarantees of trustworthiness." Whether or not a clearer line had been established, the *Roberts* approach was cast aside in 2004 when the Supreme Court decided *Crawford v. Washington*.

Focus Questions: *Crawford v. Washington*

- Based on the lessons drawn from the Raleigh case, what protections does the Confrontation Clause intend to ensure?

- Why do the lower courts in this case reach different conclusions as to the trustworthiness of the evidence? Does the answer lie in the test they apply or how they apply the facts?

- The Court offers three potential definitions of "testimonial." Which is the broadest, such that a great deal of evidence would be deemed testimonial? Which is the narrowest, such that very little evidence would be deemed testimonial?

- How does the Court's test for the admissibility of statements by the Confrontation Clause compare to the *Roberts* test for admissibility? What are the shortcomings of the *Roberts* test?

- The court fails to lay out a comprehensive definition for testimonial statements. How would you craft a definition?

Crawford v. Washington

541 U.S. 36 (2004)

SCALIA, J., delivered the opinion of the Court, in which STEVENS, KENNEDY, SOUTER, THOMAS, GINSBURG, and BREYER, JJ., joined. REHNQUIST, C. J., filed an opinion concurring in the judgment, in which O'CONNOR, J., joined.

Petitioner Michael Crawford stabbed a man who allegedly tried to rape his wife, Sylvia. At his trial, the State played for the jury Sylvia's tape-recorded statement to the police describing the stabbing, even though he had no opportunity for cross-examination. The Washington Supreme Court upheld petitioner's conviction after determining that Sylvia's statement was reliable. The question presented is whether this procedure complied with the Sixth Amendment's guarantee that, "[i]n all criminal prosecutions, the accused shall enjoy the right ... to be confronted with the witnesses against him."

I

On August 5, 1999, Kenneth Lee was stabbed at his apartment. Police arrested petitioner later that night. After giving petitioner and his wife *Miranda* warnings, detectives interrogated each of them twice. Petitioner eventually confessed that he and Sylvia had gone in search of Lee because he was upset over an earlier incident in which Lee had tried to rape her. The two had found Lee at his apartment, and a fight ensued in which Lee was stabbed in the torso and petitioner's hand was cut.

Petitioner gave the following account of the fight:

"Q. Okay. Did you ever see anything in [Lee's] hands?

"A. I think so, but I'm not positive.

"Q. Okay, when you think so, what do you mean by that?

"A. I could a swore I seen him goin' for somethin' before, right before everything happened. He was like reachin', fiddlin' around down here and stuff ... and I just ... I don't know, I think, this is just a possibility, but I think, I think that he pulled somethin' out and I grabbed for it and that's how I got cut ... but I'm not positive. I, I, my mind goes blank when things like this happen. I mean, I just, I remember things wrong, I remember things that just doesn't, don't make sense to me later."

Sylvia generally corroborated petitioner's story about the events leading up to the fight, but her account of the fight itself was arguably different—particularly with respect to whether Lee had drawn a weapon before petitioner assaulted him:

"Q. Did Kenny do anything to fight back from this assault?

"A. (pausing) I know he reached into his pocket ... or somethin'... I don't know what.

"Q. After he was stabbed?

"A. He saw Michael coming up. He lifted his hand ... his chest open, he might [have] went to go strike his hand out or something and then (inaudible).

"Q. Okay, you, you gotta speak up.

"A. Okay, he lifted his hand over his head maybe to strike Michael's hand down or something and then he put his hands in his ... put his right hand in his right pocket ... took a step back ... Michael proceeded to stab him ... then his hands were like ... how do you explain this ... open arms ... with his hands open and he fell down ... and we ran (describing subject holding hands open, palms toward assailant).

"Q. Okay, when he's standing there with his open hands, you're talking about Kenny, correct?

"A. Yeah, after, after the fact, yes.

"Q. Did you see anything in his hands at that point?

"A. (pausing) um um (no)."

The State charged petitioner with assault and attempted murder. At trial, he claimed self-defense. Sylvia did not testify because of the state marital privilege, which generally bars a spouse from testifying without the other spouse's consent. In Washington, this privilege does not extend to a spouse's out-of-court statements admissible under a hearsay exception, so the State sought to introduce Sylvia's tape-recorded statements to the police as evidence that the stabbing was not in self-defense. Noting that Sylvia had admitted she led petitioner to Lee's apartment and thus had facilitated the assault, the State invoked the hearsay exception for statements against penal interest, Wash. Rule Evid. 804(b)(3) (2003).

Petitioner countered that, state law notwithstanding, admitting the evidence would violate his federal constitutional right to be "confronted with the witnesses against him." Amdt. 6. According to our description of that right in *Ohio v. Roberts*, 448 U.S. 56, (1980), it does not bar admission of an unavailable witness's statement against a criminal defendant if the statement bears "adequate 'indicia of reliability.'" *Id.,* at 66. To meet that test, evidence must either fall within a "firmly rooted hearsay exception" or bear "particularized guarantees of trustworthiness." *Ibid.* The trial court here admitted the statement on the latter ground, offering several reasons why it was trustworthy: Sylvia was not shifting blame but rather corroborating her husband's story that he acted in self-defense or "justified reprisal"; she had direct knowledge as an eyewitness; she was describing recent events; and she was being questioned by a "neutral" law enforcement officer. The prosecution played the tape for the jury and relied on it in closing, arguing that it was "damning evidence" that "completely refutes [petitioner's] claim of self-defense." The jury convicted petitioner of assault.

The Washington Court of Appeals reversed. It applied a nine-factor test to determine whether Sylvia's statement bore particularized guarantees of trustworthiness, and noted several reasons why it did not: The statement contradicted one she had previously given; it was made in response to specific questions; and at one point she admitted she had shut her eyes during the stabbing. The court considered and rejected the State's argument that Sylvia's statement was reliable because it coincided with petitioner's to such a degree that the two "interlocked." The court determined that, although the two statements agreed about the events leading up to the stabbing, they differed on the issue crucial to petitioner's self-defense claim: "[Petitioner's] version asserts that Lee may have had something in his hand when he stabbed him; but Sylvia's version has Lee grabbing for something only after he has been stabbed."

The Washington Supreme Court reinstated the conviction, unanimously concluding that, although Sylvia's statement did not fall under a firmly rooted hearsay exception, it bore guarantees of trustworthiness: "'[W]hen a codefendant's confession is virtually identical [to, *i.e.,* interlocks with,] that of a defendant, it may be deemed reliable.'" 147 Wash.2d 424, 437 (2002). The court explained:

> "Although the Court of Appeals concluded that the statements were contradictory, upon closer inspection they appear to overlap....
>
> "[B]oth of the Crawfords' statements indicate that Lee was possibly grabbing for a weapon, but they are equally unsure when this event may have taken place. They are also equally unsure how Michael received the cut on his hand, leading the court to question when, if ever, Lee possessed a weapon. In this respect they overlap....
>
> [N]either Michael nor Sylvia clearly stated that Lee had a weapon in hand from which Michael was simply defending himself. And it is this omission by both that interlocks the statements and makes Sylvia's statement reliable." 147 Wash.2d, at 438-439.[1]

---

1. The court rejected the State's argument that guarantees of trustworthiness were unnecessary since petitioner waived his confrontation rights by invoking the marital privilege. It reasoned that "forcing the defendant to choose between the marital privilege and confronting his spouse presents an untenable Hobson's choice." 147 Wash.2d. at 432. The State has not challenged this holding here. The State also has not challenged the Court of Appeals' conclusion (not reached by the State Supreme Court) that the confrontation violation, if it occurred, was not harmless. We express no opinion on these matters.

We granted certiorari to determine whether the State's use of Sylvia's statement violated the Confrontation Clause.

II

The Sixth Amendment's Confrontation Clause provides that, "[i]n all criminal prosecutions, the accused shall enjoy the right ... to be confronted with the witnesses against him." ... Petitioner argues that [the previously discussed *Roberts*] test strays from the original meaning of the Confrontation Clause and urges us to reconsider it.

A

The Constitution's text does not alone resolve this case. One could plausibly read "witnesses against" a defendant to mean those who actually testify at trial, those whose statements are offered at trial, or something in-between. We must therefore turn to the historical background of the Clause to understand its meaning.

The right to confront one's accusers is a concept that dates back to Roman times. The founding generation's immediate source of the concept, however, was the common law. English common law has long differed from continental civil law in regard to the manner in which witnesses give testimony in criminal trials. The common-law tradition is one of live testimony in court subject to adversarial testing, while the civil law condones examination in private by judicial officers.

Nonetheless, England at times adopted elements of the civil-law practice. Justices of the peace or other officials examined suspects and witnesses before trial. These examinations were sometimes read in court in lieu of live testimony, a practice that "occasioned frequent demands by the prisoner to have his 'accusers,' *i.e.* the witnesses against him, brought before him face to face." 1 J. Stephen, History of the Criminal Law of England 326 (1883). In some cases, these demands were refused.

Pretrial examinations became routine under two statutes passed during the reign of Queen Mary in the 16th century, 1 & 2 Phil. & M., c. 13 (1554), and 2 & 3 *id.*, c. 10 (1555). These Marian bail and committal statutes required justices of the peace to examine suspects and witnesses in felony cases and to certify the results to the court. It is doubtful that the original purpose of the examinations was to produce evidence admissible at trial. Whatever the original purpose, however, they came to be used as evidence in some cases, resulting in an adoption of continental procedure.

The most notorious instances of civil-law examination occurred in the great political trials of the 16th and 17th centuries. One such was the 1603 trial of Sir Walter Raleigh for treason. Lord Cobham, Raleigh's alleged accomplice, had implicated him in an examination before the Privy Council and in a letter. At Raleigh's trial, these were read to the jury. Raleigh argued that Cobham had lied to save himself: "Cobham is absolutely in the King's mercy; to excuse me cannot avail him; by accusing me he may hope for favour." 1 D. Jardine, Criminal Trials 435 (1832). Suspecting that Cobham would recant, Raleigh demanded that the judges call him to appear, arguing that "[t]he Proof of the Common Law is by witness and jury: let Cobham be here, let him speak it. Call my accuser before my face...." 2 How. St. Tr., at 15-16. The judges refused, and, despite Raleigh's protestations that he was being tried "by the Spanish Inquisition," *id.*, at 15, the jury convicted, and Raleigh was sentenced to death.

One of Raleigh's trial judges later lamented that " 'the justice of England has never been so degraded and injured as by the condemnation of Sir Walter Raleigh.' " 1 Jardine, *supra*, at 520. Through a series of statutory and judicial reforms, English law developed a right of confrontation that limited these abuses. For example, treason statutes required witnesses to confront the accused "face to face" at his arraignment. Courts, meanwhile, developed relatively strict rules of unavailability, admitting examinations only if the witness was demonstrably unable to testify in person. Several authorities also stated that a suspect's confession could be admitted only against himself, and not against others he implicated.

One recurring question was whether the admissibility of an unavailable witness's pretrial examination depended on whether the defendant had had an opportunity to cross-examine him. In 1696, the Court of King's Bench answered this question in the affirmative, in the widely reported misdemeanor libel case of *King v. Paine*, 5 Mod. 163, 87 Eng. Rep. 584. The court ruled that, even though a witness was dead, his examination was not admissible where "the defendant not being present when [it was] taken before the mayor ... had lost the benefit of a cross-examination." *Id.*, at 165, 87 Eng. Rep., at 585. The question was also debated at length during the infamous proceedings against Sir John Fenwick on a bill of attainder. Fenwick's counsel objected to admitting the examination of a witness who had been spirited away, on the ground that Fenwick had had no opportunity to cross-examine. See *Fenwick's Case*, 13 How. St. Tr. 537, 591-592 (H.C. 1696) (Powys). The examination was nonetheless admitted on a closely divided vote after several of those present opined that the common-law rules of procedure did not apply to parliamentary attainder proceedings—one speaker even admitting that the evidence would normally be inadmissible. Fenwick was condemned, but the proceedings "must have burned into the general consciousness the vital importance of the rule securing the right of cross-examination." *Id.*, § 1364, at 22; cf. *Carmell v. Texas*, 529 U.S. 513, 526-530 (2000).

Paine had settled the rule requiring a prior opportunity for cross-examination as a matter of common law, but some doubts remained over whether the Marian statutes prescribed an exception to it in felony cases. The statutes did not identify the circumstances under which examinations were admissible, and some inferred that no prior opportunity for cross-examination was required. Many who expressed this view acknowledged that it meant the statutes were in derogation of the common law. Nevertheless, by 1791 (the year the Sixth Amendment was ratified), courts were applying the cross-examination rule even to examinations by justices of the peace in felony cases. Early 19th-century treatises confirm that requirement....

B

Controversial examination practices were also used in the Colonies. Early in the 18th century, for example, the Virginia Council protested against the Governor for having "privately issued several commissions to examine witnesses against particular men *ex parte*," complaining that "the person accused is not admitted to be confronted with, or defend himself against his defamers." A Memorial Concerning the Maladministrations of His Excellency Francis Nicholson, reprinted in 9 English Historical Documents 253, 257 (D. Douglas ed.1955)....

Many declarations of rights adopted around the time of the Revolution guaranteed a right of confrontation. The proposed Federal Constitution, however, did not. At the Massachusetts ratifying convention, Abraham Holmes objected to this omission precisely on the ground that it would lead to civil-law practices: "The mode of trial is altogether indetermined; ... whether [the defendant] is to be allowed to confront the witnesses, and have the advantage of cross-examination, we are not yet told.... [W]e shall find Congress possessed of powers enabling them to institute judicatories little less inauspicious than a certain tribunal in Spain, ... the *Inquisition*." 2 Debates on the Federal Constitution 110-111 (J. Elliot 2d ed. 1863).... The First Congress responded by including the Confrontation Clause in the proposal that became the Sixth Amendment....

III

This history supports two inferences about the meaning of the Sixth Amendment.

A

First, the principal evil at which the Confrontation Clause was directed was the civil-law mode of criminal procedure, and particularly its use of *ex parte* examinations as evidence against the accused. It was these practices that the Crown deployed in notorious treason cases like Raleigh's; that the Marian statutes invited; that English law's assertion of a right to confrontation was meant to prohibit; and that the founding-era rhetoric decried. The Sixth Amendment must be interpreted with this focus in mind....

This focus also suggests that not all hearsay implicates the Sixth Amendment's core concerns. An off-hand, overheard remark might be unreliable evidence and thus a good candidate for exclusion under hearsay rules, but it bears little resemblance to the civil-law abuses the Confrontation Clause targeted. On the other hand, *ex parte* examinations might sometimes be admissible under modern hearsay rules, but the Framers certainly would not have condoned them.

The text of the Confrontation Clause reflects this focus. It applies to "witnesses" against the accused—in other words, those who "bear testimony." 2 N. Webster, An American Dictionary of the English Language (1828). "Testimony," in turn, is typically "[a] solemn declaration or affirmation made for the purpose of establishing or proving some fact." *Ibid.* An accuser who makes a formal statement to government officers bears testimony in a sense that a person who makes a casual remark to an acquaintance does not. The constitutional text, like the history underlying the common-law right of confrontation, thus reflects an especially acute concern with a specific type of out-of-court statement.

Various formulations of this core class of "testimonial" statements exist: "*ex parte* in-court testimony or its functional equivalent—that is, material such as affidavits, custodial examinations, prior testimony that the defendant was unable to cross-examine, or similar pretrial statements that declarants would reasonably expect to be used prosecutorially," Brief for Petitioner 23; "extrajudicial statements ... contained in formalized testimonial materials, such as affidavits, depositions, prior testimony, or confessions," *White v. Illinois,* 502 U.S. 346, 365 (1992) (THOMAS, J., joined by SCALIA, J., concurring in part and concurring in judgment); "statements that were made under circumstances which would lead an objective witness reasonably to believe that the statement would be available for use at a later trial," Brief for National Association of Criminal Defense Lawyers et al. as *Amici Curiae* 3. These formulations all share a common nucleus and then define the Clause's coverage at various levels of abstraction around it. Regardless of the precise articulation, some statements qualify under any definition—for example, *ex parte* testimony at a preliminary hearing.

Statements taken by police officers in the course of interrogations are also testimonial under even a narrow standard. Police interrogations bear a striking resemblance to examinations by justices of the peace in England. The statements are not *sworn* testimony, but the absence of oath was not dispositive. Cobham's examination was unsworn, yet Raleigh's trial has long been thought a paradigmatic confrontation violation....

That interrogators are police officers rather than magistrates does not change the picture either. Justices of the peace conducting examinations under the Marian statutes were not magistrates as we understand that office today, but had an essentially investigative and prosecutorial function. England did not have a professional police force until the 19th century, so it is not surprising that other government officers performed the investigative functions now associated primarily with the police. The involvement of government officers in the production of testimonial evidence presents the same risk, whether the officers are police or justices of the peace.

In sum, even if the Sixth Amendment is not solely concerned with testimonial hearsay, that is its primary object, and interrogations by law enforcement officers fall squarely within that class.[4]

B

The historical record also supports a second proposition: that the Framers would not have allowed admission of testimonial statements of a witness who did not appear at trial unless he was unavailable to testify, and the defendant had had a prior opportunity for cross-examination. The text of the Sixth Amendment does not suggest any open-ended exceptions from the confrontation requirement to be developed by the courts. Rather, the "right ... to be confronted with the witnesses against him," Amdt. 6, is most naturally read as a reference to the right of confrontation at common law, admitting only those exceptions established at the time of the founding. See *Mattox v. United States,* 156 U.S. 237, 243 (1895). As the English authorities above reveal, the common law in 1791 conditioned admissibility of an absent witness's examination on unavailability and a prior opportunity to cross-examine. The Sixth Amendment therefore incorporates those limitations. The numerous early state decisions applying the same test confirm that these principles were received as part of the common law in this country.

We do not read the historical sources to say that a prior opportunity to cross-examine was merely a sufficient, rather than a necessary, condition for admissibility of testimonial statements. They suggest that this requirement was dispositive, and not merely one of several ways to establish reliability. This is not to deny, as THE CHIEF JUSTICE notes, that "[t]here were always exceptions to the general rule of exclusion" of hearsay evidence. Several had become well established by 1791. See 3 Wigmore § 1397, at 101; Brief for United States as *Amicus Curiae* 13, n. 5. But there is scant evidence that exceptions were invoked to admit *testimonial* statements against the accused in a *criminal* case.[6] Most of the hearsay exceptions covered statements that by their nature were not testimonial—for example, business records or statements in furtherance of a conspiracy. We do not infer from these that the Framers thought exceptions would apply even to prior testimony.[7]

---

4. We use the term "interrogation" in its colloquial, rather than any technical legal, sense. Just as various definitions of "testimonial" exist, one can imagine various definitions of "interrogation," and we need not select among them in this case. Sylvia's recorded statement, knowingly given in response to structured police questioning, qualifies under any conceivable definition.

6. The one deviation we have found involves dying declarations. The existence of that exception as a general rule of criminal hearsay law cannot be disputed. See, *e.g., Mattox v. United States,* 156 U.S. 237, 243-244 (1895). Although many dying declarations may not be testimonial, there is authority for admitting even those that clearly are. We need not decide in this case whether the Sixth Amendment incorporates an exception for testimonial dying declarations. If this exception must be accepted on historical grounds, it is *sui generis.*

7. We cannot agree with THE CHIEF JUSTICE that the fact "[t]hat a statement might be testimonial does nothing to undermine the wisdom of one of these [hearsay] exceptions." Involvement of government officers in the production of testimony with an eye toward trial presents unique potential for prosecutorial abuse-a fact borne out time and again throughout a history with which the Framers were keenly familiar. This consideration does not evaporate when testimony happens to fall within some broad, modern hearsay exception, even if that exception might be justifiable in other circumstances.

IV

Our case law has been largely consistent with these two principles. Our leading early decision, for example, involved a deceased witness's prior trial testimony. *Mattox v. United States*, 156 U.S. 237 (1895). In allowing the statement to be admitted, we relied on the fact that the defendant had had, at the first trial, an adequate opportunity to confront the witness: "The substance of the constitutional protection is preserved to the prisoner in the advantage he has once had of seeing the witness face to face, and of subjecting him to the ordeal of a cross-examination. This, the law says, he shall under no circumstances be deprived of...." *Id.*, at 244.

Our later cases conform to *Mattox's* holding that prior trial or preliminary hearing testimony is admissible only if the defendant had an adequate opportunity to cross-examine. Even where the defendant had such an opportunity, we excluded the testimony where the government had not established unavailability of the witness. We similarly excluded accomplice confessions where the defendant had no opportunity to cross-examine. In contrast, we considered reliability factors beyond prior opportunity for cross-examination when the hearsay statement at issue was not testimonial.

Even our recent cases, in their outcomes, hew closely to the traditional line. *Ohio v. Roberts*, 448 U.S., at 67-70, admitted testimony from a preliminary hearing at which the defendant had examined the witness. *Lilly v. Virginia*, 527 U.S. 116, excluded testimonial statements that the defendant had had no opportunity to test by cross-examination. And *Bourjaily v. United States*, 483 U.S. 171, 181-184 (1987), admitted statements made unwittingly to a Federal Bureau of Investigation informant after applying a more general test that did *not* make prior cross-examination an indispensable requirement.[8] ...

Our cases have thus remained faithful to the Framers' understanding: Testimonial statements of witnesses absent from trial have been admitted only where the declarant is unavailable, and only where the defendant has had a prior opportunity to cross-examine.[9]

V

Although the results of our decisions have generally been faithful to the original meaning of the Confrontation Clause, the same cannot be said of our rationales. *Roberts* conditions the admissibility of all hearsay evidence on whether it falls under a "firmly rooted hearsay exception" or bears "particularized guarantees of trustworthiness." 448 U.S., at 66. This test departs from the historical principles identified above in two respects.

---

8. One case arguably in tension with the rule requiring a prior opportunity for cross-examination when the proffered statement is testimonial is *White v. Illinois*, 502 U.S. 346 (1992), which involved, *inter alia*, statements of a child victim to an investigating police officer admitted as spontaneous declarations. It is questionable whether testimonial statements would ever have been admissible on that ground in 1791; to the extent the hearsay exception for spontaneous declarations existed at all, it required that the statements be made "immediat[ely] upon the hurt received, and before [the declarant] had time to devise or contrive any thing for her own advantage." *Thompson v. Trevanion,* Skin. 402, 90 Eng. Rep. 179 (K.B.1693). In any case, the only question presented in *White* was whether the Confrontation Clause imposed an unavailability requirement on the types of hearsay at issue. The holding did not address the question whether certain of the statements, because they were testimonial, had to be excluded *even if* the witness was unavailable. We "[took] as a given ... that the testimony properly falls within the relevant hearsay exceptions." *Id.*, at 351, n. 4.

9. ... [W]e reiterate that, when the declarant appears for cross-examination at trial, the Confrontation Clause places no constraints at all on the use of his prior testimonial statements.

First, it is too broad: It applies the same mode of analysis whether or not the hearsay consists of *ex parte* testimony. This often results in close constitutional scrutiny in cases that are far removed from the core concerns of the Clause. At the same time, however, the test is too narrow: It admits statements that *do* consist of *ex parte* testimony upon a mere finding of reliability. This malleable standard often fails to protect against paradigmatic confrontation violations.

Members of this Court and academics have suggested that we revise our doctrine to reflect more accurately the original understanding of the Clause. They offer two proposals: First, that we apply the Confrontation Clause only to testimonial statements, leaving the remainder to regulation by hearsay law—thus eliminating the overbreadth referred to above. Second, that we impose an absolute bar to statements that are testimonial, absent a prior opportunity to cross-examine—thus eliminating the excessive narrowness referred to above.

In *White,* we considered the first proposal and rejected it. 502 U.S., at 352-353. Although our analysis in this case casts doubt on that holding, we need not definitively resolve whether it survives our decision today, because Sylvia Crawford's statement is testimonial under any definition. This case does, however, squarely implicate the second proposal.

A

Where testimonial statements are involved, we do not think the Framers meant to leave the Sixth Amendment's protection to the vagaries of the rules of evidence, much less to amorphous notions of "reliability." Certainly none of the authorities discussed above acknowledges any general reliability exception to the common-law rule. Admitting statements deemed reliable by a judge is fundamentally at odds with the right of confrontation. To be sure, the Clause's ultimate goal is to ensure reliability of evidence, but it is a procedural rather than a substantive guarantee. It commands, not that evidence be reliable, but that reliability be assessed in a particular manner: by testing in the crucible of cross-examination. The Clause thus reflects a judgment, not only about the desirability of reliable evidence (a point on which there could be little dissent), but about how reliability can best be determined. Cf. 3 Blackstone, Commentaries, at 373 ("This open examination of witnesses ... is much more conducive to the clearing up of truth").

The *Roberts* test allows a jury to hear evidence, untested by the adversary process, based on a mere judicial determination of reliability. It thus replaces the constitutionally prescribed method of assessing reliability with a wholly foreign one. In this respect, it is very different from exceptions to the Confrontation Clause that make no claim to be a surrogate means of assessing reliability. For example, the rule of forfeiture by wrongdoing (which we accept) extinguishes confrontation claims on essentially equitable grounds; it does not purport to be an alternative means of determining reliability....

Dispensing with confrontation because testimony is obviously reliable is akin to dispensing with jury trial because a defendant is obviously guilty. This is not what the Sixth Amendment prescribes.

B

The legacy of *Roberts* in other courts vindicates the Framers' wisdom in rejecting a general reliability exception. The framework is so unpredictable that it fails to provide meaningful protection from even core confrontation violations.

Reliability is an amorphous, if not entirely subjective, concept. There are countless factors bearing on whether a statement is reliable; the nine-factor balancing test applied by the Court of Appeals below is representative. See, *e.g., People v. Farrell,* 34 P.3d 401, 406-407 (Colo.2001) (eight-factor test). Whether a statement is deemed reliable depends heavily on which factors the judge considers and how much weight he accords each of them. Some courts wind up attaching the same significance to opposite facts. For example, the Colorado Supreme Court held a statement more reliable because its inculpation of the defendant was "detailed," *id.,* at 407, while the Fourth Circuit found a statement more reliable because the portion implicating another was "fleeting," *United States v. Photogrammetric Data Servs., Inc.,* 259 F.3d 229, 245 (4th Cir. 2001). The Virginia Court of Appeals found a statement more reliable because the witness was in custody and charged with a crime (thus making the statement more obviously against her penal interest), *see Nowlin v. Commonwealth,* 40 Va.App. 327, 335-338, 579 S.E.2d 367, 371-372 (2003), while the Wisconsin Court of Appeals found a statement more reliable because the witness was *not* in custody and *not* a suspect, *see State v. Bintz,* 2002 WI App. 204, ¶ 13, 257 Wis.2d 177, ¶ 13, 650 N.W.2d 913, ¶ 13. Finally, the Colorado Supreme Court in one case found a statement more reliable because it was given "immediately after" the events at issue, *Farrell, supra,* at 407, while that same court, in another case, found a statement more reliable because two years had elapsed, *Stevens v. People,* 29 P.3d 305, 316 (Colo.2001).

The unpardonable vice of the *Roberts* test, however, is not its unpredictability, but its demonstrated capacity to admit core testimonial statements that the Confrontation Clause plainly meant to exclude. Despite the plurality's speculation in *Lilly,* 527 U.S., at 137, that it was "highly unlikely" that accomplice confessions implicating the accused could survive *Roberts,* courts continue routinely to admit them. One recent study found that, after *Lilly,* appellate courts admitted accomplice statements to the authorities in 25 out of 70 cases— more than one-third of the time. Kirst, Appellate Court Answers to the Confrontation Questions in *Lilly v. Virginia,* 53 Syracuse L.Rev. 87, 105 (2003). Courts have invoked *Roberts* to admit other sorts of plainly testimonial statements despite the absence of any opportunity to cross-examine. . . .

C

Roberts' failings were on full display in the proceedings below. Sylvia Crawford made her statement while in police custody, herself a potential suspect in the case. Indeed, she had been told that whether she would be released "depend[ed] on how the investigation continues." In response to often leading questions from police detectives, she implicated her husband in Lee's stabbing and at least arguably undermined his self-defense claim. Despite all this, the trial court admitted her statement, listing several reasons why it was reliable. In its opinion reversing, the Court of Appeals listed several *other* reasons why the statement was *not* reliable. Finally, the State Supreme Court relied exclusively on the interlocking character of the statement and disregarded every other factor the lower courts had considered. The case is thus a self-contained demonstration of *Roberts'* unpredictable and inconsistent application.

Each of the courts also made assumptions that cross-examination might well have undermined. The trial court, for example, stated that Sylvia Crawford's statement was reliable because she was an eyewitness with direct knowledge of the events. But Sylvia at one point told the police that she had "shut [her] eyes and . . . didn't really watch" part of the fight, and that she was "in shock." The trial court also buttressed its reliability finding by claiming that Sylvia was "being questioned by law enforcement, and, thus, the [questioner] is . . . neutral to her and not someone who would be inclined to advance her interests and shade her version of the truth unfavorably toward the defendant." The Framers would be astounded to learn that *ex parte* testimony could be admitted against a criminal defendant because it was elicited by "neutral" government officers. But even if the court's assessment of the officer's motives was accurate, it says nothing about Sylvia's perception of her situation. Only cross-examination could reveal that....

We readily concede that we could resolve this case by simply reweighing the "reliability factors" under *Roberts* and finding that Sylvia Crawford's statement falls short. But we view this as one of those rare cases in which the result below is so improbable that it reveals a fundamental failure on our part to interpret the Constitution in a way that secures its intended constraint on judicial discretion. Moreover, to reverse the Washington Supreme Court's decision after conducting our own reliability analysis would perpetuate, not avoid, what the Sixth Amendment condemns. The Constitution prescribes a procedure for determining the reliability of testimony in criminal trials, and we, no less than the state courts, lack authority to replace it with one of our own devising.

We have no doubt that the courts below were acting in utmost good faith when they found reliability. The Framers, however, would not have been content to indulge this assumption. They knew that judges, like other government officers, could not always be trusted to safeguard the rights of the people; the likes of the dread Lord Jeffreys were not yet too distant a memory. They were loath to leave too much discretion in judicial hands. Cf. U.S. Const., Amdt. 6 (criminal jury trial); Amdt. 7 (civil jury trial). By replacing categorical constitutional guarantees with open-ended balancing tests, we do violence to their design. Vague standards are manipulable, and, while that might be a small concern in run-of-the-mill assault prosecutions like this one, the Framers had an eye toward politically charged cases like Raleigh's—great state trials where the impartiality of even those at the highest levels of the judiciary might not be so clear. It is difficult to imagine *Roberts'* providing any meaningful protection in those circumstances.

    ...

Where nontestimonial hearsay is at issue, it is wholly consistent with the Framers' design to afford the States flexibility in their development of hearsay law—as does *Roberts*, and as would an approach that exempted such statements from Confrontation Clause scrutiny altogether. Where testimonial evidence is at issue, however, the Sixth Amendment demands what the common law required: unavailability and a prior opportunity for cross-examination. We leave for another day any effort to spell out a comprehensive definition of "testimonial." Whatever else the term covers, it applies at a minimum to prior testimony at a preliminary hearing, before a grand jury, or at a former trial; and to police interrogations. These are the modern practices with closest kinship to the abuses at which the Confrontation Clause was directed.

In this case, the State admitted Sylvia's testimonial statement against petitioner, despite the fact that he had no opportunity to cross-examine her. That alone is sufficient to make out a violation of the Sixth Amendment. *Roberts* notwithstanding, we decline to mine the record in search of indicia of reliability. Where testimonial statements are at issue, the only indicium of reliability sufficient to satisfy constitutional demands is the one the Constitution actually prescribes: confrontation.

The judgment of the Washington Supreme Court is reversed, and the case is remanded for further proceedings not inconsistent with this opinion.

It is so ordered.

Chief Justice REHNQUIST, with whom Justice O'CONNOR joins, concurring in the judgment.

I dissent from the Court's decision to overrule *Ohio v. Roberts,* 448 U.S. 56, (1980). I believe that the Court's adoption of a new interpretation of the Confrontation Clause is not backed by sufficiently persuasive reasoning to overrule long-established precedent. Its decision casts a mantle of uncertainty over future criminal trials in both federal and state courts, and is by no means necessary to decide the present case.

The Court's distinction between testimonial and nontestimonial statements, contrary to its claim, is no better rooted in history than our current doctrine. Under the common law, although the courts were far from consistent, out-of-court statements made by someone other than the accused and not taken under oath, unlike *ex parte* depositions or affidavits, were generally not considered substantive evidence upon which a conviction could be based....

Thus, while I agree that the Framers were mainly concerned about sworn affidavits and depositions, it does not follow that they were similarly concerned about the Court's broader category of testimonial statements. As far as I can tell, unsworn testimonial statements were treated no differently at common law than were nontestimonial statements, and it seems to me any classification of statements as testimonial beyond that of sworn affidavits and depositions will be somewhat arbitrary, merely a proxy for what the Framers might have intended had such evidence been liberally admitted as substantive evidence like it is today.

I therefore see no reason why the distinction the Court draws is preferable to our precedent. Starting with Chief Justice Marshall's interpretation as a Circuit Justice in 1807, 16 years after the ratification of the Sixth Amendment, *United States v. Burr,* 25 F.Cas. 187, 193 (No. 14,694) (CC Va. 1807), continuing with our cases in the late 19th century, *Mattox v. United States,* 156 U.S. 237, 243–244 (1895), and through today, *e.g., White v. Illinois,* 502 U.S. 346, 352–353, we have never drawn a distinction between testimonial and nontestimonial statements. And for that matter, neither has any other court of which I am aware. I see little value in trading our precedent for an imprecise approximation at this late date.

I am also not convinced that the Confrontation Clause categorically requires the exclusion of testimonial statements.... With respect to unsworn testimonial statements, there is no indication that once the hearsay rule was developed courts ever excluded these statements if they otherwise fell within a firmly rooted exception. Dying declarations are one example.

Between 1700 and 1800 the rules regarding the admissibility of out-of-court statements were still being developed. There were always exceptions to the general rule of exclusion, and it is not clear to me that the Framers categorically wanted to eliminate further ones. It is one thing to trace the right of confrontation back to the Roman Empire; it is quite another to conclude that such a right absolutely excludes a large category of evidence. It is an odd conclusion indeed to think that the Framers created a cut-and-dried rule with respect to the admissibility of testimonial statements when the law during their own time was not fully settled....

Exceptions to confrontation have always been derived from the experience that some out-of-court statements are just as reliable as cross-examined in-court testimony due to the circumstances under which they were made. We have recognized, for example, that co-conspirator statements simply "cannot be replicated, even if the declarant testifies to the same matters in court." *United States v. Inadi,* 475 U.S. 387, 395 (1986). Because the statements are made while the declarant and the accused are partners in an illegal enterprise, the statements are unlikely to be false and their admission "actually furthers the 'Confrontation Clause's very mission' which is to 'advance the accuracy of the truth-determining process in criminal trials.'" *Id.,* at 396. Similar reasons justify the introduction of spontaneous declarations, statements made in the course of procuring medical services, dying declarations, and countless other hearsay exceptions. That a statement might be testimonial does nothing to undermine the wisdom of one of these exceptions.

Indeed, cross-examination is a tool used to flesh out the truth, not an empty procedure. "[I]n a given instance [cross-examination may] be superfluous; it may be sufficiently clear, in that instance, that the statement offered is free enough from the risk of inaccuracy and untrustworthiness, so that the test of cross-examination would be a work of supererogation." 5 Wigmore § 1420, at 251. In such a case, as we noted over 100 years ago, "The law in its wisdom declares that the rights of the public shall not be wholly sacrificed in order that an incidental benefit may be preserved to the accused." *Mattox*, 156 U.S., at 243. By creating an immutable category of excluded evidence, the Court adds little to a trial's truth-finding function and ignores this longstanding guidance.

In choosing the path it does, the Court of course overrules *Ohio v. Roberts*, 448 U.S. 56, (1980), a case decided nearly a quarter of a century ago. *Stare decisis* is not an inexorable command in the area of constitutional law, but by and large, it "is the preferred course because it promotes the evenhanded, predictable, and consistent development of legal principles, fosters reliance on judicial decisions, and contributes to the actual and perceived integrity of the judicial process[.]" And in making this appraisal, doubt that the new rule is indeed the "right" one should surely be weighed in the balance. Though there are no vested interests involved, unresolved questions for the future of everyday criminal trials throughout the country surely counsel the same sort of caution. The Court grandly declares that "[w]e leave for another day any effort to spell out a comprehensive definition of 'testimonial.'" But the thousands of federal prosecutors and the tens of thousands of state prosecutors need answers as to what beyond the specific kinds of "testimony" the Court lists, is covered by the new rule. They need them now, not months or years from now. Rules of criminal evidence are applied every day in courts throughout the country, and parties should not be left in the dark in this manner.

To its credit, the Court's analysis of "testimony" excludes at least some hearsay exceptions, such as business records and official records. To hold otherwise would require numerous additional witnesses without any apparent gain in the truth-seeking process. Likewise to the Court's credit is its implicit recognition that the mistaken application of its new rule by courts which guess wrong as to the scope of the rule is subject to harmless-error analysis.

But these are palliatives to what I believe is a mistaken change of course. It is a change of course not in the least necessary to reverse the judgment of the Supreme Court of Washington in this case. The result the Court reaches follows inexorably from *Roberts* and its progeny without any need for overruling that line of cases. In *Idaho v. Wright*, 497 U.S. 805, 820-824 (1990), we held that an out-of-court statement was not admissible simply because the truthfulness of that statement was corroborated by other evidence at trial. As the Court notes, the Supreme Court of Washington gave decisive weight to the "interlocking nature of the two statements." No re-weighing of the "reliability factors," which is hypothesized by the Court is required to reverse the judgment here. A citation to *Idaho v. Wright*, would suffice. For the reasons stated, I believe that this would be a far preferable course for the Court to take here.

Focus Questions: *Davis v. Washington* and *Hammon v. Indiana*

- The Court is deciding two separate cases here—what is the distinction between the facts of each case and how do they compare in the court's application of its definition of testimonial statements?

- How does the Court further define "testimonial" than what was set out in *Crawford*? Is this sufficient direction for determining whether or not a statement is testimonial?

- The court uses the facts from *Crawford* to determine whether each case presents testimonial statements—what facts in Crawford are most important in its comparisons with the current two cases?

- Justice Thomas offers a different approach to resolving the determination of testimonial statements—how does it compare to the majority opinion approach? Which approach favors broader admissibility? How so?

Davis v. Washington
Hammon v. Indiana
547 U.S. 813 (2006)

SCALIA, J., delivered the opinion of the Court, in which ROBERTS, C. J., and STEVENS, KENNEDY, SOUTER, GINSBURG, BREYER, and ALITO, JJ., joined. THOMAS, J., filed an opinion concurring in the judgment in part and dissenting in part.

These cases require us to determine when statements made to law enforcement personnel during a 911 call or at a crime scene are "testimonial" and thus subject to the requirements of the Sixth Amendment's Confrontation Clause.

I
A

The relevant statements in *Davis v. Washington* were made to a 911 emergency operator on February 1, 2001. When the operator answered the initial call, the connection terminated before anyone spoke. She reversed the call, and Michelle McCottry answered. In the ensuing conversation, the operator ascertained that McCottry was involved in a domestic disturbance with her former boyfriend Adrian Davis, the petitioner in this case:

"911 Operator: Hello.

"Complainant: Hello.

"911 Operator: What's going on?

"Complainant: He's here jumpin' on me again.

"911 Operator: Okay. Listen to me carefully. Are you in a house or an apartment?

"Complainant: I'm in a house.

"911 Operator: Are there any weapons?

"Complainant: No. He's usin' his fists.

"911 Operator: Okay. Has he been drinking?

"Complainant: No.

"911 Operator: Okay, sweetie. I've got help started. Stay on the line with me, okay?

"Complainant: I'm on the line.

"911 Operator: Listen to me carefully. Do you know his last name?

"Complainant: It's Davis.

"911 Operator: Davis? Okay, what's his first name?

"Complainant: Adrian

"911 Operator: What is it?

"Complainant: Adrian.

"911 Operator: Adrian?

"Complainant: Yeah.

"911 Operator: Okay. What's his middle initial?

"Complainant: Martell. He's runnin' now."

As the conversation continued, the operator learned that Davis had "just r[un] out the door" after hitting McCottry, and that he was leaving in a car with someone else. McCottry started talking, but the operator cut her off, saying, "Stop talking and answer my questions." She then gathered more information about Davis (including his birthday), and learned that Davis had told McCottry that his purpose in coming to the house was "to get his stuff," since McCottry was moving. McCottry described the context of the assault, after which the operator told her that the police were on their way. "They're gonna check the area for him first," the operator said, "and then they're gonna come talk to you."

The police arrived within four minutes of the 911 call and observed McCottry's shaken state, the "fresh injuries on her forearm and her face," and her "frantic efforts to gather her belongings and her children so that they could leave the residence." 154 Wash.2d 291, 296, 111 P.3d 844, 847 (2005) (en banc).

The State charged Davis with felony violation of a domestic no-contact order. "The State's only witnesses were the two police officers who responded to the 911 call. Both officers testified that McCottry exhibited injuries that appeared to be recent, but neither officer could testify as to the cause of the injuries." *Ibid.* McCottry presumably could have testified as to whether Davis was her assailant, but she did not appear. Over Davis's objection, based on the Confrontation Clause of the Sixth Amendment, the trial court admitted the recording of her exchange with the 911 operator, and the jury convicted him. The Washington Court of Appeals affirmed. The Supreme Court of Washington, with one dissenting justice, also affirmed, concluding that the portion of the 911 conversation in which McCottry identified Davis was not testimonial, and that if other portions of the conversation were testimonial, admitting them was harmless beyond a reasonable doubt. We granted certiorari.

B

In *Hammon v. Indiana*, police responded late on the night of February 26, 2003, to a "reported domestic disturbance" at the home of Hershel and Amy Hammon. 829 N.E.2d 444, 446 (Ind.2005). They found Amy alone on the front porch, appearing "'somewhat frightened,'" but she told them that "'nothing was the matter,'" *id.*, at 446, 447. She gave them permission to enter the house, where an officer saw "a gas heating unit in the corner of the living room" that had "flames coming out of the ... partial glass front. There were pieces of glass on the ground in front of it and there was flame emitting from the front of the heating unit."

Hershel, meanwhile, was in the kitchen. He told the police "that he and his wife had 'been in an argument' but 'everything was fine now' and the argument 'never became physical.'" 829 N.E.2d, at 447. By this point Amy had come back inside. One of the officers remained with Hershel; the other went to the living room to talk with Amy, and "again asked [her] what had occurred." *Ibid.* Hershel made several attempts to participate in Amy's conversation with the police, but was rebuffed. The officer later testified that Hershel "became angry when I insisted that [he] stay separated from Mrs. Hammon so that we can investigate what had happened." *Id.*, at 34. After hearing Amy's account, the officer "had her fill out and sign a battery affidavit." *Id.*, at 18. Amy handwrote the following: "Broke our Furnace & shoved me down on the floor into the broken glass. Hit me in the chest and threw me down. Broke our lamps & phone. Tore up my van where I couldn't leave the house. Attacked my daughter." *Id.*, at 2.

The State charged Hershel with domestic battery and with violating his probation. Amy was subpoenaed, but she did not appear at his subsequent bench trial. The State called the officer who had questioned Amy, and asked him to recount what Amy told him and to authenticate the affidavit. Hershel's counsel repeatedly objected to the admission of this evidence. At one point, after hearing the prosecutor defend the affidavit because it was made "under oath," defense counsel said, "That doesn't give us the opportunity to cross examine [the] person who allegedly drafted it. Makes me mad." *Id.*, at 19. Nonetheless, the trial court admitted the affidavit as a "present sense impression," *id.*, at 20, and Amy's statements as "excited utterances" that "are expressly permitted in these kinds of cases even if the declarant is not available to testify," *id.*, at 40. The officer thus testified that Amy

> "informed me that she and Hershel had been in an argument. That he became irrate [sic] over the fact of their daughter going to a boyfriend's house. The argument became ... physical after being verbal and she informed me that Mr. Hammon, during the verbal part of the argument was breaking things in the living room and I believe she stated he broke the phone, broke the lamp, broke the front of the heater. When it became physical he threw her down into the glass of the heater.
>
> ...
>
> "She informed me Mr. Hammon had pushed her onto the ground, had shoved her head into the broken glass of the heater and that he had punched her in the chest twice I believe." *Id.*, at 17-18.

The trial judge found Hershel guilty on both charges, and the Indiana Court of Appeals affirmed in relevant part. The Indiana Supreme Court also affirmed, concluding that Amy's statement was admissible for state-law purposes as an excited utterance, 829 N.E.2d, at 449; that "a 'testimonial' statement is one given or taken in significant part for purposes of preserving it for potential future use in legal proceedings," where "the motivations of the questioner and declarant are the central concerns," *id.*, at 456, 457; and that Amy's oral statement was not "testimonial" under these standards, *id.*, at 458. It also concluded that, although the affidavit was testimonial and thus wrongly admitted, it was harmless beyond a reasonable doubt, largely because the trial was to the bench. *Id.*, at 458-459. We granted certiorari.

II

The Confrontation Clause of the Sixth Amendment provides: "In all criminal prosecutions, the accused shall enjoy the right ... to be confronted with the witnesses against him." In *Crawford v. Washington*, 541 U.S. 36, 53-54 (2004), we held that this provision bars "admission of testimonial statements of a witness who did not appear at trial unless he was unavailable to testify, and the defendant had had a prior opportunity for cross-examination." A critical portion of this holding, and the portion central to resolution of the two cases now before us, is the phrase "testimonial statements." Only statements of this sort cause the declarant to be a "witness" within the meaning of the Confrontation Clause. It is the testimonial character of the statement that separates it from other hearsay that, while subject to traditional limitations upon hearsay evidence, is not subject to the Confrontation Clause.

Our opinion in *Crawford* set forth "[v]arious formulations" of the core class of " 'testimonial' " statements, but found it unnecessary to endorse any of them, because "some statements qualify under any definition," *id.*, at 52. Among those, we said, were "[s]tatements taken by police officers in the course of interrogations," *ibid.* The questioning that generated the deponent's statement in *Crawford*—which was made and recorded while she was in police custody, after having been given *Miranda* warnings as a possible suspect herself— "qualifies under any conceivable definition" of an " 'interrogation,' " 541 U.S., at 53, n. 4. We therefore did not define that term, except to say that "[w]e use [it] … in its colloquial, rather than any technical legal, sense," and that "one can imagine various definitions…, and we need not select among them in this case." *Ibid.* The character of the statements in the present cases is not as clear, and these cases require us to determine more precisely which police interrogations produce testimony.

Without attempting to produce an exhaustive classification of all conceivable statements -or even all conceivable statements in response to police interrogation—as either testimonial or nontestimonial, it suffices to decide the present cases to hold as follows: Statements are nontestimonial when made in the course of police interrogation under circumstances objectively indicating that the primary purpose of the interrogation is to enable police assistance to meet an ongoing emergency. They are testimonial when the circumstances objectively indicate that there is no such ongoing emergency, and that the primary purpose of the interrogation is to establish or prove past events potentially relevant to later criminal prosecution.[1]

III
A

In *Crawford,* it sufficed for resolution of the case before us to determine that "even if the Sixth Amendment is not solely concerned with testimonial hearsay, that is its primary object, and interrogations by law enforcement officers fall squarely within that class." *Id.,* at 53. Moreover, as we have just described, the facts of that case spared us the need to define what we meant by "interrogations." The *Davis* case today does not permit us this luxury of indecision. The inquiries of a police operator in the course of a 911 call[2] are an interrogation in one sense, but not in a sense that "qualifies under any conceivable definition." We must decide, therefore, whether the Confrontation Clause applies only to testimonial hearsay; and, if so, whether the recording of a 911 call qualifies.

---

1. Our holding refers to interrogations because, as explained below, the statements in the cases presently before us are the products of interrogations-which in some circumstances tend to generate testimonial responses. This is not to imply, however, that statements made in the absence of any interrogation are necessarily nontestimonial. The Framers were no more willing to exempt from cross-examination volunteered testimony or answers to open-ended questions than they were to exempt answers to detailed interrogation.… And of course even when interrogation exists, it is in the final analysis the declarant's statements, not the interrogator's questions, that the Confrontation Clause requires us to evaluate.

2. If 911 operators are not themselves law enforcement officers, they may at least be agents of law enforcement when they conduct interrogations of 911 callers. For purposes of this opinion (and without deciding the point), we consider their acts to be acts of the police. As in *Crawford v. Washington,* 541 U.S. 36 (2004), therefore, our holding today makes it unnecessary to consider whether and when statements made to someone other than law enforcement personnel are "testimonial."

The answer to the first question was suggested in *Crawford,* even if not explicitly held:

> "The text of the Confrontation Clause reflects this focus [on testimonial hearsay]. It applies to 'witnesses' against the accused—in other words, those who 'bear testimony.' 1 N. Webster, An American Dictionary of the English Language (1828). 'Testimony,' in turn, is typically 'a solemn declaration or affirmation made for the purpose of establishing or proving some fact.' *Ibid.* An accuser who makes a formal statement to government officers bears testimony in a sense that a person who makes a casual remark to an acquaintance does not." 541 U.S., at 51.

A limitation so clearly reflected in the text of the constitutional provision must fairly be said to mark out not merely its "core," but its perimeter....

The question before us in *Davis,* then, is whether, objectively considered, the interrogation that took place in the course of the 911 call produced testimonial statements. When we said in *Crawford, supra,* at 53, that "interrogations by law enforcement officers fall squarely within [the] class" of testimonial hearsay, we had immediately in mind (for that was the case before us) interrogations solely directed at establishing the facts of a past crime, in order to identify (or provide evidence to convict) the perpetrator. The product of such interrogation, whether reduced to a writing signed by the declarant or embedded in the memory (and perhaps notes) of the interrogating officer, is testimonial. It is, in the terms of the 1828 American dictionary quoted in *Crawford,* " '[a] solemn declaration or affirmation made for the purpose of establishing or proving some fact.' " 541 U.S., at 51. (The solemnity of even an oral declaration of relevant past fact to an investigating officer is well enough established by the severe consequences that can attend a deliberate falsehood. See, *e.g., United States v. Stewart,* 433 F.3d 273, 288 (2nd Cir. 2006) (false statements made to federal investigators violate 18 U.S.C. § 1001)). A 911 call, on the other hand, and at least the initial interrogation conducted in connection with a 911 call, is ordinarily not designed primarily to "establis[h] or prov[e]" some past fact, but to describe current circumstances requiring police assistance.

The difference between the interrogation in *Davis* and the one in *Crawford* is apparent on the face of things. In *Davis,* McCottry was speaking about events *as they were actually happening,* rather than "describ[ing] past events," *Lilly v. Virginia,* 527 U.S. 116, 137 (1999) (plurality opinion). Sylvia Crawford's interrogation, on the other hand, took place hours after the events she described had occurred. Moreover, any reasonable listener would recognize that McCottry (unlike Sylvia Crawford) was facing an ongoing emergency. Although one *might* call 911 to provide a narrative report of a crime absent any imminent danger, McCottry's call was plainly a call for help against bona fide physical threat. Third, the nature of what was asked and answered in *Davis,* again viewed objectively, was such that the elicited statements were necessary to be able to *resolve* the present emergency, rather than simply to learn (as in *Crawford*) what had happened in the past. That is true even of the operator's effort to establish the identity of the assailant, so that the dispatched officers might know whether they would be encountering a violent felon. And finally, the difference in the level of formality between the two interviews is striking. Crawford was responding calmly, at the station house, to a series of questions, with the officer-interrogator taping and making notes of her answers; McCottry's frantic answers were provided over the phone, in an environment that was not tranquil, or even (as far as any reasonable 911 operator could make out) safe.

We conclude from all this that the circumstances of McCottry's interrogation objectively indicate its primary purpose was to enable police assistance to meet an ongoing emergency. She simply was not acting as a *witness;* she was not *testifying.* What she said was not "a weaker substitute for live testimony" at trial, *United States v. Inadi,* 475 U.S. 387, 394

(1986), like ... Sylvia Crawford's statement in *Crawford*. In each of those cases, the *ex parte* actors and the evidentiary products of the *ex parte* communication aligned perfectly with their courtroom analogues. McCottry's emergency statement does not. No "witness" goes into court to proclaim an emergency and seek help....

This is not to say that a conversation which begins as an interrogation to determine the need for emergency assistance cannot, as the Indiana Supreme Court put it, "evolve into testimonial statements," 829 N.E.2d, at 457, once that purpose has been achieved. In this case, for example, after the operator gained the information needed to address the exigency of the moment, the emergency appears to have ended (when Davis drove away from the premises). The operator then told McCottry to be quiet, and proceeded to pose a battery of questions. It could readily be maintained that, from that point on, McCottry's statements were testimonial, not unlike the "structured police questioning" that occurred in *Crawford*, 541 U.S., at 53, n. 4. This presents no great problem. Just as, for Fifth Amendment purposes, "police officers can and will distinguish almost instinctively between questions necessary to secure their own safety or the safety of the public and questions designed solely to elicit testimonial evidence from a suspect," *New York v. Quarles*, 467 U.S. 649, 658-659 (1984), trial courts will recognize the point at which, for Sixth Amendment purposes, statements in response to interrogations become testimonial. Through *in limine* procedure, they should redact or exclude the portions of any statement that have become testimonial, as they do, for example, with unduly prejudicial portions of otherwise admissible evidence. Davis's jury did not hear the *complete* 911 call, although it may well have heard some testimonial portions. We were asked to classify only McCottry's early statements identifying Davis as her assailant, and we agree with the Washington Supreme Court that they were not testimonial. That court also concluded that, even if later parts of the call were testimonial, their admission was harmless beyond a reasonable doubt. Davis does not challenge that holding, and we therefore assume it to be correct.

B

Determining the testimonial or nontestimonial character of the statements that were the product of the interrogation in *Hammon* is a much easier task, since they were not much different from the statements we found to be testimonial in *Crawford*. It is entirely clear from the circumstances that the interrogation was part of an investigation into possibly criminal past conduct—as, indeed, the testifying officer expressly acknowledged. There was no emergency in progress; the interrogating officer testified that he had heard no arguments or crashing and saw no one throw or break anything. When the officers first arrived, Amy told them that things were fine, and there was no immediate threat to her person. When the officer questioned Amy for the second time, and elicited the challenged statements, he was not seeking to determine (as in *Davis*) "what is happening," but rather "what happened." Objectively viewed, the primary, if not indeed the sole, purpose of the interrogation was to investigate a possible crime—which is, of course, precisely what the officer *should* have done.

It is true that the *Crawford* interrogation was more formal. It followed a *Miranda* warning, was tape-recorded, and took place at the station house. While these features certainly strengthened the statements' testimonial aspect—made it more objectively apparent, that is, that the purpose of the exercise was to nail down the truth about past criminal events—none was essential to the point. It was formal enough that Amy's interrogation was conducted in a separate room, away from her husband (who tried to intervene), with the officer receiving her replies for use in his "investigat[ion]." What we called the "striking resemblance" of the *Crawford* statement to civil-law *ex parte* examinations, 541 U.S., at 52, is shared by Amy's statement here. Both declarants were actively separated from the defendant—officers forcibly prevented Hershel from participating in the interrogation. Both statements deliberately recounted, in response to police questioning, how potentially criminal past events began and progressed. And both took place some time after the events described were over. Such statements under official interrogation are an obvious substitute for live testimony, because they do precisely *what a witness does* on direct examination; they are inherently testimonial.[5]

Both Indiana and the United States as *amicus curiae* argue that this case should be resolved much like *Davis*. For the reasons we find the comparison to *Crawford* compelling, we find the comparison to *Davis* unpersuasive. The statements in *Davis* were taken when McCottry was alone, not only unprotected by police (as Amy Hammon was protected), but apparently in immediate danger from Davis. She was seeking aid, not telling a story about the past. McCottry's present-tense statements showed immediacy; Amy's narrative of past events was delivered at some remove in time from the danger she described. And after Amy answered the officer's questions, he had her execute an affidavit, in order, he testified, "[t]o establish events that have occurred previously."

Although we necessarily reject the Indiana Supreme Court's implication that virtually any "initial inquiries" at the crime scene will not be testimonial, see 829 N.E.2d, at 453, 457, we do not hold the opposite—that *no* questions at the scene will yield nontestimonial answers. We have already observed of domestic disputes that "[o]fficers called to investigate ... need to know whom they are dealing with in order to assess the situation, the threat to their own safety, and possible danger to the potential victim." *Hiibel*, 542 U.S., at 186. Such exigencies may *often* mean that "initial inquiries" produce nontestimonial statements. But in cases like this one, where Amy's statements were neither a cry for help nor the provision of information enabling officers immediately to end a threatening situation, the fact that they were given at an alleged crime scene and were "initial inquiries" is immaterial.

IV

Respondents in both cases, joined by a number of their *amici*, contend that the nature of the offenses charged in these two cases—domestic violence—requires greater flexibility in the use of testimonial evidence. This particular type of crime is notoriously susceptible to intimidation or coercion of the victim to ensure that she does not testify at trial. When this occurs, the Confrontation Clause gives the criminal a windfall. We may not, however,

---

5. The dissent criticizes our test for being "neither workable nor a targeted attempt to reach the abuses forbidden by the [Confrontation] Clause," (THOMAS, J., concurring in judgment in part and dissenting in part). As to the former: We have acknowledged that our holding is not an "exhaustive classification of all conceivable statements-or even all conceivable statements in response to police interrogation," but rather a resolution of the cases before us and those like them. For *those* cases, the test is objective and quite "workable." The dissent, in attempting to formulate an exhaustive classification of its own, has not provided anything that deserves the description "workable"-unless one thinks that the distinction between "formal" and "informal" statements qualifies....

As for the charge that our holding is not a "targeted attempt to reach the abuses forbidden by the [Confrontation] Clause," which the dissent describes as the depositions taken by Marian magistrates, characterized by a high degree of formality: We do not dispute that formality is indeed essential to testimonial utterance. But we no longer have examining Marian magistrates; and we do have, as our 18th-century forebears did not, examining police officers who perform investigative and testimonial functions once performed by examining Marian magistrates. It imports sufficient formality, in our view, that lies to such officers are criminal offenses. Restricting the Confrontation Clause to the precise forms against which it was originally directed is a recipe for its extinction.

vitiate constitutional guarantees when they have the effect of allowing the guilty to go free. But when defendants seek to undermine the judicial process by procuring or coercing silence from witnesses and victims, the Sixth Amendment does not require courts to acquiesce. While defendants have no duty to assist the State in proving their guilt, they *do* have the duty to refrain from acting in ways that destroy the integrity of the criminal-trial system. We reiterate what we said in *Crawford:* that "the rule of forfeiture by wrongdoing ... extinguishes confrontation claims on essentially equitable grounds." 541 U.S., at 62. That is, one who obtains the absence of a witness by wrongdoing forfeits the constitutional right to confrontation.

We take no position on the standards necessary to demonstrate such forfeiture, but federal courts using Federal Rule of Evidence 804(b)(6), which codifies the forfeiture doctrine, have generally held the Government to the preponderance-of-the-evidence standard. State courts tend to follow the same practice. Moreover, if a hearing on forfeiture is required for instance, [one state court] observed that "hearsay evidence, including the unavailable witness's out-of-court statements, may be considered." *Commonwealth v. Edwards.,* 444 Mass. 526 at 545 (2005). The *Roberts* approach to the Confrontation Clause undoubtedly made recourse to this doctrine less necessary, because prosecutors could show the "reliability" of *ex parte* statements more easily than they could show the defendant's procurement of the witness's absence. *Crawford,* in overruling *Roberts,* did not destroy the ability of courts to protect the integrity of their proceedings.

We have determined that, absent a finding of forfeiture by wrongdoing, the Sixth Amendment operates to exclude Amy Hammon's affidavit. The Indiana courts may (if they are asked) determine on remand whether such a claim of forfeiture is properly raised and, if so, whether it is meritorious.

. . . .

We affirm the judgment of the Supreme Court of Washington. We reverse the judgment of the Supreme Court of Indiana, and remand the case to that court for proceedings not inconsistent with this opinion.

It is so ordered.

Justice THOMAS, concurring in the judgment in part and dissenting in part.

In *Crawford,* we abandoned the general reliability inquiry we had long employed to judge the admissibility of hearsay evidence under the Confrontation Clause, describing that inquiry as "*inherently,* and therefore *permanently,* unpredictable." *Id.,* at 68, n. 10 (emphasis in original). Today, a mere two years after the Court decided *Crawford,* it adopts an equally unpredictable test, under which district courts are charged with divining the "primary purpose" of police interrogations. Besides being difficult for courts to apply, this test characterizes as "testimonial," and therefore inadmissible, evidence that bears little resemblance to what we have recognized as the evidence targeted by the Confrontation Clause. Because neither of the cases before the Court today would implicate the Confrontation Clause under an appropriately targeted standard, I concur only in the judgment in *Davis v. Washington* and dissent from the Court's resolution of *Hammon v. Indiana.*

I

A

... The history surrounding the right to confrontation supports the conclusion that it was developed to target particular practices that occurred under the English bail and committal statutes passed during the reign of Queen Mary, namely, the "civil-law mode of criminal procedure, and particularly its use of *ex parte* examinations as evidence against the accused." *Crawford, supra,* at 43, 50....

In *Crawford,* we recognized that this history could be squared with the language of the Clause, giving rise to a workable, and more accurate, interpretation of the Clause. "'[W]itnesses,'" we said, are those who "'bear testimony.'" 541 U.S., at 51 (quoting 1 N. Webster, An American Dictionary of the English Language (1828)). And "'[t]estimony'" is "'[a] solemn declaration or affirmation made for the purpose of establishing or proving some fact.'" 541 U.S, at 51, (quoting Webster, *supra*). Admittedly, we did not set forth a detailed framework for addressing whether a statement is "testimonial" and thus subject to the Confrontation Clause. But the plain terms of the "testimony" definition we endorsed necessarily require some degree of solemnity before a statement can be deemed "testimonial."

This requirement of solemnity supports my view that the statements regulated by the Confrontation Clause must include "extrajudicial statements ... contained in formalized testimonial materials, such as affidavits, depositions, prior testimony, or confessions." *White, supra,* at 365, (opinion of THOMAS, J.). Affidavits, depositions, and prior testimony are, by their very nature, taken through a formalized process. Likewise, confessions, when extracted by police in a formal manner, carry sufficient indicia of solemnity to constitute formalized statements and, accordingly, bear a "striking resemblance," *Crawford, supra,* at 52, to the examinations of the accused and accusers under the Marian statutes....

The Court's standard is not only disconnected from history and unnecessary to prevent abuse; it also yields no predictable results to police officers and prosecutors attempting to comply with the law. In many, if not most, cases where police respond to a report of a crime, whether pursuant to a 911 call from the victim or otherwise, the purposes of an interrogation, viewed from the perspective of the police, are *both* to respond to the emergency situation *and* to gather evidence. Assigning one of these two "largely unverifiable motives," primacy requires constructing a hierarchy of purpose that will rarely be present—and is not reliably discernible. It will inevitably be, quite simply, an exercise in fiction.

The Court's repeated invocation of the word "objectiv[e]" to describe its test, however, suggests that the Court may not mean to reference purpose at all, but instead to inquire into the function served by the interrogation. Certainly such a test would avoid the pitfalls that have led us repeatedly to reject tests dependent on the subjective intentions of police officers. It would do so, however, at the cost of being even more disconnected from the prosecutorial abuses targeted by the Confrontation Clause. Additionally, it would shift the ability to control whether a violation occurred from the police and prosecutor to the judge, whose determination as to the "primary purpose" of a particular interrogation would be unpredictable and not necessarily tethered to the actual purpose for which the police performed the interrogation.

B

Neither the 911 call at issue in *Davis* nor the police questioning at issue in *Hammon* is testimonial under the appropriate framework. Neither the call nor the questioning is itself a formalized dialogue. Nor do any circumstances surrounding the taking of the statements render those statements sufficiently formal to resemble the Marian examinations; the statements were neither Mirandized nor custodial, nor accompanied by any similar indicia of formality. Finally, there is no suggestion that the prosecution attempted to offer the women's hearsay evidence at trial in order to evade confrontation. Accordingly, the statements at issue in both cases are nontestimonial and admissible under the Confrontation Clause.

The Court's determination that the evidence against Hammon must be excluded extends the Confrontation Clause far beyond the abuses it was intended to prevent. When combined with the Court's holding that the evidence against Davis is perfectly admissible, however, the Court's *Hammon* holding also reveals the difficulty of applying the Court's requirement that courts investigate the "primary purpose[s]" of the investigation. The Court draws a line between the two cases based on its explanation that *Hammon* involves "no emergency in progress," but instead, mere questioning as "part of an investigation into possibly criminal past conduct," and its explanation that *Davis* involves questioning for the "primary purpose" of "enabl[ing] police assistance to meet an ongoing emergency[.]" But the fact that the officer in *Hammon* was investigating Mr. Hammon's past conduct does not foreclose the possibility that the primary purpose of his inquiry was to assess whether Mr. Hammon constituted a continuing danger to his wife, requiring further police presence or action. It is hardly remarkable that Hammon did not act abusively toward his wife in the presence of the officers, and his good judgment to refrain from criminal behavior in the presence of police sheds little, if any, light on whether his violence would have resumed had the police left without further questioning, transforming what the Court dismisses as "past conduct" back into an "ongoing emergency[.]" Nor does the mere fact that McCottry needed emergency aid shed light on whether the "primary purpose" of gathering, for example, the name of her assailant was to protect the police, to protect the victim, or to gather information for prosecution. In both of the cases before the Court, like many similar cases, pronouncement of the "primary" motive behind the interrogation calls for nothing more than a guess by courts.

II

Because the standard adopted by the Court today is neither workable nor a targeted attempt to reach the abuses forbidden by the Clause, I concur only in the judgment in *Davis v. Washington,* and respectfully dissent from the Court's resolution of *Hammon v. Indiana.*

B. The Evolution of the Confrontation Clause after *Crawford* and *Davis*

Three cases subsequent to *Davis* provided further insight into the meaning of "testimonial" hearsay. The first, *Whorton v. Bocking,* 549 U.S. 406 (2007), explicitly stated what *Crawford* implied: the Confrontation Clause does not apply to nontestimonial statements. Accordingly, the mandate of *Roberts,* that hearsay offered against a criminal defendant be both necessary and reliable, did not apply to nontestimonial hearsay. Under *Crawford,* an out of court nontestimonial statement not subject to prior cross-examination is admissible even if it lacks indicia of reliability.

Giles v. California, 554 U.S. 353 (2008), involved a domestic violence scenario that eventually led to a murder. Three weeks before the murder, decedent Brenda Avie spoke to the police and told them that defendant Dwayne Giles had beaten her and threatened to kill her. On the day of the murder, Giles shot Avie but claimed that he acted in self-defense. At his murder prosecution, the prosecution sought to introduce the prior statements. The Supreme Court found her earlier statements to be testimonial, as they occurred after the assault had ended, and the police officer secured the statement to gather evidence to use in prosecuting Giles. The prosecutor argued that Giles had forfeited his

Confrontation Clause objection under FRE 804(b)(6). The Supreme Court ruled that the statements could not be admitted unless the defendant engaged in conduct **designed** to prevent the witness from testifying in the domestic assault prosecution. Therefore, as in the FRE 804(b)(6) analysis, the defendant must intend to make the declarant unavailable *as a witness* in order to forfeit his Confrontation Clause right. As the Court found no evidence of this intent, it remanded the case to determine if he possessed this intent.

In *Melendez-Diaz v. Massachusetts*, 129 S.Ct. 2527 (2009), the Supreme Court held that affidavits reporting the results of laboratory analyses are testimonial under the Confrontation Clause. In the defendant's cocaine prosecution, the prosecutor offered three affidavits reciting the chemical composition and weight of the substances seized from the defendant. The state did not, however, call the chemical analysts as witnesses. The Court found that each affidavit was a "solemn declaration or affirmation made for the purpose of establishing or proving some fact" relevant to the prosecution. *Id.* at 2532 (citing *Crawford*). Furthermore, an objective witness would recognize that the statement would be used at trial. Accordingly, these testimonial statements were subject to the Confrontation Clause and were excluded.

Whatever clarity existed after these three decisions was soon to be disrupted. In the Supreme Court's 2011 Term, two Confrontation Clause cases were decided, *Michigan v. Bryant* and *Bullcoming v. New Mexico*. The idea that reliability did, indeed, play a role in Confrontation Clause analysis was resurrected, and a more fact-intensive test for testimonial hearsay was born.

Focus Questions: *Michigan v. Bryant*

- To what extent, if any, did the Court incorporate reliability in their analysis of whether a statement is testimonial? If reliability is a factor that the Court considers, do exceptions to the hearsay rule aid in the determination of whether a statement is reliable?

- The majority and the dissent viewed the motives of the responding police officers differently. Whose argument is more convincing? To what extent should the interrogator's motive in asking the question matter?

Michigan v. Bryant
562 U.S. 344 (2011)

SOTOMAYOR, J., delivered the opinion of the Court, in which ROBERTS, C.J., and KENNEDY, BREYER, and ALITO, JJ., joined. THOMAS, J., filed an opinion concurring in the judgment. SCALIA, J., and GINSBURG, J., filed dissenting opinions. KAGAN, J., took no part in the consideration or decision of the case.

At respondent Richard Bryant's trial, the court admitted statements that the victim, Anthony Covington, made to police officers who discovered him mortally wounded in a gas station parking lot. A jury convicted Bryant of, *inter alia*, second-degree murder. On appeal, the Supreme Court of Michigan held that the Sixth Amendment's Confrontation Clause, as explained in our decisions in *Crawford v. Washington* and *Davis v. Washington* rendered Covington's statements inadmissible testimonial hearsay, and the court reversed

Bryant's conviction. We granted the State's petition for a writ of certiorari to consider whether the Confrontation Clause barred the admission at trial of Covington's statements to the police. We hold that the circumstances of the interaction between Covington and the police objectively indicate that the "primary purpose of the interrogation" was "to enable police assistance to meet an ongoing emergency." *Davis*, 547 U.S. at 822. Therefore, Covington's identification and description of the shooter and the location of the shooting were not testimonial statements, and their admission at Bryant's trial did not violate the Confrontation Clause. We vacate the judgment of the Supreme Court of Michigan and remand.

I

Around 3:25 a.m. on April 29, 2001, Detroit, Michigan police officers responded to a radio dispatch indicating that a man had been shot. At the scene, they found the victim, Anthony Covington, lying on the ground next to his car in a gas station parking lot. Covington had a gunshot wound to his abdomen, appeared to be in great pain, and spoke with difficulty.

The police asked him "what had happened, who had shot him, and where the shooting had occurred." Covington stated that "Rick" shot him at around 3 a.m. He also indicated that he had a conversation with Bryant, whom he recognized based on his voice, through the back door of Bryant's house. Covington explained that when he turned to leave, he was shot through the door and then drove to the gas station, where police found him.

Covington's conversation with the police ended within 5 to 10 minutes when emergency medical services arrived. Covington was transported to a hospital and died within hours. The police left the gas station after speaking with Covington, called for backup, and traveled to Bryant's house. They did not find Bryant there but did find blood and a bullet on the back porch and an apparent bullet hole in the back door. Police also found Covington's wallet and identification outside the house.

At trial, which occurred prior to our decisions in *Crawford* and *Davis*, the police officers who spoke with Covington at the gas station testified about what Covington had told them. The jury returned a guilty verdict on charges of second-degree murder, being a felon in possession of a firearm, and possession of a firearm during the commission of a felony....

Before the Supreme Court of Michigan, Bryant argued that Covington's statements to the police were testimonial under *Crawford* and *Davis* and were therefore inadmissible. The State, on the other hand, argued that the statements were admissible as "excited utterances" under the Michigan Rules of Evidence.... The court concluded that the circumstances "clearly indicate that the 'primary purpose' of the questioning was to establish the facts of an event that had already occurred; the 'primary purpose' was not to enable police assistance to meet an ongoing emergency."... Based on this analysis, the Supreme Court of Michigan held that the admission of Covington's statements constituted prejudicial plain error warranting reversal and ordered a new trial. The court did not address whether, absent a Confrontation Clause bar, the statements' admission would have been otherwise consistent with Michigan's hearsay rules or due process.[1]...

---

1. The Supreme Court of Michigan held that the question whether the victim's statements would have been admissible as "dying declarations" was not properly before it because at the preliminary examination, the prosecution, after first invoking both the dying declaration and excited utterance hearsay exceptions, established the factual foundation only for admission of the statements as excited utterances. The trial court ruled that the statements were admissible as excited utterances and did not

II

... The basic purpose of the Confrontation Clause was to "targe[t]" the sort of "abuses" exemplified at the notorious treason trial of Sir Walter Raleigh. Thus, the most important instances in which the Clause restricts the introduction of out-of-court statements are those in which state actors are involved in a formal, out-of-court interrogation of a witness to obtain evidence for trial. Even where such an interrogation is conducted with all good faith, introduction of the resulting statements at trial can be unfair to the accused if they are untested by cross-examination. Whether formal or informal, out-of-court statements can evade the basic objective of the Confrontation Clause, which is to prevent the accused from being deprived of the opportunity to cross-examine the declarant about statements taken for use at trial. When, as in *Davis*, the primary purpose of an interrogation is to respond to an "ongoing emergency," its purpose is not to create a record for trial and thus is not within the scope of the Clause. But there may be other circumstances, aside from ongoing emergencies, when a statement is not procured with a primary purpose of creating an out-of-court substitute for trial testimony. In making the primary purpose determination, standard rules of hearsay, designed to identify some statements as reliable, will be relevant. Where no such primary purpose exists, the admissibility of a statement is the concern of state and federal rules of evidence, not the Confrontation Clause.

Deciding this case also requires further explanation of the "ongoing emergency" circumstance addressed in *Davis*. Because *Davis* and *Hammon* arose in the domestic violence context, that was the situation "we had immediately in mind (for that was the case before us)." We now face a new context: a nondomestic dispute, involving a victim found in a public location, suffering from a fatal gunshot wound, and a perpetrator whose location was unknown at the time the police located the victim. Thus, we confront for the first time circumstances in which the "ongoing emergency" discussed in *Davis* extends beyond an initial victim to a potential threat to the responding police and the public at large. This new context requires us to provide additional clarification with regard to what Davis meant by "the primary purpose of the interrogation is to enable police assistance to meet an ongoing emergency."

III

To determine whether the "primary purpose" of an interrogation is "to enable police assistance to meet an ongoing emergency," which would render the resulting statements nontestimonial, we objectively evaluate the circumstances in which the encounter occurs and the statements and actions of the parties.

A

The Michigan Supreme Court correctly understood that this inquiry is objective. *Davis* uses the word "objective" or "objectively" no fewer than eight times in describing the relevant inquiry. "Objectively" also appears in the definitions of both testimonial and nontestimonial statements that *Davis* established.

An objective analysis of the circumstances of an encounter and the statements and actions of the parties to it provides the most accurate assessment of the "primary purpose of the interrogation." The circumstances in which an encounter occurs—e.g., at or near the scene of the crime versus at a police station, during an ongoing emergency or after-

---

address their admissibility as dying declarations.... Because of the State's failure to preserve its argument with regard to dying declarations, we similarly need not decide that question here.

wards—are clearly matters of objective fact. The statements and actions of the parties must also be objectively evaluated. That is, the relevant inquiry is not the subjective or actual purpose of the individuals involved in a particular encounter, but rather the purpose that reasonable participants would have had, as ascertained from the individuals' statements and actions and the circumstances in which the encounter occurred.

B

As our recent Confrontation Clause cases have explained, the existence of an "ongoing emergency" at the time of an encounter between an individual and the police is among the most important circumstances informing the "primary purpose" of an interrogation. The existence of an ongoing emergency is relevant to determining the primary purpose of the interrogation because an emergency focuses the participants on something other than "prov[ing] past events potentially relevant to later criminal prosecution."[8] *Davis*, 547 U.S. at 822. Rather, it focuses them on "end[ing] a threatening situation." *Id.* at 832. Implicit in *Davis* is the idea that because the prospect of fabrication in statements given for the primary purpose of resolving that emergency is presumably significantly diminished, the Confrontation Clause does not require such statements to be subject to the crucible of cross-examination.

This logic is not unlike that justifying the excited utterance exception in hearsay law. Statements "relating to a startling event or condition made while the declarant was under the stress of excitement caused by the event or condition," Fed. Rule Evid. 803(2), are considered reliable because the declarant, in the excitement, presumably cannot form a falsehood. *See Idaho v. Wright*, 497 U.S. 805, 820 (1990) ("The basis for the 'excited utterance' exception ... is that such statements are given under circumstances that eliminate the possibility of fabrication, coaching, or confabulation ..."). An ongoing emergency has a similar effect of focusing an individual's attention on responding to the emergency.[9]

Following our precedents, the court below correctly began its analysis with the circumstances in which Covington interacted with the police. But in doing so, the court construed *Davis* to have decided more than it did and thus employed an unduly narrow understanding of "ongoing emergency" that *Davis* does not require.

---

8. The existence of an ongoing emergency must be objectively assessed from the perspective of the parties to the interrogation at the time, not with the benefit of hindsight. If the information the parties knew at the time of the encounter would lead a reasonable person to believe that there was an emergency, even if that belief was later proved incorrect, that is sufficient for purposes of the Confrontation Clause. The emergency is relevant to the "primary purpose of the interrogation" because of the effect it has on the parties' purpose, not because of its actual existence.

9. Many other exceptions to the hearsay rules similarly rest on the belief that certain statements are, by their nature, made for a purpose other than use in a prosecution and therefore should not be barred by hearsay prohibitions. See, e.g., Fed. Rule Evide. 801(d)(2)(E) (statement by a co-conspirator during and in furtherance of the conspiracy); 803(4) (Statements for Purposes of Medical Diagnosis or Treatment); 803(6) (Records of Regularly Conducted Activity); 803(8) (Public Records and Reports); 803(9) (Records of Vital Statistics); 803(11) (Records of Religious Organizations); 803(12) (Marriage, Baptismal, and Similar Certificates); 803(13) (Family Records); 804(b)(3) (Statement Against Interest); *see also Melendez-Diaz v. Massachusetts*, 557 U.S. ___, ___ (2009) ("Business and public records are generally admissible absent confrontation not because they qualify under an exception to the hearsay rules, but because-having been created for the administration of an entity's affairs and not for the purpose of establishing or proving some fact at trial-they are not testimonial"); *Giles v. California*, 554 U.S., 353, 376, (2008) (noting in the context of domestic violence that "[s]tatements to friends and neighbors about abuse and intimidation and statements to physicians in the course of receiving treatment would be excluded, if at all, only by hearsay rules"); *Crawford*, 541 U.S., at 56 ("Most of the hearsay exceptions covered statements that by their nature were not testimonial-for example, business records or statements in furtherance of a conspiracy").

First, the Michigan Supreme Court repeatedly and incorrectly asserted that *Davis* "defined" "'ongoing emergency.'" In fact, *Davis* did not even define the extent of the emergency in that case. The Michigan Supreme Court erroneously read *Davis* as deciding that "the statements made after the defendant stopped assaulting the victim and left the premises did not occur during an 'ongoing emergency.'" We explicitly explained in *Davis*, however, that we were asked to review only the testimonial nature of Michelle McCottry's initial statements during the 911 call; we therefore merely assumed the correctness of the Washington Supreme Court's holding that admission of her other statements was harmless, without deciding whether those subsequent statements were also made for the primary purpose of resolving an ongoing emergency.

Second, by assuming that *Davis* defined the outer bounds of "ongoing emergency," the Michigan Supreme Court failed to appreciate that whether an emergency exists and is ongoing is a highly context-dependent inquiry. *Davis* and *Hammon* involved domestic violence, a known and identified perpetrator, and, in *Hammon*, a neutralized threat. Because *Davis* and *Hammon* were domestic violence cases, we focused only on the threat to the victims and assessed the ongoing emergency from the perspective of whether there was a continuing threat to them.

Domestic violence cases like *Davis* and *Hammon* often have a narrower zone of potential victims than cases involving threats to public safety. An assessment of whether an emergency that threatens the police and public is ongoing cannot narrowly focus on whether the threat solely to the first victim has been neutralized because the threat to the first responders and public may continue.

The Michigan Supreme Court also did not appreciate that the duration and scope of an emergency may depend in part on the type of weapon employed. The court relied on *Davis* and *Hammon*, in which the assailants used their fists, as controlling the scope of the emergency here, which involved the use of a gun. The problem with that reasoning is clear when considered in light of the assault on Amy Hammon. Hershel Hammon was armed only with his fists when he attacked his wife, so removing Amy to a separate room was sufficient to end the emergency. If Hershel had been reported to be armed with a gun, however, separation by a single household wall might not have been sufficient to end the emergency.

The Michigan Supreme Court's failure to focus on the context-dependent nature of our *Davis* decision also led it to conclude that the medical condition of a declarant is irrelevant. But *Davis* and *Hammon* did not present medical emergencies, despite some injuries to the victims. Thus, we have not previously considered, much less ruled out, the relevance of a victim's severe injuries to the primary purpose inquiry.

Taking into account the victim's medical state does not, as the Michigan Supreme Court below thought, "rende[r] non-testimonial" "all statements made while the police are questioning a seriously injured complainant." The medical condition of the victim is important to the primary purpose inquiry to the extent that it sheds light on the ability of the victim to have any purpose at all in responding to police questions and on the likelihood that any purpose formed would necessarily be a testimonial one. The victim's medical state also provides important context for first responders to judge the existence and magnitude of a continuing threat to the victim, themselves, and the public.

As the Solicitor General's brief observes, and contrary to the Michigan Supreme Court's claims, none of this suggests that an emergency is ongoing in every place or even just surrounding the victim for the entire time that the perpetrator of a violent crime is on the loose. As we recognized in *Davis*, "a conversation which begins as an interrogation to determine the need for emergency assistance" can "evolve into testimonial statements." This evolution may occur if, for example, a declarant provides police with information that makes clear that what appeared to be an emergency is not or is no longer an emergency or that what appeared to be a public threat is actually a private dispute. It could also occur if a perpetrator is disarmed, surrenders, is apprehended, or, as in *Davis*, flees with little prospect of posing a threat to the public. Trial courts can determine in the first instance when any transition from nontestimonial to testimonial occurs, and exclude "the portions of any statement that have become testimonial, as they do, for example, with unduly prejudicial portions of otherwise admissible evidence."

Finally, our discussion of the Michigan Supreme Court's misunderstanding of what *Davis* meant by "ongoing emergency" should not be taken to imply that the existence vel non of an ongoing emergency is dispositive of the testimonial inquiry. As *Davis* made clear, whether an ongoing emergency exists is simply one factor—albeit an important factor—that informs the ultimate inquiry regarding the "primary purpose" of an interrogation. Another factor the Michigan Supreme Court did not sufficiently account for is the importance of informality in an encounter between a victim and police. Formality is not the sole touchstone of our primary purpose inquiry because, although formality suggests the absence of an emergency and therefore an increased likelihood that the purpose of the interrogation is to "establish or prove past events potentially relevant to later criminal prosecution," informality does not necessarily indicate the presence of an emergency or the lack of testimonial intent. The court below, however, too readily dismissed the informality of the circumstances in this case.... As we explain further below, the questioning in this case occurred in an exposed, public area, prior to the arrival of emergency medical services, and in a disorganized fashion. All of those facts make this case distinguishable from the formal station-house interrogation in *Crawford*.

C

In addition to the circumstances in which an encounter occurs, the statements and actions of both the declarant and interrogators provide objective evidence of the primary purpose of the interrogation.... *Davis* requires a combined inquiry that accounts for both the declarant and the interrogator. In many instances, the primary purpose of the interrogation will be most accurately ascertained by looking to the contents of both the questions and the answers. To give an extreme example, if the police say to a victim, "Tell us who did this to you so that we can arrest and prosecute them," the victim's response that "Rick did it," appears purely accusatory because by virtue of the phrasing of the question, the victim necessarily has prosecution in mind when she answers.

The combined approach also ameliorates problems that could arise from looking solely to one participant. Predominant among these is the problem of mixed motives on the part of both interrogators and declarants. Police officers in our society function as both first responders and criminal investigators. Their dual responsibilities may mean that they act with different motives simultaneously or in quick succession.

Victims are also likely to have mixed motives when they make statements to the police. During an ongoing emergency, a victim is most likely to want the threat to her and to other potential victims to end, but that does not necessarily mean that the victim wants or envisions prosecution of the assailant. A victim may want the attacker to be incapacitated temporarily or rehabilitated. Alternatively, a severely injured victim may have no purpose at all in answering questions posed; the answers may be simply reflexive. The victim's injuries could be so debilitating as to prevent her from thinking sufficiently clearly to understand whether her statements are for the purpose of addressing an ongoing emergency or for the purpose of future prosecution. Taking into account a victim's injuries does not transform this objective inquiry into a subjective one. The inquiry is still objective because it focuses on the understanding and purpose of a reasonable victim in the circumstances of the actual victim—circumstances that prominently include the victim's physical state.

The dissent suggests that we intend to give controlling weight to the "intentions of the police." That is a misreading of our opinion. At trial, the declarant's statements, not the interrogator's questions, will be introduced to "establis[h] the truth of the matter asserted," *Crawford*, 541 U.S. at 60, n. 9, and must therefore pass the Sixth Amendment test. In determining whether a declarant's statements are testimonial, courts should look to all of the relevant circumstances. Even Justice SCALIA concedes that the interrogator is relevant to this evaluation, and we agree that "[t]he identity of an interrogator, and the content and tenor of his questions" can illuminate the "primary purpose of the interrogation...."

IV

As we suggested in *Davis*, when a court must determine whether the Confrontation Clause bars the admission of a statement at trial, it should determine the "primary purpose of the interrogation" by objectively evaluating the statements and actions of the parties to the encounter, in light of the circumstances in which the interrogation occurs. The existence of an emergency or the parties' perception that an emergency is ongoing is among the most important circumstances that courts must take into account in determining whether an interrogation is testimonial because statements made to assist police in addressing an ongoing emergency presumably lack the testimonial purpose that would subject them to the requirement of confrontation. As the context of this case brings into sharp relief, the existence and duration of an emergency depend on the type and scope of danger posed to the victim, the police, and the public....

We first examine the circumstances in which the interrogation occurred. The parties disagree over whether there was an emergency when the police arrived at the gas station. Bryant argues, and the Michigan Supreme Court accepted, that there was no ongoing emergency because "there ... was no criminal conduct occurring. No shots were being fired, no one was seen in possession of a firearm, nor were any witnesses seen cowering in fear or running from the scene." Bryant, while conceding that "a serious or life-threatening injury creates a medical emergency for a victim," further argues that a declarant's medical emergency is not relevant to the ongoing emergency determination.

In contrast, Michigan and the Solicitor General explain that when the police responded to the call that a man had been shot and found Covington bleeding on the gas station parking lot, "they did not know who Covington was, whether the shooting had occurred at the gas station or at a different location, who the assailant was, or whether the assailant posed a continuing threat to Covington or others."

The Michigan Supreme Court stated that the police asked Covington, "what had happened, who had shot him, and where the shooting had occurred...." The officers' testimony is essentially consistent but, at the same time, not specific. The officers basically agree on what information they learned from Covington, but not on the order in which they learned it or on whether Covington's statements were in response to general or detailed questions. They all agree that the first question was "what happened?" The answer was either "I was shot" or "Rick shot me."

As explained above, the scope of an emergency in terms of its threat to individuals other than the initial assailant and victim will often depend on the type of dispute involved. Nothing Covington said to the police indicated that the cause of the shooting was a purely private dispute or that the threat from the shooter had ended. The record reveals little about the motive for the shooting. The police officers who spoke with Covington at the gas station testified that Covington did not tell them what words Covington and Rick had exchanged prior to the shooting. What Covington did tell the officers was that he fled Bryant's back porch, indicating that he perceived an ongoing threat. The police did not know, and Covington did not tell them, whether the threat was limited to him. The potential scope of the dispute and therefore the emergency in this case thus stretches more broadly than those at issue in *Davis* and *Hammon* and encompasses a threat potentially to the police and the public.

This is also the first of our post-*Crawford* Confrontation Clause cases to involve a gun. The physical separation that was sufficient to end the emergency in *Hammon* was not necessarily sufficient to end the threat in this case; Covington was shot through the back door of Bryant's house. Bryant's argument that there was no ongoing emergency because "[n]o shots were being fired" surely construes ongoing emergency too narrowly. An emergency does not last only for the time between when the assailant pulls the trigger and the bullet hits the victim. If an out-of-sight sniper pauses between shots, no one would say that the emergency ceases during the pause. That is an extreme example and not the situation here, but it serves to highlight the implausibility, at least as to certain weapons, of construing the emergency to last only precisely as long as the violent act itself, as some have construed our opinion in *Davis*.

At no point during the questioning did either Covington or the police know the location of the shooter. In fact, Bryant was not at home by the time the police searched his house at approximately 5:30 a.m. At some point between 3 a.m. and 5:30 a.m., Bryant left his house. At bottom, there was an ongoing emergency here where an armed shooter, whose motive for and location after the shooting were unknown, had mortally wounded Covington within a few blocks and a few minutes of the location where the police found Covington.

This is not to suggest that the emergency continued until Bryant was arrested in California a year after the shooting. We need not decide precisely when the emergency ended because Covington's encounter with the police and all of the statements he made during that interaction occurred within the first few minutes of the police officers' arrival and well before they secured the scene of the shooting—the shooter's last known location.

We reiterate, moreover, that the existence vel non of an ongoing emergency is not the touchstone of the testimonial inquiry; rather, the ultimate inquiry is whether the "primary purpose of the interrogation [was] to enable police assistance to meet [the] ongoing emergency." We turn now to that inquiry, as informed by the circumstances of the ongoing emergency just described. The circumstances of the encounter provide important context for understanding Covington's statements to the police. When the police arrived at Covington's side, their first question to him was "What happened?" Covington's response was either "Rick shot me" or "I was shot," followed very quickly by an identification of "Rick" as the shooter. In response to further questions, Covington explained that the shooting occurred through the back door of Bryant's house and provided a physical description of the shooter. When he made the statements, Covington was lying in a gas station parking lot bleeding from a mortal gunshot wound to his abdomen. His answers to the police officers' questions were punctuated with questions about when emergency medical services would arrive. He was obviously in considerable pain and had difficulty breathing and talking. From this description of his condition and report of his statements, we cannot say that a person in Covington's situation would have had a "primary purpose" "to establish or prove past events potentially relevant to later criminal prosecution."

For their part, the police responded to a call that a man had been shot. As discussed above, they did not know why, where, or when the shooting had occurred. Nor did they know the location of the shooter or anything else about the circumstances in which the crime occurred. The questions they asked — "what had happened, who had shot him, and where the shooting occurred" — were the exact type of questions necessary to allow the police to " 'assess the situation, the threat to their own safety, and possible danger to the potential victim' " and to the public, including to allow them to ascertain "whether they would be encountering a violent felon." In other words, they solicited the information necessary to enable them "to meet an ongoing emergency."

Nothing in Covington's responses indicated to the police that, contrary to their expectation upon responding to a call reporting a shooting, there was no emergency or that a prior emergency had ended. Covington did indicate that he had been shot at another location about 25 minutes earlier, but he did not know the location of the shooter at the time the police arrived and, as far as we can tell from the record, he gave no indication that the shooter, having shot at him twice, would be satisfied that Covington was only wounded. In fact, Covington did not indicate any possible motive for the shooting, and thereby gave no reason to think that the shooter would not shoot again if he arrived on the scene. As we noted in *Davis*, "initial inquiries" may "often ... produce nontestimonial statements." *Id.*, at 832. The initial inquiries in this case resulted in the type of nontestimonial statements we contemplated in *Davis*.

Finally, we consider the informality of the situation and the interrogation. This situation is more similar, though not identical, to the informal, harried 911 call in *Davis* than to the structured, station-house interview in *Crawford*. As the officers' trial testimony reflects, the situation was fluid and somewhat confused: the officers arrived at different times; apparently each, upon arrival, asked Covington "what happened?"; and, contrary to the dissent's portrayal, they did not conduct a structured interrogation. The informality suggests that the interrogators' primary purpose was simply to address what they perceived to be an ongoing emergency, and the circumstances lacked any formality that would have alerted Covington to or focused him on the possible future prosecutorial use of his statements.

Because the circumstances of the encounter as well as the statements and actions of Covington and the police objectively indicate that the "primary purpose of the interrogation" was "to enable police assistance to meet an ongoing emergency," Covington's identification and description of the shooter and the location of the shooting were not testimonial hearsay. The Confrontation Clause did not bar their admission at Bryant's trial.

* * *

For the foregoing reasons, we hold that Covington's statements were not testimonial and that their admission at Bryant's trial did not violate the Confrontation Clause. We leave for the Michigan courts to decide on remand whether the statements' admission was otherwise permitted by state hearsay rules. The judgment of the Supreme Court of Michigan is vacated, and the case is remanded for further proceedings not inconsistent with this opinion.

It is so ordered.

Justice KAGAN took no part in the consideration or decision of this case.

Justice THOMAS, concurring in the judgment.

I agree with the Court that the admission of Covington's out-of-court statements did not violate the Confrontation Clause, but I reach this conclusion because Covington's questioning by police lacked sufficient formality and solemnity for his statements to be considered "testimonial." ...

Rather than attempting to reconstruct the "primary purpose" of the participants, I would consider the extent to which the interrogation resembles those historical practices that the Confrontation Clause addressed. As the majority notes, Covington interacted with the police under highly informal circumstances, while he bled from a fatal gunshot wound. The police questioning was not "a formalized dialogue," did not result in "formalized testimonial materials" such as a deposition or affidavit, and bore no "indicia of solemnity." Nor is there any indication that the statements were offered at trial "in order to evade confrontation." This interrogation bears little if any resemblance to the historical practices that the Confrontation Clause aimed to eliminate. Covington thus did not "bea[r] testimony" against Bryant, and the introduction of his statements at trial did not implicate the Confrontation Clause. I concur in the judgment.

Justice SCALIA, dissenting.

Today's tale—a story of five officers conducting successive examinations of a dying man with the primary purpose, not of obtaining and preserving his testimony regarding his killer, but of protecting him, them, and others from a murderer somewhere on the loose—is so transparently false that professing to believe it demeans this institution. But reaching a patently incorrect conclusion on the facts is a relatively benign judicial mischief; it affects, after all, only the case at hand. In its vain attempt to make the incredible plausible, however—or perhaps as an intended second goal—today's opinion distorts our Confrontation Clause jurisprudence and leaves it in a shambles. Instead of clarifying the law, the Court makes itself the obfuscator of last resort. Because I continue to adhere to the Confrontation Clause that the People adopted, as described in *Crawford v. Washington*, I dissent.

I

A

... *Crawford* and *Davis* did not address whose perspective matters—the declarant's, the interrogator's, or both—when assessing "the primary purpose of [an] interrogation." In those cases the statements were testimonial from any perspective. I think the same is true here, but because the Court picks a perspective so will I: The declarant's intent is what counts. In-court testimony is more than a narrative of past events; it is a solemn declaration made in the course of a criminal trial. For an out-of-court statement to qualify as testimonial, the declarant must intend the statement to be a solemn declaration rather than an unconsidered or offhand remark; and he must make the statement with the understanding that it may be used to invoke the coercive machinery of the State against the accused. That is what distinguishes a narrative told to a friend over dinner from a statement to the police. The hidden purpose of an interrogator cannot substitute for the declarant's intentional solemnity or his understanding of how his words may be used.

A declarant-focused inquiry is also the only inquiry that would work in every fact pattern implicating the Confrontation Clause. The Clause applies to volunteered testimony as well as statements solicited through police interrogation. An inquiry into an officer's purposes would make no sense when a declarant blurts out "Rick shot me" as soon as the officer arrives on the scene. I see no reason to adopt a different test—one that accounts for an officer's intent—when the officer asks "what happened" before the declarant makes his accusation. (This does not mean the interrogator is irrelevant. The identity of an interrogator, and the content and tenor of his questions, can bear upon whether a declarant intends to make a solemn statement, and envisions its use at a criminal trial. But none of this means that the interrogator's purpose matters.)

In an unsuccessful attempt to make its finding of emergency plausible, the Court instead adopts a test that looks to the purposes of both the police and the declarant. It claims that this is demanded by necessity, fretting that a domestic-violence victim may want her abuser briefly arrested—presumably to teach him a lesson—but not desire prosecution. I do not need to probe the purposes of the police to solve that problem. Even if a victim speaks to the police "to establish or prove past events" solely for the purpose of getting her abuser arrested, she surely knows her account is "potentially relevant to later criminal prosecution" should one ensue.

The Court also wrings its hands over the possibility that "a severely injured victim" may lack the capacity to form a purpose, and instead answer questions "reflexive[ly]." How to assess whether a declarant with diminished capacity bore testimony is a difficult question, and one I do not need to answer today. But the Court's proposed answer—to substitute the intentions of the police for the missing intentions of the declarant—cannot be the correct one. When the declarant has diminished capacity, focusing on the interrogators make less sense, not more. The inquiry under *Crawford* turns in part on the actions and statements of a declarant's audience only because they shape the declarant's perception of why his audience is listening and therefore influence his purpose in making the declaration. But a person who cannot perceive his own purposes certainly cannot perceive why a listener might be interested in what he has to say....

The Court claims one affirmative virtue for its focus on the purposes of both the declarant and the police: It "ameliorates problems that ... arise" when declarants have "mixed motives." I am at a loss to know how. Sorting out the primary purpose of a declarant with mixed motives is sometimes difficult. But adding in the mixed motives of the police only compounds the problem. Now courts will have to sort through two sets of mixed motives to determine the primary purpose of an interrogation. And the Court's solution creates a mixed-motive problem where (under the proper theory) it does not exist—viz., where the police and the declarant each have one motive, but those motives conflict. The Court does not provide an answer to this glaringly obvious problem, probably because it does not have one.

The only virtue of the Court's approach (if it can be misnamed a virtue) is that it leaves judges free to reach the "fairest" result under the totality of the circumstances. If the dastardly police trick a declarant into giving an incriminating statement against a sympathetic defendant, a court can focus on the police's intent and declare the statement testimonial. If the defendant "deserves" to go to jail, then a court can focus on whatever perspective is necessary to declare damning hearsay nontestimonial. And when all else fails, a court can mix-and-match perspectives to reach its desired outcome. Unfortunately, under this malleable approach "the guarantee of confrontation is no guarantee at all." *Giles v. California*, 554 U.S. 353, 375 (2008) (plurality).

B

Looking to the declarant's purpose (as we should), this is an absurdly easy case. Roughly 25 minutes after Anthony Covington had been shot, Detroit police responded to a 911 call reporting that a gunshot victim had appeared at a neighborhood gas station. They quickly arrived at the scene, and in less than 10 minutes five different Detroit police officers questioned Covington about the shooting. Each asked him a similar battery of questions: "what happened" and when, "who shot the victim," and "where" did the shooting take place. After Covington would answer, they would ask follow-up questions, such as "how tall is" the shooter, "[h]ow much does he weigh," what is the exact address or physical description of the house where the shooting took place, and what chain of events led to the shooting. The battery relented when the paramedics arrived and began tending to Covington's wounds.

From Covington's perspective, his statements had little value except to ensure the arrest and eventual prosecution of Richard Bryant. He knew the "threatening situation," had ended six blocks away and 25 minutes earlier when he fled from Bryant's back porch. Bryant had not confronted him face-to-face before he was mortally wounded, instead shooting him through a door. Even if Bryant had pursued him (unlikely), and after seeing that Covington had ended up at the gas station was unable to confront him there before the police arrived (doubly unlikely), it was entirely beyond imagination that Bryant would again open fire while Covington was surrounded by five armed police officers. And Covington knew the shooting was the work of a drug dealer, not a spree killer who might randomly threaten others.

Covington's knowledge that he had nothing to fear differs significantly from Michelle McCottry's state of mind during her "frantic" statements to a 911 operator at issue in *Davis*. Her "call was plainly a call for help against a bona fide physical threat" describing "events as they were actually happening." She did not have the luxuries of police protection and of time and space separating her from immediate danger that Covington enjoyed when he made his statements.

Covington's pressing medical needs do not suggest that he was responding to an emergency, but to the contrary reinforce the testimonial character of his statements. He understood the police were focused on investigating a past crime, not his medical needs. None of the officers asked Covington how he was doing, attempted more than superficially to assess the severity of his wounds, or attempted to administer first aid. They instead primarily asked questions with little, if any, relevance to Covington's dire situation. Police, paramedics, and doctors do not need to know the address where a shooting took place, the name of the shooter, or the shooter's height and weight to provide proper medical care. Underscoring that Covington understood the officers' investigative role, he interrupted their interrogation to ask "when is EMS coming?" When, in other words, would the focus shift to his medical needs rather than Bryant's crime?

Neither Covington's statements nor the colloquy between him and the officers would have been out of place at a trial; it would have been a routine direct examination. Like a witness, Covington recounted in detail how a past criminal event began and progressed, and like a prosecutor, the police elicited that account through structured questioning. Preventing the admission of "weaker substitute[s] for live testimony at trial" such as this is precisely what motivated the Framers to adopt the Confrontation Clause and what motivated our decisions in *Crawford* and in *Hammon v. Indiana*, decided with *Davis*. Ex parte examinations raise the same constitutional concerns whether they take place in a gas-station parking lot or in a police interrogation room.

C

Worse still for the repute of today's opinion, this is an absurdly easy case even if one (erroneously) takes the interrogating officers' purpose into account. The five officers interrogated Covington primarily to investigate past criminal events. None—absolutely none—of their actions indicated that they perceived an imminent threat. They did not draw their weapons, and indeed did not immediately search the gas station for potential shooters. To the contrary, all five testified that they questioned Covington before conducting any investigation at the scene. Would this have made any sense if they feared the presence of a shooter? Most tellingly, none of the officers started his interrogation by asking what would have been the obvious first question if any hint of such a fear existed: Where is the shooter?

But do not rely solely on my word about the officers' primary purpose. Listen to Sergeant Wenturine, who candidly admitted that he interrogated Covington because he "ha[d] a man here that [he] believe[d][was] dying [so he was] gonna find out who did this, period." In short, he needed to interrogate Covington to solve a crime. Wenturine never mentioned an interest in ending an ongoing emergency.

At the very least, the officers' intentions turned investigative during their 10-minute encounter with Covington, and the conversation "evolve[d] into testimonial statements." The fifth officer to arrive at the scene did not need to run straight to Covington and ask a battery of questions "to determine the need for emergency assistance." He could have asked his fellow officers, who presumably had a better sense of that than Covington—and a better sense of what he could do to assist. No, the value of asking the same battery of questions a fifth time was to ensure that Covington told a consistent story and to see if any new details helpful to the investigation and eventual prosecution would emerge. Having the testimony of five officers to recount Covington's consistent story undoubtedly helped obtain Bryant's conviction....

D

... The Court's distorted view creates an expansive exception to the Confrontation Clause for violent crimes. Because Bryant posed a continuing threat to public safety in the Court's imagination, the emergency persisted for confrontation purposes at least until the police learned his "motive for and location after the shooting." It may have persisted in this case until the police "secured the scene of the shooting" two-and-a-half hours later. (The relevance of securing the scene is unclear so long as the killer is still at large—especially if, as the Court speculates, he may be a spree-killer.) This is a dangerous definition of emergency. Many individuals who testify against a defendant at trial first offer their accounts to police in the hours after a violent act. If the police can plausibly claim that a "potential threat to ... the public" persisted through those first few hours (and if the claim is plausible here it is always plausible) a defendant will have no constitutionally protected right to exclude the uncross-examined testimony of such witnesses. His conviction could rest (as perhaps it did here) solely on the officers' recollection at trial of the witnesses' accusations.

The Framers could not have envisioned such a hollow constitutional guarantee. No framing-era confrontation case that I know of, neither here nor in England, took such an enfeebled view of the right to confrontation. For example, *King v. Brasier*, 1 Leach 199, 200, 168 Eng. Rep. 202, 202-203 (K.B.1779), held inadmissible a mother's account of her young daughter's statements "immediately on her coming home" after being sexually assaulted. The daughter needed to testify herself. But today's majority presumably would hold the daughter's account to her mother a nontestimonial statement made during an ongoing emergency. She could not have known whether her attacker might reappear to attack again or attempt to silence the lone witness against him. Her mother likely listened to the account to assess the threat to her own safety and to decide whether the rapist posed a threat to the community that required the immediate intervention of the local authorities. Utter nonsense....

II
A

But today's decision is not only a gross distortion of the facts. It is a gross distortion of the law—a revisionist narrative in which reliability continues to guide our Confrontation Clause jurisprudence, at least where emergencies and faux emergencies are concerned.

According to today's opinion, the *Davis* inquiry into whether a declarant spoke to end an ongoing emergency or rather to "prove past events potentially relevant to later criminal prosecution" is not aimed at answering whether the declarant acted as a witness. Instead, the *Davis* inquiry probes the reliability of a declarant's statements, "[i]mplicit[ly]" importing the excited-utterances hearsay exception into the Constitution. A statement during an ongoing emergency is sufficiently reliable, the Court says, "because the prospect of fabrication ... is presumably significantly diminished," so it "does not [need] to be subject to the crucible of cross-examination."

Compare that with the holding of *Crawford*: "Where testimonial statements are at issue, the only indicium of reliability sufficient to satisfy constitutional demands is the one the Constitution actually prescribes: confrontation." Today's opinion adopts, for emergencies and faux emergencies at least, the discredited logic of *White v. Illinois*, 502 U.S. 346, 355-356, and n. 8 (1992), and *Idaho v. Wright*, 497 U.S. 805, 819-820 (1990). *White* is, of course, the decision that both *Crawford* and *Davis* found most incompatible with the text and history of the Confrontation Clause. *See Davis, supra,* at 825; *Crawford, supra,* at 58, n. 8. (This is not to say that that "reliability" logic can actually justify today's result: Twenty-five minutes is plenty of time for a shooting victim to reflect and fabricate a false story.)

The Court announces that in future cases it will look to "standard rules of hearsay, designed to identify some statements as reliable," when deciding whether a statement is testimonial. *Ohio v. Roberts*, 448 U.S. 56 (1980) said something remarkably similar: An out-of-court statement is admissible if it "falls within a firmly rooted hearsay exception" or otherwise "bears adequate 'indicia of reliability.'" *Id.*, at 66. We tried that approach to the Confrontation Clause for nearly 25 years before *Crawford* rejected it as an unworkable standard unmoored from the text and the historical roots of the Confrontation Clause....

The Court attempts to fit its resurrected interest in reliability into the *Crawford* framework, but the result is incoherent. Reliability, the Court tells us, is a good indicator of whether "a statement is ... an out-of-court substitute for trial testimony." That is patently false. Reliability tells us nothing about whether a statement is testimonial. Testimonial and nontestimonial statements alike come in varying degrees of reliability. An eyewitness's statements to the police after a fender-bender, for example, are both reliable and testimonial. Statements to the police from one driver attempting to blame the other would be similarly testimonial but rarely reliable.

The Court suggests otherwise because it "misunderstands the relationship" between qualification for one of the standard hearsay exceptions and exemption from the confrontation requirement. That relationship is not a causal one. Hearsay law exempts business records, for example, because businesses have a financial incentive to keep reliable records. The Sixth Amendment also generally admits business records into evidence, but not because the records are reliable or because hearsay law says so. It admits them "because—having been created for the administration of an entity's affairs and not for the purpose of establishing or proving some fact at trial—they are not" weaker substitutes for live testimony. Moreover, the scope of the exemption from confrontation and that of the hearsay exceptions also are not always coextensive. The reliability logic of the business-record exception would extend to records maintained by neutral parties providing litigation-support services, such as evidence testing. The Confrontation Clause is not so forgiving. Business records prepared specifically for use at a criminal trial are testimonial and require confrontation....

B

The Court recedes from *Crawford* in a second significant way. It requires judges to conduct "open-ended balancing tests" and "amorphous, if not entirely subjective," inquiries into the totality of the circumstances bearing upon reliability. Where the prosecution cries "emergency," the admissibility of a statement now turns on "a highly context-dependent inquiry" into the type of weapon the defendant wielded; the type of crime the defendant committed; the medical condition of the declarant; if the declarant is injured, whether paramedics have arrived on the scene; whether the encounter takes place in an "exposed public area"; whether the encounter appears disorganized; whether the declarant is capable of forming a purpose; whether the police have secured the scene of the crime; the formality of the statement; and finally, whether the statement strikes us as reliable. This is no better than the nine-factor balancing test we rejected in *Crawford*. I do not look forward to resolving conflicts in the future over whether knives and poison are more like guns or fists for Confrontation Clause purposes, or whether rape and armed robbery are more like murder or domestic violence.

It can be said, of course, that under *Crawford* analysis of whether a statement is testimonial requires consideration of all the circumstances, and so is also something of a multifactor balancing test. But the "reliability" test does not replace that analysis; it supplements it. As I understand the Court's opinion, even when it is determined that no emergency exists (or perhaps before that determination is made) the statement would be found admissible as far as the Confrontation Clause is concerned if it is not testimonial.

In any case, we did not disavow multifactor balancing for reliability in *Crawford* out of a preference for rules over standards. We did so because it "d[id] violence to" the Framers' design....

Justice GINSBURG, dissenting.

I agree with Justice SCALIA that Covington's statements were testimonial and that "[t]he declarant's intent is what counts." Even if the interrogators' intent were what counts, I further agree, Covington's statements would still be testimonial. It is most likely that "the officers viewed their encounter with Covington [as] an investigation into a past crime with no ongoing or immediate consequences." Today's decision, Justice SCALIA rightly notes, "creates an expansive exception to the Confrontation Clause for violent crimes." In so doing, the decision confounds our recent Confrontation Clause jurisprudence, which made it plain that "[r]eliability tells us nothing about whether a statement is testimonial."

I would add, however, this observation. In *Crawford v. Washington*, this Court noted that, in the law we inherited from England, there was a well-established exception to the confrontation requirement: The cloak protecting the accused against admission of out-of-court testimonial statements was removed for dying declarations. This historic exception, we recalled in *Giles v. California*, 554 U.S. 353, 358 (2008), applied to statements made by a person about to die and aware that death was imminent. Were the issue properly tendered here, I would take up the question whether the exception for dying declarations survives our recent Confrontation Clause decisions. The Michigan Supreme Court, however, held, as a matter of state law, that the prosecutor had abandoned the issue.

Focus Questions: *Bullcoming v. New Mexico*

- How does the Court's definition of "testimonial" differ from the one in *Davis*?

- How was the surrogate testimony offered by the prosecution more limited than the testimony of the person who performed the test? If you were to cross-examine the person who performed the tests, what questions would you ask?

Would the surrogate witness be able to respond to those questions with firsthand knowledge?

- What role should an "undue burden" on the prosecution play? If the definition of "testimonial" would wreak havoc with the court system in certain circumstances, should the definition of "testimonial" be altered in those circumstances?

- To what degree did the dissenting opinion rely on the definition of "testimonial" in its analysis? To what degree did the dissent incorporate reliability in their analysis?

Bullcoming v. New Mexico

564 U.S. 647 (2011)

GINSBURG, J., delivered the opinion of the Court, except as to Part IV and footnote 6. SCALIA, J., joined that opinion in full, SOTOMAYOR and KAGAN, JJ., joined as to all but Part IV, and THOMAS, J., joined as to all but Part IV and footnote 6. SOTOMAYOR, J., filed an opinion concurring in part. KENNEDY, J., filed a dissenting opinion, in which ROBERTS, C. J., and BREYER and ALITO, JJ., joined.

In *Melendez–Diaz v. Massachusetts*, 129 S.Ct. 2527 (2009), this Court held that a forensic laboratory report stating that a suspect substance was cocaine ranked as testimonial for purposes of the Sixth Amendment's Confrontation Clause. The report had been created specifically to serve as evidence in a criminal proceeding. Absent stipulation, the Court ruled, the prosecution may not introduce such a report without offering a live witness competent to testify to the truth of the statements made in the report.

In the case before us, petitioner Donald Bullcoming was arrested on charges of driving while intoxicated (DWI). Principal evidence against Bullcoming was a forensic laboratory report certifying that Bullcoming's blood-alcohol concentration was well above the threshold for aggravated DWI. At trial, the prosecution did not call as a witness the analyst who signed the certification. Instead, the State called another analyst who was familiar with the laboratory's testing procedures, but had neither participated in nor observed the test on Bullcoming's blood sample. The New Mexico Supreme Court determined that, although the blood-alcohol analysis was "testimonial," the Confrontation Clause did not require the certifying analyst's in-court testimony. Instead, New Mexico's high court held, live testimony of another analyst satisfied the constitutional requirements.

The question presented is whether the Confrontation Clause permits the prosecution to introduce a forensic laboratory report containing a testimonial certification—made for the purpose of proving a particular fact—through the in-court testimony of a scientist who did not sign the certification or perform or observe the test reported in the certification. We hold that surrogate testimony of that order does not meet the constitutional requirement. The accused's right is to be confronted with the analyst who made the certification, unless that analyst is unavailable at trial, and the accused had an opportunity, pretrial, to cross-examine that particular scientist.

I

A

In August 2005, a vehicle driven by petitioner Donald Bullcoming rear-ended a pickup truck at an intersection in Farmington, New Mexico. When the truckdriver exited his vehicle and approached Bullcoming to exchange insurance information, he noticed that Bullcoming's eyes were bloodshot. Smelling alcohol on Bullcoming's breath, the truckdriver told his wife to call the police. Bullcoming left the scene before the police arrived, but was soon apprehended by an officer who observed his performance of field sobriety tests. Upon failing the tests, Bullcoming was arrested for driving a vehicle while "under the influence of intoxicating liquor" (DWI)....

Because Bullcoming refused to take a breath test, the police obtained a warrant authorizing a blood-alcohol analysis. Pursuant to the warrant, a sample of Bullcoming's blood was drawn at a local hospital. To determine Bullcoming's blood-alcohol concentration (BAC), the police sent the sample to the New Mexico Department of Health, Scientific Laboratory Division (SLD). In a standard SLD form titled "Report of Blood Alcohol Analysis," participants in the testing were identified, and the forensic analyst certified his finding.

SLD's report contained in the top block "information ... filled in by [the] arresting officer." This information included the "reason [the] suspect [was] stopped" (the officer checked "Accident"), and the date ("8.14.05") and time ("18:25 PM") the blood sample was drawn....

Following these segments, the report presented the "certificate of analyst," completed and signed by Curtis Caylor, the SLD forensic analyst assigned to test Bullcoming's blood sample. Caylor recorded that the BAC in Bullcoming's sample was 0.21 grams per hundred milliliters, an inordinately high level. Caylor also affirmed that "[t]he seal of th[e] sample was received intact and broken in the laboratory," that "the statements in [the analyst's block of the report] are correct," and that he had "followed the procedures set out on the reverse of th[e] report." Those "procedures" instructed analysts, *inter alia,* to "retai[n] the sample container and the raw data from the analysis," and to "not[e] any circumstance or condition which might affect the integrity of the sample or otherwise affect the validity of the analysis." Finally, in a block headed "certificate of reviewer," the SLD examiner who reviewed Caylor's analysis certified that Caylor was qualified to conduct the BAC test, and that the "established procedure" for handling and analyzing Bullcoming's sample "ha[d] been followed."

SLD analysts use gas chromatograph machines to determine BAC levels. Operation of the machines requires specialized knowledge and training. Several steps are involved in the gas chromatograph process, and human error can occur at each step....

B

The case was tried to a jury in November 2005, after our decision in *Crawford v. Washington,* 541 U.S. 36 (2004), but before *Melendez–Diaz.* On the day of trial, the State announced that it would not be calling SLD analyst Curtis Caylor as a witness because he had "very recently [been] put on unpaid leave" for a reason not revealed. A startled defense counsel objected. The prosecution, she complained, had never disclosed, until trial commenced, that the witness "out there ... [was] not the analyst [of Bullcoming's sample]." Counsel stated that, "had [she] known that the analyst [who tested Bullcoming's blood] was not available," her opening, indeed, her entire defense "may very well have been dramatically different." The State, however, proposed to introduce Caylor's finding as a "business record" during the testimony of Gerasimos Razatos, an SLD scientist who had neither observed nor reviewed Caylor's analysis.

Bullcoming's counsel opposed the State's proposal. Without Caylor's testimony, defense counsel maintained, introduction of the analyst's finding would violate Bullcoming's Sixth

Amendment right "to be confronted with the witnesses against him." The trial court overruled the objection and admitted the SLD report as a business record. The jury convicted Bullcoming of aggravated DWI, and the New Mexico Court of Appeals upheld the conviction, concluding that "the blood alcohol report in the present case was non-testimonial and prepared routinely with guarantees of trustworthiness." *State v. Bullcoming*, 144 N.M. 546, 189 P.3d 679, 685 (2008).

C

While Bullcoming's appeal was pending before the New Mexico Supreme Court, this Court decided *Melendez–Diaz*. In that case, "[t]he Massachusetts courts [had] admitted into evidence affidavits reporting the results of forensic analysis which showed that material seized by the police and connected to the defendant was cocaine." 129 S.Ct., at 2530. Those affidavits, the Court held, were " 'testimonial,' rendering the affiants 'witnesses' subject to the defendant's right of confrontation under the Sixth Amendment." *Ibid.*

In light of *Melendez–Diaz*, the New Mexico Supreme Court acknowledged that the blood-alcohol report introduced at Bullcoming's trial qualified as testimonial evidence. Like the affidavits in *Melendez–Diaz*, the court observed, the report was "functionally identical to live, in-court testimony, doing precisely what a witness does on direct examination." *State v. Bullcoming*, 147 N.M. 487, 226 P.3d 1, at 8 (2010) (quoting *Melendez–Diaz*, 129 S.Ct., at 2532). Nevertheless, for two reasons, the court held that admission of the report did not violate the Confrontation Clause.

First, the court said certifying analyst Caylor "was a mere scrivener," who "simply transcribed the results generated by the gas chromatograph machine." 226 P.3d, at 8–9. Second, SLD analyst Razatos, although he did not participate in testing Bullcoming's blood, "qualified as an expert witness with respect to the gas chromatograph machine." *Id.*, at 9. "Razatos provided live, in-court testimony," the court stated, "and, thus, was available for cross-examination regarding the operation of the … machine, the results of [Bullcoming's] BAC test, and the SLD's established laboratory procedures." *Ibid.* Razatos' testimony was crucial, the court explained, because Bullcoming could not cross-examine the machine or the written report. *Id.*, at 10. But "[Bullcoming's] right of confrontation was preserved," the court concluded, because Razatos was a qualified analyst, able to serve as a surrogate for Caylor. *Ibid.*

We granted certiorari to address this question: Does the Confrontation Clause permit the prosecution to introduce a forensic laboratory report containing a testimonial certification, made in order to prove a fact at a criminal trial, through the in-court testimony of an analyst who did not sign the certification or personally perform or observe the performance of the test reported in the certification. Our answer is in line with controlling precedent: As a rule, if an out-of-court statement is testimonial in nature, it may not be introduced against the accused at trial unless the witness who made the statement is unavailable and the accused has had a prior opportunity to confront that witness. Because the New Mexico Supreme Court permitted the testimonial statement of one witness, *i.e.*, Caylor, to enter into evidence through the in-court testimony of a second person, *i.e.*, Razatos, we reverse that court's judgment.

II

The Sixth Amendment's Confrontation Clause confers upon the accused "[i]n all criminal prosecutions, … the right … to be confronted with the witnesses against him." …
[In *Melendez–Diaz*, an] analyst's certification prepared in connection with a criminal in-

vestigation or prosecution, the Court held, is "testimonial," and therefore within the compass of the Confrontation Clause. 129 S.Ct., at 2537–2540.[6] ...

A

The New Mexico Supreme Court held surrogate testimony adequate to satisfy the Confrontation Clause in this case because analyst Caylor "simply transcribed the resul[t] generated by the gas chromatograph machine," presenting no interpretation and exercising no independent judgment. 226 P.3d, at 8. Bullcoming's "true 'accuser,'" the court said, was the machine, while testing analyst Caylor's role was that of "mere scrivener." *Id.,* at 9. Caylor's certification, however, reported more than a machine-generated number.

Caylor certified that he received Bullcoming's blood sample intact with the seal unbroken, that he checked to make sure that the forensic report number and the sample number "correspond[ed]," and that he performed on Bullcoming's sample a particular test, adhering to a precise protocol. He further represented, by leaving the "[r]emarks" section of the report blank, that no "circumstance or condition ... affect[ed] the integrity of the sample or ... the validity of the analysis." These representations, relating to past events and human actions not revealed in raw, machine-produced data, are meet for cross-examination.

... [T]he comparative reliability of an analyst's testimonial report drawn from machine-produced data does not overcome the Sixth Amendment bar. This Court settled in *Crawford* that the "obviou[s] reliab[ility]" of a testimonial statement does not dispense with the Confrontation Clause. 541 U.S., at 62 (Clause "commands, not that evidence be reliable, but that reliability be assessed in a particular manner: by testing [the evidence] in the crucible of cross-examination"). Accordingly, the analysts who write reports that the prosecution introduces must be made available for confrontation even if they possess "the scientific acumen of Mme. Curie and the veracity of Mother Teresa." *Melendez–Diaz,* 129 S.Ct., at 2537, n. 6.

B

Recognizing that admission of the blood-alcohol analysis depended on "live, in-court testimony [by] a qualified analyst," 226 P.3d, at 10, the New Mexico Supreme Court believed that Razatos could substitute for Caylor because Razatos "qualified as an expert witness with respect to the gas chromatograph machine and the SLD's laboratory procedures," *id.,* at 9. But surrogate testimony of the kind Razatos was equipped to give could not convey what Caylor knew or observed about the events his certification concerned, *i.e.,* the particular test and testing process he employed. Nor could such surrogate testimony expose any lapses or lies on the certifying analyst's part. Significant here, Razatos had no knowledge of the reason why Caylor had been placed on unpaid leave. With Caylor on the stand, Bullcoming's counsel could have asked questions designed to reveal whether incompetence, evasiveness, or dishonesty accounted for Caylor's removal from his work station. Notable in this regard, the State never asserted that Caylor was "unavailable"; the prosecution conveyed only that Caylor was on uncompensated leave. Nor did the State

---

6. To rank as "testimonial," a statement must have a "primary purpose" of "establish[ing] or prov[ing] past events potentially relevant to later criminal prosecution." *Davis v. Washington,* 547 U.S. 813, 822, (2006). See also *Bryant,* 131 S.Ct., at 1155. Elaborating on the purpose for which a "testimonial report" is created, we observed in *Melendez–Diaz* that business and public records "are generally admissible absent confrontation ... because—having been created for the administration of an entity's affairs and not for the purpose of establishing or proving some fact at trial—they are not testimonial." 129 S.Ct., at 2539–2540.

assert that Razatos had any "independent opinion" concerning Bullcoming's BAC. In this light, Caylor's live testimony could hardly be typed "a hollow formality." ...

In short, when the State elected to introduce Caylor's certification, Caylor became a witness Bullcoming had the right to confront. Our precedent cannot sensibly be read any other way. See *Melendez–Diaz*, 129 S.Ct., at 2545 (KENNEDY, J., dissenting) (Court's holding means "the ... analyst who must testify is the person who signed the certificate").

III

We turn, finally, to the State's contention that the SLD's blood-alcohol analysis reports are nontestimonial in character, therefore no Confrontation Clause question even arises in this case. *Melendez–Diaz* left no room for that argument, the New Mexico Supreme Court concluded, see 226 P.3d, at 7–8, a conclusion we find inescapable.

In *Melendez–Diaz*, a state forensic laboratory, on police request, analyzed seized evidence (plastic bags) and reported the laboratory's analysis to the police (the substance found in the bags contained cocaine). The "certificates of analysis" prepared by the analysts who tested the evidence in *Melendez–Diaz*, this Court held, were "incontrovertibly ... affirmation[s] made for the purpose of establishing or proving some fact" in a criminal proceeding. 129 S.Ct., at 2532 (internal quotation marks omitted). The same purpose was served by the certificate in question here.

The State maintains that the affirmations made by analyst Caylor were not "adversarial" or "inquisitorial"; instead, they were simply observations of an "independent scientis[t]" made "according to a non-adversarial public duty." That argument fares no better here than it did in *Melendez–Diaz*. A document created solely for an "evidentiary purpose," *Melendez–Diaz* clarified, made in aid of a police investigation, ranks as testimonial. 129 S.Ct., at 2532 (forensic reports available for use at trial are "testimonial statements" and certifying analyst is a " 'witness' for purposes of the Sixth Amendment"). ...

In all material respects, the laboratory report in this case resembles those in *Melendez–Diaz*. Here, as in *Melendez–Diaz*, a law-enforcement officer provided seized evidence to a state laboratory required by law to assist in police investigations. Like the analysts in *Melendez–Diaz*, analyst Caylor tested the evidence and prepared a certificate concerning the result of his analysis. Like the *Melendez–Diaz* certificates, Caylor's certificate is "formalized" in a signed document, *Davis*, 547 U.S., at 837, n. 2 (opinion of THOMAS, J.), headed a "report." Noteworthy as well, the SLD report form contains a legend referring to municipal and magistrate courts' rules that provide for the admission of certified blood-alcohol analyses.

In sum, the formalities attending the "report of blood alcohol analysis" are more than adequate to qualify Caylor's assertions as testimonial. ... The New Mexico Supreme Court, guided by *Melendez–Diaz*, correctly recognized that Caylor's report "fell within the core class of testimonial statements" 226 P.3d, at 7, described in this Court's leading Confrontation Clause decisions.

IV

The State and its *amici* urge that unbending application of the Confrontation Clause to forensic evidence would impose an undue burden on the prosecution. This argument, also advanced in the dissent, largely repeats a refrain rehearsed and rejected in *Melendez–Diaz*. The constitutional requirement, we reiterate, "may not [be] disregard[ed] ... at our convenience," *Melendez-Diaz*, 129 S.Ct., at 2540, and the predictions of dire consequences, we again observe, are dubious.

New Mexico law, it bears emphasis, requires the laboratory to preserve samples, which can be retested by other analysts, and neither party questions SLD's compliance with that requirement. Retesting "is almost always an option … in [DWI] cases," Brief for Public Defender Service for District of Columbia et al. as *Amici Curiae* 25 (hereinafter PDS Brief), and the State had that option here: New Mexico could have avoided any Confrontation Clause problem by asking Razatos to retest the sample, and then testify to the results of his retest rather than to the results of a test he did not conduct or observe.

Notably, New Mexico advocates retesting as an effective means to preserve a defendant's confrontation right "when the [out-of-court] statement is raw data or a mere transcription of raw data onto a public record." But the State would require the defendant to initiate retesting. The prosecution, however, bears the burden of proof. *Melendez–Diaz*, 129 S.Ct., at 2540 ("[T]he Confrontation Clause imposes a burden on the prosecution to present its witnesses, not on the defendant to bring those adverse witnesses into court."). Hence the obligation to propel retesting when the original analyst is unavailable is the State's, not the defendant's. …

We note also the "small fraction of … cases" that "actually proceed to trial." *Melendez–Diaz*, 129 S.Ct., at 2540 (citing estimate that "nearly 95% of convictions in state and federal courts are obtained via guilty plea"). And, "when cases in which forensic analysis has been conducted [do] go to trial," defendants "regularly … [stipulate] to the admission of [the] analysis." PDS Brief 20. "[A]s a result, analysts testify in only a very small percentage of cases," *id.*, at 21, for "[i]t is unlikely that defense counsel will insist on live testimony whose effect will be merely to highlight rather than cast doubt upon the forensic analysis." *Melendez–Diaz*, 129 S.Ct., at 2542. …

For the reasons stated, the judgment of the New Mexico Supreme Court is reversed, and the case is remanded for further proceedings not inconsistent with this opinion.

It is so ordered.

Justice SOTOMAYOR, concurring in part.

I agree with the Court that the trial court erred by admitting the blood alcohol concentration (BAC) report. I write separately first to highlight why I view the report at issue to be testimonial — specifically because its "primary purpose" is evidentiary — and second to emphasize the limited reach of the Court's opinion.

I

A

Under our precedents, the New Mexico Supreme Court was correct to hold that the certified BAC report in this case is testimonial.

To determine if a statement is testimonial, we must decide whether it has "a primary purpose of creating an out-of-court substitute for trial testimony." *Michigan v. Bryant*, 131 S.Ct. 1143, 1155 (2011). When the "primary purpose" of a statement is "not to create a record for trial," *ibid.*, "the admissibility of [the] statement is the concern of state and federal rules of evidence, not the Confrontation Clause," *id.*, 131 S.Ct., at 1155.

This is not the first time the Court has faced the question of whether a scientific report is testimonial. As the Court explains, in *Melendez–Diaz v. Massachusetts*, 129 S.Ct. 2527 (2009), we held that "certificates of analysis," completed by employees of the State Laboratory Institute of the Massachusetts Department of Public Health, *id.*, 129 S.Ct., at 2530–2531, were testimonial because they were "incontrovertibly … "'solemn declaration[s] or affirmation[s] made for the purpose of establishing or proving some fact,'"" *id.*, 129 S.Ct., at

2532 (quoting *Crawford v. Washington*, 541 U.S. 36, 51, (2004), in turn quoting 2 N. Webster, An American Dictionary of the English Language (1828)).

As we explained earlier this Term in *Michigan v. Bryant*, 131 S.Ct. 1143 (2011), "[i]n making the primary purpose determination, standard rules of hearsay ... will be relevant." *Id.*, 131 S.Ct., at 1155.[1] As applied to a scientific report, *Melendez–Diaz* explained that pursuant to Federal Rule of Evidence 803, "[d]ocuments kept in the regular course of business may ordinarily be admitted at trial despite their hearsay status," except "if the regularly conducted business activity is the production of evidence for use at trial." 129 S.Ct., at 2538 (citing Fed. Rule Evid. 803(6)). In that circumstance, the hearsay rules bar admission of even business records. Relatedly, in the Confrontation Clause context, business and public records "are generally admissible absent confrontation ... because—having been created for the administration of an entity's affairs and not for the purpose of establishing or proving some fact at trial—they are not testimonial." *Melendez–Diaz*, 129 S.Ct., at 2539–2540. We concluded, therefore, that because the purpose of the certificates of analysis was use at trial, they were not properly admissible as business or public records under the hearsay rules, nor were they admissible under the Confrontation Clause. The hearsay rule's recognition of the certificates' evidentiary purpose thus confirmed our decision that the certificates were testimonial under the primary purpose analysis required by the Confrontation Clause....

The formality inherent in the certification further suggests its evidentiary purpose. Although "[f]ormality is not the sole touchstone of our primary purpose inquiry," a statement's formality or informality can shed light on whether a particular statement has a primary purpose of use at trial. *Bryant*, 131 S.Ct., at 1160....

In sum, I am compelled to conclude that the report has a "primary purpose of creating an out-of-court substitute for trial testimony," *Bryant*, 131 S.Ct., at 1155, which renders it testimonial....

II

Although this case is materially indistinguishable from the facts we considered in *Melendez–Diaz*, I highlight some of the factual circumstances that this case does *not* present.

First, this is not a case in which the State suggested an alternate purpose, much less an alternate *primary* purpose, for the BAC report. For example, the State has not claimed that the report was necessary to provide Bullcoming with medical treatment....

Second, this is not a case in which the person testifying is a supervisor, reviewer, or someone else with a personal, albeit limited, connection to the scientific test at issue. Razatos conceded on cross-examination that he played no role in producing the BAC report and did not observe any portion of Curtis Caylor's conduct of the testing....

Third, this is not a case in which an expert witness was asked for his independent opinion about underlying testimonial reports that were not themselves admitted into evidence. See Fed. Rule Evid. 703 (explaining that facts or data of a type upon which experts in the field would reasonably rely in forming an opinion need not be admissible in order for the expert's opinion based on the facts and data to be admitted). As the Court notes, the State does not assert that Razatos offered an independent, expert opinion about Bullcoming's blood alcohol concentration.... We would face a different

---

1. Contrary to the dissent's characterization, *Bryant* deemed reliability, as reflected in the hearsay rules, to be "relevant," 131 S.Ct., at 1155–1156, not "essential" (opinion of KENNEDY, J.). The rules of evidence, not the Confrontation Clause, are designed primarily to police reliability; the purpose of the Confrontation Clause is to determine whether statements are testimonial and therefore require confrontation.

question if asked to determine the constitutionality of allowing an expert witness to discuss others' testimonial statements if the testimonial statements were not themselves admitted as evidence.

Finally, this is not a case in which the State introduced only machine-generated results, such as a printout from a gas chromatograph. The State here introduced Caylor's statements, which included his transcription of a blood alcohol concentration, apparently copied from a gas chromatograph printout, along with other statements about the procedures used in handling the blood sample....

This case does not present, and thus the Court's opinion does not address, any of these factual scenarios.

. . .

As in *Melendez–Diaz*, the primary purpose of the BAC report is clearly to serve as evidence. It is therefore testimonial, and the trial court erred in allowing the State to introduce it into evidence via Razatos' testimony. I respectfully concur.

Justice KENNEDY, with whom THE CHIEF JUSTICE, Justice BREYER, and Justice ALITO join, dissenting.

... Whether or not one agrees with the reasoning and the result in *Melendez–Diaz*, the Court today takes the new and serious misstep of extending that holding to instances like this one. Here a knowledgeable representative of the laboratory was present to testify and to explain the lab's processes and the details of the report; but because he was not the analyst who filled out part of the form and transcribed onto it the test result from a machine printout, the Court finds a confrontation violation. Some of the principal objections to the Court's underlying theory have been set out earlier and need not be repeated here. See *Melendez-Diaz*, 129 S.Ct., at 2544 (KENNEDY, J., dissenting). Additional reasons, applicable to the extension of that doctrine and to the new ruling in this case, are now explained in support of this respectful dissent.

I

Before today, the Court had not held that the Confrontation Clause bars admission of scientific findings when an employee of the testing laboratory authenticates the findings, testifies to the laboratory's methods and practices, and is cross-examined at trial.... Unlike *Melendez–Diaz*, where the jury was asked to credit a laboratory's findings based solely on documents that were "quite plainly affidavits," 129 S.Ct., at 2543 (THOMAS, J., concurring) (internal quotation marks omitted), here the signature, heading, or legend on the document were routine authentication elements for a report that would be assessed and explained by in-court testimony subject to full cross-examination. The only sworn statement at issue was that of the witness who was present and who testified.

The record reveals that the certifying analyst's role here was no greater than that of anyone else in the chain of custody. The information contained in the report was the result of a scientific process comprising multiple participants' acts, each with its own evidentiary significance. These acts included receipt of the sample at the laboratory; recording its receipt; storing it; placing the sample into the testing device; transposing the printout of the results of the test onto the report; and review of the results....

The representative of the testing laboratory whom the prosecution called was a scientific analyst named Mr. Razatos. He testified that he "help[ed] in overseeing the administration of these programs throughout the State," and he was qualified to answer questions concerning each of these steps.... Here, the defense used the opportunity in cross-examination to highlight the absence at trial of certain laboratory employees. Under questioning by Bullcoming's attorney, Razatos acknowledged that his name did not appear on the report; that he did not receive the sample, perform the analysis, or complete the review; and that he did not know the reason for some personnel decisions....

In these circumstances, requiring the State to call the technician who filled out a form and recorded the results of a test is a hollow formality. The defense remains free to challenge any and all forensic evidence. It may call and examine the technician who performed a test. And it may call other expert witnesses to explain that tests are not always reliable or that the technician might have made a mistake. The jury can then decide whether to credit the test, as it did here. The States, furthermore, can assess the progress of scientific testing and enact or adopt statutes and rules to ensure that only reliable evidence is admitted. Rejecting these commonsense arguments and the concept that reliability is a legitimate concern, the Court today takes a different course. It once more assumes for itself a central role in mandating detailed evidentiary rules, thereby extending and confirming *Melendez–Diaz*'s "vast potential to disrupt criminal procedures." 129 S.Ct., at 2544 (KENNEDY, J., dissenting).

II

The protections in the Confrontation Clause, and indeed the Sixth Amendment in general, are designed to ensure a fair trial with reliable evidence. But the *Crawford v. Washington* line of cases has treated the reliability of evidence as a reason to exclude it. Today, for example, the Court bars admission of a lab report because it "is formalized in a signed document." The Court's unconventional and unstated premise is that the State — by acting to ensure a statement's reliability — makes the statement more formal and therefore less likely to be admitted. That is so, the Court insists, because reliability does not animate the Confrontation Clause. Yet just this Term the Court ruled that, in another confrontation context, reliability was an essential part of the constitutional inquiry. *See Michigan v. Bryant*, 131 S.Ct. 1143, 1155–1156, 1157–1158, (2010).

Like reliability, other principles have weaved in and out of the *Crawford* jurisprudence. Solemnity has sometimes been dispositive, and sometimes not. So, too, with the elusive distinction between utterances aimed at proving past events, and those calculated to help police keep the peace.

… That the Court in the wake of *Crawford* has had such trouble fashioning a clear vision of that case's meaning is unsettling; for *Crawford* binds every judge in every criminal trial in every local, state, and federal court in the Nation. This Court's prior decisions leave trial judges to "guess what future rules this Court will distill from the sparse constitutional text," *Melendez–Diaz*, 129 S.Ct., at 2544 (KENNEDY, J., dissenting), or to struggle to apply an "amorphous, if not entirely subjective," "highly context-dependent inquiry" involving "open-ended balancing." *Bryant*, 131 S.Ct., at 1175–1176 (SCALIA, J., dissenting) (internal quotation marks omitted) (listing 11 factors relevant under the majority's approach).

III

Crawford itself does not compel today's conclusion. It is true, as *Crawford* confirmed, that the Confrontation Clause seeks in part to bar the government from replicating trial procedures outside of public view. *Crawford* explained that the basic purpose of the Clause was to address the sort of abuses exemplified at the notorious treason trial of Sir Walter Raleigh. On this view the Clause operates to bar admission of out-of-court statements obtained through formal interrogation in preparation for trial. The danger is that innocent defendants may be convicted on the basis of unreliable, untested statements by those who observed—or claimed to have observed—preparation for or commission of the crime. And, of course, those statements might not have been uttered at all or—even if spoken—might not have been true.

A rule that bars testimony of that sort, however, provides neither cause nor necessity to impose a constitutional bar on the admission of impartial lab reports like the instant one, reports prepared by experienced technicians in laboratories that follow professional norms and scientific protocols. In addition to the constitutional right to call witnesses in his own defense, the defendant in this case was already protected by checks on potential prosecutorial abuse such as free retesting for defendants; result-blind issuance of reports; testing by an independent agency; routine processes performed en masse, which reduce opportunities for targeted bias; and labs operating pursuant to scientific and professional norms and oversight....

Instead of freeing the Clause from reliance on hearsay doctrines, the Court has now linked the Clause with hearsay rules in their earliest, most rigid, and least refined formulations. In cases like *Melendez–Diaz* and this one, the Court has tied the Confrontation Clause to 18th century hearsay rules unleavened by principles tending to make those rules more sensible. As a result, the Court has taken the Clause far beyond its most important application, which is to forbid sworn, *ex parte,* out-of-court statements by unconfronted and available witnesses who observed the crime and do not appear at trial.

... [T]he States are not just at risk of having some of their hearsay rules reviewed by this Court. They often are foreclosed now from contributing to the formulation and enactment of rules that make trials fairer and more reliable. For instance, recent state laws allowing admission of well-documented and supported reports of abuse by women whose abusers later murdered them must give way, unless that abuser murdered with the specific purpose of foreclosing the testimony. Whether those statutes could provide sufficient indicia of reliability and other safeguards to comply with the Confrontation Clause as it should be understood is, to be sure, an open question. The point is that the States cannot now participate in the development of this difficult part of the law.

In short, there is an ongoing, continued, and systemic displacement of the States and dislocation of the federal structure. If this Court persists in applying wooden formalism in order to bar reliable testimony offered by the prosecution—testimony thought proper for many decades in state and federal courts committed to devising fair trial processes— then the States might find it necessary and appropriate to enact statutes to accommodate this new, intrusive federal regime. If they do, those rules could remain on State statute books for decades, even if subsequent decisions of this Court were to better implement the objectives of *Crawford*. This underscores the disruptive, long-term structural consequences of decisions like the one the Court announces today.

States also may decide it is proper and appropriate to enact statutes that require defense counsel to give advance notice if they are going to object to introduction of a report without the presence in court of the technician who prepared it. Indeed, today's opinion relies upon laws of that sort as a palliative to the disruption it is causing. It is quite unrealistic, however, to think that this will take away from the defense the incentives to insist on having the certifying analyst present. There is in the ordinary case that proceeds to trial no good reason for defense counsel to waive the right of confrontation as the Court now interprets it.

... New Mexico's experience exemplifies the problems ahead. From 2008 to 2010, subpoenas requiring New Mexico analysts to testify in impaired-driving cases rose 71%, to 1,600—or 8 or 9 every workday. New Mexico Scientific Laboratory Brief 2. In a State that is the Nation's fifth largest by area and that employs just 10 total analysts, each analyst in blood alcohol cases recently received 200 subpoenas per year. The analysts now must travel great distances on most working days. The result has been, in the laboratory's words, "chaotic." And if the defense raises an objection and the analyst is tied up in another court proceeding; or on leave; or absent; or delayed in transit; or no longer employed; or ill; or no longer living, the defense gets a windfall. As a result, good defense attorneys will object in ever-greater numbers to a prosecution failure or inability to produce laboratory analysts at trial....

Seven years after its initiation, it bears remembering that the *Crawford* approach was not preordained. This Court's missteps have produced an interpretation of the word "witness" at odds with its meaning elsewhere in the Constitution ... and at odds with the sound administration of justice. It is time to return to solid ground. A proper place to begin that return is to decline to extend *Melendez–Diaz* to bar the reliable, commonsense evidentiary framework the State sought to follow in this case.

C. The Evolution of the Confrontation Clause after *Bryant* and *Bullcoming*

In recent years, the Supreme Court has applied the holdings in *Bryant* and *Bullcoming* to broader contexts. Perhaps these decisions muddied the waters more than clarified, but they are important to our understanding of the definition of "testimonial."

Ohio v. Clark

In 2015, the Supreme Court again examined the primary purpose test in *Ohio v. Clark,* 135 S.Ct. 2173 (2015), by exploring the intent of interrogators and declarants in the context of child abuse. In *Clark,* the defendant was tried for beating a three-year-old boy. The child did not testify, but the state presented evidence that he told his teachers that Clark had assaulted him. The Court unanimously found that the child's statements were nontestimonial, even though the teachers possessed an obligation under the state's mandatory-reporting law to report suspected abuse to government authorities.

Writing for six members of the Court, Justice Alito ruled that in light of "all the relevant circumstances here, [the child's] statements clearly were not made with the primary purpose of creating evidence for Clark's prosecution." *Id.* at 2177. The Court examined a number of factors, including that the teachers' main concern was to protect the child, that the teachers did not inform the child that his answers would be used to punish the defendant, that the child never hinted that he intended for his statements to be used by the police, and that the conversation was informal and spontaneous. *Id.* at 2181. Instead, the Court found that the focus of the teachers was to end an ongoing threat and that the teachers would have acted with the same purpose whether or not they possessed a duty to report abuse.

While the Court declined to adopt a categorical rule as to whether statements to persons other than law enforcement officials are subject to the Confrontation Clause, it did note that such statements are much less likely to be testimonial as such statements are usually not made with the primary purpose of creating evidence for the prosecution. Furthermore, the Court stated that statements of very young children are unlikely to testimonial, as the declarant usually does not intend that his statements be a substitute for trial testimony.

Interestingly, two issues that remained open after *Michigan v. Bryant* were left unresolved. Throughout the opinion, Justice Alito focused on the intent of both the declarant and the teachers, noting all the participants of the conversation were not trying to gather evidence for the defendant's prosecution. At no point did the Court explicitly decided whether the test should turn on the perspective of the declarant, the interrogator, or both. Additionally, neither the majority opinion nor the two concurring opinions explored the reliability (or unreliability) of the child's statements, thus seemingly backing away from the *Bryant* analysis that considered reliability a factor in the calculus of determining a whether a statement is testimonial. A definitive answer to these two questions awaits for another day.

Williams v. Illinois

In 2012, the Supreme Court again applied *Crawford* in the forensic lab report setting in *Williams v. Illinois,* 132 S.Ct. 2221 (2012). In that case, a woman was raped and a rape kit vaginal swab was taken from the victim. The state police in Illinois sent the sample to Cellmark, a DNA research company in Maryland. Cellmark analyzed the semen on the DNA swab and sent a report of their findings back to the Illinois State Police. The Illinois State Police then searched the state DNA database and found that defendant Williams' DNA matched the Cellmark DNA profile.

At trial, Sandra Lambatos, a forensic scientist for the Illinois State Police testified that Williams' sample matched the Cellmark DNA profile. Even though Lambatos testified that Cellmark derived the DNA profile from the victim's swabs, the state did not offer the Cellmark report as evidence and did not call any witnesses from Cellmark. Thus, there was no direct evidence that the Cellmark DNA profile was in fact derived from the semen on the victim's swab and no evidence that Cellmark followed the correct procedures in analyzing the DNA. Williams was convicted and raised a Confrontation Clause objection.

The Supreme Court undertook the expected analysis: first, the Court analyzed whether the testimony of Lambatos was hearsay and then analyzed whether it was testimonial hearsay. But, the Court badly fractured in its decision. A four-member plurality found that the testimony was not offered for its truth and that no Confrontation Clause violation existed, while four dissenting justices found that the testimony was offered for its truth and that a Confrontation Clause violation existed. Justice Thomas wrote a separate opinion in which he disagreed with the plurality's reasoning; like the dissenters, Justice Thomas believed the testimony was hearsay and that forensic reports are typically testimonial, but he believed this particular forensic report was not formal enough to be testimonial. Therefore, because the Cellmark report was not testimonial, he agreed with the result and gave the four-member plurality a fifth vote.

Because the hearsay issue is inextricably intertwined with expert witness issues, it will be discussed in Section II.C of Chapter 10. For our current purposes, suffice it to say that when an expert states, "I relied on this document in my analysis," the four-member plurality believed that that statement is not offered for its truth, as it merely demonstrates what the expert relied upon in reaching her conclusions so that the fact finder can determine whether the expert is reliable in her conclusions. The four dissenters plus Justice Thomas believed that that statement is offered for its truth, because the validity of the expert's conclusions depends on the truth of the document.

Let us then move on to whether the expert's reliance on the Cellmark report was testimonial. The plurality made two arguments supporting the idea that the Cellmark report was not testimonial:

- The report is not a "witness against" the defendant. At the time that Cellmark did its analysis, no suspect had been identified (unlike *Melendez-Diaz* and *Bullcoming,* where the defendant was already arrested and charged when the forensic evidence was analyzed). Thus the initial use of the Cellmark report was to identify someone, not be a witness against a targeted individual like Williams. Accordingly, the report possessed no inculpatory, prosecutorial purpose and therefore there was no prospect of fabrication on the part of Cellmark.

- The report was so reliable that it should not be considered testimonial. After all, somehow the defendant's DNA was in Cellmark's lab, and no other evidence except the victim's swabs suggested how. The plurality stressed that DNA evidence is quite reliable, the report was crafted by an independent company (rather than a police official), and the circumstances here corroborate that Williams was, indeed, the rapist—Cellmark did not possess any other sample of Williams's DNA (so it could not have accidently analyzed his DNA), Williams's DNA matched the Cellmark report, and the victim identified Williams in a lineup after he was arrested.

The four dissenters plus Justice Thomas disagreed with both arguments:

- Any witness who testifies at trial against the defendant is a "witness against" the defendant, and that includes a hearsay declarant whose statement is offered to prove the truth of the matter in the statement. Indeed, the scope of cross-examination of any Cellmark analyst would have likely focused on whether her work was careless or incompetent, not whether Cellmark had a vendetta against Williams. In order to explore whether the work was careless or incompetent, it does not matter whether the police had a suspect at the time of the testing.

- "Corroboration" and "reliability" are not the touchstones of the analysis. The question is whether the statement is testimonial, not whether it is very reliable. If it is testimonial, the only remedy is confrontation of the witness.

As noted previously, Justice Thomas found that this particular report was not "solemn" or "formal" enough to qualify as testimonial. Thus, he disagreed with the reasoning of the plurality, but agreed with the result that Williams's conviction should be affirmed. None of the other eight justices endorsed Justice Thomas's reasoning.

As none of the plurality's reasoning received five votes, its reasoning will not be binding on future courts. Indeed, considering the even split between the plurality and the dissenters, the outcome of future cases may hinge on whether Justice Thomas considers the document "solemn" and "formal" enough to be testimonial. Moving forward, it seems that formal forensic reports will likely be deemed testimonial.

D. Synthesizing the Confrontation Clause

At present, we know that Confrontation Clause analysis boils down to three questions. First, is the statement testimonial? Second, if it is testimonial, is the declarant available for cross-examination? Third, if the declarant is not available for cross-examination, did the defendant have a prior opportunity to cross-examine the declarant?

Bryant and *Bullcoming* have muddied the waters of Confrontation Clause analysis, however. No longer is there a clear definition "testimonial," and, depending on how you interpret these cases, reliability plays a role in defining "testimonial," even though *Crawford* bemoaned the "vagaries" of the FRE and "amorphous" notions of reliability. *Davis* provided a straight-forward definition of "testimonial" in the context of police interrogations: non-testimonial interrogation means that, objectively, the primary purpose of the interrogation is to allow police assistance to an ongoing emergency. Conversely, testimonial interrogation means that, objectively, there is no ongoing emergency and the primary purpose the interrogation is to prove past events relevant for future criminal prosecution.

But *Bryant* presented a new context, one where an "ongoing emergency" extended beyond the initial victim and reached the public at large. The task now is to determine the primary purpose of the interrogation "by objectively evaluating the statements and actions of the parties to the encounter, in light of the circumstances in which the interrogation occurs." Furthermore, "standard rules of hearsay, designed to identify some statements as reliable, will be relevant" in determining a primary purpose. Why does reliability matter? Because "[i]mplicit in *Davis*" is the idea that statements meant to resolve an emergency possess a diminished prospect for fabrication and therefore "the Confrontation Clause does not require such statements to be subject to the crucible of cross-examination." So, we now possess a "context-dependent inquiry," that, according to Justice Scalia's dissent in *Bryant*, contains eleven variables and focuses on the reliability of the declarant's statement rather than "whether the declarant acted as a witness."

The unanimity of the Court in *Clark* honed the primary purpose test somewhat. The Court's concern centered on whether the primary purpose was creating evidence for a defendant's prosecution and whether the statements were meant to be a substitute for trial testimony. In terms of evaluating whether an ongoing emergency existed, the Court in both *Clark* and *Bryant* seemed to focus on factors that indicated immediacy (how close to harm was the declarant or the public?), magnitude (how great was the potential harm to the declarant or the public?), and particularity (how focused/certain was the potential harm?).

But, there was absolutely no unanimity in *Williams*, to put it mildly. In the context of forensic reports, the Court fractured in terms of defining who, precisely, is a "witness against" a criminal defendant. Do the concerns that inspired the Confrontation Clause exist when creating a scientific report when no suspect is identified? Is there really no prosecutorial purpose behind such a report, and therefore no risk of prosecutorial mischief? Even if there is no risk of prosecutorial mischief, should the defendant still be given every opportunity to explore any potential errors made by an independent criminal laboratory undertaking a scientific process?

Based on the foregoing cases, the law is far from clear. On the next page you will find a somewhat oversimplified decision tree to help guide you through a Confrontation Clause analysis, as it is currently formulated.

To analyze this decision tree, let us imagine a hypothetical: A police officer hears a gun fire and immediately pulls her car into a store's parking lot, where she observes a dead man with a gunshot wound. She exits her car and immediately asks, "Who did this?" Someone in the parking lot shouts, "It was Dirk!" In the confusion of the crime scene, the declarant leaves and remains unknown. The police officer testifies to the bystander/declarant's statement at trial. Now, let us create a second hypothetical by adding a single twist to the first: before the officer exits her vehicle and asks her question, she hears a dispatch on her vehicle's radio that states that a suspect named Dirk is in custody for the shooting. Keeping each hypothetical in mind, let us go through the decision tree.

First, we ask if this statement is offered against a defendant in a criminal case. If it is not, the Confrontation Clause does not apply. But, here, it is so offered. So, we then ask if this is admissible hearsay. Keep in mind that if it is not hearsay, it does not raise Confrontation Clause concerns, as the Confrontation Clause does not bar the use of testimonial statements for purposes other than establishing the truth of the matter asserted. In other words, a statement not offered for its truth does not "testify" to anything. Additionally,

Confrontation Clause Decision Tree

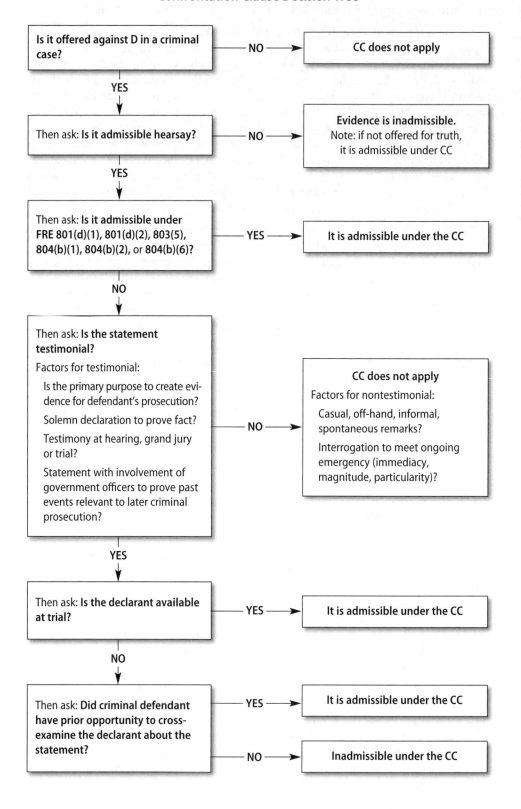

if it does not fit under a hearsay exemption/exception, then our analysis ends, as the evidence is inadmissible under FRE 802, and therefore there is no reason to continue the analysis. In our hypothetical, let us assume the statement from the bystander is offered for its truth (i.e., that Dirk did it) and satisfies the Excited Utterance exception, FRE 803(2).

Next, we must ask **how** it is admissible. Certain hearsay exemptions/exceptions satisfy the requirements of the Confrontation Clause due to an overlap between the mandates of the Confrontation Clause and the foundational requirements of the exemption/exception. In other words, by meeting the foundational requirements of these exemptions/exceptions, you have also satisfied the Confrontation Clause. Let us go through each example listed in the decision tree. FRE 801(d)(1) satisfies the Confrontation Clause because the exemption mandates that the witness be on the stand, and, therefore, the defendant may confront the witness. FRE 801(d)(2) raises no Confrontation Clause concerns because the defendant can confront his own words, and the Supreme Court has held that a defendant cannot complain of a failure to confront others speaking on his behalf. FRE 803(5) mandates that the declarant be on the stand, so the defendant may confront the declarant. FRE 804(b)(1) allows prior testimony only if the defendant had an opportunity and similar motive to examine the declarant on the prior occasion, which satisfies the Confrontation Clause. FRE 804(b)(2) was discussed in *Crawford* and appears to have been grandfathered into the Confrontation Clause as a founding-era exception. FRE 804(b)(6) was discussed in *Giles*, where the Court held that one may forfeit their Confrontation Clause right. In our hypothetical, none of these exemptions/exceptions apply.

Our next task is to determine if the statement is testimonial, as the defendant only has the right to confront witnesses regarding testimonial statements. Therefore, we must examine the factors articulated in *Crawford*, *Davis*, and *Bryant*. In the *Crawford* setting, we are concerned, in essence, with whether the statement is better characterized as a solemn declaration or a casual, off-hand remark. In the *Davis* setting, which applies only to police interrogations, we are concerned with the primary purpose the officer and declarant (Was either speaking about events actually happening? Was there an ongoing emergency? Were the statements necessary to resolve the emergency? What level of formality surrounded the statement?). In the *Bryant* setting, in which the ongoing emergency goes beyond the victim, a context-dependent inquiry emerges, examining such factors as the type of weapon, type of crime, type of danger, level of formality, and, to a degree, the reliability of the statement.

In our first version of the hypothetical, there is a strong argument that the focus of the officer's question is to respond to an ongoing emergency, as she responded immediately, there is a murder victim, and an assailant is on the loose. If that is the case, then the witness's statement would not be testimonial and would be admissible under the Confrontation Clause, as the type of crime and level of danger makes it seem unlikely that the police officer or the declarant was trying to prove past events with an eye toward a criminal trial. The context of an excited utterance makes the statement more reliable, as the Court noted in *Bryant*, due to the limited risk of fabrication. A counterargument exists, however. The victim is already dead, so the officer may have been thinking less about the emergency and more about gaining proof for trial. For all we know, the declarant may have believed that she was acting like a witness when she named Dirk as the perpetrator. In short, as in *Bryant*, the hypothetical walks the line between a structured interrogation and questioning that is meant to resolve an emergency.

In the second version of the hypothetical, however, we added the fact that defendant Dirk was already in custody when the officer shouted her question to the crowd. In this case, one could argue that she was attempting to prove past events relevant to later criminal prosecution because the defendant was already in custody, and, therefore, her motive was to obtain a testimonial statement. On the other hand, the declarant's motive might not have been testimonial, and *Bryant* made clear that both the declarant and interrogator's motives count. The declarant did not know Dirk was in custody and, arguably, did not envision his answer as giving testimony. In all likelihood, due to the diminished nature of the emergency in the second version of our hypothetical, the statement is probably testimonial.

If we are offering a testimonial statement, then the mandate from *Crawford* is clear: the declarant must be available at trial for confrontation or the defendant must have had a prior opportunity to cross-examine the unavailable declarant about the statement. If neither of these options is available, the statement is inadmissible, as it is a testimonial statement offered against a criminal defendant who was not afforded the right to confront the witness against him. Thus, in our second hypothetical, the excited utterance could not be used against the defendant, as he could not confront the declarant of the testimonial excited utterance.

Problem 8-1

On a brisk Detroit morning Samantha White and her husband Nathaniel White were having an argument. They started arguing in their house and continued their fight outside when Mr. White went to get the newspaper. As they were fighting, Jopez Johnson passed by on his daily jog. When he saw Mr. White berating Mrs. White he paused and asked Mrs. White if she was okay. Mr. White responded for Mrs. White by saying, "it's none of your f****** business — get out of here." When Mr. Johnson did not leave Mr. White went into his house and came out with a gun. As Mr. White began to shoot at Mr. Johnson, Mr. Johnson ran to a payphone to report the shots that had just been fired. When Mr. Johnson made the call he was very flustered and was shouting information at the dispatcher. The dispatcher could not understand him and had to tell Mr. Johnson to calm down so that she could understand what he was saying.

Officers Wiencek and Kue were in the area when they received a call from dispatch about the shooting and were on the scene within a few minutes. The two officers interviewed Mrs. White and Mr. Johnson separately. Both witnesses relayed the above facts. The officers had to get Mrs. White to stop crying to get her to tell them what happened. Mrs. White also told the officers that when Mr. Johnson ran to the payphone Mr. White went back into the house and to the best of her knowledge was still in there. Mrs. White then gave the officers a key to her house with permission to enter. The officers went in and conducted a sweep of the house. They found Mr. White on the second floor. After arresting Mr. White the officers spotted a bag of heroin and a gun in plain view. The gun matched the description which Mrs. White and Mr. Johnson provided the officers. Mr. White is now on trial for his actions. Neither Mrs. White nor Mr. Johnson is scheduled to testify at Mr. White's trial. Nonetheless the prosecutors want to introduce the statements made by the two witnesses when they were interviewed by Officers Wiencek and Kue in addition to Johnson's 911 phone call. Is the evidence admissible?

Problem 8-2

On July 1, 2009, Cleveland police organized a "buy-bust" operation. Detective Luther Roddy drove the confidential reliable informant ("CRI") to the buy site. Det. Roddy parked his undercover car nearby and observed the CRI approach the suspected dealer in the driveway of a home. Another officer, Detective Michael Raspberry, was also observing nearby from another undercover car. Both detectives observed the CRI engage in conversation with a man later identified as Byron Turner. The detectives observed the CRI back away from Turner and then quickly leave the scene.

The CRI returned to Det. Roddy's car in "less than a minute," and, in answer to Det. Roddy's question, "did you get anything," the CRI "immediately" answered negatively, adding, "he pulled a gun on me and told me to get the f—out of there, so I came right back to you."

Det. Roddy informed the other units, and police immediately converged on the house. Detective Frank Woyma, one of the responding officers, observed Turner quickly take a dark object from his waistband and hand it to another man, later identified as Deon Bulger. Bulger then ran into the house as the officers approached. Bulger was apprehended on the first floor, and a gun was discovered in the basement. Turner and Bulger were arrested and charged with illegal possession of a handgun.

At their trial, the CRI did not testify. Instead, Det. Roddy testified as to the CRI's statements. Are the CRI's statements admissible?

Problem 8-3

Igol Isaacs was shot on a street in Brooklyn. Police Captain Brian McGee responded to a radio call seeking assistance at the scene of the shooting. When McGee arrived at that location, there were other officers and a police van already present. McGee observed Isaacs lying face-up on the sidewalk, and a police officer with him. Without speaking with the other officers, McGee approached Isaacs, who was gasping for air. McGee knelt down beside him and asked "Who shot you?" Receiving no response, McGee then stated to Isaacs: "I don't think you're going to make it. Who shot you?" The victim responded, saying what McGee heard as "Todd shot me." When McGee sought to confirm "Todd shot you," the victim stated "[N]o. No. Tom shot me. Tom. Tom." McGee "kept asking" Isaacs "Tom, who?" but, according to McGee, it was difficult for Isaacs to breathe and he was unable to speak any further.

After McGee spoke with Isaacs, he had a conversation with another officer, but did not tell the other officer what Isaacs had said. McGee then began pushing back a crowd of people who had assembled, and set out to "preserve the crime scene." Isaacs died at the hospital sometime the same night. An autopsy revealed that he had six gunshot wounds. Three of the bullets entered Isaacs's abdomen, the right side of his back, and the left side of his back, respectively, perforated his kidney, liver, and small and large intestines, fractured two vertebrae and the spinal cord, and passed into his chest cavity, perforating the middle and lower lobes of the right lung.

Thomas Clay was subsequently charged with second-degree murder in connection with the death of Isaacs, and McGee testified to Isaacs's statements at trial. Are the statements of Isaacs admissible?

II. Due Process

As we have seen, the Confrontation Clause precludes the admission of otherwise admissible evidence due to constitutional concerns. Thus, a statement admissible under the FRE as, for example, an excited utterance, may still be inadmissible because it does not offer the defendant the opportunity to cross-examine a witness against her.

Now, we shall examine the opposite scenario: when does the Constitution require the admission of otherwise inadmissible evidence?

Chambers v. Mississippi
410 U.S. 284 (1973)

Mr. Justice POWELL delivered the opinion of the Court. WHITE, J., filed a concurring opinion. REHNQUIST, J., filed a dissenting opinion.

Petitioner, Leon Chambers, was tried by a jury in a Mississippi trial court and convicted of murdering a policeman. The jury assessed punishment at life imprisonment, and the Mississippi Supreme Court affirmed, one justice dissenting.... [T]he petition for certiorari was granted to consider whether petitioner's trial was conducted in accord with principles of due process under the Fourteenth Amendment. We conclude that it was not.

I

The events that led to petitioner's prosecution for murder occurred in the small town of Woodville in southern Mississippi. On Saturday evening, June 14, 1969, two Woodville policemen, James Forman and Aaron 'Sonny' Liberty, entered a local bar and pool hall to execute a warrant for the arrest of a youth named C. C. Jackson. Jackson resisted and a hostile crowd of some 50 or 60 persons gathered. The officers' first attempt to handcuff Jackson was frustrated when 20 or 25 men in the crowd intervened and wrestled him free. Forman then radioed for assistance and Liberty removed his riot gun, a 12-gauge sawed-off shotgun, from the car. Three deputy sheriffs arrived shortly thereafter and the officers again attempted to make their arrest. Once more, the officers were attacked by the onlookers and during the commotion five or six pistol shots were fired. Forman was looking in a different direction when the shooting began, but immediately saw that Liberty had been shot several times in the back. Before Liberty died, he turned around and fired both barrels of his riot gun into an alley in the area from which the shots appeared to have come. The first shot was wild and high and scattered the crowd standing at the face of the alley. Liberty appeared, however, to take more deliberate aim before the second shot and hit one of the men in the crowd in the back of the head and neck as he ran down the alley. That man was Leon Chambers.

Officer Forman could not see from his vantage point who shot Liberty or whether Liberty's shots hit anyone. One of the deputy sheriffs testified at trial that he was standing several feet from Liberty and that he saw Chambers shoot him. Another deputy sheriff stated that, although he could not see whether Chambers had a gun in his hand, he did see Chambers "break his arm down" shortly before the shots were fired. The officers who saw Chambers fall testified that they thought he was dead but they made no effort at that time either to examine him or to search for the murder weapon. Instead, they attended to Liberty, who was placed in the police car and taken to a hospital where he was declared dead on arrival. A subsequent autopsy showed that he had been hit with four bullets from a .22-caliber revolver.

Shortly after the shooting, three of Chambers' friends discovered that he was not yet dead. James Williams, Berkley Turner, and Gable McDonald loaded him into a car and transported him to the same hospital. Later that night, when the county sheriff discovered that Chambers was still alive, a guard was placed outside his room. Chambers was subsequently charged with Liberty's murder. He pleaded not guilty and has asserted his innocence throughout.

The story of Leon Chambers is intertwined with the story of another man, Gable McDonald. McDonald, a lifelong resident of Woodville, was in the crowd on the evening of Liberty's death. Sometime shortly after that day, he left his wife in Woodville and moved to Louisiana and found a job at a sugar mill. In November of that same year, he returned to Woodville when his wife informed him that an acquaintance of his, known as Reverend Stokes, wanted to see him. Stokes owned a gas station in Natchez, Mississippi, several miles north of Woodville, and upon his return McDonald went to see him. After talking to Stokes, McDonald agreed to make a statement to Chambers' attorneys, who maintained offices in Natchez. Two days later, he appeared at the attorneys' offices and gave a sworn confession that he shot Officer Liberty. He also stated that he had already told a friend of his, James Williams, that he shot Liberty. He said that he used his own pistol, a nine-shot .22-caliber revolver, which he had discarded shortly after the shooting. In response to questions from Chambers' attorneys, McDonald affirmed that his confession was voluntary and that no one had compelled him to come to them. Once the confession had been transcribed, signed, and witnessed, McDonald was turned over to the local police authorities and was placed in jail.

One month later, at a preliminary hearing, McDonald repudiated his prior sworn confession. He testified that Stokes had persuaded him to confess that he shot Liberty. He claimed that Stokes had promised that he would not go to jail and that he would share in the proceeds of a lawsuit that Chambers would bring against the town of Woodville. On examination by his own attorney and on cross-examination by the State, McDonald swore that he had not been at the scene when Liberty was shot but had been down the street drinking beer in a cafe with a friend, Berkley Turner. When he and Turner heard the shooting, he testified, they walked up the street and found Chambers lying in the alley. He, Turner, and Williams took Chambers to the hospital. McDonald further testified at the preliminary hearing that he did not know what had happened, that there was no discussion about the shooting either going to or coming back from the hospital, and that it was not until the next day that he learned the Chambers had been felled by a blast from Liberty's riot gun. In addition, McDonald stated that while he once owned a .22-caliber pistol he had lost it many months before the shooting and did not own or possess a weapon at that time. The local justice of the peace accepted McDonald's repudiation and released him from custody. The local authorities undertook no further investigation of his possible involvement.

Chambers' case came on for trial in October of the next year. At trial, he endeavored to develop two grounds of defense. He first attempted to show that he did not shoot

Liberty. Only one officer testified that he actually saw Chambers fire the shots. Although three officers saw Liberty shoot Chambers and testified that they assumed he was shooting his attacker, none of them examined Chambers to see whether he was still alive or whether he possessed a gun. Indeed, no weapon was ever recovered from the scene and there was no proof that Chambers had ever owned a .22-caliber pistol. One witness testified that he was standing in the street near where Liberty was shot, that he was looking at Chambers when the shooting began, and that he was sure that Chambers did not fire the shots.

Petitioner's second defense was that Gable McDonald had shot Officer Liberty. He was only partially successful, however, in his efforts to bring before the jury the testimony supporting this defense. Sam Hardin, a lifelong friend of McDonald's, testified that he saw McDonald shoot Liberty. A second witness, one of Liberty's cousins, testified that he saw McDonald immediately after the shooting with a pistol in his hand. In addition to the testimony of these two witnesses, Chambers endeavored to show the jury that McDonald had repeatedly confessed to the crime. Chambers attempted to prove that McDonald had admitted responsibility for the murder on four separate occasions, once when he gave the sworn statement to Chambers' counsel and three other times prior to that occasion in private conversations with friends.

In large measure, he was thwarted in his attempt to present this portion of his defense by the strict application of certain Mississippi rules of evidence. Chambers asserts in this Court, as he did unsuccessfully in his motion for new trial and on appeal to the State Supreme Court, that the application of these evidentiary rules rendered his trial fundamentally unfair and deprived him of due process of law. It is necessary, therefore, to examine carefully the rulings made during the trial.

II

Chambers filed a pretrial motion requesting the court to order McDonald to appear.... The trial court granted the motion.... At trial, after the State failed to put McDonald on the stand, Chambers called McDonald, laid a predicate for the introduction of his sworn out-of-court confession, had it admitted into evidence, and read it to the jury. The State, upon cross-examination, elicited from McDonald the fact that he had repudiated his prior confession. McDonald further testified, as he had at the preliminary hearing, that he did not shoot Liberty, and that he confessed to the crime only on the promise of Reverend Stokes that he would not go to jail and would share in a sizable tort recovery from the town. He also retold his own story of his actions on the evening of the shooting, including his visit to the cafe down the street, his absence from the scene during the critical period, and his subsequent trip to the hospital with Chambers.

At the conclusion of the State's cross-examination, Chambers renewed his motion to examine McDonald as an adverse witness. The trial court denied the motion, stating: "He may be hostile, but he is not adverse in the sense of the word, so your request will be overruled." On appeal, the State Supreme Court upheld the trial court's ruling, finding that "McDonald's testimony was not adverse to appellant" because "(n)owhere did he point the finger at Chambers."

Defeated in his attempt to challenge directly McDonald's renunciation of his prior confession, Chambers sought to introduce the testimony of the three witnesses to whom McDonald had admitted that he shot the officer. The first of these, Sam Hardin, would have testified that, on the night of the shooting, he spent the late evening hours with McDonald at a friend's house after their return from the hospital and that, while driving McDonald home later that night, McDonald stated that he shot Liberty. The State objected to the admission of this testimony on the ground that it was hearsay. The trial court sustained the objection.

Berkley Turner, the friend with whom McDonald said he was drinking beer when the shooting occurred, was then called to testify. In the jury's presence, and without objection, he testified that he had not been in the cafe that Saturday and had not had any beers with McDonald. The jury was then excused. In the absence of the jury, Turner recounted his conversations with McDonald while they were riding with James Williams to take Chambers to the hospital. When asked whether McDonald said anything regarding the shooting of Liberty, Turner testified that McDonald told him that he "shot him." Turner further stated that one week later, when he met McDonald at a friend's house, McDonald reminded him of their prior conversation and urged Turner not to "mess him up." Petitioner argued to the court that, especially where there was other proof in the case that was corroborative of these out-of-court statements, Turner's testimony as to McDonald's self-incriminating remarks should have been admitted as an exception to the hearsay rule. Again, the trial court sustained the State's objection.

The third witness, Albert Carter, was McDonald's neighbor. They had been friends for about 25 years. Although Carter had not been in Woodville on the evening of the shooting, he stated that he learned about it the next morning from McDonald. That same day, he and McDonald walked out to a well near McDonald's house and there McDonald told him that he was the one who shot Officer Liberty. Carter testified that McDonald also told him that he had disposed of the .22-caliber revolver later that night. He further testified that several weeks after the shooting, he accompanied McDonald to Natchez where McDonald purchased another .22 pistol to replace the one he had discarded. The jury was not allowed to hear Carter's testimony. Chambers urged that these statements were admissible, the State objected, and the court sustained the objection. On appeal, the State Supreme Court approved the lower court's exclusion of these witnesses' testimony on hearsay grounds.

In sum, then, this was Chambers' predicament. As a consequence of the combination of Mississippi's "party witness" or "voucher" rule and its hearsay rule, he was unable either to cross-examine McDonald or to present witnesses in his own behalf who would have discredited McDonald's repudiation and demonstrated his complicity. Chambers had, however, chipped away at the fringes of McDonald's story by introducing admissible testimony from other sources indicating that he had not been seen in the cafe where he said he was when the shooting started, that he had not been having beer with Turner, and that he possessed a .22 pistol at the time of the crime. But all that remained from McDonald's own testimony was a single written confession countered by an arguably acceptable renunciation. Chambers' defense was far less persuasive than it might have been had he been given an opportunity to subject McDonald's statements to cross-examination or had the other confessions been admitted.

III

The right of an accused in a criminal trial to due process is, in essence, the right to a fair opportunity to defend against the State's accusations. The rights to confront and cross-examine witnesses and to call witnesses in one's own behalf have long been recognized as essential to due process.... Both of these elements of a fair trial are implicated in the present case.

A

Chambers was denied an opportunity to subject McDonald's damning repudiation and alibi to cross-examination. He was not allowed to test the witness' recollection, to probe into the details of his alibi, or to "sift" his conscience so that the jury might judge for itself whether McDonald's testimony was worthy of belief. *Mattox v. United States*, 156 U.S. 237, 242–243 (1895). The right of cross-examination is more than a desirable rule of trial procedure. It is implicit in the constitutional right of confrontation, and helps assure the "accuracy of the truth-determining process." *Dutton v. Evans*, 400 U.S. 74, 89 (1970); *Bruton v. United States*, 391 U.S. 123, 135–137 (1968). It is, indeed, "an essential and fundamental requirement for the kind of fair trial which is this country's constitutional goal." *Pointer v. Texas*, 380 U.S. 400, 405 (1965). Of course, the right to confront and to cross-examine is not absolute and may, in appropriate cases, bow to accommodate other legitimate interests in the criminal trial process. But its denial or significant diminution calls into question the ultimate "integrity of the fact-finding process" and requires that the competing interest be closely examined. *Berger v. California*, 393 U.S. 314, 315 (1969).

In this case, petitioner's request to cross-examine McDonald was denied on the basis of a Mississippi common-law rule that a party may not impeach his own witness. The rule rests on the presumption — without regard to the circumstances of the particular case — that a party who calls a witness "vouches for his credibility." *Clark v. Lansford*, 191 So.2d 123, 125 (Miss. 1966). Although the historical origins of the "voucher" rule are uncertain, it appears to be a remnant of primitive English trial practice in which "oath-takers" or "compurgators" were called to stand behind a particular party's position in any controversy. Their assertions were strictly partisan and, quite unlike witnesses in criminal trials today, their role bore little relation to the impartial ascertainment of the facts.

Whatever validity the "voucher" rule may have once enjoyed, and apart from whatever usefulness it retains today in the civil trial process, it bears little present relationship to the realities of the criminal process. It might have been logical for the early common law to require a party to vouch for the credibility of witnesses he brought before the jury to affirm his veracity. Having selected them especially for that purpose, the party might reasonably be expected to stand firmly behind their testimony. But in modern criminal trials, defendants are rarely able to select their witnesses: they must take them where they find them. Moreover, as applied in this case, the "voucher" rule's impact was doubly harmful to Chambers' efforts to develop his defense. Not only was he precluded from cross-examining McDonald, but, as the State conceded at oral argument, he was also restricted in the scope of his direct examination by the rule's corollary requirement that the party calling the witness is bound by anything he might say. He was, therefore, effectively prevented from exploring the circumstances of McDonald's three prior oral confessions and from challenging the renunciation of the written confession.

In this Court, Mississippi has not sought to defend the rule or explain its underlying rationale. Nor has it contended that its rule should override the accused's right of confrontation. Instead, it argues that there is no incompatability between the rule and Chambers' rights because no right of confrontation exists unless the testifying witness is "adverse" to the accused....

The argument that McDonald's testimony was not "adverse" to, or "against," Chambers is not convincing. The State's proof at trial excluded the theory that more than one person participated in the shooting of Liberty. To the extent that McDonald's sworn confession tended to incriminate him, it tended also to exculpate Chambers. And, in the circumstances of this case, McDonald's retraction inculpated Chambers to the same extent that it exculpated McDonald. It can hardly be disputed that McDonald's testimony was in fact seriously adverse to Chambers. The availability of the right to confront and to cross-examine those who give damaging testimony against the accused has never been held to depend on whether the witness was initially put on the stand by the accused or by the State. We reject the notion that a right of such substance in the criminal process may be governed by that technicality or by any narrow and unrealistic definition of the word "against." The "voucher" rule, as applied in this case, plainly interfered with Chambers' right to defend against the State's charges.

B

We need not decide, however, whether this error alone would occasion reversal since Chambers' claimed denial of due process rests on the ultimate impact of that error when viewed in conjunction with the trial court's refusal to permit him to call other witnesses. The trial court refused to allow him to introduce the testimony of Hardin, Turner, and Carter. Each would have testified to the statements purportedly made by McDonald, on three separate occasions shortly after the crime, naming himself as the murderer. The State Supreme Court approved the exclusion of this evidence on the ground that it was hearsay.

The hearsay rule, which has long been recognized and respected by virtually every State, is based on experience and grounded in the notion that untrustworthy evidence should not be presented to the triers of fact. Out-of-court statements are traditionally excluded because they lack the conventional indicia of reliability: they are usually not made under oath or other circumstances that impress the speaker with the solemnity of his statements; the declarant's word is not subject to cross-examination; and he is not available in order that his demeanor and credibility may be assessed by the jury. A number of exceptions have developed over the years to allow admission of hearsay statements made under circumstances that tend to assure reliability and thereby compensate for the absence of the oath and opportunity for cross-examination. Among the most prevalent of these exceptions is the one applicable to declarations against interest — an exception founded on the assumption that a person is unlikely to fabricate a statement against his own interest at the time it is made. Mississippi recognizes this exception but applies it only to declarations against pecuniary interest. It recognizes no such exception for declarations, like McDonald's in this case, that are against the penal interest of the declarant.

This materialistic limitation on the declaration-against-interest hearsay exception appears to be accepted by most States in their criminal trial processes, although a number of States have discarded it. Declarations against penal interest have also been excluded in federal courts under the authority of *Donnelly v. United States*, 228 U.S. 243, 272 — 273 (1913), although exclusion would not be required under the newly proposed Federal Rules of Evidence. Exclusion, where the limitation prevails, is usually premised on the view that admission would lead to the frequent presentation of perjured testimony to the jury. It is believed that confessions of criminal activity are often motivated by extraneous considerations and, therefore, are not as inherently reliable as statements against pecuniary or proprietary interest.

While that rationale has been the subject of considerable scholarly criticism, we need not decide in this case whether, under other circumstances, it might serve some valid state purpose by excluding untrustworthy testimony.

The hearsay statements involved in this case were originally made and subsequently offered at trial under circumstances that provided considerable assurance of their reliability. First, each of McDonald's confessions was made spontaneously to a close acquaintance shortly after the murder had occurred. Second, each one was corroborated by some other evidence in the case — McDonald's sworn confession, the testimony of an eyewitness to the shooting, the testimony that McDonald was seen with a gun immediately after the shooting, and proof of his prior ownership of a .22-caliber revolver and subsequent purchase of a new weapon. The sheer number of independent confessions provided additional corroboration for each. Third, whatever may be the parameters of the penal-interest rationale, each confession here was in a very real sense self-incriminatory and unquestionably against interest. McDonald stood to benefit nothing by disclosing his role in the shooting to any of his three friends and he must have been aware of the possibility that disclosure would lead to criminal prosecution. Indeed, after telling Turner of his involvement, he subsequently urged Turner not to "mess him up." Finally, if there was any question about the truthfulness of the extrajudicial statements, McDonald was present in the courtroom and was under oath. He could have been cross-examined by the State, and his demeanor and responses weighed by the jury. The availability of McDonald significantly distinguishes this case from the prior Mississippi precedent ... and from the *Donnelly*-type situation, since in both cases the declarant was unavailable at the time of trial.

Few rights are more fundamental than that of an accused to present witnesses in his own defense. In the exercise of this right, the accused, as is required of the State, must comply with established rules of procedure and evidence designed to assure both fairness and reliability in the ascertainment of guilt and innocence. Although perhaps no rule of evidence has been more respected or more frequently applied in jury trials than that applicable to the exclusion of hearsay, exceptions tailored to allow the introduction of evidence which in fact is likely to be trustworthy have long existed. The testimony rejected by the trial court here bore persuasive assurances of trustworthiness and thus was well within the basic rationale of the exception for declarations against interest. That testimony also was critical to Chambers' defense. In these circumstances, where constitutional rights directly affecting the ascertainment of guilt are implicated, the hearsay rule may not be applied mechanistically to defeat the ends of justice.

We conclude that the exclusion of this critical evidence, coupled with the State's refusal to permit Chambers to cross-examine McDonald, denied him a trial in accord with traditional and fundamental standards of due process. In reaching this judgment, we establish no new principles of constitutional law. Nor does our holding signal any diminution in the respect traditionally accorded to the States in the establishment and implementation of their own criminal trial rules and procedures. Rather, we hold quite simply that under the facts and circumstances of this case the rulings of the trial court deprived Chambers of a fair trial....

Reversed and remanded.

[Concurring opinion of Justice White and dissenting opinion of Justice Rehnquist are omitted.]

Thoughts on *Chambers*

The scope of *Chambers* appears to be narrow. In *Chambers* the Supreme Court overrode the hearsay rule due, at least in part, to a strong showing of the trustworthiness of defendant's evidence. The spontaneity of the statements, their corroboration, their disserving character, their "sheer number," and their importance in the context of the defense's theory of the case all contributed to the belief that the hearsay statements were reliable and necessary. This level of reliability and necessity is very context-specific and has been found in few cases. Courts will look to the credibility of the evidence, any corroboration of the evidence, and the degree to which the evidence is so central to the defendant's case that it would be unfair not to admit the evidence (i.e., whether it would be, based on the other evidence the defendant presented, harmless error not to admit the evidence due to, for example, its cumulative nature). In short, if the court holds that the defendant's interest in introducing critical, trustworthy evidence outweighs the public interest underlying the particular exclusionary rule, then it will admit the evidence.

Problem 8-4

Robert Fortini was convicted of second degree murder for the shooting death of Ceasar Monterio. Fortini argued self-defense at his trial and testified that Monterio lunged at him before Fortini shot him. He also testified that earlier that night Monterio drove past Fortini's house and screamed curses at the occupants of the house. The trial judge excluded evidence that Monterio assaulted four men approximately five minutes before his confrontation with Fortini. Although Fortini did not know that Monterio has assaulted the four men, he argued that the prior assaults were relevant to Monterio's state of mind, as the assaults made it more likely that Monterio lunged at Fortini.

On appeal, Fortini argues that the evidence of the prior assault was relevant, trustworthy, and critical to his defense and that its exclusion violated *Chambers v. Mississippi.* How do you rule?

Professional Development Questions

- Throughout your reading of any casebook, you are in a chess match with the author, for you are trying to figure out why this particular case or problem was chosen. For example, when a case is provided in a casebook, is its purpose to articulate a rule, articulate the policy behind a rule, demonstrate the factual application of the rule, or some combination of all of these? In this chapter, try to frame the purpose of each case in developing your knowledge of the Confrontation Clause.

- More than in any other chapter of this book, this chapter focuses on what the law should be rather than what the law is. As the Confrontation Clause has evolved so quickly (and, arguably, so confusingly) since *Crawford*, has one particular Justice's approach made the most sense to you? Why?

- Where do you think the next battle line will be in Confrontation Clause jurisprudence? In other words, in what area do potentially testimonial statements play a huge role for the prosecution?

Chapter 9

Authentication and Best Evidence

I. Authentication

Relevant Rules
FRE 901

Authenticating or Identifying Evidence

(a) In General. To satisfy the requirement of authenticating or identifying an item of evidence, the proponent must produce evidence sufficient to support a finding that the item is what the proponent claims it is.

(b) Examples. The following are examples only — not a complete list — of evidence that satisfies the requirement:

(1) *Testimony of a Witness with Knowledge.* Testimony that an item is what it is claimed to be.

(2) *Nonexpert Opinion About Handwriting.* A nonexpert's opinion that handwriting is genuine, based on a familiarity with it that was not acquired for the current litigation.

(3) *Comparison by an Expert Witness or the Trier of Fact.* A comparison with an authenticated specimen by an expert witness or the trier of fact.

(4) *Distinctive Characteristics and the Like.* The appearance, contents, substance, internal patterns, or other distinctive characteristics of the item, taken together with all the circumstances.

(5) *Opinion About a Voice.* An opinion identifying a person's voice — whether heard firsthand or through mechanical or electronic transmission or recording — based on hearing the voice at any time under circumstances that connect it with the alleged speaker.

(6) *Evidence About a Telephone Conversation.* For a telephone conversation, evidence that a call was made to the number assigned at the time to:

(A) a particular person, if circumstances, including self-identification, show that the person answering was the one called; or

(B) a particular business, if the call was made to a business and the call related to business reasonably transacted over the telephone.

(7) *Evidence About Public Records.* Evidence that:

(A) a document was recorded or filed in a public office as authorized by law; or

(B) a purported public record or statement is from the office where items of this kind are kept.

(8) *Evidence About Ancient Documents or Data Compilations.* For a document or data compilation, evidence that it:

(A) is in a condition that creates no suspicion about its authenticity;

(B) was in a place where, if authentic, it would likely be; and

(C) is at least 20 years old when offered.

(9) *Evidence About a Process or System.* Evidence describing a process or system and showing that it produces an accurate result.

(10) *Methods Provided by a Statute or Rule.* Any method of authentication or identification allowed by a federal statute or a rule prescribed by the Supreme Court.

FRE 902

Evidence That Is Self-Authenticating

The following items of evidence are self-authenticating; they require no extrinsic evidence of authenticity in order to be admitted:

(1) *Domestic Public Documents That Are Signed and Sealed.* A document that bears:

(A) a seal purporting to be that of the United States; any state, district, commonwealth, territory, or insular possession of the United States; the former Panama Canal Zone; the Trust Territory of the Pacific Islands; a political subdivision of any of these entities; or a department, agency, or officer of any entity named above; and

(B) a signature purporting to be an execution or attestation.

(2) *Domestic Public Documents That Are Not Sealed but Are Signed and Certified.* A document that bears no seal if:

(A) it bears the signature of an officer or employee of an entity named in Rule 902(1)(A); and

(B) another public officer who has a seal and official duties within that same entity certifies under seal — or its equivalent — that the signer has the official capacity and that the signature is genuine.

(3) *Foreign Public Documents.* A document that purports to be signed or attested by a person who is authorized by a foreign country's law to do so. The document must be accompanied by a final certification that certifies the genuineness of the signature and official position of the signer or attester — or of any foreign official whose certificate of genuineness relates to the signature or attestation or is in a chain of certificates of genuineness relating to the signature or attestation. The certification may be made by a secretary of a United States embassy or legation; by a consul general, vice consul, or consular agent of the United States; or by a diplomatic or consular official of the foreign country assigned or accredited to the United States. If all parties have been given a reasonable opportunity to investigate the document's authenticity and accuracy, the court may, for good cause, either:

(A) order that it be treated as presumptively authentic without final certification; or

(B) allow it to be evidenced by an attested summary with or without final certification.

(4) *Certified Copies of Public Records.* A copy of an official record — or a copy of a document that was recorded or filed in a public office as authorized by law — if the copy is certified as correct by:

(A) the custodian or another person authorized to make the certification; or

(B) a certificate that complies with Rule 902(1), (2), or (3), a federal statute, or a rule prescribed by the Supreme Court.

(5) *Official Publications.* A book, pamphlet, or other publication purporting to be issued by a public authority.

(6) *Newspapers and Periodicals.* Printed material purporting to be a newspaper or periodical.

(7) *Trade Inscriptions and the Like.* An inscription, sign, tag, or label purporting to have been affixed in the course of business and indicating origin, ownership, or control.

(8) *Acknowledged Documents.* A document accompanied by a certificate of acknowledgment that is lawfully signed by a notary public or another officer who is authorized to take acknowledgments.

(9) *Commercial Paper and Related Documents.* Commercial paper, a signature on it, and related documents, to the extent allowed by general commercial law.

(10) *Presumptions Under a Federal Statute.* A signature, document, or anything else that a federal statute declares to be presumptively or prima facie genuine or authentic.

(11) *Certified Domestic Records of a Regularly Conducted Activity.* The original or a copy of a domestic record that meets the requirements of Rule 803(6)(A)–(C), as shown by a certification of the custodian or another qualified person that complies with a federal statute or a rule prescribed by the Supreme Court. Before the trial or hearing, the proponent must give an adverse party reasonable written notice of the intent to offer the record — and must make the record and certification available for inspection — so that the party has a fair opportunity to challenge them.

(12) *Certified Foreign Records of a Regularly Conducted Activity.* In a civil case, the original or a copy of a foreign record that meets the requirements of Rule 902(11), modified as follows: the certification, rather than complying with a federal statute or Supreme Court rule, must be signed in a manner that, if falsely made, would subject the maker to a criminal penalty in the country where the certification is signed. The proponent must also meet the notice requirements of Rule 902(11).

Overview Problem

At Dirk's trial for bank robbery, the prosecution offers a $20 bill with Dirk's fingerprints on it. The bill allegedly was dropped by the robber at the scene. A bank teller picked up the bill, examined it, and put it in her pocket. Unbeknownst to the teller, the bill fell out of her pocket and was missing for an unknown period of time. She eventually found the bill on the floor near her teller station and gave it to a police officer who possessed the bill until the trial. At trial, the prosecutor offered the bill into evidence and put the teller on the stand to authenticate it. What possible foundation(s) would you lay in order to admit the bill into evidence? What further facts would be helpful in this analysis?

Overview

In order for evidence to be admissible, it must be what the proponent claims it is. If the proponent wants to introduce a document allegedly written by her party-opponent, then the proponent must prove that her party-opponent in fact wrote the document or else the document is not relevant or is too confusing or misleading under FRE 403. Putting this burden on the proponent also prevents fraudulent, mistaken, and/or unreliable evidence from getting to the fact finder, thereby enhancing the reliability and accuracy of the trial. Accordingly, no evidence goes to the jury unless it is properly authenticated.

As we shall see, this requirement applies to testimony as well as documentary evidence. Thus, to cite one possible example, a party's testimony that the party-opponent called her on the phone is subject to authentication: how do you know it was the party-opponent who called you? Could you recognize the party-opponent's voice? Did the party-opponent state things that only the party-opponent knew? Did the call come from a phone to which only the party-opponent had access?

In order to authenticate evidence under FRE 901(a) the proponent must establish "by evidence sufficient to support a finding" that it is "what the proponent claims it is." This is a conditional relevance issue because the relevance of the evidence depends on a preliminary finding that the evidence is "what the proponent claims it is." The judge must therefore determine whether there is evidence sufficient to support a jury finding of authenticity of the evidence. As with all conditional relevance issues, this determination by the judge must be based on *admissible* evidence. This is so because even if the evidence is admitted, the opponent can still contest the authenticity of the evidence. Indeed, even though it is admitted, the jury is free to reject the evidence. Additionally, all other objections to the evidence (e.g., hearsay, unfair prejudice, etc.) may be used against evidence authenticated under FRE 901.

Let us build on the example of a phone call. A plaintiff alleges that the defendant called him and uttered some incriminating statements. How do we know it was in fact the defendant that called? Perhaps the plaintiff will claim he could recognize the defendant's voice and offer further evidence that he has known the defendant for over ten years. Perhaps the plaintiff will rely on his caller identification system. Perhaps the context of the call makes it readily apparent that the defendant was speaking (e.g., the defendant was stating things that only the defendant knew). The judge will examine this evidence and ask "could a reasonable jury find by a preponderance of the evidence that it was the defendant who made the phone call?" If the judge believes this test is met, then she will admit the evidence. But defense counsel may still argue to the jury that the defendant did not make the call and offer any counterproof available. At the close of evidence, the jury is free to side with the defendant's version of the facts and conclude that the defendant was not the speaker in the phone call. Put simply, just because the judge admits the evidence does not mean the jury has to accept it as true.

FRE 901(b) offers a non-exclusive list of methods to authenticate evidence. Certainly an attorney can use a method that is not on the list as long as she meets her conditional relevance burden. As we work through the problems in this section, we shall see some of the foundational elements of the FRE 901(b) methods. But, first, let us return to the overview problem.

The most common method to authenticate evidence is FRE 901(b)(1), testimony of someone with knowledge that "an item is what it is claimed to be." A bald assertion as to authenticity is not enough; the witness must typically explain how she knows the item is what she says it is. Thus, in our overview problem, the obvious problem is that at a quick glance all $20 bills look alike. The time the teller spent examining the $20 bill is therefore critical. Was there something distinctive about this particular bill that is evident on sight? Was the serial number on the bill a distinguishing characteristic that made it clear that the bill was "bait money" that the bank provided only to robbers of the bank? In other words, is there something more than a bald assertion that would allow a judge to conclude that there exists evidence sufficient to support a jury finding that this was the same $20 bill she picked up in the bank after the robber dropped it?

Compounding the authentication problem is the chain of custody issue in the overview problem. The teller dropped the bill and it was missing for an unknown period of time. Was the found bill the same as the lost bill? Was the bill in the same condition as it was at the time of the robbery? How can we be sure? Evidence which is fungible, non-distinctive, and/or likely to change in condition is often authenticated by proving a chain of custody such that each person who had custody of the evidence from the time of the event to the time of trial describes their custody of the evidence and notes that the evidence was not tampered with during their custody. Is the teller's misplacement of the bill for an unknown time fatal? Typically, the answer is that defects in the chain of custody usually affect the weight of the evidence but do not preclude admissibility. If a reasonable jury could conclude that the bill was the same item in substantially the same condition, it will be admissible, and defense counsel can attack the authenticity of the evidence at trial.

If the $20 bill had handwriting on it this could be a distinctive characteristic pursuant to FRE 901(b)(4). Additionally, pursuant for FRE 901(b)(2) a lay witness who was familiar with Dirk's handwriting could testify that the handwriting on the bill was Dirk's handwriting as long as her familiarity with Dirk's handwriting was not acquired for the purpose of litigation. An expert on handwriting could authenticate the writing as Dirk's writing under FRE 901(b)(3). And on it goes—any method listed in FRE 901(b) may be used individually or in tandem to meet the proponent's burden.

Certain evidence is said to be "self-authenticating" due to its high reliability. Thus, FRE 902 establishes certain categories where the authenticity of the evidence is sufficiently established without extrinsic evidence. Whether a writing is self-authenticating is a question for the trial judge under FRE 104(a). Like FRE 901, FRE 902 only establishes admissibility at trial. The authenticity of the evidence admitted under FRE 902 may be attacked by the opponent, and the jury is free to reject the evidence as inauthentic.

Focus Questions: *Bruther v. General Electric Co.*

- Do you agree that sufficient evidence was produced to make a showing of authenticity in this case? Should the standard be higher?

Bruther v. General Electric Co.

818 F.Supp. 1238 (S.D.Ind. 1993)

BARKER, District Judge.

.... On January 31, 1989, Plaintiff was electrocuted while changing a light bulb at his place of employment, Rexnord, Inc., in Madison, Indiana. Rexnord is now known as Envirex, Inc. According to Plaintiff, when he attempted to unscrew the bulb from its socket, the glass envelope separated from the base, exposing his right hand to an electrical current. As a result of the ensuing shock, Plaintiff apparently sustained permanent, disabling injuries; he now seeks recovery from Defendant under the full gamut of theories available in a product liability action: strict liability, negligence, breach of warranty, and failure to warn. Mrs. Bruther also seeks compensation from the Defendant for the loss of "support, services, society, love and affection and comfort of her husband ..."

Defendant has moved for summary judgment on [the ground that] ... Plaintiff cannot authenticate the bulb that he wishes to introduce into evidence....

Defendant believes that Plaintiff is unable to authenticate the bulb that he seeks to introduce into evidence because of the lack of identifying marks on the bulb, and the existence of a gap in the chain of custody which developed immediately after the accident occurred. Apparently, no one at Rexnord took care to safeguard the bulb after Plaintiff was injured. While Howard Goodin, an employee at Rexnord, later removed the bulb from the socket, it is unclear what became of the bulb after that time. It was only after Mr. James, Plaintiff's counsel, asked to examine the bulb that Don Riley, the plant safety manager, began to look for it. (The exact dates of these events is unknown). Mr. Riley found a broken bulb in a small cabinet next to the site where the accident occurred. Although he cannot positively identify the bulb as the one that was involved in the accident, Mr. Riley believes, with some reservations, that it is the bulb in question because "[w]e wouldn't keep broken bulbs; so if it was there, it had a specific purpose to be there." In addition, the record indicates that only six people had access to the area where the accident occurred and the cabinet where the bulb was found. As concerns the brand of the bulb, Plaintiff states in his affidavit:

> 4. That approximately two weeks before this incident where he was shocked, affiant had replaced these light bulbs in the same panel on which he was working when the bulb came apart on January 31, 1989. At that time, he had placed General Electric bulbs in the same two sockets that he was changing on January 31, 1989;
>
> 5. That to the best of his knowledge and belief, there have been no other brands of light bulbs ever used in that fault indicator panel other than General Electric bulbs, and he knows of no other brands of bulbs that have been stored in the area or used in that particular fault indicator panel since being employed by Rexnord (now Envirex);

Affidavit of Woodie Bruther, ¶¶ 4, 5.

The Court finds that the evidence in the record is "sufficient" within the meaning of F.R.E. 901 to support a finding that the bulb in question is the bulb that caused Plaintiff's injuries, and that the bulb was manufactured by Defendant. Of course this holding is limited only to the issue whether Plaintiff has met the threshold burden of producing enough evidence to support his allegations; the determination whether the bulb in fact is what the Plaintiff claims it is must be made by the jury when it acts in its appointed role as finder of fact. Given, however, the limited access to the area where the injury occurred and where the bulb in question was found, the proximity of the cabinet where the bulb was found to the site of the accident, Mr. Riley's statement that Rexnord would not keep a broken bulb unless there was a reason to do so, and Plaintiff's own statement that he had installed, just two weeks prior to the accident, a G.E. light bulb in the same socket where the bulb that caused Plaintiff's injuries was located, a jury considering these factors reasonably could conclude that the bulb in question is the bulb that came apart and caused Plaintiff injury.

The Defendant's arguments to the contrary are unpersuasive. Besides a frontal assault on the sufficiency of Plaintiff's evidence (*i.e.* that no one can directly identify the bulb), Defendant makes much ado about lapses in the chain of custody, and tries to persuade the Court that because the bulb in question is nondescript, akin to a blood sample, "the chain of custody requirement must be followed to the letter ..." to satisfy F.R.E. 901. That rule requires nothing of the sort. Rule 901 regulates the admissibility of evidence. The slightest research on the law in this circuit concerning the effect of gaps in the chain of custody reveals that "any discrepancies in the chain of custody go to the weight of the evidence, not its admissibility." *See U.S. v. L'Allier,* 838 F.2d 234, 242 (7th Cir.1988), *citing, United States v. Shackleford,* 738 F.2d 776, 785 (7th Cir.1984). Consequently, it is the jury, and not the Court, which must evaluate the significance of Plaintiff's inability to account for the bulb following the accident....

Because there remain genuine issues of material fact in this case, Defendant's motion for summary judgment is DENIED ...

Problem 9-1

Police received several tips that Boyd Gray (a.k.a. "Punkin"), Isreal Wilson (a.k.a. "Big Man"), and Brenda Brown were dealing heroin out of various homes in St. Louis, Missouri. One informant claimed that the transactions occurred from an apartment known as "the house." In each transaction, heroin and money would be exchanged through a hole in the door, and someone inside would record the amounts in a book. The informant said the heroin was sold either in a spoon or capsule form called "buttons."

About a month later, detectives searched "the house." They found a two-inch slit in the door, numerous capsules and syringes, and two notebooks in the bedroom. The notebooks read, on page one: "4-26-75 $112.00 cash and 21 in the bottle 24, and 60 in the plastic bags. So you started with 105, buttons." On page two: "I started with 78 buttons He brought 80, but gave me two for myself. Brenda picked up $133 Dollars for 19 buttons Brenda picked up $210 Dollars for 30 buttons, She has picked up the last $203 Dollars for 29 buttons. All total she has picked up $546 Dollars for 78 buttons." On page three: "$290 $60 Left, I'm starting with 105 buttons. Brenda picked up $210 for 30 buttons. Punkin came and got 3 buttons and $30 Dollars tonight."

The inscriptions appeared to be handwritten by one or more people, but the author or authors were never successfully identified.

The government has charged Gray, Wilson, and Brown with conspiracy to distribute drugs. It now seeks to introduce the notebooks against the defendants. The defendants claim the notebooks have not been properly authenticated. How do you rule?

Problem 9-2

On April 15, the Oglethorpe Street Branch of the Trust Company Bank in Savannah, Georgia, was robbed by a lone gunman. The robber entered the bank with a brown stocking over his face and proceeded to a teller window. The teller, upon the robber's demand, placed money into a paper bag.

That teller activated her alarm and triggered the surveillance camera mechanism. The gunman was also observed by the branch manager and secretary. The manager activated the bank's security system, including its camera.

Immediately after the robber departed, one of the tellers called the police and described the robber. The robber was immediately apprehended. The film was eventually removed from the bank camera by a technician, who gave it to an FBI agent.

Thomas Clayton was charged and convicted for the robbery. He now appeals, claiming that Government Exhibit 14 was wrongly admitted against him. Exhibit 14 consisted of five photographs prepared from the bank surveillance film and five black and white photographs of a model wearing the clothing that Clayton was allegedly wearing when he was arrested. The exhibit was prepared by FBI agent Peter Smerick, who testified as an expert witness in forensic photography.

Smerick compared the clothing taken from Clayton at the time of his arrest and those worn by the robber in the film. He used Exhibit 14 to demonstrate that the clothing was similar and to illustrate how he came to this conclusion. Although Exhibit 14 contained pictures of a model wearing the clothing, Smerick stated that his opinion was made by comparing the clothing with the film, rather than by comparing the clothed model and the film. Smerick did not take the photographs himself and could not testify to the distance between the photographer and the model or to the lighting used.

The defendant objects because Smerick did not have personal knowledge that the five photographs made from the surveillance film in Exhibit 14 were accurate representations of the bank robbery scene. Additionally, none of the bank employees present during the robbery testified that the five photographs were accurate representations of the bank. However, the bank employees testified that other photographs made from the bank surveillance film were accurate. Those photographs had been admitted as Exhibits 15, 16 and 17, and Smerick testified that Exhibit 14 came from the same roll of film.

How do you rule on Clayton's appeal?

Problem 9-3

On April 19, Emergency Services in Douglas County, Kansas received nine 911 calls from a male caller threatening to blow up local schools and City Hall. Each call was made from the same prepaid cellular phone.

Police determined that the phone was registered to a woman named Sara Little but could not find either the phone or Little at Little's registered address. The phone service provider then assisted police in "pinging" the phone to locate its approximate location. Police were then directed to Michael Parker's residence, where they discovered the phone hidden in a black recliner in the living room.

Parker was at his apartment when the police got there and said he had no idea who made the telephone calls. He said he was up late drinking with Little, another woman named Sarah Coleman, and others the night before the calls were made. He could not remember who was still at his house when he went to bed.

Coleman was located and questioned that same day. She said that she, Little, and Parker were all smoking crack at Parker's residence the night before, when at some point Parker left the apartment and she and Little were left alone. Little left during that period and never came back. Coleman left later that evening or very early the next morning and recalled seeing Little's phone on the couch when she left. Police played a tape of the 911 calls for Coleman, and Coleman identified the voice as Parker's.

Little was questioned three months after the incident, on July 4th, when she was located and apprehended for her involvement in another unrelated incident. The police played the 911 tapes for her at that time, and she also identified the voice of the caller as Parker's.

The government introduced the 911 tapes against Parker at his trial in August. They sought to authenticate the tapes through the identifications of Coleman, Little, and a third party, Detective Brown. Brown had interviewed Parker for four hours around the time of the incident. After the interview, Brown listened to the 911 tapes. He later testified that the voice of the male caller was Parker's.

Parker argues that the tapes were not properly authenticated. In regards to Coleman's testimony, Parker states that 1) Coleman had not slept for around forty hours and was under the influence of drugs and alcohol when she made the identification, and 2) when Coleman made the identification she had already been told by the police that Parker had made the 911 calls. Additionally, Parker points to the fact that Coleman could not identify his voice a month before trial, when defense counsel tested Coleman by having Parker call her and tape recording the exchange. Coleman explained that she could not identify Parker's voice at this time because she was drunk and high.

As to the other sources of authentication, Parker argues that Little's identification was faulty because it occurred months after the incident and while Little was attempting to avoid charges for an unrelated arrest. Parker challenges Detective Brown's identification because it was made only after Detective Brown interviewed him. Parker states that by this time Brown "already had it in his mind" that Parker was the caller.

The issue of authentication is now before you. How do you rule?

Problem 9-4

On June 30th, Witold Pluta, a permanent citizen of the United States, attempted to enter the U.S. from a small town in Canada. At the port of entry, a customs inspector noticed that Pluta was driving a small hatchback car filled with luggage. Yet when questioned, Pluta stated he had only been in Canada for a few days and that he had acquired nothing during his stay.

The inspector became suspicious and ordered a secondary investigation of Pluta's things. The luggage was inspected by INS Supervisory Inspector James McMillan. It was found to contain bags of women's clothing and personal effects, including a number of documents bearing the names Anna Wicijewska and Katarzyha Dybilik. The women's Polish passports were also found among the documents. Inspectors subsequently alerted border agents to be on the lookout for two Polish women who may be attempting to enter the country illegally. Wicijewska and Dybilik were eventually found hiding in the bushes in a nearby parking lot. Pluta was later charged with two counts of smuggling illegal aliens into the U.S. Part of the government's burden of proof required the government to prove Wicijewska and Dybilik were not U.S. citizens.

During Pluta's trial, the government introduced the passports to prove a connection between the women and Pluta as well as the citizenship of the women. The passports were not accompanied by any certification or affidavit of any kind. The government did, however, provide the testimony of McMillan, who had extensive knowledge in conducting passport inspections. McMillan testified as follows:

> Q. Now, based on your training, knowledge and experience in this area, do you know what those documents are?
>
> A. They're Polish passports.
>
> Q. And how do you know that, sir?
>
> A. They're identified as such right on the document.
>
> Q. Based upon your training and expertise in this area, sir, what citizenship do those passports establish?
>
> A. Polish citizenship.
>
> Q. How do you know that, sir?
>
> A. It's identified as such on the passport.

The district court admitted the passports. Pluta appeals the admission, claiming the passports were not authenticated. How do you rule?

II. The Best Evidence Rule

Relevant Rules
FRE 1001

Definitions That Apply to This Article

In this article:

(a) A "writing" consists of letters, words, numbers, or their equivalent set down in any form.

(b) A "recording" consists of letters, words, numbers, or their equivalent recorded in any manner.

(c) A "photograph" means a photographic image or its equivalent stored in any form.

(d) An "original" of a writing or recording means the writing or recording itself or any counterpart intended to have the same effect by the person who executed or issued it. For electronically stored information, "original" means any printout—or other output readable by sight—if it accurately reflects the information. An "original" of a photograph includes the negative or a print from it.

(e) A "duplicate" means a counterpart produced by a mechanical, photographic, chemical, electronic, or other equivalent process or technique that accurately reproduces the original.

FRE 1002

Requirement of the Original

An original writing, recording, or photograph is required in order to prove its content unless these rules or a federal statute provides otherwise.

FRE 1003

Admissibility of Duplicates

A duplicate is admissible to the same extent as the original unless a genuine question is raised about the original's authenticity or the circumstances make it unfair to admit the duplicate.

FRE 1004

Admissibility of Other Evidence of Content

An original is not required and other evidence of the content of a writing, recording, or photograph is admissible if:

(a) all the originals are lost or destroyed, and not by the proponent acting in bad faith;

(b) an original cannot be obtained by any available judicial process;

(c) the party against whom the original would be offered had control of the original; was at that time put on notice, by pleadings or otherwise, that the original would be a subject of proof at the trial or hearing; and fails to produce it at the trial or hearing; or

(d) the writing, recording, or photograph is not closely related to a controlling issue.

Overview Problem

In order to establish that 500 gallons of oil were delivered to a company, the driver of the oil truck took the stand. She testified that on the day in question, she drove to the company, delivered the oil, and created an internal business record of the transaction that she gave to her manager. The company objects on the ground that the business record of the transaction is the "best evidence" of the transaction, and the driver's testimony in lieu of that record is forbidden. How do you rule? Would your answer change if the manager of the oil company testified instead of the driver, and the manager's only knowledge of the transaction stemmed from the business record?

Overview

The "Best Evidence Rule" is a bit of a misnomer. In most instances, a party is free to craft its narrative through its use of evidence in the most compelling (and cost-effective) manner it visualizes. That is the essence of trial strategy. Thus, in a car accident case, the party need not show photographs of the damage to the car. It can rely on testimony describing the damage or even a drawing of the damage. The choice in narrative is theirs. However, when a party is trying **to prove the contents** of a writing, recording, or photograph, the law does require that a party produce the "best evidence" on that point. In other words, when one is trying to prove the contents of a writing, recording, or photograph, secondary evidence (e.g., testimony or an exhibit) is inadmissible—the party must provide the writing, recording, or photograph itself.

Proving the content of this type of evidence occurs in two contexts. The first context is when the writing, recording, or photograph is itself at issue in a case—its content is the thing to be proved. Perhaps a recording is alleged to violate a copyright. Perhaps a photograph is considered illegal pornography. Perhaps a document is considered libelous. In each of these instances, it is the content of the evidence that determines the parties' charge, claim, or defense. Accordingly, that recording, photograph, or document must be introduced at trial. Testimony about the document in lieu of the document itself would violate the best evidence rule, and that testimony would be inadmissible due to the independent legal significance of the document.

The second context is a bit trickier. If a witness derives her knowledge from what a document states rather than personal knowledge, the rule applies. Conversely, if a witness independently has the same knowledge as the document, the rule does not apply. Let us take a look at overview problem again. The driver of the oil truck certainly has personal knowledge of the delivery. Furthermore, the driver is not deriving her knowledge of the delivery on the internal business record. Thus, the best evidence rule does not apply—just because a record exists that reflects the personal knowledge of the witness does not mean that the record needs to be produced. On the other hand, if the manager of the oil company testified instead of the driver, the manager's testimony would violate the best evidence rule. The manager's entire knowledge of the transaction stems from the document. Therefore, lacking any firsthand evidence of the transaction, the document is the best evidence of the transaction, and the manager may not testify in lieu of the record. Put simply, the business record is incidental to the driver's testimony based on firsthand knowledge, so the best evidence rule does not apply. Lacking firsthand knowledge, the business record is not incidental to the manager's knowledge; indeed, it is central to his knowledge. The best evidence rule therefore applies to the manager.

In crafting its narrative, a party may choose to rely on a writing, recording, or photograph to prove an event. In so doing, however, the writing, recording, or photograph is being offered to prove its contents, and the best evidence rule applies. In our overview problem, let us assume that the company that received the oil signed a receipt. If the oil company decides, as a matter of strategy, that it **wants to rely** on this writing as proof of the delivery, then the best evidence rule applies. In other words, if the driver states, "The oil was delivered because a representative of the company signed a receipt to that effect," then the driver is **relying on the document to prove her point**. The driver, who has independent knowledge, has now based her testimony on the receipt, so it must be introduced. In effect, the driver has made the receipt **central** to her testimony, not **incidental** to her testimony. Rather than using the receipt to illustrate her testimony, she has made the receipt her proof, and it now has independent probative value.

When the contents of a document are to be proven, the document is truly the best evidence available. Much like the rules behind authentication, the rules behind the best evidence rule focus on getting accurate and reliable information to the fact finder. Any evidence offered instead of the document itself would run the risk of being a commentary on the document and may be (intentionally or unintentionally) vague, imprecise, incomplete, or inaccurate. Additionally, the risk of fraud is reduced when the best evidence is produced.

Now that we have examined when the rule applies, let us examine how it applies. In FRE 1001(a) and 1001(b), "writings" and "recordings" are defined as broadly as possible—"letters, words, or numbers or their equivalent." Thus, a broad mix of written and spoken language fits the definition, including drawings, designs, and musical scores. In FRE 1001(c), "photographs" are defined broadly to include things such as x-rays and motion pictures. FRE 1001(d) alerts us that there can be more than one "original," as the definition includes "any counterpart intended to have the same effect by the person who executed or issued it." For example, if a tenant and landlord execute two copies of a lease, both are considered originals. Significantly, the interplay between the definition of "duplicate" in FRE 1001(e) and the mandate of FRE 1003 ("A duplicate is admissible to the same extent as the original …") reveals that any mechanically created reproduction is admissible as a substitute for the original. A manually recreated reproduction (e.g., handwritten, typewritten, etc.) may not be substituted for the original, however, as a fear of fraud or human error exists when the human element is introduced into the copying process. Therefore, as long as the duplicate is a mechanical copy, it correctly reflects the content of its source, and the source document is authentic, the duplicate can substitute for the original in the best evidence rule.

Pursuant to FRE 1004, the production of the original may be excused, thereby allowing the admission of secondary evidence in lieu of the writing. If the original was lost or destroyed without any bad faith, secondary evidence may be used. Likewise, if the original is beyond the reach of judicial process (e.g., a subpoena is ineffective because the entity possessing the original cannot be subpoenaed or claims a privilege) or if it is in possession of the opponent who was given notice that contents would be proven at trial, secondary evidence may be used. Finally, FRE 1004(d) offers an exception when the original "is not closely related to a controlling issue." Thus, if an original would not add to the accuracy of the fact finding process because it is not central to the dispute, the lack of an original may be excused. For example, if the location of an accident is not disputed, a street sign denoting "Elm Street" is likely tangential to a product liability action that occurred on Elm Street.

Focus Questions: *Meyers v. United States*

- Why did the prosecutor prefer to offer the testimony rather than the transcript in this case?

- Was the testimony "equally competent" to the transcript?

- What degree should reliability play in a best evidence rule analysis?

Meyers v. United States

171 F.2d 800 (D.C. Cir. 1948)

WILBUR K. MILLER, Circuit Judge.

Bleriot H. Lamarre and the appellant, Bennett E. Meyers, were jointly indicted for violating the District of Columbia statute which denounces perjury and subornation, thereof. Three counts of the indictment charged Lamarre with as many separate perjuries in his testimony before a subcommittee of a committee of the United States Senate constituted to investigate the national defense program, and three more counts accused Meyers of suborning the perjuries of his codefendant.

Lamarre pleaded guilty to all three charges when he was arraigned on December 19, 1947, a few days after the return of the indictment. Meyers entered a plea of not guilty and was tried before a jury in the District Court of the United States for the District of Columbia.... Having been found guilty under each of the three counts against him, he appeals. [Meyers founded Aviation Electric Corporation and hired Lamarre, who eventually became the company's president. The company obtained contracts to furnish parts to large corporations engaged in producing aircraft for the United States Army. Meyers eventually testified before a U.S. Senate investigatory committee focusing on fraud in government contracting. Later, Lamarre was subpoenaed and testified before the committee.]

... William P. Rogers, chief counsel to the senatorial committee, who had examined Lamarre before the subcommittee and consequently had heard all the testimony given by him before that body, was permitted to testify as to what Lamarre had sworn to the subcommittee. Later in the trial the government introduced in evidence a stenographic transcript of Lamarre's testimony at the senatorial hearing.

In his brief here the appellant characterizes this as a "bizarre procedure" but does not assign as error the reception of Rogers' testimony. The dissenting opinion, however, asserts it was reversible error to allow Rogers to testify at all as to what Lamarre had said to the subcommittee, on the theory that the transcript itself was the best evidence of Lamarre's testimony before the subcommittee.

That theory is, in our view, based upon a misconception of the best evidence rule. As applied generally in federal courts, the rule is limited to cases where the contents of a writing are to be proved. Here there was no attempt to prove the contents of a writing; the issue was what Lamarre had said, not what the transcript contained. The transcript made from shorthand notes of his testimony was, to be sure, evidence of what he had said, but it was not the only admissible evidence concerning it. Rogers' testimony was equally competent, and was admissible whether given before or after the transcript was received in evidence. Statements alleged to be perjurious may be proved by any person who heard them, as well as by a reporter who recorded them in shorthand.

A somewhat similar situation was presented in *Herzig v. Swift & Co.*, 146 F.2d 444 (2d. Cir. 1945) ... In that case the trial court had excluded oral testimony concerning the earnings of a partnership on the ground that the books of account were the best evidence. After pointing out the real nature and scope of the best evidence rule, the court said, "... Here there was no attempt to prove the contents of a writing; the issue was the earnings of a partnership, which for convenience were recorded in books of account after the relevant facts occurred. Generally, this differentiation has been adopted by the courts. On the precise question of admitting oral testimony to prove matters that are contained in books of account, the courts have divided, some holding the oral testimony admissible, others excluding it. The federal courts have generally adopted the rationale limiting the 'best evidence rule' to cases where the contents of the writing are to be proved. We hold, therefore, that the district judge erred in excluding the oral testimony as to the earnings of the partnership...."

As we have pointed out, there was no issue as to the contents of the transcript, and the government was not attempting to prove what it contained; the issue was what Lamarre actually had said. Rogers was not asked what the transcript contained but what Lamarre's testimony had been....

Since we perceive no prejudicial error in appellant's trial, the judgment entered pursuant to the jury's verdict will not be disturbed.

Affirmed.

PRETTYMAN, Circuit Judge (dissenting).

... Lamarre testified before the Committee in executive session, only Senators, Mr. William P. Rogers, who was counsel to the Committee, the clerk, the reporter, and the witness being present. An official stenographic record was made of the proceedings. The testimony continued for two days, and the transcript is 315 typewritten pages.... When the trial began, the principal witness called by the Government was Mr. Rogers. He was asked by the United States Attorney, "Now, will you tell the Court and the jury in substance what the testimony was that the defendant Lamarre gave before the Committee concerning the Cadillac automobile?" Two counts of the indictment related to this automobile.

The court at once called counsel to the bench and said to the prosecutor: "Of course, technically, you have the right to proceed, the way you are doing.... I do not think that is hearsay under the hearsay rule, but it seems to me ... that, after all, when you have a prosecution based on perjury, and you have a transcript of particular testimony on which the indictment is based, that you ought to lay a foundation for it or ought to put the transcript in evidence, instead of proving what the testimony was by someone who happens to be present, who has to depend on his memory as to what was said."

... [T]he prosecutor insisted upon proceeding as he had planned with the witness. Mr. Rogers then testified: "I will try to give the substance of the testimony.... I am sure your Honor appreciates that I do not remember exactly the substance of the testimony. The substance of testimony was this, ..." And then he gave "in substance" the testimony in respect to the Cadillac car. The same process was followed in respect to the matters covered by the other counts of the indictment.... Mr. Rogers was the counsel who interrogated Lamarre before the Committee. The Committee was the actual complainant in the perjury charge. Rogers was its representative.

Thus, the sum of the practical aspect of the matter is that the prosecutor put to the jury at the opening of his case, out of the mouth of the complainant, under oath and on the stand, the complainant's interpretation of the alleged perjured testimony, translating it into approximately what the indictment attributed to the alleged perjuror. I need not elaborate the tremendous advantage thus gained by the Government....

... I realize that there is a line of authority that (absent or incompetent the original witness) a bystander who hears testimony or other conversation may testify as to what was said, even though there be a stenographic report. And there is a line of cases which holds that a stenographic transcript is not the best evidence of what was said. There is also a legal cliche that the best evidence rule applies only to documentary evidence. The trial judge in this case was confronted with that authority, and a trial court is probably not the place to inaugurate a new line of authority. But I do not know why an appellate court should perpetuate a rule clearly outmoded by scientific development. I know that courts are reluctant to do so. I recognize the view that such matters should be left to Congress. But rules of evidence were originally judge-made and are an essential part of the judicial function. I knew of no reason why the judicial branch of Government should abdicate to the legislative branch so important a part of its responsibility.

I am of opinion, and quite ready to hold, that the rules of evidence reflected by the cases to which I have just referred are outmoded and at variance with known fact, and that the courts ought to establish a new and correct rule. The rationale of the so-called "best evidence rule" requires that a party having available evidence which is relatively certain may not submit evidence which is far less certain. The law is concerned with the true fact, and with that alone; its procedures are directed to that objective, and to that alone. It should permit no procedure the sole use of which is otherwise plain and certain.... [A]s between a document itself and a description of if, the law accepts the former and excludes the latter, because the former is certain and the latter is subject to many frailties. So as between the recollection of the parties to a contract evidenced by a writing and the writing itself, the law rejects the former and accepts the latter. To be sure, the writing may be attacked for forgery, alteration or some such circumstance. But absent such impeachment, the writing is immutable evidence from the date of the event, whereas human recollection is subject to many infirmities and human recitation is subject to the vices of prejudice and interest....

The doctrine that stenographic notes are not the best evidence of testimony was established when stenography was not an accurate science.... But we have before us no such situation. Stenographic reporting has become highly developed, and official stenographic reports are relied upon in many of the most important affairs of life.... In the present instance, at least, no one has disputed the correctness of the transcript.

... Given both (1) an accurate stenographic transcription of a witness' testimony during a two-day hearing and (2) the recollection of one of the complainants as to the substance of that testimony, is the latter admissible as evidence in a trial of the witness for perjury? I think not. To say that it is, is to apply a meaningless formula and ignore crystal clear actualities. The transcript is, as a matter of simple, indisputable fact, the best evidence. The principle and not the rote of the law ought to be applied....

Problem 9-5

Richard Nano was convicted of the theft of a box of calculators. To prove that the calculators were taken by criminal means the prosecutor sought to eliminate other possibilities which would account for the disappearance. He asked the merchandise manager for the division selling calculators, " ... were they sold?" The witness answered, "They were not sold, because by checking our sales record we have not...." Defense counsel objected, "I am going to object again under the best evidence rule—checking the sales records." The trial court remarked, "Well, he testified they weren't sold. That's sufficient." Was the trial judge correct in her ruling?

Problem 9-6

Edward Conway was a train conductor. He alleges that he was injured while assisting a passenger exiting from a train with a footlocker and sued Amtrak, his employer. While Conway was assisting, the passenger let go of the footlocker and it came down on top of Conway's chest. Conway proposed to testify that he did not "have any authority to stop a passenger from boarding a train with a footlocker" according to the rules of Amtrak. Should this testimony be excluded under the Best Evidence Rule?

Problem 9-7

In 1995, singer-songwriter Crystal Cartier sued Michael Jackson for copyright infringement of her song "Dangerous," which she copyrighted in 1991. Cartier said she first wrote "Dangerous" in 1985. In 1988, she recorded "Dangerous" as part of another song, "Player." Then, in October, 1990, she recorded "Dangerous" all by itself. She copyrighted this version in 1991.

Jackson recorded a song called "Dangerous" in September, 1990. He claimed that the song grew out of another song called "Streetwalker," which he wrote with William Bottrell in 1985.

Cartier asserts that Jackson had access to her version of "Dangerous" prior to September, 1990. She alleges that in July, 1990, she distributed about twenty-five demo tapes of "Player"—which was similar to her copyrighted "Dangerous"—to various people in Los Angeles who were close to Jackson.

At trial, Cartier said she depleted her entire supply of cassettes when she distributed them in 1990. She could not provide the original recording because it was made on a rented master tape which the recording studio recycled. She said that she questioned friends and family about their copies but they could not produce the tapes given to them. She also tried to contact the record companies to whom she had distributed the tapes but said they would not speak with her.

Cartier sought to introduce secondary evidence to prove the contents of the tape, including lyric and chord charts of the version of "Dangerous" which she said appeared on her demo tapes. She also tried to introduce a recreated recording of the demo tape which she recorded from memory. Both the lyric and chord charts and the recreated recording were created in May, 1992.

Jackson's counsel moved to exclude the recreations. The district court granted the motion, finding that Cartier had not satisfied the requirements of Rule 1004(1). In particular, the trial court asserted that Cartier had not diligently searched for the originals because she had not subpoenaed the record companies for their copies.

Cartier appeals the district court's decision on two grounds. First, she claims that subpoenaing the record companies would have been futile because the companies either return the tapes immediately or destroy them to avoid liability for trademark infringement. Testimony provided by defense counsel confirmed this procedure at trial. Second, Cartier argues that the district court erred in focusing on the demo tapes as the "original" in question. She says that the original master tape was the true "original" and thus, because the master tape had been erased, she easily met the requirements of Rule 1004(1) and should be allowed to admit secondary evidence to prove its contents.

Cartier's appeal is now before you. How do you rule?

Professional Development Questions

- With so many possible ways to authenticate evidence, crafting a checklist of all the possible ways to authenticate evidence is a helpful exercise. As you craft such a list, note the interrelatedness of certain methods as well as how certain methods apply to limited types of evidence (such as documents or voices). Also, keep the rationales in mind. For example, knowing the rationale behind self-authentication may help you recognize an item that is self-authenticating, even if you have not memorized the entire list in FRE 902.
- Is the threshold for authentication too low? Why or why not?
- Documentary and real evidence play a pivotal role in many trials. Certainly the process of authenticating each and every piece of evidence that comes before the jury can be a long and tedious process. What can the attorneys and judge do to

make the process more efficient? Should stipulating to authenticity be the desired course? Will the evidence lose some of its desired weight if its authenticity is stipulated rather than proved at trial?

Chapter 10

Lay and Expert Evidence

I. Layperson Testimony

Relevant Rule
FRE 701

Opinion Testimony by Lay Witnesses

If a witness is not testifying as an expert, testimony in the form of an opinion is limited to one that is:

(a) rationally based on the witness's perception;

(b) helpful to clearly understanding the witness's testimony or to determining a fact in issue; and

(c) not based on scientific, technical, or other specialized knowledge within the scope of Rule 702.

Overview

A witness is on the stand testifying as to what she observed when a patron at a bar was attempting to leave the bar. She utters two statements: (i) "He was drunk" and (ii) "He staggered as he walked, his eyes were glassy, his breath smelled of alcohol, and he was singing the song 'I Fought the Law' at an inappropriate volume while slurring his words." Which is more helpful to the jury? Why?

The second statement, complete with concrete details, allows the jury to reach a conclusion based on the facts presented. The first statement leaves us wondering and wanting to ask follow-up questions: *How* drunk? What is your definition of "drunk"? Were his motor skills impaired? The bald conclusion of the first statement is, plainly put, less helpful to the jury.

Therefore, FRE 701 favors the fact-driven description rather than the over-arching conclusions, opinions or inferences. When we are given the underlying facts, the requirements of FRE 701 are more clearly met. The details allow the trier of fact (i) to determine if the witness's conclusion is rationally based on the witness's perception and (ii) to obtain helpful testimony to determine the fact at issue.

There are a few instances when broad opinions are allowed under FRE 701. After all, one can argue that singing at an "inappropriate volume" is a conclusion, opinion, or inference that is not very specific. But, how can the witness remedy the situation? Should the witness guess at the decibel level? Should the witness explore the distance from which the bar patron could be heard? Clearly the witness should break down conclusions to underlying facts when possible, but sometimes it is extremely difficult to do so. In these instances, an opinion by a lay witness is allowed.

A second instance when a broad lay opinion is admissible is under the "collective facts doctrine." In some instances, the sum of broken down facts does not adequately express the conclusion. A witness's testimony that a bar patron was (i) singing (ii) in a parking lot (iii) in a residential neighborhood (iv) at 2:00 a.m. (v) such that the witness could hear him from fifty yards away does not quite capture that the volume of the singing was "inappropriate." Because a lay witness would be competent to express the conclusion of "inappropriate" volume (i.e., the witness has firsthand knowledge and one needs no particular expertise to voice this opinion) and because the underlying, collective facts were explained, most judges would allow the witness to testify to the conclusion that the volume was "inappropriate." The jury gains something from the inference, and, possessing all the collective facts, the jury can evaluate the weight to give to the conclusion. Furthermore, if the opposing party does not like the conclusion, they can certainly attack it on cross-examination.

Trial judges have a great deal of discretion on when to allow a lay opinion, as they are present in the courtroom and can observe the witness and jury, but a few general principles govern these situations. First, the more a conclusion goes to a central issue in a case, the more it should be broken down. Second, the trial judge should consider the degree to which it is possible to convey the conclusion in more specific terms. As we have noted, a list of specifics may not be possible or may not adequately capture a conclusion. Third, the trial judge should consider how many facts are encapsulated in the opinion. The more facts that exist, the greater the need to break down the opinion. Finally, the trial judge should consider the jury; if the jury can draw the conclusion just as easily as the lay witness, then the lay witness should be prohibited from giving the opinion. Thus, if a car came around a curve at ninety miles per hour and hit a pedestrian who was in the middle of the road, a witness's conclusion that the pedestrian "could not have avoided the car" might be unnecessary. The jury can draw their own inference from the facts, and the lay witness's conclusion would therefore be unhelpful to the jury.

The factors in the previous paragraph all explore the helpfulness of the testimony to the jury, which is a FRE 104(a) issue for the trial judge. In addition to helpfulness, FRE 701 contains two other mandates. First, the lay opinion must be rationally based on the perception of the witness. In other words, the witness must have firsthand personal knowledge of the facts or data pertinent to her testimony. Accordingly, the opinion must be a reasonable conclusion from the underlying facts. Speculation or irrational conclusions are inadmissible under FRE 701. Second, FRE 701 prohibits lay opinions on subjects outside the realm of common experience that require special skill or knowledge. Thus, for example, a witness without the proper scientific training should not opine as to the speed of a vehicle by examining its skid marks, as her opinion lacks much probative value. Subjects requiring special skill or knowledge are in the realm of expert testimony and are expressly exempted from FRE 701.

This overview demonstrates that the discretion provided to trial judges is well-deserved. The fact-intensive nature of this analysis leaves very little room for bright line rules. Testimony that "Dirk spoke angrily" may be allowed in some instances (e.g., non-speculation, not central to trial, not easy to break down, etc.) and not allowed in others (e.g., many facts encapsulated, witness relied in part on hearsay, etc.). FRE 701 is a rule of inclusion, and cross-examination is a powerful tool for attacking a witness's unsupported opinions, but, nonetheless, unhelpful, overly broad conclusions are inadmissible.

Focus Questions: *Government of the Virgin Islands v. Knight*

- The Court notes that it is difficult to articulate all the factors that lead to the conclusion that an act was an "accident." Do you agree? What factors might be helpful in this determination?
- Do you agree with the Court's harmless error analysis?

Government of the Virgin Islands v. Knight
989 F.2d 619 (3d Cir. 1993)

Cowen, Circuit Judge

… While Henry Knight repeatedly struck Andreas Miller's head with a pistol, the gun discharged and killed Miller.… [Knight] testified that Miller grabbed his left hand, which held the pistol, and squeezed it, causing the gun accidentally to discharge. The defense supported this version of the facts with evidence that Knight's left hand was scratched. Defense counsel also elicited eyewitness testimony that Knight never pointed the gun at Miller and never threatened to shoot him. The district court permitted this factual testimony, but precluded the eyewitness, as well as the investigating police officer, from offering their opinions that the firing of the gun was an accident.… The jury found Knight guilty of voluntary manslaughter, possession of a firearm during the commission of a crime of violence, and possession of a firearm by a felon.…

Knight argues that it was reversible error to exclude an eyewitness' and an investigating officer's testimony that the firing of the gun was an accident.… Although we agree that the district court committed error by excluding the eyewitness' lay opinion, this error did not prejudice the defendant and therefore does not warrant a reversal of his conviction.

The requirement that a lay opinion be rationally based on the witness' perception requires that the witness have firsthand knowledge of the factual predicates that form the basis for the opinion. Fed.R.Evid. 701(a) advisory committee's note. The district court properly excluded the investigating police officer's opinion because he did not observe the assault. In contrast, the eyewitness obviously had first-hand knowledge of the facts from which his opinion was formed.

Having met the firsthand knowledge requirement of Rule 701(a), the eyewitness' opinion was admissible if it would help the jury to resolve a disputed fact. The "modern trend favors admissibility of opinion testimony." [*United States* v. *Leo*, 941 F.2d 181, 193 (3d Cir. 1991)]. The relaxation of the standards governing the admissibility of opinion testimony relies on cross-examination to reveal any weaknesses in the witness' conclusions. Fed.R.Evid. 701(b) advisory committee's note. If circumstances can be presented with greater clarity by stating an opinion, then that opinion is helpful to the trier of fact. Allowing witnesses to state their opinions instead of describing all of their observations has the further benefit of leaving witnesses free to speak in ordinary language.

In this case, an eyewitness' testimony that Knight fired the gun accidentally would be helpful to the jury. The eyewitness described the circumstances that led to his opinion. It is difficult, however, to articulate all of the factors that lead one to conclude a person did not intend to fire a gun. Therefore, the witness' opinion that the gunshot was accidental would have permitted him to relate the facts with greater clarity, and hence would have aided the jury. Based on an assessment of the witness' credibility, the jury then could attach an appropriate weight to this lay opinion.

Although the district court should not have excluded this opinion, the exclusion of the opinion was harmless error as it did not prejudice Knight. To find an error harmless, a court must be able to say that it is highly probable that the error did not contribute to the jury's judgment of conviction. The eyewitness was permitted to describe fully the circumstances that led to his opinion—he stated that Knight never pointed the gun at the victim and never threatened to shoot the victim. Further, Knight himself testified that although he intended to assault Miller, the discharge of the gun was accidental, and defense counsel argued this theory to the jury. The jury could infer from these circumstances that the shooting was accidental.

The opinion of an unbiased eyewitness certainly may be viewed by a jury as more credible than the opinion of a criminal defendant. In this case, however, only a modicum of evidence was necessary to prove the accident theory of the defense because the prosecution barely disputed that the shooting was an accident. Indeed, the government all but conceded this point. During the government's closing argument, the prosecutor himself stated, "[The gunshot] may have been an accident.... [The beating] resulted in an unintentional, perhaps—probably unintentional and perhaps accidental discharge of that gun." Under these circumstances, the trial court's ruling could not have significantly prejudiced Knight and a reversal of the conviction is not warranted....

Problem 10-1

Joann Tiesler was raped and murdered by a burglar in her own home near Atlanta, Georgia. The police arrested William LeCroy as he attempted to cross the border into Canada in Tiesler's car, a Ford Explorer which the police believed had been stolen from Tiesler's home by her killer. LeCroy was a troubled young man who lived in Tiesler's neighborhood and had a prior record of burglary and sexual assault. LeCroy's defense was that he did not intend to kill Tiesler.

Tiesler had been stabbed multiple times by her killer. At trial, the government called two witnesses. The first witness, Christina Anderson, discovered a shirt of Tiesler's which possessed a blood stain on the back. She will testify that the stain "looked as if someone wiped a knife blade on it." The second witness is Georgia Bureau of Investigation Agent Jeff Branyon, a crime-scene specialist who had collected evidence at Tiesler's home. Branyon will testify that he discovered a blood stain on the back of Tiesler's shirt which he believed was consistent with someone wiping a bloody knife off on the shirt. Branyon was not qualified by the court as an expert witness. The testimony of both witnesses was admitted over defense objections. LeCroy was convicted of carjacking by force "resulting in death" and sentenced to death by lethal injection. He appeals the district court's admission of Anderson's and Branyon's testimony. How do you rule? Additionally, are LeCroy's prior convictions for burglary and sexual assault admissible?

Problem 10-2

In June, 2003, Illinois police began using constant surveillance and the assistance of an informant "buyer" to catch cocaine dealer Patrick Oriedo. The surveillance worked—in a period of just over a month, police successfully documented Oriedo in five illegal drug transactions. After watching the last transaction, police stopped Oriedo in his car and searched him. The search revealed a revolver, cocaine, and a large amount of cash. Police then searched the hotel at which Oriedo was staying and found various plastic baggies left on an ironing board. Oriedo was subsequently arrested and charged.

At trial the government introduced the testimony of two federal agents. The first, Stan Reno, worked surveillance for some of the transactions for which Oriedo was tried. He testified that on one occasion he observed the "buyer" arrive at an appointed meeting place followed by two cars which appeared to be following one another. He said that, personally, the sequence of events "raised red flags" with him, as more than one car "indicates to us that there is what is called counter-surveillance occurring and they are looking for law enforcement."

The second agent, Dave Gourley, participated in the surveillance as well as the traffic stop, arrest, and search of Oriedo's hotel room. He testified about the general contents of the room as well as the baggies. He said that during the search, the baggies were significant to him because they had their corners cut off and "that's usually the way drug dealers will package the crack cocaine for resale." When asked by the prosecutor to explain how baggies are used in drug distribution, he explained how baggies were used to transport drugs, stating that based on his own observations drug dealers often take a small baggie and cut or tear the corner off, fill the baggie with the drug, and tie it in a small knot or seal it.

Oriedo was convicted. On appeal, he challenges the admission of the agents' testimony on the ground that it constituted improper lay opinion. How do you rule?

II. Expert Testimony

Relevant Rule
FRE 702

Testimony by Expert Witnesses

A witness who is qualified as an expert by knowledge, skill, experience, training, or education may testify in the form of an opinion or otherwise if:

(a) the expert's scientific, technical, or other specialized knowledge will help the trier of fact to understand the evidence or to determine a fact in issue;

(b) the testimony is based on sufficient facts or data;

(c) the testimony is the product of reliable principles and methods; and

(d) the expert has reliably applied the principles and methods to the facts of the case.

Overview Problem

John Gotti and Frank Locascio—"boss" and "consigliere," respectively, of the notorious Gambino crime family—were convicted of substantive and conspiracy violations of the Racketeer Influenced Corrupt Organizations Act ("RICO"). Both were sentenced to life imprisonment.

On appeal, Gotti and Locascio challenge the district court's admission of the expert testimony of FBI Agent Schiliro. Schiliro had been an FBI Agent for seventeen years and for five years had exclusively worked on organized crime cases.

Schiliro testified at length about the nature and function of organized crime families, explaining the roles of different members and the rules of La Cosa Nostra, or the Mafia. He testified, for example, that a "boss" must approve of all illegal activity and especially all murders, and that a "consigliere" and "underboss" are only advisory to the boss. He also listened to various taped conversations and identified the individuals speaking to the jury. He named the voice of John Gotti as the boss of the Gambino family and the various other voices, including Locascio, as consigliere. When asked about the sources of his information, Schiliro stated that over the years he had spoken to FBI agents who shared with him information about the inner workings La Cosa Nostra. Schiliro also mentioned that he had other sources of information "not before the court." The implication of this latter statement was that over the years Schiliro had spoken to countless informants and listened to many wiretapped conversations not admitted in evidence.

Gotti and Locascio argue that (i) Schiliro did not possess proper qualifications to be an expert witness, (ii) Schiliro's testimony was too broad and went beyond the scope of expert testimony, and (iii) Schiliro relied on improper, inadmissible evidence in formulating his opinion. The issue is now before you on appeal. How do you rule?

Overview to Expert Testimony

When "scientific, technical, or other specialized knowledge" is at issue in a case, a lay opinion is inappropriate because the specialized knowledge unavailable to a lay witness is crucial in establishing the validity of the opinion. Instead, the testimony of a specialist in the field, an expert, is allowed in order to help the jury resolve these difficult issues. In order to ensure the reliability of the expert testimony, an expert must possess (i) proper qualifications, (ii) a proper topic that is helpful to the jury, (iii) a proper basis for her opinion, and (iv) a proper methodology that lead to valid and reliable results. Each of these requirements will be explored in turn, and we will rely on one case, *United States v. Locascio*, 6 F.3d 924 (2nd Cir. 1993) (on which the Overview Problem is based) to explore many of these mandates.

A. Proper Qualification

Overview

An expert can be qualified through knowledge, skill, experience, training, and/or education. The proponent of the expert has the burden of proving her expertise, and typically this is done before the expert's substantive testimony commences. The opposing party may also request a voir dire examination (i.e., a preliminary examination to test the competence of a witness or evidence) to test the qualification of the expert before the substantive testimony.

In establishing expertise, formal education is not strictly required. Expertise stemming from experience is perfectly permissible. For example, a car mechanic could be deemed an expert and answer questions pertaining to that expertise (e.g., "What is the correct ignition timing on a 1955 Bel Air Chevrolet, with a 327 cubic inch engine and a four-barrel carburetor?"). But the mechanic, or any other expert, must have their expertise match their proposed testimony. Thus, an expert in mechanical engineering with no background in consumer warnings could testify as to potential defects in a product, but any testimony on the appropriate warnings for the product would exceed his expertise and would be inadmissible.

United States v. Locascio
6 F.3d 924 (2nd Cir. 1993)

Altimari, Circuit Judge

... Schiliro's Qualifications as an Expert

The defendants-appellants argue that Schiliro was not properly qualified as an expert, since his testimony required knowledge of linguistics, the sociology of crime, tape recording technology, and voice analysis. Gotti and Locascio contend that because he was not an expert in any of those areas, he was not qualified to interpret tapes or give his opinion on the Gambino Family structure.

This argument ignores the fact that Schiliro had been an FBI agent for seventeen years, and for five years had been on the FBI's Organized Crime Program, a squad that investigated only organized crime cases. For more than two years, he was the supervisor of the Organized Crime Program. Rule 702 only requires that an expert witness have "scientific, technical, or other specialized knowledge" gained through "knowledge, skill, experience, training, or education." Fed.R.Evid. 702. Because Schiliro's background qualifies as "specialized knowledge," the district court did not err in qualifying him as an expert. *See United States v. Simmons,* 923 F.2d 934, 946 (2d Cir. 1991) (holding that a veteran DEA agent was "well-suited" to offer expert testimony about coded narcotics terminology); *United States v. Roldan-Zapata,* 916 F.2d 795, 804–05 (2d Cir.1990) (holding that a narcotics investigator was properly qualified to testify about "the narcotics-related nature" of items found in a defendant's apartment and about "drug trafficking techniques generally"). Schiliro did not need to be a voice analysis expert to be able to recognize the defendants-appellants' voices on the tapes, nor did he need a linguistics degree to understand what was being said. Schiliro testified as an expert on organized crime, and he was sufficiently qualified on that basis. Although he had never before been qualified as an expert witness, even the most qualified expert must have his first day in court....

Problem 10-3

Some time before 2001, Cobbi International Food Company, a U.S. corporation, entered an agreement with Jinro America, a South Korean company, for the international trade of frozen chicken. In 2001 the deal unraveled, and

Jinro sued Cobbi for millions of dollars in damages due to breach of contract. Cobbi countered that there was no contract at all, and that the deal was really a sham which Jinro orchestrated to cover up a high-risk investment program that circumvented Korea's currency regulations.

Cobbi offered the testimony of Herbert Pelham as an expert on Korean law and business practices of Korean companies—particularly, Korean businesses' alleged propensity to engage in fraudulent activity and avoidance of Korean currency laws. Pelham has been the general manager of the Pinkerton Detective Agency's Korea Office since 1994 and acts as a private investigator for non-Korean companies doing business in Korea. He was previously an Investigations Agent with the U.S. Air Force, during which he served five tours of duty in Korea. He has lived in Korea for about 12 years.

Although Pelham had not investigated Jinro itself, Cobbi offered Pelham's testimony as to the "modus operandi" of "Korean businessmen" and their propensity to circumvent currency laws:

> A: Well, Korean businessmen don't like laws that restrict their freedom to conduct business and make money. And they certainly don't like these laws.
>
> Q: Why is that?
>
> A: Well, it—it—it restricts their ability to make investments that they may want to make and just makes it difficult to do business.

Pelham was asked whether there "are attempts made in Korea to get around these [currency] regulations." He replied, "Yes, it's 'common knowledge.'"

Pelham said he had personal knowledge of several schemes by Korean businessmen to get around the currency laws. He said that the U.S. was a "favorite safe haven" for the money for these schemes. Generally, he said the schemes are initiated "through some kind of a phony contract to get it approved through the foreign exchange bank as a trade agreement to deceive it." When prompted by defense counsel, Pelham stated that the Jinro agreement at issue was "the sort of agreement" that could have been approved by Korean banking authorities. In conclusion, he stated that he generally advised clients to be wary of oral contracts "with Koreans" because, "the prevalence of corruption and fraud in the Korean business community is very great and very extensive."

Jinro argues that Pelham was not qualified as an expert on Korean law or business practices, and that his expertise lies in the areas of investigation and security. Moreover, Jinro argues that Pelham's generalized testimony that Korean businesses engage in unlawful, unethical activities was unduly prejudicial. How do you rule?

B. Proper Topic

Relevant Rule
FRE 704

Opinion on an Ultimate Issue

(a) In General—Not Automatically Objectionable. An opinion is not objectionable just because it embraces an ultimate issue.

(b) Exception. In a criminal case, an expert witness must not state an opinion about whether the defendant did or did not have a mental state or condition that constitutes an element of the crime charged or of a defense. Those matters are for the trier of fact alone.

Overview

A proper topic for an expert witness is one that helps the trier of fact understand the evidence or determine a fact in issue. The fine line in the helpfulness analysis centers on whether a topic is so commonsensical that expert analysis would not provide any benefit to the jury. Put another way, expert testimony must be "beyond the ken" of the jurors. For example, expert testimony on the slipperiness of ice is likely unnecessary; a jury can use their own common knowledge to evaluate that topic. Furthermore, there is a risk that a jury will abdicate their role of critical assessment and merely accept the expert's word rather than analyze the issue for themselves. Yet this does not mean that expert testimony on a subject within common knowledge is automatically excluded as unhelpful. If the expert testimony can add depth to the topic (e.g., the speed at which ice forms or melts) or can disabuse a jury of any misconceptions they might have (e.g., salt is more effective than sand for melting ice), then the expert testimony is allowed.

As we will see in *United States v. Hines*, below, an expert should be providing a jury with tools which allow them to undertake factual analyses. In other words, providing the criteria that the jury should use in undertaking their analyses is preferable to providing the conclusions the jury should reach. *Hines* will discuss this point in greater detail, but, for now, it is important to note that while there is no rule that prohibits an expert from providing a conclusion, such conclusions may not be perceived as helpful by the trial judge under FRE 104(a). As such, the trial judge possesses broad discretion to exclude these conclusions.

Two areas where excluding conclusions are hotly contested are expert testimony on the law and expert testimony on the "ultimate issue" before the jury. Expert opinions on law are often excluded because they are not deemed helpful to the jury. The trial judge instructs the jury on the law, and she possesses sole dominion on the issue. Accordingly, this type of testimony conflicts with the trial judge's responsibility and could create confusion for the jury. Therefore, an expert witness should not define legal terms such as "deadly force" for the jury. Instead, the judge will explain the legal term to the jury in her jury instructions. When there exist mixed questions of fact and law, such as when an expert attempts to testify as to how the law should apply to the facts of a case (e.g., "In my opinion, the police officer unjustifiably used deadly force on the plaintiff"), a trial judge may exclude the evidence as unhelpful, for the role of the expert should not be to tell the jury what result to reach. When the application of fact to law is unavoidable in an expert's testimony, however, a trial judge may admit it with a jury instruction that the testimony was an opinion rather than a definitive statement of the law.

In terms of an expert opining on the "ultimate issue" that the jury must decide, FRE 704's Committee Notes explicitly state an expert "telling the jury what result to reach" is excludable due to its lack of helpfulness to the jury. As *Torres v. County of Oakland* discusses below, the witness cannot usurp the function of the jury (this rule on "ultimate issues" applies to both lay and expert witnesses; although the witness in *Torres* was not an expert, the rule would apply with equal force if the witness was an expert). But, if the legal term used by the witness corresponds to its lay meaning rather than its legal meaning, the conclusion is admissible. For example, expert testimony that a party acted "recklessly" could be meant to track its lay meaning (e.g., carelessly) or its legal meaning (e.g., creating a substantial and *unjustifiable* risk of harm to others with *conscious disregard* for that risk). Using the term in its lay sense is not objectionable, but using it in its legal sense usurps the function of the jury. In a reckless driving case, for example, proving "unjustifiable risk" and "conscious disregard" is the function of the jury, so expert testimony that "defendant drove recklessly" tells the jury what result to reach and is considered unhelpful. In this latter scenario, it is more helpful for the jury to have the expert give the underlying facts for her conclusion and thereby provide the jury with tools to make their determination.

Finally, FRE 704(b) provides an exception to FRE 704(a). It bans expert testimony regarding a criminal defendant's mental state or condition when that testimony is used to establish whether the accused possessed or lacked a mental state or condition that constitutes an element of, or defense to, the crime charged. Thus, an expert can testify as to whether the criminal defendant does or does not suffer from a mental disease. In providing that testimony, however, the expert may not opine on whether that mental disease affected the defendant's ability to understand the wrongfulness of her actions.

United States v. Locascio
6 F.3d 924 (2nd Cir. 1993)

Altimari, Circuit Judge

... Under the Federal Rules of Evidence, an expert is permitted to testify in the form of an opinion or otherwise when that testimony would "assist the trier of fact to understand the evidence or to determine a fact in issue." Fed.R.Evid. 702. In determining whether such evidence will assist the jury, the district court must make a "'common sense inquiry'" into "'whether the untrained layman would be qualified to determine intelligently and to the best possible degree the particular issue without enlightenment from those having a specialized understanding of the subject involved in the dispute.'" Fed.R.Evid. 702, advisory committee note. In applying this standard, the district court has broad discretion regarding the admission of expert testimony, and this Court will sustain the admission unless "manifestly erroneous." *United States v. DiDomenico,* 985 F.2d 1159, 1163 (2d Cir.1993)....

1. *Challenge to Scope of Expert Testimony*

The defendants-appellants challenge the admission of expert testimony on the inner workings of the Gambino Family as being outside the scope of expert testimony. We have, however, previously upheld the use of expert testimony to help explain the operation, structure, membership, and terminology of organized crime families. *See United States v. Daly,* 842 F.2d 1380, 1388 (2d Cir. 1988); *see also United States v. Skowronski,* 968 F.2d 242, 246 (2d Cir.1992) (upholding expert testimony of government agents explaining organized crime jargon). Other circuits considering the issue are in agreement. *See United States v. Pungitore,* 910 F.2d 1084, 1148–49 (3d Cir.1990) (upholding testimony of agent who testified about structure of organized crime families).

In *Daly,* this Court confronted a similar claim that a district court committed reversible error in admitting expert testimony on the structure of organized crime families. There, the government agent who testified "identified the five organized crime families that operate in the New York area; he described their requirements for membership, their rules of conduct and code of silence, and the meaning of certain jargon, ... and he described how, in general, organized crime has infiltrated labor unions." 842 F.2d at 1388.

Additionally, the expert identified voices on surveillance tapes. In sustaining the admission of such testimony, we explained that such expert testimony "was relevant to provide the jury with an understanding of the nature and structure of organized crime families." *Id.* We further added that there was "no question that there was much that was outside the expectable realm of knowledge of the average juror." *Id.*

We continue to believe that despite the unfortunate fact that our society has become increasingly familiar with organized crime and its activities from such sources as newspapers, movies, television, and books, it is still a reasonable assumption that jurors are not well versed in the structure and methods of organized crime families. Moreover, much of the information gleaned from such sources may be inaccurate. Consequently, the subject matter of Agent Schiliro's testimony, namely the structure and operations of organized crime families, was properly admitted.

Focus Questions: *Torres v. County of Oakland*

- In analyzing the witness's personal knowledge, what does the court mean by "outward events"? Do you agree that outward events allow someone to infer the inward feelings of another?

- Although the witness in *Torres* was not an expert, FRE 704 applies to both lay and expert testimony. What test does the court adopt in analyzing opinions on the ultimate issue? How do the Advisory Committee Notes on FRE 704 define the test?

- Do you agree that a more "carefully phrased" question could have avoided the problem of testimony containing a legal conclusion?

Torres v. County of Oakland
758 F.2d 147 (6th Cir. 1985)

CONTIE, Circuit Judge.

Belen Torres appeals a judgment entered upon a jury verdict in favor of the defendants, County of Oakland and Oakland Community Mental Health Services Board, in this employment discrimination action brought under Title VII and 42 U.S.C. § 1981. Torres' complaint alleged discriminatory treatment based on her national origin....

I.

Because Torres does not challenge the sufficiency of the evidence, the facts may be briefly stated. Torres is a Filipino by birth but has become a United States citizen. She has a Masters degree in social work and has worked for the defendants since September 1979 as a "casework supervisor."

At a meeting in February of 1980, Torres' supervisor, Norbert Birnbaum, used the term "ass" or "asshole" in reference to her. Torres offered some evidence to show that this was purely name-calling. The defendants offered evidence tending to show that, in context, the remark was that Torres would make an "ass" or "asshole" of herself if she continued to discuss subjects after the meeting's discussion had moved to other matters on the agenda.

Torres also offered evidence that her six-month evaluation was downgraded from "outstanding" to "average" in one category without consulting her. The defendants admitted that the evaluation was unilaterally downgraded, but presented evidence tending to show that the change was required by uniformly applied guidelines for attendance. The evaluation form itself reveals that in seven out of eight categories Torres did receive a rating of "outstanding"; only in the eighth category, for attendance, was she rated as "average."

In 1980, the Board decided to create a new supervisory position. Torres applied for this opening but was not promoted. The defendants did not dispute that Torres possessed the general qualifications for this position but instead presented evidence tending to show that there was a high degree of dissension in the ranks of their employees. Thus, it was advisable, in the defendants' view, to hire a new employee to fill the position rather than to promote someone from within the ranks.

II.

Torres' first argument is that the trial court erred in admitting certain testimony of Dr. Quiroga into evidence. Dr. Quiroga is the defendants' Director of Children's Services and took part in selecting the person to fill the new supervisory position. During the examination of Dr. Quiroga by the defendants, the following exchange took place:

> Q. It is true, Dr. Quiroga, that you did not believe that Ms. Torres had been discriminated against because of her national origin in that interview process?
>
> MR. KAREGA: Objection, your Honor.
>
> THE COURT: No, she may state her opinion on that.
>
> A. That is correct.

Torres argues that Dr. Quiroga's opinion testimony was not proper under Federal Rule of Evidence 701 both because it was not sufficiently based on personal perception and because it was testimony containing a legal conclusion.

… The essence of Torres' first argument is that Dr. Quiroga's testimony required her to know the intent or state of mind of Dr. Malueg, who ultimately made the decision not to promote Torres, and that an opinion on another's intent cannot be "rationally based on the perception of the witness."

The illogicality of this argument has been succinctly demonstrated by Wigmore:

> The argument has been made that, because we cannot directly see, hear, or feel the state of another person's mind, therefore testimony to another person's state of mind is based on merely conjectural and therefore inadequate data. This argument is finical enough; and it proves too much, for if valid it would forbid the jury to find a verdict upon the supposed state of a person's mind. If they are required and allowed to find such a fact, it is not too much to hear such testimony from a witness who has observed the person exhibiting in his conduct the operations of his mind.

2 J. Wigmore, *Wigmore on Evidence* § 661 (J. Chadbourn rev. 1979). Another commentator explains the requirement that a lay witness' opinion testimony must be "rationally based on the perception of the witness" as merely requiring that "the opinion or inference is one which a normal person would form on the basis of the observed facts." *See 3 J. Weinstein & M. Berger, Weinstein's Evidence* ¶ 701[03], page 701-11 (1982). Accordingly, witnesses have been allowed to give opinions on whether another person subjectively believed that he would be shot by an aggressor, *see John Hancock Mutual Life Insurance Co. v. Dutton,*

585 F.2d 1289, 1293–94 (5th Cir.1978), and, in a civil rights action, that an arrest was "motivated by racial prejudice," *see Bohannon v. Pegelow*, 652 F.2d 729, 731–32 (7th Cir.1981). As the Fifth Circuit stated in *Dutton:*

> When, as here, the witness observes first hand the altercation in question, her opinions on the feelings of the parties are based on her personal knowledge and rational perceptions and are helpful to the jury. The Rules require nothing more for admission of the testimony.

Dutton, 585 F.2d at 1294.

The record in this case clearly establishes that Dr. Quiroga was privy to the details of Dr. Malueg's selecting the new supervisor. The foundational requirement of personal knowledge of the outward events has thus been satisfied. Since we do not believe that it is beyond the ken of an ordinary person to infer from another's outward actions what his inward feelings are regarding a third person's national origin, Dr. Quiroga's testimony was rationally based on her perceptions.

Torres' second argument rests on the last clause in Rule 701, that the opinion must be "helpful" to the jury. She argues that because Dr. Quiroga's testimony was couched as a legal conclusion, it was not helpful to the jury. We agree.

At the outset, it should be noted what we do not decide. Since Federal Rule of Evidence 704 provides that "testimony ... otherwise admissible is not objectionable because it embraces the ultimate issue to be decided," Dr. Quiroga's testimony cannot be challenged as an improper conclusion on an ultimate fact. The Advisory Committee notes point out, however, that Rule 704 "does not lower the bars so as to admit all opinions." The effect of Rule 704 is merely to remove the proscription against opinions on "ultimate issues" and to shift the focus to whether the testimony is "otherwise admissible." As the Advisory Committee note explains, certain opinions which embrace an ultimate issue will be objectionable on other grounds.

> Under Rule 701 and 702, opinions must be helpful to the trier of fact, and Rule 403 provides for exclusion of evidence which wastes time. These provisions afford ample assurances against the admission of opinions which would merely tell the jury what result to reach, somewhat in the manner of the oath-helpers of an earlier day. They also stand ready to exclude opinions phrased in terms of inadequately explored legal criteria. Thus the question, "Did T have capacity to make a will?" would be excluded, while the question "Did T have sufficient mental capacity to know the nature and extent of his property and the natural objects of his bounty and formulate a rational scheme of distribution?" would be allowed.

The problem with testimony containing a legal conclusion is in conveying the witness' unexpressed, and perhaps erroneous, legal standards to the jury. This "invade[s] the province of the court to determine the applicable law and to instruct the jury as to that law." *F.A.A. v. Landy*, 705 F.2d 624, 632 (2d Cir. 1983). Although trial judges are accorded a relatively wide degree of discretion in admitting or excluding testimony which arguably contains a legal conclusion, that discretion is not unlimited. This discretion is appropriate because it is often difficult to determine whether a legal conclusion is implicated in the testimony. *See, e.g., Owen v. Kerr-McGee Corp.*, 698 F.2d 236, 240 (5th Cir.1983) ("The task of separating impermissible questions which call for overbroad or legal responses from permissible questions is not a facile one.").

The best resolution of this type of problem is to determine whether the terms used by the witness have a separate, distinct and specialized meaning in the law different from that present in the vernacular. If they do, exclusion is appropriate. *See United States v. Hearst*, 563 F.2d 1331, 1351 (9th Cir.1977) (testimony is not objectionable as containing a legal conclusion where the "average layman would understand those terms and ascribe to them essentially the same meaning intended"). Thus, when a witness was asked whether certain conduct was "unlawful," the trial court properly excluded the testimony since "terms that demand an understanding of the nature and scope of the criminal law" may be properly excluded. *See* [*United States* v. *Baskes*, 649 F.2d 471, 478 (7th Cir.1980)]. *See also Owen*, 698 F.2d at 239–40 (trial court properly excluded testimony on "cause" of the accident when there was no dispute as to the factual "cause" of the accident but only the legal "cause" of the accident); *Christiansen v. National Savings and Trust Co.*, 683 F.2d 520, 529 (D.C.Cir.1982) (inadmissibility of conclusion that defendants held a "fiduciary" relationship to plaintiffs); *Strong v. E.I. DuPont de Nemours Co.*, 667 F.2d 682, 685–86 (8th Cir. 1981) (trial court properly excluded expert's testimony that defendant's warnings were "inadequate" and that the product was therefore "unreasonably dangerous"); [*Stoler v. Penn Central Transportation Co.*, 583 F.2d 896, 898–99 (6th Cir.1978) (trial court properly excluded testimony that a railroad crossing was "extra hazardous," a legal term of art under governing law, since it "amounted to a legal opinion")].

The precise language of the question put to Dr. Quiroga was whether "Torres had been discriminated against because of her national origin." In concluding that this question called for an improper legal conclusion, we rely on several factors. First, the question tracks almost verbatim the language of the applicable statute. Title VII makes it unlawful for an employer to "discriminate against any individual ... because of such individual's ... national origin." *See* 42 U.S.C. § 2000e-2. Second, the term "discrimination" has a specialized meaning in the law and in lay use the term has a distinctly less precise meaning. *See Ward v. Westland Plastics, Inc.*, 651 F.2d 1266, 1271 (9th Cir.1980) (witness "incompetent to voice an opinion on whether that or any other conduct constituted *illegal* sex discrimination").

We emphasize that a more carefully phrased question could have elicited similar information and avoided the problem of testimony containing a legal conclusion. The defendants could have asked Dr. Quiroga whether she believed Torres' national origin "motivated" the hiring decision. This type of question would directly address the factual issue of Dr. Malueg's intent without implicating any legal terminology.

Although we hold that the trial judge should not have admitted this testimony, we conclude that this error was harmless. First, this error involved only one brief question out of a rather lengthy trial. Second, Torres admitted, upon being impeached by her deposition testimony, that she had previously stated that she did not feel that she had been discriminated against during the interview process. Under the circumstances, we hold that the admission of this testimony containing a legal conclusion was harmless error....

The judgment of the district court is Affirmed.

Focus Questions: *United States v. Hines*

- Do you agree that a jury might give heightened credence to an expert?
- How does courtroom science differ from the typical scientific method? How do those differences matter when evaluating expert testimony?
- How did this expert provide the jury with tools to assist their analysis?

United States v. Hines

55 F.Supp.2d 62 (D.Mass. 1999)

GERTNER, District Judge.

... Johannes Hines ("Hines") is charged [with] allegedly robbing the Broadway National Bank in Chelsea, Massachusetts on January 27, 1997. The government's principal evidence consisted of the eyewitness identification of the teller who was robbed, Ms. Jeanne Dunne....

Hines ... offered the testimony of Dr. Saul Kassin ("Kassin"), a psychologist who studies perception and memory, and who has been qualified as an eyewitness identification expert in other cases. The government opposed. Should I allow the testimony of [Kassin, the government seeks to counter with testimony from] Dr. Ebbe B. Ebbesen ("Ebbesen")....

I. FRAMEWORK FOR THE ANALYSIS OF EXPERT TESTIMONY

... Our evidentiary rules put a premium on firsthand observations. Opinion testimony is disfavored except under certain circumstances; hearsay is generally excluded. The jury is to draw reasonable inferences from the firsthand data. When an expert witness is called upon to draw those inferences, several concerns are raised. The rules give expert witnesses greater latitude than is afforded other witnesses to testify based on data not otherwise admissible before the jury. In addition, a certain patina attaches to an expert's testimony unlike any other witness; this is "science," a professional's judgment, the jury may think, and give more credence to the testimony than it may deserve.

Accordingly, the trial court is supposed to review expert testimony carefully. The court is to admit the testimony not only where it is relevant to the issues at bar, the usual standard under Fed.R.Evid. 401, but when certain additional requirements are met under Fed.R.Evid. 702.

The first requirement has to do with the necessity for the testimony: expert testimony may be admitted where the inferences that are sought to be drawn are inferences that a jury could not draw on its own. The inferences may be the product of specialized information, for example, beyond the ken of the lay jury. Significantly, ... expert testimony is admissible where it would "assist" the trier of fact. In the latter case, even if the inferences may be drawn by the lay juror, expert testimony may be admissible as an "aid" in that enterprise. For example, the subject *looks like* one the jury understands from every day life, but in fact, the inferences the jury may draw are erroneous. (As I describe below, eyewitness identification, and testimony about battered women syndrome fits uniquely into this category.)

The second requirement concerns the nature of the inferences to be drawn. In outlining the standards for admissibility, the [Supreme Court has] noted the difference between information gleaned in a scientific setting and information presented in a courtroom. In the former, the decision makers are professionals; there is no need to come to a definitive conclusion; the decision making process comports with certain rules established by the professional scientific community. In the courtroom, the decision makers are lay, a jury; there is a need to come to a definitive conclusion; the decision making process has to satisfy norms of due process and fairness. In our tradition, for example, the adversary system and party examination and cross examination are central. The issue then, is not only how objectively reliable the evidence is, but also the legitimacy of the process by which it is generated. It is not just how valid the data is, but how well the jury can understand it after direct and cross examination, and legal instructions....

B. *Eyewitness Identification*

The government offered the testimony of Jeanne Dunne ("Dunne"), the teller. Dunne, a white woman, gave the following identification moments after the robbery occurred: She identified the man as black with dark skin, a wide nose, and a medium build. Her description was as close to a generic identification of an African American man as one can imagine. Dunne was unable to identify Hines from a book of photographs of African American men shortly after the robbery. She picked out a few photographs, but none of them were as "dark black" as the robber. Working with a police artist, she helped construct a sketch of the robber. Immediately following, she was shown eight photographs, including one of Hines, and indicated that the Hines photograph "resembled" the robber, that it "looked like him," but she was still not sure. (Since the robber was wearing a hat, she tried to envision the man in the photograph with a baseball cap.) Months later Dunne picked Hines out of a lineup.

Hines offered the testimony of Kassin, a psychologist studying human perception at Williams College with substantial credentials, and trial experience. The government offered a similarly credentialed expert, Ebbesen. I allowed the testimony of both.

The Kassin testimony was offered to show, inter alia, the following: the decreased accuracy of cross-racial identification relative to same-race identification, the effect of stress on identification, the effect of time on memory as it relates to identification, the "confidence-accuracy" phenomenon which suggests the absence of any correlation between the amount of confidence expressed by an eyewitness in his or her memory and the accuracy of that witness' identification, the suggestiveness of subtle aspects of the identification process, such as the darkness of a particular photo as compared to others in the array, the fact that the eyewitness knows there is a suspect in the mix, the transference phenomenon by which a witness may believe that a face looks familiar but is unable to say whether her familiarity comes from seeing a previous mug shot, or from the robbery, etc.

On direct examination, Kassin identified those factors in the Dunne identification that were implicated in the studies with which he was familiar, and could undermine accuracy—the cross racial issues, the differences between the photographs of the other men and Hines' in the photo array,[24] the differences between Hines and the other men in the lineup.[25] He noted problems with what he called relative, comparative judgments: The witness would like to resolve the case and so compares the photographs of one man to another in the array, rather than attempting to compare the photographs to the man she saw. On cross, the government brought up the factors that enhanced accuracy, the nature of the lighting, the distance from the robber, the instructions that were given to the witness, especially at the lineup. The government questioned Kassin about the instructions given to Dunne at the lineup. Kassin agreed that those instructions were "ideal."

… [T]here is no question as to the scientific underpinnings of Kassin's testimony. They are based on experimental psychological studies, testing the acquisition of memory, retention, and retrieval of memory under different conditions. Indeed, the central debate before the jury, eloquently articulated by Ebbesen, the government's expert, is … whether

---

24. Kassin testified that Hines' photograph was the darkest of the eight in the array. Moreover, the numbering for his photograph was different from the others. All the others were 6 numbers, beginning with 96, Hines' number was 1234.

25. The defense pointed out that in the photograph taken of the lineup, which Dunne had indicated was a fair and accurate representation of it, Hines was the darkest man. Furthermore, Dunne could have inferred from the presence of a defense attorney that one of the men in the lineup was a suspect.

conclusions obtained in an experimental, academic, setting with college students should be applied to a real life setting. Kassin and others believe that these conclusions are appropriately applied to eyewitness identifications in court. Ebbesen disagreed.

The government claimed that the jury did not need this testimony at all, that it was not necessary under Fed.R.Evid. 702 to assist the trier of fact. I disagree. While jurors may well be confident that they can draw the appropriate inferences about eyewitness identification directly from their life experiences, their confidence may be misplaced, especially where cross-racial identification is concerned. Indeed, in this respect the rationale for the testimony tracks that for battered women syndrome experts. The jury, for example, may fault the victim for not leaving an abusive spouse, believing that they are fully capable of putting themselves in the shoes of the defendant. In fact, psychological evidence suggests that the "ordinary" response of an "ordinary" woman [is] not in play in situations of domestic violence where the victim suffers from "battered women syndrome." Common sense inferences thus may well be way off the mark.

Nor do I agree that this testimony somehow usurps the function of the jury. The function of the expert here is not to say to the jury—"you should believe or not believe the eyewitness." ... All that the expert does is provide the jury with more information with which the jury can then make a more informed decision. And only the expert can do so. In the absence of an expert, a defense lawyer, for example, may try to argue that cross racial identifications are more problematic than identifications between members of the same race, or that stress may undermine accuracy, but his voice necessarily lacks the authority of the scientific studies Kassin cited.[27]

Finally, the fact that the expert has not interviewed the particular eyewitness makes it less likely that the jury will merely accept the expert testimony and more likely that the testimony will be appropriately cabined. The witness can only be providing the jury with the tools to analyze the eyewitness; he has no more specific information. The science makes no pretensions that it can predict whether a particular witness is accurate or mistaken.

In my judgment, the accuracy of these proceedings was enormously enhanced by treating the jury to all sides of the eyewitness debate ...

II. *CONCLUSION*

Accordingly, the ... defense expert on eyewitness identification was permitted along with the testimony of the government witness.

Problem 10-4

In 1983, Hmong refugee Yia Moua immigrated to America from Laos. She and her family settled in Spokane, Washington, where there was a sizable

---

27. In the first trial, I instructed the jury as follows[:] ... One of the most important issue[s] in this case is the identification of the defendant; what we call eyewitness identification. Now, recognize that the government has the burden of proving identity beyond a reasonable doubt.... Identification testimony is an expression of belief or impression by the witness. Its value depends upon the opportunity the witness had to observe the offender at the time of the offense and then to make a reliable identification later.... In this case, the identifying witness is of a different race than the defendant. In the experience of many, it is more difficult to identify members of a different race than members of one's own. If this is also your own experience, you may consider that in evaluating the witness' testimony. This is one of the elements that you may then consider in evaluating the witness' testimony.

community of Hmong refugees. When Moua sought employment, the Washington State Employment Security Office referred her to Xiong Toyed. A state employee and Hmong refugee himself, Xiong was often enlisted by the state to help other Hmong immigrants find work.

One night, Xiong told Moua he needed to speak to her about an employment opportunity. He arrived at Moua's home, picked her up in his car, and drove her to a hotel, where he raped her. Moua eventually filed charges, stating that Xiong had raped her not once but several times, all under the premise that he wished to speak with her about an employment opportunity. Several other Hmong women eventually followed suit, alleging that Xiong had repeatedly raped them in the same manner.

Moua brought an action against Xiong under § 1983, alleging that she was deprived of her constitutional rights by someone acting under color of state law. To prove her case, Moua was required to show that Xiong abused a position of power given to him by the government. At trial Moua offered the testimony of Marshall Hurlich, an epidemiologist with the Seattle Department of Public Health who often worked with Hmong communities in the state. While epidemiologists generally study the distribution and prevention of disease throughout a population, Hurlich claimed his experience working directly with the Hmong community as a public health professional made him familiar with Hmong culture and community practices. Notably, Hmong refugees have experienced some difficulty in acclimating to the United States, particularly in their cultural clashes with western medicine. Hurlich intended to paint a picture of why Hmong female refugees were particularly susceptible to such abuse and why, given this susceptibility, Xiong had abused his power as a state employee.

The district court allowed Hurlich to testify "generally about the Hmong community," but not to the specifics of the case. Hurlich explained that Hmong women are generally submissive and raised to obey men. He described the role of Hmong women in marriage, their attitudes towards sex, discussion of sex, and extramarital affairs. Hurlich explained that upon fleeing from Laos, Hmong refugees were reliant on government officials for their needs and would not survive in the United States without government assistance. Because of this reliance on government assistance, the Hmong have developed an awe of persons in government positions.

Xiong opposed the admission of Hurlich's testimony and claims it should have been excluded because (1) it is not relevant to the facts of the case, and (2) it was unduly prejudicial. The issue is now before you on appeal. How do you rule?

Problem 10-5

Staff Sergeant Stacey Brooks and his wife would occasionally babysit for other children on their base so parents could have a night out on the town. It was later discovered that Brooks allegedly had inappropriate sexual relations with one of the children. He was court-martialed after his conviction for two counts of "indecent liberties with a female under the age of sixteen." At Brooks's trial the government called the alleged victim. Later, the prosecution called Dr. Marvin Acklin. At the time of trial, Dr. Acklin had worked in child psychology for the last 30 years. In the course of his testimony the prosecution's trial counsel asked the doctor about the cognitive functioning of younger children and their ability to distinguish truth versus lies. The following exchange took place during the direct examination of Dr. Acklin by the prosecutor:

> [Prosecutor]: In your experience, in your professional medical experience, how frequency, how frequently, excuse me, do you see cases of false allegations [sic]?

> [Dr. Acklin]: I believe I testified at the Article 32 Hearing that it's about a five percent level. That's considered to be about, interestingly enough, the level of false allegations one encounters in the business and in research. It ranges anywhere from five to twenty percent, depending on the sample that you look at, but it's generally considered to be, what's called a low base-rate phenomenon, which is ... not that infrequent. Once you take away misinterpretation, then it even drops even further, because then we're talking about the pure fabricated sex abuse allegation. And, the general sense of that in the divorce business, where they tend to occur at the greatest frequency, is it's two to five percent [sic].

The defendant objects to this testimony. How do you rule?

C. Proper Basis

Relevant Rules
FRE 703

Bases of an Expert's Opinion Testimony

An expert may base an opinion on facts or data in the case that the expert has been made aware of or personally observed. If experts in the particular field would reasonably rely on those kinds of facts or data in forming an opinion on the subject, they need not be admissible for the opinion to be admitted. But if the facts or data would otherwise be inadmissible, the proponent of the opinion may disclose them to the jury only if their probative value in helping the jury evaluate the opinion substantially outweighs their prejudicial effect.

FRE 705

Disclosing the Facts or Data Underlying an Expert's Opinion

Unless the court orders otherwise, an expert may state an opinion — and give the reasons for it — without first testifying to the underlying facts or data. But the expert may be required to disclose those facts or data on cross-examination.

Overview

FRE 703 allows expert testimony to rest on any of three grounds: (i) facts within her personal knowledge, (ii) facts presented to her at trial, or (iii) facts presented to her outside of court, but not perceived by her personally, if those facts are the type of facts reasonably relied upon by experts in her field in drawing such conclusions. The first ground concerns experts with firsthand knowledge, such as a treating physician who acts as an expert witness for her patient. The second ground allows an expert to be asked hypothetical questions at trial, which therefore permits an expert to testify even if she does not have firsthand knowledge. The expert is asked to assume certain facts are true and to comment on their ramifications. As long as the facts in the hypothetical are admitted into evidence by the close of the case, this questioning is proper. Similarly, in the second category, an expert can gain knowledge by sitting through the trial and can then be asked questions regarding the testimony she heard. Often the questions will be posed as a hypothetical: "You heard Witness X testify. Assuming what she said was true, what is your opinion on ..."

The third ground is the broadest. The expert can rely on facts or data that is neither perceived by him personally nor introduced into evidence as long as, pursuant to FRE 104(a), the trial judge finds that the facts or data are the type of facts or data relied on by experts in the field and that such reliance is reasonable in this case. In making this evaluation, the trial judge can consider the testifying expert's testimony, the opinions of other experts in the field, or other sources that the judge deems reliable.

To see how this works, let us return to the Overview Problem based on *United States v. Locascio*. As we will see in the court's analysis below, the witness relied on inadmissible hearsay of an alleged Mafia member in forming his expert opinion. The trial court thus must ask: is this the type of facts relied on by experts in Schiliro's field? Undoubtedly, experts on the Mafia must rely on information from Mafia members in order to understand a criminal organization based on secrecy. Then the trial court must ask: is this reliance reasonable? Are the facts relied on by Schiliro a close fit with the substance of his opinion *in this case*? In other words, are the hearsay statements Schiliro relied on trustworthy? If the trial court answers these questions in the affirmative, then Schiliro's *opinion* based on these facts is admissible.

But, by having an expert rely on it, can this underlying data become admissible? Could Schiliro in effect state, "My opinion is X, and it is based on hearsay statements A, B, and C?" Schiliro would argue that it would be difficult for the jury to weigh the credibility of his testimony if he can only offer unsupported opinions. Thus, he should be able to provide his underlying data to the jury so that they could better evaluate his opinions. But the prejudice here is manifest: the prosecution would be entering inadmissible hearsay for one purpose (evaluating the expert witness) while hoping that the jury would use it for an improper purpose (using the hearsay substantively to prove what it asserts). FRE 703 resolves this dilemma with a balancing test: the trial judge may admit such evidence only when the probative value substantially outweighs the danger of unfair prejudice. This "reverse 403" test clearly favors exclusion of the evidence. Accordingly, an expert cannot act as a conduit for inadmissible evidence. The expert should be focusing on what he thinks, not on what others think. Even if an expert relies on inadmissible hearsay, it is still inadmissible hearsay unless the probative value substantially outweighs the danger of unfair prejudice.

So, where does this leave the expert who relies on *inadmissible* evidence in formulating his opinion? FRE 705 provides that experts may state their opinions first, even before they explain the underlying facts and data. In fact, an unadorned conclusion is allowed by an expert, as the expert is not mandated to disclose his underlying facts on direct examination under the FRE. Of course, this type of presentation is likely to carry little weight with the jury, as they have no idea why they should believe this expert. Where the expert relies on inadmissible evidence, the trial judge can allow the evidence with a limiting instruction if it meets the "reverse 403" test of FRE 703 or the trial judge could limit the expert to discussing *types* of data relied upon rather than *specifics* of the data. Thus, in the *Locascio* case, one possible solution would be to allow the expert to testify that he relied on wiretaps of alleged Mafia members without allowing the expert to testify as to their statements.

Of course, if the expert relied on admissible evidence in formulating his opinion, that evidence could be presented to the jury to help them evaluate the expert's opinion. In that instance, the evidence would be allowed substantively and to allow the jury to evaluate the bases for the expert's opinion.

United States v. Locascio
6 F.3d 924 (2nd Cir. 1993)

Altimari, Circuit Judge

. . .

3. *Sources of Information*

Defendants-appellants next argue that because Schiliro relied upon "countless nameless informers and countless tapes not in evidence," his testimony violated Fed.R.Evid. 703 and the Confrontation Clause of the Sixth Amendment. The government responds that, although Schiliro relied upon information that was not before the court, this reliance is permitted under the rules of evidence.

According to Rule 703, the facts that form the basis for an expert's opinions or inferences need not be admissible in evidence "[i]f of a type *reasonably relied* upon by experts in the particular field." Fed.R.Evid. 703 (emphasis added). Thus, expert witnesses can testify to opinions based on hearsay or other inadmissible evidence if experts in the field reasonably rely on such evidence in forming their opinions. *See Daly,* 842 F.2d at 1387 (holding that organized crime expert can rely on otherwise inadmissible hearsay in forming his opinion). Therefore, Schiliro was entitled to rely upon hearsay as to such matters as the structure and operating rules of organized crime families and the identification of specific voices heard on tape in forming his opinion, since there is little question that law enforcement agents routinely and reasonably rely upon such hearsay in the course of their duties. An expert who meets the test of Rule 702, as Schiliro does, is assumed "to have the skill to properly evaluate the hearsay, giving it probative force appropriate to the circumstances." *In re "Agent Orange" Product Liability Litigation,* 611 F.Supp. 1223, 1245 (E.D.N.Y.1985), *aff'd,* 818 F.2d 187 (2d Cir.1987). The fact that Schiliro relied upon inadmissible evidence is therefore less an issue of admissibility for the court than an issue of credibility for the jury. *See United States v. Young,* 745 F.2d 733, 761 (2d Cir.1984) (pointing out that the defendants were free to expose the weaknesses in the prosecution's widespread use of expert testimony through cross examination).

Gotti and Locascio do not seriously contest the point that hearsay and other inadmissible evidence are often reasonably relied upon by law enforcement agents in the field, and that this reliance is anticipated by Rule 703. Rather, they argue that a district court admitting expert testimony based on inadmissible evidence must make an explicit finding that the underlying sources of information used by the expert are trustworthy. *See Barrel of Fun, Inc. v. States Farm Fire & Casualty Co.,* 739 F.2d 1028, 1033 (5th Cir.1984) (holding that an expert's testimony was inadmissible because the factual premises underlying the opinion were "inherently suspect"). We agree that a district court is not bound to accept expert testimony based on questionable data simply because other experts use such data in the field. The Supreme Court's recent decision of *Daubert v. Merrell Dow Pharmaceuticals Inc.,* 509 U.S. 579 (1993), makes this clear.... Although *Daubert* involved Rule 702 and scientific evidence, the flexibility of the federal rules also applies to Rule 703 and the determination of the trustworthiness of the sources of expert testimony. The district court has broad discretion to decide the admissibility of expert testimony based on inadmissible evidence.

We decline, however, to shackle the district court with a mandatory and explicit trustworthiness analysis. The district judge, who has the ideal vantage point to evaluate an expert's testimony during trial, already has the authority under Fed.R.Evid. 403 to conduct an explicit trustworthiness analysis should she deem one necessary. *See Shatkin v. McDonnell Douglas Corp.*, 727 F.2d 202, 208 (2d Cir.1984) (noting that the district court has the "discretionary right under Rule 703 to determine whether the expert acted reasonably in making assumptions of fact upon which he would base his testimony"). In fact, we assume that the district court consistently and continually performed a trustworthiness analysis *sub silentio* of all evidence introduced at trial. We will not, however, circumscribe this discretion by burdening the court with the necessity of making an explicit determination for all expert testimony. This is especially true in this case, because the sources relied upon by Schiliro are no different from those previously allowed by this Court. *See Daly*, 842 F.2d at 1387–88.

Problem 10-6

After causing an incident at a local VA hospital, Larry Leeson was charged with possessing a firearm as a felon and asserted an insanity defense at trial. He introduced the testimony of psychiatrist Dr. Himmelhoch, who testified that he diagnosed Leeson with Post Traumatic Stress Disorder, parietal lobe epilepsy, depression, and migraine headaches. Himmelhoch testified that on the day of Leeson's charged offense these illnesses were working together to make Leeson severely mentally ill, such that he could not understand the nature of his conduct.

The prosecution offered the testimony of psychiatrist Dr. Dana as rebuttal. Dr. Dana testified that Leeson was not suffering from any cognitive impairment on the day in question. He testified that his diagnostic assessment indicated Leeson was addicted to opiates and exhibited malingering disorder—a disorder in which an individual feigns illness or mental disorder for personal gain. If taken as true, this assessment would disqualify Leeson's insanity defense.

Dr. Dana worked at the Bureau of Prisons ("BOP") in Chicago. In addition to housing inmates as a general correctional facility, the Bureau had units of psychiatrists and other professionals working in general law enforcement and correctional capacities. When asked how he arrived at his conclusion, Dr. Dana stated that he relied on information from others in the psychiatric department as well as those outside the department:

> Q. Give us some examples of information that you utilized that came from people not within the department but still up there at the Bureau of Prisons Institution in Chicago.
>
> A. The Correctional Officers that are responsible for supervising the units, often times when they see information that is not in the realm of mainstream, not what is usually identified, they will leave messages for us, contact us of course personally about information.
>
> Q. What about other inmates, do you ever receive information from other inmates or people incarcerated at the BOP?

A. Yeah. Occasionally. Though you have to be careful about that information but in this case there were two separate inmates during the time that Mr. Leeson was there that approached the other forensic psychologist. They did not talk to me directly.

Q: Is it standard to rely on information given to you by inmates?

A: It is actually a standard in order to gather information about a person from sources and information. Again, you have to weigh the validity of all circumstances. In a situation where this was the only piece of information that I had, [I] would not generally rely on it. In situations where it's one of several pieces of information, it then becomes more reliable.

Q. And—and what information did they provide? You said there were two separate ones.

A. Yeah. They—they essentially indicated that Mr. Leeson had approached them to recruit them in assisting him in looking crazy while he was on the unit.

Q. I'm sorry?

A. And, that he had approached them and asked them to assist him in looking crazy on the unit. And one of the inmates said that he was asked by Mr. Leeson to go to the officer and tell him that an inmate in the back was acting crazy.

On appeal, Leeson argues that the district court erred in permitting Dr. Dana to testify regarding the statements of Leeson's fellow inmates at BOP Chicago. The issue is now before you. How do you rule?

Author's Note: Confrontation Clause and Expert Evidence

As you might recall from *Bullcoming v. New Mexico* in Chapter 8, Justice Sotomayor issued a concurring opinion that stressed the limited scope of the majority's holding. In particular, Justice Sotomayor made clear that the Court's holding in *Bullcoming* did not necessarily extend to a situation "in which an expert witness was asked for his independent opinion about underlying testimonial reports that were not themselves admitted into evidence." Justice Sotomayor's concurrence alluded to Federal Rule of Evidence 703, which permits a testifying expert witness to discuss "facts or data" that are not admitted into evidence as long as experts in the particular field would reasonably rely on those kinds of facts.

This scenario would play out if a prosecutor, instead of offering a testimonial written report, decided to call an expert who would base her opinion on the report without offering it into evidence. So, on the one hand, FRE 703, if its mandates were met, would allow this testimony because it is considered reliable. The Confrontation Clause, however, focuses on cross-examination, not reliability, as its procedural mandate. As the author of the testimonial report is not being cross-examined, the Confrontation Clause would seem to be violated. So, if an expert formulates her opinions based upon reliable, but testimonial, hearsay, how should the court resolve this dilemma?

Courts have responded to this dilemma by drawing a distinction between an expert's hearsay that is based on general knowledge and an expert's hearsay relating to case-specific facts. Experts usually acquire the general knowledge in their field through hearsay, such as when a medical doctor learns how generally to treat a broken wrist through knowledge obtained from textbooks or medical journals. Typically, this general knowledge has not been subject to exclusion on hearsay grounds. Therefore, an expert can allude to this hearsay in her testimony (e.g., "It is generally accepted that the best way to treat a broken wrist is with a cast for six weeks").

Case-specific facts are treated differently, however. A case-specific fact is one that relates to the particular events and participants alleged to have been involved in the case being tried, such as how, when, and/or where a particular plaintiff broke his wrist. When an expert has no personal knowledge of a case-specific fact, then an expert has traditionally been precluded from relating it to the finder of fact. Instead, a party must establish case-specific facts by calling witnesses with personal knowledge of those facts. An expert may then testify about more generalized information to help jurors understand the significance of those case-specific facts.

An expert's attempt to discuss case-specific facts for which she had no personal knowledge was the focus of the Supreme Court in *Williams v. Illinois*, 132 S.Ct. 2221 (2012). *Williams* is a confusing decision, but in the recent case of *People v. Sanchez*, 63 Cal.4th 665 (2016), the California Supreme Court explained the *Williams* decision quite well:

> *Williams* was a rape prosecution in which the identity of the attacker was disputed. Semen samples were collected from the rape victim and sent to a Cellmark laboratory for DNA analysis. Cellmark produced a DNA profile purporting to be an accurate profile of the unknown semen donor. Independent of the rape investigation, a sample of Williams's DNA had been acquired and entered in the state's database. That "known" sample from Williams was tested and a profile produced. At trial, a prosecution expert testified that she compared Williams's known profile to the Cellmark profile and, in her opinion, they matched. Williams objected that the Cellmark results, related to the factfinder by the expert, constituted hearsay because they were out-of-court statements by the report writer and were offered to prove their truth: that the profile was, indeed, an accurate profile of the man who committed the rape for which Williams was being tried.
>
> Considering the hearsay question, a four-member plurality of the *Williams* court concluded statements in the Cellmark report were not admitted for their truth, but only to allow the judge, sitting as factfinder, to evaluate the testimony of the expert who opined that the two profiles matched. The plurality acknowledged that the prosecution expert "lacked personal knowledge that the profile produced by Cellmark was based on the vaginal swabs taken from the victim," but reasoned the expert was testifying in the manner of a hypothetical question and any linkage between the sample from the victim to the DNA profile created by Cellmark "was a mere premise of the prosecutor's question, and [the expert] simply assumed that premise to be true when she gave her answer indicating that there was a match between the two DNA profiles. There is no reason to think that the trier of fact took [the expert's] answer as substantive evidence to establish where the DNA profiles came from."
>
> Five justices, the four-member dissent and Justice Thomas writing separately, specifically rejected this approach. In doing so, they called into question the continuing validity of relying on a not-for-the-truth analysis in the expert witness context. Justice Thomas observed that the expert relied upon, as substantive

evidence, Cellmark's representation that, in fact, the sample it tested was that taken from the victim: "[The prosecution expert] opined that petitioner's DNA profile matched the male profile derived from [the victim's] vaginal swabs. In reaching that conclusion, [the expert] relied on Cellmark's out-of-court statements that the profile it reported was in fact derived from [the victim's] swabs, rather than from some other source. *Thus, the validity of [the expert's] opinion ultimately turned on the truth of Cellmark's statements.* The plurality's assertion that Cellmark's statements were merely relayed to explain 'the assumptions on which [the expert's] opinion rest[ed],' overlooks that the value of [the expert's] testimony *depended on the truth of those very assumptions.*"

The dissent also identified another hearsay problem. In addition to asserting that there was a link between the victim's sample and the Cellmark profile, the expert also asserted, as fact, that the Cellmark test was reliable: "Nothing in [the expert's] testimony indicates that she was making an assumption or considering a hypothesis. To the contrary, [the expert] affirmed, without qualification, that the Cellmark report showed a 'male DNA profile found in semen from the vaginal swabs of [the victim].' Had she done otherwise, this case would be different. There was nothing wrong with [the expert's] testifying that two DNA profiles — the one shown in the Cellmark report and the one derived from Williams's blood — matched each other; that was a straightforward application of [her] expertise. Similarly, [the expert] could have added that *if* the Cellmark report resulted from scientifically sound testing of [the victim's] vaginal swab, *then* it would link Williams to the assault. What [the expert] could not do was what she did: indicate that the Cellmark report *was* produced in this way by saying that [the victim's] vaginal swab contained DNA matching Williams's."

This reasoning points out the flaw in the not-for-the-truth limitation when applied to case-specific facts. When an expert relies on hearsay to provide case-specific facts, considers the statements as true, and relates them to the jury as a reliable basis for the expert's opinion, it cannot logically be asserted that the hearsay content is not offered for its truth. In such a case, "the validity of [the expert's] opinion ultimately turn[s] on the truth" of the hearsay statement. If the hearsay that the expert relies on and treats as true is *not* true, an important basis for the opinion is lacking. In *Williams,* the expert's opinion that the Cellmark profile matched the defendant's known profile could not prove that Williams was the semen donor unless the Cellmark profile was, in truth, linked to the victim and was scientifically accurate.... If the hearsay statements about the linkage and accuracy of the Cellmark profile were not *true,* the fact that the two profiles matched would have been irrelevant. That is, the fact that they matched could not have had a tendency in reason to prove the disputed fact of the rapist's identity.

Id. at 681–83.

Therefore, according to *Williams,* if an expert testifies to case-specific out-of-court statements to explain the basis of her opinion, those statements are offered for their truth and are hearsay. The proponent of the evidence must either (i) find an applicable hearsay exception or (ii) admit the evidence through a different witness (which would then allow the expert witness to be asked a hypothetical question based on the evidence). *Id.* at 684.

Let us unfold a hypothetical on this tricky issue. Assume in a vehicular manslaughter case, the prosecution offers an expert to testify that, based on the skid marks of the car, the car was travelling at fifty miles per hour. At trial, the expert explains that accident reconstruction experts rely on a mathematical formula to determine speed based on the length of the skid mark. Is this testimony hearsay? No, it is not; it is general knowledge that is not excluded.

Now assume that the expert then testifies that the skid mark in question was 100 feet long and that the expert is aware of this fact because a police officer who measured the skid mark told him the measurement. Is this testimony hearsay? Yes, according to five members of the *Williams* court, it is. This case-specific fact is offered for its truth because the validity of the expert's opinion on the speed of the car turns on the truth of the statement made by the officer. If the skid mark is not 100 feet long, then the expert's conclusion as to the speed of the vehicle is incorrect. So, the prosecution has two options. First, they can try to find a hearsay exception for the police officer's statement, which would allow the expert to testify to that statement in court. Second, they could bring in the evidence through another means, such as putting the police officer on the stand to testify as to her measurements. After the police officer has testified the expert can be asked a hypothetical questions based on the evidence, such as, "if you assume that the skid mark was 100 feet long, how fast was the car moving?"

Note the Confrontation Clause implications of those two paths. If the police officer testifies as to her measurements, she will not be relying on hearsay and can be cross-examined. If the expert testifies as to the police officer's hearsay statement, the defendant cannot cross-examine the police officer. As this statement is likely testimonial (because it is a police officer relaying information to a prosecution expert for use at trial), we have a violation of the Confrontation Clause if the officer is unavailable and the defendant did not have a prior opportunity for cross-examination. Therefore, even if the police officer's statement satisfies a hearsay exception, it will be inadmissible.

Accordingly, FRE 703 encompasses many variables when an expert attempts to disclose facts upon which the expert relied. Remember to ask yourself whether the fact is general knowledge or case-specific. Then, if it is case-specific, you must determine whether the expert had independent knowledge of the fact or if the expert received the fact through an out-of-court statement. If it is an out-of-court statement, you must assess whether it is being offered for its truth, and, if so, you must find an appropriate hearsay exception. Once you have found a hearsay exception, you still must determine whether the hearsay statement is testimonial. If it is, it must meet the mandates of the Confrontation Clause.

Problem 10-7

As part of California's efforts to control gang activity, police officers issue what are known as "STEP notices" to individuals associating with known gang members. The purpose of the notice is to both provide and gather information. The notice informs the recipient that he is associating with a known gang; that the gang engages in criminal activity; and that, if the recipient commits certain crimes with gang members, he may face increased penalties for his conduct. Accordingly, the STEP notice serves a community outreach effort to dissuade gang members and associates from continuing to engage in gang behavior by apprising them of the potential penalties they faced if they continued to do so. The issuing officer records the date and time the notice is given, along with other identifying information like descriptions and tattoos, and the identification of the recipient's associates. Additionally, the issuing officer signs the notice under penalty of perjury and often record statements made at the time of the interaction.

Marcos Arturo Sanchez was arrested for possession of a firearm by a felon, possession of drugs while armed with a loaded firearm, and commission of a felony for the benefit of a street gang. For the latter crime, the prosecution offered a police officer who was a gang expert to testify that Sanchez was a member of the Delhi gang. On his direct examination, the gang expert testified generally about gang culture, how one joins a gang, and about the Delhi gang in particular. He quoted from a STEP notice from the previous year that Sanchez received for associating with the Delhi gang as the basis of his opinion that Sanchez was a member of the Delhi gang. On cross-examination, the gang expert conceded that he had never met Sanchez and that he was not present when Sanchez was given the STEP notice.

Sanchez argues on appeal that the testimony violated his Sixth Amendment Confrontation Clause right. How do you rule?

D. Proper Methodology

Overview

As will be discussed in *Daubert v. Merrell Dow Pharmaceuticals*, below, for many years courts relied on the test from *Frye v. United States*, 293 Fed. 1013 (D.C.Cir.1923), to determine whether novel scientific theories were admissible. *Frye* mandated that the proponent of the evidence must prove that the scientific theory is "generally accepted" in the relevant scientific community in order to be admissible. Therefore any type of "junk science" which lacked sufficient support in relevant scientific circles was inadmissible. The key issue in *Daubert* thus became whether the *Frye* test survived the adoption of the FRE.

One quick note about the Supreme Court's analysis in *Daubert*: FRE 702 was amended to its current form in 2000. From the current rule we can see a reliable methodology has three components: (i) the expert must base the opinion on sufficient facts or data; (ii) the expert must ground the opinion in reliable principles and methods; and (iii) the expert must apply those principles and methods to the facts of the case in a reliable manner. But the version of FRE 702 when *Daubert* was decided looked much different:

Testimony by Experts. If scientific, technical, or otherwise specialized knowledge will assist the trier of fact to understand the evidence or to determine a fact in issue, a witness qualified as an expert by knowledge, skill, experience, training, or education, may testify thereto in the form of an opinion or otherwise.

Keep this version of the rule in mind when you read *Daubert*.

Focus Questions: *Daubert v. Merrell Dow*

- In stressing that expert evidence must be reliable, the Court emphasizes the requirement of "scientific ... knowledge." What does "scientific" connote to the Court? What does "knowledge" connote to the Court?

- What language of FRE 702 does the Court emphasize in determining that expert evidence must be relevant? How does this relate to the idea of "fit"?

- Are the so-called "*Daubert* factors" dicta? Are any of the factors more important than the others?

Daubert v. Merrell Dow Pharmaceuticals
509 U.S. 579 (1993)

BLACKMUN, J., delivered the opinion for a unanimous Court with respect to Parts I and II–A, and the opinion of the Court with respect to Parts II–B, II–C, III, and IV, in which WHITE, O'CONNOR, SCALIA, KENNEDY, SOUTER, and THOMAS, JJ., joined. REHNQUIST, C.J., filed an opinion concurring in part and dissenting in part, in which STEVENS, J., joined.

In this case we are called upon to determine the standard for admitting expert scientific testimony in a federal trial.

I

Petitioners Jason Daubert and Eric Schuller are minor children born with serious birth defects. They and their parents sued respondent in California state court, alleging that the birth defects had been caused by the mothers' ingestion of Bendectin, a prescription antinausea drug marketed by respondent. Respondent removed the suits to federal court on diversity grounds.

After extensive discovery, respondent moved for summary judgment, contending that Bendectin does not cause birth defects in humans and that petitioners would be unable to come forward with any admissible evidence that it does. In support of its motion, respondent submitted an affidavit of Steven H. Lamm, physician and epidemiologist, who is a well-credentialed expert on the risks from exposure to various chemical substances. Doctor Lamm stated that he had reviewed all the literature on Bendectin and human birth defects—more than 30 published studies involving over 130,000 patients. No study had found Bendectin to be a human teratogen (*i.e.,* a substance capable of causing malformations in fetuses). On the basis of this review, Doctor Lamm concluded that maternal use of Bendectin during the first trimester of pregnancy has not been shown to be a risk factor for human birth defects.

Petitioners did not (and do not) contest this characterization of the published record regarding Bendectin. Instead, they responded to respondent's motion with the testimony of eight experts of their own, each of whom also possessed impressive credentials. These experts had concluded that Bendectin can cause birth defects. Their conclusions were based upon "in vitro" (test tube) and "in vivo" (live) animal studies that found a link between Bendectin and malformations; pharmacological studies of the chemical structure of Bendectin that purported to show similarities between the structure of the drug and that of other substances known to cause birth defects; and the "reanalysis" of previously published epidemiological (human statistical) studies.

The District Court granted respondent's motion for summary judgment.... The United States Court of Appeals for the Ninth Circuit affirmed. 951 F.2d 1128 (1991). Citing *Frye v. United States,* 293 F. 1013, 1014 (D.C.Cir.1923), the court stated that expert opinion based on a scientific technique is inadmissible unless the technique is "generally accepted" as reliable in the relevant scientific community. The court declared that expert opinion based on a methodology that diverges "significantly from the procedures accepted by recognized authorities in the field ... cannot be shown to be 'generally accepted as a reliable technique.'" [951 F.2d] at 1130.

The court emphasized that other Courts of Appeals considering the risks of Bendectin had refused to admit reanalyses of epidemiological studies that had been neither published nor subjected to peer review. 951 F.2d, at 1130–1131. Those courts had found unpublished reanalyses "particularly problematic in light of the massive weight of the original published studies supporting [respondent's] position, all of which had undergone full scrutiny from the scientific community." *Id.,* at 1130. Contending that reanalysis is generally accepted by the scientific community only when it is subjected to verification and scrutiny by others in the field, the Court of Appeals rejected petitioners' reanalyses as "unpublished, not subjected to the normal peer review process and generated solely for use in litigation." *Id.,* at 1131. The court concluded that petitioners' evidence provided an insufficient foundation to allow admission of expert testimony that Bendectin caused their injuries and, accordingly, that petitioners could not satisfy their burden of proving causation at trial....

II
A

In the 70 years since its formulation in the *Frye* case, the "general acceptance" test has been the dominant standard for determining the admissibility of novel scientific evidence at trial. Although under increasing attack of late, the rule continues to be followed by a majority of courts, including the Ninth Circuit.

The *Frye* test has its origin in a short and citation-free 1923 decision concerning the admissibility of evidence derived from a systolic blood pressure deception test, a crude precursor to the polygraph machine. In what has become a famous (perhaps infamous) passage, the then Court of Appeals for the District of Columbia described the device and its operation and declared:

"Just when a scientific principle or discovery crosses the line between the experimental and demonstrable stages is difficult to define. Somewhere in this twilight zone the evidential force of the principle must be recognized, and while courts will go a long way in admitting expert testimony deduced from a well-recognized scientific principle or discovery, *the thing from which the deduction is made must be sufficiently established to have gained general acceptance in the particular field in which it belongs.*" 293 F. at 1014 (emphasis added).

... The merits of the *Frye* test have been much debated, and scholarship on its proper scope and application is legion. Petitioners' primary attack, however, is not on the content but on the continuing authority of the rule. They contend that the *Frye* test was superseded by the adoption of the Federal Rules of Evidence. We agree.

... Here there is a specific Rule that speaks to the contested issue. Rule 702, governing expert testimony, provides:

"If scientific, technical, or other specialized knowledge will assist the trier of fact to understand the evidence or to determine a fact in issue, a witness qualified as an expert by knowledge, skill, experience, training, or education, may testify thereto in the form of an opinion or otherwise."

Nothing in the text of this Rule establishes "general acceptance" as an absolute prerequisite to admissibility. Nor does respondent present any clear indication that Rule 702 or the Rules as a whole were intended to incorporate a "general acceptance" standard. The drafting history makes no mention of *Frye*, and a rigid "general acceptance" requirement would be at odds with the "liberal thrust" of the Federal Rules and their "general approach of relaxing the traditional barriers to 'opinion' testimony." *Beech Aircraft Corp. v. Rainey*, 488 U.S. 153, 169 (1988). Given the Rules' permissive backdrop and their inclusion of a specific rule on expert testimony that does not mention " 'general acceptance,' " the assertion that the Rules somehow assimilated *Frye* is unconvincing. *Frye* made "general acceptance" the exclusive test for admitting expert scientific testimony. That austere standard, absent from, and incompatible with, the Federal Rules of Evidence, should not be applied in federal trials.

B

That the *Frye* test was displaced by the Rules of Evidence does not mean, however, that the Rules themselves place no limits on the admissibility of purportedly scientific evidence. Nor is the trial judge disabled from screening such evidence. To the contrary, under the Rules the trial judge must ensure that any and all scientific testimony or evidence admitted is not only relevant, but reliable.

The primary locus of this obligation is Rule 702, which clearly contemplates some degree of regulation of the subjects and theories about which an expert may testify. "*If scientific,* technical, or other specialized *knowledge will assist the trier of fact* to understand the evidence or to determine a fact in issue" an expert "may testify *thereto.*" (Emphasis added.) The subject of an expert's testimony must be "scientific ... knowledge."[8] The adjective " scientific" implies a grounding in the methods and procedures of science. Similarly, the word "knowledge" connotes more than subjective belief or unsupported speculation. The term "applies to any body of known facts or to any body of ideas inferred from such facts or accepted as truths on good grounds." Webster's Third New International Dictionary 1252 (1986). Of course, it would be unreasonable to conclude that the subject of scientific testimony must be "known" to a certainty; arguably, there are no certainties in science. See, *e.g.,* Brief for Nicolaas Bloembergen et al. as *Amici Curiae* 9 ("Indeed, scientists do not assert that they know what is immutably 'true'—they are committed to searching for new, temporary, theories to explain, as best they can, phenomena"); Brief for American Association for the Advancement of Science et al. as *Amici Curiae* 7–8 ("Science is not an encyclopedic body of knowledge about the universe. Instead, it represents a *process* for proposing and refining theoretical explanations about the world that are subject to further testing and refinement" (emphasis in original)). But, in order to qualify as "scientific knowledge," an inference or assertion must be derived by the scientific method. Proposed testimony must be supported by appropriate validation—*i.e.,* "good grounds," based on what is known. In short, the requirement that an expert's testimony pertain to "scientific knowledge" establishes a standard of evidentiary reliability.[9]

---

8. Rule 702 also applies to "technical, or other specialized knowledge." Our discussion is limited to the scientific context because that is the nature of the expertise offered here.

9. We note that scientists typically distinguish between "validity" (does the principle support what it purports to show?) and "reliability" (does application of the principle produce consistent results?). Although "the difference between accuracy, validity, and reliability may be such that each is distinct from the other by no more than a hen's kick," Starrs, *Frye v. United States* Restructured and Revitalized: A Proposal to Amend Federal Evidence Rule 702, 26 Jurimetrics J. 249, 256 (1986), our reference here is to *evidentiary* reliability—that is, trustworthiness. In a case involving scientific evidence, *evidentiary reliability* will be based upon *scientific validity.*

Rule 702 further requires that the evidence or testimony "assist the trier of fact to understand the evidence or to determine a fact in issue." This condition goes primarily to relevance. "Expert testimony which does not relate to any issue in the case is not relevant and, ergo, non-helpful." [3 J. Weinstein & M. Berger, Weinstein's Evidence ¶ 702[02], p. 702-18 (1988)] The consideration has been aptly described by Judge Becker as one of "fit." *United States v. Downing*, 753 F.2d 1224, 1242 (3d Cir. 1985). "Fit" is not always obvious, and scientific validity for one purpose is not necessarily scientific validity for other, unrelated purposes. The study of the phases of the moon, for example, may provide valid scientific "knowledge" about whether a certain night was dark, and if darkness is a fact in issue, the knowledge will assist the trier of fact. However (absent creditable grounds supporting such a link), evidence that the moon was full on a certain night will not assist the trier of fact in determining whether an individual was unusually likely to have behaved irrationally on that night. Rule 702's "helpfulness" standard requires a valid scientific connection to the pertinent inquiry as a precondition to admissibility.

That these requirements are embodied in Rule 702 is not surprising. Unlike an ordinary witness, see Rule 701, an expert is permitted wide latitude to offer opinions, including those that are not based on firsthand knowledge or observation. See Rules 702 and 703. Presumably, this relaxation of the usual requirement of firsthand knowledge—a rule which represents "a 'most pervasive manifestation' of the common law insistence upon 'the most reliable sources of information,'" Advisory Committee's Notes on Fed.Rule Evid. 602—is premised on an assumption that the expert's opinion will have a reliable basis in the knowledge and experience of his discipline.

C

Faced with a proffer of expert scientific testimony, then, the trial judge must determine at the outset, pursuant to Rule 104(a), whether the expert is proposing to testify to (1) scientific knowledge that (2) will assist the trier of fact to understand or determine a fact in issue.[11] This entails a preliminary assessment of whether the reasoning or methodology underlying the testimony is scientifically valid and of whether that reasoning or methodology properly can be applied to the facts in issue. We are confident that federal judges possess the capacity to undertake this review. Many factors will bear on the inquiry, and we do not presume to set out a definitive checklist or test. But some general observations are appropriate.

Ordinarily, a key question to be answered in determining whether a theory or technique is scientific knowledge that will assist the trier of fact will be whether it can be (and has been) tested. "Scientific methodology today is based on generating hypotheses and testing them to see if they can be falsified; indeed, this methodology is what distinguishes science from other fields of human inquiry." Green, Expert Witnesses and Sufficiency of Evidence in Toxic Substances Litigation: The Legacy of Agent Orange and Bendectin Litigation, 86 Nw. U. L. Rev. 643, 645 (1992). See also C. Hempel, Philosophy of Natural Science 49 (1966) ("[T]he statements constituting a scientific explanation must be capable of empirical test"); K. Popper, Conjectures and Refutations: The Growth of Scientific Knowledge 37

---

11. Although the *Frye* decision itself focused exclusively on "novel" scientific techniques, we do not read the requirements of Rule 702 to apply specially or exclusively to unconventional evidence. Of course, well-established propositions are less likely to be challenged than those that are novel, and they are more handily defended. Indeed, theories that are so firmly established as to have attained the status of scientific law, such as the laws of thermodynamics, properly are subject to judicial notice under Federal Rule of Evidence 201.

(5th ed. 1989) ("[T]he criterion of the scientific status of a theory is its falsifiability, or refutability, or testability") (emphasis deleted).

Another pertinent consideration is whether the theory or technique has been subjected to peer review and publication. Publication (which is but one element of peer review) is not a *sine qua non* of admissibility; it does not necessarily correlate with reliability, and in some instances well-grounded but innovative theories will not have been published. Some propositions, moreover, are too particular, too new, or of too limited interest to be published. But submission to the scrutiny of the scientific community is a component of "good science," in part because it increases the likelihood that substantive flaws in methodology will be detected. The fact of publication (or lack thereof) in a peer reviewed journal thus will be a relevant, though not dispositive, consideration in assessing the scientific validity of a particular technique or methodology on which an opinion is premised.

Additionally, in the case of a particular scientific technique, the court ordinarily should consider the known or potential rate of error, and the existence and maintenance of standards controlling the technique's operation.

Finally, "general acceptance" can yet have a bearing on the inquiry. A "reliability assessment does not require, although it does permit, explicit identification of a relevant scientific community and an express determination of a particular degree of acceptance within that community." *United States v. Downing*, 753 F.2d, at 1238. Widespread acceptance can be an important factor in ruling particular evidence admissible, and "a known technique which has been able to attract only minimal support within the community," *Downing*, 753 F.2d, at 1238, may properly be viewed with skepticism.

The inquiry envisioned by Rule 702 is, we emphasize, a flexible one. Its overarching subject is the scientific validity—and thus the evidentiary relevance and reliability—of the principles that underlie a proposed submission. The focus, of course, must be solely on principles and methodology, not on the conclusions that they generate.

Throughout, a judge assessing a proffer of expert scientific testimony under Rule 702 should also be mindful of other applicable rules. Rule 703 provides that expert opinions based on otherwise inadmissible hearsay are to be admitted only if the facts or data are "of a type reasonably relied upon by experts in the particular field in forming opinions or inferences upon the subject." Rule 706 allows the court at its discretion to procure the assistance of an expert of its own choosing. Finally, Rule 403 permits the exclusion of relevant evidence "if its probative value is substantially outweighed by the danger of unfair prejudice, confusion of the issues, or misleading the jury...." Judge Weinstein has explained: "Expert evidence can be both powerful and quite misleading because of the difficulty in evaluating it. Because of this risk, the judge in weighing possible prejudice against probative force under Rule 403 of the present rules exercises more control over experts than over lay witnesses." Weinstein, 138 F.R.D., at 632.

III

We conclude by briefly addressing what appear to be two underlying concerns of the parties and *amici* in this case. Respondent expresses apprehension that abandonment of "general acceptance" as the exclusive requirement for admission will result in a "free-for-all" in which befuddled juries are confounded by absurd and irrational pseudoscientific assertions. In this regard respondent seems to us to be overly pessimistic about the capabilities of the jury and of the adversary system generally. Vigorous cross-examination, presentation of contrary evidence, and careful instruction on the burden of proof are the traditional and appropriate means of attacking shaky but admissible evidence. Additionally, in the event the trial court concludes that the scintilla of evidence presented supporting a position is insufficient to allow a reasonable juror to conclude that the position more likely than not is true, the court remains free to direct a judgment, Fed.Rule Civ.Proc. 50(a), and likewise to grant summary judgment, Fed.Rule Civ.Proc. 56. These conventional devices, rather than wholesale exclusion under an uncompromising "general acceptance" test, are the appropriate safeguards where the basis of scientific testimony meets the standards of Rule 702.

Petitioners and, to a greater extent, their *amici* exhibit a different concern. They suggest that recognition of a screening role for the judge that allows for the exclusion of "invalid" evidence will sanction a stifling and repressive scientific orthodoxy and will be inimical to the search for truth. It is true that open debate is an essential part of both legal and scientific analyses. Yet there are important differences between the quest for truth in the courtroom and the quest for truth in the laboratory. Scientific conclusions are subject to perpetual revision. Law, on the other hand, must resolve disputes finally and quickly. The scientific project is advanced by broad and wide-ranging consideration of a multitude of hypotheses, for those that are incorrect will eventually be shown to be so, and that in itself is an advance. Conjectures that are probably wrong are of little use, however, in the project of reaching a quick, final, and binding legal judgment—often of great consequence—about a particular set of events in the past. We recognize that, in practice, a gatekeeping role for the judge, no matter how flexible, inevitably on occasion will prevent the jury from learning of authentic insights and innovations. That, nevertheless, is the balance that is struck by Rules of Evidence designed not for the exhaustive search for cosmic understanding but for the particularized resolution of legal disputes.

IV

To summarize: "General acceptance" is not a necessary precondition to the admissibility of scientific evidence under the Federal Rules of Evidence, but the Rules of Evidence— especially Rule 702—do assign to the trial judge the task of ensuring that an expert's testimony both rests on a reliable foundation and is relevant to the task at hand. Pertinent evidence based on scientifically valid principles will satisfy those demands.

The inquiries of the District Court and the Court of Appeals focused almost exclusively on "general acceptance," as gauged by publication and the decisions of other courts. Accordingly, the judgment of the Court of Appeals is vacated, and the case is remanded for further proceedings consistent with this opinion.

It is so ordered.

Chief Justice REHNQUIST, with whom Justice STEVENS joins, concurring in part and dissenting in part.

... The Court concludes, correctly in my view, that the *Frye* rule did not survive the enactment of the Federal Rules of Evidence, and I therefore join Parts I and II-A of its opinion. The ... Court ... proceeds to construe Rules 702 and 703 very much in the abstract, and then offers some "general observations."

"General observations" by this Court customarily carry great weight with lower federal courts, but the ones offered here suffer from the flaw common to most such observations—they are not applied to deciding whether particular testimony was or was not admissible, and therefore they tend to be not only general, but vague and abstract. This is particularly unfortunate in a case such as this, where the ultimate legal question depends on an appreciation of one or more bodies of knowledge not judicially noticeable, and subject to different interpretations in the briefs of the parties and their *amici....*

The various briefs filed in this case are markedly different from typical briefs, in that large parts of them do not deal with decided cases or statutory language—the sort of material we customarily interpret. Instead, they deal with definitions of scientific knowledge, scientific method, scientific validity, and peer review—in short, matters far afield from the expertise of judges. This is not to say that such materials are not useful or even necessary in deciding how Rule 703 should be applied; but it is to say that the unusual subject matter should cause us to proceed with great caution in deciding more than we have to, because our reach can so easily exceed our grasp.

But even if it were desirable to make "general observations" not necessary to decide the questions presented, I cannot subscribe to some of the observations made by the Court. In Part II-B, the Court concludes that reliability and relevancy are the touchstones of the admissibility of expert testimony.... Questions arise simply from reading this part of the Court's opinion, and countless more questions will surely arise when hundreds of district judges try to apply its teaching to particular offers of expert testimony. Does all of this *dicta* apply to an expert seeking to testify on the basis of "technical or other specialized knowledge"—the other types of expert knowledge to which Rule 702 applies— or are the "general observations" limited only to "scientific knowledge"? What is the difference between scientific knowledge and technical knowledge; does Rule 702 actually contemplate that the phrase "scientific, technical, or other specialized knowledge" be broken down into numerous subspecies of expertise, or did its authors simply pick general descriptive language covering the sort of expert testimony which courts have customarily received? The Court speaks of its confidence that federal judges can make a "preliminary assessment of whether the reasoning or methodology underlying the testimony is scientifically valid and of whether that reasoning or methodology properly can be applied to the facts in issue." The Court then states that a "key question" to be answered in deciding whether something is "scientific knowledge" "will be whether it can be (and has been) tested." Following this sentence are three quotations from treatises, which not only speak of empirical testing, but one of which states that the "'criterion of the scientific status of a theory is its falsifiability, or refutability, or testability.'"

I defer to no one in my confidence in federal judges; but I am at a loss to know what is meant when it is said that the scientific status of a theory depends on its "falsifiability," and I suspect some of them will be, too.

I do not doubt that Rule 702 confides to the judge some gatekeeping responsibility in deciding questions of the admissibility of proffered expert testimony. But I do not think it imposes on them either the obligation or the authority to become amateur scientists in order to perform that role. I think the Court would be far better advised in this case to decide only the questions presented, and to leave the further development of this important area of the law to future cases.

Author's Note: Thoughts on *Daubert*

Daubert was a landmark case, and, shortly after it was decided, many practitioners and scholars wondered whether it had loosened or tightened the standard for scientific evidence. On the one hand, the standard seemed looser in that evidence that was not "generally accepted" was now potentially admissible. On the other hand, *Daubert* emphasized a deeper analysis of multiple criteria, thus implying that "junk science" would not make it past the trial judge's gatekeeper role; even if the science was generally accepted, that did not necessarily make it admissible. Some studies found that the exclusion rate for scientific evidence increased after *Daubert*. One thing is certain, however: Not all states rushed to embrace *Daubert*. Many states decided not to apply *Daubert's* reasoning to their rules of evidence and instead maintained the *Frye* general acceptance test.

The law continued to evolve after *Daubert*. Courts added to the non-exclusive list of *Daubert* factors to determine reliability, including such factors as whether the expert testimony is based on research the expert has conducted independent of litigation, whether there is an analytical gap between the data and the opinion, the experience of the expert, whether the expert has accounted for alternative explanations, whether the expert utilized appropriate professional care, and whether the field is known to reach reliable results in the area of the proposed testimony.

The issues presented by FRE 702 are FRE 104(a) issues for the judge to determine. The burden of satisfying the rule and the *Daubert* requirements are on the proponent of the witness. In making this decision, the judge is free to request affidavits, deposition transcripts, oral argument, or even live testimony from expert witnesses (often called a *Daubert* hearing).

The Supreme Court further clarified the scope of *Daubert* in *Kumho Tire*, below. In addition to determining whether *Daubert* applied to all expert testimony (rather than just scientific testimony), the Supreme Court also stressed that courts have broad discretion in deciding how to determine reliability.

Focus Questions: *Kumho Tire Company v. Carmichael*

- Does the Court add another layer of analysis in addition to weighing the *Daubert* factors? Is this approach more ad hoc? Is it more or less friendly to admission of expert evidence?

- Does *Kumho Tire* vest too much power in the trial judge's decision making? Does the fact that a trial judge's determination is evaluated on an abuse of discretion standard influence your answer?

- How does an expert avoid an *ipse dixit* situation?

Kumho Tire Company v. Carmichael
526 U.S. 137 (1999)

BREYER, J., delivered the opinion of the Court, Parts I and II of which were unanimous, and Part III of which was joined by REHNQUIST, C.J., and O'CONNOR, SCALIA, KENNEDY, SOUTER, THOMAS, and GINSBURG, JJ. SCALIA, J., filed a concurring opinion, in which O'CONNOR and THOMAS, JJ., joined. STEVENS, J., filed an opinion concurring in part and dissenting in part.

... This case requires us to decide how *Daubert* [*v. Merrell Dow Pharmaceuticals, Inc.*, 509 U.S. 579 (1993)] applies to the testimony of engineers and other experts who are not scientists. We conclude that *Daubert's* general holding—setting forth the trial judge's general "gatekeeping" obligation—applies not only to testimony based on "scientific" knowledge, but also to testimony based on "technical" and "other specialized" knowledge.

See Fed. Rule Evid. 702. We also conclude that a trial court *may* consider one or more of the more specific factors that *Daubert* mentioned when doing so will help determine that testimony's reliability. But, as the Court stated in *Daubert,* the test of reliability is "flexible," and *Daubert's* list of specific factors neither necessarily nor exclusively applies to all experts or in every case. Rather, the law grants a district court the same broad latitude when it decides *how* to determine reliability as it enjoys in respect to its ultimate reliability determination. See *General Electric Co. v. Joiner,* 522 U.S. 136, 143 (1997) (courts of appeals are to apply "abuse of discretion" standard when reviewing district court's reliability determination). Applying these standards, we determine that the District Court's decision in this case—not to admit certain expert testimony—was within its discretion and therefore lawful.

I

On July 6, 1993, the right rear tire of a minivan driven by Patrick Carmichael blew out. In the accident that followed, one of the passengers died, and others were severely injured. In October 1993, the Carmichaels brought this diversity suit against the tire's maker and its distributor, whom we refer to collectively as Kumho Tire, claiming that the tire was defective. The plaintiffs rested their case in significant part upon deposition testimony provided by an expert in tire failure analysis, Dennis Carlson, Jr., who intended to testify in support of their conclusion.

Carlson's depositions relied upon certain features of tire technology that are not in dispute. A steel-belted radial tire like the Carmichaels' is made up of a "carcass" containing many layers of flexible cords, called "plies," along which (between the cords and the outer tread) are laid steel strips called "belts." Steel wire loops, called "beads," hold the cords together at the plies' bottom edges. An outer layer, called the "tread," encases the carcass, and the entire tire is bound together in rubber, through the application of heat and various chemicals. The bead of the tire sits upon a "bead seat," which is part of the wheel assembly. That assembly contains a "rim flange," which extends over the bead and rests against the side of the tire.

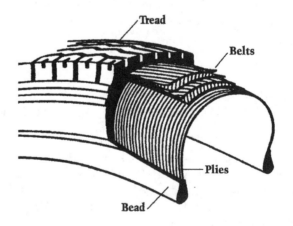

Radial-Ply Tire Construction

Carlson's testimony also accepted certain background facts about the tire in question. He assumed that before the blowout the tire had traveled far. (The tire was made in 1988 and had been installed some time before the Carmichaels bought the used minivan in March 1993; the Carmichaels had driven the van approximately 7,000 additional miles in the two months they had owned it.) Carlson noted that the tire's tread depth, which was 11/32 of an inch when new, had been worn down to depths that ranged from 3/32 of an inch along some parts of the tire, to nothing at all along others. He conceded that the tire tread had at least two punctures which had been inadequately repaired.

Despite the tire's age and history, Carlson concluded that a defect in its manufacture or design caused the blowout. He rested this conclusion in part upon three premises which, for present purposes, we must assume are not in dispute: First, a tire's carcass should stay bound to the inner side of the tread for a significant period of time after its tread depth has worn away. Second, the tread of the tire at issue had separated from its inner steel-belted carcass prior to the accident. Third, this "separation" caused the blowout.

Carlson's conclusion that a defect caused the separation, however, rested upon certain other propositions, several of which the defendants strongly dispute. First, Carlson said that if a separation is *not* caused by a certain kind of tire misuse called "overdeflection" (which consists of underinflating the tire or causing it to carry too much weight, thereby generating heat that can undo the chemical tread/carcass bond), then, ordinarily, its cause is a tire defect. Second, he said that if a tire has been subject to sufficient overdeflection to cause a separation, it should reveal certain physical symptoms. These symptoms include (a) tread wear on the tire's shoulder that is greater than the tread wear along the tire's center; (b) signs of a "bead groove," where the beads have been pushed too hard against the bead seat on the inside of the tire's rim; (c) sidewalls of the tire with physical signs of deterioration, such as discoloration; and/or (d) marks on the tire's rim flange. Third, Carlson said that where he does not find *at least two* of the four physical signs just mentioned (and presumably where there is no reason to suspect a less common cause of separation), he concludes that a manufacturing or design defect caused the separation.

Carlson added that he had inspected the tire in question. He conceded that the tire to a limited degree showed greater wear on the shoulder than in the center, some signs of "bead groove," some discoloration, a few marks on the rim flange, and inadequately filled puncture holes (which can also cause heat that might lead to separation). But, in each instance, he testified that the symptoms were not significant, and he explained why he believed that they did not reveal overdeflection. For example, the extra shoulder wear, he said, appeared primarily on one shoulder, whereas an overdeflected tire would reveal equally abnormal wear on both shoulders. Carlson concluded that the tire did not bear at least two of the four overdeflection symptoms, nor was there any less obvious cause of separation; and since neither overdeflection nor the punctures caused the blowout, a defect must have done so.

Kumho Tire moved the District Court to exclude Carlson's testimony on the ground that his methodology failed Rule 702's reliability requirement. The court agreed with Kumho that it should act as a *Daubert*-type reliability "gatekeeper," even though one might consider Carlson's testimony as "technical," rather than "scientific." The court then examined Carlson's methodology in light of the reliability-related factors that *Daubert* mentioned, such as a theory's testability, whether it "has been a subject of peer review or publication," the "known or potential rate of error," and the "degree of acceptance … within the relevant scientific community." The District Court found that all those factors argued against the reliability of Carlson's methods, and it granted the motion to exclude the testimony (as well as the defendants' accompanying motion for summary judgment).

The plaintiffs, arguing that the court's application of the *Daubert* factors was too "inflexible," asked for reconsideration. And the court granted that motion. After reconsidering the matter, the court agreed with the plaintiffs that *Daubert* should be applied flexibly, that its four factors were simply illustrative, and that other factors could argue in favor of admissibility. It conceded that there may be widespread acceptance of a "visual-inspection method" for some relevant purposes. But the court found insufficient indications of the reliability of "the component of Carlson's tire failure analysis which most concerned the Court, namely, the methodology employed by the expert in analyzing the data obtained in the visual inspection, and the scientific basis, if any, for such an analysis." It consequently affirmed its earlier order declaring Carlson's testimony inadmissible and granting the defendants' motion for summary judgment.

The Eleventh Circuit reversed.... It noted that "the Supreme Court in *Daubert* explicitly limited its holding to cover only the 'scientific context,' " adding that "a *Daubert* analysis" applies only where an expert relies "on the application of scientific principles," rather than "on skill- or experience-based observation." It concluded that Carlson's testimony, which it viewed as relying on experience, "falls outside the scope of *Daubert*," that "the district court erred as a matter of law by applying *Daubert* in this case," and that the case must be remanded for further (non-*Daubert*-type) consideration under Rule 702.

... We granted certiorari in light of uncertainty among the lower courts about whether, or how, *Daubert* applies to expert testimony that might be characterized as based not upon "scientific" knowledge, but rather upon "technical" or "other specialized" knowledge.

II
A

In *Daubert,* this Court held that Federal Rule of Evidence 702 imposes a special obligation upon a trial judge to "ensure that any and all scientific testimony ... is not only relevant, but reliable." 509 U.S. at 589. The initial question before us is whether this basic gatekeeping obligation applies only to "scientific" testimony or to all expert testimony. We, like the parties, believe that it applies to all expert testimony.

For one thing, Rule 702 itself says:

> "If scientific, technical, or other specialized knowledge will assist the trier of fact to understand the evidence or to determine a fact in issue, a witness qualified as an expert by knowledge, skill, experience, training, or education, may testify thereto in the form of an opinion or otherwise."

This language makes no relevant distinction between "scientific" knowledge and "technical" or "other specialized" knowledge. It makes clear that any such knowledge might become the subject of expert testimony. In *Daubert,* the Court specified that it is the Rule's word "knowledge," not the words (like "scientific") that modify that word, that "establishes a standard of evidentiary reliability." Hence, as a matter of language, the Rule applies its reliability standard to all "scientific," "technical," or "other specialized" matters within its scope. We concede that the Court in *Daubert* referred only to "scientific" knowledge. But as the Court there said, it referred to "scientific" testimony "because that [wa]s the nature of the expertise" at issue.

Neither is the evidentiary rationale that underlay the Court's basic *Daubert* "gatekeeping" determination limited to "scientific" knowledge. *Daubert* pointed out that Federal Rules 702 and 703 grant expert witnesses testimonial latitude unavailable to other witnesses on the "assumption that the expert's opinion will have a reliable basis in the knowledge and experience of his discipline." *Id.*, at 592 (pointing out that experts may testify to opinions, including those that are not based on firsthand knowledge or observation). The Rules grant that latitude to all experts, not just to "scientific" ones.

Finally, it would prove difficult, if not impossible, for judges to administer evidentiary rules under which a gatekeeping obligation depended upon a distinction between "scientific" knowledge and "technical" or "other specialized" knowledge. There is no clear line that divides the one from the others. Disciplines such as engineering rest upon scientific knowledge. Pure scientific theory itself may depend for its development upon observation and properly engineered machinery. And conceptual efforts to distinguish the two are unlikely to produce clear legal lines capable of application in particular cases.

Neither is there a convincing need to make such distinctions. Experts of all kinds tie observations to conclusions through the use of what Judge Learned Hand called "general truths derived from ... specialized experience." Hand, Historical and Practical Considerations Regarding Expert Testimony, 15 Harv. L.Rev. 40, 54 (1901). And whether the specific expert testimony focuses upon specialized observations, the specialized translation of those observations into theory, a specialized theory itself, or the application of such a theory in a particular case, the expert's testimony often will rest "upon an experience confessedly foreign in kind to [the jury's] own." *Ibid.* The trial judge's effort to assure that the specialized testimony is reliable and relevant can help the jury evaluate that foreign experience, whether the testimony reflects scientific, technical, or other specialized knowledge.

We conclude that *Daubert*'s general principles apply to the expert matters described in Rule 702. The Rule, in respect to all such matters, "establishes a standard of evidentiary reliability." 509 U.S., at 590. It "requires a valid ... connection to the pertinent inquiry as a precondition to admissibility." *Id.*, at 592. And where such testimony's factual basis, data, principles, methods, or their application are called sufficiently into question, see Part III, *infra*, the trial judge must determine whether the testimony has "a reliable basis in the knowledge and experience of [the relevant] discipline." 509 U.S., at 5926.

B

Petitioners ask more specifically whether a trial judge determining the "admissibility of an engineering expert's testimony" *may* consider several more specific factors that *Daubert* said might "bear on" a judge's gatekeeping determination. Brief for Petitioners i. These factors include:

-Whether a "theory or technique ... can be (and has been) tested";

-Whether it "has been subjected to peer review and publication";

-Whether, in respect to a particular technique, there is a high "known or potential rate of error" and whether there are "standards controlling the technique's operation"; and

-Whether the theory or technique enjoys " 'general acceptance' " within a " 'relevant scientific community.' " 509 U.S., at 592–594.

Emphasizing the word "may" in the question, we answer that question yes.

Engineering testimony rests upon scientific foundations, the reliability of which will be at issue in some cases. In other cases, the relevant reliability concerns may focus upon personal knowledge or experience. As the Solicitor General points out, there are many different kinds of experts, and many different kinds of expertise. Our emphasis on the word "may" thus reflects *Daubert*'s description of the Rule 702 inquiry as "a flexible one."

509 U.S., at 594. *Daubert* makes clear that the factors it mentions do *not* constitute a "definitive checklist or test." *Id.*, at 593. And *Daubert* adds that the gatekeeping inquiry must be "'tied to the facts'" of a particular "case." *Id.*, at 591. We agree with the Solicitor General that "[t]he factors identified in *Daubert* may or may not be pertinent in assessing reliability, depending on the nature of the issue, the expert's particular expertise, and the subject of his testimony." Brief for United States as *Amicus Curiae* 19. The conclusion, in our view, is that we can neither rule out, nor rule in, for all cases and for all time the applicability of the factors mentioned in *Daubert*, nor can we now do so for subsets of cases categorized by category of expert or by kind of evidence. Too much depends upon the particular circumstances of the particular case at issue.

Daubert itself is not to the contrary. It made clear that its list of factors was meant to be helpful, not definitive. Indeed, those factors do not all necessarily apply even in every instance in which the reliability of scientific testimony is challenged. It might not be surprising in a particular case, for example, that a claim made by a scientific witness has never been the subject of peer review, for the particular application at issue may never previously have interested any scientist. Nor, on the other hand, does the presence of *Daubert's* general acceptance factor help show that an expert's testimony is reliable where the discipline itself lacks reliability, as, for example, do theories grounded in any so-called generally accepted principles of astrology or necromancy.

At the same time, and contrary to the Court of Appeals' view, some of *Daubert's* questions can help to evaluate the reliability even of experience-based testimony. In certain cases, it will be appropriate for the trial judge to ask, for example, how often an engineering expert's experience-based methodology has produced erroneous results, or whether such a method is generally accepted in the relevant engineering community. Likewise, it will at times be useful to ask even of a witness whose expertise is based purely on experience, say, a perfume tester able to distinguish among 140 odors at a sniff, whether his preparation is of a kind that others in the field would recognize as acceptable.

We must therefore disagree with the Eleventh Circuit's holding that a trial judge may ask questions of the sort *Daubert* mentioned only where an expert "relies on the application of scientific principles," but not where an expert relies "on skill- or experience-based observation." We do not believe that Rule 702 creates a schematism that segregates expertise by type while mapping certain kinds of questions to certain kinds of experts. Life and the legal cases that it generates are too complex to warrant so definitive a match.

To say this is not to deny the importance of *Daubert's* gatekeeping requirement. The objective of that requirement is to ensure the reliability and relevancy of expert testimony. It is to make certain that an expert, whether basing testimony upon professional studies or personal experience, employs in the courtroom the same level of intellectual rigor that characterizes the practice of an expert in the relevant field. Nor do we deny that, as stated in *Daubert*, the particular questions that it mentioned will often be appropriate for use in determining the reliability of challenged expert testimony. Rather, we conclude that the trial judge must have considerable leeway in deciding in a particular case how to go about determining whether particular expert testimony is reliable. That is to say, a trial court should consider the specific factors identified in *Daubert* where they are reasonable measures of the reliability of expert testimony.

C

The trial court must have the same kind of latitude in deciding *how* to test an expert's reliability, and to decide whether or when special briefing or other proceedings are needed to investigate reliability, as it enjoys when it decides *whether or not* that expert's relevant testimony is reliable. Our opinion in *Joiner* makes clear that a court of appeals is to apply an abuse-of-discretion standard when it "review[s] a trial court's decision to admit or exclude expert testimony." 522 U.S., at 138–139. That standard applies as much to the trial court's decisions about how to determine reliability as to its ultimate conclusion. Otherwise, the trial judge would lack the discretionary authority needed both to avoid unnecessary "reliability" proceedings in ordinary cases where the reliability of an expert's methods is properly taken for granted, and to require appropriate proceedings in the less usual or more complex cases where cause for questioning the expert's reliability arises.... Thus, whether *Daubert's* specific factors are, or are not, reasonable measures of reliability in a particular case is a matter that the law grants the trial judge broad latitude to determine....

III

We further explain the way in which a trial judge "may" consider *Daubert's* factors by applying these considerations to the case at hand, a matter that has been briefed exhaustively by the parties and their 19 *amici*. The District Court did not doubt Carlson's qualifications, which included a masters degree in mechanical engineering, 10 years' work at Michelin America, Inc., and testimony as a tire failure consultant in other tort cases. Rather, it excluded the testimony because, despite those qualifications, it initially doubted, and then found unreliable, "the methodology employed by the expert in analyzing the data obtained in the visual inspection, and the scientific basis, if any, for such an analysis." After examining the transcript in "some detail," and after considering respondents' defense of Carlson's methodology, the District Court determined that Carlson's testimony was not reliable. It fell outside the range where experts might reasonably differ, and where the jury must decide among the conflicting views of different experts, even though the evidence is "shaky." *Daubert,* 509 U.S., at 596. In our view, the doubts that triggered the District Court's initial inquiry here were reasonable, as was the court's ultimate conclusion.

For one thing, and contrary to respondents' suggestion, the specific issue before the court was not the reasonableness *in general* of a tire expert's use of a visual and tactile inspection to determine whether overdeflection had caused the tire's tread to separate from its steel-belted carcass. Rather, it was the reasonableness of using such an approach, along with Carlson's particular method of analyzing the data thereby obtained, to draw a conclusion regarding *the particular matter to which the expert testimony was directly relevant.* That matter concerned the likelihood that a defect in the tire at issue caused its tread to separate from its carcass. The tire in question, the expert conceded, had traveled far enough so that some of the tread had been worn bald; it should have been taken out of service; it had been repaired (inadequately) for punctures; and it bore some of the very marks that the expert said indicated, not a defect, but abuse through overdeflection. The relevant issue was whether the expert could reliably determine the cause of *this* tire's separation.

Nor was the basis for Carlson's conclusion simply the general theory that, in the absence of evidence of abuse, a defect will normally have caused a tire's separation. Rather, the expert employed a more specific theory to establish the existence (or absence) of such abuse. Carlson testified precisely that in the absence of *at least two* of four signs of abuse (proportionately greater tread wear on the shoulder; signs of grooves caused by the beads; discolored sidewalls; marks on the rim flange), he concludes that a defect caused the separation. And his analysis depended upon acceptance of a further implicit proposition, namely, that his visual and tactile inspection could determine that the tire before him had not been abused despite some evidence of the presence of the very signs for which he looked (and two punctures).

For another thing, the transcripts of Carlson's depositions support both the trial court's initial uncertainty and its final conclusion. Those transcripts cast considerable doubt upon the reliability of both the explicit theory (about the need for two signs of abuse) and the implicit proposition (about the significance of visual inspection in this case). Among other things, the expert could not say whether the tire had traveled more than 10, or 20, or 30, or 40, or 50 thousand miles, adding that 6,000 miles was "about how far" he could "say with any certainty." The court could reasonably have wondered about the reliability of a method of visual and tactile inspection sufficiently precise to ascertain with some certainty the abuse-related significance of minute shoulder/center relative tread wear differences, but insufficiently precise to tell "with any certainty" from the tread wear whether a tire had traveled less than 10,000 or more than 50,000 miles. And these concerns might have been augmented by Carlson's repeated reliance on the "subjective[ness]" of his mode of analysis in response to questions seeking specific information regarding how he could differentiate between a tire that actually had been overdeflected and a tire that merely looked as though it had been. They would have been further augmented by the fact that Carlson said he had inspected the tire itself for the first time the morning of his first deposition, and then only for a few hours. (His initial conclusions were based on photographs.)

Moreover, prior to his first deposition, Carlson had issued a signed report in which he concluded that the tire had "not been ... overloaded or underinflated," not because of the absence of "two of four" signs of abuse, but simply because "the rim flange impressions ... were normal." That report also said that the "tread depth remaining was 3/32 inch," *id.*, at 336, though the opposing expert's (apparently undisputed) measurements indicate that the tread depth taken at various positions around the tire actually ranged from .5/32 of an inch to 4/32 of an inch, with the tire apparently showing greater wear along *both* shoulders than along the center.

Further, in respect to one sign of abuse, bead grooving, the expert seemed to deny the sufficiency of his own simple visual-inspection methodology. He testified that most tires have some bead groove pattern, that where there is reason to suspect an abnormal bead groove he would ideally "look at a lot of [similar] tires" to know the grooving's significance, and that he had not looked at many tires similar to the one at issue.

Finally, the court, after looking for a defense of Carlson's methodology as applied in these circumstances, found no convincing defense. Rather, it found (1) that "none" of the *Daubert* factors, including that of "general acceptance" in the relevant expert community, indicated that Carlson's testimony was reliable, (2) that its own analysis "revealed no countervailing factors operating in favor of admissibility which could outweigh those identified in *Daubert*"; and (3) that the "parties identified no such factors in their briefs." For these three reasons *taken together*, it concluded that Carlson's testimony was unreliable.

... [T]he question before the trial court was specific, not general. The trial court had to decide whether this particular expert had sufficient specialized knowledge to assist the jurors "in deciding the particular issues in the case." ... The particular issue in this case concerned the use of Carlson's two-factor test and his related use of visual/tactile inspection to draw conclusions on the basis of what seemed small observational differences. We have found no indication in the record that other experts in the industry use Carlson's two-factor test or that tire experts such as Carlson normally make the very fine distinctions about, say, the symmetry of comparatively greater shoulder tread wear that were necessary, on Carlson's own theory, to support his conclusions. Nor, despite the prevalence of tire testing, does anyone refer to any articles or papers that validate Carlson's approach. Indeed, no one has argued that Carlson himself, were he still working for Michelin, would have concluded in a report to his employer that a similar tire was similarly defective on grounds identical to those upon which he rested his conclusion here. Of course, Carlson himself claimed that his method was accurate, but, as we pointed out in *Joiner,* "nothing in either *Daubert* or the Federal Rules of Evidence requires a district court to admit opinion evidence that is connected to existing data only by the *ipse dixit* of the expert." 522 U.S., at 146....

In sum, Rule 702 grants the district judge the discretionary authority, reviewable for its abuse, to determine reliability in light of the particular facts and circumstances of the particular case. The District Court did not abuse its discretionary authority in this case. Hence, the judgment of the Court of Appeals is

Reversed.

[Concurring opinion by Scalia, J., and concurring and dissenting opinion by Stevens, J., omitted.]

Author's Note: Thoughts on *Kumho Tire*

Kumho Tire established that all the *Daubert* factors would not necessarily apply to every case and that the process should remain flexible based upon the issue presented in the case. Let us now examine one example of the flexibility afforded by *Kumho Tire* to give better context to the scope of that opinion.

Focus Questions: *Hernandez v. City of Albuquerque*

- What could the expert have done differently in order to satisfy the Court that his testimony was relevant and reliable? To what degree should plaintiff's attorney have better prepared his expert witness?

- Why does the witness's lack of specialization affect the admissibility, and not just the weight, of his opinion? Should his lack of specialization go solely to weight?

Hernandez v. City of Albuquerque
2004 WL 5520000 (D.N.M. 2004)

JAMES O. BROWNING, District Judge.

THIS MATTER comes before the Court on the Defendant Tom Benard's Motion in Limine to Exclude Portions of the Testimony of Dr. Alan J. Watts; or in the Alternative, Motion for a Daubert Hearing, filed December 9, 2003.... The primary issue is whether the Court should exclude Watts from testifying at trial that the head wound the Plaintiff, Robert Hernandez, received is consistent with a blow by an asp [which is a telescoping, expandable baton commonly possessed by police officers]. Because Watts assumes that there was a blow by a blunt object, and that assumption involves the ultimate issue the jury will need to decide, the Court is not persuaded that his testimony will be helpful to the jury on the issues at trial. Accordingly, the Court will grant the motion and exclude Watts as a witness at trial.

BACKGROUND

[Hernandez refused to pull his car over for the police and a high speed chase involving several officers ensued. He claims that, after the police stopped him, took him to the ground, and handcuffed him, Albuquerque police officer Benard physically assaulted him.] Hernandez alleges that Benard violated his constitutional rights when Benard used excessive force against him, striking him with an asp. Hernandez suffered a 1/2 inch wound to his head. Hernandez retained Watts, a physicist with 34 years of experience to review the facts, determine, and subsequently testify whether the injuries to Hernandez' head are consistent with the allegations that he makes in the Complaint.

Watts possesses a Ph.D. in Physics, a science that deals with matter and energy, and their interactions in the field of mechanics. Watts is an accredited physicist with practical experience dealing in force analysis, shock physics, impact damage effects, and biomechanics. Watts has given expert testimony in body force analysis and biomechanics in almost every judicial district in New Mexico, as well as in the Federal District Court of New Mexico. He has also testified in several foreign jurisdictions. Many attorneys have consulted and/or retained Watts in the past, including Benard's counsel. Watts has authored and/or co-authored numerous scientific papers and articles, as well as a book in which at least one chapter deals with impact injuries to the head and brain.

Watts' earlier career focused on the area of weapons research and design. Later, Watts began to focus on biomechanics in the context of legal consulting. Watts is not a trained medical doctor, a neurologist, or a forensic pathologist. Indeed, he has no formal medical or forensic training. Watts also testified that he is not an expert in police procedures and has no knowledge of correct or incorrect police operating procedures. He has no experience as a law enforcement officer or in the use or handling of an asp, nor has he witnessed someone struck by an asp.

The Court held a *Daubert* hearing on December 29, 2003. In addition to hearing arguments from counsel, the Court heard testimony and cross-examination of Watts....

ANALYSIS

Hernandez wants Watts to testify about his scientific knowledge, but the issue is whether what he says will be of any assistance to the jury. While Watts has the expertise to testify about the speed of an asp blow, the Court does not think he can say much more. Watts does not appear qualified to testify regarding the other opinions that he offers. And if Watts can properly testify only to the speed of an asp blow, the question is whether that is really helpful to the fact finder.

I. *ALL PROPOSED EXPERT TESTIMONY MUST SATISFY THE REQUIREMENTS AS EXPRESSED IN RULE 702, DAUBERT, AND KUMHO TIRE TO ENSURE THAT THE EXPERT'S TESTIMONY IS BOTH RELEVANT AND RELIABLE.*

... As discussed in *Daubert v. Merrell Dow Pharms., Inc.,* 509 U.S. 579 (1993), and as refined in *Kumho Tire Co., Ltd. v. Carmichael,* 526 U.S. 137 (1999), the purpose of rule 702 is to ensure that all expert testimony is both relevant and reliable. Thus, the Court must perform a "gatekeeping inquiry ... tied to the facts of a particular case" to determine if the proposed expert testimony is properly admitted. *See Kumho Tire Co., Ltd. v. Carmichael,* 526 U.S. at 150 (internal quotation marks and citation omitted).

The Supreme Court significantly clarified the scope of *Daubert v. Merrell Dow Pharms., Inc.* in *Kumho Tire,* holding the district court's rule 702 gatekeeping duties apply to all expert testimony, whether the expert bases his or her testimony on scientific, technical, or other specialized knowledge. The purpose of the *Daubert* gatekeeping function is not to measure every expert by an inflexible set of criteria, but to undertake whatever inquiry is necessary to "make certain that an expert, whether basing testimony upon professional studies or personal experience, employs in the courtroom the same level of intellectual rigor that characterizes the practice of an expert in the relevant field." The trial judge in all cases of proffered expert testimony must find that it is properly grounded, well reasoned, and not speculative before he or she admits the evidence.

First and foremost, to determine whether Watts may testify at trial, the Court must determine whether he is competent to testify as an expert. Additionally, to be reliable under *Daubert*, the expert must derive his or her inference or assertion by a proper method and must support his or her opinion by appropriate validation—i.e., good grounds, based on what is known. Hernandez must show that "the method employed by [Watts] in reaching the conclusion is scientifically sound and that the opinion is based on facts which satisfy Rule 702's reliability requirements." *Dodge v. Cotter Corp.,* 328 F.3d 1212, 1222 (10th Cir.2003) (citation omitted).

While expert opinions "must be based on facts which enable [the expert] to express a reasonably accurate conclusion as opposed to conjecture or speculation, ... absolute certainty is not required." *Id.* Hernandez need not prove that Watts is undisputably correct or that his conclusions/opinions are generally accepted. Instead, Hernandez need only show that the method which Watts used in reaching his conclusion is sound and that the opinions are based on facts which satisfy rule 702's reliability requirements.

In *Daubert v. Merrell Dow Pharms., Inc.,* the court set forth five non-exhaustive factors to aid the court's function in ensuring reliability: (i) whether the theory or scientific technique can be tested or has been tested; (ii) whether the theory or technique has been subjected to peer review and publication; (iii) whether there is a known or potential rate of error associated with the methodology; (iv) whether there are standards controlling the technique's operation and whether they were maintained; and (v) whether the theory or technique is generally accepted within the relevant community. *See Daubert v. Merrell Dow Pharms., Inc.,* 509 U.S. at 593-94. The Court "may" apply these factors if necessary, but the "specific factors neither necessarily nor exclusively appl[y] to all experts or in every case." *Kumho Tire Co., Ltd. v. Carmichael,* 526 U.S. at 141. District courts have broad discretion to consider a variety of other factors.

II. *WATTS' TESTIMONY WILL NOT BE HELPFUL TO THE JURY IN DECIDING THE ISSUES IN THIS CASE.*

To arrive at his general opinion on causation, Watts reviewed scientific literature, drew general propositions therefrom, and then combined those propositions to conclude that an asp blow could have caused the injury to Hernandez' head. His proposed testimony, however, has an important limitation: Watts will not testify that the asp blow caused the injury, but only that the wound is consistent with an asp blow or that the asp blow could have caused the wound. What is in dispute is whether the asp caused the head wound. And Watts testifies that he cannot determine whether blunt trauma caused the wound.

Watts does not know what object caused Hernandez' head wound. And because he is not medically trained or trained as a pathologist, he cannot and should not testify about the nature of the injury. Thus, all that Watts can say is that the wound is consistent with a strike by an asp.

Watts did not attempt to determine what caused Hernandez' head wound. Rather, Watts assumes that there was a blow by a blunt object. Specifically, he assumes that the wound was caused by a blunt object and not by a sharp object. He did not make that determination himself. He simply relied upon what he was told.

Thus, Watts assumes what needs to be determined. His testimony does not help the jury do what it needs to do—that is, decide what caused the wound. After the jury decides whether Benard hit Hernandez in the head, they can use Watts' testimony to tell them the wound is consistent with an asp blow. That testimony will not be helpful to the jury.

The Court might still be persuaded to admit this marginally helpful testimony as harmless except that Watts also says that the wound is consistent with a cut. Watts admits that he did not see a photograph of the wound after it was cleaned up. He also testified that he did not investigate whether a cut, which requires less energy than an asp blow, could have caused the head wound. Hence, Watts not only cannot say with any certainty what caused the wound, but he also cannot rule out other possible causes. Thus, the Court does not think that will be helpful to the task before the jury at trial, and will exclude the testimony.

Further, the Court is concerned that, because Watts does have impressive credentials, an impressive presence and manner, and is a highly qualified expert in certain fields, his testimony on an issue that is not helpful will convey the impression that he thinks an asp did cause the wound. That would be unfair to Benard. Thus, the unfair prejudice of the testimony substantially outweighs the probative value of the proposed testimony.

III. *WATTS' PROPOSED TESTIMONY FAILS TO SATISFY THE RELIABILITY REQUIREMENT OF DAUBERT AND KUMHO TIRE.*

Benard argues that the Court should exclude Watts' testimony for four reasons: (i) his opinion is based upon unsound and incomplete scientific principles regarding the alleged ASP strike; (ii) he is not a medical doctor and cannot offer testimony regarding the nature of wound that Hernandez sustained, blood spatter or pooling, and/or injuries that would occur as a result of a head strike; (iii) he is not an expert in police procedures and the Court should thus not allow him to testify regarding the officers' conduct at the scene; and (iv) he cannot state that the alleged ASP strike was the only source of trauma to Hernandez' head, because he does not have all of the factual evidence. The Court will start with the last argument first.

A. INCOMPLETE FACTUAL EVIDENCE

Benard argues that the factual information that Hernandez provided to Watts surrounding the April, 2000 incident was incomplete. Watts bases his opinion, in part, on the fact that Hernandez could not have sustained it during the motor vehicle chase or the vehicle accident. But as discussed above, Watts assumes the issue that the jury must decide. Watts' speed calculations assume that a blunt object, i.e., an asp, caused the wound. Again, Watts does not help the jury determine whether Benard hit Hernandez in the head with an asp. Watts assumes that he did.

Watts testified at his deposition that he did not do any calculations concerning the speed of impact of Hernandez' vehicle because he "wasn't provided any data" allowing him to do that. Watts was aware that Hernandez' vehicle struck and obliterated a lamp post, and then struck a wall before his vehicle came to rest.

Nevertheless, Watts did not measure these forces or consider such forces in formulating his opinions. Watts testified that he cannot rule out these forces "but [he] saw nothing in the description of the accident that would lead [him] to believe that the crash itself was the cause of any problem" and that he "would need to know the specifics of how the crash occurred before [he] could really give a serious answer to that."

Hernandez asserts Watts, using the principles of physics, explained in great detail why, in his opinion, the head injury did not result from the vehicle crash. The extent of Watts' explanation, however, appears to be that because Hernandez' head and body would move forward as a result of the impact, one would not expect this type of injury to the back of the head. This explanation is not helpful to the jury. The Court does not believe that it is beyond the scope of an average juror's knowledge. Moreover, Watts testified that Hernandez would "rebound slightly" after impacting the air bag. He does not, however, address whether the injury could have been inflicted at that point.

The Court will exclude Watts' testimony. If he did not do any calculations concerning the speed of the vehicle when it crashed, the Court does not understand how he can conclude the vehicle impact did not cause the injury to Hernandez' head. As a result, this case is one in which too great an analytical gap exists between the data and opinion. Watts has not provided a sufficient factual or other basis to state that the impacts which Hernandez sustained during the motor vehicle chase could not have caused the alleged head injury. The evidentiary rules require more than speculation. Accordingly, Watts' methodology to determine the speed of an asp in this case may be scientifically sound under the principles of physics, but his opinion, which suggests that an asp was the only object that could have caused Hernandez' wound, does not reasonably flow from the data upon which he relies.

B. UNSOUND AND INCOMPLETE SCIENTIFIC PRINCIPLES.

Watts formulated his opinion that Benard struck Hernandez in the head with an asp, in part, based upon how fast an average person can swing various objects. Specifically, Watts testified that his "analysis implied certain inferred speeds that ... were well within the capability of a typical adult," relying upon a book entitled "The Science and Folklore of Baseball," by Robert Watts and Terry Bahill. The basis of his analysis is how fast an average adult can swing a baseball bat, i.e., the inferred speed, not an expandable baton or an asp.

Watts' proposed opinion is problematic, because Watts does not calculate the force necessary to create certain injuries. For example, he does not calculate the force necessary to create a laceration to the head. Rather than doing these calculations of other forces that might cause a head wound, Watts "read the literature that quote such forces" and adopts its findings. Watts does not rely, however, upon any literature that discusses the force or speed necessary to inflict an injury by an asp or the speeds at which an average adult can swing an asp. Watts testified in relation to swinging an asp or expandable baton:

> Q: Do you have any information on how fast an asp can be brought down, at what speed a typical person or a normal person would do it? Is there any data on that?
>
> A: I'm not aware of any, but treating it as a variation of a bat, the answer is you could easily swing it at up to 60 or 70 miles an hour....

Thus, Watts is unaware of any existing data concerning the speed at which typical adult can swing an asp. He does, however, explain how he reached his conclusion. He pointed to an objective source to show that he followed the scientific method, as it is practiced by at least a recognized minority of scientists in Watts' field.

Benard argues that Watts' testimony fails to satisfy the *Daubert* factors because: (i) he has not provided the Court with the assurance that the data regarding speeds and forces applicable to baseball bats are readily applied to expandable batons or asps; (ii) he has not assured the Court that such application has been tested and/or accepted within the relevant community; and (iii) he has not established that he is qualified to give such opinions assuming such an analogy is appropriate. But Benard does not object to Watts' qualifications to testify as an expert in the field of biomechanics.

And Watts' credentials generally qualify him as an expert to give testimony as to the relationship between impact and injury. Case law supports allowing such testimony. *See, e.g., Arnold v. Riddell, Inc.,* 882 F.Supp. 979, 989–90 (D.Kan.1995) (permitting biomechanical engineer to testify about causation of injury from various forces). And Watts has been qualified to give expert opinion testimony regarding body force analysis, biomechanics and blood spatters, and holds a Ph.D. in physics.

As Watts testified, while the specifics of each case will differ, the physics is the same in all cases. Accordingly, it boils down to applying the laws of mechanics to the human body. Mechanics is a part of physics. To arrive at specific causation, Watts looked at how much energy would be required to cause Hernandez' injury, took into account the weight and dimensions of the asp, the contact area, and then calculated the impact speed required to account for the injury.

Under *Daubert,* Watts' opinion about the speed of the asp which was allegedly brought down on Hernandez' head is reliable. When Watts testifies about the speed of the asp, he is within the reasonable confines of his subject matter. He is qualified as an expert pursuant to rule 702 on biomechanics. He can testify about the speed of an asp blow. The Court is not convinced, however, that this testimony is helpful to the jury.

Apparently realizing that problem, Watts suggests that he might be able to go further. Somewhat inconsistent with some of the testimony discussed above, Watts testified that he considered all plausible causes of Hernandez' injury—the motor vehicle accident, the passenger door frame, a gun, items on Benard's utility belt, etc .—and then, based on the force and speed necessary to produce the injury, ruled out the least plausible causes until only the most likely cause remained—a deliberate asp blow. As explained above, Watts does not adequately explain the basis for his conclusion that the head wound could not have occurred during the vehicle crash. With respect to each other alternative, Watts dismisses the possibility based on his assumption that Hernandez' wound was caused by blunt trauma rather than by a sharp object. That assumption, however, rests entirely upon other people's characterization of the wound. Such a basis does not satisfy *Daubert's* reliability standard, and the Court will exclude testimony regarding the speed of an asp strike and the likelihood that alternative sources did not cause Hernandez' wound.

C. IMPROPER MEDICAL AND/OR FORENSIC PATHOLOGY OPINIONS.

Watts also proposes to testify about the resulting injury, but the Court does not believe that his opinion on the injury is reliable. Despite his lack of medical and forensic training, Watts bases his conclusions upon medical or forensic principles:

The existence of some limited blood spatter to the right of Mr. Hernandez strongly suggests that a *second* blow was delivered. The logic is as follows. During a short-lived blunt impact the blood does *not* immediately flow profusely (this only occurs due to sharp instrument penetration into arteries, or due to bullets, etc.). Rather, the blood starts to "well up" and forms a pool at the injury strike point. However, if a subsequent blow is then delivered onto the same region the pooling blood can now be spattered. Based upon his testimony, however, Watts is not qualified to discuss injuries that may or may not occur from an asp strike or what object would cause immediate blood flow or a blood pool beneath the skin.

Hernandez nevertheless contends that Watts' opinion regarding blood spatter and causation of the wound are proper and admissible. Hernandez contends that a witness may be qualified as an expert on the basis of "knowledge, skill, experience [or] training." Fed.R.Evid. 702. In reaching his conclusion, Watts reviewed scientific literature regarding blood stain evidence; reviewed photographs showing the pooling of blood and blood spots to the right side of Hernandez with small "tails" pointing away from Hernandez; and concluded that a blow delivered at his previously calculated impact speed of 23 to 38 mph would give the observed "low velocity" splatter.

Watts' lack of specialization as a medical doctor, a neurologist, or a forensic pathologist affects the admissibility of this opinion, not just the weight the jury would give to that opinion. He has read a book on blood spatters, and while spatters may be a matter of physics, Watts cannot eliminate causes; he can only tell the jury that Hernandez' wound is consistent with the physics of a second asp blow. While the movement of fluids is generally within the realm of physics, Watts proposed testimony regarding blood spatter is outside his area of expertise.

Watts testified that the blood spatters could be consistent with Hernandez shaking his head. Watts testified that the blood spatters are consistent with Hernandez' body being moved. The spatter could have been consistent with a blow into existing pool of blood. The spatter could have come from blood dripping off something.

The Court does not think Watts' opinion tells the jury what it needs to determine the issue here, i.e., whether Hernandez was struck by a blunt object. Watts does not know what caused the blood spatters. While, on cross-examination, opposing counsel can usually use his or her opportunity to ferret out any weakness in a party's evidence to ensure the jury properly evaluates the testimony's weight and credibility, the Court has a special role in screening experts that it does not have with other evidence. *See Goebel v. Denver & Rio Grande Western R. Co.*, 346 F.3d 987, 994 (10th Cir.2003) (noting that vigorous cross-examination, presentation of contrary evidence, and careful instruction on the burden of proof are the traditional and appropriate means of attacking shaky but admissible evidence) (citing *Daubert v. Merrell Dow Pharms., Inc.*, 509 U.S. at 596). Accordingly, the Court will not permit Hernandez to admit Watts' testimony regarding blood splatter.

The Court is also not convinced that Watts is qualified to give opinions discussing injuries resulting from an alleged strike to the head, such as the dizziness Hernandez alleges. Such an opinion should be reserved for a medical doctor or someone with specialized training in symptoms. Watts does not have any more training or knowledge on physical symptoms than the average juror.

The Court will also preclude Watts from testifying about the nature of the wound that Hernandez sustained. Watts suggested that an asp caused the wound on Hernandez' head because it would not be possible to sustain such a wound by any other means. Benard contends that Watts misinterpreted the term "laceration" as something different than a "cut." Watts testified that he looked up the two terms in standard dictionaries and forensic pathology books and found that the term "cut" is used to describe any parting of the skin. If the injury is inflicted with a sharp object it is called an "incision." The term "laceration" is used when the skin is crushed or torn to produce a ragged cut. For the purposes of his analysis and opinions, Watts assumed that Hernandez' head wound was a "laceration" resulting from blunt trauma rather than a sharp object. Hernandez argues that Watts properly relied on these interpretations and definitions to conclude that Hernandez' injuries were the result of blunt trauma—i.e., an asp blow.

The inappropriateness of Watts' testimony is underscored by the deposition testimony of Dr. Mark Berger, Hernandez' expert and a physician. Berger testified that a laceration and a cut, medically, are the same thing. Berger also testified that Hernandez' wound, whether caused by a blunt trauma, a jagged cut, or a smooth surgical cut, would fall within the term laceration. There is the very real possibility that Watts improperly interpreted medical reports and medical terms to formulate his opinions. Dr. Berger's deposition testimony shows that medically trained experts would likely reach a different conclusion than Watts.

The Court need not and should not decide on this motion whether Watts correctly interpreted the difference between a laceration and/or a cut. All the Court needs to decide is that the reasoning behind Watts' opinion requires some basis in medical principles. For example, Watts assumes or decides that blunt trauma caused Hernandez' wound to the head and that the wound was a laceration versus a cut. At his deposition, Watts testified:

Q: [S]ince you can't determine whether it was a blunt trauma or a sharp trauma, if you take out the fact that you believe this was a blunt trauma, then that could explain an eight-tenths of an inch cut on the back of the head?

A: Well, the catch for that logic … is you just showed me an exhibit which was the medical exhibit which, itself, described it as blunt trauma, not a cut.

Q: Where does it say blunt trauma? In which exhibit? Show me where it says blunt trauma.

A: The one you showed me just now.

Q: This one, the hospital record says "blunt trauma?"

A: Yes, sir.

Q: Now, is that reporting what Mr. Hernandez said he was hit in the back of the head with a blunt object, or is that the medical? Where do you see blunt trauma?

A: Evaluation and management. It calls it "blunt contact."

Q: And that's based upon the history that Mr. Hernandez gave?

A: Well, I'm assuming the emergency medical boys would state it wasn't if they disagreed. They keep referring to it as blunt trauma.

Q: Where else did they refer to it as blunt trauma?

A: Well, they're calling it a laceration, to start with, which is not what you mean by a sharp object.

…

Q: So you have ruled out that causing the cut or the laceration without even knowing what objects could have come in contact with him; is that correct?

A: On the basis that it's blunt trauma and not a sharp cut.

…

Q: Now, you're assuming laceration means that it couldn't be a cut. That's how you interpret that medical term; is that correct?

A: My understanding is that's how the medics interpret that medical term.

Q: But you're not a medic?

A: No.

Q: You've never written a medical report?

A. No, sir. But I have books on medicine, and that's the way they describe it.

Watts is thus interpreting medical reports and medical terms to formulate his opinions. Watts does not have the expertise to conduct such interpretation. Moreover, Watts' opinions are unreliable to the extent that he does not consider the possibility that a sharp object caused Hernandez' head wound. Accordingly, the Court will exclude Watts' opinions that rely upon medical or forensic principles.

D. ALBUQUERQUE POLICE DEPARTMENT AND POLICIES.

Watts also expresses opinions that rely upon police procedures and policies. For instance, Watts concludes that the officers at the scene "were anxious to quickly hand-cuff [Hernandez] and 'secure' him," leading to high adrenaline levels. Watts also stated that Benard "was probably 'running on adrenaline' and failed to follow correct procedure."

Hernandez concedes that Watts is not an expert in police procedure and relied on what Hernandez gave him in the form of quotes from other police officers coupled with common sense to conclude that Benard failed to follow correct procedure. Hence, given that Watts is not an expert in police procedures and has no knowledge about police operating procedures, the Court will not allow Watts to testify concerning police procedures, similar to those described above. Likewise, the Court will not permit Watts to comment on the conduct of any of the officers at the scene, specifically whether the conduct was appropriate or inappropriate. He also should not testify to the psychological or physiological effects of an officer responding to stimuli during the effectuation of an arrest.

IT IS THEREFORE ORDERED that Defendant Tom Benard's Motion in Limine to Exclude Portions of the Testimony of Dr. Alan J. Watts ... is granted. The Court will exclude the proposed testimony of Dr. Watts at trial.

Professional Development Questions

- What steps would you take to convince a court to allow expert testimony on a novel scientific concept that has not achieved general acceptance in the relevant scientific community? Does your answer change based on whether you are representing the plaintiff or defendant?

- As you near the end of this book, you now realize that certain evidence may result in multiple objections. For example, a document may arguably be irrelevant, unauthenticated, and littered with hearsay. What other areas of evidence law may yield successful objections to an expert witness?

- When choosing an expert witness, you must anticipate how that witness will be cross-examined. What factors would you consider when choosing an expert witness? What aspects of her background and/or testimony would be particularly susceptible to cross-examination?

- Additionally, when choosing an expert witness, one must bear in mind how persuasive her presentation will be on direct examination. What factors would you consider in this regard? For example, would you favor a witness with an outstanding qualifications but weak public speaking skills over a witness with less impressive qualifications but a much stronger delivery? Does your answer change depending on the topic of the opinion?

Chapter 11

Privileges

I. Overview to Privileges

Relevant Rule
FRE 501

Privilege in General

The common law — as interpreted by United States courts in the light of reason and experience — governs a claim of privilege unless any of the following provides otherwise:

- the United States Constitution;

- a federal statute; or

- other rules prescribed by the Supreme Court.

But in a civil case, state law governs privilege regarding a claim or defense for which state law supplies the rule of decision.

Overview

Privileges occupy an odd corner of evidence law: potentially relevant and reliable evidence is screened from the jury. The rationale behind any particular privilege is to protect the privacy of a socially important relationship, such as those between marital partners, between attorneys and their clients, and between psychotherapists and their patients. In each of the three previously-articulated relationships, a federal privilege exists in order to encourage the open exchange of information. As we shall see, those relationships would suffer if the participants in the relationship believed that their words (to and from their spouse, their lawyer, or their psychotherapist) could surface in a court of law. The sense of trust and privacy essential to those relationships could very well erode if the words that make up those relationships are not protected.

With that understanding of the rationale behind privileges comes an important caveat: it is the words of the relationship, the *communications*, that are protected. The underlying facts behind those communications are not shielded just because we tell them to, for example, our lawyer. Thus, if a criminal defendant is asked if she was at the murder scene, she cannot object by stating "That's privileged because I told my lawyer." While it is improper to ask the witness *to recount the conversation she had with her lawyer*, it is perfectly permissible to ask about underlying facts. In other words, sharing a communication with a person with whom a privileged relationship exists does not make the fact go away. It is still available for exploration as long as privileged conversations are not broached. In this way, the privilege does not exceed its scope: only the relationship's conversations are protected, which is the purpose behind the privilege.

When Article V of the Federal Rules of Evidence was first proposed, it contained a total of thirteen rules with nine separate privileges. For a variety of reasons, the rules were controversial, and Congress decided to pass only a revised version of FRE 501. As you can see from the language of FRE 501, privileges shall be governed by the principles of the common law as interpreted "in the light of reason and experience[.]" Thus, Congress turned its back to the idea of codified privileges and decided that its evolution will be governed largely by federal common law. Federal privilege law controls in federal criminal prosecutions and federal civil cases not based on diversity jurisdiction, but state privilege law governs in diversity cases and other claims founded on state law.

Finally, as we undertake our analysis of privileges, please note one commonality to all of them: the burden of establishing a privilege falls on the party asserting it. This is only fair, as the party asserting the privilege is the one attempting to withhold potentially relevant and reliable evidence from the finder of fact.

II. Attorney-Client Privilege

Relevant Rule
FRE 502

Attorney-Client Privilege and Work Product; Limitations on Waiver

The following provisions apply, in the circumstances set out, to disclosure of a communication or information covered by the attorney-client privilege or work-product protection.

(a) Disclosure Made in a Federal Proceeding or to a Federal Office or Agency; Scope of a Waiver. When the disclosure is made in a federal proceeding or to a federal office or agency and waives the attorney-client privilege or work-product protection, the waiver extends to an undisclosed communication or information in a federal or state proceeding only if:

(1) the waiver is intentional;

(2) the disclosed and undisclosed communications or information concern the same subject matter; and

(3) they ought in fairness to be considered together.

(b) Inadvertent Disclosure. When made in a federal proceeding or to a federal office or agency, the disclosure does not operate as a waiver in a federal or state proceeding if:

(1) the disclosure is inadvertent;

(2) the holder of the privilege or protection took reasonable steps to prevent disclosure; and

(3) the holder promptly took reasonable steps to rectify the error, including (if applicable) following Federal Rule of Civil Procedure 26(b)(5)(B).

(c) Disclosure Made in a State Proceeding. When the disclosure is made in a state proceeding and is not the subject of a state-court order concerning waiver, the disclosure does not operate as a waiver in a federal proceeding if the disclosure:

(1) would not be a waiver under this rule if it had been made in a federal proceeding; or

(2) is not a waiver under the law of the state where the disclosure occurred.

(d) Controlling Effect of a Court Order. A Federal court may order that the privilege or protection is not waived by disclosure connected with the litigation pending before the court— in which event the disclosure is also not a waiver in any other federal or state proceeding.

(e) Controlling Effect of a Party Agreement. An agreement on the effect of disclosure in a federal proceeding is binding only on the parties to the agreement, unless it is incorporated into a court order.

(f) Controlling Effect of this Rule. Notwithstanding Rules 101 and 1101, this rule applies to state proceedings and to federal court-annexed and federal court-mandated arbitration proceedings, in the circumstances set out in the rule. And notwithstanding Rule 501, this rule applies even if state law provides the rule of decision.

(g) Definitions. In this rule:

(1) "attorney-client privilege" means the protection that applicable law provides for confidential attorney-client communications; and

(2) "work-product protection" means the protection that applicable law provides for tangible material (or its intangible equivalent) prepared in anticipation of litigation or for trial.

Overview

Before we dive into FRE 502 and the idea of waiving the attorney-client privilege, let us get a better picture of what the attorney-client privilege is. Most courts mandate that there be a (i) communication, (ii) made in confidence, (iii) between privileged parties, (iv) for the purpose of obtaining or providing legal assistance for the client. The rationale for the attorney-client privilege is to encourage full and open discussions between a lawyer and client so that the lawyer can provide the best advice possible without fear that those words could become public. The client is the holder of the privilege, and therefore the attorney cannot reveal the communication without the client's consent. The privilege continues even after the attorney-client relationship has terminated, and it may be asserted even after the death of the client. The burden of establishing the existence of the privilege rests on the party who asserts it.

A. Communication

As noted in Section I, there is no privilege for the underlying facts contained in a communication between an attorney and client, and there is no privilege for a client's knowledge. A communication covers oral statements, written communications, and assertive conduct (e.g., nodding one's head to assert "yes") by both the client and the lawyer. However, a communication in the attorney-client privilege context does not include acts and observations. For example, witnessing a client hide a gun would not be considered a communication, as it is based on observation rather than conversation.

B. Made in Confidence

When a client communicates information to an attorney, the client must have a reasonable expectation that the information will remain confidential. Thus an eavesdropper would only destroy confidentiality if no reasonable precautions were taken to ensure confidentiality. In the context of an eavesdropper, if reasonable precautions are not taken, the lack of those precautions may indicate that no intent to keep the conversation confidential existed.

Statements may also lose their confidentiality if, while being expressed, the client intended that the lawyer publicize the comment to the public, even if they were never disclosed to the public. Thus, advising your lawyer that the statement could be released to the press or could be used in a public document destroys the privilege, as the comment was never meant to be confidential.

C. Between Privileged Parties

Confidentiality is lost if non-essential persons to the attorney-client relationship hear the communication. Persons whose presence is reasonably necessary in the furtherance of the consultation are considered "essential," so employees of the attorney (e.g., paralegals, secretaries, etc.) and necessary agents of the client (e.g., translators, accountants, etc.) would not destroy the privilege if the client reasonably believed that the discussion was confidential. The privilege also protects communications to a lawyer representing another client in a matter of common interest.

One must keep in mind the type of client in order to determine the client's necessary agents. A client may be an individual or any type of entity (e.g., governmental units, corporations, etc.). For an individual, an essential representative would include those who have authority to obtain or act on advice of an attorney, such as a parent for her child. For an entity, employees of the entity may be considered "representatives of the client" if (i) their communications were made for the purpose of securing legal advice, (ii) the employee was acting at the behest of his manager, (iii) the communications were within the scope of the employee's duties, and (iv) the communications were considered confidential when made. Meeting this test is often a critical issue in litigation, because if the employee was not a privileged party, then the employee's statements are discoverable. If this test is satisfied, the privilege belongs to the client and not the employee who qualifies as a "representative" of the client.

For example, in the case of *United States v. Upjohn*, 449 U.S. 383 (1981), the Supreme Court ruled that government investigators could ask corporate employees what they knew about illegal payments, but they could not ask the employees what they told corporate counsel about illegal payments. (*Upjohn* will be discussed in greater detail in *Sandra T.E. v. South Berwyn School District 100*, below). Nonetheless, when dealing with a corporate client, often a lawyer will ask a corporate client to craft summaries of information. To keep such information confidential, the lawyer should ensure that the employees know that the purpose behind the request is obtain legal advice for the corporation; the employees should be told to keep the information confidential and should be asked for information that is limited to matters within the scope of employment. In this way, the communications themselves will be immunized from discovery, even if the underlying facts would not be.

A statement to an expert retained by the attorney may defeat confidentiality if the communication between the expert and the client is meant to help the expert testify at trial. In that instance, it is expected that the client's words will be used at trial, so no privilege applies. If the expert was retained *solely* to assist the attorney in *preparing* the case, however, any statements to the expert will be confidential.

If an attorney represents multiple clients in a matter, the privilege attaches to each of their communications. However, if later litigation between those same parties erupts, the privilege is waived, as the multiple clients demonstrated the lack of an intent to keep their communications confidential among themselves when they made the decision to hire joint counsel.

D. Legal Assistance

The client's intent to obtain legal services can sometimes be a murky element. A preliminary discussion with a lawyer who decides not to take the case would be covered under the attorney-client privilege, but communications made after the attorney has declined the client's case are not privileged. Communications to a lawyer as a friend or business partner would not be covered. The services must be legal in nature, which can be a very fact-intensive issue, and the burden is on the party seeking the privilege to establish that the attorney was acting in a professional legal capacity. Thus, if an attorney serves a dual role for a client that includes non-legal services (e.g., attorney/investigator, attorney/business advisor, etc.), the legal aspect must predominate in the communication for it to be protected by the privilege. Furthermore, even if a lawyer is retained for a legal purpose, not all facts about the retention are privileged. Information about whether the lawyer is retained and the identity of the lawyer's client are typically not privileged. Similarly, the payment of a lawyer's fee is not typically privileged unless providing the information would divulge a confidential communication or somehow incriminate the client.

E. Exceptions/Waiver

Exceptions exist to the attorney-client privilege. Communications relevant to an issue of breach of duty either by the lawyer to the client (e.g., malpractice) or by the client to the lawyer (e.g., failure to pay a fee) are excepted. Other exceptions include communications relevant to a dispute in which both parties claim through the same deceased client, communications relevant to an issue concerning an attested document to which the lawyer was an attesting witness, and communications relevant to a dispute between two or more clients who jointly consulted an attorney on a matter of common interest. The most litigated exception is the crime-fraud exception, which holds that no privilege exists if a client seeks advice from a lawyer to facilitate an *ongoing or future* crime or fraud. The privilege applies to attorney-client communications concerning crimes or frauds already committed by the client but which are not ongoing. The party seeking to take advantage of the exception carries the burden, and fishing expeditions are not allowed. Therefore, the party alleging that communications relate to a future crime or fraud must have a good faith, reasonable basis for their allegation.

Finally, we come to the issue of waiver, which can occur intentionally or by accident. An intentional disclosure occurs when a party to the communication reveals the attorney-client communication to a third party. Thus, a client telling a friend that "I told my lawyer that I have an alibi" waives any attorney-client protections for that statement. As we discussed in the introductory section to privileges, it is the *communications* between the privileged parties that is protected, not the underlying facts. Therefore, by stating "I told my lawyer" or "I told my client" to a non-privileged party, the communication itself has been waived by revealing it to someone outside the relationship.

Mistaken disclosure may occur in the eavesdropper context we discussed above. It may also occur when documents or information are accidently released to an opponent. FRE 502 governs the latter situation, and it was passed in 2008 in an attempt to limit the risk of accidental disclosure of documents or information protected by the attorney-client privilege. In essence, an inadvertent disclosure does not amount to a waiver if the party took reasonable steps to prevent the disclosure and then took prompt and reasonable steps to rectify the inadvertent disclosure. Courts typically examine the volume of documents and time constraints involved in the situation to determine the reasonableness of the steps taken. Even if a party does not meet these requirements and the disclosure is deemed a waiver, the waiver will only extend to the material actually disclosed. Thus, only in rare occasions will the waiver be deemed a "subject matter waiver" (i.e., a waiver as to all undisclosed protected communications and information on the same subject matter).

Focus Questions: *Sandra T.E. v. South Berwyn School District 100*

- What factors indicate that attorneys are conducting an investigation *as attorneys* rather than as non-attorney investigators?

- What steps can the attorney and client take to make clear that the attorney is being retained for legal services?

Sandra T.E. v. South Berwyn School District 100
600 F.3d 612 (7th Cir. 2010)

SYKES, Circuit Judge.

. . .

I. Background

In January 2005 police arrested Robert Sperlik, an elementary-school band teacher employed by District 100, on charges that he had repeatedly sexually abused numerous female students ages nine to twelve.... Sperlik eventually confessed to the crimes and was convicted and sentenced to 20 years in prison. Some of Sperlik's victims told police they had reported the abuse to the school principal after it occurred, but the principal failed to take appropriate action against Sperlik. On January 26, 2005, shortly after Sperlik's arrest, some of the victims and their families filed this civil lawsuit against District 100 and the school principal who was alleged to have been deliberately indifferent to the ongoing sexual abuse; they asserted claims under 42 U.S.C. § 1983, 20 U.S.C. § 1681 (Title IX of the Education Amendments of 1972), and various state laws.

As news of Sperlik's arrest became known, the families of District 100 students were understandably outraged at the extent and duration of the teacher's crimes and the possibility that the school administration knew about the sexual abuse but had failed to respond. Reacting to the criminal charges, the public outcry, and the filing of the civil lawsuit, the School Board retained the law firm of Sidley Austin LLP (then Sidley Austin Brown & Wood LLP) to conduct an internal investigation. The School Board wanted Sidley to review the criminal charges filed against Sperlik, investigate the actions of school administrators in response to the allegations of sexual abuse, examine whether any district employees had failed to comply with district policies or federal or state law, and analyze the effectiveness of the District's existing compliance procedures. According to the February 4, 2005 engagement letter between Sidley and the School Board, Sidley was to "investigate the response of the school administration to allegations of sexual abuse of students" and to "provide legal services in connection with" the investigation. Scott Lassar, a partner at Sidley and a former U.S. Attorney for the Northern District of Illinois, spearheaded the investigation.

On the same day the engagement letter was issued, the School Board president and superintendent of schools sent a joint letter to parents announcing the District's retention of Lassar to conduct the investigation. Ten days later the superintendent sent another more detailed letter to parents explaining that the investigation had begun and would be completed as soon as possible. As the investigation proceeded, attorneys from Sidley interviewed many school-district employees, including current and former principals, social workers, administrative employees, and members of the School Board. Sidley also interviewed a handful of third parties who had never been employed by the School District. None of the interviews were recorded. Instead, the attorneys took notes of the witnesses' answers and later prepared written memoranda memorializing the interviews for future use in Sidley's legal advice to the Board. These notes and memoranda are the subject of the present discovery dispute.

Lassar and a Sidley colleague delivered an oral report of the firm's findings at a closed executive session of the Board in April 2005, and later that month delivered a written "Executive Summary"—marked "Privileged and Confidential," "Attorney-Client Communication," and "Attorney Work Product"—to the Board. This concluded Sidley's engagement; other lawyers have represented the defendants throughout this litigation.

In the fall of 2006, the plaintiffs launched a discovery effort aimed at forcing the disclosure of the contents of Sidley's investigation. They subpoenaed Lassar to appear for a deposition and to produce documents in the firm's possession relating to Sidley's work for the School Board.

After a motion to quash was denied, Sidley turned over more than a thousand pages of documents. But the firm withheld its notes and memoranda from the witness interviews and other internal legal memoranda prepared in connection with the investigation. These documents, Sidley asserted, were protected by the attorney-client privilege and the work-product doctrine. The plaintiffs moved to compel production of the missing documents. After a series of hearings—of which Sidley had only informal notice and no opportunity to file a brief—the district court ordered the School Board to disclose any documents relating to Sidley's investigation that it had in its possession. The judge concluded that the Board hired Lassar "as an investigator, not as an attorney," and therefore the attorney-client privilege did not apply. The court later deferred ruling on the question of the documents in Sidley's possession: "If the plaintiffs insist that there [are] other documents or other information which they are entitled to which you have not turned over to the board, that's a different issue. We haven't gotten to that issue."

When it became clear that Sidley, not the School Board, had the documents the plaintiffs wanted, the plaintiffs turned their attention back to Sidley. They served a second subpoena on Lassar, essentially a duplicate of the first. Sidley responded by again asserting that the documents were protected by the attorney-client privilege and the work-product doctrine. The plaintiffs then filed a Motion for a Rule to Show Cause asking the court to hold Lassar in contempt. This time the court solicited briefing on the privilege and work-product claims, and the engagement letter between Sidley and the Board and other evidence about the nature of Sidley's engagement was brought before the court. After another hearing the court declined to commence contempt proceedings because Sidley had not yet been ordered to comply with the subpoena. But the court summarily rejected Sidley's attorney-client privilege and work-product claims and ordered the firm to produce the documents: "[T]he Court's prior ruling [regarding] attorney client privilege [will] stand.... The materials requested by Plaintiffs [should] be produced in accordance with the Court's prior ruling." Sidley moved for reconsideration, but this motion was denied. Sidley and District 100 appealed.

II. Discussion ...

B. Attorney-Client Privilege and Work-Product Doctrine

Sidley claims that the interview notes and legal memoranda its attorneys prepared in connection with the District 100 investigation are protected from disclosure by both the attorney-client privilege and the work-product doctrine. The attorney-client privilege protects communications made in confidence by a client and a client's employees to an attorney, acting as an attorney, for the purpose of obtaining legal advice. *See Upjohn Co. v. United States,* 449 U.S. 383, 394-99 (1981). The privilege belongs to the client, although an attorney may assert the privilege on the client's behalf. The work-product doctrine protects documents prepared by attorneys in anticipation of litigation for the purpose of analyzing and preparing a client's case. *See* Fed.R.Civ.P. 26(b)(3). Unlike the attorney-client privilege, the attorney has an independent privacy interest in his work product and may assert the work-product doctrine on his own behalf; the doctrine's protection is not waived simply because the attorney shared the information with his client.

To determine if a communication falls within the protection of the attorney-client privilege, we ask: (1) whether "legal advice of any kind [was] sought ... from a professional legal adviser in his capacity as such"; and (2) whether the communication was "relat[ed] to that purpose" and "made in confidence ... by the client." *United States v. Evans,* 113 F.3d 1457, 1461 (7th Cir.1997). It appears that the district court assumed that when an attorney performs investigative work, he is not acting as an attorney for purposes of the privilege; this raises a legal issue about the scope of the privilege, so our review is de novo.

The judge's decision in this case developed over a series of hearings and numerous minute orders. As we have noted, Sidley was not provided formal notice and an opportunity to present a case for the privilege prior to the first two of these hearings; only after the plaintiffs moved for a contempt sanction against Lassar was Sidley given formal notice and an opportunity to brief the issue. It appears the judge was influenced in the earlier hearings by the letters the school superintendent and Board president sent to parents reassuring them of the District's desire to discover the truth about the circumstances surrounding Sperlik's abuse and announcing the Board's decision to retain Lassar to "conduct a thorough investigation." In the judge's view, these statements pointed to the conclusion that Sidley was hired as an investigator, and as such, the privilege did not apply.

Later on, in the proceedings on the plaintiffs' Motion for a Rule to Show Cause against Lassar, the judge all but ignored the engagement letter, which should have been the most important piece of evidence. The engagement letter between Sidley and the School Board explained that Sidley had been hired to "investigate the response of the school administration to allegations of sexual abuse of students" *and* "provide legal services in connection with the specific representation." There is no indication that the judge actually considered the engagement letter when it was brought to the court's attention in these later proceedings;

rather, the judge simply reiterated his earlier ruling that Sidley had been hired as an investigator and the privilege therefore did not apply.

This oversight was a mistake; the engagement letter brings this case squarely within the Supreme Court's decision in *Upjohn,* which explained that factual investigations performed by attorneys *as attorneys* fall comfortably within the protection of the attorney-client privilege. In *Upjohn* a corporation's in-house counsel investigated the role of some of the corporation's employees in making potentially illegal payments to foreign governmental officials; this investigation included interviews with corporate officers and employees. A separate federal tax inquiry into the alleged misconduct was pending, and federal investigators attempted to obtain the results of the corporation's internal investigation by issuing a summons for documents memorializing the employees' interviews with the corporation's in-house counsel. The Supreme Court held that the attorney-client privilege applied. *Upjohn,* 449 U.S. at 401.

The Court began by noting that "[t]he first step in the resolution of any legal problem is ascertaining the factual background and sifting through the facts with an eye to the legally relevant." *Id.* at 390-91. The Court held that because "[t]he communications at issue were made by Upjohn employees to counsel for Upjohn acting as such, at the direction of corporate superiors in order to secure legal advice from counsel," the "communications must be protected against compelled disclosure." *Upjohn,* 449 U.S. at 394-95. The federal investigators could not force disclosure of the notes and other documents made by the in-house counsel to discover what the employees had said but instead must interview the employees themselves. *Id.* at 396.

Following *Upjohn,* other circuits have concluded that when an attorney conducts a factual investigation in connection with the provision of legal services, any notes or memoranda documenting client interviews or other client communications in the course of the investigation are fully protected by the attorney-client privilege. For example, in *In re Allen,* 106 F.3d 582 (4th Cir. 1997), the Fourth Circuit confronted a district-court ruling virtually identical to the one at issue in this case. There, the district court had concluded that a special counsel hired by the West Virginia Attorney General to conduct an investigation into alleged misconduct within the state Department of Justice was acting as an investigator and not an attorney because various client letters described the attorney's work as an "investigation." In reversing, the Fourth Circuit noted that "clients often do retain lawyers to perform investigative work because they want the benefit of a lawyer's expertise and judgment," and "if a client retains an attorney to use her legal expertise to conduct an investigation, that lawyer is indeed performing legal work." *Id.* at 604.

The same is true here. The engagement letter spells out that the Board retained Sidley to provide legal services in connection with developing the School Board's response to Sperlik's sexual abuse of his students. Sidley's investigation of the factual circumstances surrounding the abuse was an integral part of the package of legal services for which it was hired and a necessary prerequisite to the provision of legal advice about how the District should respond. Although an engagement letter cannot reclassify nonprivileged communications as "legal services" in order to invoke the attorney-client privilege, *see Burden-Meeks v. Welch,* 319 F.3d 897, 899 (7th Cir.2003) (business advice cannot be considered legal services), the conduct of Sidley attorneys during the investigation confirms that they were acting in their capacity as attorneys. During the confidential interviews with school-district employees, the attorneys provided so-called "*Upjohn* warnings" emphasizing that Sidley represented the School Board and not the employee and that the

School Board had control over whether the conversations remained privileged. No third parties attended the interviews, the School Board received Lassar's report of the firm's findings during an executive session not open to the public, and the written executive summary that Sidley turned over to the Board was marked "Privileged and Confidential," "Attorney-Client Communication," and "Attorney Work Product." If more were needed, affidavits submitted into the record by Lassar, his Sidley colleagues, and the School Board president emphasized that Sidley had been hired to provide legal advice in the context of the facts it uncovered during the internal investigation. Because the Sidley lawyers were hired in their capacity as lawyers to provide legal services — including a factual investigation — the attorney-client privilege applies to the communications made and documents generated during that investigation.

The fact that the privilege is invoked to protect communications made by employees of a governmental entity rather than a private party does not change the analysis. The plaintiffs suggest that shielding the contents of Sidley's interviews with school-district personnel—paid for by the taxpayers and involving a matter of grave public concern—is contrary to the public interest and should not be permitted. We have previously held that the privilege does not apply to communications between a state officeholder and his state-government attorney when the attorney is subpoenaed to give testimony before a federal grand jury. *See In re Witness Before the Special Grand Jury 2000-2,* 288 F.3d 289 (7th Cir.2002) (general counsel to Illinois governor could not assert attorney-client privilege to avoid giving grand-jury testimony against governor). But we did not articulate in *In re Witness* a generally applicable exception for communications between governmental employees and taxpayer-paid counsel.

This is a civil case for damages against a local unit of government and certain individual public employees, not a grand-jury proceeding. Although the allegations are very serious and there are important public as well as private interests at stake, we think the policies underlying the attorney-client privilege have their normal application. *See Ross v. City of Memphis,* 423 F.3d 596, 603 (6th Cir.2005) ("The civil context presents different concerns because government[al] entities are frequently exposed to civil liability. The risk of extensive civil liability is particularly acute for municipalities, which do not enjoy sovereign immunity."). Of course, the attorney-client privilege protects not only the attorney-client relationship in imminent or ongoing litigation but also the broader attorney-client relationship outside the litigation context. Confidential legal advising promotes the public interest "by advising clients to conform their conduct to the law and by addressing legal concerns that may inhibit clients from engaging in otherwise lawful and socially beneficial activities." *United States v. BDO Seidman, LLP,* 492 F.3d 806, 815 (7th Cir.2007). This is true for public clients no less than private ones. The public interest is best served when agencies of the government have access to the confidential advice of counsel regarding the legal consequences of their past and present activities and how to conform their future operations to the requirements of the law....

[The Court also concluded that the work-product doctrine also prevented disclosure of the documents, because the doctrine applies to attorney-led investigations when the documents at issue can fairly be said to have been prepared or obtained because of the prospect of litigation. Furthermore, the plaintiffs could not establish a substantial need for the documents or that they could not obtain equivalent materials without undue hardship. The Court noted that it was "extremely reluctant" to allow discovery of attorney work product solely for impeachment evidence.]

Reversed.

Focus Questions: *United States v. Lentz*

- The Court states that a client's waiver of the attorney-client privilege can be implied by conduct—how did the defendant's conduct imply a waiver here?

- What is the standard of proving a purported crime or fraud under the crime-fraud exception? Is this a low or high hurdle? Should the standard of proof be higher or lower?

United States v. Lentz

419 F.Supp.2d 820 (E.D. Va. 2005)

ELLIS, District Judge.

In this remanded kidnapping for murder prosecution, the defendant seeks suppression of certain tape-recorded telephone communications between defendant Jay E. Lentz ("Lentz") and his attorney regarding a murder-for-hire plot to eliminate key witnesses and the prosecutor in defendant's case. At issue is ... whether the tape recordings are protected by the attorney-client privilege....

I.

The facts relevant to this motion to suppress occurred following remand of this case for retrial and while Lentz was incarcerated at Northern Neck Regional Jail (NNRJ) awaiting the retrial. Yet, a brief synopsis of the underlying kidnapping for murder prosecution and the procedural history of this case provides the context essential to a full understanding of the questions presented.

Lentz is charged with kidnapping for murder in violation of 18 U.S.C. § 1201(a) for the disappearance and murder of his ex-wife, Doris Lentz ("Doris"). Because neither Doris' body nor a murder weapon were ever found, the government's case against Lentz in the first trial in June 2003 was largely circumstantial. In this regard, the government presented evidence at trial tending to show, *inter alia,* (i) that Lentz had physically and verbally abused Doris during their marriage; (ii) that, based on a prior arrangement between Doris and Lentz, Doris had gone to Lentz's house to pick up their daughter, Julia, on the day Doris disappeared; (iii) that Doris had told her mother, boyfriend, aunt, and friend that she was going to Lentz's house in Maryland to pick up Julia on the day she disappeared; (iv) that within days of Doris' disappearance, her car was found abandoned in a District of Columbia parking lot, unlocked, and with her purse and keys in plain view; (v) that there were blood stains in the car's interior, nearly all of which contained Doris' DNA; (vi) that one of the blood stains in Doris' car was a match for Lentz's DNA; and (vii) that the driver's seat of Doris' car had been adjusted to fit someone who (like Lentz) was much taller than Doris. [The Fourth Circuit Court of Appeals reversed a trial court ruling and remanded the case for a new trial.] ...

During the interim between the remand of this case and the originally scheduled July 11 trial date, the case took a surprising twist. On May 19, 2005, the government, in an *ex parte,* under seal pleading, represented that it had information from inmate Christopher Jackmon ("Jackmon"), who was incarcerated with Lentz at NNRJ from late 2004 until early 2005, concerning Lentz's murder-for-hire plot. Specifically, Jackmon was prepared to testify that Lentz had discussed his case with him and ultimately had solicited Jackmon's help in a plot to kill (i) certain key prosecution witnesses Lentz believed had provided especially damaging testimony in his first trial; and (ii) one or both of the prosecutors in his case, namely Assistant United States Attorneys Steven D. Mellin and Patricia M. Haynes. Most relevant here, the government also represented that it had obtained tape recordings of three telephone conversations that occurred on January 10, 2005 between Lentz and his attorney, Frank Salvato, that the government believes corroborates Jackmon's story.[2]

These three telephone calls occurred between 9:39 a.m. and 10:26 a.m. on January 10, 2005, and were placed by Lentz to his counsel from a telephone located in "C Pod," the pod that included Lentz's cell at NNRJ. The record convincingly establishes that during the period in question, all outgoing telephone calls from NNRJ were recorded and subject to monitoring by jail officials and that Lentz and his counsel knew this was so. At the pretrial evidentiary hearing on this issue, Major Ted Hull, the assistant superintendent for the NNRJ, testified (i) that all outgoing telephone calls placed by inmates at NNRJ are placed through the same telephone system; (ii) that all such calls are subject to monitoring and recording; and (iii) that prior to connecting each outgoing call, the system plays a pre-recorded message, heard by both parties, stating that the call is subject to monitoring and recording.[3] Accordingly, NNRJ has a recording of all outgoing inmate calls, including those made by Lentz on the day in question and, prior to connecting the parties, both Lentz and his counsel received the pre-recorded message advising them that the call would be recorded and was subject to monitoring. Indeed, Lentz and his counsel essentially acknowledged as much during the course of their conversations.[4]

The content of the three telephone calls at issue merits a brief description. During the first call, Lentz asked Mr. Salvato what he knew about "a guy named Ridley [who] got murdered at the Springfield Mall." When Mr. Salvato inquired why this murder was relevant to Lentz's case, Lentz explicitly refused to answer. Immediately following this exchange, Lentz began to press Mr. Salvato for details about Jackmon. In this regard, at one point Lentz explicitly stated to Mr. Salvato, "I'm asking you to certify some information. This is important." Presumably, what Lentz meant by this was that the purpose of his calls was to determine whether Jackmon had been telling Lentz the truth about being

---

2. According to the government, it obtained these recordings, in part, to ascertain whether Mr. Salvato had advised Lentz to destroy any corroborating evidence of the murder-for hire plot. The government suspected this might have occurred because a search of Lentz's cell that same afternoon had failed to disclose certain documents relating to the murder-for-hire plot Jackmon claimed he had seen in Lentz's possession shortly before January 10, and because shortly after the telephone conversations, Lentz had abruptly canceled a meeting with an FBI undercover agent, posing as a "hit man," to discuss the plot. In fact, the telephone conversations do not reflect that Mr. Salvato directed Lentz to destroy any evidence.

3. Major Hull testified that owing to an inadvertent error by NNRJ's telephone service provider, toll-free calls placed from the jail to the Richmond and Alexandria Federal Public Defenders's (FPD) Offices from approximately October 2003 until May or June of 2005 were not preceded by this warning. Only calls from NNRJ to these FPD offices were affected by this error. Because none of the calls at issue were made to the FPD, the evidence is undisputed that each of the calls at issue was preceded a notice that calls were recorded and subject to monitoring. Accordingly, Lentz's claim, by counsel, that the warnings played "sporadically at best" is unsupported by the record.

4. In one instance, in response to a statement by Mr. Salvato concerning the hypothetical killing of a witness, the transcript of the call suggests that Lentz feigned ignorance on the matter, asking Mr. Salvato, "Why are you carrying on here? What if this thing was recorded?" In response, Mr. Salvato stated, "Oh, my God. All the [outgoing inmate] phone calls are recorded Jay.... They're all recorded."

released from prison soon because a key witness in the case against Jackmon had been murdered. Lentz apparently believed that this murder was the handiwork of a "hit man" Jackmon had hired, and that the murder had taken place at Springfield Mall. During the third call, when Mr. Salvato inquired how Jackmon would be able to help Lentz, Lentz replied that Jackmon would be able to help Lentz secure a hit man "in case [Lentz] need[ed] something like that to happen in [his] case." The context of this statement leaves no doubt that the "something like that" to which Lentz referred was a murder-for-hire arrangement. Moreover, during these calls Lentz specifically directed Mr. Salvato not to call him by name, but to use an alias, "Bucks," instead. Over the course of these conversations, Mr. Salvato repeatedly asked Lentz if he was kidding about hiring a hit man. In response, Lentz stated that "[he doesn't] joke at 9 in the morning." Presumably to entice Mr. Salvato to empathize with him, Lentz stated that he was "sitting in the bowels of hell," that he was "at the end of his rope," and that "[he's] gotta do what [he's] gotta do to survive."

In sum, the three calls in question focus chiefly on whether Jackmon could be trusted regarding Lentz's possible use of a hit man to murder witnesses and perhaps a prosecutor prior to his forthcoming retrial. The contents of these calls, taken as a whole, invite the inference that Lentz was seriously considering a murder-for-hire plot, and was calling Mr. Salvato to inquire about Jackmon's reliability with respect to information Jackmon had provided Lentz about his own case.

On May 19, 2005, the government filed an *ex parte,* under seal motion seeking an order permitting the government team investigating the taped calls to disclose the transcripts of those calls as well as the recordings of the calls themselves, to both the prosecutors assigned to conduct the *Lentz* retrial and the team of prosecutors investigating the murder-for-hire plot. That motion was denied, and the government was directed instead to deliver promptly to defense counsel a copy of the government's under seal motion and its attachments, which included the telephone call transcripts. Lentz was then allowed a period of time to investigate the matter, after which he moved, by counsel, to suppress all transcripts and recordings of his telephone conversations with his attorney. In Lentz's view, the telephone calls and their contents ... are protected by the attorney-client privilege ... [and are inadmissible] for any purpose, including offering them at the retrial as evidence of Lentz's consciousness of guilt with respect to Doris' murder.

II.

Few principles of law are as well-settled as the attorney-client privilege; it is a bedrock principle of the adversary system. In essence, the privilege's purpose is to encourage full and frank communication between attorneys and clients by according court-enforced protection against disclosure of such communications when the client invokes the privilege. The privilege recognizes that sound legal advice and informed advocacy serves the public interest, that such advice or advocacy depends upon the lawyer's being fully informed by the client, and that this occurs only where the client feels secure that communications with counsel will not be disclosed.

While recognizing the fundamental importance of the privilege, courts have nonetheless been careful not to stretch its application to circumstances beyond its rationale. This is so because the attorney-client privilege, like all privileges, "impedes [the] full and free discovery of the truth," and is "in derogation of the public's 'right to every man's evidence.'" *In re Grand Jury Proceedings,* 727 F.2d 1352, 1355 (4th Cir.1984) (quoting *Weil v. Investment/Indicators, Research & Management, Inc.,* 647 F.2d 18, 24 (9th Cir.1981)). Accordingly, courts carefully construe the privilege to apply only to those situations in which the party invoking the privilege consulted an attorney for the purpose of securing a legal opinion or services, and in connection with that consultation, communicated information intended to be kept confidential. Thus, in this circuit and elsewhere, the boundaries of the attorney-client privilege are clearly demarcated and well-settled. The privilege applies only if:

> (1) the asserted holder of the privilege is or sought to become a client; (2) the person to whom the communication was made (a) is a member of the bar of a court, or his subordinate and (b) in connection with this communication is acting as a lawyer; (3) the communication relates to a fact of which the attorney was informed (a) by his client (b) without the presence of strangers (c) for the purpose of securing primarily either (i) an opinion on law or (ii) legal services or (iii) assistance in some legal proceeding, and not (d) for the purpose of committing a crime or tort; and (4) the privilege has been (a) claimed and (b) not waived by the client.

And importantly, the burden is on the proponent of the attorney-client privilege to demonstrate its applicability. Specifically, the proponent must establish "not only that an attorney-client relationship existed, but also that the particular communications at issue are privileged and that the privilege was not waived." *In re Grand Jury Subpoena*, 341 F.3d 331, 335 (4th Cir.2003). And, it is also well-settled that a client waives the attorney-client privilege by voluntarily disclosing otherwise privileged communications to a third party. In fact, this requirement of confidentiality is so central to any claim of privilege that the privilege may be lost even by an inadvertent disclosure to a third party. *See In re Grand Jury Proceedings*, 727 F.2d at 1356 (holding that the privilege is lost where the party did not take "reasonable steps to insure and maintain [the] confidentiality [of the communications.]"); *see also id.* (noting that the presence of eavesdroppers in certain circumstances may destroy the privilege). Waiver need not be explicit; the client waives the privilege by conduct "which implies a waiver of the privilege or a consent to disclosure." *U.S. v. Dakota*, 197 F.3d 821, 825 (6th Cir.1999). *See also Hanson v. U.S. Agency for Intern. Development*, 372 F.3d 286, 293–94 (4th Cir.2004) ("A client can waive an attorney-client privilege expressly or through his own conduct.").

These principles, applied here, compel the conclusion that an inmate's telephone conversations with counsel are not protected by the attorney-client privilege where, as here, the inmate is notified at the outset that the calls are recorded and subject to monitoring. In these circumstances, Lentz could not reasonably have assumed that his conversations with Mr. Salvato would be confidential. His decision to proceed with the conversations, despite notification that the conversations were being recorded and were subject to monitoring, is no different from Lentz electing to proceed with these conversations notwithstanding the known presence of a third party within earshot of the conversation.[16]

---

16. Nor is it persuasive to argue, as Lentz does, that Mr. Salvato told him that their conversations were privileged, because the monitoring and recording notice that preceded each of the calls destroyed any reasonable expectation of privilege. During the third call, Mr. Salvato stated to Lentz that "this is a privileged call, but they're all recorded." Mr. Salvato's suggestion that the attorney-client privilege would apply to a call that was being recorded by a third party is simply mistaken and cannot serve to rescue the waived privilege. What is more, it is clear from the contents of these calls that Lentz understood that the calls were recorded, which confirms the waiver. *See supra* note 4. Even assuming that Mr. Salvato's erroneous advice with respect to privilege relieved Lentz's concern regarding the NNRJ's recording and monitoring of the calls, it is worth noting that Lentz made many of the incriminating statements at issue prior to Mr. Salvato's mistaken statement. Thus, Lentz cannot claim that any such statement was induced by Mr. Salvato's misstatement, nor would it matter had it been otherwise, for it is simply unreasonable for Lentz to believe the conversations would remain private. *See United States v. Dornau*, 491 F.2d 473, 480–81 (2d Cir.1974) (upholding admission of defendant's

The Fourth Circuit has not yet squarely addressed the question whether inmates waive any privilege protection for telephone conversations when they choose to proceed with these conversations in the face of notice that the calls are being recorded and subject to monitoring. Significantly, however, the three circuits that have done so have uniformly held that such notice destroys any expectation of privilege. Particularly instructive in this regard is the Eight Circuit's opinion in *United States v. Hatcher*, 323 F.3d 666, 674 (8th Cir. 2003) in which the panel held that:

> The presence of the prison recording device destroyed the attorney-client privilege. Because the inmates and their lawyers were aware that their conversations were being recorded, they could not reasonably expect that their conversations would remain private. The presence of the recording device was the functional equivalent of the presence of a third party. These conversations were not privileged. *Hatcher,* 323 F.3d at 674.

Similarly, Lentz here could not "reasonably expect that ... [his] conversations would remain private." *Id.* It follows that Lentz's recorded conversations with his attorney, like the recorded conversations in *Hatcher,* were not privileged. Lentz attempts to distinguish *Hatcher* on the ground that the monitoring notice at NNRJ was not played before all calls and that, as a result, he reasonably believed that his calls to Mr. Salvato were confidential or protected by the privilege. This argument fails. Contrary to Lentz's argument, the record establishes that ... the NNRJ system automatically and unfailingly provided the recording and monitoring notice before each call was connected, and that this occurred with respect to the three calls at issue here. Thus, Lentz and Mr. Salvato received the notice before each of the three calls and Lentz's decision to proceed with the conversations under these circumstances constituted a waiver of the attorney-client privilege. *See U.S. v. Dakota,* 197 F.3d 821, 825 (6th Cir.1999) (stating that client's waiver of privilege can be implied from conduct inconsistent with the assertion of that privilege). Moreover, as noted previously, Lentz's concern that the calls might be recorded suggests that he did not, in fact, believe that the calls were privileged.[19] If Lentz truly believed that his conversations with Mr. Salvato were privileged, then he would have been unconcerned about any possible recording, since it would be inadmissible.[20]

In sum, then, the notice at the beginning of each call, as well as Lentz's statements during the calls, make clear that Lentz could not reasonably have expected the conversations to be confidential. Accordingly, the telephone calls between Lentz and Mr. Salvato are not privileged.

III.

A separate and independent ground for the result reached here is the well-established crime fraud exception to the attorney-client privilege. Thus, assuming, *arguendo,* that Lentz had a reasonable expectation that his conversations with Mr. Salvato would be confidential, they nonetheless would not be privileged because communications made for

---

incriminatory statements over defendant's objection that the statements were induced by a mistaken "express assurance" from his counsel regarding their admissibility); *United States v. Mendelsohn,* 896 F.2d 1183, 1188–89 (9th Cir.1990) (upholding district court's conclusion that defendant waived the attorney-client privilege by making certain incriminatory statements to authorities, even though defendant's attorney allegedly told defendant that the conduct at issue was not illegal)[.]

19. *See supra* note 4 (noting that Lentz feigned ignorance to Mr. Salvato's questions concerning the hypothetical murder of a witness, stating, "Why are you carrying on here? What if this thing was recorded?").

20. Lentz's request that Mr. Salvato call him by a false name is further evidence that Lentz was aware that the calls were recorded and monitored.

an unlawful purpose or to further an illegal scheme are not privileged. The crime-fraud exception applies only to communications about ongoing or future activities. Communications concerning past crimes or frauds are privileged unless the privilege has otherwise been waived. *In re Grand Jury Subpoena Duces Tecum*, 731 F.2d 1032, 1041 (2nd Cir.1984) (stating that communications with respect to past frauds are privileged).

The rationale for the crime-fraud exception is closely tied to the policies underlying the attorney-client privilege. Whereas confidentiality of communications facilitates the rendering of sound legal advice, which is to be encouraged, it cannot be said that advice in furtherance of a fraudulent or unlawful goal is sound, nor is it to be encouraged. Rather, advice in furtherance of such goals is anathema to our system of justice; hence, a client's communications seeking such advice are not worthy of protection. It is immaterial whether the attorney knew that the client was seeking his advice for illegal purposes or whether the attorney joined in, or, as here, counseled against the illegal activity. The attorney's knowledge and intent are not material to the operation of the crime fraud exception; only the client's knowledge and intent are material in this regard. It is similarly immaterial whether the defendant actually succeeded in completing the crime or fraud in question; rather, solicitation alone triggers the exception.

The party asserting the crime-fraud exception to the privilege—here, the government—bears the burden to establish a prima facie case that the communications in question fall outside the scope of the privilege. To overcome an established privilege using the crime-fraud exception, the government must show that the communications (i) were made for an unlawful purpose or to further an illegal scheme and (ii) reflect an ongoing or future unlawful or illegal scheme or activity. Importantly, the purported crime or fraud need not be proved either by a preponderance or beyond a reasonable doubt. Rather, the proof "must be such as to subject the opposing party to the risk of non-persuasion of the evidence as to the disputed fact is left unrebutted." *See Union Camp Corp. v. Lewis*, 385 F.2d 143, 144–45 (4th Cir. 1967). Finally, when making its prima facie showing, the government is not limited to admissible evidence; it may rely on any relevant evidence, including hearsay, that has been lawfully obtained that is not otherwise privileged.

These principles, applied here, make clear that the government has made a prima facie showing that the crime-fraud exception applies to the conversations in question. In this case, the contents of the telephone calls, viewed as a whole, leave no doubt that Lentz's primary purpose in calling Mr. Salvato was to discuss Lentz's murder-for-hire plot. Specifically, Lentz sought to corroborate certain things that Jackmon had told him, including (i) whether Jackmon's release from prison was imminent and (ii) whether Jackmon's release was related to the murder of a witness in his case. When Mr. Salvato asked Lentz why this was relevant, Lentz replied that Jackmon might help him "in case [Lentz] needed something like that to happen on [his] case." The conversations in general, and this comment in particular, leave no doubt that Lentz's purpose in calling Mr. Salvato was to get information that would assist Lentz in the planning and carrying out the murder-for-hire plot.

In sum, then, Lentz called Mr. Salvato in order to assess the validity of what Jackmon had told him, which would in turn help Lentz decide whether he should continue to trust Jackmon and involve Jackmon in the planning and/or execution of Lentz's murder-for-hire plot. Accordingly, there can be little doubt that Lentz, in contacting Mr. Salvato, was seeking aid and information from his attorney to further his nascent murder-for-hire plot.[27]

---

27. Lentz argues the government cannot meet this first element of the crime-fraud exception because Lentz "never took proactive steps to plan a crime, and any plans that were made were made

Given that the government has more than met its burden to show that the calls at issue fall within the crime-fraud exception, it falls to Lentz to rebut this showing. He has failed to do so; he offers no plausible justification or argument for why the conversations at issue should escape the crime-fraud exception to the privilege. Therefore, because the crime-fraud exception strips the conversations at issue of any privilege protection, the contents of the calls between Lentz and Mr. Salvato would not be protected by the privilege even had they been confidential. . . .

An appropriate Order will issue.

Problem 11-1

Clarence Robinson was arrested by the DEA for drug-related offenses. When he was arrested, roughly $3500 of assets was seized. About a month later the DEA sent Robinson a notice of the seizure at the jail were Robinson was housed. Later that month Robinson met with attorney Mike Thomas. At that time Robinson showed Thomas the note of the forfeiture to explain his situation and asked Thomas if he would represent him in his forfeiture trial. Thomas declined, so Robinson asked Thomas to pass the seizure notice to attorney Ruth Cantrell, who had worked for Robinson in the past. Thomas made a copy of the letter, sent the copy to Cantrell, and gave the original back to Robinson. Cantrell later declined to represent Robinson due to her lack of expertise on the issue. Robinson therefore decided to represent himself. He testified that that the DEA never gave him notice that they had seized $3500 worth of his assets at the time of his arrest.

The next day the Assistant United States Attorney (AUSA) assigned to Robinson's forfeiture proceeding contacted Thomas and asked him about the veracity of Robinson's testimony. Thomas produced the copy of the notice of the seizure and the letters exchanged by Thomas and Cantrell regarding the notice of the seizure. Robinson is now on trial for perjury and argues that his receipt of the notice and the letters between Thomas and Cantrell are subject to the attorney-client privilege. How do you rule?

Problem 11-2

After a widely publicized trial, in March 1982, socialite Claus von Bulow was convicted, but later acquitted, of assault with intent to murder for allegedly injecting his wife Martha with insulin, causing her to lapse into an irreversible coma. Harvard Law professor Alan M. Dershowitz represented von Bulow on appeal. Shortly after the acquittal, von Bulow's children sued von Bulow on behalf of their mother, alleging common law assault, negligence, fraud, and RICO violations. These claims arose out of the same facts and circumstances as the criminal prosecution.

---

by Jackmon." Even assuming that Lentz was simply along for the ride in a scheme solely concocted by Jackmon, the disjunctive phrasing of the standard indicates that the government can still meet its burden by showing only that Lentz was "engaged in" a criminal or fraudulent scheme. *See In re Grand Jury Proceedings # 5*, 401 F.3d 247, 251(4th Cir. 2005) ("[T]he party invoking the crime-fraud exception must make a prima facie showing that the client was engaged in *or* planning a criminal or fraudulent scheme. . . .") (emphasis added).

In May 1986, with von Bulow's permission, Dershowitz published a book entitled "Reversal of Fortune: Inside the von Bulow Case." The book chronicles the events surrounding the criminal trial, the successful appeal, and von Bulow's acquittal, and contains several conversations von Bulow had with his attorneys. Von Bulow and Dershowitz appeared together on several television and radio shows to promote the book. After obtaining an advance copy of the book, the plaintiffs' attorney notified von Bulow that the plaintiffs would treat publication as a waiver of the attorney-client privilege. Von Bulow's attorney responded that no waiver had occurred.

Plaintiffs moved to compel discovery of certain discussions between von Bulow and his attorneys. The district court found a waiver of the attorney-client privilege with respect to the contents of the published conversations and all communications between von Bulow and Dershowitz or other attorneys relating to the published conversations, and ordered von Bulow and his attorneys to comply with the discovery request. Was the court's ruling correct?

Problem 11-3

In 1972, the defendant, Marcus Junior Clanton, pleaded guilty to two charges of bank robbery, one in Atlanta and one in Miami. Clanton had previous psychological evaluations and had been found both mentally competent and mentally incompetent at various times. On appeal, Clanton claimed he was not mentally competent when he entered the guilty plea. He argued that the district court erroneously admitted testimony by Clanton's trial attorney concerning Clanton's mental competence, in violation of Clanton's attorney-client privilege. Clanton's trial attorney, M. C. Mykel, had been a state juvenile court probation officer and a social worker and had had extensive training with psychiatrists and psychologists. He testified that there was nothing to indicate that Clanton was incompetent or could not fully cooperate with him, that he believed Clanton was mentally competent when he entered his guilty pleas, and that he would not have permitted his client to plead guilty knowing he was not mentally competent. Did the district court err in allowing Clanton's attorney to testify as to Clanton's competence?

Problem 11-4

HPD is a company that develops, manufactures, and sells toilet cleaning products. One of its successful products was 2000 Flushes, a chlorine bleach tablet. In September 1999, HPD sued its competitor Clorox for false advertisement, unfair competition, and patent infringement of 2000 Flushes through its marketing and sale of its product Rain Clean. HPD alleged that Rain Clean did not contain an effective chlorine bleaching agent, yet Clorox advertised Rain Clean as a bleach-containing toilet cleaner. HPD claimed that it suffered diminished sales as a result of Clorox's deceptive marketing, ostensibly because consumers purchased Rain Clean over 2000 Flushes under the mistaken belief that the two products were equivalents.

In a contentious discovery standoff, HPD requested the production of various documents prepared by Karen Peeff, a longtime paralegal in Clorox's in-house legal department. Clorox employees routinely conferred with Peeff on marketing, regulatory matters, and other issues. Peeff took part in many discussions with

Clorox employees concerning Rain Clean. She raised several questions for consideration and provided advice in her capacity as a legal specialist on advertising and regulatory matters. These communications were embodied in several meeting minutes and emails, and HPD requested these documents during discovery. Peeff did not consult with attorneys in the Clorox legal department regarding the issues or communications embodied in these documents.

Clorox opposed the production of documents on the basis that the attorney-client privilege insulated them from disclosure. How should the court have ruled on the discovery issue?

Problem 11-5

Jane Dill lived with her young daughter and her boyfriend, Paul Beard. In 2003, the ATF raided her home and found marijuana, drug paraphernalia and a pistol with the serial number shaved off. Dill acted extremely surprised that the contraband was present in her home. Based on her surprise, the Special Agents at the scene did not arrest her and instead arrested Beard. She later signed a sworn affidavit in which she stated that she had never seen the gun or drug paraphernalia before and testified consistently with the affidavit before a grand jury. In December, 2003, Beard was indicted by a grand jury and was appointed counsel.

The following year the attorney appointed as counsel met repeatedly with Beard and Dill in preparation for Beard's defense. In their first couple of conversations, Dill maintained that the story which she told to the ATF was true. Months later, she informed counsel that she wanted to change her story because the punishment she would receive would be less than what Beard would face, even with the potential perjury charge. The attorney informed them that he thought this would probably get Beard acquitted, but that changing her story would amount to perjury and that he, as an attorney, could not perpetrate a fraud on the court.

One year later Beard informed the judge via letter that his counsel would not allow him to put on the defense he wished to pursue. Soon after the letter was sent, Beard's counsel asked for permission to withdraw, and the judge accepted counsel's request. In March of 2004, Dill came forward and told the ATF that she had lied in her sworn affidavit out of a fear that she would be separated from her child.

In April, 2004, the prosecution sent Beard's former counsel a grand jury subpoena for all documents which the attorney possessed in relation to his representation of Beard. The attorney refused to do so on the grounds that the documents were covered by the attorney-client privilege. Was Beard's attorney correct? What procedures should the court follow in making this determination?

III. Marital Privileges

Two marital privileges exist. For both, their purpose is to protect marital harmony by shielding adverse testimony at trial from one's spouse and/or shielding the communications one shares with one's spouse. Let us focus on each in turn and then compare them.

A. The Spousal Testimonial Privilege

The spousal testimonial privilege, will be discussed in *Trammel v. United States*, below. It allows the spouse of an accused in a criminal case to refuse to take the stand to testify *adversely* against her spouse (while some states apply the privilege to civil cases, federal jurisdictions limit it to criminal cases only). Thus, favorable testimony from a spouse can be forced. The spousal testimonial privilege applies to *all* testimony by the spouse, even if the matters do not concern the marital relations, marital communications, or domestic issues. The testifying spouse is essentially deemed incompetent to testify as to any matter. The privilege ends, however, when the marriage does. Either a divorce or legal separation that occurs before the trial ends the privilege. A former spouse may testify against her former spouse on any matter except for confidential marital communications that occurred during the marriage.

Numerous exceptions to the privilege exist which could force a spouse to testify adversely against his or her spouse. The privilege does not apply when the spouses are adversaries in a legal proceeding or when the testimony concerns the abuse of a child of the household. Some courts hold that the privilege also does not apply when the spouses were joint participants in a crime, but the majority view is that the privilege continues even if both spouses were involved in criminal activity.

B. The Marital Communications Privilege

The marital communications privilege shields confidences that occur during a marriage between spouses in both civil and criminal cases. The rationale for the privilege is to encourage private communications between spouses without the fear that those communications will surface in legal proceedings. The privileges requires a (i) confidential (ii) communication (iii) that occurred during a marriage. Like the attorney-client privilege, it can be waived as to statements made in the presence of third parties (such as children who are old enough to understand the statement) and does not apply to observations. In terms of observations, the privilege is limited to utterances or expressions intended by one spouse to convey a message to the other. Therefore even acts that are done in the privacy of the material home are not covered if there was no intent to communicate.

Eavesdroppers may not testify as to marital confidences, subject to a similar subjective/objective test applicable to attorney-client privilege: First, did the parties subjectively intend for the statement to be confidential? Second, did they take reasonable precautions to make the statement confidential? If so, the eavesdropper may not testify. Like the attorney-client privilege, the parties to the marital communication must each make efforts that are reasonably designed to protect and preserve the privilege.

The marital communications privilege continues even after a marriage ends, on the theory that allowing divorce to void the privilege may prevent spouses from sharing confidences with each other. Either party can prevent the other from testifying as to the communications that occurred during the marriage (although some jurisdictions limit the holder to the person who actually made the communication). Thus, even if one spouse is eager to testify to a marital confidence, the other spouse may prevent the testimony as to the marital confidence.

Furthermore, a non-consensual disclosure by one spouse does not normally waive the privilege. For example, if a wife shares a marital confidence with a neighbor without the consent of the husband (e.g., "My husband told me last night that he robbed a bank"), then the husband can prevent both the wife and the neighbor from testifying if the husband's initial statement to the wife was a confidential communication that occurred during a marriage.

Exceptions to the marital communications privilege mirror those to the marital testimonial privilege. It does not apply in legal actions between a husband and wife or when a spouse or child of the household is a victim of the other spouse in a criminal action. Also, a crime-fraud exception exists if the spouses' communication seeks to perpetuate a wrong on a third party. This includes one spouse becoming an accessory after the fact to the crime of the other spouse — if a spouse actively participates in the fruits of the crime and engages in a cover up, the privilege will not apply.

C. Comparison of the Privileges

Based on the foregoing, certain key differences exist between the two marital privileges, as exemplified in the chart below. Most of the differences can be explained by focusing on the rationales behind the privileges. The adverse spousal testimonial privilege exists to protect the current marriage and, in order to do so, deems the holder incompetent to testify about anything adversarial to their spouse. The marital communications privilege is meant to foster open communication during a marriage, and, therefore, protects both parties by privileging the information even if the marriage ends. It does not deem a witness incompetent to testify, and, accordingly, non-communications (such as actions and observations) are not covered.

	Testimonial	Communications
Case	Criminal only	Criminal and Civil
Marital Status	Currently Married	Married or Divorced
Duration	During Marriage only	Applies During and After Marriage
Pre-marital communications covered?	Yes	No
Actions or observations covered?	Yes	No
Holder	Witness-Spouse	Both Spouses

Focus Questions: *Trammel v. United States*

- What is the Court's major criticism of the *Hawkins* case?
- What limitations does the Court place on a spouse's ability to prevent adverse spousal testimony?

Trammel v. United States

445 U.S. 40 (1980)

Mr. Chief Justice BURGER delivered the opinion of the Court. STEWART, J., filed a concurring opinion.

We granted certiorari to consider whether an accused may invoke the privilege against adverse spousal testimony so as to exclude the voluntary testimony of his wife. This calls for a re-examination of *Hawkins v. United States*, 358 U.S. 74 (1958).

I

On March 10, 1976, petitioner Otis Trammel was indicted with two others, Edwin Lee Roberts and Joseph Freeman, for importing heroin into the United States from Thailand and the Philippine Islands and for conspiracy to import heroin ... The indictment also named six unindicted co-conspirators, including petitioner's wife Elizabeth Ann Trammel.

According to the indictment, petitioner and his wife flew from the Philippines to California in August 1975, carrying with them a quantity of heroin. Freeman and Roberts assisted them in its distribution. Elizabeth Trammel then traveled to Thailand where she purchased another supply of the drug. On November 3, 1975, with four ounces of heroin on her person, she boarded a plane for the United States. During a routine customs search in Hawaii, she was searched, the heroin was discovered, and she was arrested. After discussions with Drug Enforcement Administration agents, she agreed to cooperate with the Government.

Prior to trial on this indictment, petitioner ... advised the court that the Government intended to call his wife as an adverse witness and asserted his claim to a privilege to prevent her from testifying against him. At a hearing on the motion, Mrs. Trammel was called as a Government witness under a grant of use immunity. She testified that she and petitioner were married in May 1975 and that they remained married.[1] She explained that her cooperation with the Government was based on assurances that she would be given lenient treatment. She then described, in considerable detail, her role and that of her husband in the heroin distribution conspiracy.

After hearing this testimony, the District Court ruled that Mrs. Trammel could testify in support of the Government's case to any act she observed during the marriage and to any communication "made in the presence of a third person"; however, confidential communications between petitioner and his wife were held to be privileged and inadmissible....

At trial, Elizabeth Trammel testified within the limits of the court's pretrial ruling; her testimony, as the Government concedes, constituted virtually its entire case against petitioner. He was found guilty on both the substantive and conspiracy charges and sentenced to an indeterminate term of years....

In the Court of Appeals petitioner's only claim of error was that the admission of the adverse testimony of his wife, over his objection, contravened this Court's teaching in *Hawkins v. United States*, *supra*, and therefore constituted reversible error. The Court of Appeals rejected this contention....

---

1. In response to the question whether divorce was contemplated, Mrs. Trammel testified that her husband had said that "I would go my way and he would go his."

II

The privilege claimed by petitioner has ancient roots. Writing in 1628, Lord Coke observed that "it hath beene resolved by the Justices that a wife cannot be produced either against or for her husband." 1 E. Coke, A Commentarie upon Littleton 6b (1628). *See, generally*, 8 J. Wigmore, Evidence § 2227 (McNaughton rev. 1961). This spousal disqualification sprang from two canons of medieval jurisprudence: first, the rule that an accused was not permitted to testify in his own behalf because of his interest in the proceeding; second, the concept that husband and wife were one, and that since the woman had no recognized separate legal existence, the husband was that one. From those two now long-abandoned doctrines, it followed that what was inadmissible from the lips of the defendant-husband was also inadmissible from his wife.

Despite its medieval origins, this rule of spousal disqualification remained intact in most common-law jurisdictions well into the 19th century.... Indeed, it was not until 1933, in *Funk v. United States*, 290 U.S. 371, that this Court abolished the testimonial disqualification in the federal courts, so as to permit the spouse of a defendant to testify in the defendant's behalf. *Funk*, however, left undisturbed the rule that either spouse could prevent the other from giving adverse testimony. The rule thus evolved into one of privilege rather than one of absolute disqualification.

The modern justification for this privilege against adverse spousal testimony is its perceived role in fostering the harmony and sanctity of the marriage relationship. Notwithstanding this benign purpose, the rule was sharply criticized. Professor Wigmore termed it "the merest anachronism in legal theory and an indefensible obstruction to truth in practice." 8 Wigmore § 2228, at 221. The Committee on Improvements in the Law of Evidence of the American Bar Association called for its abolition. In its place, Wigmore and others suggested a privilege protecting only private marital communications, modeled on the privilege between priest and penitent, attorney and client, and physician and patient.[5]

These criticisms influenced the American Law Institute, which, in its 1942 Model Code of Evidence advocated a privilege for marital confidences, but expressly rejected a rule vesting in the defendant the right to exclude all adverse testimony of his spouse. In 1953 the Uniform Rules of Evidence, drafted by the National Conference of Commissioners on Uniform State Laws, followed a similar course; it limited the privilege to confidential communications and "abolishe[d] the rule, still existing in some states, and largely a sentimental relic, of not requiring one spouse to testify against the other in a criminal action." Several state legislatures enacted similarly patterned provisions into law.

In *Hawkins v. United States*, 358 U.S. 74 (1958), this Court considered the continued vitality of the privilege against adverse spousal testimony in the federal courts. There the District Court had permitted petitioner's wife, over his objection, to testify against him. With one questioning concurring opinion, the Court held the wife's testimony inadmissible; it took note of the critical comments that the common-law rule had engendered, but chose not to abandon it. Also rejected was the Government's suggestion that the Court modify the privilege by vesting it in the witness-spouse, with freedom to testify or not

---

5. This Court recognized just such a confidential marital communications privilege in *Wolfle v. United States*, 291 U.S. 7 (1934) and in *Blau v. United States*, 340 U.S. 332 (1951). In neither case, however, did the Court adopt the Wigmore view that the communications privilege be substituted *in place of* the privilege against adverse spousal testimony. The privilege as to confidential marital communications is not at issue in the instant case; accordingly, our holding today does not disturb *Wolfle* and *Blau*.

independent of the defendant's control. The Court viewed this proposed modification as antithetical to the widespread belief, evidenced in the rules then in effect in a majority of the States and in England, "that the law should not force or encourage testimony which might alienate husband and wife, or further inflame existing domestic differences."

Hawkins, then, left the federal privilege for adverse spousal testimony where it found it, continuing "a rule which bars the testimony of one spouse against the other unless both consent." *Id.*, at 78. Accord, *Wyatt v. United States*, 362 U.S. 525 (1960).[7] However, in so doing, the Court made clear that its decision was not meant to "foreclose whatever changes in the rule may eventually be dictated by 'reason and experience.'" 358 U.S. at 79.

III
A

The Federal Rules of Evidence acknowledge the authority of the federal courts to continue the evolutionary development of testimonial privileges in federal criminal trials "governed by the principles of the common law as they may be interpreted ... in the light of reason and experience." Fed.Rule Evid. 501.... In rejecting the proposed Rules and enacting Rule 501, Congress manifested an affirmative intention not to freeze the law of privilege. Its purpose rather was to "provide the courts with the flexibility to develop rules of privilege on a case-by-case basis," 120 Cong.Rec. 40891 (1974) (statement of Rep. Hungate), and to leave the door open to change.

Although Rule 501 confirms the authority of the federal courts to reconsider the continued validity of the *Hawkins* rule, the long history of the privilege suggests that it ought not to be casually cast aside. That the privilege is one affecting marriage, home, and family relationships—already subject to much erosion in our day—also counsels caution. At the same time, we cannot escape the reality that the law on occasion adheres to doctrinal concepts long after the reasons which gave them birth have disappeared and after experience suggest the need for change. This was recognized in *Funk* where the Court "decline[d] to enforce ... ancient rule[s] of the common law under conditions as they now exist." 290 U.S., at 382. For, as Mr. Justice Black admonished in another setting, "[w]hen precedent and precedent alone is all the argument that can be made to support a court-fashioned rule, it is time for the rule's creator to destroy it." *Francis v. Southern Pacific Co.*, 333 U.S. 445, 471 (1948) (dissenting opinion).

B

Since 1958, when *Hawkins* was decided, support for the privilege against adverse spousal testimony has been eroded further. Thirty-one jurisdictions, including Alaska and Hawaii, then allowed an accused a privilege to prevent adverse spousal testimony. 358 U.S., at 81, n. 3 (STEWART, J., concurring). The number has now declined to 24. In 1974, the National Conference on Uniform State Laws revised its Uniform Rules of Evidence, but again rejected the *Hawkins* rule in favor of a limited privilege for confidential communications.... The trend in state law toward divesting the accused of the privilege to bar adverse spousal testimony has special relevance because the laws of marriage and domestic relations are concerns traditionally reserved to the states. Scholarly criticism of the *Hawkins* rule has also continued unabated.

---

7. The decision in *Wyatt* recognized an exception to *Hawkins* for cases in which one spouse commits a crime against the other. This exception, placed on the ground of necessity, was a longstanding one at common law. It has been expanded since then to include crimes against the spouse's property, and in recent years crimes against children of either spouse. Similar exceptions have been found to the confidential marital communications privilege. See 8 Wigmore § 2338.

C

Testimonial exclusionary rules and privileges contravene the fundamental principle that "'the public ... has a right to every man's evidence.'" *United States v. Bryan*, 339 U.S. 323, 331 (1950). As such, they must be strictly construed and accepted "only to the very limited extent that permitting a refusal to testify or excluding relevant evidence has a public good transcending the normally predominant principle of utilizing all rational means for ascertaining truth." *Elkins v. United States*, 364 U.S. 206, 234 (Frankfurter, J., dissenting). Here we must decide whether the privilege against adverse spousal testimony promotes sufficiently important interests to outweigh the need for probative evidence in the administration of criminal justice.

It is essential to remember that the *Hawkins* privilege is not needed to protect information privately disclosed between husband and wife in the confidence of the marital relationship—once described by this Court as "the best solace of human existence." *Stein v. Bowman*, 13 Pet., at 223. Those confidences are privileged under the independent rule protecting confidential marital communications. The *Hawkins* privilege is invoked, not to exclude private marital communications, but rather to exclude evidence of criminal acts and of communications made in the presence of third persons....

No other testimonial privilege sweeps so broadly.... The *Hawkins* rule ... is not limited to confidential communications; rather it permits an accused to exclude all adverse spousal testimony. As Jeremy Bentham observed more than a century and a half ago, such a privilege goes far beyond making "every man's house his castle," and permits a person to convert his house into "a den of thieves." 5 Rationale of Judicial Evidence 340 (1827). It "secures, to every man, one safe and unquestionable and every ready accomplice for every imaginable crime." *Id.*, at 338.

The ancient foundations for so sweeping a privilege have long since disappeared. Nowhere in the common-law world—indeed in any modern society—is a woman regarded as chattel or demeaned by denial of a separate legal identity and the dignity associated with recognition as a whole human being. Chip by chip, over the years those archaic notions have been cast aside so that "[n]o longer is the female destined solely for the home and the rearing of the family, and only the male for the marketplace and the world of ideas." *Stanton v. Stanton*, 421 U.S. 7, 14-15 (1975).

The contemporary justification for affording an accused such a privilege is also unpersuasive. When one spouse is willing to testify against the other in a criminal proceeding—whatever the motivation—their relationship is almost certainly in disrepair; there is probably little in the way of marital harmony for the privilege to preserve. In these circumstances, a rule of evidence that permits an accused to prevent adverse spousal testimony seems far more likely to frustrate justice than to foster family peace.[12] Indeed, there is reason to believe that vesting the privilege in the accused could actually undermine the marital relationship. For example, in a case such as this the Government is unlikely to offer a wife immunity and lenient treatment if it knows that her husband can prevent her from giving adverse testimony. If the Government is dissuaded from making such an offer, the privilege can have the untoward effect of permitting one spouse to escape justice at the

---

12. It is argued that abolishing the privilege will permit the Government to come between husband and wife, pitting one against the other. That, too, misses the mark. Neither *Hawkins*, nor any other privilege, prevents the Government from enlisting one spouse to give information concerning the other or to aid in the other's apprehension. It is only the spouse's testimony in the courtroom that is prohibited.

expense of the other. It hardly seems conducive to the preservation of the marital relation to place a wife in jeopardy solely by virtue of her husband's control over her testimony.

IV

Our consideration of the foundations for the privilege and its history satisfy us that "reason and experience" no longer justify so sweeping a rule as that found acceptable by the Court in *Hawkins*. Accordingly, we conclude that the existing rule should be modified so that the witness-spouse alone has a privilege to refuse to testify adversely; the witness may be neither compelled to testify nor foreclosed from testifying. This modification— vesting the privilege in the witness-spouse—furthers the important public interest in marital harmony without unduly burdening legitimate law enforcement needs.

Here, petitioner's spouse chose to testify against him. That she did so after a grant of immunity and assurances of lenient treatment does not render her testimony involuntary. Accordingly, the District Court and the Court of Appeals were correct in rejecting petitioner's claim of privilege, and the judgment of the Court of Appeals is

Affirmed.

[Concurring opinion by Stewart, J., omitted.]

Problem 11-6

On December 2, 1973, government agents detained and searched Lee Vernon Smith and his wife, Geraldine, after they arrived at the Des Moines, Iowa, airport on a flight from California. The agents found 1.3 grams of heroin in Lee's briefcase and 120 grams in a package in Geraldine's underclothing.

At trial, Geraldine testified that her husband placed the package in her underclothing. Lee was subsequently convicted for constructive possession of the heroin concealed on his wife. On appeal, Lee argues that his wife's testimony was protected by the marital communications privilege and should have been excluded. How do you rule?

Problem 11-7

In December, 1981, Marcia Neal agreed to allow the FBI to listen to and record her telephone conversations with her husband, Jake. Jake was wanted for a robbery in which he allegedly assaulted a female teller. Marcia agreed to a grant of immunity in exchange for helping with the telephone conversations.

Marcia had three telephone conversations with her husband at the FBI's request. She began the first with the question, "Is there somewhere I can talk to you without anybody bothering us?" In all the conversations, she adopted the tone of a frightened, dependant wife. She told Jake that she was worried that the police were following her and sought his reassurances and support. In all the conversations, Marcia also asked Jake questions that the FBI had crafted to elicit incriminating answers. Jake showed great reluctance to respond to the potentially incriminating questions; he lowered his voice during the conversations and changed phones several times. Are the conversations admissible at Jake's trial?

Problem 11-8

Return to the facts of *United States v. Neal*, described *supra*, in Problem 11-7. Along with allowing the FBI to record conversations with her husband, Marcia Neal also testified at trial about the events that occurred on the night of the robbery. Marcia stated that her husband, Jake, came home with a pillowcase filled with loose bills and some bills wrapped with rubber bands around them, at around 10:00 p.m.; that he emptied the pillowcase out onto their bed; that they talked about where the money came from; that she helped Jake sort out the bills; that she spent some of the money herself, including $2,000 on her current boyfriend; and that she burned the money wrappers and anything else in the house which was related to the stolen money.

Jake claims that Marcia's testimony is privileged and was wrongly admitted. How do you rule?

Problem 11-9

Jack Lavin became head of BT Securities' Chicago office in January 1994. About a month later, Lavin set up a system to routinely tape telephone conversations that he and his employees had with customers. Later, Lavin discovered that the system was taping his private line as well as his office line. He requested that the taping of his private line cease, and it did cease by September 2, 1994.

In mid-November, 1994, Lavin's lawyer was notified that BT was being investigated for securities fraud. As part of the investigation, BT had produced thousands of tapes of employee conversations to the Federal Reserve Bank. Included in the production were tapes of seven conversations that Lavin had with his wife on his private line. Lavin, through his lawyer, immediately asserted the marital communications privilege as to the conversations between him and his wife. BT notified the Federal Reserve that the privilege had been invoked. Lavin also secured an agreement with BT that it would give him notice and an opportunity to seek judicial relief prior to any further disclosure.

The SEC eventually subpoenaed the tapes. The district court found that although the privilege applied to the conversations, Lavin had subsequently waived the privilege by not seeking physical control over the tapes after he learned of their existence. The issue is now before you on appeal. How do you rule?

IV. The Doctor and Psychotherapist Privileges

The Supreme Court recognized the psychotherapist-patient privilege in *Jaffee v. Redmond*, below. As you will see, the purpose behind the privilege is to facilitate the treatment of patients by removing the risk that the patient's comments to her psychotherapist could be revealed to third parties. The patient is the holder of the privilege, and, as with most professional privileges, it covers only confidential communications that occur during a professional relationship. Thus, a communication made without the purpose of seeking treatment would not be covered. Certain facts that do not involve communications, such as the identity of the patient or the time of treatment, may not be covered. *See In re Zuniga,* 714 F.2d 632, 640 (6th Cir. 1983). On the question of whether the identity of a client is privileged, it is important to note that the relationship between a psychotherapist and patient is not necessarily analogous to the relationship between a lawyer and client. Divulging a patient's use of a psychotherapist's services may harm the relationship, as the client may have multiple reasons for keeping the relationship a secret.

Exceptions to the psychotherapist-patient are jurisdiction-specific. A great divergence in the parameters of the exceptions exists, and many jurisdictions have adopted exceptions for civil commitment proceedings, court-ordered examinations, lawsuits between the patient and psychotherapist, and when a serious threat of harm to the patient or others exists. Additionally, a patient can waive the privilege by voluntarily disclosing confidential communications to third parties.

There is no doctor-patient privilege in federal practice, and proposed (but unenacted) FRE 504 focused exclusively on the psychotherapist-patient relationship. Many states have adopted the doctor-patient privilege, but, again, its parameters are very jurisdiction-specific. The rationale for the doctor-patient privilege mirrors that of the psychotherapist-patient privilege: effective treatment is enhanced when a patient openly discloses information. This rationale may be somewhat weaker in the doctor-patient context than in the psychotherapist-patient context, however. Even without the privilege, almost all patients will be candid with their doctor in order to gain the best treatment. Furthermore, the goal of patient privacy can be effectuated through other means, such as patient privacy legislation.

Those jurisdictions that have adopted a doctor-patient privilege typically mirror the requirements of the psychotherapist-patient privilege. The patient is the holder, the confidential communication must be made in the course of seeking medical treatment, and facts that do not involve communications, such as identity, are usually not covered. In many jurisdictions, the term "doctor" includes the doctor's medical personnel (e.g., nurses, receptionists, etc.), and the term "patient" includes people with a close relationship to that patient (e.g., spouses, parents, etc.). Many different exceptions have been crafted by jurisdictions which have adopted the physician-patient privilege. Thus, some jurisdictions mandate the reporting of elder or child abuse and gunshot wounds. Other jurisdictions create exceptions in criminal cases, will contests, and patient-doctor litigation. Many jurisdictions hold that if a person files a lawsuit that puts a specific medical condition at issue, then that person has waived their doctor-patient privilege as to the medical records relevant to that condition. For example, if a plaintiff sues over a knee injury he suffered, he has waived his privilege regarding his treatment for that knee injury as well as other knee injuries the plaintiff may have suffered in the past. By putting his medical condition at issue, it is only fair that the defendant be able to explore seriousness and extent of the plaintiff's injury.

Focus Questions: *Jaffee v. Redmond*

- What public good is advanced by the psychotherapist-client privilege? What costs are associated with the privilege? How does the Court balance them?
- How much training should a psychotherapist possess before the privilege applies to him or her? Do any factors counterbalance applying the privilege to a psychotherapist with minimal training?

- The dissent notes that the privilege will lead to injustice? What injustice could occur based on the facts of this case? What injustices could occur generally under this privilege?

Jaffee v. Redmond

518 U.S. 1 (1996)

STEVENS, J., delivered the opinion of the Court, in which O'CONNOR, KENNEDY, SOUTER, THOMAS, GINSBURG, and BREYER, JJ., joined. SCALIA, J., filed a dissenting opinion, in which REHNQUIST, C.J., joined as to Part III.

After a traumatic incident in which she shot and killed a man, a police officer received extensive counseling from a licensed clinical social worker. The question we address is whether statements the officer made to her therapist during the counseling sessions are protected from compelled disclosure in a federal civil action brought by the family of the deceased. Stated otherwise, the question is whether it is appropriate for federal courts to recognize a "psychotherapist privilege" under Rule 501 of the Federal Rules of Evidence.

I

... On June 27, 1991, Redmond was the first officer to respond to a "fight in progress" call at an apartment complex. As she arrived at the scene, two of Allen's sisters ran toward her squad car, waving their arms and shouting that there had been a stabbing in one of the apartments. Redmond testified at trial that she relayed this information to her dispatcher and requested an ambulance. She then exited her car and walked toward the apartment building. Before Redmond reached the building, several men ran out, one waving a pipe. When the men ignored her order to get on the ground, Redmond drew her service revolver. Two other men then burst out of the building, one, Ricky Allen, chasing the other. According to Redmond, Allen was brandishing a butcher knife and disregarded her repeated commands to drop the weapon. Redmond shot Allen when she believed he was about to stab the man he was chasing. Allen died at the scene. Redmond testified that before other officers arrived to provide support, "people came pouring out of the buildings," and a threatening confrontation between her and the crowd ensued.

Petitioner filed suit in Federal District Court alleging that Redmond had violated Allen's constitutional rights by using excessive force during the encounter at the apartment complex.... At trial, petitioner presented testimony from members of Allen's family that conflicted with Redmond's version of the incident in several important respects. They testified, for example, that Redmond drew her gun before exiting her squad car and that Allen was unarmed when he emerged from the apartment building.

During pretrial discovery petitioner learned that after the shooting Redmond had participated in about 50 counseling sessions with Karen Beyer, a clinical social worker licensed by the State of Illinois and employed at that time by the Village of Hoffman Estates. Petitioner sought access to Beyer's notes concerning the sessions for use in cross-examining Redmond. Respondents vigorously resisted the discovery. They asserted that the contents of the conversations between Beyer and Redmond were protected against involuntary disclosure by a psychotherapist-patient privilege. The district judge rejected this argument. Neither Beyer nor Redmond, however, complied with his order to disclose the contents of Beyer's notes. At depositions and on the witness stand both either refused to answer certain questions or professed an inability to recall details of their conversations.

In his instructions at the end of the trial, the judge advised the jury that the refusal to turn over Beyer's notes had no "legal justification" and that the jury could therefore presume that the contents of the notes would have been unfavorable to respondents. The jury awarded petitioner $45,000 on the federal claim and $500,000 on her state-law claim.

The Court of Appeals for the Seventh Circuit reversed and remanded for a new trial. Addressing the issue for the first time, the court concluded that "reason and experience," the touchstones for acceptance of a privilege under Rule 501 of the Federal Rules of Evidence, compelled recognition of a psychotherapist-patient privilege. 51 F.3d 1346, 1355 (1995). "Reason tells us that psychotherapists and patients share a unique relationship, in which the ability to communicate freely without the fear of public disclosure is the key to successful treatment." *Id.*, at 1355-1356. As to experience, the court observed that all 50 States have adopted some form of the psychotherapist-patient privilege. *Id.*, at 1356. The court attached particular significance to the fact that Illinois law expressly extends such a privilege to social workers like Karen Beyer. *Id.*, at 1357. The court also noted that, with one exception, the federal decisions rejecting the privilege were more than five years old and that the "need and demand for counseling services has skyrocketed during the past several years." *Id.*, at 1355-1356.

The Court of Appeals qualified its recognition of the privilege by stating that it would not apply if, "in the interests of justice, the evidentiary need for the disclosure of the contents of a patient's counseling sessions outweighs that patient's privacy interests." *Id.*, at 1357. Balancing those conflicting interests, the court observed, on the one hand, that the evidentiary need for the contents of the confidential conversations was diminished in this case because there were numerous eyewitnesses to the shooting, and, on the other hand, that Officer Redmond's privacy interests were substantial. *Id.*, at 1358. Based on this assessment, the court concluded that the trial court had erred by refusing to afford protection to the confidential communications between Redmond and Beyer....

II

Rule 501 of the Federal Rules of Evidence authorizes federal courts to define new privileges by interpreting "common law principles ... in the light of reason and experience."... The Rule thus did not freeze the law governing the privileges of witnesses in federal trials at a particular point in our history, but rather directed federal courts to "continue the evolutionary development of testimonial privileges." *Trammel v. United States*, 445 U.S. 40, 47 (1980).

The common-law principles underlying the recognition of testimonial privileges can be stated simply. "'For more than three centuries it has now been recognized as a fundamental maxim that the public ... has a right to every man's evidence. When we come to examine the various claims of exemption, we start with the primary assumption that there is a general duty to give what testimony one is capable of giving, and that any exemptions which may exist are distinctly exceptional, being so many derogations from a positive general rule.'" *United States v. Bryan*, 339 U.S. 323 (1950) (citation omitted). Exceptions from the general rule disfavoring testimonial privileges may be justified, however, by a "'public good transcending the normally predominant principle of utilizing all rational means for ascertaining truth.'" *Trammel*, 445 U.S., at 50....

III

Like the spousal and attorney-client privileges, the psychotherapist-patient privilege is "rooted in the imperative need for confidence and trust." *Ibid.* Treatment by a physician for physical ailments can often proceed successfully on the basis of a physical examination, objective information supplied by the patient, and the results of diagnostic tests. Effective psychotherapy, by contrast, depends upon an atmosphere of confidence and trust in which the patient is willing to make a frank and complete disclosure of facts, emotions, memories, and fears. Because of the sensitive nature of the problems for which individuals consult psychotherapists, disclosure of confidential communications made during counseling sessions may cause embarrassment or disgrace. For this reason, the mere possibility of disclosure may impede development of the confidential relationship necessary for successful treatment....

Our cases make clear that an asserted privilege must also "serv[e] public ends." *Upjohn Co. v. United States*, 449 U.S. 383, 389 (1981). Thus, the purpose of the attorney-client privilege is to "encourage full and frank communication between attorneys and their clients and thereby promote broader public interests in the observance of law and administration of justice." *Ibid.* And the spousal privilege, as modified in *Trammel*, is justified because it "furthers the important public interest in marital harmony," 445 U.S., at 53. The psychotherapist privilege serves the public interest by facilitating the provision of appropriate treatment for individuals suffering the effects of a mental or emotional problem. The mental health of our citizenry, no less than its physical health, is a public good of transcendent importance.

In contrast to the significant public and private interests supporting recognition of the privilege, the likely evidentiary benefit that would result from the denial of the privilege is modest. If the privilege were rejected, confidential conversations between psychotherapists and their patients would surely be chilled, particularly when it is obvious that the circumstances that give rise to the need for treatment will probably result in litigation. Without a privilege, much of the desirable evidence to which litigants such as petitioner seek access—for example, admissions against interest by a party—is unlikely to come into being. This unspoken "evidence" will therefore serve no greater truth-seeking function than if it had been spoken and privileged.

That it is appropriate for the federal courts to recognize a psychotherapist privilege under Rule 501 is confirmed by the fact that all 50 States and the District of Columbia have enacted into law some form of psychotherapist privilege. We have previously observed that the policy decisions of the States bear on the question whether federal courts should recognize a new privilege or amend the coverage of an existing one. Because state legislatures are fully aware of the need to protect the integrity of the factfinding functions of their courts, the existence of a consensus among the States indicates that "reason and experience" support recognition of the privilege. In addition, given the importance of the patient's understanding that her communications with her therapist will not be publicly disclosed, any State's promise of confidentiality would have little value if the patient were aware that the privilege would not be honored in a federal court. Denial of the federal privilege therefore would frustrate the purposes of the state legislation that was enacted to foster these confidential communications....

The uniform judgment of the States is reinforced by the fact that a psychotherapist privilege was among the nine specific privileges recommended by the Advisory Committee in its proposed privilege rules.... In rejecting the proposed draft that had specifically identified each privilege rule and substituting the present more open-ended Rule 501, the Senate Judiciary Committee explicitly stated that its action "should not be understood as disapproving any recognition of a psychiatrist-patient ... privileg[e] contained in the [proposed] rules." S.Rep. No. 93-1277, at 13, U.S.Code Cong. & Admin.News 1974, pp. 7051, 7059.

Because we agree with the judgment of the state legislatures and the Advisory Committee that a psychotherapist-patient privilege will serve a "public good transcending the normally predominant principle of utilizing all rational means for ascertaining truth," *Trammel,* 445 U.S., at 50, we hold that confidential communications between a licensed psychotherapist and her patients in the course of diagnosis or treatment are protected from compelled disclosure under Rule 501 of the Federal Rules of Evidence.

IV

All agree that a psychotherapist privilege covers confidential communications made to licensed psychiatrists and psychologists. We have no hesitation in concluding in this case that the federal privilege should also extend to confidential communications made to licensed social workers in the course of psychotherapy. The reasons for recognizing a privilege for treatment by psychiatrists and psychologists apply with equal force to treatment by a clinical social worker such as Karen Beyer. Today, social workers provide a significant amount of mental health treatment. Their clients often include the poor and those of modest means who could not afford the assistance of a psychiatrist or psychologist but whose counseling sessions serve the same public goals. Perhaps in recognition of these circumstances, the vast majority of States explicitly extend a testimonial privilege to licensed social workers. We therefore agree with the Court of Appeals that "[d]rawing a distinction between the counseling provided by costly psychotherapists and the counseling provided by more readily accessible social workers serves no discernible public purpose." 51 F.3d, at 1358, n. 19.

We part company with the Court of Appeals on a separate point. We reject the balancing component of the privilege implemented by that court and a small number of States. Making the promise of confidentiality contingent upon a trial judge's later evaluation of the relative importance of the patient's interest in privacy and the evidentiary need for disclosure would eviscerate the effectiveness of the privilege. As we explained in *Upjohn,* if the purpose of the privilege is to be served, the participants in the confidential conversation "must be able to predict with some degree of certainty whether particular discussions will be protected. An uncertain privilege, or one which purports to be certain but results in widely varying applications by the courts, is little better than no privilege at all." 449 U.S., at 393.

These considerations are all that is necessary for decision of this case. A rule that authorizes the recognition of new privileges on a case-by-case basis makes it appropriate to define the details of new privileges in a like manner. Because this is the first case in which we have recognized a psychotherapist privilege, it is neither necessary nor feasible to delineate its full contours in a way that would "govern all conceivable future questions in this area." Id., at 386.

V

The conversations between Officer Redmond and Karen Beyer and the notes taken during their counseling sessions are protected from compelled disclosure under Rule 501 of the Federal Rules of Evidence. The judgment of the Court of Appeals is affirmed.

It is so ordered.

Justice SCALIA, with whom THE CHIEF JUSTICE joins as to Part III, dissenting.

The Court has discussed at some length the benefit that will be purchased by creation of the evidentiary privilege in this case: the encouragement of psychoanalytic counseling. It has not mentioned the purchase price: occasional injustice. That is the cost of every rule which excludes reliable and probative evidence—or at least every one categorical enough to achieve its announced policy objective. In the case of some of these rules, such as the one excluding confessions that have not been properly "Mirandized," *see Miranda v. Arizona*, 384 U.S. 436 (1966), the victim of the injustice is always the impersonal State or the faceless "public at large." For the rule proposed here, the victim is more likely to be some individual who is prevented from proving a valid claim—or (worse still) prevented from establishing a valid defense....

The Court today ignores this traditional judicial preference for the truth, and ends up creating a privilege that is new, vast, and ill defined. I respectfully dissent.

I

The case before us involves confidential communications made by a police officer to a state-licensed clinical social worker in the course of psychotherapeutic counseling. Before proceeding to a legal analysis of the case, I must observe that the Court makes its task deceptively simple by the manner in which it proceeds. It begins by characterizing the issue as "whether it is appropriate for federal courts to recognize a 'psychotherapist privilege'" and devotes almost all of its opinion to that question. Having answered that question (to its satisfaction) in the affirmative, it then devotes less than a page of text to answering in the affirmative the small remaining question whether "the federal privilege should also extend to confidential communications made to licensed social workers in the course of psychotherapy."

Of course the prototypical evidentiary privilege analogous to the one asserted here—the lawyer-client privilege—is not identified by the broad area of advice giving practiced by the person to whom the privileged communication is given, but rather by the professional status of that person. Hence, it seems a long step from a lawyer-client privilege to a tax advisor-client or accountant-client privilege. But if one recharacterizes it as a "legal advisor" privilege, the extension seems like the most natural thing in the world. That is the illusion the Court has produced here: It first frames an overly general question ("Should there be a psychotherapist privilege?") that can be answered in the negative only by excluding from protection office consultations with professional psychiatrists (i.e., doctors) and clinical psychologists. And then, having answered that in the affirmative, it comes to the only question that the facts of this case present ("Should there be a social worker-client privilege with regard to psychotherapeutic counseling?") with the answer seemingly a foregone conclusion. At that point, to conclude against the privilege one must subscribe to the difficult proposition, "Yes, there is a psychotherapist privilege, but not if the psychotherapist is a social worker."

Relegating the question actually posed by this case to an afterthought makes the impossible possible in a number of wonderful ways. For example, it enables the Court to treat the Proposed Federal Rules of Evidence developed in 1972 by the Judicial Conference Advisory Committee as strong support for its holding, whereas they in fact counsel clearly and directly against it. The Committee did indeed recommend a "psychotherapist privilege" of sorts; but more precisely, and more relevantly, it recommended a privilege for psychotherapy conducted by "a person authorized to practice medicine" or "a person licensed or certified as a psychologist," Proposed Rule of Evidence 504, which is to say that it recommended against the privilege at issue here....

II

... Effective psychotherapy undoubtedly is beneficial to individuals with mental problems, and surely serves some larger social interest in maintaining a mentally stable society. But merely mentioning these values does not answer the critical question: Are they of such importance, and is the contribution of psychotherapy to them so distinctive, and is the application of normal evidentiary rules so destructive to psychotherapy, as to justify making our federal courts occasional instruments of injustice? ...

When is it, one must wonder, that the psychotherapist came to play such an indispensable role in the maintenance of the citizenry's mental health? For most of history, men and women have worked out their difficulties by talking to, inter alios, parents, siblings, best friends, and bartenders—none of whom was awarded a privilege against testifying in court. Ask the average citizen: Would your mental health be more significantly impaired by preventing you from seeing a psychotherapist, or by preventing you from getting advice from your mom? I have little doubt what the answer would be. Yet there is no mother-child privilege.

How likely is it that a person will be deterred from seeking psychological counseling, or from being completely truthful in the course of such counseling, because of fear of later disclosure in litigation? And even more pertinent to today's decision, to what extent will the evidentiary privilege reduce that deterrent? The Court does not try to answer the first of these questions; and it cannot possibly have any notion of what the answer is to the second, since that depends entirely upon the scope of the privilege, which the Court amazingly finds it "neither necessary nor feasible to delineate." If, for example, the psychotherapist can give the patient no more assurance than "A court will not be able to make me disclose what you tell me, unless you tell me about a harmful act," I doubt whether there would be much benefit from the privilege at all. That is not a fanciful example, at least with respect to extension of the psychotherapist privilege to social workers.

Even where it is certain that absence of the psychotherapist privilege will inhibit disclosure of the information, it is not clear to me that that is an unacceptable state of affairs. Let us assume the very worst in the circumstances of the present case: that to be truthful about what was troubling her, the police officer who sought counseling would have to confess that she shot without reason, and wounded an innocent man. If (again to assume the worst) such an act constituted the crime of negligent wounding under Illinois law, the officer would of course have the absolute right not to admit that she shot without reason in criminal court. But I see no reason why she should be enabled both not to admit it in criminal court (as a good citizen should), and to get the benefits of psychotherapy by admitting it to a therapist who cannot tell anyone else. And even less reason why she should be enabled to deny her guilt in the criminal trial—or in a civil trial for negligence-while yet obtaining the benefits of psychotherapy by confessing guilt to a social worker who cannot testify. It seems to me entirely fair to say that if she wishes the benefits of telling the truth she must also accept the adverse consequences....

The Court confidently asserts that not much truth-finding capacity would be destroyed by the privilege anyway, since "[w]ithout a privilege, much of the desirable evidence to which litigants such as petitioner seek access ... is unlikely to come into being." If that is so, how come psychotherapy got to be a thriving practice before the "psychotherapist privilege" was invented? Were the patients paying money to lie to their analysts all those years? ...

The Court suggests one last policy justification: since psychotherapist privilege statutes exist in all the States, the failure to recognize a privilege in federal courts "would frustrate the purposes of the state legislation that was enacted to foster these confidential communications." This is a novel argument indeed. A sort of inverse pre-emption: The truth-seeking functions of federal courts must be adjusted so as not to conflict with the policies of the States....

The Court concedes that there is "divergence among the States concerning the types of therapy relationships protected and the exceptions recognized." To rest a newly announced federal common-law psychotherapist privilege, assertable from this day forward in all federal courts, upon "the States' unanimous judgment that some form of psychotherapist privilege is appropriate," is rather like announcing a new, immediately applicable, federal common law of torts, based upon the States' "unanimous judgment" that some form of tort law is appropriate. In the one case as in the other, the state laws vary to such a degree that the parties and lower federal judges confronted by the new "common law" have barely a clue as to what its content might be.

III

Turning from the general question that was not involved in this case to the specific one that is: The Court's conclusion that a social-worker psychotherapeutic privilege deserves recognition is even less persuasive. In approaching this question, the fact that five of the state legislatures that have seen fit to enact "some form" of psychotherapist privilege have elected not to extend any form of privilege to social workers ought to give one pause. So should the fact that the Judicial Conference Advisory Committee was similarly discriminating in its conferral of the proposed Rule 504 privilege....

A licensed psychiatrist or psychologist is an expert in psychotherapy—and that may suffice (though I think it not so clear that this Court should make the judgment) to justify the use of extraordinary means to encourage counseling with him, as opposed to counseling with one's rabbi, minister, family, or friends. One must presume that a social worker does not bring this greatly heightened degree of skill to bear, which is alone a reason for not encouraging that consultation as generously. Does a social worker bring to bear at least a significantly heightened degree of skill—more than a minister or rabbi, for example? I have no idea, and neither does the Court. The social worker in the present case, Karen Beyer, was a "licensed clinical social worker" in Illinois a job title whose training requirements consist of a "master's degree in social work from an approved program," and "3,000 hours of satisfactory, supervised clinical professional experience." Ill. Comp. Stat., ch. 225, § 20/9 (1994). It is not clear that the degree in social work requires any training in psychotherapy.... With due respect, it does not seem to me that any of this training is comparable in its rigor (or indeed in the precision of its subject) to the training of the other experts (lawyers) to whom this Court has accorded a privilege, or even of the experts (psychiatrists and psychologists) to whom the Advisory Committee and this Court proposed extension of a privilege in 1972. Of course these are only Illinois' requirements for "social workers." Those of other States, for all we know, may be even less demanding. Indeed, I am not even sure there is a nationally accepted definition of "social worker," as there is of psychiatrist and psychologist. It seems to me quite irresponsible to extend the so-called "psychotherapist privilege" to all licensed social workers, nationwide, without exploring these issues....

In its consideration of this case, the Court was the beneficiary of no fewer than 14 amicus briefs supporting respondents, most of which came from such organizations as the American Psychiatric Association, the American Psychoanalytic Association, the American Association of State Social Work Boards, the Employee Assistance Professionals Association, Inc., the American Counseling Association, and the National Association of Social Workers. Not a single amicus brief was filed in support of petitioner. That is no surprise. There is no self-interested organization out there devoted to pursuit of the truth in the federal courts. The expectation is, however, that this Court will have that interest prominently—indeed, primarily—in mind. Today we have failed that expectation, and that responsibility. It is no small matter to say that, in some cases, our federal courts will be the tools of injustice rather than unearth the truth where it is available to be found. The common law has identified a few instances where that is tolerable. Perhaps Congress may conclude that it is also tolerable for the purpose of encouraging psychotherapy by social workers. But that conclusion assuredly does not burst upon the mind with such clarity that a judgment in favor of suppressing the truth ought to be pronounced by this honorable Court. I respectfully dissent.

Problem 11-10

Dona Vanderbilt had been working as an administrative assistant for the town of Chilmark for three years when she discovered that a co-worker—a male administrative assistant with the same qualifications and work experience—was paid more than her. Dona asked Chilmark to increase her pay and that of another female administrative assistant several times, but Chilmark refused. The wage disparity continued for the next several years.

Vanderbilt is now suing Chilmark for gender discrimination. As part of her claim, she is seeking damages for emotional distress. In response to Vanderbilt's claims for emotional distress, Chilmark has filed a motion to compel Vanderbilt to (1) produce her psychiatric and psychotherapeutic records, (2) answer questions at a deposition concerning the substance of any psychiatric treatment, counseling, or psychotherapy she may have undergone, and (3) allow the deposition of any mental health professionals who have treated her.

How should the judge rule?

V. Other Privileges

Many other privileges exist, but they vary dramatically from jurisdiction to jurisdiction. Their scope, definitions of privileged parties, and decision as to who holds the privilege vary greatly. Accordingly, this section will provide a brief overview on some of these privileges, both private and governmental.

Proposed (but never adopted) FRE 506 concerned a clergy-penitent privilege. The goal is to allow the penitent to be open and candid to their clergy in order to obtain spiritual counseling. The holder for this privilege is usually the penitent, although some states allow the clergyperson to hold the privilege as well. A clergyperson does not include self-denominated clergy but rather focuses on clergy who are regularly engaged in some type of organized ministry. The communication need not necessarily be a confession in the doctrinal sense, but it must involve obtaining spiritual guidance. Some jurisdictions have crafted exceptions whereby the clergy must report matters that endanger others, such as child abuse.

A journalist privilege has been adopted by numerous states. The goal is to protect the identity of a source in order to encourage the free flow of information to a journalist. In *Branzburg v. Hayes,* 408 U.S. 665 (1972), the Supreme Court ruled that the First Amendment's guarantee of freedom of the press did not require the recognition of a journalist's privilege. Nonetheless, some federal courts have allowed a qualified privilege whereby the interest of the journalist is balanced against a criminal defendant's right to a fair trial. Thus, courts examine whether the privileged information is relevant, whether it can be obtained by other means, and whether there exists a compelling interest in the information.

Other private privileges have gained little traction in federal or state jurisdictions. Although it has not been recognized federally, some states have enacted an accountant-client privilege. Most jurisdictions have rejected a "researcher" privilege whereby information would be privileged if it is part of scholarly study and a need for confidentiality exists. Some courts have recognized a trade secrets privilege whereby the owner of a trade secret may refuse to disclose it as long as the privilege will not conceal fraud or otherwise work injustice. A peer review privilege for deliberations regarding university hiring, promotion, and tenure decisions has failed due to the strength of the counterbalancing need to determine whether illegal discrimination has occurred. A parent-child privilege has been accepted in very few states. Some jurisdictions have accepted a privilege for self-critical analysis whereby an entity's attempt to candidly evaluate its actions (e.g., a medical review board) are privileged. Some states have passed statutes privileging communications in guidance counselor-student relationships. A privilege for comments made to probation officers has also been recognized.

A number of government privileges have been proposed as well. For example, in order to protect the safety of confidential informants, a qualified privilege exists protecting the identity of informants. The government, not the informant, is the holder of the privilege, and the privilege protects only the identity of the informant, not her communications (unless, of course, the communications reveal the identity of the informant). Sometimes, however, the identity of the informant is essential to a fair determination of defendant's case. Thus, the court qualifies the privilege by requiring a balancing between the government's interest in protecting the informant and the defendant's right to prepare her defense. Such factors as the informant's degree of involvement in the crime, the helpfulness of the disclosure to the defense, and the strength of the government's interest are balanced. The burden of proof is on the defendant.

The government is also the holder of a state (including military) secrets privilege that covers secrets relating to the national defense or the international relations of the United States. The privilege applies once the government makes a showing of reasonable likelihood that the evidence will disclose a secret of state. If this threshold is met, there is no balancing of the state's interest against the opposing party's interest — the privilege cannot be overcome. Although the law is unsettled on the point, it appears that the trial court makes the final determination concerning the applicability of the privilege, and it cannot rely exclusively on representations of the head of a responsible government agency. *See e.g., Doe v. Tenet,* 329 F.3d 1135, 1151-54 (9th Cir. 2003), *rev'd on other grounds,* 544 U.S. 1 (2005). The dismissal of a claim or defense on the grounds of the state secret should be the last possible resort for the court.

Even if the information does not rise to the level of a "state secret," the government may claim a deliberative process privilege. The privilege seeks to protect information which, if disclosed, would be adverse to the public interest because revealing the information would damage government decision making. For example, revealing a preliminary position paper on a hotly contested issue might make the decision makers less likely to be candid in their evaluation of the issue if they knew their preliminary thoughts would be released. Similarly, citizens who provide information might be less likely to do so if they knew their thoughts would be released. On the executive level, similar concerns regarding the ability to receive candid advice justify an executive privilege. Thus, the public interest is served by privileging the communications of presidential advisors in the course of preparing advice for the President.

Professional Development Questions

- Privileges prevent the introduction of relevant and reliable evidence. Have the courts drawn the line on the admissibility of this evidence in the right places? Is one particular privilege that we discussed too broad or too narrow?

- As you approach the end of this book, you will want to incorporate trial advocacy techniques to deepen your understanding of evidence law. One trial attorney adage is that a jury can respond negatively to winning objections, as the jury feels the attorney is trying to keep important evidence from them. So, the thinking goes, if the answer will not hurt your case, you should not object to an objectionable question or answer. Do you agree?

- Another aspect of trial advocacy is the tone that you adopt before the jury. Undoubtedly, you should not try to be someone you are not before the jury, as they may very well sense that you are not being sincere. How would you characterize your "style" as trial advocate? Adversarial? Professorial? Kind? Would your style change depending on the stage of trial (e.g., adopting a different style for cross-examination rather than direct examination)?

- Now is good time to revisit a professional development question offered near the midpoint of this book: If you began this semester with a strong interest in being a trial attorney, how has learning the rules of evidence influenced your desire? If you had limited or no interest in trial work as the semester began, has that interest changed or stayed the same? Has your interest changed as the semester progressed? What was the source of that change?

Appendix

Federal Rules of Evidence

Effective July 1, 1975, as amended to December 1, 2017

ARTICLE I. GENERAL PROVISIONS

Rule 101. Scope; Definitions

(a) **Scope.** These rules apply to proceedings in United States courts. The specific courts and proceedings to which the rules apply, along with exceptions, are set out in Rule 1101.

(b) **Definitions.** In these rules:

(1) "civil case" means a civil action or proceeding;

(2) "criminal case" includes a criminal proceeding;

(3) "public office" includes a public agency;

(4) "record" includes a memorandum, report, or data compilation;

(5) a "rule prescribed by the Supreme Court" means a rule adopted by the Supreme Court under statutory authority; and

(6) a reference to any kind of written material or any other medium includes electronically stored information.

Rule 102. Purpose

These rules should be construed so as to administer every proceeding fairly, eliminate unjustifiable expense and delay, and promote the development of evidence law, to the end of ascertaining the truth and securing a just determination.

Rule 103. Rulings on Evidence

(a) **Preserving a Claim of Error.** A party may claim error in a ruling to admit or exclude evidence only if the error affects a substantial right of the party and:

(1) if the ruling admits evidence, a party, on the record:

(A) timely objects or moves to strike; and

(B) states the specific ground, unless it was apparent from the context; or

(2) if the ruling excludes evidence, a party informs the court of its substance by an offer of proof, unless the substance was apparent from the context.

(b) **Not Needing to Renew an Objection or Offer of Proof.** Once the court rules definitively on the record—either before or at trial—a party need not renew an objection or offer of proof to preserve a claim of error for appeal.

(c) **Court's Statement About the Ruling; Directing an Offer of Proof.** The court may make any statement about the character or form of the evidence, the objection made, and the ruling. The court may direct that an offer of proof be made in question and-answer form.

(d) Preventing the Jury from Hearing Inadmissible Evidence. **To the extent practicable, the court must conduct a jury trial so that inadmissible evidence is not suggested to the jury by any means.**

(e) **Taking Notice of Plain Error.** A court may take notice of a plain error affecting a substantial right, even if the claim of error was not properly preserved.

Rule 104. Preliminary Questions

(a) **In General.** The court must decide any preliminary question about whether a witness is qualified, a privilege exists, or evidence is admissible. In so deciding, the court is not bound by evidence rules, except those on privilege.

(b) **Relevance that Depends on a Fact.** When the relevance of evidence depends on whether a fact exists, proof must be introduced sufficient to support a finding that the fact does exist. The court may admit the proposed evidence on the condition that the proof be introduced later.

(c) **Conducting a Hearing so that the Jury Cannot Hear It.** The court must conduct any hearing on a preliminary question so that the jury cannot hear it if:

(1) the hearing involves the admissibility of a confession;

(2) a defendant in a criminal case is a witness and so requests; or

(3) justice so requires.

(d) **Cross-Examining a Defendant in a Criminal Case.** By testifying on a preliminary question, a defendant in a criminal case does not become subject to cross-examination on other issues in the case.

(e) **Evidence Relevant to Weight and Credibility.** This rule does not limit a party's right to introduce before the jury evidence that is relevant to the weight or credibility of other evidence.

Rule 105. Limiting Evidence That Is Not Admissible Against Other Parties or for Other Purposes

If the court admits evidence that is admissible against a party or for a purpose—but not against another party or for another purpose—the court, on timely request, must restrict the evidence to its proper scope and instruct the jury accordingly.

Rule 106. Remainder of or Related Writings or Recorded Statements

If a party introduces all or part of a writing or recorded statement, an adverse party may require the introduction, at that time, of any other part—or any other writing or recorded statement—that in fairness ought to be considered at the same time.

ARTICLE II. JUDICIAL NOTICE

Rule 201. Judicial Notice of Adjudicative Facts

(a) **Scope.** This rule governs judicial notice of an adjudicative fact only, not a legislative fact.

(b) **Kinds of Facts that May Be Judicially Noticed.** The court may judicially notice a fact that is not subject to reasonable dispute because it:

(1) is generally known within the trial court's territorial jurisdiction; or

(2) can be accurately and readily determined from sources whose accuracy cannot reasonably be questioned.

(c) **Taking Notice.** The court:

(1) may take judicial notice on its own; or

(2) must take judicial notice if a party requests it and the court is supplied with the necessary information.

(d) **Timing.** The court may take judicial notice at any stage of the proceeding.

(e) **Opportunity to be Heard.** On timely request, a party is entitled to be heard on the propriety of taking judicial notice and the nature of the fact to be noticed. If the court takes judicial notice before notifying a party, the party, on request, is still entitled to be heard.

(f) **Instructing the Jury.** In a civil case, the court must instruct the jury to accept the noticed fact as conclusive. In a criminal case, the court must instruct the jury that it may or may not accept the noticed fact as conclusive.

ARTICLE III. PRESUMPTIONS IN CIVIL CASES

Rule 301. Presumptions in Civil Cases Generally

In a civil case, unless a federal statute or these rules provide otherwise, the party against whom a presumption is directed has the burden of producing evidence to rebut the presumption. But this rule does not shift the burden of persuasion, which remains on the party who had it originally.

Rule 302. Applying State Law to Presumptions in Civil Cases

In a civil case, state law governs the effect of a presumption regarding a claim or defense for which state law supplies the rule of decision.

ARTICLE IV. RELEVANCE AND ITS LIMITS

Rule 401. Test for Relevant Evidence

Evidence is relevant if:

(a) it has any tendency to make a fact more or less probable than it would be without the evidence; and

(b) the fact is of consequence in determining the action.

Rule 402. General Admissibility of Relevant Evidence

Relevant evidence is admissible unless any of the following provides otherwise:

- the United States Constitution;
- a federal statute;
- these rules; or
- other rules prescribed by the Supreme Court.

Irrelevant evidence is not admissible.

Rule 403. Excluding Relevant Evidence for Prejudice, Confusion, Waste of Time, or Other Reasons

The court may exclude relevant evidence if its probative value is substantially outweighed by a danger of one or more of the following: unfair prejudice, confusing the issues, misleading the jury, undue delay, wasting time, or needlessly presenting cumulative evidence.

Rule 404. Character Evidence; Crimes or Other Acts

(a) Character Evidence.

(1) *Prohibited Uses.* Evidence of a person's character or character trait is not admissible to prove that on a particular occasion the person acted in accordance with the character or trait.

(2) *Exceptions for a Defendant or Victim in a Criminal Case.* The following exceptions apply in a criminal case:

(A) a defendant may offer evidence of the defendant's pertinent trait, and if the evidence is admitted, the prosecutor may offer evidence to rebut it;

(B) subject to the limitations in Rule 412, a defendant may offer evidence of an alleged victim's pertinent trait, and if the evidence is admitted, the prosecutor may:

(i) offer evidence to rebut it; and

(ii) offer evidence of the defendant's same trait; and

(C) in a homicide case, the prosecutor may offer evidence of the alleged victim's trait of peacefulness to rebut evidence that the victim was the first aggressor.

(3) *Exceptions for a Witness.* Evidence of a witness's character may be admitted under Rules 607, 608, and 609.

(b) Crimes, Wrongs, or Other Acts.

(1) *Prohibited Uses.* Evidence of a crime, wrong, or other act is not admissible to prove a person's character in order to show that on a particular occasion the person acted in accordance with the character.

(2) *Permitted Uses; Notice in a Criminal Case.* This evidence may be admissible for another purpose, such as proving motive, opportunity, intent, preparation, plan, knowledge, identity, absence of mistake, or lack of accident. On request by a defendant in a criminal case, the prosecutor must:

(A) provide reasonable notice of the general nature of any such evidence that the prosecutor intends to offer at trial; and

(B) do so before trial—or during trial if the court, for good cause, excuses lack of pretrial notice.

Rule 405. Methods of Proving Character

(a) By Reputation or Opinion. When evidence of a person's character or character trait is admissible, it may be proved by testimony about the person's reputation or by testimony in the form of an opinion. On cross-examination of the character witness, the court may allow an inquiry into relevant specific instances of the person's conduct.

(b) By Specific Instances of Conduct. When a person's character or character trait is an essential element of a charge, claim, or defense, the character or trait may also be proved by relevant specific instances of the person's conduct.

Rule 406. Habit; Routine Practice

Evidence of a person's habit or an organization's routine practice may be admitted to prove that on a particular occasion the person or organization acted in accordance with the habit or routine practice. The court may admit this evidence regardless of whether it is corroborated or whether there was an eyewitness.

Rule 407. Subsequent Remedial Measures

When measures are taken that would have made an earlier injury or harm less likely to occur, evidence of the subsequent measures is not admissible to prove:

- negligence;

- culpable conduct;

- a defect in a product or its design; or

- a need for a warning or instruction.

But the court may admit this evidence for another purpose, such as impeachment or— if disputed—proving ownership, control, or the feasibility of precautionary measures.

Rule 408. Compromise Offers and Negotiations

(a) **Prohibited Uses.** Evidence of the following is not admissible—on behalf of any party— either to prove or disprove the validity or amount of a disputed claim or to impeach by a prior inconsistent statement or a contradiction:

(1) furnishing, promising, or offering—or accepting, promising to accept, or offering to accept—a valuable consideration in compromising or attempting to compromise the claim; and

(2) conduct or a statement made during compromise negotiations about the claim— except when offered in a criminal case and when the negotiations related to a claim by a public office in the exercise of its regulatory, investigative, or enforcement authority.

(b) **Exceptions.** The court may admit this evidence for another purpose, such as proving a witness's bias or prejudice, negating a contention of undue delay, or proving an effort to obstruct a criminal investigation or prosecution.

Rule 409. Offers to Pay Medical and Similar Expenses

Evidence of furnishing, promising to pay, or offering to pay medical, hospital, or similar expenses resulting from an injury is not admissible to prove liability for the injury.

Rule 410. Pleas, Plea Discussions, and Related Statements

(a) **Prohibited Uses.** In a civil or criminal case, evidence of the following is not admissible against the defendant who made the plea or participated in the plea discussions:

(1) a guilty plea that was later withdrawn;

(2) a nolo contendere plea;

(3) a statement made during a proceeding on either of those pleas under Federal Rule of Criminal Procedure 11 or a comparable state procedure; or

(4) a statement made during plea discussions with an attorney for the prosecuting authority if the discussions did not result in a guilty plea or they resulted in a later-withdrawn guilty plea.

(b) **Exceptions.** The court may admit a statement described in Rule 410(a)(3) or (4):

(1) in any proceeding in which another statement made during the same plea or plea discussions has been introduced, if in fairness the statements ought to be considered together; or

(2) in a criminal proceeding for perjury or false statement, if the defendant made the statement under oath, on the record, and with counsel present.

Rule 411. Liability Insurance

Evidence that a person was or was not insured against liability is not admissible to prove whether the person acted negligently or otherwise wrongfully. But the court may admit this evidence for another purpose, such as proving a witness's bias or prejudice or proving agency, ownership, or control.

Rule 412. Sex-Offense Cases: The Victim's Sexual Behavior or Predisposition

(a) Prohibited Uses. The following evidence is not admissible in a civil or criminal proceeding involving alleged sexual misconduct:

(1) evidence offered to prove that a victim engaged in other sexual behavior; or

(2) evidence offered to prove a victim's sexual predisposition.

(b) Exceptions.

(1) *Criminal Cases.* The court may admit the following evidence in a criminal case:

(A) evidence of specific instances of a victim's sexual behavior, if offered to prove that someone other than the defendant was the source of semen, injury, or other physical evidence;

(B) evidence of specific instances of a victim's sexual behavior with respect to the person accused of the sexual misconduct, if offered by the defendant to prove consent or if offered by the prosecutor; and

(C) evidence whose exclusion would violate the defendant's constitutional rights.

(2) *Civil Cases.* In a civil case, the court may admit evidence offered to prove a victim's sexual behavior or sexual predisposition if its probative value substantially outweighs the danger of harm to any victim and of unfair prejudice to any party. The court may admit evidence of a victim's reputation only if the victim has placed it in controversy.

(c) Procedure to Determine Admissibility.

(1) *Motion.* If a party intends to offer evidence under Rule 412(b), the party must:

(A) file a motion that specifically describes the evidence and states the purpose for which it is to be offered;

(B) do so at least 14 days before trial unless the court, for good cause, sets a different time;

(C) serve the motion on all parties; and

(D) notify the victim or, when appropriate, the victim's guardian or representative.

(2) *Hearing.* Before admitting evidence under this rule, the court must conduct an in camera hearing and give the victim and parties a right to attend and be heard. Unless the court orders otherwise, the motion, related materials, and the record of the hearing must be and remain sealed.

(d) Definition of "Victim." In this rule, "victim" includes an alleged victim.

Rule 413. Similar Crimes in Sexual-Assault Cases

(a) Permitted Use. In a criminal case in which a defendant is accused of a sexual assault, the court may admit evidence that the defendant committed any other sexual assault. The evidence may be considered on any matter to which it is relevant.

(b) Disclosure to the Defendant. If the prosecutor intends to offer this evidence, the prosecutor must disclose it to the defendant, including witnesses' statements or a summary of the expected testimony. The prosecutor must do so at least 15 days before trial or at a later time that the court allows for good cause.

(c) Effect on Other Rules. This rule does not limit the admission or consideration of evidence under any other rule.

(d) Definition of "Sexual Assault." In this rule and Rule 415, "sexual assault" means a crime under federal law or under state law (as "state" is defined in 18 U.S.C. §513) involving:

(1) any conduct prohibited by 18 U.S.C. chapter 109A;

(2) contact, without consent, between any part of the defendant's body—or an object—and another person's genitals or anus;

(3) contact, without consent, between the defendant's genitals or anus and any part of another person's body;

(4) deriving sexual pleasure or gratification from inflicting death, bodily injury, or physical pain on another person; or

(5) an attempt or conspiracy to engage in conduct described in subparagraphs (1)–(4).

Rule 414. Similar Crimes in Child-Molestation Cases

(a) Permitted Uses. In a criminal case in which a defendant is accused of child molestation, the court may admit evidence that the defendant committed any other child molestation. The evidence may be considered on any matter to which it is relevant.

(b) Disclosure to the Defendant. If the prosecutor intends to offer this evidence, the prosecutor must disclose it to the defendant, including witnesses' statements or a summary of the expected testimony. The prosecutor must do so at least 15 days before trial or at a later time that the court allows for good cause.

(c) Effect on Other Rules. This rule does not limit the admission or consideration of evidence under any other rule.

(d) Definition of "Child" and "Child Molestation." In this rule and Rule 415:

(1) "child" means a person below the age of 14; and

(2) "child molestation" means a crime under federal law or under state law (as "state" is defined in 18 U.S.C. §513) involving:

(A) any conduct prohibited by 18 U.S.C. chapter 109A and committed with a child;

(B) any conduct prohibited by 18 U.S.C. chapter 110;

(C) contact between any part of the defendant's body—or an object—and a child's genitals or anus;

(D) contact between the defendant's genitals or anus and any part of a child's body;

(E) deriving sexual pleasure or gratification from inflicting death, bodily injury, or physical pain on a child; or

(F) an attempt or conspiracy to engage in conduct described in subparagraphs (A)–(E).

Rule 415. Similar Acts in Civil Cases Involving Sexual Assault or Child Molestation

(a) Permitted Uses. In a civil case involving a claim for relief based on a party's alleged sexual assault or child molestation, the court may admit evidence that the party committed any other sexual assault or child molestation. The evidence may be considered as provided in Rules 413 and 414.

(b) Disclosure to the Opponent. If a party intends to offer this evidence, the party must disclose it to the party against whom it will be offered, including witnesses' statements or a summary of the expected testimony. The party must do so at least 15 days before trial or at a later time that the court allows for good cause.

(c) Effect on Other Rules. This rule does not limit the admission or consideration of evidence under any other rule.

ARTICLE V. PRIVILEGES

Rule 501. Privilege in General

The common law—as interpreted by United States courts in the light of reason and experience—governs a claim of privilege unless any of the following provides otherwise:

- the United States Constitution;
- a federal statute; or
- rules prescribed by the Supreme Court.

But in a civil case, state law governs privilege regarding a claim or defense for which state law supplies the rule of decision.

Rule 502. Attorney-Client Privilege and Work Product; Limitations on Waiver

The following provisions apply, in the circumstances set out, to disclosure of a communication or information covered by the attorney-client privilege or work-product protection.

(a) Disclosure Made in a Federal Proceeding or to a Federal Office or Agency; Scope of a Waiver. When the disclosure is made in a federal proceeding or to a federal office or agency and waives the attorney-client privilege or work-product protection, the waiver extends to an undisclosed communication or information in a federal or state proceeding only if:

(1) the waiver is intentional;

(2) the disclosed and undisclosed communications or information concern the same subject matter; and

(3) they ought in fairness to be considered together.

(b) Inadvertent Disclosure. When made in a federal proceeding or to a federal office or agency, the disclosure does not operate as a waiver in a federal or state proceeding if:

(1) the disclosure is inadvertent;

(2) the holder of the privilege or protection took reasonable steps to prevent disclosure; and

(3) the holder promptly took reasonable steps to rectify the error, including (if applicable) following Federal Rule of Civil Procedure 26(b)(5)(B).

(c) Disclosure Made in a State Proceeding. When the disclosure is made in a state proceeding and is not the subject of a state-court order concerning waiver, the disclosure does not operate as a waiver in a federal proceeding if the disclosure:

(1) would not be a waiver under this rule if it had been made in a federal proceeding; or

(2) is not a waiver under the law of the state where the disclosure occurred.

(d) Controlling Effect of a Court Order. A federal court may order that the privilege or protection is not waived by disclosure connected with the litigation pending before the court—in which event the disclosure is also not a waiver in any other federal or state proceeding.

(e) **Controlling Effect of a Party Agreement.** An agreement on the effect of disclosure in a federal proceeding is binding only on the parties to the agreement, unless it is incorporated into a court order.

(f) **Controlling Effect of this Rule.** Notwithstanding Rules 101 and 1101, this rule applies to state proceedings and to federal court-annexed and federal court-mandated arbitration proceedings, in the circumstances set out in the rule. And notwithstanding Rule 501, this rule applies even if state law provides the rule of decision.

(g) **Definitions.** In this rule:

(1) "attorney-client privilege" means the protection that applicable law provides for confidential attorney-client communications; and

(2) "work-product protection" means the protection that applicable law provides for tangible material (or its intangible equivalent) prepared in anticipation of litigation or for trial.

ARTICLE VI. WITNESSES

Rule 601. Competency to Testify in General

Every person is competent to be a witness unless these rules provide otherwise. But in a civil case, state law governs the witness's competency regarding a claim or defense for which state law supplies the rule of decision.

Rule 602. Need for Personal Knowledge

A witness may testify to a matter only if evidence is introduced sufficient to support a finding that the witness has personal knowledge of the matter. Evidence to prove personal knowledge may consist of the witness's own testimony. This rule does not apply to a witness's expert testimony under Rule 703.

Rule 603. Oath or Affirmation to Testify Truthfully

Before testifying, a witness must give an oath or affirmation to testify truthfully. It must be in a form designed to impress that duty on the witness's conscience.

Rule 604. Interpreter

An interpreter must be qualified and must give an oath or affirmation to make a true translation.

Rule 605. Judge's Competency as a Witness

The presiding judge may not testify as a witness at the trial. A party need not object to preserve the issue.

Rule 606. Juror's Competency as a Witness

(a) **At the Trial.** A juror may not testify as a witness before the other jurors at the trial. If a juror is called to testify, the court must give a party an opportunity to object outside the jury's presence.

(b) **During an Inquiry into the Validity of a Verdict or Indictment.**

(1) *Prohibited Testimony or Other Evidence.* During an inquiry into the validity of a verdict or indictment, a juror may not testify about any statement made or incident that occurred during the jury's deliberations; the effect of anything on that juror's or

another juror's vote; or any juror's mental processes concerning the verdict or indictment. The court may not receive a juror's affidavit or evidence of a juror's statement on these matters.

(2) *Exceptions.* A juror may testify about whether:

(A) extraneous prejudicial information was improperly brought to the jury's attention;

(B) an outside influence was improperly brought to bear on any juror; or

(C) a mistake was made in entering the verdict on the verdict form.

Rule 607. Who May Impeach a Witness

Any party, including the party that called the witness, may attack the witness's credibility.

Rule 608. A Witness's Character for Truthfulness or Untruthfulness

(a) **Reputation or Opinion Evidence.** A witness's credibility may be attacked or supported by testimony about the witness's reputation for having a character for truthfulness or untruthfulness, or by testimony in the form of an opinion about that character. But evidence of truthful character is admissible only after the witness's character for truthfulness has been attacked.

(b) **Specific Instances of Conduct.** Except for a criminal conviction under Rule 609, extrinsic evidence is not admissible to prove specific instances of a witness's conduct in order to attack or support the witness's character for truthfulness. But the court may, on cross-examination, allow them to be inquired into if they are probative of the character for truthfulness or untruthfulness of:

(1) the witness; or

(2) another witness whose character the witness being cross-examined has testified about.

By testifying on another matter, a witness does not waive any privilege against self-incrimination for testimony that relates only to the witness's character for truthfulness.

Rule 609. Impeachment by Evidence of a Criminal Conviction

(a) **In General.** The following rules apply to attacking a witness's character for truthfulness by evidence of a criminal conviction:

(1) for a crime that, in the convicting jurisdiction, was punishable by death or by imprisonment for more than one year, the evidence:

(A) must be admitted, subject to Rule 403, in a civil case or in a criminal case in which the witness is not a defendant; and

(B) must be admitted in a criminal case in which the witness is a defendant, if the probative value of the evidence outweighs its prejudicial effect to that defendant; and

(2) for any crime regardless of the punishment, the evidence must be admitted if the court can readily determine that establishing the elements of the crime required proving—or the witness's admitting—a dishonest act or false statement.

(b) **Limit on Using the Evidence After 10 Years.** This subdivision (b) applies if more than 10 years have passed since the witness's conviction or release from confinement for it, whichever is later. Evidence of the conviction is admissible only if:

(1) its probative value, supported by specific facts and circumstances, substantially outweighs its prejudicial effect; and

(2) the proponent gives an adverse party reasonable written notice of the intent to use it so that the party has a fair opportunity to contest its use.

(c) Effect of a Pardon, Annulment, or Certificate of Rehabilitation. Evidence of a conviction is not admissible if:

(1) the conviction has been the subject of a pardon, annulment, certificate of rehabilitation, or other equivalent procedure based on a finding that the person has been rehabilitated, and the person has not been convicted of a later crime punishable by death or by imprisonment for more than one year; or

(2) the conviction has been the subject of a pardon, annulment, or other equivalent procedure based on a finding of innocence.

(d) Juvenile Adjudications. Evidence of a juvenile adjudication is admissible under this rule only if:

(1) it is offered in a criminal case;

(2) the adjudication was of a witness other than the defendant;

(3) an adult's conviction for that offense would be admissible to attack the adult's credibility; and

(4) admitting the evidence is necessary to fairly determine guilt or innocence.

(e) Pendency of an Appeal. A conviction that satisfies this rule is admissible even if an appeal is pending. Evidence of the pendency is also admissible.

Rule 610. Religious Beliefs or Opinions

Evidence of a witness's religious beliefs or opinions is not admissible to attack or support the witness's credibility.

Rule 611. Mode and Order of Examining Witnesses and Presenting Evidence

(a) Control by the Court; Purposes. The court should exercise reasonable control over the mode and order of examining witnesses and presenting evidence so as to:

(1) make those procedures effective for determining the truth;

(2) avoid wasting time; and

(3) protect witnesses from harassment or undue embarrassment.

(b) Scope of Cross-Examination. Cross-examination should not go beyond the subject matter of the direct examination and matters affecting the witness's credibility. The court may allow inquiry into additional matters as if on direct examination.

(c) Leading Questions. Leading questions should not be used on direct examination except as necessary to develop the witness's testimony. Ordinarily, the court should allow leading questions:

(1) on cross-examination; and

(2) when a party calls a hostile witness, an adverse party, or a witness identified with an adverse party.

Rule 612. Writing Used to Refresh a Witness's Memory

(a) Scope. This rule gives an adverse party certain options when a witness uses a writing to refresh memory:

(1) while testifying; or

(2) before testifying, if the court decides that justice requires the party to have those options.

(b) Adverse Party's Options; Deleting Unrelated Matter. Unless 18 U.S.C. § 3500 provides otherwise in a criminal case, an adverse party is entitled to have the writing produced at the hearing, to inspect it, to cross-examine the witness about it, and to introduce in evidence any portion that relates to the witness's testimony. If the producing party claims that the writing includes unrelated matter, the court must examine the writing in camera, delete any unrelated portion, and order that the rest be delivered to the adverse party. Any portion deleted over objection must be preserved for the record.

(c) Failure to Produce or Deliver the Writing. If a writing is not produced or is not delivered as ordered, the court may issue any appropriate order. But if the prosecution does not comply in a criminal case, the court must strike the witness's testimony or—if justice so requires—declare a mistrial.

Rule 613. Witness's Prior Statement

(a) Showing or Disclosing the Statement During Examination. When examining a witness about the witness's prior statement, a party need not show it or disclose its contents to the witness. But the party must, on request, show it or disclose its contents to an adverse party's attorney.

(b) Extrinsic Evidence of a Prior Inconsistent Statement. Extrinsic evidence of a witness's prior inconsistent statement is admissible only if the witness is given an opportunity to explain or deny the statement and an adverse party is given an opportunity to examine the witness about it, or if justice so requires. This subdivision (b) does not apply to an opposing party's statement under Rule 801(d)(2).

Rule 614. Court's Calling or Examining a Witness

(a) Calling. The court may call a witness on its own or at a party's request. Each party is entitled to cross-examine the witness.

(b) Examining. The court may examine a witness regardless of who calls the witness.

(c) Objections. A party may object to the court's calling or examining a witness either at that time or at the next opportunity when the jury is not present.

Rule 615. Excluding Witnesses

At a party's request, the court must order witnesses excluded so that they cannot hear other witnesses' testimony. Or the court may do so on its own. But this rule does not authorize excluding:

> (a) a party who is a natural person;

> (b) an officer or employee of a party that is not a natural person, after being designated as the party's representative by its attorney;

> (c) a person whose presence a party shows to be essential to presenting the party's claim or defense; or

> (d) a person authorized by statute to be present.

ARTICLE VII. OPINIONS AND EXPERT TESTIMONY

Rule 701. Opinion Testimony by Lay Witnesses

If a witness is not testifying as an expert, testimony in the form of an opinion is limited to one that is:

> (a) rationally based on the witness's perception;

> (b) helpful to clearly understanding the witness's testimony or to determining a fact in issue; and

(c) not based on scientific, technical, or other specialized knowledge within the scope of Rule 702.

Rule 702. Testimony by Expert Witnesses

A witness who is qualified as an expert by knowledge, skill, experience, training, or education may testify in the form of an opinion or otherwise if:

(a) the expert's scientific, technical, or other specialized knowledge will help the trier of fact to understand the evidence or to determine a fact in issue;

(b) the testimony is based on sufficient facts or data;

(c) the testimony is the product of reliable principles and methods; and

(d) the expert has reliably applied the principles and methods to the facts of the case.

Rule 703. Bases of an Expert's Opinion Testimony

An expert may base an opinion on facts or data in the case that the expert has been made aware of or personally observed. If experts in the particular field would reasonably rely on those kinds of facts or data in forming an opinion on the subject, they need not be admissible for the opinion to be admitted. But if the facts or data would otherwise be inadmissible, the proponent of the opinion may disclose them to the jury only if their probative value in helping the jury evaluate the opinion substantially outweighs their prejudicial effect.

Rule 704. Opinion on an Ultimate Issue

(a) **In General—Not Automatically Objectionable.** An opinion is not objectionable just because it embraces an ultimate issue.

(b) **Exception.** In a criminal case, an expert witness must not state an opinion about whether the defendant did or did not have a mental state or condition that constitutes an element of the crime charged or of a defense. Those matters are for the trier of fact alone.

Rule 705. Disclosing the Facts or Data Underlying an Expert's Opinion

Unless the court orders otherwise, an expert may state an opinion—and give the reasons for it—without first testifying to the underlying facts or data. But the expert may be required to disclose those facts or data on cross-examination.

Rule 706. Court-Appointed Expert Witnesses

(a) **Appointment Process.** On a party's motion or on its own, the court may order the parties to show cause why expert witnesses should not be appointed and may ask the parties to submit nominations. The court may appoint any expert that the parties agree on and any of its own choosing. But the court may only appoint someone who consents to act.

(b) **Expert's Role.** The court must inform the expert of the expert's duties. The court may do so in writing and have a copy filed with the clerk or may do so orally at a conference in which the parties have an opportunity to participate. The expert:

(1) must advise the parties of any findings the expert makes;

(2) may be deposed by any party;

(3) may be called to testify by the court or any party; and

(4) may be cross-examined by any party, including the party that called the expert.

(c) **Compensation.** The expert is entitled to a reasonable compensation, as set by the court. The compensation is payable as follows:

(1) in a criminal case or in a civil case involving just compensation under the Fifth Amendment, from any funds that are provided by law; and

(2) in any other civil case, by the parties in the proportion and at the time that the court directs—and the compensation is then charged like other costs.

(d) Disclosing the Appointment to the Jury. The court may authorize disclosure to the jury that the court appointed the expert.

(e) Parties' Choice of Their Own Experts. This rule does not limit a party in calling its own experts.

ARTICLE VIII. HEARSAY

Rule 801. Definitions That Apply to This Article; Exclusions from Hearsay

(a) Statement. "Statement" means a person's oral assertion, written assertion, or nonverbal conduct, if the person intended it as an assertion.

(b) Declarant. "Declarant" means the person who made the statement.

(c) Hearsay. "Hearsay" means a statement that:

(1) the declarant does not make while testifying at the current trial or hearing; and

(2) a party offers in evidence to prove the truth of the matter asserted in the statement.

(d) Statements That Are Not Hearsay. A statement that meets the following conditions is not hearsay:

(1) *A Declarant-Witness's Prior Statement.* The declarant testifies and is subject to cross-examination about a prior statement, and the statement:

(A) is inconsistent with the declarant's testimony and was given under penalty of perjury at a trial, hearing, or other proceeding or in a deposition;

(B) is consistent with the declarant's testimony and is offered:

(i) to rebut an express or implied charge that the declarant recently fabricated it or acted from a recent improper influence or motive in so testifying; or

(ii) to rehabilitate the declarant's credibility as a witness when attacked on another ground; or

(C) identifies a person as someone the declarant perceived earlier.

(2) *An Opposing Party's Statement.* The statement is offered against an opposing party and:

(A) was made by the party in an individual or representative capacity;

(B) is one the party manifested that it adopted or believed to be true;

(C) was made by a person whom the party authorized to make a statement on the subject;

(D) was made by the party's agent or employee on a matter within the scope of that relationship and while it existed; or

(E) was made by the party's coconspirator during and in furtherance of the conspiracy.

The statement must be considered but does not by itself establish the declarant's authority under (C); the existence or scope of the relationship under (D); or the existence of the conspiracy or participation in it under (E).

Rule 802. The Rule Against Hearsay

Hearsay is not admissible unless any of the following provides otherwise:

- a federal statute;
- these rules; or
- other rules prescribed by the Supreme Court.

Rule 803. Exceptions to the Rule Against Hearsay — Regardless of Whether the Declarant Is Available as a Witness

The following are not excluded by the rule against hearsay, regardless of whether the declarant is available as a witness:

(1) *Present Sense Impression.* A statement describing or explaining an event or condition, made while or immediately after the declarant perceived it.

(2) *Excited Utterance.* A statement relating to a startling event or condition, made while the declarant was under the stress of excitement that it caused.

(3) *Then-Existing Mental, Emotional, or Physical Condition.* A statement of the declarant's then-existing state of mind (such as motive, intent, or plan) or emotional, sensory, or physical condition (such as mental feeling, pain, or bodily health), but not including a statement of memory or belief to prove the fact remembered or believed unless it relates to the validity or terms of the declarant's will.

(4) *Statement Made for Medical Diagnosis or Treatment.* A statement that:

(A) is made for—and is reasonably pertinent to—medical diagnosis or treatment; and

(B) describes medical history; past or present symptoms or sensations; their inception; or their general cause.

(5) *Recorded Recollection.* A record that:

(A) is on a matter the witness once knew about but now cannot recall well enough to testify fully and accurately;

(B) was made or adopted by the witness when the matter was fresh in the witness's memory; and

(C) accurately reflects the witness's knowledge.

If admitted, the record may be read into evidence but may be received as an exhibit only if offered by an adverse party.

(6) *Records of a Regularly Conducted Activity.* A record of an act, event, condition, opinion, or diagnosis if:

(A) the record was made at or near the time by—or from information transmitted by—someone with knowledge;

(B) the record was kept in the course of a regularly conducted activity of a business, organization, occupation, or calling, whether or not for profit;

(C) making the record was a regular practice of that activity;

(D) all these conditions are shown by the testimony of the custodian or another qualified witness, or by a certification that complies with Rule 902 (11) or (12) or with a statute permitting certification; and

(E) the opponent does not show that the source of information or the method or circumstances of preparation indicate a lack of trustworthiness.

(7) *Absence of a Record of a Regularly Conducted Activity.* Evidence that a matter is not included in a record described in paragraph (6) if:

(A) the evidence is admitted to prove that the matter did not occur or exist;

(B) a record was regularly kept for a matter of that kind; and

(C) the opponent does not show that the possible source of the information or other circumstances indicate a lack of trustworthiness.

(8) *Public Records.* A record or statement of a public office if:

(A) it sets out:

(i) the office's activities;

(ii) a matter observed while under a legal duty to report, but not including, in a criminal case, a matter observed by law-enforcement personnel; or

(iii) in a civil case or against the government in a criminal case, factual findings from a legally authorized investigation; and

(B) the opponent does not show that the source of information or other circumstances indicate a lack of trustworthiness.

(9) *Public Records of Vital Statistics.* A record of a birth, death, or marriage, if reported to a public office in accordance with a legal duty.

(10) *Absence of a Public Record.* Testimony — or a certification under Rule 902 — that a diligent search failed to disclose a public record or statement if:

(A) the testimony or certification is admitted to prove that

(i) the record or statement does not exist; or

(ii) a matter did not occur or exist, if a public office regularly kept a record or statement for a matter of that kind; and

(B) in a criminal case, a prosecutor who intends to offer a certification provides written notice of that intent at least 14 days before trial, and the defendant does not object in writing within 7 days of receiving the notice — unless the court sets a different time for the notice or the objection.

(11) *Records of Religious Organizations Concerning Personal or Family History.* A statement of birth, legitimacy, ancestry, marriage, divorce, death, relationship by blood or marriage, or similar facts of personal or family history, contained in a regularly kept record of a religious organization.

(12) *Certificates of Marriage, Baptism, and Similar Ceremonies.* A statement of fact contained in a certificate:

(A) made by a person who is authorized by a religious organization or by law to perform the act certified;

(B) attesting that the person performed a marriage or similar ceremony or administered a sacrament; and

(C) purporting to have been issued at the time of the act or within a reasonable time after it.

(13) *Family Records.* A statement of fact about personal or family history contained in a family record, such as a Bible, genealogy, chart, engraving on a ring, inscription on a portrait, or engraving on an urn or burial marker.

(14) *Records of Documents That Affect an Interest in Property.* The record of a document that purports to establish or affect an interest in property if:

(A) the record is admitted to prove the content of the original recorded document, along with its signing and its delivery by each person who purports to have signed it;

(B) the record is kept in a public office; and

(C) a statute authorizes recording documents of that kind in that office.

(15) *Statements in Documents That Affect an Interest in Property.* A statement contained in a document that purports to establish or affect an interest in property if the matter stated was relevant to the document's purpose—unless later dealings with the property are inconsistent with the truth of the statement or the purport of the document.

(16) *Statements in Ancient Documents.* A statement in a document that is at least 20 years old and whose authenticity is established.

(17) *Market Reports and Similar Commercial Publications.* Market quotations, lists, directories, or other compilations that are generally relied on by the public or by persons in particular occupations.

(18) *Statements in Learned Treatises, Periodicals, or Pamphlets.* A statement contained in a treatise, periodical, or pamphlet if:

(A) the statement is called to the attention of an expert witness on cross-examination or relied on by the expert on direct examination; and

(B) the publication is established as a reliable authority by the expert's admission or testimony, by another expert's testimony, or by judicial notice.

If admitted, the statement may be read into evidence but not received as an exhibit.

(19) *Reputation Concerning Personal or Family History.* A reputation among a person's family by blood, adoption, or marriage—or among a person's associates or in the community—concerning the person's birth, adoption, legitimacy, ancestry, marriage, divorce, death, relationship by blood, adoption, or marriage, or similar facts of personal or family history.

(20) *Reputation Concerning Boundaries or General History.* A reputation in a community—arising before the controversy—concerning boundaries of land in the community or customs that affect the land, or concerning general historical events important to that community, state, or nation.

(21) *Reputation Concerning Character.* A reputation among a person's associates or in the community concerning the person's character.

(22) *Judgment of a Previous Conviction.* Evidence of a final judgment of conviction if:

(A) the judgment was entered after a trial or guilty plea, but not a nolo contendere plea;

(B) the conviction was for a crime punishable by death or by imprisonment for more than a year;

(C) the evidence is admitted to prove any fact essential to the judgment; and

(D) when offered by the prosecutor in a criminal case for a purpose other than impeachment, the judgment was against the defendant.

The pendency of an appeal may be shown but does not affect admissibility.

(23) *Judgments Involving Personal, Family, or General History, or a Boundary.* A judgment that is admitted to prove a matter of personal, family, or general history, or boundaries, if the matter:

(A) was essential to the judgment; and

(B) could be proved by evidence of reputation.

(24) [*Other Exceptions.*] [Transferred to Rule 807.]

Rule 804. Exceptions to the Rule Against Hearsay — When the Declarant Is Unavailable as a Witness

(a) Criteria for Being Unavailable. A declarant is considered to be unavailable as a witness if the declarant:

(1) is exempted from testifying about the subject matter of the declarant's statement because the court rules that a privilege applies;

(2) refuses to testify about the subject matter despite a court order to do so;

(3) testifies to not remembering the subject matter;

(4) cannot be present or testify at the trial or hearing because of death or a then-existing infirmity, physical illness, or mental illness; or

(5) is absent from the trial or hearing and the statement's proponent has not been able, by process or other reasonable means, to procure:

(A) the declarant's attendance, in the case of a hearsay exception under Rule 804(b)(1) or (6); or

(B) the declarant's attendance or testimony, in the case of a hearsay exception under Rule 804(b)(2), (3), or (4).

But this subdivision (a) does not apply if the statement's proponent procured or wrongfully caused the declarant's unavailability as a witness in order to prevent the declarant from attending or testifying.

(b) The Exceptions. The following are not excluded by the rule against hearsay if the declarant is unavailable as a witness:

(1) *Former Testimony.* Testimony that:

(A) was given as a witness at a trial, hearing, or lawful deposition, whether given during the current proceeding or a different one; and

(B) is now offered against a party who had — or, in a civil case, whose predecessor in interest had — an opportunity and similar motive to develop it by direct, cross-, or redirect examination.

(2) *Statement Under the Belief of Imminent Death.* In a prosecution for homicide or in a civil case, a statement that the declarant, while believing the declarant's death to be imminent, made about its cause or circumstances.

(3) *Statement Against Interest.* A statement that:

(A) a reasonable person in the declarant's position would have made only if the person believed it to be true because, when made, it was so contrary to the declarant's proprietary or pecuniary interest or had so great a tendency to invalidate the declarant's claim against someone else or to expose the declarant to civil or criminal liability; and

(B) is supported by corroborating circumstances that clearly indicate its trustworthiness, if it is offered in a criminal case as one that tends to expose the declarant to criminal liability.

(4) *Statement of Personal or Family History.* A statement about:

(A) the declarant's own birth, adoption, legitimacy, ancestry, marriage, divorce, relationship by blood, adoption, or marriage, or similar facts of personal or family history, even though the declarant had no way of acquiring personal knowledge about that fact; or

(B) another person concerning any of these facts, as well as death, if the declarant was related to the person by blood, adoption, or marriage or was so intimately associated with the person's family that the declarant's information is likely to be accurate.

(5) [*Other Exceptions.*] [Transferred to Rule 807.]

(6) *Statement Offered Against a Party That Wrongfully Caused the Declarant's Unavailability.* A statement offered against a party that wrongfully caused—or acquiesced in wrongfully causing—the declarant's unavailability as a witness, and did so intending that result.

Rule 805. Hearsay Within Hearsay

Hearsay within hearsay is not excluded by the rule against hearsay if each part of the combined statements conforms with an exception to the rule.

Rule 806. Attacking and Supporting the Declarant's Credibility

When a hearsay statement—or a statement described in Rule 801(d)(2)(C), (D), or (E)—has been admitted in evidence, the declarant's credibility may be attacked, and then supported, by any evidence that would be admissible for those purposes if the declarant had testified as a witness. The court may admit evidence of the declarant's inconsistent statement or conduct, regardless of when it occurred or whether the declarant had an opportunity to explain or deny it. If the party against whom the statement was admitted calls the declarant as a witness, the party may examine the declarant on the statement as if on cross-examination.

Rule 807. Residual Exception

(a) In General. Under the following circumstances, a hearsay statement is not excluded by the rule against hearsay even if the statement is not specifically covered by a hearsay exception in Rule 803 or 804:

(1) the statement has equivalent circumstantial guarantees of trustworthiness;

(2) it is offered as evidence of a material fact;

(3) it is more probative on the point for which it is offered than any other evidence that the proponent can obtain through reasonable efforts; and

(4) admitting it will best serve the purposes of these rules and the interests of justice.

(b) Notice. The statement is admissible only if, before the trial or hearing, the proponent gives an adverse party reasonable notice of the intent to offer the statement and its particulars, including the declarant's name and address, so that the party has a fair opportunity to meet it.

ARTICLE IX. AUTHENTICATION AND IDENTIFICATION

Rule 901. Authenticating or Identifying Evidence

(a) In General. To satisfy the requirement of authenticating or identifying an item of evidence, the proponent must produce evidence sufficient to support a finding that the item is what the proponent claims it is.

(b) Examples. The following are examples only—not a complete list—of evidence that satisfies the requirement:

(1) *Testimony of a Witness with Knowledge.* Testimony that an item is what it is claimed to be.

(2) *Nonexpert Opinion About Handwriting.* A nonexpert's opinion that handwriting is genuine, based on a familiarity with it that was not acquired for the current litigation.

(3) *Comparison by an Expert Witness or the Trier of Fact.* A comparison with an authenticated specimen by an expert witness or the trier of fact.

(4) *Distinctive Characteristics and the Like.* The appearance, contents, substance, internal patterns, or other distinctive characteristics of the item, taken together with all the circumstances.

(5) *Opinion About a Voice.* An opinion identifying a person's voice—whether heard firsthand or through mechanical or electronic transmission or recording—based on hearing the voice at any time under circumstances that connect it with the alleged speaker.

(6) *Evidence About a Telephone Conversation.* For a telephone conversation, evidence that a call was made to the number assigned at the time to:

(A) a particular person, if circumstances, including selfidentification, show that the person answering was the one called; or

(B) a particular business, if the call was made to a business and the call related to business reasonably transacted over the telephone.

(7) *Evidence About Public Records.* Evidence that:

(A) a document was recorded or filed in a public office as authorized by law; or

(B) a purported public record or statement is from the office where items of this kind are kept.

(8) *Evidence About Ancient Documents or Data Compilations.* For a document or data compilation, evidence that it:

(A) is in a condition that creates no suspicion about its authenticity;

(B) was in a place where, if authentic, it would likely be; and

(C) is at least 20 years old when offered.

(9) *Evidence About a Process or System.* Evidence describing a process or system and showing that it produces an accurate result.

(10) *Methods Provided by a Statute or Rule.* Any method of authentication or identification allowed by a federal statute or a rule prescribed by the Supreme Court.

Rule 902. Evidence That Is Self-Authenticating

The following items of evidence are self-authenticating; they require no extrinsic evidence of authenticity in order to be admitted:

(1) *Domestic Public Documents That Are Sealed and Signed.* A document that bears:

(A) a seal purporting to be that of the United States; any state, district, commonwealth, territory, or insular possession of the United States; the former Panama Canal Zone; the Trust Territory of the Pacific Islands; a political subdivision of any of these entities; or a department, agency, or officer of any entity named above; and

(B) a signature purporting to be an execution or attestation.

(2) *Domestic Public Documents That Are Not Sealed but Are Signed and Certified.* A document that bears no seal if:

    (A) it bears the signature of an officer or employee of an entity named in Rule 902(1)(A); and

    (B) another public officer who has a seal and official duties within that same entity certifies under seal—or its equivalent—that the signer has the official capacity and that the signature is genuine.

(3) *Foreign Public Documents.* A document that purports to be signed or attested by a person who is authorized by a foreign country's law to do so. The document must be accompanied by a final certification that certifies the genuineness of the signature and official position of the signer or attester—or of any foreign official whose certificate of genuineness relates to the signature or attestation or is in a chain of certificates of genuineness relating to the signature or attestation. The certification may be made by a secretary of a United States embassy or legation; by a consul general, vice consul, or consular agent of the United States; or by a diplomatic or consular official of the foreign country assigned or accredited to the United States. If all parties have been given a reasonable opportunity to investigate the document's authenticity and accuracy, the court may, for good cause, either:

    (A) order that it be treated as presumptively authentic without final certification; or

    (B) allow it to be evidenced by an attested summary with or without final certification.

(4) *Certified Copies of Public Records.* A copy of an official record—or a copy of a document that was recorded or filed in a public office as authorized by law—if the copy is certified as correct by:

    (A) the custodian or another person authorized to make the certification; or

    (B) a certificate that complies with Rule 902(1), (2), or (3)

    a federal statute, or a rule prescribed by the Supreme Court.

(5) *Official Publications.* A book, pamphlet, or other publication purporting to be issued by a public authority.

(6) *Newspapers and Periodicals.* Printed material purporting to be a newspaper or periodical.

(7) *Trade Inscriptions and the Like.* An inscription, sign, tag, or label purporting to have been affixed in the course of business and indicating origin, ownership, or control.

(8) *Acknowledged Documents.* A document accompanied by a certificate of acknowledgment that is lawfully executed by a notary public or another officer who is authorized to take acknowledgments.

(9) *Commercial Paper and Related Documents.* Commercial paper, a signature on it, and related documents, to the extent allowed by general commercial law.

(10) *Presumptions Under a Federal Statute.* A signature, document, or anything else that a federal statute declares to be presumptively or prima facie genuine or authentic.

(11) *Certified Domestic Records of a Regularly Conducted Activity.* The original or a copy of a domestic record that meets the requirements of Rule 803(6)(A)–(C), as shown by a certification of the custodian or another qualified person that complies with a federal statute or a rule prescribed by the Supreme Court. Before the trial or hearing, the pro-

ponent must give an adverse party reasonable written notice of the intent to offer the record—and must make the record and certification available for inspection—so that the party has a fair opportunity to challenge them.

(12) *Certified Foreign Records of a Regularly Conducted Activity.* In a civil case, the original or a copy of a foreign record that meets the requirements of Rule 902(11), modified as follows: the certification, rather than complying with a federal statute or Supreme Court rule, must be signed in a manner that, if falsely made, would subject the maker to a criminal penalty in the country where the certification is signed. The proponent must also meet the notice requirements of Rule 902(11).

Rule 903. Subscribing Witness's Testimony

A subscribing witness's testimony is necessary to authenticate a writing only if required by the law of the jurisdiction that governs its validity.

ARTICLE X. CONTENTS OF WRITINGS, RECORDINGS, AND PHOTOGRAPHS

Rule 1001. Definitions That Apply to This Article

In this article:

(a) A "writing" consists of letters, words, numbers, or their equivalent set down in any form.

(b) A "recording" consists of letters, words, numbers, or their equivalent recorded in any manner.

(c) A "photograph" means a photographic image or its equivalent stored in any form.

(d) An "original" of a writing or recording means the writing or recording itself or any counterpart intended to have the same effect by the person who executed or issued it. For electronically stored information, "original" means any printout—or other output readable by sight—if it accurately reflects the information. An "original" of a photograph includes the negative or a print from it.

(e) A "duplicate" means a counterpart produced by a mechanical, photographic, chemical, electronic, or other equivalent process or technique that accurately reproduces the original.

Rule 1002. Requirement of the Original

An original writing, recording, or photograph is required in order to prove its content unless these rules or a federal statute provides otherwise.

Rule 1003. Admissibility of Duplicates

A duplicate is admissible to the same extent as the original unless a genuine question is raised about the original's authenticity or the circumstances make it unfair to admit the duplicate.

Rule 1004. Admissibility of Other Evidence of Content

An original is not required and other evidence of the content of a writing, recording, or photograph is admissible if:

(a) all the originals are lost or destroyed, and not by the proponent acting in bad faith;

(b) an original cannot be obtained by any available judicial process;

(c) the party against whom the original would be offered had control of the original; was at that time put on notice, by pleadings or otherwise, that the original would be a subject of proof at the trial or hearing; and fails to produce it at the trial or hearing; or

(d) the writing, recording, or photograph is not closely related to a controlling issue.

Rule 1005. Copies of Public Records to Prove Content

The proponent may use a copy to prove the content of an official record—or of a document that was recorded or filed in a public office as authorized by law—if these conditions are met: the record or document is otherwise admissible; and the copy is certified as correct in accordance with Rule 902(4) or is testified to be correct by a witness who has compared it with the original. If no such copy can be obtained by reasonable diligence, then the proponent may use other evidence to prove the content.

Rule 1006. Summaries to Prove Content

The proponent may use a summary, chart, or calculation to prove the content of voluminous writings, recordings, or photographs that cannot be conveniently examined in court. The proponent must make the originals or duplicates available for examination or copying, or both, by other parties at a reasonable time and place. And the court may order the proponent to produce them in court.

Rule 1007. Testimony or Statement of a Party to Prove Content

The proponent may prove the content of a writing, recording, or photograph by the testimony, deposition, or written statement of the party against whom the evidence is offered. The proponent need not account for the original.

Rule 1008. Functions of the Court and Jury

Ordinarily, the court determines whether the proponent has fulfilled the factual conditions for admitting other evidence of the content of a writing, recording, or photograph under Rule 1004 or 1005. But in a jury trial, the jury determines—in accordance with Rule 104(b)—any issue about whether:

(a) an asserted writing, recording, or photograph ever existed;

(b) another one produced at the trial or hearing is the original; or

(c) other evidence of content accurately reflects the content.

ARTICLE XI. MISCELLANEOUS RULES

Rule 1101. Applicability of the Rules

(a) **To Courts and Judges.** These rules apply to proceedings before:

- United States district courts;
- United States bankruptcy and magistrate judges;
- United States courts of appeals;
- the United States Court of Federal Claims; and
- the district courts of Guam, the Virgin Islands, and the Northern Mariana Islands.

(b) **To Cases and Proceedings.** These rules apply in:

- civil cases and proceedings, including bankruptcy, admiralty, and maritime cases;
- criminal cases and proceedings; and
- contempt proceedings, except those in which the court may act summarily.

(c) **Rules on Privilege.** The rules on privilege apply to all stages of a case or proceeding.

(d) **Exceptions.** These rules—except for those on privilege—do not apply to the following:

(1) the court's determination, under Rule 104(a), on a preliminary question of fact governing admissibility;

(2) grand-jury proceedings; and

(3) miscellaneous proceedings such as:

- extradition or rendition;
- issuing an arrest warrant, criminal summons, or search warrant;
- a preliminary examination in a criminal case;
- sentencing;
- granting or revoking probation or supervised release; and
- considering whether to release on bail or otherwise.

(e) Other Statutes and Rules. A federal statute or a rule prescribed by the Supreme Court may provide for admitting or excluding evidence independently from these rules.

Rule 1102. Amendments

These rules may be amended as provided in 28 U.S.C. § 2072.

Rule 1103. Title

These rules may be cited as the Federal Rules of Evidence.

Index